PEARSON CUSTOM SOCIOLOGY

Formerly published as Intersections, Crossroads & Inequalities

EDITORS

KATHLEEN A. TIEMANN
University of North Dakota
Introduction to Sociology, Social Problems & Issues, Inequalities & Diversity

RALPH B. MCNEAL, JR.
University of Connecticut
Introduction to Sociology

BETSY LUCAL
Indiana University South Bend
Inequalities & Diversity

MORTEN G. ENDER
United States Military Academy, West Point
Inequalities & Diversity

COMPILED BY:

PEARSON

Senior Vice President, Editorial: Patrick F. Boles
Editor: Ana Díaz-Caneja
Development Editor: Abbey Lewis
Editorial Assistant: Hannah Coker
Operations Manager: Eric M. Kenney
Production Manager: Jennifer Berry
Rights Manager: Michael E. Mushlitz
Art Director: Renée Sartell
Cover Designer: Renée Sartell

Cover Art: "Figures," courtesy of Eugenie Lewalski Berg; "Abstract Crowd," courtesy of Diana Ong/Superstock; "R&B Figures," courtesy of Diana Ong/Superstock; "Bramante's Staircase," courtesy of Veer/Photodisc Photography; "Hand Prints," courtesy of Veer/Photodisc Photography; "People Running-Falling," courtesy of Veer/Campbell Laird; "Sunbathers on Beach," courtesy of Veer/Scott Barrow; "Parada Gay, Florianapolis_25 (colorful balloons being set free)," courtesy of Paul Mansfield Photography/Getty Images; "Family Tree, Relatives," courtesy of Kudryashka/iStockphoto.com.

Printed in the United States of America.
 V092
Please visit our website at *www.pearsonlearningsolutions.com*.

Attention bookstores: For permission to return any unsold stock, contact us at *pe-uscustomreturns@pearson.com*.

Pearson Learning Solutions, 501 Boylston Street, Suite 900, Boston, MA 02116
A Pearson Education Company
www.pearsoned.com

ISBN 10: 1-256-56238-6
ISBN 13: 978-1-256-56238-2

Table of Contents

Sociology: Perspective, Theory, and Method

Sociology: Perspective, Theory, and Method

- What makes the sociological perspective a new and exciting way of seeing the world?

- Why is sociology an important tool for your future career?

- How do sociologists conduct research to learn about the social world?

Watch the *Core Concepts in Sociology* video "Sociologists at Work" on **mysoclab.com**

This chapter introduces the discipline of sociology. The most important skill to gain from this course is the ability to use what we call the *sociological perspective*. The chapter next introduces *sociological theory*, which helps us build understanding from what we see using the sociological perspective. The chapter continues by explaining how sociologists "do" sociology, describing three approaches to conducting research and four methods of data collection.

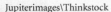

Jupiterimages\Thinkstock

From the moment he first saw Tonya, as they both stepped off the subway train, Duane knew she was "the one." As the two walked up the stairs to the street and entered the building where they were both taking classes, Duane tried to get Tonya to stop and talk. At first, she ignored him. But after class, they met again, and she agreed to join him for coffee. That was three months ago. Today, they are engaged to be married.

If you were to ask people in the United States, "Why do couples like Tonya and Duane marry?" it is a safe bet that almost everyone would reply, "People marry because they fall in love." Most of us find it hard to imagine a marriage being happy without love; for the same reason, when people fall in love, we expect them to think about getting married.

But is the decision about whom to marry really just a matter of personal feelings? There is plenty of evidence that if love is the key to marriage, Cupid's arrow is carefully aimed by the society around us.

Society has many "rules" about whom we should and should not marry. In all states but Massachusetts, Vermont, New Hampshire, Connecticut, and Iowa, along with the District of Columbia, the law rules out half the population, banning people from marrying someone of the same sex, even if the couple is deeply in love. But there are other rules as well. Sociologists have found that people, especially when they are young, are very likely to marry someone close in age, and people of all ages typically marry someone of the same race, of similar social class background, of much the same level of education, and with the same degree of physical attractiveness (Schwartz & Mare, 2005; Schoen & Cheng, 2006; Feng Hou & Myles, 2008; Chapter 13, "Family and Religion," gives details). People end up making choices about whom to marry, but society narrows the field long before they do.

When it comes to love, our decisions do not simply result from what philosophers call "free will." Sociology teaches us that our social world guides our life choices in much the same way that the seasons influence our choice of clothing.

The Sociological Perspective

Sociology is *the systematic study of human society*. At the heart of this discipline is a distinctive point of view called the *sociological perspective*.

Seeing the General in the Particular

Years ago, Peter Berger (1963) described the **sociological perspective** as *seeing the general in the particular*. By this he meant that sociology helps us see *general* patterns in the behavior of *particular* people. Although every individual is unique, society shapes the lives of people in various *categories* (such as children and adults, women and men, the rich and the poor) very differently. We begin to see the world sociologically by realizing how the general categories into which we fall shape our particular life experiences.

This text explores the power of society to guide our actions, thoughts, and feelings. We may think that marriage results simply from the personal feeling of love. Yet the sociological perspective shows us that factors such as our sex, age, race, and social class guide our selection of a partner. It might be more accurate to think of love as a feeling we have for others who match up with what society teaches us to want in a mate.

Seeing the Strange in the Familiar

At first, using the sociological perspective may seem like *seeing the strange in the familiar*. Consider how you would react if someone were to say to you, "You fit all the right categories, which means you would make a wonderful spouse!" We are used to thinking that people fall in love and decide to marry based on personal feelings. But the sociological perspective reveals to us the initially strange idea that society shapes what we think and do.

Because we live in an individualistic society, learning to see how society affects us may take a bit of practice. Consider the decision by women to bear children. Like the selection of a mate, the choice

Sociology: Perspective, Theory, and Method

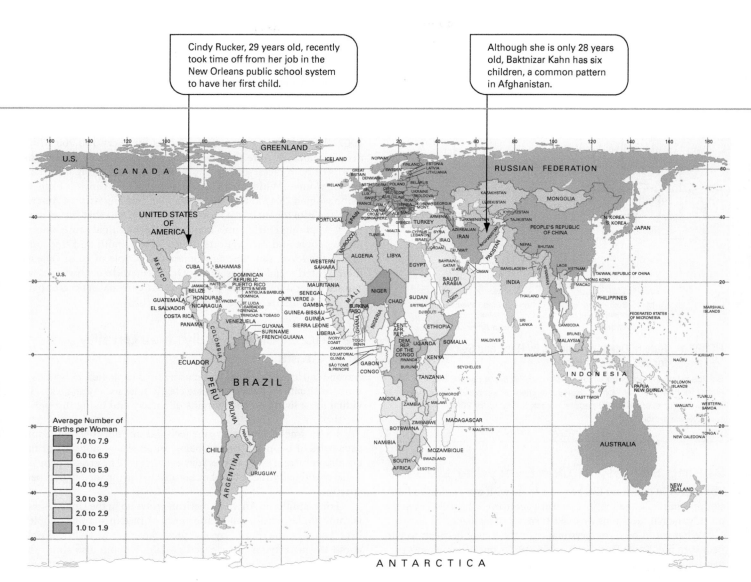

Window on the World

GLOBAL MAP 1   **Women's Childbearing in Global Perspective**

Is childbearing simply a matter of personal choice? A look around the world shows that it is not. In general, women living in poor countries have many more children than women in rich nations. Can you point to some of the reasons for this global disparity? In simple terms, such differences mean that if you had been born into another society (whether you are female or male), your life might be quite different from what it is now.

Sources: Data from Hamilton, Martin, & Ventura (2009), Population Reference Bureau (2009), United Nations Development Programme (2009), and Central Intelligence Agency (2009). Map projection from *Peters Atlas of the World* (1990).

of having a child—or how many to have—would seem to be very personal. Yet there are social patterns here as well. As shown in Global Map 1, the average woman in the United States has about two children during her lifetime. In the Philippines, however, the "choice" is about three; in Guatemala, about four; in Ethiopia, about five; in Afghanistan, about six; and in Niger, about seven.

What accounts for these striking differences? Because poor countries provide women with less schooling and fewer economic opportunities, women's lives are centered in the home, and they are less likely to use contraception. The strange truth is that society has much to do with the familiar decisions that women and men make about childbearing.

sociology the systematic study of human society

sociological perspective the special point of view of sociology that sees general patterns of society in the lives of particular people

Diversity Snapshot

White men are more than 12 times more likely than black women to commit suicide.

FIGURE 1 **Rate of Death by Suicide, by Race and Sex, for the United States**

Suicide rates are higher for white people than for black people and higher for men than for women. Rates indicate the number of deaths by suicide for every 100,000 people in each category for 2007.

Source: Xu et al. (2010).

Seeing Society in Our Everyday Lives

The society in which we live has a lot to do with our choices in food, clothing, music, schooling, jobs, and just about everything else. Even the most "personal" decisions we make turn out to be shaped by society.

What could be more personal than the lonely decision to end your own life? Emile Durkheim (1858–1917), one of sociology's pioneers, showed that social forces are at work even in such an intensely personal action as suicide. Examining official records in and around his native France, Durkheim (1966, orig. 1897) found that some categories of people were more likely than others to take their own lives. He found that men, Protestants, wealthy people, and the unmarried each had much higher suicide rates than women, Catholics and Jews, the poor, and married people. Durkheim explained these differences in terms of *social integration*: Categories of people with strong social ties had low suicide rates, and more individualistic people had high suicide rates.

In Durkheim's time, men had much more freedom than women. But despite its advantages, freedom weakens social ties and thus increases the rate of suicide. Likewise, more individualistic Protestants were more likely to commit suicide than more tradition-bound Catholics and Jews, whose rituals encourage stronger social ties. The wealthy have much more freedom than the poor—but once again, at the cost of a higher suicide rate.

A century later, Durkheim's analysis still holds true. Figure 1 shows suicide rates for four categories of the U.S. population. In

2007, there were 12.9 recorded suicides for every 100,000 white people, which is more than twice the rate for African Americans (4.9). For both races, suicide was more common among men than among women. White men (20.5) are almost four times as likely as white women (5.4) to take their own lives. Among African Americans, the rate for men (8.4) was almost five times that for women (1.7). Applying Durkheim's logic, the higher suicide rate among white people and men reflects their greater wealth and freedom, just as the lower rate among women and people of color reflects their limited social choices. Just as Durkheim did a century ago, we can see general sociological patterns in the personal actions of particular individuals. ● Go to **mysoclab.com**

Seeing Sociologically: Marginality and Crisis

Anyone can learn to see the world using the sociological perspective. But two situations help people see clearly how society shapes individual lives: living on the margins of society and living through a social crisis.

From time to time, everyone feels like an "outsider." For some categories of people, however, being an *outsider*—not part of the dominant category—is an everyday experience. The greater people's social marginality, the better they are able to use the sociological perspective.

For example, no African American grows up in the United States without understanding the importance of race in shaping people's lives. Songs by the rapper Jay-Z express the anger he feels, not only about the poverty he experienced growing up, but also about the many innocent lives he has seen lost to violence in a society of such wide racial disparities. His lyrics, and those of many similar artists, which are spread throughout the world by the mass media, show that some people of color—especially African Americans living in the inner city—feel like their hopes and dreams are crushed by society. But white people, as the dominant majority, think less often about race and the privileges it provides, believing that race affects only people of color and not themselves as well. People at the margins of social life, including women, gays and lesbians, people with disabilities, and the very old, are aware of social patterns that others rarely think about. To become better at using the sociological perspective, we must step back from our familiar routines and look at our lives with a new curiosity.

Periods of change or crisis make everyone feel a little off balance, encouraging us to use the sociological perspective. The sociologist C. Wright Mills (1959) illustrated this idea using the Great Depression of the 1930s. As the unemployment rate soared to 25 percent, people without jobs could not help but see general social forces at work in their particular lives. Rather than saying, "Something is wrong with

Sociology: Perspective, Theory, and Method

Go to the Multimedia Library at mysoclab.com to hear author John Macionis answer the question "How Do You Know Something Is True?"

global perspective the study of the larger world and our society's place in it

high-income countries	**middle-income countries**	**low-income countries**
the nations with the highest overall standards of living	nations with a standard of living about average for the world as a whole	nations with a low standard of living in which most people are poor

me; I can't find a job," they took a sociological approach and realized, "The economy has collapsed; there are no jobs to be found!" Mills believed that using what he called the "sociological imagination" in this way helps people understand their society and how it affects their own lives. The Seeing Sociology in Everyday Life box takes a closer look.

The Importance of a Global Perspective

As new information technology draws even the farthest reaches of the planet closer together, many academic disciplines are taking a **global perspective,** *the study of the larger world and our society's place in it.* What is the importance of a global perspective for sociology?

First, global awareness is a logical extension of the sociological perspective. Sociology shows us that our place in society shapes our life experiences. It stands to reason, then, that the position of our society in the larger world system affects everyone in the United States.

The world's 194 nations can be divided into three broad categories according to their level of economic development. **High-income countries** are *the nations with the highest overall standards of living.* The sixty-seven nations in this category include the United States and Canada, Argentina, the nations of Western Europe, Israel, Saudi Arabia, Japan, and Australia. Taken together, these nations generate most of the world's goods and services, and the people who live in them own most of the planet's wealth. Economically speaking, people in these countries are very well off, not because they are smarter or work harder than anyone else but because they were lucky enough to be born in a rich region of the world.

A second category is **middle-income countries,** *nations with a standard of living about average for the world as a whole.* People living in any of these seventy-one nations—many of the countries of Eastern Europe, South Africa and some other

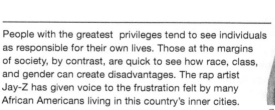

People with the greatest privileges tend to see individuals as responsible for their own lives. Those at the margins of society, by contrast, are quick to see how race, class, and gender can create disadvantages. The rap artist Jay-Z has given voice to the frustration felt by many African Americans living in this country's inner cities.

Gary He\AP Wide World Photos

African nations, and almost all of Latin America and Asia—are as likely to live in rural villages as in cities and to walk or ride tractors, scooters, bicycles, or animals as to drive automobiles. On average, they receive eight to ten years of schooling. Most middle-income countries also have considerable social inequality within their borders, meaning that some people are extremely rich (members of the business elite in nations across North Africa, for example) but many more lack safe housing and adequate nutrition (people living in the shanty settlements that surround Lima, Peru, or Mumbai, India).

The remaining fifty-six nations of the world are **low-income countries,** *nations with a low standard of living in which most people are poor.* Most of the poorest countries in the world are in Africa, and a few are in Asia. Here again, a few people are very rich, but the majority struggle to get by with poor housing, unsafe water, too little food, and perhaps most serious of all, little chance to improve their lives.

Later we will explain the causes and consequences of global wealth and poverty. We will make comparisons between the United States and other nations for four reasons:

1. **Where we live shapes the lives we lead.** As you saw in Global Map 1, women living in rich and poor nations have very different lives, as suggested by the number of children they have. To understand ourselves and appreciate how others live, we must understand something about how countries differ, which is easy to do by paying attention to the global maps found throughout this text.

2. **Societies throughout the world are increasingly interconnected.** Historically, people in the United States took only passing note of the countries beyond our own borders. In recent decades, however, the United States and the rest of the world have become linked as never before. Electronic technology now transmits pictures, sounds, and written documents around the globe in seconds.

One effect of this new technology is that people all over the world now share many of the same tastes in food, clothing, movies, and music. Rich countries such as the United States influence other nations, whose people are ever more likely to gobble up our Big Macs and Whoppers, dance to the latest hip-hop music, and speak English.

But the larger world also has an impact on us. We all know the contributions of famous immigrants such as Arnold Schwarzenegger (who came to the United States from Austria) and Gloria Estefan (who came from Cuba). More than 1.5 million immigrants enter the United States

Sociology: Perspective, Theory, and Method

○ Making the Grade

Mills used the term "sociological imagination" to mean the same thing as the term "sociological perspective" used by Peter Berger and others.

○ Making the Grade

The box below suggests that C. Wright Mills hoped the sociological imagination would spark social change toward a more equal society.

SEEING SOCIOLOGY IN EVERYDAY LIFE

The Sociological Imagination: Turning Personal Problems into Public Issues

As Mike opened the envelope, he felt the tightness in his chest. The letter he dreaded was in his hands—his job was finished at the end of the day. After eleven years! Years in which he had worked hard, sure that he would move up in the company. All those hopes and dreams were now suddenly gone. Mike felt like a failure. Anger at himself—for not having worked even harder, for having wasted so many years of his life in what had turned out to be a dead-end job—swelled up inside him.

But as he returned to his workstation to pack his things, Mike soon realized that he was not alone. Almost all his colleagues in the tech support group had received the same letter. Their jobs were moving to India, where the company was able to provide telephone tech support for less than half the cost of employing workers in California.

By the end of the weekend, Mike was sitting in the living room with a dozen other ex-employees. Comparing notes and sharing ideas, they now realized that they were simply a few of the victims of a massive outsourcing of jobs that is part of what analysts call the "globalization of the economy."

In good times and bad, the power of the sociological perspective lies in making sense of our individual lives. We see that many of our particular problems (and our successes as well) are not unique to us but are the result of larger social

trends. Half a century ago, the sociologist C. Wright Mills pointed to the power of what he called the sociological imagination to help us understand everyday events. As he saw it, society—not people's personal failings—is the main cause of poverty and other social problems. By turning personal problems into public issues, the sociological imagination is also the key to bringing people together to create needed change. In this excerpt,* Mills (1959:3–5) explains the need for a sociological imagination:

When society becomes industrialized, a peasant becomes a worker; a feudal lord is liquidated or becomes a businessman. When classes rise or fall, a man is employed or unemployed; when the rate of investment goes up or down, a man takes new heart or goes broke. When wars happen, an insurance salesman becomes a rocket launcher; a store clerk, a radar man; a wife lives alone; a child grows up without a father. Neither the life of an individual nor the history of a society can be understood without understanding both.

Yet men do not usually define the troubles they endure in terms of historical

---

*In this excerpt, Mills uses "man" and male pronouns to apply to all people. As far as gender was concerned, even this outspoken critic of society reflected the conventional writing practices of his time.

change. . . . The well-being they enjoy, they do not usually impute to the big ups and downs of the society in which they live. Seldom aware of the intricate connection between the patterns of their own lives and the course of world history, ordinary men do not usually know what this connection means for the kind of men they are becoming and for the kinds of history-making in which they might take part. They do not possess the quality of mind essential to grasp the interplay of men and society, of biography and history, of self and world. . . .

What they need . . . is a quality of mind that will help them [see] what is going on in the world and . . . what may be happening within themselves. It is this quality . . . [that] may be called the sociological imagination.

WHAT DO YOU THINK?

1. As Mills sees it, how are personal troubles different from public issues? Explain this difference in terms of what happened to Mike.

2. Living in the United States, why do we often blame ourselves for the personal problems we face?

3. By using the sociological imagination, how do we gain the power to change the world?

---

each year, bringing their skills and talents along with their fashions and foods, greatly increasing the racial and cultural diversity of this country.

Trade across national boundaries has also created a global economy. Large corporations make and market goods worldwide. Stock traders in New York pay close attention to the financial markets in Tokyo and Hong Kong even as wheat farmers in Kansas watch the price of grain in the former Soviet republic of Georgia. Because most new U.S. jobs involve international trade, greater global understanding has never been more important.

3. **Many social problems that we face in the United States are far more serious elsewhere.** Poverty is a serious problem in this country, but, poverty in Latin America, Africa, and Asia is both more common and more serious. In the same way, although women have lower social standing than men in the United States, gender inequality is much greater in the world's poor countries.

4. **Thinking globally helps us learn more about ourselves.** We cannot walk the streets of a distant city without thinking about what it means to live in the United States. Comparing life in various settings often leads to unexpected lessons. For instance, a

Sociology: Perspective, Theory, and Method

○ Making the Grade

Think of the global perspective as an extension of the sociological perspective. Here at home, where we are "placed" within society affects how we act, think, and feel. Expanding our vision shows that our nation's place in the world affects the lives of all who live in this country.

○ Seeing Sociology
in Everyday Life

How would your life be different if you had been born into a family in a poor farming village in Asia? What might you be doing right now instead of reading this text?

Minh-Thu Pham

Caroline Penn\CORBIS- NY

Paul Liebhardt\Paul W. Liebhardt

Paul Liebhardt\Paul W. Liebhardt

Paul Liebhardt\Paul W. Liebhardt

UpperCut Images\SuperStock, Inc.

We can easily see the power of society over the individual by imagining how different our lives would be had we been born in place of any of these children from, respectively, Bolivia, Ethiopia, Thailand, Mali, South Korea, and India.

squatter settlement in Chennai, India. There, despite a desperate lack of basic material goods, people thrive in the love and support of family members. Why, then, are so many poor people in the United States angry and alone? Are material things—so central to our definition of a "rich" life—the best way to measure human well-being?

In sum, in an increasingly interconnected world, we can understand ourselves only to the extent that we understand others. Sociology is an invitation to learn a new way of looking at the world around us. Is this invitation worth accepting? What are the benefits of applying the sociological perspective?

Applying the Sociological Perspective

Applying the sociological perspective is useful in many ways. First, sociology is at work guiding many of the laws and policies that shape our lives. Second, on an individual level, making use of the sociological perspective leads to important personal growth and expanded awareness. Third, studying sociology is excellent preparation for the world of work.

Sociology and Public Policy

Sociologists have helped shape public policy—the laws and regulations that guide how people in communities live and work—in countless ways, from racial desegregation and school busing to laws regulating divorce. For example, in her study of how divorce affects people's income, the sociologist Lenore Weitzman (1985, 1996) discovered that women who leave marriages typically experience a dramatic loss of income. Recognizing this fact, many states passed laws that have increased women's claims to marital property and enforced fathers' obligations to provide support for women raising their children.

Sociology and Personal Growth

By applying the sociological perspective, we are likely to become more active and aware and to think more critically in our everyday lives. Using sociology pays off in four ways:

1. **The sociological perspective helps us assess the truth of "common sense."** We all take many things for granted, but that does not make them true. One good example is the idea that we are free individuals who are personally responsible for our lives. If

Sociology: Perspective, Theory, and Method

Seeing Sociology in Everyday Life

This discussion shows you that using the sociological perspective is valuable for changing society by shaping public policy, for your personal enrichment, and for advancing your career.

Go to the Multimedia Library at **mysoclab.com** to view the slideshow "The Functions of Sociologists"

we think we decide our own fate, we may be quick to praise successful people as superior and consider others with fewer achievements personally deficient. A sociological approach, by contrast, encourages us to ask whether common beliefs are really true and, to the extent that they are not, why they are so widely held.

2. **The sociological perspective helps us see the opportunities and constraints in our lives.** Sociological thinking leads us to see that in the game of life, we have a say in how to play our cards, but it is society that deals us the hand. The more we understand the game, the better players we will be. Sociology helps us learn more about the world around us so that we can pursue our goals more effectively.

3. **The sociological perspective empowers us to be active participants in our society.** The better we understand how society operates, the more effective citizens we become. As C. Wright Mills explained, it is the sociological perspective that turns a private problem (such as being out of work) into a public issue (a lack of good jobs). As we come to see how society affects us, we may decide to support society as it is, or we may set out with others to change it.

4. **The sociological perspective helps us live in a diverse world.** North Americans represent just 5 percent of the world's population, and much of the other 95 percent lives very differently than we do. Still, like people everywhere, we tend to view our own way of life as "right," "natural," and "better." The sociological perspective prompts us to think critically about the strengths and weaknesses of all ways of life, including our own.

Careers: The "Sociology Advantage"

Most students at colleges and universities today are very interested in getting a good job. A background in sociology is excellent preparation for the working world. Of course, completing a bachelor's degree in sociology is the right choice for people who decide they would like to go on to graduate work and eventually become a professor or researcher in this field. Throughout the United States, tens of thousands of men and women teach sociology in universities, colleges, and high schools. But just as many professional sociologists work as researchers for government agencies or private foundations and businesses, gathering important information on how people live, what they think, and how they spend their money. In today's cost-conscious world, agencies and companies want to be sure that the products, programs, and policies they create get the job done at the lowest cost. Sociologists, especially those with advanced research skills, are in high demand for this type of evaluation research (Deutscher, 1999).

In addition, a smaller but increasing number of people work as clinical sociologists. These women and men work, much as clinical psychologists do, with the goal of improving the lives of troubled clients. A basic difference is that sociologists focus on difficulties not in the personality but in the individual's web of social relationships. ● Go to mysoclab.com

But sociology is not just for people who want to be sociologists. People who work in criminal justice—including jobs in police departments, probation offices, and correction facilities—also gain the "sociology advantage" by learning what categories of people are most at risk of becoming criminals or victims, how effective various policing policies and programs are at preventing crime, and why people turn to crime in the first place. Similarly, people who work in the health care field—including physicians, nurses, and technicians—also gain a sociology advantage by learning about patterns of health and illness within the population, as well as how factors such as race, ethnicity, gender, and social class affect human health.

The American Sociological Association (2007) reports that sociology is also excellent preparation for jobs in dozens of fields, including advertising, banking, business, education, government, journalism, law, public relations, and social work. In almost any type of work, success depends on understanding how various categories of people differ in beliefs, family patterns, and other ways of life.

Steve Liss\Getty Images/Time Life Pictures

Just about every job in today's economy involves working with people. For this reason, studying sociology is good preparation for your future career. In what ways does having "people skills" help police officers perform their job?

Sociology: Perspective, Theory, and Method

Making the Grade

Looking back, we can see that sociology developed when and where social change was greatest.

positivism a scientific approach to knowledge based on "positive" facts as opposed to mere speculation

Unless you have a job that never involves dealing with people, you should consider the workplace benefits of taking courses in sociology.

The Origins of Sociology

Like the "choices" people make, major historical events rarely just "happen." Even sociology itself is the result of powerful social forces.

Social Change and Sociology

Striking changes in Europe during the eighteenth and nineteenth centuries made people think more about society and their place in it, spurring the development of sociology. Three kinds of changes were especially important in the development of sociology: the rise of a factory-based economy, the explosive growth of cities, and new ideas about democracy and political rights.

A New Industrial Economy

During the Middle Ages, most people in Europe plowed fields near their homes or engaged in small-scale *manufacturing* (a term derived from Latin words meaning "to make by hand"). By the end of the eighteenth century, inventors were using new sources of energy—the power of moving water and then steam—to operate large machines in mills and factories. As a result, instead of laboring at home or in tightly knit groups, workers became part of a large and anonymous labor force, under the control of strangers who owned the factories. This change in the system of production took people away from their homes, weakening the traditions that had guided community life for centuries.

The Growth of Cities

Across Europe, landowners took part in what historians call the *enclosure movement*—they fenced off more and more farmland to create grazing areas for sheep, the source of wool for the thriving textile mills. Without land, countless tenant farmers had little choice but to head to the cities in search of work in the new factories.

As cities grew larger, these urban migrants faced many social problems, including pollution, crime, and homelessness. Moving through streets crowded with strangers, they faced a new, impersonal social world.

Political Change

Economic development and the growth of cities also brought new ways of thinking. In the writings of Thomas Hobbes (1588–1679), John Locke (1632–1704), and Adam Smith (1723–1790), we see a shift in focus from people's moral duties to God and king to the pursuit of self-interest. Philosophers now spoke of *personal liberty* and *individual rights*. Echoing these sentiments, our own Declaration of Independence

What we see depends on our point of view. When gazing at the stars, lovers see romance, but scientists see thermal reactions. How does using the sociological perspective change what we see in the world around us?

Frank Zullo/Photo Researchers, Inc.

clearly states that each citizen has "certain unalienable rights," including "life, liberty, and the pursuit of happiness."

The French Revolution, which began in 1789, was an even greater break with political and social tradition. As the French social analyst Alexis de Tocqueville (1805–1859) declared, the change in society in the wake of the French Revolution amounted to "nothing short of the regeneration of the whole human race" (1955:13, orig. 1856). As the new industrial economy, enormous cities, and fresh political ideas combined to draw attention to society, the new discipline known as sociology developed in France, Germany, and England, the countries where these changes were greatest.

Science and Sociology

Throughout history, the nature of society has fascinated people, including the brilliant philosophers K'ung Fu-tzu, or Confucius (551–479 B.C.E.), in China and Plato (427–347 B.C.E.) and Aristotle (384–322 B.C.E.) in Greece.[1] Later, the Roman emperor Marcus Aurelius (121–180), the medieval thinkers Saint Thomas Aquinas (c. 1225–1274) and Christine de Pizan (c. 1363–1431), and the great English playwright William Shakespeare (1564–1616) wrote about the workings of society.

---

[1]The abbreviation B.C.E. means "before the common era." We use this throughout the text instead of the traditional B.C. ("before Christ") to reflect the religious diversity of our society. Similarly, in place of the traditional A.D. (*anno Domini*, "in the year of our Lord"), we use the abbreviation C.E. ("common era").

Sociology: Perspective, Theory, and Method

Winston-Salem Journal

Back to School: In Poor Economy, Laid-off Workers Flocking to Community Colleges

By LISA O'DONNELL
February 10, 2009

Scores of laid-off workers are going back to the classroom, leading to an increase in enrollment in community colleges across North Carolina.

Historically, people have flocked to community colleges during recessions to learn new job skills. This time around, they are taking classes in such fields as health care and technical education, administrators said.

"At Forsyth Tech, and community colleges in general, we have an inverse relationship with the economy," said Gary Green, the president of Forsyth Technical Community College. "When you get a downturn, the job market tightens up and people look to community colleges to prop themselves up and get the skills they need to get back into the work force or to solidify their place in the work force. That's what we're seeing occur."

Mary Sue Antonucci of Pilot Mountain returned to the classroom last year because her job painting houses was not providing enough income. She is pursuing an associate's degree in art and hopes to open her own business.

"I realized, of course, that the job was not going to sustain me," said Antonucci, 50. "I knew I would not be able to take care of myself if I had no degree."

Although official full-time enrollment figures for degree-seeking students aren't yet available for the spring semester, administrators estimate that 12,500 new students enrolled in the state's fifty-eight community colleges this academic year, a 6.2 percent jump in enrollment from last year.

Typically, more students enroll in community colleges in the fall, but not this year, said Kennon Briggs, the executive vice president for the state's community-college system.

"Most companies gave their layoff notices in January and February rather than October or November," Briggs said. "We think for the first time in history that our spring-semester enrollment is going to be bigger than the fall's."

At Forsyth Tech, the number of students in fall 2008 increased 9.5 percent compared with fall 2007. For the spring semester, enrollment is up about 11.4 percent compared with last spring, Green said.

Colleges are being forced to serve more students with less money, Briggs said.

A few months ago, the governor's office asked the community-college system to trim 5 percent —$45 million—from its budget for the current fiscal year.

"What makes this a challenge is that we're growing at that rate at a time when we've been asked to return 5 percent of our current budget because state revenues have not materialized," Briggs said.

To compensate for the loss in funds, some colleges have increased class sizes and asked their faculty to teach more courses, Briggs said.

Forsyth Tech is dealing with the enrollment increase by offering some classes at 7 a.m. and adding part-time instructors, Green said.

Class sizes have not increased for the most part, Green said, because it would reduce the quality of instruction.

"We've had to work with the facilities we have and the personnel resources we have," he said.

Both Briggs and Green said they expect enrollment to continue to expand for at least another academic year based on the bleak economic forecast. . . .

WHAT DO YOU THINK?

1. This article describes the recent surge in community college enrollments in North Carolina, and a similar trend is occurring all across the country. How does this rise in community college enrollments reflect not just personal choices by individuals but also larger changes in society?

2. Can you point to other personal choices people have been making that may be linked to the weaker economy? What are they?

3. Did the weakening economy affect your life in terms of work? What about your decision to attend college? Explain.

Yet these thinkers were more interested in imagining the ideal society than they were in studying society as it really was. It was the French social thinker Auguste Comte (1798–1857) who coined the term *sociology* in 1838 to describe this new way of thinking. This makes sociology among the youngest of the academic disciplines— far newer than history, physics, or economics, for example.

Comte (1975, orig. 1851–54) saw sociology as the product of three stages of historical development. During the earliest *theological stage*, from the beginning of human history up to the end of the European Middle Ages about 1350 C.E., people took the religious view that society expressed God's will.

With the dawn of the Renaissance in the fifteenth century, Comte explained, the theological stage gave way to a *metaphysical stage* in which people came to see society as a natural rather than supernatural phenomenon. The English philosopher Thomas Hobbes (1588–1679), for example, suggested that society reflected not the perfection of God so much as the failings of selfish human nature.

What Comte called the *scientific stage* began with the work of early scientists such as the Polish astronomer Copernicus (1473–1543), the Italian astronomer and physicist Galileo (1564–1642), and the English physicist and mathematician Isaac Newton (1642–1727). Comte's contribution came in applying the scientific approach, originally used to analyze the physical world, to the study of society.[2]

Comte's approach is called **positivism**, *a scientific approach to knowledge based on "positive" facts as opposed to mere speculation.* Comte thought that knowledge based on tradition or metaphysics was really only speculation. A positivist approach to knowledge, however, is based on *science*. As a positivist, Comte believed that society operates according to certain laws, just as the physical world operates

---

[2]Illustrating Comte's stages, the ancient Greeks and Romans viewed the planets as gods; Renaissance metaphysical thinkers saw them as astral influences (giving rise to astrology); by the time of Galileo, scientists understood planets as natural objects moving according to natural laws.

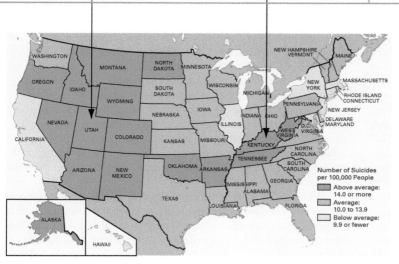

In the Plains and Mountain regions, and across the mountainous Appalachian region of the country, population density is very low, so people are more isolated. This isolation contributes to a higher rate of suicide.

Explore population density in your own state and across the United States on mysoclab.com. What conclusions can you draw about the relation between population density and suicide rate?

Seeing Ourselves

NATIONAL MAP 1

Suicide Rates across the United States

This map shows which states have high, average, and low suicide rates. Look for patterns. By and large, high suicide rates occur where people live far apart from one another. More densely populated states have low suicide rates. Do these data support or contradict Durkheim's theory of suicide? Why?

Explore on mysoclab.com

Source: Xu et al. (2010).

Number of Suicides per 100,000 People

- Above average: 14.0 or more
- Average: 10.0 to 13.9
- Below average: 9.9 or fewer

according to gravity and other laws of nature. Comte believed that by using science, people could come to understand the laws not only of the physical world but of society as well.

By the beginning of the twentieth century, sociology had taken hold in the United States and showed the influence of Comte's ideas. Today, most sociologists continue to consider science a crucial part of sociology, but we now realize that human behavior is far more complex than the movement of planets. We are creatures of imagination and spontaneity, so human behavior can never be explained by any rigid "laws of society." In addition, early sociologists such as Karl Marx (1818–1883) were troubled by the striking inequalities of the new industrial society. They hoped that the new discipline of sociology would not just help us understand society but also lead to change toward greater social justice.

Sociological Theory

The desire to translate observations into understanding brings us to the important part of sociology known as *theory*. A **theory** is *a statement of how and why specific facts are related*. The job of sociological theory is to explain social behavior in the real world. For example, recall Durkheim's theory that categories of people with low social integration (men, Protestants, the wealthy, and the unmarried) are at higher risk of suicide. Seeing Sociology in the News explains one consequence for young people of the recent economic recession.

Sociologists conduct research to test and refine their theories. National Map 1 shows the suicide rates for each of the fifty states and gives you a chance to do some theorizing of your own.

In building theory, sociologists face two basic questions: What issues should we study? And how should we connect the facts? In answering these questions, sociologists look to one or more theoretical approaches as "road maps." Think of a **theoretical approach** as *a basic image of society that guides thinking and research*. Sociologists make use of three theoretical approaches: the *structural-functional approach*, the *social-conflict approach*, and the *symbolic-interaction approach*.

The Structural-Functional Approach

The **structural-functional approach** is *a framework for building theory that sees society as a complex system whose parts work together to promote solidarity and stability*. As its name suggests, this approach points to **social structure,** *any relatively stable pattern of social behavior.* Social structure gives our lives shape in families, the workplace, or the college classroom. This approach also looks for each structure's **social functions,** *the consequences of a social pattern for the operation of society as a whole.* All social patterns, from a simple handshake to complex religious rituals, function to tie people together and to keep society going, at least in its present form.

The structural-functional approach owes much to Auguste Comte, who pointed out the need to keep society unified when many traditions were breaking down. Emile Durkheim, who helped establish sociology in French universities, also based his work on this approach. A third structural-functional pioneer was the English sociologist Herbert Spencer (1820–1903). Spencer compared society to the human body: Just as the structural parts of the human body—the skeleton, muscles, and internal organs—function together to help the entire organism survive, social structures work together to preserve society. The structural-functional approach, then, leads sociologists to identify various structures of society and investigate their functions.

The U.S. sociologist Robert K. Merton (1910–2003) expanded our understanding of social function by pointing out that any social structure probably has many functions, some more obvious than others. He distinguished between **manifest functions,** *the recognized and intended consequences of any social pattern*, and **latent functions,** *the unrecognized and unintended consequences of any social pattern*. For example, the obvious function of this country's system of higher education is to give young people the information and skills they will need to hold jobs after graduation. Perhaps just as important, although less often acknowledged, is college's function as a "marriage broker," bringing together young people of similar social backgrounds. Another latent function of higher education is to limit unemployment by keeping millions of people out of the labor market, where many of them might not easily find jobs.

But Merton also recognized that not all the effects of social structure are good. Thus a **social dysfunction** is *any social pattern that may disrupt the operation of society*. Globalization of the economy, a rising flow of immigrants, and increasing inequality of income are all factors that—in the eyes of some people—disrupt existing social patterns. As these examples suggest, what is helpful and what is harmful for society is a matter about which people often disagree. In addition, what is functional for one category of people (say, a banking system that provides high profits for Wall Street executives) may well be dysfunctional for other categories of people (workers who lose pension funds invested in banks that fail or people who cannot pay their mortgages and end up losing their homes).

○ **CRITICAL REVIEW** The main idea of the structural-functional approach is its vision of society as stable and orderly. The main goal of sociologists who use this approach, then, is to figure out "what makes society tick."

In the mid-1900s, most sociologists favored the structural-functional approach. In recent decades, however, its influence has declined. By focusing attention on social stability and unity, critics point out, structural-functionalism ignores inequalities of social class, race, ethnicity, and gender, which cause tension and conflict. In general, its focus on stability at the expense of conflict makes this approach somewhat conservative. As a critical response, sociologists developed the social-conflict approach.

○ **CHECK YOUR LEARNING** How do manifest functions differ from latent functions? Give an example of a manifest function and a latent function of automobiles in the United States.

The Social-Conflict Approach

The **social-conflict approach** is *a framework for building theory that sees society as an arena of inequality that generates conflict and change*. Unlike the structural-functional emphasis on solidarity and stability, this approach highlights how factors such as class, race, ethnicity, gender, and age are linked to inequality in terms of money, power, education, and social prestige. A conflict analysis rejects the idea that social structure promotes the operation of society as a whole, focusing instead on how any social pattern benefits some people while hurting others.

Sociologists using the social-conflict approach look at ongoing conflict between dominant and disadvantaged categories of people—the rich in relation to the poor, white people in relation to people of color, and men in relation to women. Typically, people on top try to protect their privileges while the disadvantaged try to gain more for themselves.

A conflict analysis of our educational system shows how schooling reproduces class inequality from one generation to the next. For example, secondary schools assign students to either college preparatory or vocational training programs. From a structural-functional point of view, such "tracking" benefits everyone by providing schooling that fits students' abilities. But conflict analysis argues that tracking often has less to do with talent than with social background, meaning that well-to-do students are placed in higher tracks while poor children end up in lower tracks.

In this way, young people from privileged families get the best schooling, which leads them to college and later to high-income careers. The children of poor families, by contrast, are not prepared for college and, like their parents before them, typically get stuck in low-paying jobs. In both cases, the social standing of one generation is passed on to the next, with schools justifying the practice in terms of individual merit (Bowles & Gintis, 1976; Oakes, 1982, 1985).

Many sociologists use social-conflict analysis not just to understand society but also to reduce inequality. Karl Marx championed the cause of workers in what he saw as their battle against factory owners. In a well-known statement (inscribed on his monument in London's Highgate Cemetery), Marx declared, "The philosophers have only interpreted the world, in various ways; the point, however, is to change it."

Feminism and the Gender-Conflict Approach

One important type of conflict analysis is the **gender-conflict approach,** *a point of view that focuses on inequality and conflict between women and men*. The gender-conflict approach is closely linked to **feminism,** *support of social equality for women and men*.

The importance of the gender-conflict approach lies in making us aware of the many ways in which our society places men in positions of power over women, in the home (where men are usually considered the "head of the household"), in the workplace (where men earn more income and hold most positions of power), and in the mass media (how many hip-hop stars are women?).

Another contribution of the gender-conflict approach is making us aware of the importance of women to the development of sociology. Harriet Martineau (1802–1876) is regarded as the first woman sociologist. Born to a wealthy English family, Martineau made her mark in 1853 by translating the writings of Auguste Comte from French into English. She later documented the evils of slavery and argued for laws to protect factory workers, defending workers' right to unionize. She was particularly concerned about the position of women in society and fought for changes in education policy so that women could look forward to more in life than marriage and raising children.

In the United States, Jane Addams (1860–1935) was a sociological pioneer who in 1899 helped found Hull House, a Chicago settlement house that provided assistance to immigrant families. Although widely published—Addams wrote eleven books and hundreds of articles—she chose the life of a public activist over that of a university sociologist, speaking out on issues involving inequality, immigration, and the pursuit of peace. Though her pacifism during World War I was the subject of much controversy, she was awarded the Nobel Peace Prize in 1931.

The Race-Conflict Approach

Another important type of social-conflict analysis is the **race-conflict approach,** *a point of view that focuses on inequality and conflict between people of different racial and ethnic categories.* Just as men have power over women, white people have numerous social advantages over people of color, including, on average, higher incomes, more schooling, better health, and longer life expectancy.

The race-conflict approach also points out the contributions to the development of sociology made by people of color. Ida Wells Barnett (1862–1931) was born to slave parents but rose to become a teacher and then a journalist and newspaper publisher. She campaigned tirelessly for racial equality and, especially, to put an end to the lynching of black people. She wrote and lectured about racial inequality throughout her life (Lengermann & Niebrugge-Brantley, 1998).

An important contribution to understanding race in the United States was made by William Edward Burghardt Du Bois (1868–1963). Born to a poor Massachusetts family, Du Bois enrolled at Fisk University in Nashville, Tennessee, and then at Harvard University, where he earned the first doctorate awarded by that university to a person of color. Du Bois then founded the Atlanta Sociological Laboratory, which was an important center of sociological research in the early decades of the last century. Like most people who follow the social-conflict approach (whether focusing on class,

Courtesy of the Library of Congress

We can use the sociological perspective to look at sociology itself. All of the most widely recognized pioneers of the discipline were men. This is because in the nineteenth century, it was all but unheard of for women to be college professors, and few women took a central role in public life. But Jane Addams was an early sociologist in the United States, who founded Hull House, a Chicago settlement house where she spent many hours helping young people.

gender, or race), Du Bois believed that scholars should not simply learn about society's problems but also try to solve them. He therefore studied the black communities across the United States, pointing to numerous social problems ranging from educational inequality, a political system that denied people their right to vote, and the terrorist practice of lynching. Du Bois spoke out against racial inequality and participated in the founding of the National Association for the Advancement of Colored People (NAACP) (E. Wright, 2002a, 2002b). The Thinking About Diversity box takes a closer look at the ideas of W. E. B. Du Bois.

○ **CRITICAL REVIEW** The various social-conflict approaches have gained a large following in recent decades, but like other approaches, they have met with criticism. Because any conflict analysis focuses on inequality, it largely ignores how shared values and interdependence can unify members of a society. In addition, say critics, to the extent that it pursues political goals, a social-conflict approach cannot claim scientific objectivity. Supporters of social-conflict analysis respond that *all* theoretical approaches have political consequences.

macro-level orientation a broad focus on social structures that shape society as a whole

> **structural-functional approach**
> **social-conflict approach**

micro-level orientation a close-up focus on social interaction in specific situations

> **symbolic-interaction approach** a framework for building theory that sees society as the product of the everyday interactions of individuals

THINKING ABOUT DIVERSITY: RACE, CLASS, & GENDER

W. E. B. Du Bois: A Pioneer in Sociology

One of sociology's pioneers in the United States, William Edward Burghardt Du Bois saw sociology as a key to solving society's problems, especially racial inequality. Du Bois earned a Ph.D. in sociology from Harvard University and established the Atlanta Sociological Laboratory, one of the first centers of sociological research in the United States. He helped his colleagues in sociology—and people everywhere—see the deep racial divisions in the United States. White people can simply be "Americans," Du Bois explained, but African Americans have a "double consciousness," reflecting their status as citizens who are never able to escape identification based on the color of their skin.

In his sociological classic *The Philadelphia Negro: A Social Study* (1899), Du Bois explored Philadelphia's African American community, identifying both the strengths and the weaknesses of people wrestling with overwhelming social problems on a day-to-day basis. He challenged the belief—widespread at that time—that blacks were inferior to whites, and he blamed white prejudice for the problems African Americans faced. He also criticized successful people of color for being so eager to win white acceptance

that they gave up all ties with the black community, which needed their help.

Despite notable achievements, Du Bois gradually grew impatient with academic study, which he felt was too detached from the everyday struggles of people of color. Du Bois wanted change. It was the hope of sparking public action against racial separation that led Du Bois, in 1909, to participate in the founding of the National Association for the Advancement of Colored People (NAACP), an organization that has been active in supporting racial equality for more than a century. As the editor of the organization's magazine, *Crisis*, Du Bois worked

Art Resource/Schomburg Center for Research in Black Culture

tirelessly to challenge laws and social customs that deprived African Americans of the rights and opportunities enjoyed by the white majority.

Du Bois described race as the major problem facing the United States in the twentieth century. Early in his career, as a sociological researcher, he made enormous contributions to the study of racial inequality. Later, as an activist, he believed political reform might overcome deep racial divisions. But by the end of his life, he had grown bitter, believing that little had changed. At the age of ninety-three, Du Bois left the United States for the African nation of Ghana, where he died two years later.

WHAT DO YOU THINK?

1. If he were alive today, do you think that Du Bois would still consider race a major problem in the twenty-first century? Why or why not?

2. How much do you think African Americans today experience "double consciousness"?

3. In what ways can sociology help us understand and reduce racial conflict?

Sources: Based on Baltzell (1967), Du Bois (1967, orig. 1899), Wright (2002a, 2002b), and personal communication with Earl Wright II.

A final criticism of both the structural-functional and social-conflict approaches is that they paint society in broad strokes—in terms of "family," "social class," "race," and so on. A third theoretical approach views society less in general terms and more as the specific, everyday experiences of individual people.

○ **CHECK YOUR LEARNING** Why do you think sociologists characterize the social-conflict approach as "activist"? What is it actively trying to achieve?

The Symbolic-Interaction Approach

The structural-functional and social-conflict approaches share a **macro-level orientation,** meaning *a broad focus on social structures that shape*

society as a whole. Macro-level sociology takes in the big picture, rather like observing a city from a helicopter and seeing how highways help people move from place to place or how housing differs from rich to poor neighborhoods. Sociology also uses a **micro-level orientation,** *a close-up focus on social interaction in specific situations.* Exploring city life in this way occurs at street level, where you might watch how children invent games on a school playground or observe how pedestrians respond to homeless people they pass on the street. The **symbolic-interaction approach,** then, is *a framework for building theory that sees society as the product of the everyday interactions of individuals.*

How does "society" result from the ongoing experiences of tens of millions of people? One answer, is that society is nothing more than the reality that people construct for themselves as they interact

○ Making the Grade

The Applying Theory table summarizes the three major theoretical approaches in sociology. Study the table to be sure you understand each one.

● Seeing Sociology
in Everyday Life

How would a structural-functional and a social-conflict analysis provide different answers to the question "What categories of people are you most likely to date and eventually marry?" How does a micro-level understanding of "romance" differ from a macro-level understanding?

● APPLYING THEORY ●

Major Theoretical Approaches

	Structural-Functional Approach	Social-Conflict Approach	Symbolic-Interaction Approach
What is the level of analysis?	Macro-level	Macro-level	Micro-level
What image of society does the approach have?	Society is a system of interrelated parts that is relatively stable. Each part works to keep society operating in an orderly way. Members generally agree about what is morally right and morally wrong.	Society is a system of social inequalities based on class (Marx), gender (feminism and gender-conflict approach), and race (race-conflict approach). Society operates to benefit some categories of people and harm others. Social inequality causes conflict that leads to social change.	Society is an ongoing process. People interact in countless settings using symbolic communications. The reality people experience is variable and changing.
What core questions does the approach ask?	How is society held together? What are the major parts of society? How are these parts linked? What does each part do to help society work?	How does society divide a population? How do advantaged people protect their privileges? How do disadvantaged people challenge the system seeking change?	How do people experience society? How do people shape the reality they experience? How do behavior and meaning change from person to person and from one situation to another?

with one another. That is, we human beings live in a world of symbols, and we attach meaning to virtually everything, from the words on this page to the wink of an eye. We create "reality," therefore, as we define our surroundings, decide what we think of others, and shape our own identities.

The symbolic-interaction approach has roots in the thinking of Max Weber (1864–1920), a German sociologist who emphasized understanding a particular setting from the point of view of the people in it. Since Weber's time, sociologists have taken micro-level sociology in a number of directions. George Herbert Mead (1863-1931) explored how our personalities develop as a result of social experience. Erving Goffman's (1922-1982) *dramaturgical analysis* describes how we resemble actors on a stage as we play out our various roles. Other contemporary sociologists, including George Homans and Peter Blau, have developed *social-exchange analysis*, the idea that interaction is guided by what each person stands to gain and lose from others. In the ritual of courtship, for example, people seek mates who can offer them at least as much—in terms of physical attractiveness, intelligence, and social background—as they offer in return.

○ **CRITICAL REVIEW** Without denying the existence of macro-level social structures such as the family and social class, the symbolic-interaction approach reminds us that society basically amounts to *people interacting*. That is, micro-level sociology shows us how individuals construct and experience society. However, by emphasizing what is unique in each social scene, this approach risks overlooking the widespread influence of culture, as well as structural factors such as class, gender, and race.

○ **CHECK YOUR LEARNING** How does a micro-level analysis differ from a macro-level analysis? Provide an explanation of a social pattern at both levels.

The Applying Theory table summarizes the structural-functional, social-conflict, and symbolic-interaction approaches. Keep in mind that each is helpful in answering particular types of questions. As the next Seeing Sociology in Everyday Life box shows, the fullest understanding of society comes from using all three approaches.

positivist sociology the study of society based on scientific observation of social behavior

empirical evidence information we can verify with our senses

science a logical system that develops knowledge from direct, systematic observation

Seeing Sociology in Everyday Life

Think of three commonsense ideas that you were brought up to believe and that you later realized (perhaps thinking sociologically) were not entirely true.

SEEING SOCIOLOGY IN EVERYDAY LIFE

Sports: Playing the Theory Game

Who doesn't enjoy sports? Children and teens may play as many as two or three organized sports. For adults who don't participate themselves, weekend television is filled with sporting events, and whole sections of our newspapers are devoted to teams and players and scores. What can we learn by applying sociology's three theoretical approaches to this familiar element of life in the United States?

Structural-Functional Approach According to the structural-functional approach, the manifest functions of sports include recreation, getting in shape, and letting off steam in a relatively harmless way. Sports have important latent functions as well, from building social relationships to creating jobs. Perhaps the most important latent function of sports is to encourage competition, which is central to our society's way of life.

Of course, sports also have dysfunctional consequences. For example, colleges and universities that try to field winning teams sometimes recruit students for their athletic skill rather than their academic ability. This practice not only lowers a school's academic standards but also shortchanges athletes, who spend little time doing the academic work that will prepare them for future careers (Upthegrove, Roscigno, & Charles, 1999).

Social-Conflict Approach A social-conflict analysis points out how sports are linked to social inequality. Some sports—

tennis, swimming, golf, skiing—are expensive, so participation is largely limited to the well-to-do. Football, baseball, and basketball, however, are accessible to people at almost all income levels. Thus the games people play are not simply a matter of choice but also a reflection of their social standing.

Throughout history, men have dominated the world of sports. The first modern Olympic Games, held in 1896, excluded women from competition. Through most of the twentieth century, Little League teams barred girls based on the traditional ideas that girls lack the strength and the stamina to play sports and that they risk losing their femininity if they do. Both the

All Olympic games involve outstanding athletes. However, the sports that are central to the summer games, including track and field events, have a higher share of athletes of color. By contrast, the winter Olympics have fewer minorities and more well-to-do athletes. Can you explain why?

PCN Photography\Alamy Images

Olympics and the Little League are now open to females as well as males, but even today, women still take a back seat to men, particularly in sports with the greatest earnings and social prestige.

Although our society long excluded people of color from professional sports, opportunities have expanded in recent decades. In 1947, Jackie Robinson crossed the "color line" to become the first African American player in Major League Baseball. More than fifty years later, professional baseball retired the legendary Robinson's number 42 on *all* teams. In 2008, African Americans (12.8 percent of the U.S. population) accounted for 10.2 percent of Major League Baseball players, 67 percent of National Football League (NFL) players, and 77 percent of National Basketball Association (NBA) players (Lapchick, 2009).

But racial discrimination still exists in professional sports. For one thing, race is linked to the positions athletes play on the field, a pattern called "stacking." The figure shows the results of a 2009 study of race in Major League Baseball. Notice that white players are most concentrated in the central "thinking" positions of pitcher (66 percent white) and catcher (62 percent white). By contrast, African Americans represented only 5 percent of pitchers, and there were no black catchers. At the same time, 9 percent of infielders are African Americans, as are 32 percent of outfielders (positions characterized as requiring "speed and reactive ability") (Lapchick, 2009).

Three Ways to Do Sociology

All sociologists want to learn about the social world. But just as some may prefer one theoretical approach to another, many sociologists favor one research orientation. The following sections describe three ways to do sociological research: positivist, interpretive, and critical sociology.

Positivist Sociology

One popular way to do sociological research is **positivist sociology,** which is *the study of society based on scientific observation of social*

behavior. As explained earlier, positivist research discovers facts through the use of **science,** *a logical system that develops knowledge from direct, systematic observation.* Positivist sociology is sometimes called *empirical sociology* because it is based on **empirical evidence,** which is *information we can verify with our senses.*

Scientific research often challenges what we accept as "common sense." Here are three examples of widely held beliefs that are not supported by scientific evidence:

1. **"Differences in the behavior of females and males are just 'human nature.'"** Wrong. Much of what we call "human

Go to MySocLibrary at mysoclab.com to read
"Names, Logos, Mascots, and Flags: The Contradictory
Use of Sports Symbols" by Stanley D. Eitzen

○ Making the Grade

The pattern of "stacking," shown in the figure below, illustrates a
social-conflict approach to understanding.

More broadly, African Americans have a large share of players in only five major sports: basketball, football, baseball, boxing, and track. And across all professional sports, the vast majority of managers, head coaches, and team owners are still white (Lapchick, 2009).

Who benefits most from professional sports? Although some players get sky-high salaries and millions of fans follow their teams, the vast profits sports generate are controlled by a small number of people—predominantly white men. In sum, sports in our country are bound up with inequalities based on gender, race, and wealth.
○ Go to mysoclab.com

Symbolic-Interaction Approach At the micro-level, a sporting event is a complex, face-to-face interaction. In part, play is guided by the players' assigned positions and the rules of the game. But players are also spontaneous and unpredictable. Following the symbolic-interaction approach, we see sports less as a system and more as an ongoing process.

From this point of view, too, we would also expect each player to understand the game a little differently. Some players enjoy stiff competition; for others, love of the game may be greater than the need to win. In addition, the behavior of any single player is likely to change over time. A rookie in professional baseball, for example, may feel self-conscious during the

Diversity Snapshot

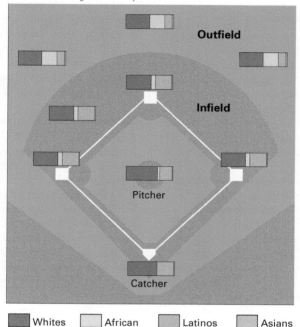

Outfield

Infield

Pitcher

Catcher

■ Whites □ African Americans ■ Latinos ■ Asians

"Stacking" in Professional Baseball

Does race play a part in professional sports? Looking at the various positions in professional baseball, we see that white players are more likely to play the central positions in the infield, while people of color are more likely to play in the outfield. What do you make of this pattern?

Source: Lapchick (2009).

first few games in the big leagues but go on to develop a comfortable sense of fitting in with the team. Coming to feel at home on the field was slow and painful for Jackie Robinson, who knew that many white players and millions of white fans resented his presence. In time, however, his outstanding ability and his confident, cooperative manner won him the respect of the entire nation.

The three theoretical approaches provide different insights into sports, and none is entirely correct. Applied to any issue, each approach provides part of a complex picture. To fully appreciate the power of the sociological perspective, you should become familiar with all three.

WHAT DO YOU THINK?

1. Describe how a macro-level approach to sports differs from a micro-level approach. Which theoretical approaches are macro-level, and which one is micro-level?

2. Make up three questions about sports that reflect the focus of each of the three theoretical approaches.

3. How might you apply the three approaches to other social patterns, such as the workplace or family life?

nature" is constructed by the society in which we live. We know this because researchers have found that definitions of "feminine" and "masculine" change over time and vary from one society to another.

2. **"The United States is a middle-class society in which most people are more or less equal."** Not true. The richest 5 percent of U.S. families control more than 60 percent of the country's wealth, while almost half of all families have scarcely any wealth at all (Wolff, 2009).

3. **"People marry because they are in love."** Not exactly. In U.S. society, as already discussed, many social rules guide the selection of mates. Around the world, research indicates that marriages in most societies are arranged by parents and have little to do with love.

These examples confirm the old saying that "it's not what we *don't* know that gets us into trouble as much as the things we *do* know that *just aren't so.*" The next Seeing Sociology in Everyday Life box explains why we also need to think critically about the "facts" we find in the popular media and on the Internet.

concept a mental construct that represents some aspect of the world in a simplified form

variable a concept whose value changes from case to case

measurement a procedure for determining the value of a variable in a specific case

reliability consistency in measurement

validity actually measuring exactly what you intend to measure

correlation a relationship in which two (or more) variables change together

cause and effect a relationship in which change in one variable (the independent variable) causes change in another (the dependent variable)

We have all been brought up hearing many widely accepted "truths," being bombarded by "expert" advice in the popular media, and feeling pressure to accept the opinions of those around us. As adults, we need to evaluate more critically what we see, read, and hear. Sociology can help us do that. Sociologists (and everyone else) can use science to assess many kinds of information.

Concepts, Variables, and Measurement

Let's take a closer look at how science works. A basic element of science is the **concept,** *a mental construct that represents some aspect of the world in a simplified form.* Sociologists use concepts to label aspects of social life, including "the family" and "the economy," and to categorize people in terms of their "gender" or "social class."

A **variable** is *a concept whose value changes from case to case.* The familiar variable "height," for example, has a value that varies from person to person. The concept "social class" can describe people's social standing using the values "upper-class," "middle-class," "working-class," and "lower-class."

The use of variables depends on **measurement,** *a procedure for determining the value of a variable in a specific case.* Some variables are easy to measure, as when a nurse checks our blood pressure. But measuring sociological variables can be far more difficult. For example, how would you measure a person's social class? You might start by looking at the clothing people wear, listening to how they speak, or noting where they live. Or trying to be more precise, you might ask about income, occupation, and education. Because there are many ways to measure a complex variable like social class, researchers must make decisions about how to *operationalize* a variable, stating exactly what they are measuring.

Statistics

Sociologists also face the problem of dealing with large numbers of people. For example, how do you report income for thousands or even millions of individuals? Listing streams of numbers would carry little meaning and tell us nothing about the people as a whole. To solve this problem, sociologists use *descriptive statistics* to state what is "average" for a large population. The most commonly used descriptive statistics are the *mean* (the arithmetic average of all measures, which you calculate by adding all the values and dividing by the number of cases), the *median* (the score at the halfway point in a listing of numbers from lowest to highest), and the *mode* (the score that occurs most often).

Reliability and Validity

For a measurement to be useful, it must be reliable and valid. **Reliability** refers to *consistency in measurement.* A measurement is reliable if repeated measurements give the same result time after time. But consistency does not guarantee **validity,** which is *actually meas-uring exactly what you intend to measure.* Valid measurement means more than hitting the same spot somewhere on a target again and again; it means hitting the exact target, the bull's-eye.

Say you want to know just how religious the students at your college are. You might ask students how often they attend religious services. But is going to a house of worship really the same thing as being religious? Maybe not, because people take part in religious rituals for many reasons, some of them having little to do with religion; in addition, some strong believers avoid organized religion altogether. Thus even when a measure yields consistent results (meaning that it is reliable), it can still miss the intended target (and therefore lack validity). Good sociological research depends on careful measurement, which is always a challenge to researchers.

Correlation and Cause

The real payoff in scientific research is determining how variables are related. **Correlation** means *a relationship in which two (or more) variables change together.* But sociologists want to know not just how variables change but which variable changes the other. The scientific ideal is to determine **cause and effect,** *a relationship in which change in one variable causes change in another.* As noted earlier, Emile Durkheim found that the degree of social integration (the cause) affected the suicide rate (the effect) among categories of people. Scientists refer to the cause as the *independent variable* and the effect as the *dependent variable.* Understanding cause and effect is valuable because it allows researchers to *predict* how one pattern of behavior will produce another.

Just because two variables change together does not necessarily mean that they have a cause-and-effect relationship. For instance, the marriage rate in the United States falls to its lowest point in January, which also happens to be the month when the national death rate is highest. Does this mean that people drop dead because they don't marry or that they don't marry because they die? Of course not. More likely, it is the cold and often stormy weather across much of the country in January (perhaps combined with the postholiday blues) that is responsible for both the low marriage rate and the high death rate.

When two variables change together but neither one causes the other, sociologists describe the relationship as a *spurious,* or false, correlation. A spurious correlation between two variables usually results from some third factor. For example, delinquency rates are high where young people live in crowded housing, but this is not because crowded housing causes youngsters to "turn bad." Both crowded housing and delinquency result from a third factor: poverty. To be sure of a real cause-and-effect relationship, we must show that (1) variables are correlated, (2) the independent (causal) variable occurs before the dependent variable, and (3) there is no evidence that a third variable has been overlooked, causing a spurious correlation.

Seeing Sociology in Everyday Life

Why do you think many doctors, teachers, and police officers avoid working professionally with their own children?

SEEING SOCIOLOGY IN EVERYDAY LIFE

Is What We Read in the Popular Press True? The Case of Extramarital Sex

Every day, we see stories in newspapers and magazines that tell us what people think and how they behave. But a lot of what you might read turns out to be misleading or worse.

Take the issue of extramarital sex, meaning married people having sex with someone other than their spouse. A look at the cover of many of the "women's magazines" you find in the checkout aisle at the supermarket or a quick reading of the advice column in your local newspaper might lead you to think that extramarital sex is a major issue facing married couples.

The "pop" media seem full of stories about how to keep your spouse from "cheating" or pointing out the clues that tip you off when your spouse is having an affair. Most of the studies reported in the popular press and on Internet Web sites suggest that more than half of married people—women as well as men—cheat on their spouse.

But is extramarital sex really that widespread? No. Researchers who conduct sound sociological investigation have found that in any given year, only 3 to 4 percent of married people have an extramarital relationship, and no more than 15 to 20 percent of married people have *ever* done so. Why, then, do surveys in the popular media report rates of extramarital sex that are so much higher? We can answer this question by taking a look at who fills out pop surveys.

First, it is people with a personal interest in some topic who are most likely to respond to an offer in the popular media or online to complete a survey. For this reason, people who have some personal experience with extramarital sex (either their own behavior or their partner's) are more likely to show up in these studies. In contrast, studies correctly done by skilled researchers carefully select subjects so that the results are representative of the entire population.

Second, because the readership of the magazines and online sources that conduct these surveys is, on average, young, their surveys end up attracting a high proportion of young respondents. And one thing we know about young people—married or unmarried—is that they are more likely to have sex. For example, the typical married person who is thirty years of age is more than twice as likely to have had an extramarital relationship than the typical married person over age sixty.

Third, women are much more likely than men to read the popular magazines that feature sex

August 2010

TRIXIE

"How Much Cheating? New Survey Tells All!"

"10 Tips for a Sexy You!"

Vic Bider\PhotoEdit Inc.

surveys. Therefore, women are more likely to fill out the surveys. In recent decades, the share of women, especially younger women, who have had extramarital sex has gone up. Why are today's younger women more likely than women a generation or two earlier to have had extramarital sex? Probably because women today are working out of the home and many are traveling as part of their job. In general, today's women have a wider social network that brings them into contact with more men.

Remember that a lot of what you read in the popular media and online may not be as true as some people think.

WHAT DO YOU THINK?

1. Can you think of other issues on which pop media surveys may give misleading information? What are they?

2. Explain why we should have more trust in the results of sound research carried out by skilled sociologists than in the surveys conducted by the popular media.

3. Do you think companies are likely to sell more magazines or newspapers if they publish "research" results that distort the truth? Explain.

Sources: T. W. Smith (2006), Black (2007), Parker-Pope (2008).

The Ideal of Objectivity

A guiding principle of science is *objectivity*, or personal neutrality, in conducting research. Ideally, objective research allows the facts to speak for themselves and not be influenced by the personal values and biases of the researcher. In reality, of course, achieving total neutrality is impossible for anyone. But carefully observing the rules of scientific research will maximize objectivity. Go to mysoclab.com

The German sociologist Max Weber noted that people usually choose *value-relevant* research topics—topics they care about. But once their work is under way, he cautioned, researchers should try to be *value-free*. That is, we must be dedicated to finding truth as it *is* rather than as we think it *should be*. For Weber, this difference sets science apart from politics. Researchers (unlike politicians) must stay open-minded and be willing to accept whatever results come from their work, whether they personally agree with them or not.

Weber's argument still carries much weight in sociology, although most researchers realize that we can never be completely value-free or even aware of all our biases (Demerath, 1996). In addition, keep in mind that sociologists are not "average" people: Most are highly educated white men and women who are more politically

research orientations

positivist sociology
the study of society based on
systematic observation of
social behavior

interpretive sociology
the study of society that
focuses on discovering the
meanings people attach to
their social world

critical sociology
the study of society that
focuses on the need for
social change

 Go to the Multimedia Library at mysoclab.com to view
the *Core Concepts in Sociology* video "Qualitative vs.
Quantitative Research"

liberal than the population as a whole. Sociologists need to remember that they, too, are influenced by their social backgrounds.

Interpretive Sociology

Not all sociologists agree that science is the only way—or even the best way—to study human society. This is because, unlike planets or other elements of the natural world, humans do not simply move around as objects that can be measured. On the contrary, people are active creatures who attach *meaning* to their actions, and meaning is not easy to observe directly. Therefore, sociologists have developed a second research orientation, known as **interpretive sociology,** *the study of society that focuses on discovering the meanings people attach to their social world.* Max Weber, the pioneer of this framework, argued that the proper focus of sociology is *interpretation*, or understanding the meanings people create in their everyday lives.

The Importance of Meaning

Interpretive sociology differs from positivist sociology in three ways. First, positivist sociology focuses on action—on what people do—because this is what we can observe directly. Interpretive sociology, focuses on people's understanding of their actions and their surroundings. Second, positivist sociology claims that objective reality exists "out there"; interpretive sociology counters that reality is subjective, constructed by people in the course of their everyday lives. Third, positivist sociology tends to favor *quantitative* data, numerical measurements of outward behavior; interpretive sociology favors *qualitative* data, researchers' perceptions of how people understand their world. In sum, the positivist orientation, close to science, is well suited for research in a laboratory, where investigators stand back and take careful measurements of what people do. The interpretive orientation, while not rejecting science outright, claims that we learn more by interacting with people, focusing on subjective meaning, and learning how people make sense of their everyday lives. This type of research is best carried out in a natural setting. ● Go to mysoclab.com

Weber's Concept of *Verstehen*

Max Weber claimed that the key to interpretive sociology lies in *Verstehen* (pronounced "fair-SHTAY-en"), the German word for "understanding." It is the interpretive sociologist's job not just to observe *what* people do but also to share in their world of meaning, coming to appreciate *why* they act as they do. Subjective thoughts and feelings, which scientists tend to dismiss because they are difficult to measure, are the focus of the interpretive sociologist's attention.

Critical Sociology

Like the interpretive orientation, critical sociology developed in reaction to what many sociologists saw as the limitations of positivist

sociology. In this case, however, the problem involves the central principle of scientific research: objectivity. Positivist sociology holds that reality is "out there" and that the researcher's job is to study and document how society works. But Karl Marx, who founded the critical orientation, rejected the idea that society exists as a "natural" system. To assume that society is somehow "fixed," he claimed, is the same as saying that society cannot be changed. Positivist sociology, in his view, ends up supporting the status quo. **Critical sociology,** by contrast, is *the study of society that focuses on the need for social change.*

The Importance of Change

Rather than asking the positivist question "How does society work?" critical sociologists ask moral and political questions, especially "Should society exist in its present form?" Their answer, typically, is that it should not. Critical sociology does not reject science completely—Marx (like critical sociologists today) used scientific methods to learn about inequality. But critical sociology does reject the scientific neutrality that requires researchers to try to be "objective" and limit their work to studying the status quo.

One recent account of the critical orientation, echoing Marx, claims that the point of this type of sociology is "not just to research the social world but to change it in the direction of democracy and social justice" (Feagin & Hernán, 2001:1). In making value judgments about how society should be changed, critical sociology rejects Weber's goal that sociology be a value-free science and emphasizes instead that sociologists should be activists in pursuit of greater social equality.

Sociologists using the critical orientation seek to change not only society but also the character of research itself. They often identify personally with their research subjects and encourage them to help decide what to study and how to do the work. Often researchers and subjects use their findings to provide a voice for less powerful people and advance the political goal of a more equal society (Hess, 1999; Feagin & Hernán, 2001; Perrucci, 2001).

Sociology as Politics

Positivist sociologists object to taking sides in this way, claiming that critical sociology (whether feminist, Marxist, or of some other critical orientation) becomes political, lacks scientific objectivity, and cannot correct for its own biases. Critical sociologists respond that *all* research is political in that either it calls for change or it does not; sociologists thus have no choice about their work being political, but they can choose *which* positions to support.

Critical sociology is an activist approach that ties knowledge to action and seeks not just to understand the world as it exists but also to improve it. In general, positivist sociology tends to appeal to researchers who try to be nonpolitical or who have more conservative political views; critical sociology appeals to those whose politics ranges from liberal to radical left.

Sociology: Perspective, Theory, and Method

Imagine that you are a positivist sociologist. How might you criticize
critical sociology? Now imagine that you are a critical sociologist.
How might you criticize positivist sociology?

gender   the personal traits and social positions that members of
a society attach to being female or male

SUMMING UP

Three Research Orientations in Sociology

	Positivist Sociology	Interpretive Sociology	Critical Sociology
What is reality?	Society is an orderly system. There is an objective reality "out there."	Society is ongoing interaction. People construct reality as they attach meanings to their behavior.	Society is patterns of inequality. Reality is that some categories of people dominate others.
How do we conduct research?	Using a scientific orientation, the researcher carefully observes behavior, gathering empirical, ideally quantitative, data. Researcher tries to be a neutral observer.	Seeking to look "deeper" than outward behavior, the researcher focuses on subjective meaning. The researcher gathers qualitative data, discovering the subjective sense people make of their world. Researcher is a participant.	Seeking to go beyond positivism's focus on studying the world as it is, the researcher is guided by politics and uses research as a strategy to bring about desired social change. Researcher is an activist.
Corresponding theoretical approach	Structural-functional approach	Symbolic-interaction approach	Social-conflict approach

Research Orientations and Theory

Is there a link between research orientations and sociological theory? There is no precise connection, but each of the three ways to do sociology—positivist, interpretive, and critical—does stand closer to one of the theoretical approaches presented earlier in this chapter. The positivist orientation is linked to the structural-functional approach (because both are concerned with the scientific goal of understanding society as it is), the interpretive orientation to the symbolic-interaction approach (because both focus on the meanings people attach to their social world), and the critical orientation to the social-conflict approach (because both seek to reduce social inequality). The Summing Up table provides a quick review of the differences among the three ways to do sociology. Many sociologists favor one orientation over another; however, because each provides useful insights, it is a good idea to become familiar with all three.

Gender and Research

In recent years, sociologists have become aware that research is affected by **gender,** *the personal traits and social positions that members of a society attach to being female or male.* Gender can affect sociological research in five ways (Eichler, 1988; Giovannini, 1992):

1. **Androcentricity.** *Androcentricity* (literally, "focus on the male") means approaching an issue from a male perspective. Some-

times researchers act as if only men's activities are important, ignoring what women do. For years, sociologists studying occupations focused on the paid labor of men and overlooked the housework and child care traditionally performed by women. Research that tries to explain human behavior cannot ignore half of humanity.

   Gynocentricity—seeing the world from a female perspective—can also limit good sociological investigation. However, in our male-dominated society, this problem arises less often.

2. **Overgeneralizing.** This problem occurs when sociologists gather data only from men but then use that information to draw conclusions about all people. For example, a researcher might speak to a handful of male public officials and then form conclusions about an entire community.

3. **Gender blindness.** Failing to consider gender at all is called *gender blindness.* The lives of men and women differ in many ways. A study of growing old in the United States might suffer from gender blindness if it overlooked the fact that most elderly men live with spouses but elderly women generally live alone.

4. **Double standards.** Researchers must be careful not to judge men and women by different standards. For example, a family researcher who labels a couple "man and wife" may define the man as the "head of the household" and treat him as important while assuming that the woman simply engages in family "support work."

5. **Interference.** Another way gender can distort a study is if a subject reacts to the sex of the researcher, interfering with the

● Seeing Sociology
in Everyday Life

Think of three research topics about U.S. society that might be
affected by the gender of the researcher. In each case, explain why.

Go to the Multimedia Library at **mysoclab.com**
to see Jeff Lucas discuss "Experiments"

If you ask only male subjects about their attitudes or actions, you may be
able to support conclusions about "men" but not more generally about
"people." What would a researcher have to do to ensure that research data
support conclusions about all of society?

research operation. While studying a small community in
Sicily, for instance, Maureen Giovannini (1992) found that
many men treated her as a *woman* rather than as a *researcher*.
Some thought it inappropriate for an unmarried woman to
speak privately with a man. Others denied Giovannini access
to places they considered off-limits to women.

There is nothing wrong with focusing research on people of one
sex or the other. But all sociologists, as well as people who read their
work, should be mindful of how gender can affect an investigation.

Research Ethics

Like all other scientific investigators, sociologists must be aware that
their work can harm as well as help subjects and communities. For this
reason, the American Sociological Association—the major profes-

sional organization of sociologists in North America—has established
formal guidelines for conducting research (1997).

Sociologists must try to be skillful and fair-minded in their work.
They must disclose all research findings without omitting significant data. They should make their results available to other sociologists who may want to conduct a similar study.

Sociologists must also make sure that subjects taking part in a
research project are not harmed, and they must stop work right away
if they suspect that any subject is at risk of harm. Researchers are also
required to protect the privacy of individuals involved in a research
project, even if they come under pressure from authorities, such as the
police or the courts, to release confidential information. Researchers
must also get the *informed consent* of participants, which means that
the subjects must fully understand their responsibilities and the risks
that the research involves and agree to take part before the work begins.

Another guideline concerns funding. Sociologists must include in
their published reports all sources of financial support. They must avoid
accepting money from a source if there is any question about a conflict
of interest. Researchers must never accept funding from any organization that seeks to influence the research results for its own purposes.

The federal government also plays a part in research ethics. Every
college and university that seeks federal funding for research involving human subjects must have an *institutional review board* (IRB)
that examines grant applications and ensures that research will not
violate ethical standards.

Finally, there are global dimensions to research ethics. Before beginning work in another country, an investigator must become familiar
enough with that society to understand what people *there* are likely to
regard as a violation of privacy or a source of personal danger. In a
diverse society such as our own, the same rule applies to studying people whose cultural background differs from that of the researcher. The
Thinking About Diversity box offers tips on the sensitivity outsiders
should apply when studying Hispanic communities.

Research Methods

A **research method** is *a systematic plan for doing research*. Four widely
used methods of sociological investigation are experiments, surveys,
participant observation, and the use of existing sources. None is better or worse than any other. Rather, just as a carpenter chooses a
particular tool for a particular job, researchers select a method according to whom they want to study and what they want to learn.

Testing a Hypothesis: The Experiment

The **experiment** is *a research method for investigating cause and effect
under highly controlled conditions*. Experiments closely follow the logic
of science, testing a specific *hypothesis*, a statement of how two (or

research method a systematic plan for doing research

experiment
a research method for investigating cause and effect under highly controlled conditions

survey
a research method in which subjects respond to a series of statements or questions on a questionnaire or in an interview

participant observation
a research method in which investigators systematically observe people while joining them in their routine activities

use of existing sources

THINKING ABOUT DIVERSITY: RACE, CLASS, & GENDER

Studying the Lives of Hispanics

JORGE: If you are going to include Latinos in your research, you need to learn a little about their culture.

MARK: I'm interviewing lots of different families. What's special about interviewing Latinos?

JORGE: Sit down and I'll tell you a few things you need to know. . . .

Because our society is socially diverse, sociologists often find themselves studying people who differ from themselves. Learning, in advance, the ways of life of any category of people can ease the research process and ensure that no hard feelings are caused along the way.

Gerardo Marín and Barbara Van Oss Marín (1991) have identified five areas of concern when conducting research with Hispanic people, currently the largest minority in the United States.

1. **Be careful with terms.** The Maríns point out that "Hispanic" is a label of convenience used by the U.S. Census Bureau. Few people from Spanish- and Portuguese-speaking cultures think of themselves as "Hispanic"; most identify with a particular country, such as Peru, Cuba, Argentina, or Spain.

2. **Be aware of cultural differences.** By and large, the U.S. population is individualistic and competitive. Many Hispanics, by contrast, place more value on cooperation and community. An outsider may judge the behavior of a Hispanic subject as

conformist or overly trusting when in fact the person is simply trying to be helpful. Researchers should also realize that Hispanic respondents might agree with a particular statement merely out of politeness.

3. **Anticipate family dynamics.** Hispanic cultures have strong family loyalties. Asking subjects to reveal information about another family member may make them uncomfortable or even angry. The Maríns add that a researcher's request to speak privately with a Hispanic woman in the home may provoke suspicion or outright disapproval from her husband or father.

4. **Take your time.** Spanish cultures, the Maríns explain, tend to place the quality of relationships above simply getting a job done. A non-Hispanic researcher who tries to hurry an interview with a Hispanic family out of a desire not to delay the family's dinner may be

Ter Foxx\Alamy Images

considered rude for not proceeding at a more sociable and relaxed pace.

5. **Think about personal space.** Finally, Hispanics typically maintain closer physical contact than many non-Hispanics. Therefore, researchers who seat themselves across the room from their subjects may seem standoffish. Researchers might also wrongly label Hispanics "pushy" if they move closer than a non-Hispanic researcher finds comfortable.

Of course, Hispanics differ among themselves just as people in any category do, and these generalizations apply to some more than to others. But investigators should be aware of cultural dynamics when carrying out any research, especially in the United States, where hundreds of distinctive categories of people make up our multicultural society.

WHAT DO YOU THINK?

1. Give a specific example of damage to a study that might occur if researchers are not sensitive to the culture of their subjects.

2. What do researchers need to do to avoid the kinds of problems noted in this box?

3. Discuss the research process with classmates from various cultural backgrounds. In what ways are the concerns raised by people of different cultural backgrounds similar? In what ways do they differ?

more) variables are related. A hypothesis is really an educated guess about how variables are linked, usually expressed as an *if-then* statement: *If* this particular thing were to happen, *then* that particular thing will result. 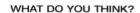 Go to mysoclab.com

An experimenter gathers the evidence needed to reject or not to reject the hypothesis in four steps: (1) State which variable is the *independent variable* (the "cause" of the change) and which is the *dependent variable* (the "effect," the thing that is changed). (2) Measure the initial value of the dependent variable. (3) Expose the

dependent variable to the independent variable (the "cause" or "treatment"). (4) Measure the dependent variable again to see what change, if any, took place. If the expected change took place, the experiment supports the hypothesis; if not, the hypothesis must be modified.

Successful experiments depend on careful control of all factors that might affect what the experiment is trying to measure. Control is easiest in a research laboratory. But experiments in an everyday location—"in the field," as sociologists say—have the advantage of letting researchers observe subjects in their natural settings.

Sociology: Perspective, Theory, and Method

Go to the Multimedia Library at mysoclab.com to view the video "The Stanford Prison Experiment"

○ Making the Grade

Sociologists use various research methods. Which one is chosen depends on the question being asked and also what resources are available for the study.

Illustration of an Experiment: The "Stanford County Prison"

Prisons can be violent settings, but is this due simply to the "bad" people who end up there? Or as Philip Zimbardo suspected, does prison itself somehow cause violent behavior? To answer this question, Zimbardo devised a fascinating experiment, which he called the "Stanford County Prison" (Zimbardo, 1972; Haney, Banks, & Zimbardo, 1973).

Zimbardo thought that once inside a prison, even emotionally healthy people are likely to engage in violence. So Zimbardo treated the *prison setting* as the independent variable capable of causing *violence*, the dependent variable.

To test this hypothesis, Zimbardo and his research team first constructed a realistic-looking "prison" in the basement of the psychology building on the campus of Stanford University. Then they placed an ad in a local newspaper, offering to pay young men to help with a two-week research project. To each of the seventy who responded they administered a series of physical and psychological tests and then selected the healthiest twenty-four.

The next step was to assign randomly half the men to be "prisoners" and half to be "guards." The plan called for the guards and prisoners to spend the next two weeks in the mock prison. The prisoners began their part of the experiment when real police officers "arrested" them at their homes. After searching and handcuffing the men, the police drove them to the local police station, where they were fingerprinted. Then police transported their captives to the Stanford prison, where the guards locked them up. Zimbardo started his video camera rolling and watched to see what would happen next. ● Go to mysoclab.com

The experiment turned into more than anyone had bargained for. Both guards and prisoners soon became embittered and hostile toward one another. Guards humiliated the prisoners by assigning them jobs such as cleaning toilets with their bare hands. The prisoners resisted and insulted the guards. Within four days, the researchers had removed five prisoners who displayed signs of "extreme emotional depression, crying, rage and acute anxiety" (Hanley, Banks, & Zimbardo, 1973:81). Before the end of the first week, the situation had become so bad that the researchers had to end the experiment.

The events that unfolded at the "Stanford County Prison" supported Zimbardo's hypothesis that prison violence is rooted in the social character of jails themselves, not in the personalities of individual guards and prisoners. This finding raised questions about our society's prisons, leading to some basic reforms. Zimbardo's experiment also shows the potential of research to threaten the physical and mental well-being of subjects. Such dangers are not always as obvious as they were in this case. Therefore, researchers must carefully consider the potential harm to subjects at all stages of their work and halt any study, as Zimbardo did, if subjects suffer harm of any kind.

○ **CRITICAL REVIEW** In carrying out the "Stanford County Prison" study, the researchers chose to do an experiment because they were interested in testing a hypothesis. In this case, Zimbardo and his colleagues wanted to find out if the prison setting itself (rather than the personalities of individual guards and prisoners) is the cause of prison violence. The fact that the "prison" erupted in violence—even using guards and prisoners with "healthy" profiles—supports their hypothesis.

○ **CHECK YOUR LEARNING** How might Zimbardo's findings help explain the abuse of Iraqi prisoners by U.S. soldiers after the 2003 invasion?

Asking Questions: Survey Research

A **survey** is *a research method in which subjects respond to a series of statements or questions on a questionnaire or in an interview.* The most widely used of all research methods, the survey is well suited to studying what cannot be observed directly, such as political attitudes or religious beliefs.

A survey targets some *population*, for example, unmarried mothers or adults living in rural counties in Wisconsin. Sometimes every adult in the country is the survey population, as in polls taken during national political campaigns. Of course, contacting a vast number of people is all but impossible, so researchers usually study a *sample*, a much smaller number of subjects selected to represent the entire population. Surveys using samples of as few as 1,500 people commonly give accurate estimates of public opinion for the entire country.

Beyond selecting subjects, the survey must have a specific plan for asking questions and recording answers. The most common way to do this is to give subjects a *questionnaire* with a series of written statements or questions. Often the researcher lets subjects choose possible responses to each item, as on a multiple-choice test. Sometimes, though, a researcher may want subjects to respond freely, to permit all opinions to be expressed. Of course, this free-form approach means that the researcher later has to make sense out of what can be a bewildering array of answers.

In an *interview*, a researcher personally asks subjects a series of questions, thereby solving one problem common to the questionnaire method: the failure of some subjects to return the questionnaire to the researcher. A further difference is that interviews give participants freedom to respond as they wish. Researchers often ask follow-up questions to clarify an answer or to probe a bit more deeply. In doing this, however, a researcher must avoid influencing the subject even in subtle ways, such as by raising an eyebrow as the subject offers an answer.

Sociology: Perspective, Theory, and Method

Illustration of Survey Research: Studying the African American Elite

Do highly successful African Americans escape the sting of racism? The sociologist Lois Benjamin—herself a successful college professor and the first African American faculty member at the University of Tampa—thought the answer was no. To investigate the effects of racism on talented African American men and women, Benjamin set out to conduct survey research.

Benjamin (1991) chose to interview subjects rather than distribute a questionnaire because she wanted to enter into a conversation with her subjects, to ask follow-up questions, and to be able to pursue topics that might come up in conversation. A second reason Benjamin favored interviews over questionnaires is that racism is a sensitive topic. A supportive researcher can make it easier for subjects to answer painful questions more freely.

Because conducting interviews takes a great deal of time, Benjamin had to limit the number of people in her study. She settled for 100 men and women. Even this small number kept Benjamin busy for more than two years of scheduling, traveling, and meeting with respondents. She spent another two years transcribing the tapes of her interviews, sorting out what the hours of talk told her about racism, and writing up her results.

Benjamin began by interviewing people she knew and asking them to suggest others. This strategy is called *snowball sampling* because the number of individuals included grows rapidly over time. Snowball sampling is appealing because it is an easy way to do research: We begin with familiar people, who provide introductions to their friends and colleagues. The drawback, however, is that snowball sampling rarely produces a sample that is representative of the larger population. Benjamin's sample probably contained many like-minded individuals, and it was certainly biased toward people willing to talk openly about race. She understood these problems and tried to include in her sample people of both sexes, of different ages, and representing different regions of the country. The next Thinking About Diversity box presents a statistical profile of Benjamin's respondents along with some tips on how to read tables.

Benjamin based all her interviews on a series of questions and allowed her subjects to answer however they wished. As usually happens, the interviews took place in a wide range of settings. She met subjects in offices (hers or theirs), in hotel rooms, and in cars. In each case, Benjamin tape-recorded the conversation, which lasted from two-and-one-half to three hours, so that she would not be distracted by taking notes.

As research ethics demand, Benjamin offered complete anonymity to participants. Even so, many of the women and men in her study—including notables such as Vernon E. Jordan Jr., the former president of the National Urban League, and Yvonne Walker-

Focus groups are a type of survey in which a small number of people representing a target population are asked for their opinions about some issue or product. Here a sociology professor asks students to evaluate textbooks for use in her introductory class.

Jupiter Images/Polka Dot/Alamy Images Royalty Free

Taylor, the first woman president of Wilberforce University—were accustomed to being in the public eye and permitted Benjamin to use their names.

What surprised Benjamin most about her research was how eagerly many subjects responded to her request for an interview. These normally busy men and women appeared to go out of their way to contribute to her project. Furthermore, once the interviews were under way, many of her subjects became very emotional. Benjamin reports that at some point in the conversation, about 40 of her 100 subjects cried. For them, apparently, the research provided an opportunity to release feelings and share experiences they had never revealed to anyone before. How did Benjamin respond to the expression of such sentiments? She reports that she cried along with her respondents.

Of the research orientations described earlier in this chapter, you will see that Benjamin's research fits best under interpretive sociology (she wanted to find out what race meant to her subjects) and critical sociology (she undertook the study partly to show that racial prejudice still exists). Many of her subjects reported fearing that race might someday undermine their success, and others spoke of a race-based "glass ceiling" preventing them from reaching the highest positions in U.S. society. Summarizing her findings, Benjamin concluded that despite the improving social standing of African Americans, black people in the United States still suffer the sting of racial hostility.

Seeing Sociology
in Everyday Life

Suggest a research topic that might lead a researcher to use a
questionnaire. What about a topic that would call for interviews?

Go to the Multimedia Library at mysoclab.com to
view the slideshow "How to Read a Table"

THINKING ABOUT DIVERSITY: RACE, CLASS, & GENDER

Lois Benjamin's African American Elite: Using Tables in Research

Say you want to present a lot of information about a diverse population. How do you do it quickly and easily? The answer is by using a table. A table provides a lot of information in a small amount of space, so learning to read tables can increase your reading efficiency. When you spot a table, look first at the title to see what information it contains. The title of the table presented here provides a profile of the 100 subjects participating in Lois Benjamin's research. Across the top of the table, you will see eight variables that describe these men and women. Reading down each column, note the categories within each variable; the percentages in each column add up to 100.

Starting at the top left, we see that Benjamin's sample was mostly men (63 percent, versus 37 percent women). In terms of age, most of the respondents (68 percent) were in the middle stage of life, and most grew up in a predominantly black community in the South or in the North or Midwest region of the United States.

These individuals are indeed a professional elite. Notice that half have earned either a doctorate (32 percent) or a medical or law degree (17 percent). Given their extensive education (and Benjamin's own position as a professor), we should not be surprised that the largest share (35 percent) work in academic institutions. In terms of income, these are wealthy individuals, with most (64 percent) earning

Reuben Burrell/ Hampton University/Lois Benjamin

more than $50,000 annually back in 1990 (a salary that only 39 percent of full-time workers make even today).

Finally, we see that these 100 individuals are generally left of center in their political views. In part, this reflects their extensive schooling (which encourages progressive thinking) and the tendency of academics to fall on the liberal side of the political spectrum.

Go to mysoclab.com

WHAT DO YOU THINK?

1. Why are statistical data, such as those in this table, an efficient way to convey a lot of information?

2. Looking at the table, can you determine how long it took most people to become part of this elite? Explain your answer.

3. Do you see any ways in which this African American elite might differ from a comparable white elite? If so, what are they?

CRITICAL REVIEW Professor Benjamin chose the survey as her method because she wanted to ask a lot of questions and gather information from her subjects. Certainly, some of the information she collected could have been obtained using a questionnaire. But she decided to carry out interviews because she was dealing with a complex and sensitive topic. Interacting with her subjects one on one for several hours, Benjamin could put them at ease, discuss personal matters, and ask them follow-up questions.

CHECK YOUR LEARNING Could this research have been carried out by a white sociologist? Why or why not?

In the Field: Participant Observation

Participant observation is *a research method in which investigators systematically observe people while joining them in their routine activities.* This method lets researchers study everyday social life in any natural setting, from a nightclub to a religious seminary. Cultural anthropologists use participant observation to study other societies, calling this method *fieldwork.*

At the beginning of a field study, most researchers do not have a specific hypothesis in mind. In fact, they may not yet realize what the important questions will turn out to be. This makes most participant observation *exploratory* and *descriptive*, falling within interpretive sociology and producing mostly qualitative, rather than quantitative, data. Compared with experiments and surveys, participant observation has few hard-and-fast rules. But this flexibility allows investigators to explore the unfamiliar and adapt to the unexpected.

Participant observers try to gain entry into a setting without disturbing the routine behavior of others. Their role is twofold: To gain an insider's viewpoint, they must become participants in the setting, "hanging out" for months or even years, trying to act, think, and even feel the same way as the people they are observing; at the same time, they must remain observers, standing back from the action and applying the sociological perspective to social patterns that others take for granted.

Because the personal impressions of a single researcher play such a central role, critics claim that participant observation falls short of scientific standards. Yet its personal approach is also a strength: Where a high-profile team of sociologists administering a formal survey

The Talented 100: Lois Benjamin's African American Elite

Sex	Age	Childhood Racial Setting	Childhood Region	Highest Educational Degree	Job Sector	Income	Political Orientation
Male 63%	35 or younger 6%	Mostly black 71%	West 6%	Doctorate 32%	College or university 35%	More than $50,000 64%	Radical left 13%
Female 37%	36 to 54 68%	Mostly white 15%	North or Midwest 32%	Medical or law 17%	Private, for-profit 17%	$35,000 to $50,000 18%	Liberal 38%
	55 or older 26%	Racially mixed 14%	South 38%	Master's 27%	Private, nonprofit 9%	$20,000 to $34,999 12%	Moderate 28%
			Northeast 12%	Bachelor's 13%	Government 22%	Less than $20,000 6%	Conservative 5%
			Other 12%	Less 11%	Self-employed 14%		Depends on issue 14%
					Retired 3%		Unknown 2%
100%	100%	100%	100%	100%	100%	100%	100%

Source: Adapted from Lois Benjamin, *The Black Elite: Facing the Color Line in the Twilight of the Twentieth Century* (Chicago: Nelson-Hall, 1991), p. 276.

might disrupt a setting, a sensitive participant observer often can gain important insight into people's behavior.

Illustration of Participant Observation: *Street Corner Society*

Did you ever wonder what everyday life was like in an unfamiliar neighborhood? In the late 1930s, a young graduate student at Harvard University named William Foote Whyte (1914–2000) set out to study social life in a rather rundown section of Boston. His curiosity led him to carry out four years of participant observation in this neighborhood, which he called "Cornerville."

At the time, Cornerville was home to first- and second-generation Italian immigrants. Most were poor, and many Bostonians considered Cornerville a place to avoid, a slum inhabited by criminals. Wanting to learn the truth, Whyte set out to discover for himself exactly what life was like inside this community. His celebrated book, *Street Corner Society* (1981, orig. 1943), describes Cornerville as a community with its own code of values, complex social patterns, and particular social conflicts.

To start, Whyte considered a range of research methods. He could have taken questionnaires to one of Cornerville's community centers and asked local people to fill them out. Or he could have invited members of the community to come to his Harvard office for interviews. But it is easy to see that such formal strategies would have gained little cooperation from the local people and produced few insights. Whyte decided, therefore, to ease into Cornerville life and slowly build a personal understanding of this rather mysterious place.

Soon enough, Whyte discovered the challenges of even getting started in field research. As an upper-middle-class WASP graduate student from Harvard, he stood out on the streets of Cornerville. Even a friendly overture from such an outsider could seem pushy and rude. Early on, Whyte dropped in at a local bar, hoping to buy a woman a drink and encourage her to talk about Cornerville. Looking around the room, he could find no woman alone. He thought he might have an opportunity when he saw a man sit down with two women. He walked over and asked, "Pardon me. Would you mind if I joined you?" Instantly, he realized his mistake:

> There was a moment of silence while the man stared at me. Then he offered to throw me down the stairs. I assured him that this would not be necessary, and demonstrated as much by walking right out of there without any assistance. (1981:289)

Sociology: Perspective, Theory, and Method

Seeing Sociology in Everyday Life

As the photo below suggests, conducting participant observation requires researchers to adapt to unfamiliar surroundings.

Read an account of participant observation research, "Hanging Tongues: A Social Encounter with the Assembly Line" by William E. Thompson, on mysoclab.com

Michael Doolittle\The Image Works

Participant observation is a method of sociological research that allows a researcher to investigate people as they go about their everyday lives in some "natural" setting. At its best, participant observation makes you a star in your own reality show, but living in what may be a strange setting far from home for months at a time is always challenging.

As this incident suggests, gaining entry to a community is the vital—and sometimes hazardous—first step in field research. "Breaking in" requires patience, ingenuity, and a little luck. Whyte's big break came in the form of a young man named "Doc," whom he met in a local social service agency. Whyte complained to Doc about how hard it was to make friends in Cornerville. Doc responded by taking Whyte under his wing and introducing him to others in the community. With Doc's help, Whyte soon became a neighborhood regular.

Whyte's friendship with Doc illustrates the importance of a *key informant* in field research. Such people not only introduce a researcher to a community but often remain a source of information and help. But using a key informant also has its risks. Because any person has a particular circle of friends, a key informant's guidance is certain to "spin" the study in one way or another. Moreover, in the eyes of others, the reputation of the key informant, for better or worse, usually rubs off on the investigator. So although a key informant is helpful early on, a participant observer must seek a broader range of contacts.

Having entered the Cornerville world, Whyte quickly learned another lesson: A field researcher needs to know when to speak and when to shut up. One evening, he joined a group discussing neighborhood gambling. Wanting to get the facts straight, Whyte asked innocently, "I suppose the cops were all paid off?"

> The gambler's jaw dropped. He glared at me. Then he denied vehemently that any policeman had been paid off and immediately switched the conversation to another subject. For the rest of that evening I felt very uncomfortable.

The next day, Doc offered some sound advice:

> "Go easy on that 'who,' 'what,' 'why,' 'when,' 'where' stuff, Bill. You ask those questions and people will clam up on you. If people accept you, you can just hang around, and you'll learn the answers in the long run without even having to ask the questions." (1981:303)

In the months and years that followed, Whyte became familiar with everyday life in Cornerville and even married a local woman with whom he would spend the rest of his life. In the process, he learned that the common stereotypes were wrong. In Cornerville, most people worked hard, many were quite successful, and some even boasted of sending children to college. Even today, Whyte's book makes for fascinating reading about the deeds, dreams, and disappointments of immigrants and their children living in one ethnic community, and it contains the rich detail that can only come from years of participant observation.

CRITICAL REVIEW To study the community he called Cornerville, Professor Whyte chose participant observation—a good choice because he did not have a specific hypothesis to test, nor did he know at the outset exactly what the questions were. By moving into this community for several years, Whyte was able to come to know the place and to paint a complex picture of social life there. Read on mysoclab.com

CHECK YOUR LEARNING Give an example of a topic for sociological research that would be best studied using (1) an experiment, (2) a survey, and (3) participant observation.

Using Available Data: Existing Sources

Not all research requires that investigators collect new data. Sometimes sociologists make use of existing sources, data collected by others.

The data most widely used by researchers are gathered by government agencies such as the U.S. Census Bureau. Data about other nations in the world are found in various publications of the United Nations and the World Bank.

Using available information saves time and money. This method has special appeal to sociologists with low budgets. And in fact, government data are usually more extensive and more accurate than what researchers could obtain on their own.

But using available data has problems of its own. Data may not be available in the exact form that is needed. For example, you may be able to find the average salaries paid to professors at your school but not separate figures for the amounts paid to women and men. Further, there are always questions about how accurate the existing data are. In his nineteenth-century study of suicide, described earlier, Emile Durkheim used official records. But Durkheim had no way to know if a death classified as a suicide was really an accident or vice versa.

Sociology: Perspective, Theory, and Method

┌─○ Making the Grade

Using existing sources—especially in clever and creative ways, as
Baltzell did—is the key to conducting historical research in sociology.

┌─○ Making the Grade

Can you describe a research project that might be carried out on your
campus using existing sources? Explain your research question and
what documents you would use.

Illustration of the Use of Existing Sources:
A Tale of Two Cities

Why might one city have been home to many famous people and
another have produced hardly any famous people at all? To those of
us living in the present, historical data offer a key to unlocking secrets
of the past. The award-winning study *Puritan Boston and Quaker
Philadelphia*, by E. Digby Baltzell (1979), shows how a researcher can
use available data to do historical research.

The story begins with Baltzell making a chance visit to Bowdoin
College in Maine. As he walked into the college library, he saw on the
wall three portraits—of the celebrated author Nathaniel Hawthorne,
the famous poet Henry Wadsworth Longfellow, and Franklin Pierce,
the fourteenth president of the United States. He soon learned that all
three men were members of the same class at Bowdoin, graduating in
1825. How could it be, Baltzell wondered, that this small college had
graduated more famous people in a single year than his own, much
bigger University of Pennsylvania had graduated in its entire history?
To answer this question, Baltzell was soon paging through historical
documents to see whether the New England states had indeed produced more famous people than his native Pennsylvania.

What were Baltzell's data? He turned to the *Dictionary of American Biography*, twenty volumes profiling more than 13,000 outstanding men and women in fields such as politics, law, and the arts. The
dictionary told Baltzell who was great, and he realized that the longer
the biography, the more important the person is thought to be.

By the time Baltzell had identified the seventy-five individuals
with the longest biographies, he saw a striking pattern. Massachusetts
had the most by far, with twenty-one of the seventy-five top achievers.
The New England states, combined, claimed thirty-one entries. By
contrast, Pennsylvania could boast of only two, and all the states in
the Middle Atlantic region had just twelve. Looking more closely,
Baltzell discovered that most of New England's great achievers had
grown up in and around the city of Boston. Again, in stark contrast,
almost no one of comparable standing came from his own Philadelphia,
a city with many more people than Boston.

What could explain this remarkable pattern? Baltzell drew inspiration from the German sociologist Max Weber (1958, orig.
1904–05), who argued that a region's record of achievement was
influenced by its major religious beliefs. In the religious differences
between Boston and Philadelphia, Baltzell found the answer to his
puzzle. Boston was a Puritan settlement, founded by people who
highly valued the pursuit of excellence and public achievement.
Philadelphia, by contrast, was settled by Quakers, who believed in
equality and avoided public notice.

Both the Puritans and the Quakers had fled religious persecution
in England, but once people settled in the new land, the two religious traditions produced quite different cultural patterns. Convinced of humanity's innate sinfulness, Boston Puritans built a rigid

society in which family, church, and school regulated people's behavior. They celebrated hard work as a means of glorifying God and
viewed public success as a reassuring sign of God's blessing. In short,
Puritanism fostered a disciplined and ambitious life in which people
both sought and respected achievement.

Philadelphia's Quakers, by contrast, built their way of life on the
belief that all human beings are basically good. They saw little need
for strong social institutions to "save" people from sinfulness. They
believed in equality, so even those who became rich considered themselves no better than anyone else. Thus rich and poor alike lived mod-
estly and discouraged one another from standing out by seeking fame
or running for public office.

In Baltzell's sociological imagination, Boston and Philadelphia
took the form of two social "test tubes": Puritanism was poured into
one, Quakerism into the other. Centuries later, we can see that different "chemical reactions" occurred in each case. The two belief systems apparently led to different attitudes toward personal
achievement, which in turn shaped the history of each region. Today,
we can see that Boston's Kennedys (despite being Catholic) are only
one of that city's many families that exemplify the Puritan pursuit of
recognition and leadership. By contrast, there has never been even
one family with such stature in the entire history of Philadelphia.

Baltzell's study uses scientific logic, but it also illustrates the
interpretive approach by showing how people make sense of their
world. His research reminds us that sociological investigation often
involves mixing research orientations to fit a particular problem.
The Summing Up table provides a quick review of the four major
methods of sociological investigation.

┌─○ **CRITICAL REVIEW** The main reason Professor Baltzell
chose to use existing sources is that this is a good way to learn
about history. The *Dictionary of American Biography* offers a great
deal of information about people who lived long ago and obviously are not available for an interview. At the same time, existing
sources were not created with the purpose of answering a modern-
day sociologist's questions. For this reason, using such documents requires a critical eye and a good deal of creative thinking.

└─○ **CHECK YOUR LEARNING** What other questions about
life in the past might you wish to answer using existing sources?

Putting It All Together: Ten Steps in Sociological Research

The following ten questions will guide you through a research project in sociology:

1. **What is your topic?** Being curious and using the sociological
   perspective can generate ideas for social research at any time

○ Making the Grade

The ten steps listed below are a summary of what is needed to conduct good sociological research.

○ Making the Grade

Study the Summing Up table below to be sure that you understand the four major research methods.

SUMMING UP

Four Research Methods

	Experiment	Survey	Participant Observation	Existing Sources
Application	For explanatory research that specifies relationships between variables Generates quantitative data	For gathering information about issues that cannot be directly observed, such as attitudes and values Useful for descriptive and explanatory research Generates quantitative or qualitative data	For exploratory and descriptive study of people in a "natural" setting Generates qualitative data	For exploratory, descriptive, or explanatory research whenever suitable data are available
Advantages	Provides the greatest opportunity to specify cause-and-effect relationships Replication of research is relatively easy	Sampling, using questionnaires, allows surveys of large populations Interviews provide in-depth responses	Allows study of "natural" behavior Usually inexpensive	Saves time and expense of data collection Makes historical research possible
Limitations	Laboratory settings have an artificial quality Unless the research environment is carefully controlled, results may be biased	Questionnaires must be carefully prepared and may yield a low return rate Interviews are expensive and time-consuming	Time-consuming Replication of research is difficult Researcher must balance roles of participant and observer	Researcher has no control over possible biases in data Data may only partially fit current research needs

and in any place. Pick a topic you find interesting and that you think is important to study.

2. **What have others already learned?** You are probably not the first person with an interest in some issue. Visit the library and search the Internet to see what theories and methods other researchers have applied to your topic. In reviewing the existing research, note problems that have come up to avoid repeating past mistakes.

3. **What, exactly, are your questions?** Are you seeking to explore an unfamiliar setting? To describe some category of people? To investigate cause and effect between variables? Clearly state the goals of your research, and operationalize all variables.

4. **What will you need to carry out research?** How much time and money are available to you? What special equipment or skills does the research require? Can you do all the work yourself?

5. **Are there ethical concerns?** Might the research harm anyone? How can you minimize the chances for injury? Will you promise your subjects anonymity? If so, how will you ensure that anonymity will be maintained?

6. **What method will you use?** Consider all major research strategies and combinations of methods. The most suitable method will depend on the kinds of questions you are asking and the resources available to you.

7. **How will you record the data?** The research method you use guides your data collection. Be sure to record information accurately and in a way that will make sense to you later on (it may be months before you write up the results of your work). Watch out for any personal bias that may creep into your work.

8. **What do the data tell you?** Determine what the data say about your initial questions. If your study involves a specific hypothesis, you should be able to confirm, reject, or modify it on the basis of your findings. Keep in mind that there will be several ways to interpret your results, depending on the theoretical approach you apply, and you should consider them all.

9. **What are your conclusions?** Prepare a final report explaining what you have learned. Also, evaluate your own work. What problems arose during the research process? What questions were left unanswered?

Sociology: Perspective, Theory, and Method

stereotype a simplified description applied to every person in some category

CONTROVERSY & DEBATE

Is Sociology Nothing More Than Stereotypes?

JENA: (*raising her eyes from her notebook*) Today, in sociology class, we talked about stereotypes.

MARCIA: (*trying to focus on her science lab*) OK, here's one: Roommates don't like to be disturbed when they're studying.

JENA: Seriously, my studious friend, we all have stereotypes, even professors.

MARCIA: (*becoming faintly interested*) Like what?

JENA: Professor Chandler said today in class that Protestants are most likely to kill themselves. And later Yannina—this girl from, I think, Ecuador—said something like "You Americans are rich, but you don't take marriage seriously, and you love to divorce!"

MARCIA: My brother said to me last week that "everybody knows you have to be black to play professional basketball." Now there's a stereotype!

College students, like everyone else, are quick to make generalizations about people. As this chapter explains, sociologists, too, love to generalize by looking for social patterns in everyday life. However, beginning students of sociology may wonder if sociological generalizations aren't really the same thing as stereotypes. For example, are the statements reported by Jena and Marcia true generalizations or false stereotypes?

A **stereotype** is *a simplified description applied to every person in some category.* Each of the statements the students made is a stereotype that is false, for three reasons. First, rather than describing averages, each statement describes every person in some category in exactly the same way; second, even though many stereotypes often contain an element of truth, each of these three statements leaves out relevant

facts and distorts reality; and third, each statement is motivated by bias, spoken more as a put-down than as a fair-minded observation.

Good sociology makes generalizations, but they must meet three conditions. First, sociologists do not carelessly apply any generalization to everyone in a category. Second, sociologists make sure that a generalization squares with all available facts. And third, sociologists make generalizations fair-mindedly, in the interest of getting at the truth.

Jena recalled her professor saying that the suicide rate among Protestants is higher than the rate among Catholics or Jews. However, the statement "Protestants are most likely to kill themselves" is not a fair generalization because most Protestants take no such action. It would be just as wrong to jump to the conclusion that a particular friend, because he is a Protestant, is about to end his own life. (Imagine refusing to lend money to a roommate, who happens to be

Photodisc/Getty Images

A sociology classroom is a good place to get at the truth behind common stereotypes.

a Baptist, explaining, "Well, given your risk of suicide, I might never get paid back!")

Second, sociologists shape their generalizations to available facts. A more factual version of the statement Yannina made is that by world standards, the U.S. population has a very high standard of living, that almost everyone in our society does marry at some point with every intention of staying married, and that even though our divorce rate is among the world's highest, few people take pleasure in divorcing.

Third, sociologists try to be fair-minded and want to get at the truth. The statements made by Marcia's brother about African Americans and basketball is a stereotype and therefore not good sociology for two reasons. First, it is simply not true, and second, it seems motivated by racial bias rather than truth-seeking.

The bottom line, then, is that good sociological generalizations are *not* the same as stereotyping. But a college sociology course is an excellent setting for getting at the truths behind common stereotypes. The classroom encourages discussion and offers the factual information you need to decide whether a particular statement is a valid sociological generalization or a harmful or unfair stereotype.

WHAT DO YOU THINK?

1. Can you think of a common stereotype of sociologists? What is it? After reading this box, do you still think it is valid?

2. Do you think taking a sociology course can help correct people's stereotypes? Why or why not?

3. Can you think of a stereotype of your own that might be challenged by sociological analysis?

---

10. **How can you share what you have learned?** Consider making a presentation to a class or maybe even to a meeting of professional sociologists. The important point is to share what you have learned with others and to let them respond to your work.

The Controversy & Debate box discusses the use of the sociological perspective and reviews many of the ideas presented in this chapter. This box will help you apply what you have learned to the important question of how the generalizations made by sociologists differ from the common stereotypes we hear every day.

Sociology: Perspective, Theory, and Method

Seeing Sociology in Everyday Life

The Sociological Perspective

"Why do couples marry?"

We asked this question at the beginning of this chapter. The commonsense answer is that people marry because they are in love. But as this chapter has explained, society guides our everyday lives, affecting what we do, think, and feel. Look at the three photographs, each showing a couple who, we can assume, is "in love." In each case, can you provide some of the rest of the story? By looking at the categories that the people involved represent, explain how society is at work in bringing the two people together.

> **HINT** Society is at work on many levels. Consider (1) rules about same-sex and other-sex marriage, (2) laws defining the number of people who may marry, (3) the importance of race and ethnicity, (4) the importance of social class, (5) the importance of age, and (6) the importance of social exchange (what each partner offers the other). All societies enforce various rules that state who should or should not marry whom.

Jada Pinkett met Will Smith in 1995 when she auditioned for a part on his hit show, *The Fresh Prince of Bel Air*. Two years later, they married. What social patterns do you see?

Victor Malafronte/Getty Images Inc. - Hulton Archive Photos

In 1997, during the fourth season of her hit TV show, *Ellen*, Ellen DeGeneres "came out" as a lesbian, which put her on the cover of *Time* magazine. Since then, she has been an activist on behalf of gay and lesbian issues. Following California's brief legalization of same-sex marriage in 2008, she married her longtime girlfriend, Australian actress Portia de Rossi.

In 2000, at the age of fifty-six, Michael Douglas ended a twenty-three-year marriage in order to marry actress Catherine Zeta-Jones, who was then thirty-one. How likely is it that a fifty-six-year-old woman would marry a thirty-one-year-old man?

Applying SOCIOLOGY in Everyday Life

1. Analyze the marriages of your parents, other family members, and friends in terms of class, race, age, and other factors. What evidence can you find that society guides the feeling we call "love"?

2. Research the U.S. divorce rate over the past century. Using the sociological perspective, and try to identify societal factors that caused the divorce rate to rise or fall.

3. Explore your local area, and draw a sociological map of the community. Include the types of buildings (for example, "big, single-family homes," "rundown business district," "new office buildings," "student apartments") found in various places, and guess at the categories of people who live or work there. What patterns do you see?

Making the Grade

Sociology: Perspective, Theory, and Method

 Watch on mysoclab.com

What Is the Sociological Perspective?

The **SOCIOLOGICAL PERSPECTIVE** reveals the power of society to shape individual lives.
- C. Wright Mills called this point of view the "sociological imagination," which transforms personal troubles into public issues.
- Being an outsider or experiencing social crisis can encourage the sociological perspective.

APPLYING THE SOCIOLOGICAL PERSPECTIVE has many benefits:
- helping us understand the barriers and opportunities in our lives
- giving us an advantage in our careers
- guiding public policy

✓ Global awareness is an important part of the sociological perspective because our society's place in the world affects us all.

sociology the systematic study of human society

sociological perspective the special point of view of sociology that sees general patterns of society in the lives of particular people

global perspective the study of the larger world and our society's place in it

high-income countries the nations with the highest overall standards of living

middle-income countries nations with a standard of living about average for the world as a whole

low-income countries nations with a low standard of living in which most people are poor

Origins of Sociology

RAPID SOCIAL CHANGE helped trigger the development of sociology:
- rise of an industrial economy
- explosive growth of cities
- new political ideas

AUGUSTE COMTE named sociology in 1838.
- Early philosophers tried to describe the ideal society, but Comte wanted to understand society as it really is.
- Karl Marx and many later sociologists used sociology to try to make society better.

✓ The countries that experienced the most rapid social change were those in which sociology developed first.

positivism a scientific approach to knowledge based on "positive" facts as opposed to mere speculation

theory a statement of how and why specific facts are related

theoretical approach a basic image of society that guides thinking and research

structural-functional approach a framework for building theory that sees society as a complex system whose parts work together to promote solidarity and stability

social structure any relatively stable pattern of social behavior

social functions the consequences of a social pattern for the operation of society as a whole

manifest functions the recognized and intended consequences of any social pattern

latent functions the unrecognized and unintended consequences of any social pattern

social dysfunction any social pattern that may disrupt the operation of society

social-conflict approach a framework for building theory that sees society as an arena of inequality that generates conflict and change

gender-conflict approach a point of view that focuses on inequality and conflict between women and men

feminism support of social equality for women and men

race-conflict approach a point of view that focuses on inequality and conflict between people of different racial and ethnic categories

macro-level orientation a broad focus on social structures that shape society as a whole

micro-level orientation a close-up focus on social interaction in specific situations

symbolic-interaction approach a framework for building theory that sees society as the product of the everyday interactions of individuals

Theory: Linking Facts to Create Meaning

 macro-level

The **STRUCTURAL-FUNCTIONAL APPROACH** explores how social structures work together to help society operate.
- Auguste Comte, Emile Durkheim, and Herbert Spencer helped develop the structural-functional approach.

The **SOCIAL-CONFLICT APPROACH** shows how inequality creates conflict and causes change.
- Two important types of conflict analysis are the **gender-conflict approach**, linked to **feminism**, and the **race-conflict approach**.
- Karl Marx helped develop the social-conflict approach.

Explore on mysoclab.com

 micro-level

The **SYMBOLIC-INTERACTION APPROACH** studies how people, in everyday interaction, construct reality.
- Max Weber and George Herbert Mead helped develop the symbolic-interaction approach.

See the Applying Theory table.

✓ To get the full benefit of the sociological perspective, apply all three approaches.

Research: Doing Sociology

POSITIVIST SOCIOLOGY uses the logic of science to understand how variables are related.

- tries to establish cause and effect
- demands that researchers try to be objective

INTERPRETIVE SOCIOLOGY focuses on the meanings that people attach to behavior.

- People construct reality in their everyday lives.
- Weber's *Verstehen* is learning how people understand their world.

CRITICAL SOCIOLOGY uses research to bring about social change.

- focuses on inequality
- rejects the principle of objectivity, claiming that all research is political

See the Summing Up table.

✓ Gender, involving both researcher and subjects, can affect all research.

✓ All researchers must follow professional ethical guidelines for conducting research .

positivist sociology the study of society based on systematic observation of social behavior

science a logical system that develops knowledge from direct, systematic observation

empirical evidence information we can verify with our senses

concept a mental construct that represents some aspect of the world in a simplified form

variable a concept whose value changes from case to case

measurement a procedure for determining the value of a variable in a specific case

reliability consistency in measurement

validity actually measuring exactly what you intend to measure

correlation a relationship in which two (or more) variables change together

cause and effect a relationship in which change in one variable (the independent variable) causes change in another (the dependent variable)

interpretive sociology the study of society that focuses on discovering the meanings people attach to their social world

critical sociology the study of society that focuses on the need for social change

gender the personal traits and social positions that members of a society attach to being female or male

Methods: Strategies for Doing Research

The **EXPERIMENT** allows researchers to study cause and effect between two or more variables in a controlled setting.

- example of an experiment: Zimbardo's "Stanford County Prison"

SURVEY research uses questionnaires or interviews to gather subjects' responses to a series of questions.

- example of a survey: Benjamin's "Talented 100"

Through **PARTICIPANT OBSERVATION**, researchers join with people in a social setting for an extended period of time.

- example of participant observation: Whyte's *Street Corner Society*

Researchers use data collected by others from **EXISTING SOURCES** to save time and money.

- example of using existing sources: Baltzell's *Puritan Boston and Quaker Philadelphia*

research method a systematic plan for doing research

experiment a research method for investigating cause and effect under highly controlled conditions

survey a research method in which subjects respond to a series of statements or questions on a questionnaire or in an interview

participant observation a research method in which investigators systematically observe people while joining them in their routine activities

stereotype a simplified description applied to every person in some category

See the Summing Up table.

▣ Read on mysoclab.com

✓ Which method the researcher uses depends on the question being asked.

✓ Researchers combine these methods, depending on the specific goals of their study.

Sample Test Questions

Multiple-Choice Questions

1. **What does the sociological perspective show us about whom any individual chooses to marry?**
   a. There is no explaining personal feelings like love.
   b. People's actions reflect human free will.
   c. The operation of society guides many of our personal choices.
   d. In the case of love, opposites attract.

2. **The personal value of studying sociology includes**
   a. seeing the opportunities and constraints in our lives.
   b. the fact that it is good preparation for a number of careers.
   c. becoming more active participants in society.
   d. All of the above are correct.

3. **The discipline of sociology first developed in**
   a. countries experiencing rapid social change.
   b. countries with strong traditions.
   c. countries with a history of warfare.
   d. the world's poorest countries.

4. **Which early sociologist coined the term *sociology* in 1838?**
   a. Karl Marx
   b. Auguste Comte
   c. Adam Smith
   d. Herbert Spencer

5. **Sociology's social-conflict approach draws attention to**
   a. how structure contributes to the overall operation of society.
   b. how people construct meaning through interaction.
   c. patterns of social inequality.
   d. the stable aspects of society.

6. **Empirical evidence refers to**
   a. quantitative rather than qualitative data.
   b. what people consider "common sense."
   c. information we can verify with our senses.
   d. patterns found in every known society.

7. **When trying to measure people's "social class," you would have to keep in mind that**
   a. no measurement can ever be both reliable and valid.
   b. there are several ways to operationalize this variable.
   c. there is no way to measure "social class."
   d. in the United States, everyone agrees on what "social class" means.

8. **Interpretive sociology is a research orientation that**
   a. focuses on people's actions.
   b. sees an objective reality "out there."
   c. seeks to increase social justice.
   d. focuses on the meanings people attach to behavior.

9. **In research using participant observation, the problem of "breaking in" to a setting is often solved with the help of a**
   a. key informant.
   b. research assistant.
   c. bigger budget.
   d. sample.

10. **The critical sociology research orientation is linked most closely to which theoretical approach?**
    a. structural-functional approach
    b. social-conflict approach
    c. symbolic-interaction approach
    d. None of the above is correct.

ANSWERS: 1(c); 2(d); 3(a); 4(b); 5(c); 6(c); 7(b); 8(d); 9(a); 10(b).

Essay Questions

1. Explain why using the sociological perspective can make us seem less in control of our lives. In what ways does it actually give us greater power over our lives?

2. Guided by the discipline's three major theoretical approaches, come up with sociological questions about (a) television, (b) war, and (c) colleges and universities.

3. Discuss positivist sociology, interpretive sociology, and critical sociology so that you present each orientation clearly. Why might a sociologist prefer one orientation to another? Why is it important for a student of sociology to understand all three?

Promoting Bad Statistics

Joel Best

Who decides what is a social problem and which of many social problems will have our attention? Why do we believe that missing children, the homeless, domestic violence, and environmental illness are social problems? Why do we ignore other issues that are equally as serious and compelling? In this article, sociologist Joel Best explains how statistics, even dubious ones, are used to make cases for the importance of particular social problems and to gain the attention of the media, politicians, and the public.

In contemporary society, social problems must compete for attention. To the degree that one problem gains media coverage, moves to the top of politicians' agendas, or becomes the subject of public concern, others will be neglected. Advocates find it necessary to make compelling cases for the importance of particular social problems. They choose persuasive wording and point to disturbing examples, and they usually bolster their case with dramatic statistics.

Statistics have a fetish-like power in contemporary discussions about social problems. We pride ourselves on rational policy making, and expertise and evidence guide our rationality. Statistics become central to the process, numbers evoke science and precision; they seem to be nodules of truth, facts that distill the simple essence of apparently complex social processes. In a culture that treats facts and opinions as dichotomous terms, numbers signify truth—what we call "hard facts." In virtually every debate about social problems, statistics trump "mere opinion."

Reprinted from *Society* (March-April, 2001), reprinted by permission from Springer Science and Business Media.

Yet social problems statistics often involve dubious data. While critics occasionally call some number into question, it generally is not necessary for a statistic to be accurate—or even plausible—in order to achieve widespread acceptance. Advocates seeking to promote social problems often worry more about the processes by which policy makers, the press, and the public come to focus on particular problems, than about the quality of their figures. I seek here to identify some principles that govern this process. They are, if you will, guidelines for creating and disseminating dubious social problems statistics.

Although we talk about facts as though they exist independently of people, patiently awaiting discovery, someone has to produce—or construct—all that we know. Every social statistic reflects the choices that go into producing it The key choices involve definition and methodology. Whenever we count something, we must first define what it is we hope to count, and then choose the methods by which we will go about counting. In general, the press regards statistics as facts, little bits of truth. The human choices behind every number are forgotten; the very presentation of a number gives each claim credibility. In this sense, statistics are like fetishes.

◉ Any Number is Better than No Number

By this generous standard, a number need not bear close inspection, or even be remotely plausible. To choose an example first brought to light by Christina Hoff Sommers, a number of recent books, both popular and scholarly, have repeated the garbled claim that anorexia kills 150,000 women annually. (The figure seems to have originated from an estimate for the total number of women who are anorexic; only about 70 die each year from the disease.) It should have been obvious that something was wrong with this figure. Anorexia typically affects *young* women. Each year, roughly 8,500 females aged 15–24 die from all causes; another 47,000 women aged 25–44 also die. What are the chances, then, that there could be 150,000 deaths from anorexia each year? But, of course, most of us have no idea how many young women die each year—("It must be a lot. . . ."). When we hear that anorexia kills 150,000 young women per year, we assume that whoever cites the number must know that it is true. It is, after all, a number and therefore presumably factual.

Oftentimes, social problems statistics exist in splendid isolation. When there is only one number, that number has the weight of authority. It is accepted and repeated. People treat the statistic as authoritative because it is a statistic. Often, these lone numbers come from activists seeking to draw attention to neglected social phenomena. One symptom of societal neglect is that no one has bothered to do much research or compile careful records; there often are no official statistics or other sources for more accurate numbers. When reporters cover the story, they want to report facts. When activists have the only available figures, their numbers look like facts, so, in the absence of other numbers, the media simply report the activists' statistics.

Once a number appears in one news report, that story becomes a potential source for everyone seeking information about the social problem; officials, experts, activists, and other reporters routinely repeat figures that appear in press reports.

☻ Numbers Take on Lives of Their Own

David Luckenbill has referred to this as "number laundering." A statistic's origin—perhaps simply as someone's best guess—is soon forgotten, and through repetition, the figure comes to be treated as a straightforward fact—accurate and authoritative. The trail becomes muddy, and people lose track of the estimate's original source, but they become confident that the number must be correct because it appears everywhere.

It barely matters if critics challenge a number, and expose it as erroneous. Once a number is in circulation, it can live on, regardless of how thoroughly it may have been discredited. Today's improved methods of information retrieval—electronic indexes, full-text databases, and the Internet—make it easier than ever to locate statistics. Anyone who locates a number can, and quite possibly will, repeat it. That annual toll of 150,000 anorexia deaths has been thoroughly debunked, yet the figure continues to appear in occasional newspaper stories. Electronic storage has given us astonishing, unprecedented access to information, but many people have terrible difficulty sorting through what's available and distinguishing good information from bad. Standards for comparing and evaluating claims seem to be wanting. This is particularly true for statistics that are, after all, numbers and therefore factual, requiring no critical evaluation. Why not believe and repeat a number that everyone else uses? Still, some numbers do have advantages.

◉ Big Numbers are Better than Little Numbers

Remember: social problems claims must compete for attention; there are many causes and a limited amount of space on the front page of the *New York Times*. Advocates must find ways to make their claims compelling: they favor melodrama—terrible villains, sympathetic, vulnerable victims, and big numbers. Big numbers suggest that there is a big problem, and big problems demand attention, concern, action. They must not be ignored.

Advocates seeking to attract attention to a social problem soon find themselves pressed for numbers. Press and policy makers demand facts ("You say it's a problem? Well, how big a problem is it?"). Activists believe in the problem's seriousness, and they often spend much of their time talking to others who share that belief. They know that the problem is much more serious, much more common than generally recognized ("The cases we know about are only the tip of the iceberg."). When asked for figures, they thus offer their best estimates, educated guesses, guesstimates, ballpark figures, or stabs in the dark. Mitch Snyder, the most visible spokesperson for the homeless in the early 1980s, explained on ABC's "Nightline" how activists arrived at the figure of three million homeless: "Everybody demanded it. Everybody said we want a number. . . . We got on the phone, we made a lot of calls, we talked to a lot of people, and we said, 'Okay, here are some numbers.' They have no meaning, no value." Because activists sincerely believe that the new problem is big and important, and because they suspect that there is a very large dark figure of unreported or unrecorded cases, activists' estimates tend to be high, and to err on the side of exaggeration.

This helps explain the tendency to estimate the scope of social problems in large, suspiciously round figures. There are, we are told, one million victims of elder abuse each year, two million missing children, three million homeless, 60 million functionally illiterate Americans; child pornography may be, depending on your source, a $1 billion or $46 billion industry, and so on. Often, these estimates are the only available numbers.

The mathematician John Allen Paulos argues that innumeracy—the mathematical counterpart to illiteracy—is widespread and consequential. He suggests that innumeracy particularly shapes the way we deal with large numbers. Most of us understand hundreds, even thousands, but soon the orders of magnitude blur into a single category. "It's a lot." Even the most implausible figures can gain widespread acceptance When missing-children advocates charged that nearly two million children are missing each year, anyone might have done the basic math; there are about 60 million children under 18; if two million are missing, that would be one in 30, that is, every year, the equivalent of one child in every American schoolroom would be missing. A 900-student school would have 30 children missing from its student body each year. To be sure, the press debunked this statistic in 1985, but only four years after missing children became a highly publicized issue and the two-million estimate gained wide circulation. And, of course, having been discredited, the number survives and can still be encountered on occasion.

It is remarkable how often contemporary discussions of social problems make no effort to define what is at issue. Often, were given a dramatic, compelling example, perhaps a tortured, murdered child, then told that this terrible case is an example of a social problem—in this case, child abuse—and finally given a statistic: "There are more than three million reports of child abuse each year." The example, coupled with the problem's name, seems sufficient to make the definition self-evident. However, definitions cannot always be avoided.

◉ Definitions: Better Broad than Narrow

Because broad definitions encompass more kinds of cases, they justify bigger numbers, and we have already noted the advantages of big numbers. No definition is perfect; there are two principal ways definitions of social problems can be flawed. On the one hand, a definition might be too broad and encompass more than it ought to include. That is, broad definitions tend to identify what methodologists call false positives; they include some cases that arguably ought not to be included as part of the problem. On the other hand, a definition that is too narrow may exclude false negatives, cases that perhaps ought to be included as part of the problem.

In general, activists trying to promote a new social problem view false negatives as more troubling than false positives. Activists often feel frustrated trying to get people concerned about some social condition that has been ignored. The general failure to recognize and acknowledge that something is wrong is part of what the activists want to correct; therefore, they may be especially careful not to make things worse by defining the problem too narrowly. A definition that is too narrow fails to recognize a problem's full extent; in doing so, it helps perpetuate the history of neglecting the problem. Some activists favor definitions broad enough to encompass every case that ought to be included; that is, they promote broad definitions in hopes of eliminating all false negatives.

However, broad definitions may invite criticism. They include cases that not everyone considers instances of social problems; that is, while they minimize false negatives, they do so at the cost of maximizing cases that critics may see as false positives. The rejoinder to this critique returns us to the idea of neglect and the harm it causes. Perhaps, advocates acknowledge, their definitions may seem to be too broad, to encompass cases that seem too trivial to be counted as instances of the social problem. But how can we make that judgment? Here advocates are fond of pointing to terrible examples, to the victim whose one, brief, comparatively mild experience had terrible personal consequences; to the child who, having been exposed to a flasher, suffers a lifetime of devastating psychological consequences. Perhaps, advocates say, other victims with similar experiences suffer less or at least seem to suffer less. But is it fair to define a problem too narrowly to include everyone who suffers? Shouldn't our statistics measure the problem's full extent? While social problems statistics often go unchallenged, critics occasionally suggest that some number is implausibly large, or that a definition is too broad.

◉ Defending Numbers by Attacking Critics

When activists have generated a statistic as part of a campaign to arouse concern about some social problem, there is a tendency for them to conflate the number with the cause. Therefore, anyone who questions a statistic can be suspected of being unsympathetic to the larger claims, indifferent to the victims' suffering, and so on. *Ad hominem* attack on the motives of individuals challenging numbers is a standard response to statistical confrontations. These attacks allow advocates to refuse to budge; making *ad hominem* arguments lets them imply that their opponents don't want to acknowledge the truth, that their statistics are derived from ideology, rather than methodology. If the advocates' campaign has been reasonably successful, they can argue that there is now widespread appreciation that this is a big, serious problem, after all, the advocates' number has been widely accepted and repeated, surely it must be correct. A fallback stance—useful in those rare cases where public scrutiny leaves one's own numbers completely discredited—is to treat the challenge as meaningless nitpicking. Perhaps our statistics were flawed, the advocates acknowledge, but the precise number hardly makes a difference ("After all, even one victim is too many.").

Similarly, criticizing definitions for being too broad can provoke angry reactions. For advocates, such criticisms seem to deny victim's suffering, minimize the extent of the problem, and by extension endorse the status quo. If broader definitions reflect progress, more sensitive appreciation of the true scope of social problems, then calls for narrowing definitions are retrograde, insensitive refusals to confront society's flaws.

Of course, definitions must be operationalized if they are to lead to statistics. It is necessary to specify how the problem will be measured and the statistic produced. If there is to be a survey, who will be sampled? And how will the questions be worded? In what order will they be asked? How will the responses be coded? Most of what we call social-scientific methodology requires choosing how to measure social phenomena. Every statistic depends upon these choices. Just as advocates' preference for large numbers leads them to favor broad definitions, the desirability of broad definitions shapes measurement choices.

◉ Measures: Better Inclusive than Exclusive

Most contemporary advocates have enough sociological sophistication to allude to the dark figure—that share of a social problem that goes unreported and unrecorded. Official statistics, they warn, inevitably underestimate the size of social problems. This undercounting helps justify advocates' generous estimates (recall all those references to "the tip of the iceberg"). Awareness of the dark figure also justifies measurement decisions that maximize researchers' prospects for discovering and counting as many cases as possible.

Consider the first federally sponsored National Incidence Studies of Missing, Abducted, Runaway, and Thrownaway Children (NIS-MART). This was an attempt to produce an accurate estimate for the numbers of missing children. To estimate family abductions (in which a family member kidnaps a child) researchers conducted a telephone survey of households. The researchers made a variety of inclusive measurement decisions: an abduction could involve moving a child as little as 20 feet; it could involve the child's complete cooperation; there was no minimum time that the abduction had to last; those involved may not have considered what happened an abduction; and there was no need that the child's whereabouts be unknown (in most family abductions identified by NISMART, the child was not with someone who had legal custody, but everyone knew where the child was). Using these methods of measurement, a non-custodial parent who took a child for an unauthorized visit, or who extended an authorized visit for an extra night, was counted as having committed a "family abduction." If the same parent tried to conceal the taking or to prevent the custodial parent's contact with the child, the abduction was classified in the most serious ("policy-focal") category. The NISMART researchers concluded that there were 163,200 of these more serious family abductions each year, although evidence from states with the most thorough missing-children reporting systems suggests that only about 9,000 cases per year come to police attention. In other words, the researchers' inclusive measurement choices led to a remarkably high estimate. Media coverage of the family-abduction problem coupled this high figure with horrible examples—cases of abductions lasting years, involving long-term sexual abuse, ending in homicide, and so on. Although most of the episodes identified by NISMART's methods were relatively minor, the press implied that very serious cases were very common ("It's a big number!").

There is nothing atypical about the NISMART example. Advocacy research has become an important source of social problems statistics. Advocates hope research will produce large numbers, and they tend to believe that broad definitions are justified. They deliberately adopt inclusive research measurements that promise to minimize false negatives and generate large numbers. These measurement decisions almost always occur outside public scrutiny and only rarely attract attention. When the media report numbers, percentages, and rates, they almost never explain the definitions and measurements used to produce those statistics.

While many statistics seem to stand alone, occasions do arise when there are competing numbers or contradictory statistical answers to what seems to be the same question. In general, the media tend to treat such competing numbers with a sort of even-handedness.

◉ Competing Numbers are Equally Good

Because the media tend to treat numbers as factual, and to ignore definitions and measurement choices, inconsistent numbers pose a problem. Clearly, both numbers cannot be correct. Where a methodologist might try to ask how different advocates arrived at different numbers (in hopes of showing that one figure is more accurate than another, or at least of understanding how the different numbers might be products of different methods), the press is more likely to account for any difference in terms of the competitors' conflicting ideologies or agendas.

Consider the case of the estimates for the crowd size at the 1995 Million Man March. The event's very name set a standard for its success: as the date for the March approached, its organizers insisted that it would attract a million people, while their critics predicted that the crowd would never reach that size. On the day of the march, the organizers announced success: there were, they said, 1.5 to 2 million people present. Alas, the National Park Service Park Police, charged by Congress with estimating the size of demonstrations on the Capitol Mall, calculated that the march drew only 400,000 people (still more than any previous civil rights demonstration). The Park Police knew the Mall's dimensions, took aerial photos, and multiplied the area covered by the crowd by a multiplier based on typical crowd densities. The organizers, like the organizers of many previous demonstrations on the Mall, insisted that the Park Police estimate was far too low. Enter a team of aerial photo analysts from Boston University who eventually calculated that the crowd numbered 837,000 plus or minus 25 percent (i.e., they suggested there might have been a million people in the crowd).

The press covered these competing estimates in standard "he said-she said" style. Few reporters bothered to ask why the two estimates were different. The answer was simple: the BU researchers used a different multiplier. Where the Park Police estimated that there was one demonstrator per 3.6 square feet (actually a fairly densely-packed crowd), the BU researchers calculated that there was a person for every 1.8 square feet (the equivalent of being packed in a crowded elevator). But rather than trying to compare or evaluate the processes by which people arrived at the different estimates, most press reports treated the numbers as equally valid, and implied that the explanation for the difference lay in the motives of those making the estimates.

The March organizers (who wanted to argue that the demonstration had been successful) produced a high number; the Park Police (who, the March organizers insisted, were biased against the March) produced a low one, and the BU scientists (presumably impartial and authoritative) found something in between. The BU estimate quickly found favor in the media: it let the organizers save face (because the BU team conceded the crowd might have reached one million); it seemed to split the difference between the high and low estimates; and it apparently came from experts. There was no effort to judge the competing methods and assumptions behind the different numbers, for example, to ask whether it was likely that hundreds of thousands of men stood packed as close together as the BU researchers imagined for the hours the demonstration lasted.

This example, like those discussed earlier, reveals that public discussions of social statistics are remarkably unsophisticated. Social scientists advance their careers by using arcane inferential statistics to interpret data. The standard introductory undergraduate statistics textbook tends to zip through descriptive statistics on the way to inferential statistics. But it is descriptive statistics—simple counts, averages, percentages, rates, and the like—that play the key role is public discussions over social problems and social policy. And the level of those discussions is not terribly advanced. There is too little critical thinking about social statistics. People manufacture, and other people repeat, dubious figures. While this can involve deliberate attempts to deceive and manipulate, this need not be the case. Often, the people who create the numbers—who, as it were, make all those millions—believe in them. Neither the advocates who create statistics, nor the reporters who repeat them, nor the larger public questions the figures.

What Paulos calls innumeracy is partly to blame—many people aren't comfortable with basic ideas of numbers and calculations. But there is an even more fundamental issue: many of us do not appreciate that every number is a social construction, produced by particular people using particular methods. The naive, but widespread, tendency is to treat statistics as fetishes, that is, as almost magical nuggets of fact, rather than as someone's efforts to summarize, to simplify complexity. If we accept the statistic as a fetish, then several of the guidelines I have outlined make perfect sense. Any number is better than no number, because the number represents truth. Numbers take on lives of their own because they are true, and their truth justifies their survival. The best way to defend a number is to attack its critics' motives, because anyone who questions a presumably true number must have dubious reasons for doing so. And, when we are confronted with competing numbers, those numbers are equally good, because, after all, they are somehow equivalent bits of truth. At the same time, the guidelines offer those who must produce numbers justifications for favoring big numbers, broad definitions, and inclusive methods. Again, this need not be cynical. Often, advocates are confident that they know the truth, and they approach collecting statistics as a straightforward effort to generate the numbers needed to document what they, after all, know to be true.

Any effort to improve the quality of public discussion of social statistics needs to begin with the understanding that numbers are socially constructed. Statistics are not nuggets of objective fact that we discover, rather, they are people's creations. Every statistic reflects people's decisions to count, their choices of what to count and how to go about counting it, and so on. These choices inevitably shape the resulting numbers.

Public discussions of social statistics need to chart a middle path between naivete (the assumption that numbers are simply true) and cynicism (the suspicion that figures are outright lies told by people with bad motives). This middle path needs to be critical. It needs to recognize that every statistic has to be created, to acknowledge that every statistic is imperfect, yet to appreciate that statistics still offer an essential way of summarizing complex information. Social scientists have a responsibility to promote this critical stance in the public, within the press, and among advocates.

Suggested Further Readings

Best, Joel. *Damned Lies and Statistics*. Berkeley, CA: University of California Press, 2001.

Loseke, Donileen R. *Thinking about Social Problems*. Hawthorne, NY. Aldine de Gruyter, 1999.

Paulos, John Allen. *Innumeracy*. New York. Random House, 1988.

☻ ☻ ☻

Questions

1. Why are statistics so powerful? What is their role in the market-place of competing social problems?

2. Explain why big numbers are better than little numbers or no numbers at all. How is this related to innumeracy?

3. Best argues, "Statistics are not nuggets of objective fact that we discover; rather they are people's creations." Explain what he means by this statement.

4. Use the lessons that Best provided to create an argument for something you find objectionable being a social problem worthy of public attention.

Culture

Culture

- What is culture?

- Why is it so important to understand people's cultural differences?

- How does culture support social inequality?

Watch the *Core Concepts in Sociology* video "A Society of Consumers" on **mysoclab.com**

Chapter Overview

This chapter focuses on the concept of "culture," which refers to a society's entire way of life. Notice that the root of the word "culture" is the same as that of the word "cultivate," suggesting that people living together actually "grow" their way of life over time.

Reprinted by permission of Charles Schwab Corporation

It's late on a Tuesday night, but Fang Lin gazes intently at her computer screen. Dong Wang, who is married to Fang, walks up behind her chair.

"I'm trying to finish organizing our investments," Fang explains, speaking in Chinese.

"I didn't realize that we could do all this online in our own language," Dong says, reading the screen. "That's great. I like that a lot."

Fang and Dong are not alone in feeling this way. Back in 1990, executives of Charles Schwab & Co., a large investment brokerage corporation, gathered in a conference room at the company's headquarters in San Francisco to discuss ways to expand their business. They came up with the idea that the company would profit by giving greater attention to the increasing cultural diversity of the United States. Why? Pointing to data collected by researchers at the U.S. Census Bureau, they saw that the number of Asian Americans was rising rapidly, not just in San Francisco but all over the country. The data also showed company officials that Asian Americans, on average, are doing pretty well, with half of families earning more than $65,000 a year (in today's dollars).

Based on such data, Schwab launched a diversity initiative, assigning executives to work just on building awareness of the company among Asian Americans. Since then, the scope of the program has grown so that Schwab now employs more than 300 people who speak Chinese, Japanese, Korean, Vietnamese, or some other Asian language. Having account executives who speak languages other than English is important because research shows that most immigrants who come to the United States prefer to communicate in their first language, especially when dealing with important matters like investing their money. In addition, the company has launched Web sites using Korean, Chinese, and other Asian languages. Fang Lin and Dong Wang are just two of the millions of people who have opened accounts with companies that reach out to them in a familiar language other than English.

This initiative has been extremely successful for Schwab, which now manages a much larger share of investments made by Asian Americans. Asian Americans spent $250 billion in 2008, so any company would be smart to follow the lead Schwab has taken. Other racial and ethnic categories that represent even larger markets in the United States are Hispanic Americans and African Americans (each spending more than $500 billion in 2008) (Fattah, 2002; Karrfalt, 2003; U.S. Census Bureau, 2009; U.S. Bureau of Labor Statistics, 2009).

Businesses like Schwab have learned that the United States is the most *multicultural* of all the world's nations. This cultural diversity reflects our long history of receiving immigrants from all over the world. The ways of life found around the world differ not only in terms of languages and forms of dress but also in preferred foods, musical tastes, family patterns, and beliefs about right and wrong. Some of the world's people have many children, while others have few; some honor the elderly, while others seem to glorify youth. Some societies are peaceful and others warlike, and they embrace thousands of different religious beliefs and ideas about what is polite and rude, beautiful and ugly, pleasant and repulsive. This amazing human capacity for so many different ways of life is a matter of human culture. ● Go to **mysoclab.com**

What Is Culture?

Culture is *the ways of thinking, ways of acting, and material objects that together form a people's way of life.* When studying culture, sociologists consider both thoughts and things. *Nonmaterial culture* consists of the ideas created by members of a society, ranging from art

culture the ways of thinking, the ways of acting, and the material objects that together form a people's way of life

society people who interact in a defined territory and share a culture

culture shock personal disorientation when experiencing an unfamiliar way of life

Go to the Multimedia Library at **mysoclab.com** to view the video "Sociologists and Culture"

Paul W. Liebhardt

Boaz Rottem\Alamy Images

Marvin Dembinsky Photo Associates\Alamy Images

Paul W. Liebhardt

Jon Arnold Images Ltd.\Alamy.com

Hubertus Kanus\Photo Researchers, Inc.

Photononstop\SuperStock, Inc.

Suzy Bennett\Alamy Images

Getty Images, Inc - Stockbyte Royalty Free

Human beings around the globe create diverse ways of life. Such differences begin with outward appearance: Contrast the women shown here from Ethiopia, India, Kenya, Thailand, South Yemen, and the United States and the men from Taiwan (Republic of China), Ecuador, and Papua New Guinea. Less obvious but of even greater importance are internal differences, since culture also shapes our goals in life, our sense of justice, and even our innermost personal feelings.

Go to the Multimedia Library at mysoclab.com to explore the strange rituals of the Nacirema

● Seeing Sociology in Everyday Life

Can you describe specific practices or patterns familiar to us in the United States that would shock people living in some other part of the world? Explain your response.

Hazel Thompson/The New York Times

All societies contain cultural differences that can provoke a mild case of culture shock. This woman traveling on a British subway is not sure what to make of the woman sitting next to her, who is wearing the Muslim full-face veil known as the *niqab*.

to Zen; *material culture* refers to physical things, everything from arm-chairs to zippers.

The terms "culture" and "society" obviously go hand in hand, but their precise meanings differ. Culture is a shared way of life or social heritage; **society** refers to *people who interact in a defined territory and share a culture*. Neither society nor culture could exist without the other.

Culture shapes not only what we do but also what we think and how we feel—elements of what we commonly but wrongly describe as "human nature." The warlike Yąnomamö of the Brazilian rain forest think aggression is natural, but halfway around the world, the Semai of Malaysia live quite peacefully. The cultures of the United States and Japan both stress achievement and hard work, but members of our society value individualism more than the Japanese, who value collective harmony. ● Go to mysoclab.com

Given the extent of cultural differences in the world and people's tendency to view their own way of life as "natural," it is no wonder that we often feel **culture shock,** *personal disorientation when experiencing an unfamiliar way of life.* People can experience culture shock right here in the United States when, say, African Americans shop in an Iranian neighborhood in Los Angeles, college students visit the Amish countryside in Ohio, or New Yorkers travel through small towns in the Deep South. But culture shock can be intense when we travel abroad. The Thinking Globally box tells the story of a U.S.

researcher making his first visit to the home of the Yąnomamö people living in the Amazon region of South America.

> **January 2, high in the Andes Mountains of Peru.** In the rural highlands, people are poor and depend on one another. The culture is built on cooperation among families and neighbors who have lived nearby for many generations. Today, we spend an hour watching a new house being built. A young couple invited their families and friends, who arrived about 6:30 in the morning, and right away everyone began building. By midafternoon, most of the work had been done, and the couple then provided a large meal, drinks, and music that continued for the rest of the day.

No particular way of life is "natural" to humans, even though most people around the world view their own behavior that way. The cooperation that comes naturally in small communities high in the Andes Mountains of Peru is very different from the competitive lifestyle that is natural to so many people living in, say, Chicago or New York. Such variations come from the fact that we are creatures of culture who join together to create our own way of life. Every other animal, from ants to zebras, behaves very much the same all around the world because their behavior is determined by instincts, biological programming over which the species has no control. A few animals—notably chimpanzees and related primates—have some capacity for culture, as researchers have learned by observing them using tools and teaching simple skills to their offspring. But the creative power of humans is far greater than that of any other form of life. In short, *only humans rely on culture rather than instinct to ensure their survival* (Harris, 1987; Morell, 2008). To understand how human culture came to be, we need to look back at the history of our species.

Culture and Human Intelligence

Scientists tell us that our planet is 4.5 billion years old . Life appeared about 1 billion years later. Fast-forward another 2 to 3 billion years, and we find dinosaurs ruling Earth. It was only after these giant creatures disappeared—some 65 million years ago—that our history took a crucial turn with the appearance of the animals we call primates.

The importance of primates is that they have the largest brains relative to body size of all living creatures. About 12 million years ago, primates began to evolve along two different lines, leading humans away from the great apes, our closest relatives. Some 3 million years ago, our distant human ancestors climbed down from the trees of Central Africa to move around in the tall grasses. There, walking upright, they learned the advantages of hunting in groups and made use of fire, tools, and weapons; built simple shelters; and fashioned basic clothing. These Stone Age achievements mark the

Culture

THINKING GLOBALLY

Confronting the Yąnomamö: The Experience of Culture Shock

A small aluminum motorboat chugged steadily along the muddy Orinoco River, deep within South America's vast tropical rain forest. The anthropologist Napoleon Chagnon was nearing the end of a three-day journey to the home territory of the Yąnomamö, one of the most technologically simple societies on Earth.

Some 12,000 Yąnomamö live in villages scattered along the border of Venezuela and Brazil. Their way of life could hardly be more different from our own. The Yąnomamö wear little clothing and live without electricity, cars, or other conveniences most people in the United States take for granted. They use bows and arrows for hunting and warfare, as they have for centuries. Many of the Yąnomamö have had little contact with the outside world, so Chagnon would be as strange to them as they would be to him.

By 2:00 in the afternoon, Chagnon had almost reached his destination. The hot sun and humid air were becoming unbearable. Chagnon's clothes were soaked with sweat, and his face and hands were swollen from the bites of gnats swarming around him. But he scarcely noticed, so focused was he on the fact that in just a few moments, he would be face to face with people unlike any he had ever known.

Chagnon's heart pounded as the boat slid onto the riverbank. He and his guide climbed from the boat and walked toward the Yąnomamö village, stooping as they pushed their way through the dense undergrowth. Chagnon describes what happened next:

I looked up and gasped when I saw a dozen burly, naked, sweaty, hideous men staring at us down the shafts of their drawn arrows! Immense wads of green tobacco were stuck between their lower teeth and lips, making them look even more hideous, and strands of dark green slime dripped or hung from their nostrils—strands so long that they clung to their [chests] or drizzled down their chins.

Herve Collart\CORBIS- NY

My next discovery was that there were a dozen or so vicious, underfed dogs snapping at my legs, circling me as if I were to be their next meal. I just stood there holding my notebook, helpless and pathetic. Then the stench of the decaying vegetation and filth hit me and I almost got sick. I was horrified. What kind of welcome was this for the person who came here to live with you and learn your way of life, to become friends with you? (1992:11–12)

Fortunately for Chagnon, the Yąnomamö villagers recognized his guide and lowered their weapons. Reassured that he would survive the afternoon, Chagnon still was shaken by his inability to make any sense of these people. And this was to be his home for a year and a half! He wondered why he had given up physics to study human culture in the first place.

WHAT DO YOU THINK?

1. As they came to know Chagnon, might the Yąnomamö, too, have experienced culture shock? Why?

2. Can you think of an experience you had that is similar to the one described here?

3. How can studying sociology help reduce the experience of culture shock?

point at which our ancestors embarked on a distinct evolutionary course, making culture their primary strategy for survival. By about 250,000 years ago, our species, *Homo sapiens*—Latin for "intelligent person"—had emerged. Humans continued to evolve so that by about 40,000 years ago, people who looked more or less like us roamed the planet. With larger brains, these "modern" *Homo sapiens* developed culture rapidly, as the wide range of tools and cave art that have survived from this period suggests.

By 12,000 years ago, the founding of permanent settlements and the creation of specialized occupations in the Middle East (in portions of modern-day Iraq and Egypt) marked a turning point. About this time, the biological forces we call instincts had almost disappeared, replaced by a more efficient survival scheme: *fashioning the natural environment to our purposes.* Ever since, humans have made and remade their world in countless ways, resulting in today's fascinating cultural diversity.

How Many Cultures?

How many cultures are there in the United States? One indicator of culture is language; the Census Bureau lists more than 300 languages spoken in this country, most of which were brought by immigrants from nations around the world (U.S. Census Bureau, 2007).

Culture

symbol anything that carries a particular meaning recognized by people who
share a culture

Margo Silver/Stone/Getty Images

People throughout the world communicate not just with spoken words
but also with bodily gestures. Because gestures vary from culture to
culture, they can occasionally be the cause of misunderstandings. For
instance, the commonplace "thumbs up" gesture we use to express
"Good job!" can get a person from the United States into trouble in
Greece, Iran, and a number of other countries, where people take it to
mean "Up yours!"

Globally, experts document almost 7,000 languages, suggesting
the existence of as many distinct cultures. Yet the number of languages
spoken around the world is declining, and more than half are now
spoken by fewer than 10,000 people (Lewis, 2009). Experts expect
that the coming decades may see the disappearance of hundreds of
these languages, including Gullah, Pennsylvania German, and Pawnee
(all spoken in the United States), Han (northwestern Canada), Oro in
the Amazon region (Brazil), Sardinian (Sardinia, Italy), Aramaic (the
language of Jesus of Nazareth in the Middle East), Nu Shu (a language of southern China that is the only one known to be spoken
exclusively by women), and Wakka Wakka and several other Aborig-
inal tongues spoken in Australia. What accounts for the decline? Likely
reasons include high-technology communication, increasing international migration, and an expanding global economy, all of which
are reducing global cultural diversity (UNESCO, 2001; Barovick, 2002;
Hayden, 2003).

The Elements of Culture

Although cultures vary greatly, they all have common elements,
including symbols, language, values, and norms. We begin our discussion with the one that is the basis for all the others: symbols.

Symbols

Like all creatures, human beings sense the surrounding world, but
unlike others, we also give the world *meaning*. Humans transform
the elements of the world into *symbols*. A **symbol** is *anything
that carries a particular meaning recognized by people who share
a culture*. A word, a whistle, a wall of graffiti, a flashing red light,
a raised fist—all serve as symbols. The human capacity to create
and manipulate symbols is almost limitless—think of the variety of
meanings associated with the simple act of winking an eye, which can
convey such messages as interest, understanding, or insult.

Societies create new symbols all the time. The Seeing Sociology in
Everyday Life box describes some of the "cyber-symbols" that have developed along with our increasing use of computers for communication.

We are so dependent on our culture's symbols that we often take
them for granted. We become keenly aware of the importance of a
symbol, however, when it is used in an unconventional way, as when
someone burns a U.S. flag during a political demonstration. Entering
an unfamiliar culture also reminds us of the power of symbols; culture
shock is really the inability to "read" meaning in unfamiliar surroundings. Not understanding the symbols of a culture leaves a person feeling lost and isolated, unsure of how to act, and sometimes frightened.

Culture shock is a two-way process. On one hand, the traveler
experiences culture shock when meeting people whose way of life is
dramatically different. For example, North Americans who consider
dogs beloved household pets might be put off by the Masai of eastern
Africa, who ignore dogs and never feed them. The same travelers might
be horrified to find that in parts of Indonesia and in the northern
regions of the People's Republic of China, people roast dogs for dinner.

On the other hand, a traveler can *inflict* culture shock on others
by acting in ways that offend them. The North American who asks
for a steak in an Indian restaurant is likely to offend Hindus working there because they consider cows sacred and never to be eaten.
Global travel provides endless opportunities for misunderstanding.

Symbolic meanings also vary within a single society. In the
debate about flying the Confederate flag over the South Carolina
state house a few years ago, some people saw the flag as a symbol of
regional pride or family heritage, while others saw it as a symbol of
racial oppression.

Language

The heart of a symbolic system is **language,** *a system of symbols that
allows people to communicate with one another.* Humans have created
many alphabets to express the hundreds of languages we speak; several examples are shown in Figure 1. Even rules for writing differ:
Most people in Western societies write from left to right, people in
northern Africa and western Asia write from right to left, and people
in eastern Asia write from top to bottom. Global Map 1 shows where

Culture

Anything can serve as a symbol; what makes something a symbol is simply that humans attach meaning to it.

language a system of symbols that allows people to communicate with one another

cultural transmission the process by which one generation passes culture to the next

Sapir-Whorf thesis the idea that people see and understand the world through the cultural lens of language

SEEING SOCIOLOGY IN EVERYDAY LIFE — New Symbols in the World of Instant Messaging

MOLLY: gr8 2 c u!
GREG: u 2
MOLLY: jw about next time
GREG: idk, lotta work
MOLLY: no prb, xoxoxo
GREG: thanx, bcnu

The world of symbols changes all the time. One reason that people create new symbols is that we develop new ways to communicate. Today, more than 135 million people in the United States (most of them young and many of them students) use mobile text-messaging on a regular basis (Nielsen, 2008).

Here are some of the most common text-messaging symbols:

b   be
bc   because
b4   before
b4n   'bye for now
bbl   be back later
bcnu   be seeing you
brb   be right back
cu   see you
def   definitely
g2g   got to go
gal   get a life
gmta   great minds think alike
gr8   great
hagn   have a good night
h&k   hugs and kisses
idc   I don't care

idt   I don't think
idk   I don't know
imbl   it must be love
jk   just kidding
jw   just wondering
j4f   just for fun
kc   keep cool
l8r   later
lmao   laugh my ass off
ltnc   long time no see
myob   mind your own business
no prb   no problem
omg   oh my gosh
pcm   please call me
plz   please
prbly   probably

qpsa   ¿Que pasa?
rt   right
thanx   thanks
u   you
ur   you are
w/   with
w/e   whatever
w/o   without
wan2   want to
wtf   what the freak
y   why
2l8   too late
?   question
2   to, too, two
4   for, four

Fancy/Veer\Corbis RF

WHAT DO YOU THINK?

1. What does the creation of symbols such as these suggest about culture?

2. Do you think that using such symbols is a good way to communicate? Does it lead to confusion or misunderstanding? Why or why not?

3. What other kinds of symbols can you think of that are new to your generation?

Sources: J. Rubin (2003), Berteau (2005), and Bacher (2009).

in the world we find the three most widely spoken languages, English, Chinese, and Spanish.

Language allows much more than communication; it is the key to **cultural transmission,** *the process by which one generation passes culture to the next.* Just as our bodies contain the genes of our ancestors, our cultural heritage contains countless symbols created by those who came before us. Language is the key that unlocks centuries of accumulated wisdom.

Language skills may link us to the past, but they also spark the human imagination to connect symbols in new ways, creating an almost limitless range of future possibilities. Language sets humans apart as the only creatures who are self-conscious, aware of our limitations and our ultimate mortality, yet are able to dream and hope for a future better than the present.

Does Language Shape Reality?

Does someone who speaks Cherokee, an American Indian language, experience the world differently from other North Americans who think in Spanish or English? Edward Sapir and Benjamin Whorf claimed that the answer is yes, because each language has its own

● Seeing Sociology
in Everyday Life

Think about the games you played when you were growing up, like Tag or Capture the Flag, or board games, like Monopoly or Chutes and Ladders. What cultural values do they teach? What about video games like Grand Theft Auto, God of War, or Rainbow Six Vegas?

FIGURE 1   Human Languages: A Variety of Symbols
Here the English word "read" is written in twelve of the hundreds of languages humans use to communicate with one another.

distinct symbols that serve as the building blocks of reality (Sapir, 1929, 1949; Whorf, 1956, orig. 1941). Further, they noted that each symbolic system has words or expressions not found in any other symbolic system. Finally, all languages connect symbols with distinctive emotions, so as multilingual people know, a single idea may "feel" different when it is expressed in Spanish rather than in English or Chinese.

Formally, the **Sapir-Whorf thesis** holds that *people see and understand the world through the cultural lens of language*. In the decades since Sapir and Whorf published their work, however, scholars have taken issue with this proposition. Current thinking is that although we do fashion reality out of our symbols, evidence does not support the notion that language *determines* reality in the way Sapir and Whorf claimed. For example, we know that children understand the idea of "family" long before they learn that word; similarly, adults can imagine new ideas or things before devising a name for them (Kay & Kempton, 1984; Pinker, 1994).

Values and Beliefs

What accounts for the popularity of movie characters such as James Bond, Neo, Erin Brockovich, Lara Croft, and Rocky Balboa? Each is ruggedly individualistic, going it alone and relying on personal skill and savvy to challenge "the system." In admiring such characters, we are supporting certain **values,** *culturally defined standards that people use to decide what is desirable, good, and beautiful and that serve as broad guidelines for social living*. Values are what people who share a culture use to make choices about how to live.

Values are broad principles that underlie **beliefs,** *specific ideas that people hold to be true*. In other words, values are abstract standards

of goodness, and beliefs are particular matters that people accept as true or false. For example, because most U.S. adults share the value of providing equal opportunity for all, they believe that a qualified woman could serve as president of the United States, as the 2008 presidential campaign of Hillary Rodham Clinton demonstrated (NORC, 2009:326).

Key Values of U.S. Culture

The sociologist Robin Williams Jr. (1970) identified ten values as central to our way of life:

1. **Equal opportunity.** People in the United States believe in not *equality of condition* but *equality of opportunity*. This means that society should provide everyone with the chance to get ahead according to individual talents and efforts.

2. **Individual achievement and personal success.** Our way of life encourages competition so that each person's rewards should reflect personal merit. A successful person is given the respect due a "winner."

3. **Material comfort.** Success in the United States generally means making money and enjoying what it will buy. Although people sometimes remark that "money won't buy happiness," most of us pursue wealth all the same.

4. **Activity and work.** Our heroes, from Olympic gold medalists to the winners of television's *American Idol*, are "doers" who get the job done. Our culture values action over reflection and taking control of events over passively accepting fate.

5. **Practicality and efficiency.** We value the practical over the theoretical, "doing" over "dreaming." "Major in something that will help you get a job!" parents tell their college-age children.

6. **Progress.** We are an optimistic people who, despite waves of nostalgia, believe that the present is better than the past. We celebrate progress, viewing the "very latest" as the "very best."

7. **Science.** We expect scientists to solve problems and to improve our lives. We believe that we are rational people, which probably explains our cultural tendency (especially among men) to devalue emotion and intuition as sources of knowledge.

8. **Democracy and free enterprise.** Members of our society recognize numerous individual rights that governments should not take away. We believe that a just political system is based on free elections in which adults select government leaders and on an economy that responds to the choices of individual consumers.

9. **Freedom.** We favor individual initiative over collective conformity. While we know that everyone has responsibilities to others, we believe that people should be free to pursue their personal goals.

Seeing Sociology in Everyday Life

How many languages are spoken by people on your campus? See if you can find out the extent of language diversity at your college.

Window on the World

GLOBAL MAP 1

Language in Global Perspective

Chinese (including Mandarin, Cantonese, and dozens of other dialects) is the native tongue of nearly one-fifth of the world's people, almost all of whom live in Asia. Although all Chinese people read and write with the same characters, they use several dozen dialects. The "official" dialect, taught in schools throughout the People's Republic of China and the Republic of Taiwan, is Mandarin (the dialect of Beijing, China's capital). Cantonese, the language of Canton, is the second most common Chinese dialect; it differs in sound from Mandarin roughly the way French differs from Spanish.

Chinese
- Official language
- Widely spoken second language

English
- Official language
- Widely spoken second language

English is the native tongue or official language in several world regions (spoken by 5 percent of humanity) and has become the preferred second language in most of the world.

Spanish
- Official language
- Widely spoken second language

The largest concentration of Spanish speakers is in Latin America and, of course, Spain. Spanish is also the second most widely spoken language in the United States.

Sources: *Peters Atlas of the World* (1990), Lewis (2009), and World Factbook (2009).

Culture

● Seeing Sociology
in Everyday Life

Would you say that physical fitness is an emerging cultural value? Why
or why not?

norms rules and expectations by which a society guides the behavior of its members

mores norms that are widely observed
and have great moral significance

folkways norms for routine or casual
interaction

Twentieth Century-Fox Film CorpThe Kobal Collection.The Pictur\Picture Desk,
Inc./Kobal Collection

Every culture is a work in progress in that cultural values change over time. In
the 2010 film *Avatar*, the "traditional" values of our own society are evident in the
humans' efforts to exploit the resources of the planet Pandora, as well as their
willingness to use force to accomplish this goal. At the same time, a competing
set of values held by the native Pandora people—who live peacefully and simply
by honoring the natural world—is now emerging among members of our society.

10. **Racism and group superiority.** Despite strong ideas about
individualism and freedom, most people in the United States
still judge others according to gender, race, ethnicity, and social
class. In general, U.S. culture values males over females, whites
over people of color, people with northwestern European backgrounds over those whose ancestors came from other parts of
the world, and rich over poor. Although we describe ourselves
as a nation of equals, there is little doubt that some of us are
"more equal" than others.

Values: Often in Harmony, Sometimes in Conflict

In many ways, cultural values go together. Williams's list includes
examples of *value clusters* in our way of life. For instance, we value
activity and work because we expect effort to lead to achievement
and success and result in material comfort.

Sometimes, however, one core cultural value contradicts another.
Take the first and last items on Williams's list, for example: Members of our society say they believe in equality of opportunity, yet
many also look down on others because of their sex or race. Value
conflict causes strain and often leads to awkward balancing acts in
our beliefs. Sometimes we decide that one value is more important

than another by, for example, supporting equal opportunity while
opposing same-sex marriage. In these cases, we simply learn to
live with the contradictions.

Emerging Values

Like all elements of culture, values change over time. People in the
United States have always valued hard work. In recent decades,
however, we have placed increasing importance on leisure—having
time off from work to do things such as reading, travel, or community service that provide enjoyment and satisfaction. Similarly,
although the importance of material comfort remains strong, more
people are seeking personal growth through meditation and other
spiritual activity.

Values: A Global Perspective

Values vary from culture to culture around the world. In general,
the values that are important in higher-income countries differ
somewhat from those in lower-income countries.

People in lower-income nations develop cultures that value survival. This means that people place a great deal of importance on
physical safety and economic security. They worry about having
enough to eat and a safe place to sleep at night. In addition, lower-
income nations tend to be traditional, with values that celebrate the
past and emphasize the importance of family and religious beliefs.
These nations, in which men have most of the power, typically discourage or forbid practices such as divorce and abortion.

People in higher-income countries develop cultures that value
individualism and self-expression. These countries are rich enough
that most of the people take survival for granted, focusing their attention instead on which "lifestyle" they prefer and how to achieve the
greatest personal happiness. In addition, these cultures tend to be
secular and rational, placing less emphasis on family ties and
religious beliefs and more on people thinking for themselves and
being tolerant of others who differ from them. In higher-income
nations, women have social standing more equal to men, and there
is widespread support for practices such as divorce and abortion
(World Values Survey, 2008). Figure 2 shows how selected countries
of the world compare in terms of cultural values.

Norms

Most people in the United States are eager to gossip about "who's hot"
and "who's not." Members of American Indian societies, however,
typically condemn such behavior as rude and divisive. Both patterns
illustrate the operation of **norms,** *rules and expectations by which a
society guides the behavior of its members.* In everyday life, people
respond to each other with *sanctions,* rewards or punishments that
encourage conformity to cultural norms.

Culture

● Seeing Sociology
in Everyday Life

Give two examples of campus folkways and two examples of campus
mores. What are the likely consequences of violating each type of norm?

● Seeing Sociology
in Everyday Life

Figure 2 shows that as a rich nation, the United States ranks high in
terms of self-expression but is more traditional than many other high-
income nations, such as those in Europe. Can you point to specific beliefs
or practices that set us apart from Europeans as more traditional?

William Graham Sumner (1959, orig. 1906), an early U.S. sociologist, coined the term **mores** (pronounced "MORE-ayz") to refer to *norms that are widely observed and have great moral significance.* Certain mores include *taboos,* such as our society's insistence that adults not engage in sexual relations with children.

People pay less attention to **folkways,** *norms for routine or casual interaction.* Examples include ideas about appropriate greetings and proper dress. A man who does not wear a tie to a formal dinner party may raise an eyebrow for violating folkways or "etiquette." If he were to arrive at the dinner party wearing *only* a tie, however, he would violate cultural mores and invite a more serious response.

As we learn cultural norms, we gain the capacity to evaluate our own behavior. Doing wrong (say, downloading a term paper from the Internet) can cause both *shame*—the painful sense that others disapprove of our actions—and also *guilt*—a negative judgment we make of ourselves. Only cultural creatures can experience shame and guilt. This is what the writer Mark Twain had in mind when he remarked that people "are the only animals that blush—or need to."

Ideal and Real Culture

Values and norms do not describe actual behavior so much as they suggest how we *should* behave. We must remember that *ideal culture* always differs from *real culture,* which is what actually occurs in everyday life. For example, most women and men agree on the importance of sexual faithfulness in marriage. Even so, in one study, 17 percent of married people reported having been sexually unfaithful to their spouse at some point in the marriage (NORC, 2009:1955). But a culture's moral standards are important all the same, calling to mind the old saying "Do as I say, not as I do."

Global Snapshot

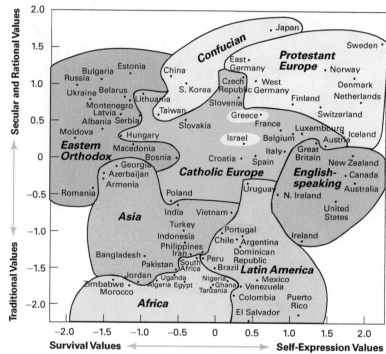

FIGURE 2 Cultural Values of Selected Countries

A general global pattern is that higher-income countries tend to be secular and rational and favor self-expression. By contrast, the cultures of lower-income countries tend to be more traditional and concerned with economic survival. Each region of the world, however, has distinctive cultural patterns, including religious traditions, that affect values. Looking at the figure, what patterns can you see?

Sources: Inglehart & Welzel (2005) and Inglehart (2009).

Technology and Culture

In addition to symbolic elements such as values and norms, every culture includes a wide range of physical human creations called *artifacts.* The Chinese eat with chopsticks rather than knives and forks, the Japanese place mats rather than rugs on the floor, and many men and women in India prefer flowing robes to the close-fitting clothing common in the United States. The material culture of a people can seem as strange to outsiders as their language, values, and norms.

A society's artifacts partly reflect underlying cultural values. The warlike Yąnomamö carefully craft their weapons and prize the poison tips on their arrows. By contrast, our society's embrace of individuality and independence goes a long way toward explaining our high regard for the automobile: We own about 250 million motor vehicles—more than one for every licensed driver—and even in an age of high gasoline prices, many of these are the large sport utility vehicles that we might expect rugged, individualistic people to choose.

In addition to expressing values, material culture also reflects a society's level of **technology,** *knowledge that people use to make a way of life in their surroundings.* The more complex a society's technology, the easier it is for members of that society to shape the world for themselves.

● Seeing Sociology
in Everyday Life

Do some research in your own home: Look at the photographs that
are displayed, and try to understand who is shown, what makes the
event important, and what these photographs suggest about
patterns of culture.

● Seeing Sociology
in Everyday Life

If archaeologists dig up our civilization 50,000 years from now,
based on the artifacts they find, what kind of people will they think
we were? Point to specific artifacts (such as SUVs, cell phones, and
credit cards) and what they say about us.

Monty Brinton/CBS\Getty Images Inc.

What would it be like to live in a society with simple technology? That's the premise of the
television show *Survivor*. What advantages do societies with simple technology afford their
members? What disadvantages do you see?

the primary food source for these peoples—
while men do most of the hunting. Because the
tasks they perform are of equal value, the two
sexes are regarded as having about the same
social importance (Leacock, 1978).

Hunters and gatherers do not have formal
leaders. They may look to one person as a
shaman, or priest, but holding such a position
does not excuse the person from the daily work
of finding food. Overall, hunting and gathering is
a simple and egalitarian way of life.

Limited technology leaves hunters and gatherers vulnerable to the forces of nature. Storms
and droughts can easily destroy their food supply,
and they have few effective ways to respond to
accidents or disease. Looking back at these societies, we see that many children died in childhood, and only half lived to the age of twenty.

As people with powerful technology steadily
close in on them, hunting and gathering societies
are vanishing. Fortunately, studying their way of
life has provided us with valuable information
about our sociocultural history and our fundamental ties to the natural environment.

Gerhard Lenski argued that a society's level of technology is crucial in determining what cultural ideas and artifacts emerge or are
even possible (Nolan & Lenski, 2007). He pointed to the importance
of *sociocultural evolution*—the historical changes in culture brought
about by new technology—which unfolds in terms of four major
levels of development: hunting and gathering, horticulture and pastoralism, agriculture, and industry.

Hunting and Gathering

The oldest and most basic way of living is **hunting and gathering,**
the use of simple tools to hunt animals and gather vegetation for food.
From the time of our earliest human ancestors 3 million years ago
until about 1800, most people in the world lived as hunters and gatherers. Today, however, this technology supports only a few societies,
including the Kaska Indians of northwestern Canada, the Pygmies of
Central Africa, the Khoisan of southwestern Africa, the Aborigines of
Australia, and the Semai of Malaysia. Typically, hunters and gatherers
spend most of their time searching for game and edible plants. Their
societies are small, generally with several dozen people living in a
nomadic, familylike group, moving on as they use up an area's vegetation or follow migratory animals.

Everyone helps search for food, with the very young and the
very old doing what they can. Women usually gather vegetation—

Horticulture and Pastoralism

Horticulture, *the use of hand tools to raise crops*, appeared around
10,000 years ago. The hoe and the digging stick (used to punch holes
in the ground for planting seeds) first turned up in fertile regions of
the Middle East and Southeast Asia, and by 6,000 years ago, these
tools were in use from Western Europe to China. Central and South
Americans also learned to cultivate plants, but rocky soil and mountainous land forced members of many societies to continue to hunt
and gather even as they adopted this new technology (Fisher, 1979;
Chagnon, 1992).

In especially dry regions, societies turned not to raising crops
but to **pastoralism,** *the domestication of animals.* Throughout the
Americas, Africa, the Middle East, and Asia, many societies combine
horticulture and pastoralism.

Growing plants and raising animals allows societies to feed hundreds of members. Pastoral peoples remain nomadic, but horticul-
turalists make permanent settlements. In a horticultural society, a
material surplus means that not everyone has to produce food; some
people are free to make crafts, become traders, or serve as full-time
priests. Compared with hunters and gatherers, pastoral and horticultural societies are more unequal, with some families operating as
a ruling elite.

technology knowledge that people use to make a way of life in their surroundings

| **hunting and gathering** the use of simple tools to hunt animals and gather vegetation for food | → | **horticulture** the use of hand tools to raise crops **pastoralism** the domestication of animals | → | **agriculture** large-scale cultivation using plows harnessed to animals or more powerful energy sources | → | **industry** the production of goods using advanced sources of energy to drive large machinery | → | **postindustrialism** the production of information using computer technology |

Because hunters and gatherers have little control over nature, they generally believe that the world is inhabited by spirits. As they gain the power to raise plants and animals, however, people come to believe in one God as the creator of the world. The pastoral roots of Judaism and Christianity are evident in the term "pastor" and the common view of God as a "shepherd" who stands watch over all.

Agriculture

Around 5,000 years ago, technological advances led to **agriculture,** *large-scale cultivation using plows harnessed to animals or more powerful energy sources.* Agrarian technology first appeared in the Middle East and gradually spread throughout the world. The invention of the animal-drawn plow, the wheel, writing, numbers, and new metals changed societies so much that historians call this era the "dawn of civilization."

By turning the soil, plows allow land to be farmed for centuries, so agrarian people can live in permanent settlements. With large food surpluses that can be transported by animal-powered wagons, populations grow into the millions. As members of agrarian societies become more and more specialized in their work, money is used as a form of common exchange, replacing the earlier system of barter. Although the development of agrarian technology expands human choices and fuels urban growth, it also makes social life more individualistic and impersonal.

Agriculture also brings about a dramatic increase in social inequality. Most people live as serfs or slaves, but a few elites are freed from labor to cultivate a "refined" way of life based on the study of philosophy, art, and literature. At all levels, men gain pronounced power over women.

People with only simple technology live much the same the world over, with minor differences caused by regional variations in climate. But agrarian technology gives people enough control over the world that cultural diversity dramatically increases (Nolan & Lenski, 2007).

Industry

Industrialization occurred as societies replaced the muscles of animals and humans with new forms of power. Formally, **industry** is *the production of goods using advanced sources of energy to drive large machinery.* The introduction of steam power, starting in England about 1775, greatly boosted productivity and transformed culture in the process.

Agrarian people work in or near their homes, but most people in industrial societies work in large factories under the supervision of strangers. In this way, industrialization pushes aside the traditional cultural values that guided family-centered agrarian life for centuries.

Industry also made the world seem smaller. In the nineteenth century, railroads and steamships carried people across land and sea faster and farther than ever before. In the twentieth century, this process continued with the invention of the automobile, the airplane, radio, television, and computers.

Industrial technology also raises living standards and extends the human life span. Schooling becomes the rule because industrial jobs demand more and more skills. In addition, industrial societies reduce economic inequality and steadily extend political rights.

It is easy to see industrial societies as "more advanced" than those relying on simpler technology. After all, industry raises living standards and stretches life expectancy to the seventies and beyond— about twice that of the Yanomamö. But as industry intensifies individualism and expands personal freedom, it weakens human community. Also, industry has led people to abuse the natural environment, which threatens us all. And although advanced technology gives us laborsaving machines and miraculous forms of medical treatment, it also contributes to unhealthy levels of stress and has created weapons capable of destroying in a flash everything that our species has achieved.

Postindustrial Information Technology

Going beyond the four categories discussed by Lenski, we see that many industrial societies, including the United States, have now entered a postindustrial era in which more and more economic production makes use of *new information technology.* **Postindustrialism** refers to *the production of information using computer technology.* Production in industrial societies centers on factories that make *things,* but postindustrial production centers on computers and other electronic devices that create, process, store, and apply *ideas and information.*

The emergence of an information economy changes the skills that define a way of life. No longer are mechanical abilities the only key to success. People find that they must learn to work with symbols by speaking, writing, computing, and creating images and sounds. One result of this change is that our society now has the capacity to create symbolic culture on an unprecedented scale as people work with computers to generate new words, music, and images.

Cultural Diversity

In the United States, we are aware of our cultural diversity when we hear several different languages being spoken while riding a subway in New York, Washington, D.C., or Los Angeles. Compared to a country such as Japan, whose historical isolation makes it the most *monocultural* of all high-income nations, centuries of heavy immigration have made the United States the most *multicultural* of all high-income countries.

Read "Gangstas, Thugs, and Hustlas: The Code of the Street in Rap Music" by Charis E. Kubrin on mysoclab.com

Sometimes the distinction between high culture and popular is not so clear. Bonham's Auction House in England recently featured spray-painted works by the graffiti artist Banksy. This particular one was expected to be sold for more than $250,000.

Between 1820 (when the government began keeping track of immigration) and 2009, more than 76 million people came to our shores. This cultural mix continues to increase as more than 1.5 million people arrive each year. A century ago, almost all immigrants came from Europe; today, the majority of newcomers arrive from Latin America and Asia. To understand the reality of life in the United States, we must move beyond shared cultural patterns to consider cultural diversity.

High Culture and Popular Culture

Cultural diversity can involve social class. In fact, in everyday talk, we usually use the term "culture" to mean art forms such as classical literature, music, dance, and painting. We describe people who attend the opera or the theater as "cultured," thinking that they appreciate the "finer things in life."

We speak less kindly of ordinary people, assuming that everyday culture is somehow less worthy. So we are tempted to judge the music of Haydn as "more cultured" than hip-hop, couscous as better than cornbread, and polo as more polished than Ping-Pong.

These differences arise because many cultural patterns are readily available to only some members of a society. Sociologists use the term **high culture** to refer to *cultural patterns that distinguish a society's elite* and **popular culture** to describe *cultural patterns that are widespread among a society's population.*

Common sense may suggest that high culture is superior to popular culture, but sociologists are uneasy with such judgments, for two reasons. First, neither elites nor ordinary people share all the same tastes and interests; people in both categories differ in numerous ways. Second, do we praise high culture because it is really better than popular culture or simply because its supporters have more money, power, and prestige? For example, there is no difference between a violin and a fiddle; however, we name the instrument one way when it is used to produce a type of music typically enjoyed by a person of higher position and the other way when it produces music appreciated by people with lower social standing.

Subculture

The term **subculture** refers to *cultural patterns that set apart some segment of a society's population.* People who ride "chopper" motorcycles, traditional Korean Americans, New England "Yankees," Ohio State football fans, the southern California "beach crowd," Elvis impersonators, and wilderness campers all display subcultural patterns.

It is easy but often inaccurate to put people in subcultural categories because almost everyone participates in many subcultures without having much commitment to any one of them. In some cases, ethnicity and religion can be strong enough to set people apart from one another, with tragic results. Consider the former nation of Yugoslavia in southeastern Europe. The 1990s' civil war there was fueled by extreme cultural diversity. This *one* small country with a population about equal to the Los Angeles metropolitan area made use of *two* alphabets, embraced *three* major religions, spoke *four* major languages, was home to *five* major nationalities, was divided into *six* separate republics, and absorbed the cultural influences of *seven* surrounding countries. The cultural conflict that plunged this nation into civil war shows that subcultures are a source not only of pleasing variety but also of tension and even violence. Read on mysoclab.com

Many people view the United States as a melting pot where many nationalities blend into a single "American" culture (Gardyn, 2002). But given so much cultural diversity, how accurate is the melting pot image? For one thing, subcultures involve not just *difference* but also *hierarchy.* Too often what we view as dominant or "mainstream" culture are the patterns favored by powerful segments of the population, and we view the lives of disadvantaged people as "subculture." But are the cultural patterns of rich skiers on the mountains of Aspen, Colorado, any less a subculture than the

Culture

multiculturalism a perspective recognizing the cultural diversity of the United States and promoting equal standing for all cultural traditions

Eurocentrism the dominance of European (especially English) cultural patterns

Afrocentrism emphasizing and promoting African cultural patterns

Making the Grade

State several arguments in favor of our society sharing a common culture; state several arguments in favor of our society recognizing cultural diversity.

Michael Buckner/Discovery Channel\Getty Images Inc.

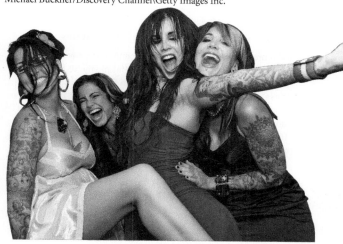

A generation ago, most people regarded tattoos as a mark of low social status. Today, this cultural pattern is gaining popularity among people at all social class levels. Kat Von D is a tattoo artist on the nationwide television show *L.A. Ink.*

cultural patterns of skateboarders on the streets of Los Angeles? Some sociologists therefore prefer to level the playing field of society by emphasizing multiculturalism.

Multiculturalism

Multiculturalism is *a perspective recognizing the cultural diversity of the United States and promoting equal standing for all cultural traditions.* Multiculturalism represents a sharp change from the past, when U.S. society downplayed cultural diversity, defining itself in terms of its European and especially English immigrants. Today there is spirited debate about whether we should continue to focus on historical traditions or highlight contemporary diversity.

E pluribus unum, the Latin phrase that appears on each U.S. coin, means "out of many, one." This motto symbolizes not only our national political union but also the idea that the varied experiences of immigrants from around the world come together to form a new way of life.

But from the outset, the many cultures did not melt together as much as harden into a hierarchy. At the top were the English, who formed a majority and established English as the nation's dominant language. Further down, people of other backgrounds were advised to model themselves after "their betters" so that the "melting" was really a process of Anglicization—adoption of English ways. As multiculturalists see it, early in its history, U.S. society set up the English

way of life as an ideal that everyone else should imitate and by which everyone should be judged.

Since then, historians have reported events from the point of view of the English and others of European ancestry, paying little attention to the perspectives and accomplishments of Native Americans and people of African and Asian descent. Multiculturalists criticize this as **Eurocentrism,** *the dominance of European (especially English) cultural patterns.* Molefi Kete Asante, a supporter of multiculturalism, argues that like "the fifteenth-century Europeans who could not cease believing that the Earth was the center of the universe, many [people] today find it difficult to cease viewing European culture as the center of the social universe" (1988:7).

One controversial issue involves language. Some people believe that English should be the official language of the United States; by 2009, legislatures in thirty states had enacted laws making it the official language. But more than 55 million men and women—one in five—speak a language other than English at home. Spanish is the second most commonly spoken language in the United States, and several hundred other tongues are heard across the country, including Italian, German, French, Filipino, Japanese, Korean, Vietnamese, Russian, and a host of Native American languages. National Map 1 shows where in the United States large numbers of people speak a language other than English at home.

Supporters of multiculturalism say it is a way of coming to terms with our country's increasing social diversity. With the Asian American and Hispanic American populations increasing rapidly, some analysts predict that today's children will live to see people of African, Asian, and Hispanic ancestry become the *majority* of this country's population.

Supporters also claim that multiculturalism is a good way to strengthen the academic achievement of African American children. To counter Eurocentrism, some multicultural educators are calling for **Afrocentrism,** *emphasizing and promoting African cultural patterns,* which they see as a strategy for correcting centuries of ignoring the cultural achievements of African societies and African Americans.

Although multiculturalism has found favor in recent years, it has drawn criticism as well. Opponents say it encourages divisiveness rather than unity because it urges people to identify with only their own category rather than with the nation as a whole. In addition, critics say, multiculturalism actually harms minorities themselves. Multicultural policies (from African American studies departments to all-black dorms) seem to support the same racial separation that our nation has struggled so long to overcome. Furthermore, in the early grades, an Afrocentric curriculum may deny children important knowledge and skills by forcing them to study only certain topics from a single point of view.

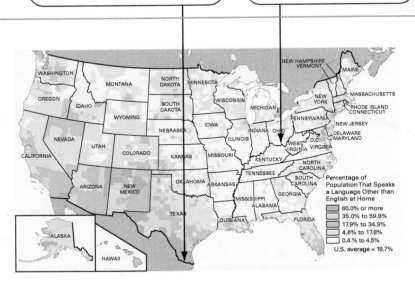

Elvira Martinez lives in Zapata County, Texas, where about three-quarters of the people in her community speak Spanish at home.

Jeffrey Steen lives in Adams County, Ohio, where almost none of his neighbors speaks a language other than English.

Explore the percentage of foreign-born people in your local community and in counties across the United States on mysoclab.com

Percentage of Population That Speaks a Language Other than English at Home
- 60.0% or more
- 35.0% to 59.9%
- 17.9% to 34.9%
- 4.6 % to 17.8%
- 0.4 % to 4.5%

U.S. average = 19.7%

Seeing Ourselves

NATIONAL MAP 1

Language Diversity across the United States

Of more than 283 million people age five or older in the United States, the Census Bureau reports that nearly 56 million (20 percent) speak a language other than English at home. Of these, 62 percent speak Spanish and 15 percent use an Asian language (the Census Bureau lists thirty-nine languages and language categories, each of which is favored by more than 100,000 people). The map shows that non–English speakers are concentrated in certain regions of the country. Which ones? What do you think accounts for this pattern?

Explore on mysoclab.com

Sources: U.S. Census Bureau (2003, 2009).

Finally, the global war on terrorism has drawn the issue of multiculturalism into the spotlight. In 2005, British Prime Minister Tony Blair responded to a terrorist attack in London, stating, "It is important that the terrorists realize [that] our determination to defend our values and our way of life is greater than their determination to . . . impose their extremism on the world." He went on to warn that the British government would expel Muslim clerics who encouraged hatred and terrorism (Barone, 2005). In a world of cultural difference and conflict, we have much to learn about tolerance and peacemaking.

Counterculture

Cultural diversity also includes outright rejection of conventional ideas or behavior. **Counterculture** refers to *cultural patterns that strongly oppose those widely accepted within a society.*

During the 1960s, for example, a youth-oriented counterculture rejected mainstream culture as too competitive, self-centered, and materialistic. Instead, hippies and other counterculturalists favored a collective and cooperative lifestyle in which "being" was more important than "doing" and the capacity for personal growth—or "expanded consciousness"—was prized more highly than material possessions like fancy homes and cars. Such differences led some people to "drop out" of the larger society and join countercultural communities.

Countercultures are still flourishing. At the extreme, small militaristic communities (made up of people born and bred in this country) or bands of religious militants (from other countries) exist in the United States, some of them engaging in violence intended to threaten our way of life.

Cultural Change

Perhaps the most basic human truth is that "all things shall pass." Even the dinosaurs, which thrived on this planet for 160 million years, exist today only as fossils. Will humanity survive for millions of years to come? All we can say with certainty is that given our reliance on culture, the human record will show continuous change.

Figure 3 shows changes in student attitudes that have occurred between 1969 (the height of the 1960s' counterculture) and 2009. Some attitudes have changed only slightly: Today, as a generation ago, most men and women look forward to raising a family. But today's students are much less concerned than those of the 1960s with developing a philosophy of life and are much more interested in making money.

Change in one dimension of a cultural system usually sparks changes in others. For example, today's college women are far more interested in making money because women are much more likely to be in the labor force than their mothers or grandmothers were. Working for income may not change their interest in having a family, but it does increase their age at first marriage and the divorce rate. Such connections illustrate the principle of **cultural integration,** *the close relationships among various elements of a cultural system.*

Some parts of a cultural system change faster than others. William Ogburn (1964) observed that technology moves quickly, generating new elements of material culture (such as test-tube babies) faster than nonmaterial culture (such as ideas about parenthood) can keep up with them. Ogburn called this inconsistency **cultural lag,** *the fact that some cultural elements change more quickly than others, disrupting a cultural system.* In a world in which a woman can give birth to a child by using another woman's egg, which has

Culture

cultural integration the close relationships among various elements of a cultural system

cultural lag the fact that some cultural elements change more quickly than others, disrupting a cultural system

been fertilized in a laboratory with the sperm of a total stranger, how are we to apply traditional ideas about motherhood and fatherhood?

Cultural changes are set in motion in three ways. The first is *invention*, the process of creating new cultural elements, such as the telephone (1876), the airplane (1903), and the computer (late 1940s), each of which changed our way of life. The process of invention goes on all the time, as indicated by the thousands of applications submitted every year to the U.S. Patent Office. The timeline inside the back cover of this book shows other inventions that have helped change our culture.

Discovery, a second cause of change, involves recognizing and understanding more fully something already in existence, from a distant star to the foods of another culture to women's athletic ability. Many discoveries result from painstaking scientific research, and others happen by a stroke of luck, as in 1898 when Marie Curie unintentionally left a rock on a piece of photographic paper, noticed that emissions from the rock had exposed the paper, and thus discovered radium.

The third cause of cultural change is *diffusion*, the spread of objects or ideas from one society to another. Because new technology sends information around the globe in seconds, cultural diffusion has never been greater than it is today.

Our own way of life has contributed many significant cultural elements to the world, ranging from computers to jazz music. Of course, diffusion works the other way, too, so that much of what we assume is "American" actually comes from elsewhere. Most of the clothing we wear and the furniture we use, as well as the watch we carry and the money we spend, all had their origins in other cultures (Linton, 1937a).

It is certainly correct to talk about "American culture," especially when we are comparing our way of life to the culture of some other society. But this discussion of cultural change shows us that culture is always complex and always changing. The Thinking About Diversity box on the following two pages offers a good example of the diverse and dynamic character of culture with a brief look at the history of rock-and-roll music.

Ethnocentrism and Cultural Relativism

December 10, a small village in Morocco. Watching many of our fellow travelers browsing through a tiny ceramics factory, we have little doubt that North Americans are among the world's greatest shoppers. We delight in surveying hand-woven carpets in China or India, inspecting finely crafted metals in Turkey, or collecting the beautifully colored porcelain tiles we find here in Morocco. Of course, all these items are wonderful bargains. But one major reason for the low prices is unsettling to people living in rich countries: Many products from the world's low- and

Compared to college students 40 years ago, today's students are less interested in developing a philosophy of life and more interested in making money.

Student Snapshot

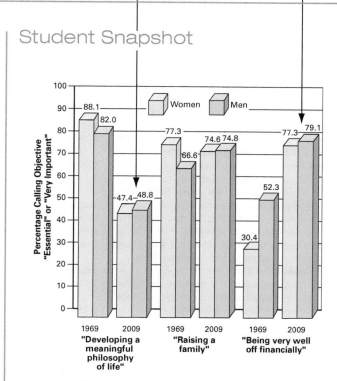

FIGURE 3   **Life Objectives of First-Year College Students, 1969 and 2009**

Researchers have surveyed first-year college students every year since 1969. While attitudes about some things such as the importance of family have stayed about the same, attitudes about other life goals have changed dramatically.

Sources: Astin et al. (2002) and Pryor et al. (2009).

middle-income countries are made by children—some as young as five or six—who work long days for pennies per hour.

We think of childhood as a time of innocence and freedom from adult burdens such as work. In poor countries throughout the world, however, families depend on income earned by their children. So what people in one society think of as right and natural, people elsewhere find puzzling or even immoral. Perhaps the Chinese philosopher Confucius had it right when he noted that "all people are the same; it's only their habits that are different."

Just about every imaginable idea or behavior is commonplace somewhere in the world, and this cultural variation causes travelers both excitement and distress. Australians flip light switches down to

Youth cultures tend to develop as societies industrialize because young people gain more independence from parents and have more money to spend on their own interests.

ethnocentrism the practice of judging another culture by the standards of one's own culture

cultural relativism the practice of judging a culture by its own standards

THINKING ABOUT DIVERSITY: RACE, CLASS, & GENDER

Early Rock-and-Roll: Race, Class, and Cultural Change

In the 1950s, rock-and-roll emerged as part of U.S. popular culture. Rock soon grew to become a cultural tide that swept away musical tastes and traditions and changed the country in ways we still experience today.

Early in the 1950s, mainstream "pop" music was largely aimed at white adults. Songs were written by professional composers, recorded by long-established record labels, and performed by well-known artists including Perry Como, Eddie Fisher, Doris Day, and Patti Page. Just about every big-name performer was white.

In the United States, the 1950s was a time of rigid racial segregation. This racial separation meant that the cultures of white people and black people were different. In the subcultural world of African Americans, music had different sounds and rhythms, reflecting jazz, gospel singing, and rhythm and blues. All of these musical styles were the creations of African American com-posers and performers working with black-owned record companies and broadcast on radio stations to an almost entirely black audience.

Class, too, divided the musical world of the 1950s, even among whites. A second musical subculture was country and western, a musical style popular among poorer whites, especially people living in the South. Like rhythm and blues, country and western music had its own composers and performers, its own record labels, and its own radio stations.

In the early 1950s, there were a variety of musical worlds in U.S. society, separated by the walls of race and class. There was little "crossover" music, meaning that very rarely, if ever, did performers or songs from one world gain popularity in another.

This musical segregation began to break down about 1955 with the birth of rock-and-roll. Rock was a new mix of many existing musical patterns, drawing on mainstream pop but including country and western and, especially, rhythm and blues.

The new rock-and-roll music drew together musical traditions, but it soon divided society in a new way—by age. Rock-and-roll was the first music clearly linked to the emergence of a youth culture—rock was all the rage among teenagers but was little appreciated or even understood by their parents. One reason for this age split was that in the prosperous 1950s, young people had more money to spend, and record companies realized that they could make a fortune selling music to the new "youth market."

Within a few years, the new youth culture presented young people with many new musical stars, and many definitely were not people who looked or acted like their parents. The rock-and-roll performers were men (and a few women) who looked young and took a rebellious stand

Carlos Rene Perez\AP Wide World Photos

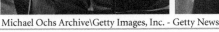
Michael Ochs Archive\Getty Images, Inc. - Getty News

© Bettmann/CORBIS

Elvis Presley (*center*) drew together the music of rhythm and blues singers, such as Big Mama Thornton (*left*), and country and western stars, including Carl Perkins (*right*). The development of rock-and-roll illustrates the ever-changing character of U.S. culture.

turn them on, but North Americans flip them up. The Japanese name city blocks; North Americans name city streets. Egyptians stand very close to others in conversation; North Americans are used to maintaining several feet of "personal space." Bathrooms lack toilet paper in much of rural Morocco, causing considerable discomfort for North Americans, who recoil at the thought of using the left hand for bathroom hygiene, as the locals do.

Given that a particular culture is the basis for everyday experiences, it is no wonder that people everywhere exhibit **ethnocentrism,** *the practice of judging another culture by the standards of one's own culture.* Some small degree of ethnocentrism is necessary for people to be emotionally attached to their way of life. But ethnocentrism can also generate misunderstanding and sometimes even leads to conflict.

Culture

○ Making the Grade

During the 1950s, rock-and-roll helped bring together black and white musical styles, but because this music was popular among the young, it also divided people by age.

○ Seeing Sociology in Everyday Life

Just for fun, go to http://www.TheSociologyPage.com, where you can hear one of the author's "cover" performances of oldies rock-and-roll.

against "adult" culture. The typical rocker was a young man who looked like what parents might have called a "juvenile delinquent" and who claimed to be "cool," an idea that most parents did not even understand.

The first band to make it big in rock-and-roll was Bill Haley and the Comets. These men (Haley lowered his stated age to gain greater acceptance) came out of the country and western tradition (his earlier bands included the Down Homers and the Saddlemen). Haley's first big hits in 1954—"Shake, Rattle, and Roll" and "Rock around the Clock"—were recordings of earlier rhythm and blues songs.

Very quickly, however, young people began to lose interest in older performers such as Bill Haley and turned their attention to younger performers who had a stronger juvenile delinquent image—musicians sporting sideburns, turned-up collars, and black leather jackets. By the end of 1955, the unquestioned star of rock-and-roll was a poor white southern boy from Tupelo, Mississippi, named Elvis Aron Presley. From his rural roots, Elvis knew country and western music, and after he moved to his adopted hometown of Memphis, Tennessee, he learned all about black gospel and rhythm and blues.

Before the 1950s ended, Presley had become the first superstar of rock-and-roll—not only because he had talent but also because he had great crossover power. With early hits including "Hound Dog" (a rhythm and blues song originally recorded by Big Mama Thornton) and "Blue Suede Shoes" (written by country and western star Carl Perkins), Presley broke down many of the walls of race and class in the music of the United States.

Elvis went on to a twenty-year career as "the King." But during that time, illustrating the expanding and changing character of culture, popular music developed in many new and different directions. By the end of the 1950s, popular musical styles included soft rock (Ricky Nelson, Pat Boone), rockabilly (Johnny Cash), and dozens of doo-wop groups, both black and white (often named for birds—the Falcons, the Penguins, and the Flamingos—or cars—the Imperials, the Impalas, the Fleetwoods).

During the 1960s, rock music grew even more popular and more diverse, including folk music (the Kingston Trio; Peter, Paul, and Mary; Bob Dylan), surf music (the Beach Boys, Jan and Dean), and the "British invasion" led by the Beatles.

At first, the Beatles were very close to the clean-cut, pop side of rock, but they soon shared the spotlight with another British band that was proud of its "delinquent" clothing and street fighter looks—the Rolling Stones. During the 1960s, the hard rock of the Beatles and Stones was joined by softer "folk rock" performed by the Byrds, Buffalo Springfield, the Mamas and the Papas, Simon and Garfunkel, and Crosby, Stills, and Nash. Mainstream rock continued with bands like the Who, and rhythm and blues gave birth to "Motown" (named after the "motor city," Detroit), as well as "soul" music, creating dozens of African American stars, including Aretha Franklin, James Brown, the Four Tops, the Temptations, and Diana Ross and the Supremes.

On the West Coast, San Francisco developed a different, more political rock music per-

formed by Jefferson Airplane, the Grateful Dead, and Janis Joplin. West Coast spin-off musical styles included "acid rock," influenced by drug use, performed by the Doors and Jimi Hendrix. The jazz influence also returned to the world of rock, creating such "jazz rock" groups as Chicago and Blood, Sweat, and Tears.

This brief look at the early decades of rock-and-roll shows the power of race and class to divide and separate people, shaping different subcultural patterns. It also shows the power of music to bring people together. We also see that the production of culture—in terms of music as well as movies and music videos—has become a megabusiness. But most of all, it shows us that culture is not a rigid system that stands still but is better described as a living process, changing, adapting, and reinventing itself over time.

WHAT DO YOU THINK?

1. Many dimensions of our way of life shaped rock-and-roll. In what ways do you think the emergence of rock-and-roll changed U.S. culture?

2. Throughout this period of musical change, most musical performers were men. What does this tell us about our way of life? Is popular music still dominated by men today?

3. Can you carry on the story of musical change in the United States to the present? (Think of disco, heavy metal, punk rock, rap, and hip-hop.)

Source: Based on Stuessy & Lipscomb (2008).

Even language is culturally biased. Years ago, people in North America or Europe referred to China as the "Far East." But this term, unknown to the Chinese, is an ethnocentric term for a region that is far east *of us*. The Chinese name for their country translates as "Central Kingdom," suggesting that they, like us, see their society as the center of the world.

The alternative to ethnocentrism is **cultural relativism,** *the practice of judging a culture by its own standards.* Cultural relativism can

be difficult for travelers to adopt: It requires not only openness to unfamiliar values and norms but also the ability to put aside cultural standards we have known all our lives. Even so, as people of the world increasingly come into contact with one another, the importance of understanding other cultures will become ever greater.

Widespread ethnocentrism in the world certainly contributes to armed conflict between nations. At the same time, today's military is

Associated Press

U.S. Troops Train for Both Combat and Conversation

BY DAN ELLIOTT
March 29, 2010

FORT CARSON, Colo.—Two young American soldiers in combat gear sit at a small table in a concrete block building, politely but insistently questioning a 66-year-old Afghan actor playing the role of a village elder.

Outside, in the thick red mud of a remote Fort Carson valley, other soldiers crouch in defensive positions, peering into their rifle sights in the cold morning. But inside, the soldiers are learning to negotiate, rather than shoot, trying to coax information from the Afghan elder about bomb-makers in a nearby village.

The soldiers are among about 4,000 members of Fort Carson's 1st Brigade Combat Team and supporting units who will deploy to Afghanistan this summer. They're practicing counterinsurgency tactics, cultivating trust and cooperation with the Afghan people at the same time they wage war on the insurgents.

The Army's top commanders and planners say that strategy is the key to success in Afghanistan.

"Understanding the culture, and the impact of your actions on the culture, is so essential to mission success that you won't succeed without it," Gen. George W. Casey, the Army chief of staff, said during a visit to Fort Carson this month.

The strategy, detailed in a 2006 Army manual, is a dramatic change in U.S. counterinsurgency doctrine, shifting the focus from the enemy to the population, said Conrad Crane, director of the Army Military History Institute at the Army War College at Carlisle Barracks, Pa.

"If you work with the people, the people are going to give you the intelligence you need for the next operation," said Crane, the lead author of the new doctrine. "It's a revolutionary type of intelligence."

The success of the approach will be measured by how much support and information the soldiers get, he said. "Are they telling you where the explosives are, are they telling you where the bad guys are?"

The strategy is getting its first major test in Afghanistan in Helmand province, where 10,000 U.S., NATO and Afghan troops pushed the Taliban out of the town of Marjah in February.

The allies are now trying to win over the townspeople with good governance, public services and aid.

Making it work in the long run will be tough, said Rick "Ozzie" Nelson, a counterterrorism expert at the Center for Strategic and International Studies.

The basic level of cultural knowledge and language skills the soldiers are getting might not be enough to navigate through Afghanistan's intricate web of ethnic and tribal groups, he said.

But any level of skills will help, Nelson said, noting, "There didn't used to be any cultural training."

At Fort Carson, several hundred soldiers from the 1st Brigade are being schooled in the details of Afghan religion, history, geography and tribal structure and taking lessons in Dari, one of Afghanistan's languages.

They'll learn between 600 and 1,500 Dari words, including basic greetings, requests for IDs

Aurora Photos\Alamy Images

often called upon not only to fight but to win the hearts and minds of the local people in an unfamiliar setting. Seeing Sociology in the News explains how the U.S. Army is training combat soldiers to understand the culture of tribal people in rural Afghanistan.

As the opening to this chapter explained, businesses in the United States are learning the value of marketing to a culturally diverse population. Similarly, businesses now know that success in the global economy depends on awareness of cultural patterns around the world. IBM, for example, now provides technical support for its products on Web sites in more than thirty languages (IBM, 2009).

This embrace of difference is a change from the past, when many companies used marketing strategies that lacked sensitivity to cultural diversity. The translation of Coors beer's phrase "Turn It Loose" startled Spanish-speaking customers by proclaiming that the beer would cause diarrhea. Braniff Airlines translated its slo-

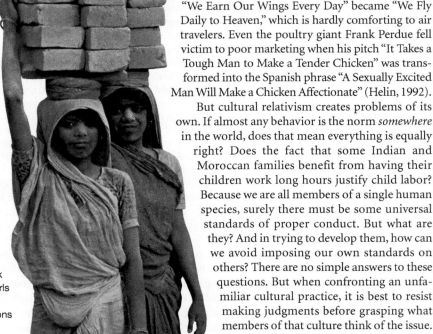

In the world's low-income countries, most children must work to provide their families with needed income. These young girls work long hours in a brick factory in the Kathmandu Valley, Nepal. Is it ethnocentric for people living in high-income nations to condemn the practice of child labor because we think youngsters belong in school? Why or why not?

gan "Fly in Leather" into Spanish so carelessly that it read "Fly Naked"; similarly, Eastern Airlines' slogan "We Earn Our Wings Every Day" became "We Fly Daily to Heaven," which is hardly comforting to air travelers. Even the poultry giant Frank Perdue fell victim to poor marketing when his pitch "It Takes a Tough Man to Make a Tender Chicken" was transformed into the Spanish phrase "A Sexually Excited Man Will Make a Chicken Affectionate" (Helin, 1992).

But cultural relativism creates problems of its own. If almost any behavior is the norm *somewhere* in the world, does that mean everything is equally right? Does the fact that some Indian and Moroccan families benefit from having their children work long hours justify child labor? Because we are all members of a single human species, surely there must be some universal standards of proper conduct. But what are they? And in trying to develop them, how can we avoid imposing our own standards on others? There are no simple answers to these questions. But when confronting an unfamiliar cultural practice, it is best to resist making judgments before grasping what members of that culture think of the issue. Remember also to think about your own

Culture

74

and friendly questions like "How are you doing" and "How is your family," said Mowafiq Al-Anazi, an associate dean at the Defense Language Institute in Monterey, Calif.

"We see language and culture very inextricably intertwined," said Army Col. Sue Ann Sandusky, commandant at the institute. "You're learning a language in order to be able to communicate and understand communication, and to do that you have to be able to place the words and language in the cultural context."

The soldiers still train for combat, too. After meeting with the village elder in the Fort Carson exercise, the platoon was ambushed a few miles away by other soldiers playing the role of Taliban fighters. In a chaotic gun battle waged with blanks, the shouting and cursing platoon overcame the attackers and summoned a Black Hawk helicopter to evacuate a soldier with a make-believe wound. . . .

Veterans and relative newcomers in the 1st Brigade say both combat training and cultural training will help when they get to Afghanistan.

"If you get the people on your side, the enemy will go away," said Command Sgt. Maj. Martin Kelley, a 24-year Army veteran who has served three deployments to Iraq as well as previous stints in Bosnia and Kuwait.

Second Lt. Richard Groat, who negotiated with the village elder and then led the platoon as it fought off the mock Taliban attack, said it was his first patrol and felt like the real thing.

"This process provides experience for me that I don't have," he said.

Ahmad Shah Alam, who played the role of the village elder in the negotiation exercise, said the scenario was realistic, and that the brushy hills and snowy mountain backdrop of Fort Carson give the soldiers a good sense of what it's like to be in Afghanistan.

"I feel like I was home," said Alam, a professional actor who appeared in the 2007 movie "Kite Runner" in a role called "man in the park." . . .

He said he feels it's his duty to help the Americans fighting insurgents in Afghanistan.

"This is very tough," he said. "I do not wish to be an American soldier."

WHAT DO YOU THINK?

1. In what ways is cultural knowledge an important part of what today's military calls "counterinsurgency tactics"? Provide examples from the article.

2. One military officer claims, "If you get the people on your side, the enemy will go away." Do you think that combat soldiers in a foreign land can realistically expect to do that? Why or why not?

3. If the people of the world were able to greatly increase cultural understanding, do you think we might expect to put an end to war? Why or why not?

way of life as others might see it. After all, what we gain most from studying others is better insight into ourselves.

A Global Culture?

Today more than ever, we can observe many of the same cultural patterns the world over. Walking the streets of Seoul, South Korea; Kuala Lumpur, Malaysia; Chennai, India; Cairo, Egypt; or Casablanca, Morocco, we see people wearing jeans, hear familiar music, and read ads for many of the same products we use at home.

Societies around the world now have more contact with one another than ever before, thanks to the flow of goods, information, and people:

1. **Global economy: The flow of goods.** International commerce is at an all-time high. The global economy has spread many consumer goods—from cars and TV shows to music and fashion—throughout the world.

2. **Global communications: The flow of information.** The Internet and satellite-assisted communications enable people to experience events taking place thousands of miles away, often as they happen. In addition, English has long been the dominant language of the Internet, helping spread the English language around the world. It was not until late in 2009 that a person could register a Web address in Korean, Chinese, Arabic, or another language that uses a non-Latin script. Recall from Global Map 1 that English is now the preferred second language in most parts of the world.

3. **Global migration: The flow of people.** Knowledge about the rest of the world motivates people to move where they imagine life will be better, and modern transportation technology, especially air travel, makes relocating easier than ever before. As a result, in most countries, significant numbers of people were born elsewhere (including some 38 million people in the United States, 12.5 percent of the population).

These global links help make the cultures of the world more similar. But there are three important limitations to the global culture thesis. First, the flow of information, goods, and people is uneven in different parts of the world. Generally speaking, urban areas (centers of commerce, communication, and people) have stronger ties to one another, and rural villages remain isolated. In addition, the greater economic and military power of North America and Western Europe means that nations in these regions influence the rest of the world more than the rest of the world influences them.

Second, the global culture thesis assumes that people everywhere are able to *afford* the new goods and services. Desperate poverty in much of the world deprives people of even the basic necessities of a safe and secure life.

Third, although many cultural elements have spread throughout the world, people everywhere do not attach the same meanings to them. Do children in Tokyo draw the same lessons from reading the Harry Potter books as children in London or New York? Similarly, we

○ Making the Grade

One good piece of evidence supporting the claim that a global culture is emerging is the widespread use of English as a second language almost everywhere in the world (see Global Map 1).

cultural universals traits that are part of every known culture

sociobiology a theoretical approach that explores ways in which human biology affects how we create culture

enjoy foods from around the world while knowing little about the lives of the people who created them. In short, people everywhere look at the world through their own cultural lenses.

Theoretical Analysis of Culture

Sociologists investigate how culture helps us make sense of ourselves and the surrounding world. Here we will examine several macro-level theoretical approaches to understanding culture.

The Functions of Culture: Structural-Functional Analysis

The structural-functional approach explains culture as a complex strategy for meeting human needs. Drawing from the philosophical doctrine of *idealism*, this approach considers values to be the core of a culture (Parsons, 1966; R. M. Williams, 1970). In other words, cultural values direct our lives, give meaning to what we do, and bind people together. Countless other cultural traits have various functions that support the operation of society.

Thinking functionally helps us understand unfamiliar ways of life. Consider the Amish farmer in central Ohio plowing hundreds of acres with a team of horses. His methods may violate the U.S. cultural value of efficiency, but from the Amish point of view, hard work functions to develop the discipline necessary for a devoutly religious way of life. Long days of working together not only make the Amish self-sufficient but also strengthen family ties and unify local communities.

Of course, Amish practices have dysfunctions as well. The hard work and strict religious discipline are too demanding for some, who end up leaving the community. Also, strong religious beliefs sometimes prevent compromise, and as a result, slight differences in religious practices have caused the Amish to divide into different communities (Kraybill, 1989; Kraybill & Olshan, 1994).

If cultures are strategies for meeting human needs, we would expect to find many common patterns around the world. **Cultural universals** are *traits that are part of every known culture.* Comparing hundreds of cultures, George Murdock (1945) identified dozens of cultural universals. One common element is the family, which functions everywhere to control sexual reproduction and to oversee the care of children. Funeral rites, too, are found everywhere because all human communities cope with the reality of death. Jokes are another cultural universal, serving as a safe means of releasing social tensions.

○ **CRITICAL REVIEW** The strength of structural-functional analysis lies in showing how culture operates to meet human needs. Yet by emphasizing a society's dominant cultural patterns, this approach largely ignores cultural diversity. Also, because this approach emphasizes cultural stability, it downplays the importance of change. In short, cultural systems are neither as stable nor as universal as structural-functional analysis leads us to believe. The Applying Theory table summarizes this theoretical approach's main lessons about culture and places it alongside two other approaches that we consider next.

○ **CHECK YOUR LEARNING** In the United States, what are some of the functions of sports, July Fourth celebrations, and Black History Month?

Inequality and Culture: Social-Conflict Analysis

The social-conflict approach draws attention to the link between culture and inequality. From this point of view, any cultural trait benefits some members of society at the expense of others.

Why do certain values dominate a society in the first place? Many conflict theorists, especially Marxists, argue that culture is shaped by a society's system of economic production. Social-conflict theory, then, is rooted in the philosophical doctrine of *materialism*, which holds that a society's system of material production (such as our own capitalist economy) has a powerful effect on the rest of the culture. This materialist approach contrasts with the idealistic leanings of structural-functionalism.

Social-conflict analysis ties our society's cultural values of competitiveness and material success to our country's capitalist economy, which serves the interests of the nation's wealthy elite. The culture of capitalism teaches us to think that rich and powerful people work harder or longer than others and that they therefore deserve their wealth and privileges. It also encourages us to view capitalism as somehow "natural," discouraging us from trying to reduce economic inequality.

Eventually, however, the strains of inequality erupt into movements for social change. Two examples are the civil rights movement and the women's movement. Both sought greater equality, and both encountered opposition from defenders of the status quo.

○ **CRITICAL REVIEW** The social-conflict approach suggests that cultural systems do not address human needs equally, allowing some people to dominate others. This inequality in turn generates pressure toward change.

Yet by stressing the divisiveness of culture, this approach understates ways in which cultural patterns integrate members of a society. Thus we should consider both social-conflict and structural-functional insights for a fuller understanding of culture.

Making the Grade

The concept "cultural universal" is an older concept linked to the structural-functional approach. It is based on the idea that if some cultural trait is found everywhere, it must be very useful for society.

Making the Grade

Because multiculturalism supports greater social equality for people of various cultural backgrounds, this theory falls within sociology's social-conflict approach.

●APPLYING THEORY●

Culture

	Structural-Functional Approach	Social-Conflict Approach	Sociobiology Approach
What is the level of analysis?	Macro-level	Macro-level	Macro-level
What is culture?	Culture is a system of behavior by which members of societies cooperate to meet their needs.	Culture is a system that benefits some people and disadvantages others.	Culture is a system of behavior that is partly shaped by human biology.
What is the foundation of culture?	Cultural patterns are rooted in a society's core values and beliefs.	Cultural patterns are rooted in a society's system of economic production.	Cultural patterns are rooted in humanity's biological evolution.
What core questions does the approach ask?	How does a cultural pattern help society operate? What cultural patterns are found in all societies?	How does a cultural pattern benefit some people and harm others? How does a cultural pattern support social inequality?	How does a cultural pattern help a species adapt to its environment?

CHECK YOUR LEARNING How might a social-conflict analysis of college fraternities and sororities differ from a structural-functional analysis?

Evolution and Culture: Sociobiology

We know that culture is a human creation, but does human biology influence how this process unfolds? A third way of thinking, standing with one leg in biology and the other in sociology, is **sociobiology,** *a theoretical approach that explores ways in which human biology affects how we create culture.*

Sociobiology rests on the theory of evolution proposed by Charles Darwin in his book *On the Origin of Species* (1859). Darwin asserted that living organisms change over long periods of time as a result of *natural selection*, a matter of four simple principles. First, all living things live to reproduce themselves. Second, the blueprint for reproduction is in the genes, the basic units of life that carry traits of one generation into the next. Third, some random variation in genes allows each species to "try out" new life patterns in a particular environment. This variation enables some organisms to survive better than others and to pass on their advantageous genes to their offspring. Fourth and finally, over thousands of generations, the genes that promote reproduction survive and become dominant. In this way, as biologists say, a species *adapts* to its environment, and dominant traits emerge as the "nature" of the organism.

Sociobiologists claim that the large number of cultural universals reflects the fact that all humans are members of a single biological species. It is our common biology that underlies, for example, the apparently universal "double standard" of sexual behavior. As the sex researcher Alfred Kinsey put it, "Among all people everywhere in the world, the male is more likely than the female to desire sex with a variety of partners" (quoted in Barash, 1981:49). But why?

We all know that children result from joining a woman's egg with a man's sperm. But the biological significance of a single sperm is very different from that of a single egg. For healthy men, sperm is a "renewable resource" produced by the testes throughout most of the life course. A man releases hundreds of millions of sperm in a single ejaculation (Barash, 1981:47). A newborn girl's ovaries, however, contain her entire lifetime supply of follicles, or immature eggs. A woman releases a single egg cell from the ovaries each month. So although men are biologically capable of fathering thousands of offspring, a woman is able to bear only a relatively small number of children.

Given this biological difference, men reproduce their genes most efficiently by being promiscuous—readily engaging in sex. But women look at reproduction differently. Each of a woman's pregnancies demands that she carry the child, give birth, and provide care for some time afterward. Efficient reproduction on the part of the woman therefore depends on selecting a man whose qualities (beginning with the likelihood that he will simply stay around) will contribute to her child's survival and, later, successful reproduction.

○ Making the Grade

Theories dealing with how biology affects human behavior do not have wide support in sociobiology. Sociobiology is a theory— supported by some sociologists, not by others—that has one foot in biology and the other in sociology.

● Seeing Sociology in Everyday Life

What might be a sociobiological analysis of sibling rivalry? In other words, why do siblings often fight? Why do siblings often join forces when threatened by an "outsider"?

The double standard certainly involves more than biology and is tangled up with the historical domination of women by men. But sociobiology suggests that this cultural pattern, like many others, has an underlying "bio-logic." Simply put, the double standard exists around the world because women and men everywhere tend toward distinctive reproductive strategies.

○ **CRITICAL REVIEW** Sociobiology has generated intriguing insights into the biological roots of some cultural patterns. But this approach remains controversial for two reasons.

First, some critics fear that sociobiology may revive the biological arguments of a century ago that claimed the superiority of one race or sex. But defenders counter that sociobiology rejects the past pseudoscience of racial and gender superiority. In fact, they say, sociobiology unites all humanity because all people share a single evolutionary history. Sociobiology does assert that men and women differ biologically in some ways that culture cannot easily overcome. But far from claiming that males are somehow more important than females, sociobiology emphasizes that both sexes are vital to human reproduction and survival.

GoGo Images Corporation\Alamy Images

Using an evolutionary perspective, sociobiologists explain that different reproductive strategies give rise to a double standard: Men treat women as sexual objects more than women treat men that way. While this may be so, many sociologists counter that behavior—such as that shown here—is more correctly understood as resulting from a culture of male domination.

Second, say the critics, sociobiologists have little evidence to support their theories. Research to date suggests that biological forces do not *determine* human behavior in any rigid sense. Rather, humans *learn* behavior within a culture. The contribution of sociobiology, then, includes explaining why some cultural patterns are more common and seem easier to learn than others (Barash, 1981).

○ **CHECK YOUR LEARNING** Using the sociobiology approach, explain why some cultural patterns, such as sibling rivalry (the fact that children in the same family often compete and even fight with each other), are widespread.

Because any analysis of culture requires a broad focus on the workings of society, the three approaches discussed in this chapter are macrolevel in scope.

Culture and Human Freedom

This entire chapter leads us to ask an important question: To what extent are human beings, as cultural creatures, free? Does culture bind us to each other and to the past? Or does it enhance our capacity for individual thought and independent choice?

As symbolic creatures, humans cannot live without culture. But the capacity for culture does have some drawbacks. We may be the only animals who name ourselves, but living in a symbolic world means that we are also the only creatures who experience alienation. In addition, culture is largely a matter of habit, which limits our choices and drives us to repeat troubling patterns, such as racial prejudice and gender discrimination, in each new generation.

Our society's emphasis on personal achievement urges us toward excellence, yet this same competitive behavior also isolates us from one another. Material things comfort us in some ways but divert us from the security and satisfaction that come from close relationships and spiritual strength.

For better and worse, human beings are cultural creatures, just as ants and bees are prisoners of their biology. But there is a crucial difference. Biological instincts create a ready-made world; culture forces us to choose as we make and remake a world for ourselves. No better evidence of this freedom exists than the cultural diversity of our own society and the even greater human diversity around the world.

Learning about this cultural diversity is one goal shared by sociologists. The Thinking Globally box offers some contrasts between the cultures of the United States and Canada. Wherever we may live, the better we understand the workings of the surrounding culture, the better prepared we will be to use the freedom it offers us.

Culture

THINKING GLOBALLY

The United States and Canada: Two National Cultures or One?

The United States and Canada are two of the largest high-income nations in the world, and they share a common border of about 4,000 miles. But do the United States and Canada share the same culture?

One important point to make right away is that both nations are *multicultural*. Not only do both countries have hundreds of Native American societies, but immigration has also brought people from all over the world to both the United States and Canada. In both countries, most early immigrants came from Europe, but in recent years, most immigrants have come from nations in Asia and Latin America. The Canadian city of Vancouver, for example, has a Chinese community about the same size as the Latino community in Los Angeles.

Canada differs from the United States in one important respect—historically, Canada has had *two* dominant cultures: French (about 16 percent of the population) and British (roughly 36 percent). Almost one-third of people in the provinces of Quebec (where French is the official language) and New Brunswick (which is officially bilingual) claim some French ancestry.

Are the dominant values of Canada much the same as those we have described for the United States? Seymour Martin Lipset (1985) finds that they differ to some degree. The United States declared its independence from Great Britain in 1776; Canada did not formally separate from Great Britain until 1982, and the British monarch is still Canada's official head of state. Thus, Lipset continues, the dominant culture of Canada lies between the culture of the United States and that of Great Britain.

The culture of the United States is more individualistic, and Canada's is more collective. In the United States, individualism is seen in the historical importance of the cowboy, a self-sufficient loner, and even outlaws such as Jesse James and Billy the Kid are regarded as heroes because they challenged authority. In Canada, it is the Mountie—Canada's well-known police officer on horseback—who is looked on with

great respect. Canada's greater emphasis on collective life is also evident in stronger unions: Canadian workers are almost three times as likely to be members of a union as workers in the United States (Steyn, 2008).

Politically, people in the United States tend to think that individuals ought to do things for themselves. In Canada, much as in Great Britain, there is a strong sense that government should look after the interests of everyone. The U.S. Constitution emphasizes the importance of "life, liberty, and the pursuit of happiness" (words that place importance on the individual), while Canadian society is based on "peace, order, and good government" (words that place importance on the government) (Steyn, 2008). One clear result of this difference today is that Canada has a much broader social welfare system (including universal health care) than the United States (the only high-income nation without such a program). It also helps explain the

fact that about one-third of all households in the United States own one or more guns, and the idea that individuals are entitled to own a gun, although controversial, is widespread. In Canada, by contrast, few households have a gun, and the government restricts gun ownership, as in Great Britain.

WHAT DO YOU THINK?

1. Why do you think some Canadians feel that their way of life is overshadowed by that of the United States?

2. Ask your friends to name the capital city of Canada (the correct answer is Ottawa, in the province of Ontario). Are you surprised by how few know the answer? Why or why not?

3. Why do many people in the United States not know very much about either Canada or Mexico, countries with which we share long borders?

The individuals that a society celebrates as heroic are a good indication of that society's cultural values. In the United States, outlaws such as Jesse James (and later, Bonnie and Clyde) were regarded as heroes because they represented the individual standing strong against authority. In Canada, by contrast, people have always looked up to the Mountie, who symbolizes society's authority over the individual.

Culture

Seeing Sociology in Everyday Life

What clues do we have to a society's cultural values?

The values of any society—that is, what that society thinks is important—are reflected in various aspects of everyday life, including the things people have and the ways they behave. An interesting way to "read" our own culture's values is to look at the "superheroes" that we celebrate. Take a look at the characters in the three photos below, and in each case, describe what makes the character special and what each character represents in cultural terms.

Superman first appeared in an *Action Comic* book in 1938, as the United States struggled to climb out of economic depression and faced the rising danger of war. Since then, Superman has been featured in a television show as well as in a string of Hollywood films. One trait of most superheroes is that they have a secret identity; in this case, Superman's everyday identity is "mild-mannered news reporter" Clark Kent.

Buffy, the Vampire Slayer, a more recent star of television, film, comic books, and video games, is a rare example of a woman playing a superhero character.

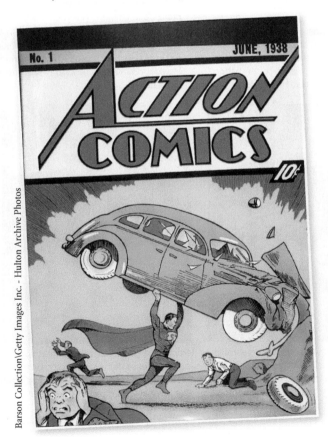

Barson Collection\Getty Images Inc. – Hulton Archive Photos

20th Century Fox Television\Picture Desk, Inc./Kobal Collection

Superman (as well as Spider-Man and Buffy) defines our society as good; after all, Superman fights for "truth, justice, and the American way." Many superheroes have stories that draw on great people in our cultural history, including religious figures such as Moses and Jesus: They have mysterious origins (we never really know their true families), they are "tested" through great moral challenges, and they finally succeed in overcoming all obstacles. (Today's superheroes, however, are likely to win the day using force and often violence.) Having a "secret identity" means that superheroes can lead ordinary lives (and means we ordinary people can imagine being superheroes). But to keep their focus on fighting evil, superheroes must place their work ahead of any romantic interests ("Work comes first!"). Buffy also illustrates the special challenge to "do it all" faced by women in our society: Constantly called on to fight evil, she still must make time for her studies as well as her friends.

Another longtime superhero important to our culture is Spider-Man. In all three *Spider-Man* movies, Peter Parker (who transforms into Spider-Man when he confronts evil) is secretly in love with Mary Jane Watson, but—in true superhero style—he does not allow himself to follow his heart.

Marvel/Sony Pictures\Picture Desk, Inc./Kobal Collection

Applying SOCIOLOGY in Everyday Life

1. What traits define popular culture "heroes" such as Clint Eastwood's film character Dirty Harry, Sylvester Stallone's film characters Rocky and Rambo, and Arnold Schwarzenegger's character The Terminator?

2. Ask someone in the class who has lived in another country how the culture of that nation differs from the way of life here. Look for ways in which this person sees or understands U.S. culture differently from people who have lived here all their lives.

3. Watch a Disney film such as *Finding Nemo*, *The Lion King*, *The Little Mermaid*, *Aladdin*, or *Pocahontas*. One reason for the popularity of these films is that they all share culture themes that are important to our society. Using the list of key values of U.S. culture in this chapter, explain what makes any of these films "American."

Making the Grade

Culture

What Is Culture?

👁 Watch on mysoclab.com

Culture is a **WAY OF LIFE**.
- Culture is shared by members of a society.
- Culture shapes how we act, think, and feel.

Culture is a **HUMAN TRAIT**.
- Although several species display a limited capacity for culture, only human beings rely on culture for survival.

Culture is a **PRODUCT OF EVOLUTION**.
- As the human brain evolved, culture replaced biological instincts as our species' primary strategy for survival.

culture the ways of thinking, the ways of acting, and the material objects that together form a people's way of life

society people who interact in a defined territory and share a culture

culture shock personal disorientation when experiencing an unfamiliar way of life

- We experience **CULTURE SHOCK** when we enter an unfamiliar culture and are not able to "read" meaning in our new surroundings.
- We create culture shock for others when we act in ways they do not understand.

✓ *Approximately 200 different cultures exist in the United States. Worldwide, there are roughly 7,000 different cultures.*

The Elements of Culture

Culture relies on **SYMBOLS** in the form of words, gestures, and actions to express meaning.

LANGUAGE is the symbolic system by which one generation transmits culture to the next.

symbol anything that carries a particular meaning recognized by people who share a culture

language a system of symbols that allows people to communicate with one another

cultural transmission the process by which one generation passes culture to the next

Sapir-Whorf thesis the idea that people see and understand the world through the cultural lens of language

values culturally defined standards that people use to decide what is desirable, good, and beautiful and that serve as broad guidelines for social living

VALUES are abstract standards of what ought to be (for example, equality of opportunity).
BELIEFS are specific statements that people who share a culture hold to be true (for example, "A qualified woman could be elected president").

NORMS, which guide human behavior, are of two types:
- **mores** (for example, sexual taboos), which have great moral significance
- **folkways** (for example, greetings or dining etiquette), which are matters of everyday politeness

beliefs specific ideas that people hold to be true

norms rules and expectations by which a society guides the behavior of its members

mores norms that are widely observed and have great moral significance

folkways norms for routine or casual interaction

✓ *Values and norms (standards for how we should behave) reflect **ideal culture**, which differs from **real culture** (what actually occurs in everyday life).*

Technology and Culture

Culture is shaped by **TECHNOLOGY**. We understand technological development in terms of stages of **SOCIOCULTURAL EVOLUTION**:
- hunting and gathering
- horticulture and pastoralism
- agriculture
- industry
- postindustrial information technology

technology knowledge that people use to make a way of life in their surroundings

hunting and gathering the use of simple tools to hunt animals and gather vegetation for food

horticulture the use of hand tools to raise crops

pastoralism the domestication of animals

agriculture large-scale cultivation using plows harnessed to animals or more powerful energy sources

industry the production of goods using advanced sources of energy to drive large machinery

postindustrialism the production of information using computer technology

✓ *Members of societies that possess sophisticated technology should be careful not to judge cultures with simpler technology as inferior.*

Cultural Diversity

We live in a **CULTURALLY DIVERSE SOCIETY**.
- This diversity is due to our history of immigration.
- Diversity reflects regional differences.
- Diversity reflects differences in social class that set off **high culture** (available only to elites) from **popular culture** (available to average people).

A number of values are central to our way of life. But **CULTURAL PATTERNS** are not the same throughout our society.
- **Subculture** is based on differences in interests as well as life experiences.
- **Multiculturalism** is an effort to enhance appreciation of cultural diversity.
- **Counterculture** is strongly at odds with conventional ways of life.

high culture cultural patterns that distinguish a society's elite

popular culture cultural patterns that are widespread among a society's population

subculture cultural patterns that set apart some segment of a society's population

multiculturalism a perspective recognizing the cultural diversity of the United States and promoting equal standing for all cultural traditions

Eurocentrism the dominance of European (especially English) cultural patterns

Afrocentrism emphasizing and promoting African cultural patterns

counterculture cultural patterns that strongly oppose those widely accepted within a society

cultural integration the close relationships among various elements of a cultural system

cultural lag the fact that some cultural elements change more quickly than others, disrupting a cultural system

ethnocentrism the practice of judging another culture by the standards of one's own culture

cultural relativism the practice of judging a culture by its own standards

CULTURAL CHANGE results from
- **invention** (examples include the telephone and the computer)
- **discovery** (for example, the recognition that women are capable of political leadership)
- **diffusion** (for example, the growing popularity of various ethnic foods and musical styles)

CULTURAL LAG results when some parts of a cultural system change faster than others.

How do we understand cultural differences?
- **ETHNOCENTRISM** links people to their society but can cause misunderstanding and conflict between societies.
- **CULTURAL RELATIVISM** is increasingly important as people of the world come into more and more contact with each other.

Read on mysoclab.com

Explore on mysoclab.com

✓ Global cultural patterns result from the worldwide flow of goods, information, and people.

Theoretical Analysis of Culture

The **STRUCTURAL-FUNCTIONAL APPROACH** views culture as a relatively stable system built on core values. All cultural patterns play some part in the ongoing operation of society.

The **SOCIAL-CONFLICT APPROACH** sees culture as a dynamic arena of inequality and conflict. Cultural patterns benefit some categories of people more than others.

SOCIOBIOLOGY explores how the long history of evolution has shaped patterns of culture in today's world.

cultural universals traits that are part of every known culture

sociobiology a theoretical approach that explores ways in which human biology affects how we create culture

See the Applying Theory table.

Culture and Human Freedom

- Culture can limit the choices we make.
- As cultural creatures, we have the capacity to shape and reshape our world to meet our needs and pursue our dreams.

Sample Test Questions

Multiple-Choice Questions

1. Of all the world's countries, the United States is the most
   a. multicultural.
   b. culturally uniform.
   c. slowly changing.
   d. resistant to cultural diversity.

2. Ideas created by members of a society are part of
   a. high culture.
   b. material culture.
   c. norms.
   d. nonmaterial culture.

3. Sociologists define a symbol as
   a. any gesture that creates conflict within a population.
   b. any element of material culture.
   c. anything that has meaning to people who share a culture.
   d. any pattern that causes culture shock.

4. U.S. culture holds a strong belief in
   a. the traditions of the past.
   b. individuality.
   c. equality of condition for all.
   d. "being" rather than "doing."

5. Cheating on a final examination is an example of violating campus
   a. folkways.
   b. symbols.
   c. mores.
   d. high culture.

6. Which of the following phrases describes the concept of ethnocentrism?
   a. taking pride in your ethnicity
   b. judging an unfamiliar culture using the standards of your own culture
   c. seeing another culture as better than your own
   d. judging another culture by its own standards

7. *Subculture* refers to
   a. a part of the population lacking culture.
   b. elements of popular culture.
   c. people who embrace high culture.
   d. cultural patterns that set apart a segment of a society's population.

8. Which region of the United States has the largest share of people who speak a language other than English at home?
   a. the Southwest
   b. the Northeast
   c. the Northwest
   d. the South

9. In human history, the "dawn of civilization" took place with the development of
   a. hunting and gathering.
   b. pastoralism.
   c. industry.
   d. agriculture.

10. Which theoretical approach focuses on the link between culture and social inequality?
    a. the structural-functional approach
    b. the social-conflict approach
    c. the symbolic-interaction approach
    d. the sociobiology approach

ANSWERS: 1(a); 2(d); 3(c); 4(b); 5(c); 6(b); 7(d); 8(a); 9(d); 10(b).

Essay Questions

1. In the United States, hot dogs, hamburgers, French fries, and ice cream have long been considered national favorites. What cultural patterns help explain this country's love of these foods?

2. From what you have learned in this chapter, do you think that a global culture is emerging? Do you think the idea of global culture is positive or negative? Explain your answer.

Social Interaction
in Everyday Life

Social Interaction
in Everyday Life

- How do we create reality in our face-to-face interactions?

- Why do employers try to control their workers' feelings on the job as well as their behavior?

- What makes something funny?

Watch the *Core Concepts in Sociology* video "Social Interaction and Social Roles" on **mysoclab.com**

Chapter Overview

This chapter takes a micro-level look at society, examining patterns of everyday social interaction. First, the chapter identifies important social structures, including status and role. Then it explains how we construct reality in social interaction. Finally, it applies the lessons learned to three everyday experiences: emotion, gender, and humor.

Ingram Publishing\SuperStock, Inc.

Harold and Sybil are on their way to another couple's home in an unfamiliar area near Fort Lauderdale, Florida. For the last twenty minutes, as Sybil sees it, they have been driving in circles, searching in vain for Coconut Palm Road.

"Look, Harold," says Sybil. "There are some people up ahead. Let's ask for directions."

Harold, gripping the wheel ever more tightly, begins muttering under his breath. "I know where I am. I don't want to waste time talking to strangers. Just let me get us there."

"I'm sure you know where you are, Harold," Sybil responds, looking straight ahead. "But I don't think you know where you're going."

Harold and Sybil are lost in more ways than one: Not only can't they find where their friends live, but they also cannot understand why they are growing angrier with each other with each passing minute.

What's going on? Like most men, Harold cannot stand getting lost. The longer he drives around, the more incompetent he feels. Sybil can't understand why Harold doesn't pull over to ask someone the way to Coconut Palm Road. If she were driving, she thinks to herself, they would already be comfortably settled in with their friends.

Why don't men like to ask for directions? Because men value their independence, they are uncomfortable asking for any type of help and are reluctant to accept it. To ask another person for assistance is the same as saying, "You know something I don't know." If it takes Harold a few more minutes to find Coconut Palm Road on his own—and to keep his sense of being in control—he thinks that's the way to go.

Women are more in tune with others and strive for connectedness. From Sybil's point of view, asking for help is right because sharing information builds social bonds and at the same time gets the job done. Asking for directions seems as natural to her as searching on his own is to Harold. Obviously, getting lost is sure to create conflict for Harold and Sybil as long as neither one of them understands the other's point of view.

Such everyday social patterns are the focus of this chapter. The central concept is **social interaction,** *the process by which people act and react in relation to others.* We begin by presenting the rules and building blocks of everyday experience and then explore the almost magical way in which face-to-face interaction creates the reality in which we live.

Social Structure: A Guide to Everyday Living

October 21, Ho Chi Minh City, Vietnam. This morning we leave the ship and make our way along the docks toward the center of Ho Chi Minh City, known to an earlier generation as Saigon. Government security officers wave us through the heavy iron gates. Pressed against the fence are dozens of men who operate cyclos (bicycles with small carriages attached to the front), the Vietnamese version of taxicabs. We spend the next twenty minutes shaking our heads at several persistent drivers who pedal alongside us, pleading for our business. The pressure is uncomfortable. We decide to cross the street but realize suddenly that there are no stop signs or signal lights—and the street is an unbroken stream of bicycles, cyclos, motorbikes, and small trucks. The locals don't bat an eye; they just walk at a steady pace across the street, parting waves of vehicles that immediately close in again behind them. Walk right into traffic? With our small children on our backs? Yup, we did it; that's the way it works in Vietnam.

Members of every society rely on social structure to make sense out of daily situations. As our family's introduction to the streets of

social interaction the process by which people act and react in relation to others

status a social position that a person holds

ascribed status a social position a person receives at birth or takes on involuntarily later in life

achieved status a social position a person takes on voluntarily that reflects personal ability and effort

status set all the statuses a person holds at a given time

master status a status that has special importance for social identity, often shaping a person's entire life

Vietnam suggests, the world can be disorienting, even frightening, when society's rules are unclear. Let's take a closer look at the ways in which society organizes everyday life.

Status

In every society, people build their lives using the idea of **status,** *a social position that a person holds.* In everyday use, the word "status" generally refers to prestige, as when a college president is said to have more "status" than a newly hired assistant professor. But sociologically speaking, both "president" and "professor" are statuses, or positions, within the collegiate organization.

Status is part of our social identity and defines our relationships to others. As Georg Simmel (1950:307, orig. 1902), one of the founders of sociology, pointed out, before we can deal with anyone, we need to know who the person is.

Each of us holds many statuses at once. The term **status set** refers to *all the statuses a person holds at a given time,* A teenage girl may be a daughter to her parents, a sister to her brother, a student at her school, and a goalie on her soccer team.

Status sets change over the life course. A child grows up to become a parent, a student graduates to become a lawyer, and a single person marries to become a husband or a wife, sometimes becoming single again as a result of death or divorce. Joining an organization or finding a job enlarges our status set; retirement or withdrawing from activities makes it smaller. Over a lifetime, people gain and lose dozens of statuses.

Ascribed and Achieved Status

Sociologists classify statuses in terms of how people attain them. An **ascribed status** is *a social position a person receives at birth or takes on involuntarily later in life.* Exam-

Members of our society celebrate the achievement of Olympic athletes such as Apolo Ohno not only because he has won eight medals in speed skating (not to mention winning in the reality television show *Dancing with the Stars*), but because he was able to do all this even after a challenging childhood during which his parents divorced, he lost contact with his mother, and his father had to spend long hours working.

 zumasportsworld\Newscom

ples of ascribed statuses are being a daughter, a Cuban, a teenager, or a widower. Ascribed statuses are matters about which we have little or no choice.

By contrast, an **achieved status** refers to *a social position a person takes on voluntarily that reflects personal ability and effort.* Achieved statuses in the United States include honors student, Olympic athlete, software writer, and thief.

In the real world, of course, most statuses involve a combination of ascription and achievement. That is, people's ascribed statuses influence the statuses they achieve. People who achieve the status of lawyer, for example, are likely to share the ascribed benefit of being born into relatively well-off families. By the same token, many less desirable statuses, such as convicted criminal, drug addict, or unemployed worker, are more easily achieved by people who were born into poverty.

Master Status

Some statuses matter more than others. A **master status** is *a status that has special importance for social identity, often shaping a person's entire life.* For most people, a job is a master status because it reveals a great deal about social background, education, and income. In a few cases, a person's name is a master status; being in the Bush or Kennedy family attracts attention and creates opportunities.

A master status can be negative as well as positive. Consider serious illness. Sometimes people, even lifelong friends, avoid cancer patients or people with AIDS because of their illnesses. As another example, the fact that all societies limit opportunities for women makes gender a master status.

Sometimes a physical disability can serve as a master status to the point that we dehumanize people by seeing them only in terms of their disability. The Thinking About Diversity box on the next page shows how.

Role

A second important social structure is **role,** *behavior expected of someone who holds a particular status.* A person *holds* a status and *performs* a role (Linton, 1937b). For example, holding the status of student leads you to perform the role of attending classes and completing assignments.

Social Interaction in Everyday Life

THINKING ABOUT DIVERSITY: RACE, CLASS, & GENDER

Physical Disability as a Master Status

Physical disability works in much the same way as class, gender, or race in defining people in the eyes of others. In the following interviews, two women explain how a physical disability can become a master status—a trait that overshadows everything else about them. The first voice is of twenty-nine-year-old Donna Finch, who lives with her husband and son in Muskogee, Oklahoma, and holds a master's degree in social work. She is also blind.

Most people don't expect handicapped people to grow up; they are always supposed to be children. . . . You aren't supposed to date; you aren't supposed to have a job; somehow you're just supposed to disappear. I'm not saying this is true of anyone else, but in my own case I think I was more intellectually mature than most children, and more emotionally immature. I'd say that not until the last four or five years have I felt really whole.

Rose Helman is an elderly woman who has retired and lives near New York City. She suffers from spinal meningitis and is also blind.

You ask me if people are really different today than in the '20s and '30s. Not too

much. They are still fearful of the handicapped. I don't know if fearful is the right word, but uncomfortable at least. But I can

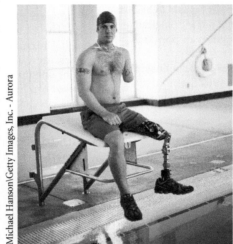

Michael Hanson\Getty Images, Inc. - Aurora

Modern technology means that most soldiers who lose limbs in war now survive. How do you think the loss of an arm or a leg affects a person's social identity and sense of self?

understand it somewhat; it happened to me. I once asked a man to tell me which staircase to use to get from the subway out to the street. He started giving me directions that were confusing, and I said, "Do you mind taking me?" He said, "Not at all." He grabbed me on the side with my dog on it, so I asked him to take my other arm. And he said, "I'm sorry, I have no other arm." And I said, "That's all right, I'll hold onto the jacket." It felt funny hanging onto the sleeve without the arm in it.

WHAT DO YOU THINK?

1. Have you ever had a disease or disability that became a master status? If so, how did others react?

2. How might such a master status affect someone's personality?

3. Can being very fat or very thin serve as a master status? Why or why not?

Source: Based on Orlansky & Heward (1981).

Both statuses and roles vary by culture. In the United States, the status "uncle" refers to a brother of either mother or father; in Vietnam, however, the word for "uncle" is different when referring to the mother's or father's side of the family, and the two men have different responsibilities. In every society, actual role performance varies according to a person's unique personality, although some societies permit more individual expression of a role than others.

Because we hold many statuses at once in our status set, everyday life is a mix of many roles. Robert Merton (1968) introduced the term **role set** to identify *a number of roles attached to a single status.*

Figure 1 shows four statuses of one person, each linked to a different role set. First, as a professor, this woman interacts with students (the teacher role) and other academics (the colleague role). Second, as a researcher, she gathers and analyzes data (the fieldwork role) that she uses in her publications (the author role). Third,

the same woman holds the status of "wife," with a marital role (such as confidante and sexual partner) toward her spouse, with whom she shares a domestic role toward the household. Fourth, she holds the status of "mother," with routine responsibilities for her children (the maternal role) as well as involvement in their school and other organizations (the civic role).

A global perspective shows us that the roles people use to define their lives differ from society to society. In low-income countries, people spend fewer years as students, and family roles are typically very important to social identity. In high-income nations, people spend more years as students, and family roles may or may not be very important to social identity. Another dimension of difference involves housework. As Global Map 1 shows, especially in poor nations of the world, doing housework is an important role that falls heavily on women. ● Go to **mysoclab.com**

Social Interaction in Everyday Life

Remember that *status* refers to a social position and *role* refers to behavior. We *hold* a status and *perform* a role.

role behavior expected of someone who holds a particular status

role set a number of roles attached to a single status

role conflict conflict among the roles connected to two or more statuses

role strain tension among the roles connected to a single status

Role Conflict and Role Strain

People in modern, high-income countries juggle many responsibilities demanded by their various statuses and roles. As most mothers can testify, being a parent and working outside the home both involve physically and emotionally draining roles. Sociologists thus recognize **role conflict** as *conflict among the roles connected to two or more statuses*.

We experience role conflict when we find ourselves pulled in various directions as we try to respond to the many statuses we hold. One response to role conflict is deciding that "something has to go." More than one politician, for example, has decided not to run for office because of the conflicting demands of a hectic campaign schedule and family life. In other cases, people put off having children in order to stay on the "fast track" for career success.

Even roles linked to a single status can make competing demands on us. **Role strain** is *tension among the roles connected to a single status*. A college professor may enjoy being friendly with students. At the same time, however, the professor must maintain the personal distance needed to evaluate students objectively and fairly. In short, performing the roles of even a single status can be something of a balancing act.

One strategy for minimizing role conflict is separating parts of our lives so that we perform roles for one status at one time and place and carry out roles for another status in a completely different setting. A familiar example of this pattern is deciding to "leave the job at work" before heading home to the family.

Role Exit

After she left the life of a Catholic nun to become a university sociologist, Helen Rose Fuchs Ebaugh began to study her own experience of *role exit*, the process by which people disengage from important social roles. In studying a range of "exes," including ex-nuns, ex-doctors, ex-husbands, and ex-alcoholics, Ebaugh saw a pattern in the process of becoming an "ex."

According to Ebaugh (1988), the process begins as people come to doubt their ability to continue in a certain role. As they imagine alternative roles, they ultimately reach a tipping point when they decide to pursue a new life. Even at this point, however, a past role can continue to influence their lives. Exes carry with them a self-image shaped by an earlier role, which can interfere with building a new sense of self. For example, an ex-nun may hesitate to wear stylish clothing and makeup.

Exes must also rebuild relationships with people who knew them in their earlier life. Learning new social skills is another challenge. For example, Ebaugh reports, ex-nuns who enter the dating scene after decades in the church are often surprised to learn that today's sexual norms are very different from those they knew when they were teenagers.

FIGURE 1   Status Set and Role Sets

A status set includes all the statuses a person holds at a given time. The status set defines *who we are* in society. The many roles linked to each status define *what we do*.

The Social Construction of Reality

In 1917, the Italian playwright Luigi Pirandello wrote a play titled *The Pleasure of Honesty*, about a character named Angelo Baldovino, a brilliant man with a checkered past. Baldovino enters the fashionable home of the Renni family and introduces himself in a peculiar way:

> Inevitably we construct ourselves. Let me explain. I enter this house and immediately I become what I have to become, what I can become: I construct myself. That is, I present myself to you in a form suitable to the relationship I wish to achieve with you. And, of course, you do the same with me. (act 1, scene 1)

Baldovino suggests that although behavior is guided by status and role, we have considerable ability to shape what happens from moment to moment. In other words, "reality" is not as fixed as we may think.

The **social construction of reality** is *the process by which people creatively shape reality through social interaction*. This idea is the foundation of the symbolic-interaction approach. As Baldovino's remark

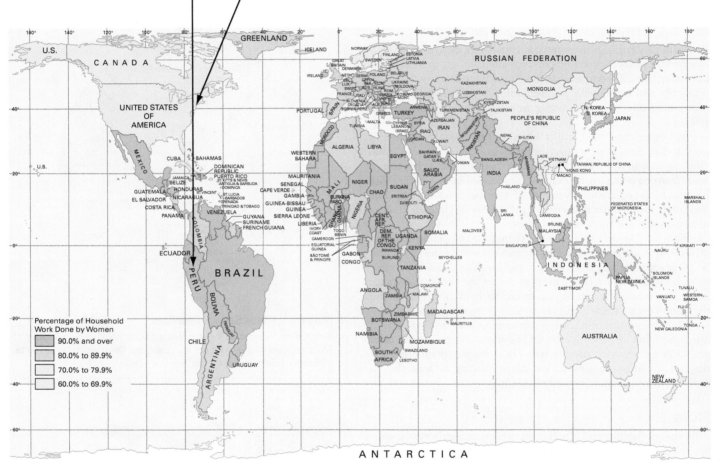

Window on the World

GLOBAL MAP 1   **Housework in Global Perspective**

Throughout the world, housework is a major part of women's routines and identities. This is especially true in poor nations of Latin America, Africa, and Asia, where the social position of women is far below that of men. But our society also defines housework and child care as "feminine" activities, even though women and men have the same legal rights and most women work outside the home.

Source: *Peters Atlas of the World* (1990); updated by the author.

suggests, quite a bit of "reality" remains unclear in everyone's mind, especially in unfamiliar situations. So we present ourselves in terms that suit the setting and our purposes, and as others do the same, reality takes shape.

Social interaction, then, is a complex negotiation that builds reality. Most everyday situations involve at least some agreement about what's going on. But how people see events depends on their different backgrounds, interests, and intentions. One example of changing patterns in everyday interaction involves greeting another person. Seeing Sociology in the News takes a look at how young people have embraced hugging as a form of greeting, replacing the handshakes that are common among their parents.

social construction of reality the process by which people creatively shape reality through social interaction

Thomas theorem W. I. Thomas's claim that situations defined as real are real in their consequences

ethnomethodology Harold Garfinkel's term for the study of the way people make sense of their everyday surroundings

Explore how education shapes reality construction on www.mysoclab.com

"Street Smarts"

What people commonly call "street smarts" is actually a form of constructing reality. In his autobiography, *Down These Mean Streets,* Piri Thomas recalls moving to a new apartment in Spanish Harlem. Returning home one evening, young Piri found himself cut off by Waneko, the leader of the local street gang, who was flanked by a dozen others.

> "Whatta ya say, Mr. Johnny Gringo," drawled Waneko.
>
> *Think man,* I told myself, *think your way out of a stomping. Make it good.* "I hear you 104th Street coolies are supposed to have heart," I said. "I don't know this for sure. You know there's a lot of streets where a whole 'click' is made out of punks who can't fight one guy unless they all jump him for the stomp." I hoped this would push Waneko into giving me a fair one. His expression didn't change.
>
> "Maybe we don't look at it that way."
>
> *Crazy, man,* I cheer inwardly, *the* cabron *is falling into my setup.* . . . "I wasn't talking to you," I said. "Where I come from, the pres is president 'cause he got heart when it comes to dealing."
>
> Waneko was starting to look uneasy. He had bit on my worm and felt like a sucker fish. His boys were now light on me. They were no longer so much interested in stomping me as seeing the outcome between Waneko and me. "Yeah," was his reply. . . .
>
> I knew I'd won. Sure, I'd have to fight; but one guy, not ten or fifteen. If I lost, I might still get stomped, and if I won I might get stomped. I took care of this with my next sentence. "I don't know you or your boys," I said, "but they look cool to me. They don't feature as punks."
>
> I had left him out purposely when I said "they."

Now his boys were in a separate class. I had cut him off. He would have to fight me on his own, to prove his heart to himself, to his boys, and most important, to his turf. He got away from the stoop and asked, "Fair one, Gringo?" (1967:56–57)

This situation reveals the drama—sometimes subtle, sometimes savage—by which human beings creatively build everyday reality. Of course, not everyone enters a situation with equal power. Should a police officer on patrol have come upon the fight that took place between Piri and Waneko, both young men might have ended up in jail.

Explore on mysoclab.com

Flirting is an everyday experience in reality construction. Each person offers information to the other and hints at romantic interest. Yet the interaction proceeds with a tentative and often humorous air so that either individual can withdraw at any time without further obligation.

The Thomas Theorem

By using his wits and fighting with Waneko until they both tired, Piri Thomas won acceptance by the gang. What took place that evening in Spanish Harlem is an example of the **Thomas theorem,** named after W. I. Thomas and Dorothy Thomas (1928; Thomas, 1966:301, orig. 1931): *Situations that are defined as real are real in their consequences.*

Applied to social interaction, the Thomas theorem means that although reality is "soft" as it is being shaped, it can become "hard" in its effects. In the situation just described, local gang members saw Piri Thomas act in a worthy way, so in their eyes, he *became* worthy.

Ethnomethodology

Most of the time, we take social reality for granted. To become more aware of the social world we help create, Harold Garfinkel (1967) came up with **ethnomethodology,** *the study of the way people make sense of their everyday surroundings.* This approach begins by pointing out that everyday behavior rests on a number of assumptions. For instance, when you ask someone the simple question "How are you?" you usually want to know how someone is doing in general, but you might be wondering how a person is dealing with a specific physical, mental, spiritual, or financial challenge. However, the person being asked probably assumes that you are not really interested in the details about any of these things and that you are just "being polite."

One good way to investigate the assumptions we make about everyday reality is to break the rules. For example, the next time someone asks, "How are you?" offer details from your last physical examination or explain all the good and bad things that have happened since you woke up that morning and see how the person reacts.

The results are predictable, because we all have some idea of what the "rules" of everyday interaction are. The person will most likely become confused or irritated by your unexpected behavior—a reaction that helps us see not only what the rules are but how important they are to everyday reality.

Goodshoot\Thinkstock

Social Interaction in Everyday Life

The New York Times

For Teenagers, Hello Means "How About a Hug?"

BY SARAH KERSHAW
May 28, 2009

There is so much hugging at Pascack Hills High School in Montvale, New Jersey, that students have broken down the hugs by type:

There is the basic friend hug, probably the most popular, and the bear hug, of course. But now there is also the bear claw, when a boy embraces a girl awkwardly with his elbows poking out.

There is the hug that starts with a high-five, then moves into a fist bump, followed by a slap on the back and an embrace.

There's the shake and lean; the hug from behind; and, the newest addition, the triple—any combination of three girls and boys hugging at once.

"We're not afraid, we just get in and hug," said Danny Schneider, a junior at the school, where hallway hugging began shortly after 7 a.m. on a recent morning as students arrived. "The guy friends, we don't care. You just get right in there and jump in."

There are romantic hugs, too, but that is not what these teenagers are talking about.

Girls embracing girls, girls embracing boys, boys embracing each other—the hug has become the favorite social greeting when teenagers meet or part these days. Teachers joke about "one hour" and "six hour" hugs, saying that students hug one another all day as if they were separated for the entire summer.

A measure of how rapidly the ritual is spreading is that some students complain of peer pressure to hug to fit in. And schools from Hillsdale, New Jersey, to Bend, Oregon, wary in a litigious era about sexual harassment or improper touching—or citing hallway clogging and late arrivals to class—have banned hugging or imposed a three-second rule.

Parents, who grew up in a generation more likely to use the handshake, the low-five or the high-five, are often baffled by the close physical contact. "It's a wordless custom, from what I've observed," wrote Beth J. Harpaz, the mother of two boys, 11 and 16, and a parenting columnist

for The Associated Press, in a new book, *13 Is the New 18*.

"And there doesn't seem to be any other overt way in which they acknowledge knowing each other," she continued, describing the scene at her older son's school in Manhattan. "No hi, no smile, no wave, no high-five—just the hug. Witnessing this interaction always makes me feel like I am a tourist in a country where I do not know the customs and cannot speak the language."

For teenagers, though, hugging is hip. And not hugging?

"If somebody were to not hug someone, to never hug anybody, people might be just a little wary of them and think they are weird or peculiar," said Gabrielle Brown, a freshman at Fiorello H. LaGuardia High School in Manhattan.

Comforting as the hug may be, principals across the country have clamped down. "Touching and physical contact is very dangerous territory," said Noreen Hajinlian, the principal of George G. White School, a junior high school in Hillsdale, New Jersey, who banned hugging two years ago. . . .

Reality Building: Class and Culture

People do not build everyday experience out of thin air. In part, how we act or what we see in our surroundings depends on our interests. Gazing at the sky on a starry night, for example, lovers discover romance and scientists see hydrogen atoms fusing into helium. Social background also affects what we see, which is why the residents of Spanish Harlem experience a different world than people living on Manhattan's pricey Upper East Side.

In global perspective, reality construction varies even more. Consider these everyday situations: People waiting for a bus in London typically "queue up" in a straight line; people in New York City are rarely so orderly. The law in Saudi Arabia forbids women to drive cars, a ban unthinkable in the United States. In this country, a "short walk" means a few blocks or a few minutes; in the Andes Mountains of Peru, this same phrase means a few miles.

The point is that people build reality from the surrounding culture. For example, people the world over find different meanings in specific gestures, so inexperienced travelers can find themselves building an unexpected and unwelcome reality. Similarly, in a study of popular culture, JoEllen Shively (1992) screened films set in the American West to men of European descent and to Native American men. The men in both categories claimed to enjoy the films, but for different reasons. White men interpreted the films as praising

People build reality from their surrounding culture. Yet because cultural systems are marked by diversity and even outright conflict, reality construction always involves tensions and choices. Turkey is a nation with a mostly Muslim population, but it has also embraced Western culture. Here, women confront starkly different definitions of what is "feminine."

Staton R. Winter, *The New York Times*.

Staton R. Winter/The New York Times

But pro-hugging students say it is not a romantic or sexual gesture, simply the "hello" of their generation. "We like to get cozy," said Katie Dea, an eighth grader at Claire Lilienthal Alternative School in San Francisco. "The high-five is, like, boring."

Some sociologists said that teenagers who grew up in an era of organized play dates and close parental supervision are more cooperative with one another than previous generations—less cynical and individualistic and more loyal to the group.

But Amy L. Best, a sociologist at George Mason University, said the teenage embrace is more a reflection of the overall evolution of the American greeting, which has become less formal since the 1970s. "Without question, the boundaries of touch have changed in American culture," she said. "We display bodies more readily, there are fewer rules governing body touch and a lot more permissible access to other people's bodies."

Hugging appears to be a grass-roots phenomenon and not an imitation of a character or custom on TV or in movies. The prevalence of boys' nonromantic hugging (especially of other boys) is most striking to adults. Experts say that over the last generation, boys have become more comfortable expressing emotion, as embodied by the MTV show "Bromance," which is now a widely used term for affection between straight male friends.

But some sociologists pointed out that African American boys and men have been hugging as part of their greeting for decades, using the word "dap" to describe a ritual involving handshakes, slaps on the shoulders and, more recently, a hug, also sometimes called the gangsta hug among urban youth. . . .

There are, too, some young critics of hugging.

Amy Heaton, a freshman at Bethesda-Chevy Chase High School in Bethesda, Maryland, said casual social hugging seemed disingenuous to her. . . . "It's like air-kissing. It's really superficial."

But Carrie Osbourne, a sixth-grade teacher at Claire Lilienthal Alternative School, said hugging was a powerful and positive sign that children are inclined to nurture one another, breaking down barriers. "And it gets to that core that every person wants to feel cared for, regardless of your age or how cool you are or how cool you think you are," she said.

WHAT DO YOU THINK?

1. The handshake of the adult world has been replaced by the hug of the teenage world. Can you think of other everyday life gestures that differ from one generation to another? Explain.

2. Have you ever felt "not hip" for not hugging someone? If so, explain what happened.

3. Why do you think many older people consider hugging (or other physical touching) "dangerous territory," while younger people seem more casual about this?

rugged people striking out for the frontier and conquering the forces of nature. Native American men saw in the same films a celebration of land and nature. Given their different cultures, it is as if people in the two categories saw two different films.

Films also have an effect on the reality we all experience. The 2009 film *Adam,* for example, about a young man with Asperger syndrome, is one of a series of recent films that have changed people's awareness of the struggle of coping with mental disorders.

Dramaturgical Analysis: The "Presentation of Self"

Erving Goffman (1922–1982) was another sociologist who analyzed social interaction, explaining how people live their lives much like actors performing on a stage. If we imagine ourselves as directors observing what goes on in the theater of everyday life, we are doing what Goffman called **dramaturgical analysis,** *the study of social interaction in terms of theatrical performance.*

Dramaturgical analysis offers a fresh look at the concepts of status and role. A status is like a part in a play, and a role is a script, supplying dialogue and action for the characters. Goffman described each person's performance as the **presentation of self,** *a person's efforts to create specific impressions in the minds of others.* This process, sometimes called *impression management,* begins with the idea of personal performance (Goffman, 1959, 1967).

Performances

As we present ourselves in everyday situations, we reveal information to others both consciously and unconsciously. Our performances include the way we dress (in theatrical terms, our costume), the objects we carry (props), and our tone of voice and the way we carry ourselves (our demeanor). In addition, we vary our performances according to where we happen to be (the set). We may joke loudly in a restaurant or at a sporting event, for example, but we lower our voices when entering a house of worship. People design settings, such as homes or offices, to bring about desired reactions in others.

An Application: The Doctor's Office

Consider how the operation of a physician's office conveys important information to an audience of patients. The fact that medical doctors enjoy high prestige and power in the United States is clear upon entering a doctor's office. First, the doctor is nowhere to be seen. Instead, in what Goffman describes as the "front region" of the setting, the patient encounters a receptionist, who works as a gatekeeper, deciding whether and when the patient can meet the doctor. A simple

● Seeing Sociology
in Everyday Life

Members of every culture have rules about how close people should stand while talking. To see what the rules are in your social world, during a conversation, slowly move closer and closer to the other person and see what happens.

Nonverbal Communication

The novelist William Sansom describes the performance of a character named Mr. Preedy, an English vacationer on a beach in Spain:

> He took care to avoid catching anyone's eye. First, he had to make it clear to those potential companions of his holiday that they were of no concern to him whatsoever. He stared through them, round them, over them—eyes lost in space. The beach might have been empty. If by chance a ball was thrown his way, he looked surprised; then let a smile of amusement light his face (Kindly Preedy), looked around dazed to see that there were people on the beach, tossed it back with a smile to himself and not a smile *at* the people. . . .
>
> [He] then gathered together his beach-wrap and bag into a neat sand-resistant pile (Methodical and Sensible Preedy), rose slowly to stretch his huge frame (Big-Cat Preedy), and tossed aside his sandals (Carefree Preedy, after all). (1956:230–31)

Without saying a single word, Mr. Preedy offers a great deal of information about himself to anyone watching him. This is the process of **nonverbal communication,** *communication using body movements, gestures, and facial expressions rather than speech.*

Many parts of the body can be used to generate *body language,* that is, to convey information to others. Facial expressions are the most significant form of body language. Smiling, for example, shows pleasure, although we distinguish among the deliberate smile of Kindly Preedy on the beach, a spontaneous smile of joy at seeing a friend, a pained smile of embarrassment, and the full, unrestrained smile of self-satisfaction we often associate with winning some important contest.

Eye contact is another crucial element of nonverbal communication. Generally, we use eye contact to invite social interaction. Someone across the room "catches our eye," sparking a conversation. Avoiding another's eyes, by contrast, discourages communication. Hands also speak for us. Common hand gestures within our culture convey, among other things, an insult, a request for a ride, an invitation for someone to join us, or a demand that others stop in their tracks. Gestures also add meaning to spoken words. For example, pointing in a threatening way gives greater emphasis to a word of warning, shrugging the shoulders adds an air of indifference to the phrase "I don't know," and rapidly waving the arms lends urgency to the single word "Hurry!"

Body Language and Deception

As any actor knows, it is very difficult to pull off a perfect performance in front of others. In everyday life, unintended body language can contradict our planned meaning: A teenage boy explains why he is getting home so late, for example, but his mother doubts his words because he avoids looking her in the eye; the movie star on a television talk show claims that her recent flop at the box office is "no big deal," but the nervous swing of her leg suggests otherwise. Because

I didn't ask you to undress so I could examine you. I asked you to undress because it's essential to the doctor-patient relationship that I be fully clothed and you be sitting there in your underwear.

SIPRESS

glance around the doctor's waiting room, with patients (often impatiently) waiting to be invited into the inner sanctum, leaves little doubt that the doctor and staff are in charge.

The "back region" is composed of the examination rooms as well as the doctor's private office. Once inside the office, the patient can see a wide range of props, such as medical books and framed degrees, that give the impression that the doctor has the specialized knowledge necessary to call the shots. The doctor is usually seated behind a desk—the larger and grander the desk, the greater the statement of power—and the patient is given only a chair.

The doctor's appearance and manner offer still more information. The usual white lab coat (costume) may have the practical function of keeping clothes from becoming dirty, but its social function is to let others know the physician's status at a glance. A stethoscope around the neck and a black medical bag in hand (more props) have the same purpose. The doctor uses highly technical language that is often mystifying to the patient, again emphasizing that the doctor is in charge. Finally, patients use the title "doctor," but they, in turn, are often addressed only by their first names, which further shows the doctor's dominant position. The overall message of a doctor's performance is clear: "I will help you, but you must allow me to take charge." ● Read on **mysoclab.com**

nonverbal communication is hard to control, it provides clues to deception, in much the same way that changes in breathing, pulse rate, perspiration, and blood pressure recorded on a lie detector suggest that a person is lying.

Recognizing dishonest performances is difficult because no single bodily gesture tells us for sure that someone is lying. But because any performance involves so many bits of body language, few people can keep up a lie without some slip-up, raising the suspicions of a careful observer. Therefore, the key to detecting lies is to view the whole performance with an eye for inconsistencies.

Gender and Performances

Because women are socialized to respond to others, they tend to be more sensitive than men to nonverbal communication. In fact, gender is a central element in personal performances.

Demeanor

Demeanor—the way we act and carry ourselves—is a clue to social power. Simply put, powerful people enjoy more personal freedom in how they act. Off-color remarks, swearing, or putting one's feet on the desk may be acceptable for the boss but rarely for employees. Similarly, powerful people can interrupt others, but less powerful people are expected to show respect through silence (Smith-Lovin & Brody, 1989; Henley, Hamilton, & Thorne, 1992; C. Johnson, 1994).

Because women generally occupy positions of less power, demeanor is a gender issue as well. Forty percent of all working women in the United States hold secretarial or service jobs under the control of supervisors who are usually men. Women, then, learn to craft their personal performances more carefully than men and defer to men more often in everyday interaction.

Use of Space

How much space does a personal performance require? Power plays a key role here; the more power you have, the more space you use. Men typically command more space than women, whether pacing back and forth before an audience or casually stretching out on a bench. Why? Our culture has traditionally measured femininity by how *little* space women occupy—the standard of "daintiness"—and masculinity by how *much* territory a man controls—the standard of "turf" (Henley, Hamilton, & Thorne, 1992).

For both sexes, **personal space** is *the surrounding area over which a person makes some claim to privacy.* In the United States, people generally stay several feet apart when speaking; throughout the Middle East, by contrast, people stand much closer. But just about everywhere, men (with their greater social power) often intrude into

apaphotos\Newscom

When we observe the performances of other people, we are often aware that what we see is not completely "real." In the 2009 film *Surrogates,* people of the future are able to buy robots that look just like themselves—only without any human flaws—and allow these "surrogates" to live for them while they remain electronically linked to the action in the safety of their homes. Why do you think this film was so popular with audiences?

women's personal space. If a woman moves into a man's personal space, however, he is likely to take it as a sign of sexual interest.

Staring, Smiling, and Touching

Eye contact encourages interaction. In conversations, women hold eye contact more than men. But men have their own brand of eye contact: staring. When men stare at women, they are claiming social dominance and defining women as sexual objects.

Although it often shows pleasure, smiling can also be a sign of trying to please someone or of submission. In a male-dominated world, it is not surprising that women smile more than men (Henley, Hamilton, & Thorne, 1992).

Finally, mutual touching suggests intimacy and caring. Apart from close relationships, however, touching is generally something men do to women (but rarely, in our culture, to other men). A male doctor touches the shoulder of his female nurse as they examine a report, a young man touches the back of his woman friend as he guides her across the street, or a male instructor touches the arms of young women as he teaches them to ski. In such examples, the intent of the touching may be harmless and may bring little response, but it

Paul W. Liebhardt

Paul W. Liebhardt

Paul W. Liebhardt

Hand gestures vary widely from one culture to another. Yet people everywhere chuckle, grin, or smirk to indicate that they don't take another person's performance seriously. Therefore, the world over, people who cannot restrain their mirth tactfully cover their faces.

amounts to a subtle ritual by which men claim dominance over women.

Idealization

People behave the way they do for many, often complex reasons. Even so, Goffman suggests, we construct performances to *idealize* our intentions. That is, we try to convince others (and perhaps ourselves) that our actions reflect ideal cultural standards rather than selfish motives.

Idealization is easily illustrated by returning to the world of doctors and patients. In a hospital, doctors engage in a performance known as "making rounds." Upon entering a patient's room, the doctor often stops at the foot of the bed and silently examines the patient's chart. Afterward, doctor and patient talk briefly. In ideal terms, this routine represents a personal visit to check on a patient's condition.

In reality, the picture is not so perfect. A doctor may see dozens of patients a day and remember little about many of them. Reading the chart is a chance to recall the patient's name and medical problems, but revealing the impersonality of the patient's care would undermine the cultural ideal of the doctor as deeply concerned about the welfare of others.

Doctors, college professors, and other professionals typically idealize their motives for entering their chosen careers. They are quick to describe their work as "making a contribution to science," "serving the community," or even "answering a call from God." Rarely do people admit the more common, less honorable motives: the income, power, prestige, and leisure time that these occupations provide.

We all use idealization to some degree. When was the last time you smiled and made polite remarks to someone you did not like? Such little lies ease our way through social interactions. Even when we suspect that others are putting on an act, we are unlikely to challenge their performance, for reasons that we shall examine next.

Embarrassment and Tact

The famous speaker giving a campus lecture keeps mispronouncing the college's name; the visiting ambassador rises from the table to speak, unaware of the napkin that still hangs from his neck; the president becomes ill at a state dinner. As carefully as people may craft their performances, slip-ups of all kinds happen. The result is *embarrassment,* or discomfort after a spoiled performance. Goffman describes embarrassment as "losing face."

Embarrassment is an ever-present danger because idealized performances typically contain some deception. In addition, most performances involve juggling so many elements that one thoughtless moment can shatter the intended impression.

A curious fact is that an audience often overlooks flaws in a performance, allowing the actor to avoid embarrassment. If we do point out a misstep ("Excuse me, but your fly is open"), we do it quietly and only to help someone avoid even greater loss of face. In Hans Christian Andersen's classic fable "The Emperor's New Clothes," the child who blurts out the truth, that the emperor is parading about naked, is scolded for being rude.

Often members of an audience actually help the performer recover from a flawed performance. *Tact* is helping someone "save face." After hearing a supposed expert make an embarrassingly inaccurate remark, for example, we might ignore the comment, as if it

Barbara Penoya\Getty Images, Inc.- Photodisc./Royalty Free   David Young-Wolff\ PhotoEdit Inc.   Andy Crawford © Dorling Kindersley   Lucian Coman\ Shutterstock   Jupiter Images - Thinkstock Images Royalty Free   Thinkstock Royalty Free

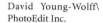

To most people in the United States, these expressions convey anger, fear, disgust, happiness, surprise, and sadness. But do people elsewhere in the world define them in the same way? Research suggests that all human beings experience the same basic emotions and display them to others in the same basic ways. But culture plays a part by specifying the situations that trigger one emotion or another.

had never been spoken. Or with mild laughter we could treat what was said as a joke. Or we could simply respond, "I'm sure you didn't mean that," hearing the statement but not allowing it to destroy the performance. With these options in mind, it is easier to understand Abraham Lincoln's observation that "tact is the ability to describe others the way they see themselves."

Why is tact so common? Embarrassment creates discomfort not only for the actor but also for everyone else. Just as the entire audience feels uneasy when an actor forgets a line, people who observe the awkward behavior of others are reminded of how fragile their own performances often are. Socially constructed reality thus functions like a dam holding back a sea of chaos. Should one person's performance spring a leak, others tactfully help make repairs. After all, everyone lends a hand in building reality, and no one wants it suddenly swept away.

In sum, Goffman's research shows that although behavior is spontaneous in some respects, it is more patterned than we like to think. Almost 400 years ago, William Shakespeare captured this idea in lines that still ring true:

All the world's a stage,
And all the men and women merely players:
They have their exits and their entrances;
And one man in his time plays many parts.

(*As You Like It*, act 2, scene 7)

Interaction in Everyday Life: Three Applications

The final sections of this chapter illustrate the major elements of social interaction by focusing on three important dimensions of everyday life: emotions, language, and humor.

Emotions: The Social Construction of Feeling

Emotions, more commonly called *feelings,* are an important dimension of everyday life. Indeed, what we *do* often matters less than how we *feel* about it. Emotions seem very personal because they are "inside." Even so, just as society guides our behavior, it guides our emotional life.

The Biological Side of Emotions

Studying the social interaction of men and women all over the world, Paul Ekman (1980a, 1980b) reported that people everywhere express six basic emotions: happiness, sadness, anger, fear, disgust, and surprise. In addition, Ekman found that people in every society use much the same facial expressions to show these emotions. To help us understand this universal problem, Ekman explains that some emotional responses seem to be "wired" into human beings; that is, they are biologically programmed in our facial features, muscles, and central nervous system.

Why? Over centuries of evolution, emotions developed in the human species because they serve a social purpose: supporting group life. Emotions are powerful forces that allow us to overcome our individualism and build connections with others. Thus the capacity for emotion arose in our ancestors along with the capacity for culture (Turner, 2000).

The Cultural Side of Emotions

But culture does play an important role in guiding human emotions. First, Ekman explains, culture defines *what triggers* an emotion. Whether people define the departure of an old friend as joyous (causing happiness), insulting (arousing anger), a loss (creating sadness), or mystical (causing surprise and awe) has a lot to do with the culture.

● Seeing Sociology
in Everyday Life

What emotions are (or are not) expected of a college professor in front of a class?

● Seeing Sociology
in Everyday Life

What are the "emotional scripts" that students might apply to college graduation? That is, why might people see this event in positive or negative terms?

CONTROVERSY & DEBATE

Managing Feelings: Women's Abortion Experiences

LIZ: I just *can't* be pregnant! There's no way I can deal with a baby at this point in my life! I'm going to see my doctor tomorrow about an abortion.

JEN: I can't believe you'd do that, Liz! How are you going to feel in a couple of years when you think of what that *child* would be doing if you'd let it live?

Few issues today generate as much emotion as abortion. In a study of women's abortion experiences, the sociologist Jennifer Keys (2002) discovered emotional scripts or "feeling rules" that guide how women feel about ending a pregnancy.

Keys explains that different emotional scripts arise from the political controversy surrounding abortion. The antiabortion movement defines abortion as a personal tragedy, the "killing of an unborn child." Given this definition, which we see in Jen's comment above, women who end a preg-

nancy through abortion are doing something very wrong and can expect to feel grief, guilt,

The words that doctors and nurses use guide whether a woman having an abortion defines the experience in positive or negative terms.

and regret. So intense are these feelings, according to supporters of this position, that such women often suffer from "postabortion syndrome."

Those who take the pro-choice position have an opposing view of abortion. From this point of view, illustrated by Liz's comment, the woman's problem is the *unwanted pregnancy*; abortion is an acceptable medical solution. Therefore, the emotion to be expected in a woman who ends a pregnancy is not guilt but relief.

In her research, Keys conducted in-depth interviews with forty women who had recently had abortions and found that all of them used such scripts to "frame" their situation in an antiabortion or pro-choice manner. In part, this construction of reality reflects the woman's own attitude about abortion. In addition, however, women's partners and friends typically encouraged specific feelings

Second, culture provides rules for the *display* of emotions. For example, most people in the United States express emotions more freely with family members than with others in the workplace. Similarly, we expect children to express emotions to parents, although parents tend to hide their emotions from their children. Third, culture guides how we *value* emotions. Some societies encourage the expression of emotion, while others expect members to control their feelings and maintain a "stiff upper lip." Gender also plays a part; traditionally at least, many cultures expect women to show emotions while condemning emotional expression by men as a sign of weakness. In some cultures, of course, this pattern is less pronounced or even reversed.

Emotions on the Job

In the United States, most people are freer to express their feelings at home than on the job. This is because, as Arlie Russell Hochschild (1979, 1983) explains, the typical corporation or other place of busi-

ness does indeed try to control not only the behavior of its employees but also their emotions. Take the case of an airline flight attendant who offers passengers a drink, a snack, and a smile. Do you think that this smile might convey real pleasure at serving the customer? It may. But Hochschild's study of flight attendants points to a different conclusion: The smile is an emotional script demanded by the airline as the right way to do the job. Therefore, from Hochschild's research we see an added dimension of the "presentation of self" described by Erving Goffman. Not only do our everyday life presentations to others involve surface acting but they also involve the "deep acting" of emotions.

With these patterns in mind, it is easy to see that we socially construct our emotions as part of our everyday reality, a process sociologists call *emotion management*. The Controversy & Debate box relates the very different emotions displayed by women who decide to have an abortion, depending on their personal view of terminating a pregnancy.

○ Making the Grade

The language we use has the effect of reflecting and reinforcing patterns of male dominance.

about the event. Ivy, one young woman in the study, had a close friend who was also pregnant. "Congratulations!" she exclaimed when she learned of Ivy's condition. "We're going to be having babies together!" Such a statement established one "feeling rule"—having a baby is *good*—which sent the message to Ivy that her planned abortion should trigger guilt. Working in the other direction, Jo's partner was horrified at the news that she was pregnant. Doubting his own ability to be a father, he blurted out, "I would rather put a gun to my head than have this baby!" His panic not only defined having the child as a mistake but alarmed Jo as well. Clearly, her partner's reaction made the decision to end the pregnancy a matter of relief from a terrible problem.

Medical personnel also play a part in the process of reality construction by using specific terms. Nurses and doctors who talk about "the baby" encourage the antiabortion framing of abortion and provoke grief and guilt. On the other hand, those who use language such as "pregnancy tissue," "fetus," or "the contents of the uterus" encourage the pro-choice framing of abortion as a simple medical procedure leading to relief. Olivia began using the phrase "products of conception," which she picked up from her doctor. Denise spoke of her procedure as "taking the extra cells out of my body. Yeah, I did feel some guilt when I thought that this was the beginning of life, but my body is full of life— you have lots of cells in you."

After the procedure, most women reported actively trying to manage their feelings. Explained Ivy, "I never used the word 'baby.' I kept saying to myself that it was not formed yet. There was nothing there yet. I kept that in my mind." On the other hand, Keys found that all of the women in her study who had undergone abortions but nevertheless leaned toward the antiabortion position did use the term "baby." When interviewed, Gina explained, "I do think of it as a baby. The truth is that I ended my baby's life and I should not have done that. Thinking that makes me feel guilty. But—considering what I did—maybe I *should* feel guilty." Believing that what she had done was wrong, in other words, Gina actively called out the feeling of guilt—in part, Keys concluded, to punish herself.

WHAT DO YOU THINK?

1. In your own words, explain "emotional scripts" or "feeling rules."

2. Can you apply the idea of "scripting feelings" to the experience of getting married?

3. In light of this discussion, to what extent is it correct to say that our feelings are not as personal as we may think they are?

Language: The Social Construction of Gender

Language is the thread that weaves members of a society in the symbolic web we call culture. Language conveys not only a surface message but also deeper levels of meaning. One important level involves gender. Language defines men and women differently in terms of both power and value (Henley, Hamilton, & Thorne, 1992; Thorne, Kramarae, & Henley, 1983).

Language and Power

A young man proudly rides his new motorcycle up his friend's driveway and asks, "Isn't she a beauty?" On the surface, the question has little to do with gender. Yet why does he use the pronoun *she* rather than *he* or *it* to refer to his prized possession?

The answer is that language helps men establish control over their surroundings. That is, a man attaches a female pronoun to a motorcycle (or car, boat, or other object) because doing so reflects *ownership*. Perhaps this is also why, in the United States and elsewhere, traditionally a woman who marries takes the last name of her husband. But some women today (currently about 18 percent) are asserting their independence by keeping their own name or combining the two family names.

Language and Value

Typically, the English language treats as masculine whatever has greater value, force, or significance. For instance, the adjective *virtuous*, meaning "morally worthy" or "excellent," is derived from the Latin word *vir*, meaning "man." On the other hand, the adjective *hysterical*, meaning "emotionally out of control" comes from the Greek word *hyster*, meaning "uterus."

In many familiar ways, language also confers a different value on the two sexes. Traditional masculine terms such as *king* or *lord* have a positive meaning, while comparable terms, such as *queen, madam,* or *dame,* can have negative meanings. Similarly, the use of the suffixes *-ess* and *-ette* to indicate femininity usually devalues the words

Kevpix\Alamy Images

Many of us think emotions are simply part of our biological makeup. While there is a biological foundation to human emotion, sociologists have demonstrated that what triggers an emotion—as well as when, where, and to whom the emotion is displayed—is shaped by culture. For example, many occupations not only regulate a worker's on-the-job behavior but also expect workers to display a particular emotion, as in the case of the always-smiling airline flight attendant. Can you think of other jobs that regulate emotions in this way?

to which they are added. For example, a *major* has higher standing than a *majorette,* as does a *host* in relation to a *hostess* or a *master* to a *mistress.* Thus language both mirrors social attitudes and helps perpetuate them.

Given the importance of gender to social interaction in everyday life, perhaps we should not be surprised that women and men sometimes have trouble communicating with each other. In the Thinking About Diversity box, Harold and Sybil, whose misadventures finding their friends' home were described in the opening to this chapter, return to illustrate how the two sexes often seem to be speaking different languages.

Reality Play: The Social Construction of Humor

Humor plays an important part in everyday life. Everyone laughs at a joke, but few people think about what makes something funny. We can apply many of the ideas developed in this chapter to explain how, by using humor, we "play with reality" (Macionis, 1987).

The Foundation of Humor

Humor is produced by the social construction of reality; specifically, it arises as people create and contrast two different realities. Generally, one reality is *conventional,* that is, what people in a specific situation expect. The other reality is *unconventional,* an unexpected violation of cultural patterns. In short, humor arises from the contradictions, ambiguities, and double meanings found in differing definitions of the same situation.

There are countless ways to mix realities and thereby generate humor. Contrasting realities emerge from statements that contradict themselves, such as "Nostalgia is not what it used to be"; statements that repeat themselves, such as Yogi Berra's line "It's *déjà vu* all over again"; or statements that mix up words, such as Oscar Wilde's line, "Work is the curse of the drinking class." Even switching around syllables does the trick, as in the case of the country song "I'd Rather Have a Bottle in Front of Me than a Frontal Lobotomy."

You can also build a joke the other way around, leading the audience to expect an unconventional answer and then delivering a very ordinary one. When a reporter asked the famous criminal Willy Sutton why he robbed banks, for example, he replied dryly, "Because that's where the money is." Regardless of how a joke is constructed, the greater the opposition or difference between the two definitions of reality, the greater the humor.

When telling jokes, the comedian uses various strategies to strengthen this opposition and make the joke funnier. One common technique is to present the first, conventional remark in conversation with another actor but then turn toward the audience or the camera to deliver the second, unexpected line. In a Marx Brothers movie, Groucho remarks, "Outside of a dog, a book is a man's best friend." Then, raising his voice and turning to the camera, he adds, "And *inside* of a dog, it's too dark to read!" Such "changing channels" emphasizes the difference between the conventional and unconventional realities. Following the same logic, many stand-up comedians also "reset" the audience to conventional expectations by adding "But seriously, folks, . . ." between jokes. Monty Python comedian John Cleese did this with his trademark line, "And now for something completely different."

Comedians pay careful attention to their performances—the precise words they use and the timing with which they deliver their

THINKING ABOUT DIVERSITY: RACE, CLASS, & GENDER

Gender and Language: "You Just Don't Understand!"

In the story that opened this chapter, Harold and Sybil faced a situation that rings all too true to many people: When they are lost, men grumble to themselves and perhaps blame their partners but avoid asking for directions. For their part, women can't understand why men refuse help when they need it.

Deborah Tannen (1990) explains that men typically define most everyday encounters as competitive. Therefore, getting lost is bad enough without asking for help, which lets someone else get "one up." By contrast, because women have traditionally had a subordinate position, they find it easy to ask for help. Sometimes, Tannen points out, women ask for assistance even when they don't need it.

A similar gender-linked pattern involves what women consider "trying to be helpful" and men call "nagging." Consider the following exchange (adapted from Adler, 1990):

SYBIL: What's wrong, honey?

HAROLD: Nothing.

SYBIL: Something is bothering you. I can tell.

HAROLD: I told you nothing is bothering me. Leave me alone.

SYBIL: But I can see that something is wrong.

HAROLD: OK. Just why do you think something is bothering me?

SYBIL: Well, for one thing, you're bleeding all over your shirt.

HAROLD: (*now irritated*) Yeah, well, it doesn't bother me.

SYBIL: (*losing her temper*) WELL, IT SURE IS BOTHERING ME!

HAROLD: (*walking away*) Fine. I'll go change my shirt.

The problem couples face in communicating is that what one partner *intends* by a comment is not always what the other *hears* in the words. To Sybil, her opening question is an effort at cooperative problem solving. She can see that something is wrong with Harold (who has cut himself while doing yard work), and she wants to help him. But Harold interprets her pointing out his problem as belittling him and tries to close off the discussion. Sybil, confident that Harold would be more positive toward her if he just understood that she only wants to be helpful, repeats her question. This sets in motion a vicious circle in which Harold, thinking his wife is trying to make him feel incapable of looking after himself, responds by digging in his heels. This, in turn, makes his wife all the more sure that she needs to do something. And around it goes until somebody gets really angry.

In the end, Harold agrees to change his shirt but still refuses to discuss the original problem. Defining his wife's concern as "nagging," Harold just wants Sybil to leave him alone. For her part, Sybil fails to understand her husband's view of the situation and walks away convinced that he is a stubborn grouch.

WHAT DO YOU THINK?

1. Based on this box, how would you describe the basic difference between the way men and women talk?
2. What are the reasons for any gender differences in language?
3. Do you think that understanding Tannen's conclusions would help female-male couples communicate better? Why or why not?

Photodisc/Getty Images

lines. A joke is well told if the comic times the lines to create the sharpest possible opposition between the realities; in a careless performance, the joke falls flat. Because the key to humor lies in the collision of realities, we can see why the climax of a joke is termed the "*punch* line."

The Dynamics of Humor: "Getting It"

After hearing a joke, did you ever say, "I don't get it"? To "get" humor, members of an audience must understand the two realities involved well enough to appreciate their difference. A comedian may make getting the joke harder by leaving out some important information. In such cases, the audience must pay attention to the stated elements of the joke and fill in the missing pieces. As a simple example, consider the comment of movie producer Hal Roach upon reaching his hundredth birthday: "If I had known I would live to be one hundred, I would have taken better care of myself!" Here, getting the joke depends on realizing the unstated fact that Roach must have taken pretty good care of himself because he did make it to one hundred.

○ Seeing Sociology
in Everyday Life

Can you remember some of the first jokes you ever heard as a child? Can you explain why very young people's humor focuses on certain topics?

Dana Edelson\AP Wide World Photos

Humor provides an opportunity to express sentiments that are potentially dangerous or disruptive. For this reason, people in every society use humor when they talk about those in power. With this thought in mind, can you explain why just about every president has been the target of jokes? Here, Dwayne "The Rock" Johnson impersonates President Obama on *Saturday Night Live*.

Or take one of W. C. Fields's lines: "Some weasel took the cork out of my lunch!" "What a lunch!" we think to ourselves to "finish" the joke.

Here is an even more complex joke: What do you get if you cross an insomniac, a dyslexic, and an agnostic? Answer: A person who stays up all night wondering if there is a dog. To get this one, you must know that insomnia is an inability to sleep, that dyslexia causes a person to reverse letters in words, and that an agnostic doubts the existence of God.

Why would a comedian require the audience to make this sort of effort to understand a joke? Our enjoyment of a joke is increased by the pleasure of figuring out all the pieces needed to "get it." In addition, "getting" the joke makes you an "insider" compared to

those who don't get it. We have all experienced the frustration of not getting a joke: fear of being judged stupid, coupled with a sense of being excluded from a pleasure shared by others. Sometimes someone may tactfully explain a joke so the other person doesn't feel left out. But as the old saying goes, if a joke has to be explained, it isn't very funny.

The Topics of Humor

All over the world, people smile and laugh, making humor a universal element of human culture. But because the world's people live in different cultures, humor rarely travels well.

October 1, Kobe, Japan. Can you share a joke with people who live halfway around the world? At dinner, I ask two Japanese college women to tell me a joke. "You know 'crayon'?" Asako asks. I nod. "How do you ask for a crayon in Japanese?" I respond that I have no idea. She laughs out loud as she says what sounds like "crayon crayon." Her companion Mayumi laughs too. My wife and I sit awkwardly, straight-faced. Asako relieves some of our embarrassment by explaining that the Japanese word for "give me" is kureyo, which sounds like "crayon." I force a smile.

What is humorous to the Japanese, then, may be lost on the Chinese, Brazilians, or people in the United States. Even the social diversity of this country means that people will find humor in different situations. New Englanders, southerners, and westerners have their own brands of humor, as do Latinos and Anglos, fifteen- and fifty-year-olds, Wall Street bankers and rodeo riders.

But for everyone, topics that lend themselves to double meanings or controversy generate humor. For example, in the United States, the first jokes many of us learned as children concerned bodily functions kids are not supposed to talk about. The mere mention of "unmentionable acts" or certain parts of the body can dissolve young faces in laughter.

Are there jokes that can break through the cultural barrier? Yes, but they must touch on universal human experiences such as, say, turning on a friend:

I think of a number of jokes, but none seems likely to work. Understanding jokes about the United States is difficult for people who know little about our culture. Is there something more universal? Inspiration: "Two men are walking in the woods

Seeing Sociology in Everyday Life

Humor is most common among people with roughly the same social standing. Why is it risky to joke with people who have more power than you do? What about joking with people who have less power?

Making the Grade

Why would comedians doing "blue-collar humor" have to look and sound like "Larry the cable guy"?

and come upon a huge bear. One guy leans over and tightens up the laces on his running shoes. 'Jake,' says the other, 'what are you doing? You can't outrun that bear!' 'I don't have to outrun the bear,' responds Jake. 'I just have to outrun you!'" Smiles all around.

The controversy found in humor often walks a fine line between what is funny and what is "sick." During the Middle Ages, people used the word "humors" (derived from the Latin *humidus,* meaning "moist") to mean a balance of bodily fluids that regulated a person's health. Researchers today document the power of humor to reduce stress and improve health. One recent study of cancer patients, for example, found that the greater a patient's sense of humor, the greater the odds of surviving the disease. Such findings confirm the old saying "Laughter is the best medicine" (Bakalar, 2005; Sven Svebak, cited in M. Elias, 2007). At the extreme, however, people who always take conventional reality lightly risk being defined as deviant or even mentally ill (a common stereotype shows insane people laughing uncontrollably, and for a long time mental hospitals were known as "funny farms").

Then, too, every social group considers certain topics too sensitive for humorous treatment. If you joke about such things, you risk criticism for telling a "sick" joke (and being labeled "sick" yourself). People's religious beliefs, tragic accidents, or appalling crimes are some of the subjects of "sick" jokes or no jokes at all. Even years later, there have been no jokes about the victims of the September 11, 2001, terrorist attacks.

The Functions of Humor

Humor is found everywhere because it works as a safety valve for potentially disruptive statements and ideas. Put another way, humor provides an acceptable way to discuss a sensitive topic without appearing to be serious or being offensive. Having said something controversial, people often use humor to defuse the situ-

Chris Rock is an African American comedian who likes to make jokes involving race, sometimes at the expense of black people. No doubt, many whites have commented, "If I made a joke like that, wow . . ." All people make fun of themselves. But when people of one racial category (especially those who have historically been dominant) make fun of people of another race, their humor can easily seem like a racially insensitive "put down."

zumawirewestphotos\Newscom

ation by simply stating, "I didn't mean anything by what I said—it was just a joke!"

People also use humor to relieve tension in uncomfortable situations. One study of medical examinations found that most patients try to joke with doctors to ease their own nervousness (Baker et al., 1997).

Humor and Conflict

Humor holds the potential to liberate those who laugh, but it can also be used to put down other people. Men who tell jokes about women, for example, are typically expressing some measure of hostility toward them. Similarly, jokes about gay people reveal tensions about sexual orientation. Real conflict can be masked by humor when people choose not to bring the conflict out into the open (Primeggia & Varacalli, 1990).

"Put-down" jokes make one category of people feel good at the expense of another. After collecting and analyzing jokes from many societies, Christie Davies (1990) confirmed that ethnic conflict is a driving force behind humor in most of the world. The typical ethnic joke makes fun of some disadvantaged category of people, at the same time making the joke teller feel superior. Given the Anglo-Saxon traditions of U.S. society, Poles and other ethnic and racial minorities have long been the butt of jokes, as have Newfoundlanders in eastern Canada, Scots in England, Irish in Scotland, Sikhs in India, Turks in Germany, Hausas in Nigeria, Tasmanians in Australia, and Kurds in Iraq.

Disadvantaged people also make fun of the powerful, although usually with some care. Women in the United States joke about men, just as African Americans find humor in white people's ways and poor people poke fun at the rich. Throughout the world, people target their leaders with humor, and officials in some countries take such jokes seriously enough to arrest those who do not show proper respect (Speier, 1998).

In sum, humor is much more important than we may think. It is a means of mental escape from a conventional world that is not entirely to our liking (Flaherty, 1984, 1990; Yoels & Clair, 1995). This fact helps explain why so many of our nation's comedians come from the ranks of historically marginalized peoples, including Jews and African Americans. As long as we maintain a sense of humor, we assert our freedom and are never prisoners of reality. By putting a smile on our faces, we change ourselves and the world just a little and for the better.

Seeing Sociology in Everyday Life

Social Interaction in Everyday Life

How do we all construct the reality we experience?

This chapter suggests that Shakespeare might have had it right when he said "All the world's a stage." And if so, then the Internet may be the latest and greatest stage so far. When we use Web sites such as Facebook, as Goffman explains, we present ourselves as we want others to see us. Everything we write about ourselves as well as how we arrange our page creates an impression in the mind of anyone interested in "checking us out." Take a look at the Facebook page below, paying careful attention to all the details. What is the young man explicitly saying about himself? What can you read "between the lines"? That is, what information can you identify that he may be trying to conceal or at least purposely not be mentioning? How honest do you think his "presentation of self" is? Why? Do a similar analysis of the young woman's Facebook profile shown on the next page.

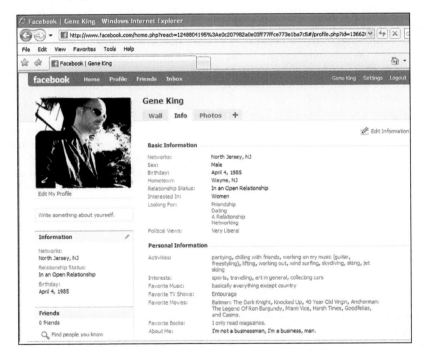

HINT Just about every element of a presentation conveys information about us to others, so all the information found on a Web site like this one is significant. Some information is intentional—for example, what people write about themselves and the photos they choose to post. Other information may be unintentional but is nevertheless picked up by the careful viewer, who may be noting the following things:

- The length and tone of the person's profile (Is it a long-winded list of talents and accomplishments or humorous and modest?)
- The language used (Poor grammar may be a clue to educational level.)
- What hour of the day or night the person wrote the material (A person creating his profile at 11 o'clock on a Saturday night may not be quite the party person he describes himself to be.).

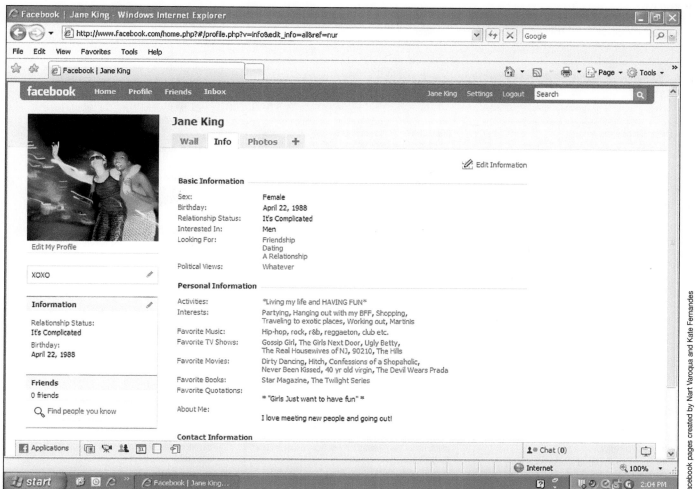

George Doyle\Getty Images – Stockbyte

Facebook pages created by Nart Varoqua and Kate Fernandes

Applying SOCIOLOGY in Everyday Life

1. Identify five important ways in which you present yourself to others, including, for example, the way you decorate your dorm room, apartment, or house; the way you dress; and the way you behave in the classroom. In each case, think about what you are trying to say about yourself. Have your presentations changed in recent years? If so, how, and why?

2. During one full day, every time somebody asks, "How are you?" or "How's it goin'?" stop and actually give a com-

plete, truthful answer. What happens when you respond to a polite question in an honest way? Listen to how people respond, and also watch their body language. What can you conclude?

3. Stroll around downtown or at a local mall. Pay attention to how many women and men you find at each location. From your observations, are there stores that are "gendered" so that there are "female spaces" and "male spaces"? How and why are spaces "gendered"?

Making the Grade

Social Interaction in Everyday Life

What Is Social Structure?

◉─[Watch on mysoclab.com

SOCIAL STRUCTURE refers to social patterns that guide our behavior in everyday life. The building blocks of social structure are
- **STATUS**—a social position that is part of our social identity and that defines our relationships to others
- **ROLE**—the action expected of a person who holds a particular status

✓ *A person holds a status and performs a role.*

A status can be either an
- **ASCRIBED STATUS**, which is involuntary (for example, being a teenager, an orphan, or a Mexican American), or an
- **ACHIEVED STATUS**, which is earned (for example, being an honors student, a pilot, or a thief).

A **MASTER STATUS**, which can be either ascribed or achieved, has special importance for a person's identity (for example, being blind, a doctor, or a Kennedy).

ROLE CONFLICT results from tension among roles linked to two or more statuses (for example, a woman who juggles her responsibilities as a mother and a corporate CEO).

ROLE STRAIN results from tension among roles linked to a single status (for example, the college professor who enjoys personal interaction with students but at the same time knows that social distance is necessary in order to evaluate students fairly).

social interaction the process by which people act and react in relation to others

status a social position that a person holds

status set all the statuses a person holds at a given time

ascribed status a social position a person receives at birth or takes on involuntarily later in life

achieved status a social position a person takes on voluntarily that reflects personal ability and effort

master status a status that has special importance for social identity, often shaping a person's entire life

role behavior expected of someone who holds a particular status

role set a number of roles attached to a single status

role conflict conflict among the roles connected to two or more statuses

role strain tension among the roles connected to a single status

✓ *A person's status set changes over the life course.*

✓ *The role sets attached to a single status vary from society to society around the world.*

The Social Construction of Reality

Through **SOCIAL INTERACTION**, we construct the reality we experience.
- For example, two people interacting both try to shape the reality of their situation.

◉─[Explore on mysoclab.com

The **THOMAS THEOREM** says that the reality people construct in their interaction has real consequences for the future.
- For example, a teacher who believes a certain student to be intellectually gifted may well encourage exceptional academic performance.

social construction of reality the process by which people creatively shape reality through social interaction

Thomas theorem W. I. Thomas's claim that situations defined as real are real in their consequences

ethnomethodology Harold Garfinkel's term for the study of the way people make sense of their everyday surroundings

ETHNOMETHODOLOGY is a strategy to reveal the assumptions people have about their social world.
- We can expose these assumptions by intentionally breaking the "rules" of social interaction and observing the reactions of other people.

Both **CULTURE** and **SOCIAL CLASS** shape the reality people construct.
- For example, a "short walk" for a New Yorker is a few city blocks, but for a peasant in Latin America, it could be a few miles.

✓ *Through the social construction of reality, people creatively shape their social world.*

Dramaturgical Analysis: The "Presentation of Self"

DRAMATURGICAL ANALYSIS explores social interaction in terms of theatrical performance: A status operates as a part in a play and a role is a script.
PERFORMANCES are the way we present ourselves to others.

- Performances are both conscious (intentional action) and unconscious (nonverbal communication).
- Performances include costume (the way we dress), props (objects we carry), and demeanor (tone of voice and the way we carry ourselves).

Read on mysoclab.com

GENDER affects performances because men typically have greater social power than women. Gender differences involve *demeanor, use of space*, and *staring, smiling, and touching*.

- **DEMEANOR**—With greater social power, men have more freedom in how they act.
- **USE OF SPACE**—Men typically command more space than women.
- **STARING** and **TOUCHING** are generally done by men to women.
- **SMILING**, as a way to please another, is more commonly done by women.

IDEALIZATION of performances means we try to convince others that our actions reflect ideal culture rather than selfish motives.

EMBARRASSMENT is the "loss of face" in a performance. People use **TACT** to help others "save face."

dramaturgical analysis Erving Goffman's term for the study of social interaction in terms of theatrical performance

presentation of self Erving Goffman's term for a person's efforts to create specific impressions in the minds of others

nonverbal communication communication using body movements, gestures, and facial expressions rather than speech

personal space the surrounding area over which a person makes some claim to privacy

Interaction in Everyday Life: Three Applications

EMOTIONS: The Social Construction of **FEELING**

The same basic emotions are biologically programmed into all human beings, but culture guides what triggers emotions, how people display emotions, and how people value emotions. In everyday life, the presentation of self involves managing emotions as well as behavior.

LANGUAGE: The Social Construction of **GENDER**

Gender is an important element of everyday interaction. Language defines women and men as different types of people, reflecting the fact that society attaches greater power and value to what is viewed as masculine.

REALITY PLAY: The Social Construction of **HUMOR**

Humor results from the difference between conventional and unconventional definitions of a situation. Because humor is a part of culture, people around the world find different situations funny.

Sample Test Questions

Multiple-Choice Questions

1. **Which of the following concepts defines who we are in relation to others?**
   a. role
   b. status
   c. role set
   d. role strain

2. **In U.S. society, which of the following is typically a master status?**
   a. occupation
   b. age
   c. sex
   d. physical or mental disability

3. *Role set* **refers to**
   a. all the roles found in any one society.
   b. a number of roles attached to a single status.
   c. a number of roles that are more or less the same.
   d. the leadership roles within any one organization.

4. **Frank excels at football at his college, but with the time sports demands, he doesn't have enough time to study. He is experiencing the problem of**
   a. role set.
   b. role strain.
   c. role conflict.
   d. role exit.

5. **The Thomas theorem states that**
   a. our statuses and roles are the key to our personality.
   b. most people rise to their level of incompetence.
   c. people know the world only through their language.
   d. situations defined as real are real in their consequences.

6. **Which of the following is the correct meaning of "presentation of self"?**
   a. efforts to create impressions in the minds of others
   b. acting out a master status

   c. thinking back over the process of role exit
   d. trying to draw attention away from others

7. **Research supports the conclusion that people around the world**
   a. rarely display any emotion when "on the job."
   b. are prompted by the same "triggers" to display emotions.
   c. experience the same six basic emotions.
   d. follow the same rules about when and where to display emotions.

8. **In terms of dramaturgical analysis, tact is understood as**
   a. helping someone take on a new role.
   b. helping someone "save face."
   c. making it difficult for someone to perform a role.
   d. negotiating a situation to get your own way.

9. **In her study of human emotion, Arlie Hochschild explains that many companies**
   a. try to regulate the emotions of workers.
   b. want workers to lack all emotion.
   c. encourage workers to express their true emotions.
   d. profit from making customers more emotional.

10. **People are likely to "get" a joke when they**
    a. know something about more than one culture.
    b. have a different social background than the joke teller.
    c. understand the two different realities being presented.
    d. know why someone wants to tell the joke.

ANSWERS: 1(b); 2(d); 3(b); 4(c); 5(d); 6(a); 7(c); 8(b); 9(a); 10(c).

Essay Questions

1. Explain Erving Goffman's claim that we engage in a "presentation of self." What are the elements of this presentation? Apply this approach to an analysis of a college professor teaching a class.

2. In what ways are human emotions rooted in our biology? In what ways are emotions guided by culture?

Groups and Organizations

Groups and Organizations

- How do groups affect how we behave?

- Why can "who you know" be as important as "what you know"?

- In what ways have large business organizations changed in recent decades?

Watch the *Core Concepts in Sociology* video "Organizational Culture: Norms and Values" on **mysoclab.com**

This chapter analyzes social groups, both small and large, highlighting the differences between them. Then the focus shifts to formal organizations that carry out various tasks in our modern society and provide most of us with jobs.

Historic Site of the Original McDonalds

With the workday over, Juan and Jorge pushed through the doors of the local McDonald's restaurant. "Man, am I hungry," announced Juan, heading right into line. "Look at all the meat I'm gonna eat." But Jorge, a recent immigrant from a small village in Guatemala, is surveying the room with a sociological eye. "There is much more than food to see here. This place is all about America!"

And so it is, as we shall see. But back in 1948, when the story of McDonald's began, people in Pasadena, California, paid little attention to the opening of a new restaurant by brothers Maurice and Richard McDonald. The McDonald brothers' basic concept, which was soon called "fast food," was to serve meals quickly and cheaply to large numbers of people. The brothers trained employees to do highly specialized jobs: One person grilled hamburgers while others "dressed" them, made French fries, whipped up milkshakes, and handed the food to the customers in assembly-line fashion.

As the years went by, the McDonald brothers prospered, and they opened several more restaurants, including one in San Bernardino. It was there, in 1954, that Ray Kroc, a traveling blender and mixer salesman, paid them a visit.

Kroc was fascinated by the efficiency of the McDonald brothers' system and saw the potential for expanding into a nationwide chain of fast-food restaurants. The three launched the plan as partners. Soon Kroc bought out the McDonalds (who returned to running their original restaurant) and went on to become one of the greatest success stories of all time. Today, McDonald's is one of the mostly widely known brand names in the world, with 32,000 restaurants serving 58 million people daily throughout the United States and in 117 other countries.

The success of McDonald's points to more than just the popularity of hamburgers and French fries. The organizational principles that guide this company are coming to dominate social life in the United States and elsewhere. As Jorge correctly observed, this one small business not only transformed the restaurant industry but also changed our way of life.

We begin this chapter by looking at *social groups,* the clusters of people with whom we interact in our daily lives. As you will learn, the scope of group life expanded greatly during the twentieth century. From a world of families, local neighborhoods, and small businesses, our society now relies on the operation of huge corporations and other bureaucracies that sociologists describe as *formal organizations.* Understanding this expansion of social life and appreciating what it means for us as individuals are the main objectives of this chapter.

Social Groups

Almost everyone wants a sense of belonging, which is the essence of group life. A **social group** is *two or more people who identify with and interact with one another.* Human beings come together as couples, families, circles of friends, churches, clubs, businesses, neighborhoods, and large organizations. Whatever the form, groups contain people with shared experiences, loyalties, and interests. While keeping their individuality, members of social groups also think of themselves as a special "we."

Not every collection of individuals forms a group. People with a status in common, such as women, African Americans, homeowners, soldiers, millionaires, college graduates, and Roman Catholics, are not a group but a *category.* Though they know that others hold the same status, most are strangers to one another. Similarly, students sitting in a large stadium interact to a very limited extent. Such a loosely formed collection of people in one place is a *crowd* rather than a group.

However, the right circumstances can quickly turn a crowd into a group. Events from power failures to terrorist attacks can make people bond quickly with strangers.

Primary and Secondary Groups

People often greet one another with a smile and a simple "Hi! How are you?" The response is usually "Fine, thanks. How about you?" This

social group two or more people who identify with and interact with one another

primary group a small social group whose members share personal and lasting relationships

secondary group a large and impersonal social group whose members pursue a specific goal or activity

Seeing Sociology in Everyday Life

List all the groups in your life that you think of as "we." Is each a primary or secondary group?

answer is often more scripted than sincere. Explaining how you are *really* doing might make people feel so awkward that they would beat a hasty retreat.

Social groups are of two types, based on their members' degree of genuine personal concern for one another. According to Charles Horton Cooley, a **primary group** is *a small social group whose members share personal and lasting relationships.* Joined by *primary relationships,* people spend a great deal of time together, engage in a wide range of activities, and feel that they know one another pretty well. In short, they show real concern for one another. The family is every society's most important primary group.

Cooley called personal and tightly integrated groups "primary" because they are among the first groups we experience in life. In addition, family and friends have primary importance in the socialization process, shaping our attitudes, behavior, and social identity.

Members of primary groups help one another in many ways, but they generally think of their group as an end in itself rather than as a means to other ends. In other words, we tend to think that family and friendship link people who "belong together." Members of a primary group also tend to view each other as unique and irreplaceable. Especially in the family, we are bound to others by emotion and loyalty. Brothers and sisters may not always get along, but they always remain "family."

In contrast to the primary group, the **secondary group** is *a large and impersonal social group whose members pursue a specific goal or activity.* In most respects, secondary groups have characteristics opposite those of primary groups. *Secondary relationships* involve weak emotional ties and little personal knowledge of one another. Many secondary groups exist for only a short time, beginning and ending without particular significance. Students enrolled in the same course at a large university—people who may or may not see one another after the semester ends—are one example of a secondary group.

Secondary groups include many more people than primary groups. For example, dozens or even hundreds of people may work in the same company, yet most of them pay only passing attention to one another. Sometimes the passage of time transforms a group from secondary to primary, as with co-workers who share an office for many years and develop closer relationships. But generally, members of a secondary group do not think of themselves as "we." Secondary ties need not be hostile or cold, of course. Interactions among students, co-workers, and business associates are often quite pleasant even if they are impersonal.

Unlike members of primary groups, who display a *personal orientation,* people in secondary groups have a *goal orientation.* Primary group members define each other according to *who* they are in

Michael Newman\PhotoEdit Inc.

As human beings, we live our lives as members of groups. Such groups may be large or small, temporary or long-lasting, and can be based on kinship, cultural heritage, or some shared interest.

terms of family ties or personal qualities, but people in secondary groups look to one another for *what* they are, that is, what they can do for each other. In secondary groups, we tend to "keep score," aware of what we give others and what we receive in return. This goal orientation means that secondary group members usually remain formal and polite. It is in a secondary relationship, therefore, that we ask the question "How are you?" without expecting a truthful answer.

The Summing Up table on the next page reviews the characteristics of primary and secondary groups. Keep in mind that these traits define two types of groups in ideal terms; most real groups contain elements of both. For example, a women's group on a university campus may be quite large (and therefore secondary), but its members may identify strongly with one another and provide lots of mutual support (making it seem primary).

Many people think that small towns and rural areas emphasize primary relationships and that large cities are characterized by secondary ties. This generalization is partly true, but some urban neighborhoods—especially those populated by people of a single ethnic or religious category—can be very tightly knit.

Group Leadership

How do groups operate? One important element of group dynamics is leadership. Although a small circle of friends may have no leader at all, most large secondary groups place leaders in a formal chain of command.

Look closely at the Summing Up table below to be sure you understand how primary and secondary groups differ. The arrows at the top indicate that these two concepts form a continuum—that is, any particular group is primary and secondary to some degree.

instrumental leadership group leadership that focuses on the completion of tasks

expressive leadership group leadership that focuses on the group's well-being

SUMMING UP

Primary Groups and Secondary Groups

	Primary Group ←——————→	Secondary Group
Quality of relationships	Personal orientation	Goal orientation
Duration of relationships	Usually long-term	Variable; often short-term
Breadth of relationships	Broad; usually involving many activities	Narrow; usually involving few activities
Perception of relationships	Ends in themselves	Means to an end
Examples	Families, circles of friends	Co-workers, political organizations

Two Leadership Roles

Groups typically benefit from two kinds of leadership. **Instrumental leadership** refers to *group leadership that focuses on the completion of tasks.* Members look to instrumental leaders to make plans, give orders, and get things done. **Expressive leadership,** by contrast, is *group leadership that focuses on the group's well-being.* Expressive leaders take less of an interest in achieving goals and focus on promoting the well-being of members and minimizing tension and conflict among members.

Because they concentrate on performance, instrumental leaders usually have formal, secondary relationships with other members. These leaders give orders and reward or punish people according to how much they contribute to the group's efforts. Expressive leaders build more personal, primary ties. They offer sympathy to members going through tough times, keep the group united, and lighten serious moments with humor. Typically, successful instrumental leaders enjoy more *respect* from members and expressive leaders generally receive more personal *affection.*

Three Leadership Styles

Sociologists also describe leadership in terms of its decision-making style. *Authoritarian leadership* focuses on instrumental concerns, takes personal charge of decision making, and demands that group members obey orders. Although this leadership style may win little affection from the group, a fast-acting authoritarian leader is appreciated in a crisis.

Democratic leadership is more expressive, making a point of including everyone in the decision-making process. Although less successful in a crisis situation, when there is little time for discussion, democratic leaders generally draw on the ideas of all members to develop creative solutions to problems.

Laissez-faire leadership allows the group to function more or less on its own (*laissez-faire* in French means "leave it alone"). This style is typically the least effective in promoting group goals (White & Lippitt, 1953; Ridgeway, 1983).

Group Conformity

Groups influence the behavior of their members, often promoting conformity. "Fitting in" provides a secure feeling of belonging, but at the extreme, group pressure can be unpleasant and even dangerous. Interestingly, as experiments by Solomon Asch and Stanley Milgram showed, even strangers can encourage group conformity.

Asch's Research

Solomon Asch (1952) recruited students for what he told them was a study of visual perception. Before the experiment began, he explained to all but one member of a small group that their real purpose was to put pressure on the remaining person. Placing six to eight students around a table, Asch showed them a "standard" line, as drawn on Card 1 in Figure 1, and asked them to match it to one of the three lines on Card 2.

Anyone with normal vision can see that the line marked "A" on Card 2 is the correct choice. Initially, as planned, everyone made the matches correctly. But then Asch's secret accomplices began answering incorrectly, leaving the uninformed student (seated at the table so as to answer next to last) bewildered and uncomfortable.

What happened? Asch found that one-third of all subjects chose to conform by answering incorrectly. Apparently, many of us are willing to compromise our own judgment to avoid the discomfort of being different, even from people we do not know.

Go to the Multimedia Library at mysoclab.com
to view the video "Milgram Obedience Study Today"

groupthink the tendency of group members to conform, resulting in a narrow view of some issue

Milgram's Research

Stanley Milgram, a former student of Solomon Asch's, conducted conformity experiments of his own. In Milgram's controversial study (1963, 1965; A. G. Miller, 1986), a researcher explained to male recruits that they would be taking part in a study of how punishment affects learning. One by one, he assigned them to the role of teacher and placed another person—actually an accomplice of Milgram's—in a connecting room to pose as a learner.

The teacher watched as the learner sat down in what looked like an electric chair. The researcher applied electrode paste to one of the learner's wrists, explaining that this would "prevent blisters and burns." The researcher then attached an electrode to the wrist and secured the leather straps, explaining that they would "prevent excessive movement while the learner was being shocked." Although the shocks would be painful, the researcher reassured the teacher, they would cause "no permanent tissue damage."

The researcher then led the teacher back into the adjoining room, pointing out that the "electric chair" was connected to a "shock generator," actually a phony but realistic-looking piece of equipment with a label that read "Shock Generator, Type ZLB, Dyson Instrument Company, Waltham, Mass." On the front was a dial that supposedly regulated electric current from 15 volts (labeled "Slight Shock") to 300 volts ("Intense Shock") to 450 volts ("Danger: Severe Shock"). ● Go to mysoclab.com

Seated in front of the "shock generator," the teacher was told to read aloud pairs of words. Then the teacher was to repeat the first word of each pair and wait for the learner to recall the second word. Whenever the learner failed to answer correctly, the teacher was told to apply an electric shock.

The researcher directed the teacher to begin at the lowest level (15 volts) and to increase the shock by 15 volts every time the learner made a mistake. And so the teacher did. At 75, 90, and 105 volts, the teacher heard moans from the learner; at 120 volts, shouts of pain; by 270 volts, screams; at 315 volts, pounding on the wall; after that, dead silence. Only a few of the forty subjects assigned to the role of teacher during the initial research even questioned the procedure before reaching the dangerous level of 300 volts, and twenty-six of the subjects—almost two-thirds—went all the way to the potentially lethal 450 volts. Even Milgram was surprised at how readily people obeyed authority figures.

Milgram (1964) then modified his research to see whether ordinary people—not authority figures—could pressure strangers to administer electrical shocks, in the same way that Asch's groups had pressured individuals to match lines incorrectly.

This time, Milgram formed a group of three teachers, two of whom were his accomplices. Each of the teachers was to suggest a shock level when the learner made an error; the rule was that the group would then administer the *lowest* of the three suggested

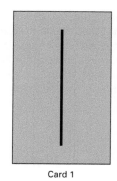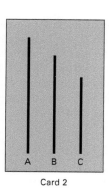

Card 1   Card 2

FIGURE 1 Cards Used in Asch's Experiment in Group Conformity
In Asch's experiment, subjects were asked to match the line on Card 1 to one of the lines on Card 2. Many subjects agreed with the wrong answers given by others in their group.
Source: Asch (1952).

levels. This arrangement gave the person who was not in on the experiment the power to deliver a lesser shock regardless of what the others said.

The accomplices suggested increasing the shock level with each error the learner made, putting pressure on the third person to do the same. The subjects in these groups applied voltages three to four times higher than those applied by subjects acting alone. Thus Milgram's research suggests that people are likely to follow the directions not only of legitimate authority figures but also of groups of ordinary individuals, even if doing so means harming another person.

Janis's "Groupthink"

Experts also cave in to group pressure, says Irving Janis (1972, 1989). Janis argues that a number of U.S. foreign policy blunders, including the failure to foresee the Japanese attack on Pearl Harbor during World War II and our ill-fated involvement in the Vietnam War, resulted from group conformity among our highest-ranking political leaders.

Common sense tells us that group discussion improves decision making. Janis counters that group members often seek agreement that closes off other points of view. Janis called this process **groupthink,** *the tendency of group members to conform, resulting in a narrow view of some issue.*

A classic example of groupthink resulted in the disastrous U.S. invasion of the Bay of Pigs in Cuba in 1961. Looking back, Arthur Schlesinger Jr., an adviser to President Kennedy at the time, confessed

Seeing Sociology in Everyday Life

In terms of in-groups and out-groups, explain what happens when people who may not like each other discover that they have a common enemy.

feeling guilty "for having kept so quiet during those crucial discussions in the Cabinet Room," adding that the group discouraged anyone from challenging what, in hindsight, Schlesinger considered "nonsense" (quoted in Janis, 1972:30, 40). Groupthink may also have been a factor in the U.S. invasion of Iraq in 2003, when U.S. leaders were led to believe—erroneously—that Iraq had stockpiles of weapons of mass destruction.

Reference Groups

How do we assess our own attitudes and behavior? Frequently, we use a **reference group,** *a social group that serves as a point of reference in making evaluations and decisions.*

A young man who imagines his family's response to a woman he is dating is using his family as a reference group. A supervisor who tries to predict her employees' reaction to a new vacation policy is using them in the same way. As these examples suggest, reference groups can be primary or secondary. In either case, our need to conform shows how others' attitudes affect us.

We also use groups we do *not* belong to for reference. Being well prepared for a job interview means showing up dressed the way people in that company dress for work. Conforming to groups we do not belong to is a strategy to win acceptance and illustrates the process of *anticipatory socialization.*

Stouffer's Research

Samuel Stouffer and his colleagues (1949) conducted a classic study of reference groups during World War II. Researchers asked soldiers to rate their own, or any competent soldier's, chances of promotion in their army unit. You might guess that soldiers serving in outfits with high promotion rates would be optimistic about advancement. Yet Stouffer's research pointed to the opposite conclusion: Soldiers in army units with low promotion rates were actually more positive about their chances to move ahead.

The key to understanding Stouffer's results lies in the groups against which soldiers measured themselves. Those assigned to units with lower promotion rates looked around them and saw people making no more headway than they were. Although they had not been promoted, neither had many others, so they did not feel deprived. However, soldiers in units with higher promotion rates could think of many people who had been promoted sooner or more often than they had. With such people in mind, even soldiers who had been promoted themselves were likely to feel shortchanged.

The point is that we do not make judgments about ourselves in isolation, nor do we compare ourselves with just anyone. Regardless of our situation in *absolute* terms, we form a subjective sense of our well-being by looking at ourselves *relative* to specific reference groups (Merton, 1968; Mirowsky, 1987).

In-Groups and Out-Groups

Each of us favors some groups over others, whether because of political outlook, social prestige, or just manner of dress. On some college campuses, for example, left-leaning student activists may look down on fraternity members, whom they view as conservative; fraternity members, in turn, may snub the "nerds" who work too hard. People in just about every social setting make similar positive and negative evaluations of members of other groups.

Such judgments illustrate another key element of group dynamics: the opposition of in-groups and out-groups. An **in-group** is *a social group toward which a member feels respect and loyalty.* An **out-group,** by contrast, is *a social group toward which a person feels a sense of competition or opposition.* In-groups and out-groups are based on the idea that "we" have valued traits that "they" lack.

Tensions between groups sharpen the groups' boundaries and give people a clearer social identity. However, members of in-groups generally hold overly positive views of themselves and unfairly negative views of various out-groups.

Power also plays a part in intergroup relations. A powerful in-group can define others as a lower-status out-group. Historically, in countless U.S. cities and towns, many white people viewed people of color as an out-group and subordinated them socially, politically, and economically. Internalizing these negative attitudes, minorities often struggled to overcome negative self-images. In this way, in-groups and out-groups foster loyalty but also generate conflict (Tajfel, 1982; Bobo & Hutchings, 1996).

Group Size

The next time you go to a party, try to arrive first. If you do, you will be able to observe some fascinating group dynamics. Until about six people enter the room, every person who arrives usually joins in a single conversation. As more people arrive, the group divides into two or more clusters, and it divides again and again as the party grows. This process shows that group size plays a crucial role in how group members interact.

To understand why, note the mathematical number of relationships possible among two to seven people. As shown in Figure 2, two people form a single relationship; adding a third person results in three relationships; a fourth person yields six. Increasing the number of people further boosts the number of relationships much more rapidly because every new individual can interact with everyone already there. Thus by the time seven people join one conversation, twenty-one "channels" connect them. With so many open channels, at this point the group usually divides into smaller conversation groups.

The Dyad

The German sociologist Georg Simmel (1858–1918) explored the dynamics in the smallest social groups. Simmel (1950, orig. 1902)

Making the Grade

Is a network a group? No, because there is no common identification or frequent interaction among members. But fuzzy or not, networks are a valuable resource, which is probably the best reason to understand a little about how they work.

used the term **dyad** (Greek for "pair") to designate *a social group with two members.* Simmel explained that social interaction in a dyad is typically more intense than in larger groups because neither member must share the other's attention with anyone else. In the United States, love affairs, marriages, and the closest friendships are dyadic.

But like a stool with only two legs, dyads are unstable. Both members of a dyad must work to keep the relationship going; if either withdraws, the group collapses. To make marriage more stable, society supports the marital dyad with legal, economic, and often religious ties.

The Triad

Simmel also studied the **triad,** *a social group with three members.* A triad contains three relationships, each of which unites two of the three people. A triad is more stable than a dyad because one member can act as a mediator if relations between the other two become strained. This analysis of group dynamics helps explain why members of a dyad (say, spouses having conflict) often seek out a third person (such as a marriage counselor) to discuss tensions between them.

On the other hand, two of the three can pair up to press their views on the third, or two may intensify their relationship, leaving the other feeling left out. For example, when two of the three members of a triad develop a romantic interest in each other, they will come to understand the meaning of the old saying, "Two's company, three's a crowd."

As groups grow beyond three people, they become more stable and capable of withstanding the loss of one or more members. At the same time, increases in group size reduce the intense interaction possible in only the smallest groups. This is why larger groups are based less on personal attachments and more on formal rules and regulations.

Social Diversity: Race, Class, and Gender

Race, ethnicity, class, and gender each play a part in group dynamics. Peter Blau (1977; Blau, Blum, & Schwartz, 1982; South & Messner, 1986) points out three ways in which social diversity influences intergroup contact:

1. **Large groups turn inward.** Blau explains that the larger a group is, the more likely its members are to concentrate relationships among themselves. Say a college is trying to enhance social diversity by increasing the number of international students. These students may add a dimension of difference, but as their numbers rise, they become more likely to form their own social group. Thus efforts to promote social diversity may have the unintended effect of promoting separatism.

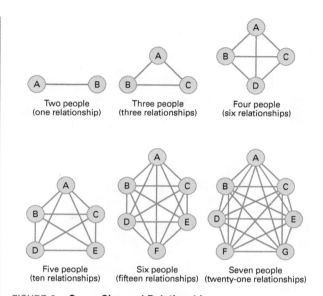

Two people (one relationship)

Three people (three relationships)

Four people (six relationships)

Five people (ten relationships)

Six people (fifteen relationships)

Seven people (twenty-one relationships)

FIGURE 2   Group Size and Relationships

As the number of people in a group increases, the number of relationships that link them increases much faster. By the time six or seven people share a conversation, the group usually divides into two. Why are relationships in smaller groups typically more intense?

2. **Heterogeneous groups turn outward.** The more socially diverse a group is, the more likely its members are to interact with outsiders. Campus groups that recruit people of both sexes and various social backgrounds typically have more intergroup contact than those with members of one social category.

3. **Physical boundaries create social boundaries.** To the extent that a social group is physically segregated from others (by having its own dorm or dining area, for example), its members are less likely to interact with other people.

Networks

A **network** is *a web of weak social ties.* Think of a network as a "fuzzy" group containing people who come into occasional contact but lack a sense of boundaries and belonging. If you think of a *group* as a "circle of friends," think of a *network* as a "social web" expanding outward, often reaching great distances and including large numbers of people.

The largest network of all is the World Wide Web of the Internet. But the Internet has expanded much more in some global regions than in others. Global Map 1 shows that Internet use is high in rich countries and far less common in poor nations.

Go to the Multimedia Library at mysoclab.com to listen to the NPR report "Scientists Debate Six Degrees of Separation"

formal organizations large secondary groups organized to achieve their goals efficiently

The triad, illustrated by Jonathan Green's painting *Friends,* includes three people. A triad is more stable than a dyad because conflict between any two persons can be mediated by the third member. Even so, should the relationship between any two become more intense in a positive sense, those two are likely to exclude the third.

Jonathan Green, *Friends,* 1992. Oil on masonite, 14 in. × 11 in. © Jonathan Green. http://www.jonathangreenstudios.com

Some networks come close to being groups, as in the case of college friends who stay in touch years after graduation by e-mail and telephone. More commonly, however, a network includes people we know of or who know of us but with whom we interact rarely, if at all. As one woman known as a community organizer puts it, "I get calls at home, [and] someone says, 'Are you Roseann Navarro? Somebody told me to call you. I have this problem . . .'" (Kaminer, 1984:94).

Network ties often give us the sense that we live in a "small world." In a classic experiment, Stanley Milgram (1967; Watts, 1999) gave letters to subjects in Kansas and Nebraska intended for specific people in Boston who were unknown to the original subjects. No addresses were given, and the subjects in the study were told to send the letters to others they knew personally who might know the target people. Milgram found that the target people received the letters

with, on average, six people passing them on. This result led Milgram to claim that everyone is connected to everyone else by "six degrees of separation." Later research, however, has cast doubt on Milgram's claim. Examining Milgram's original data, Judith Kleinfeld noted that most of Milgram's letters (240 out of 300) never arrived at all (Wildavsky, 2002). Most of those that did reach their destination had been given to people who were wealthy, a fact that led Kleinfeld to conclude that rich people are better connected across the country than ordinary men and women. ● Go to mysoclab.com

Network ties may be weak, but they can be a powerful resource. For immigrants trying to become established in a new community, businesspeople seeking to expand their operations, or new college graduates looking for a job, *whom* you know often is just as important as *what* you know (Hagan, 1998; Petersen, Saporta, & Seidel, 2000).

Networks are based on people's colleges, clubs, neighborhoods, political parties, religious organizations, and personal interests. Obviously, some networks are made up of people with more wealth, power, and prestige than others; that explains the importance of being "well connected." The networks of more privileged categories of people—such as the members of a country club—are a valuable form of "social capital," which is more likely to lead people in these categories to higher-paying jobs (Green, Tigges, & Diaz, 1999; Lin, Cook, & Burt, 2001).

Some people also have denser networks than others; that is, they are connected to more people. Typically, the largest social networks include people who are young, well educated, and living in large cities (Fernandez & Weinberg, 1997; Podolny & Baron, 1997).

Gender also shapes networks. Although the networks of men and women are typically of the same size, women include more relatives (and more women) in their networks, and men include more co-workers (and more men). Women's ties, therefore, may not be quite as powerful as typical "old boy" networks. But research suggests that as gender equality increases in the United States, the networks of men and women are becoming more alike (Reskin & McBrier, 2000; Torres & Huffman, 2002).

Formal Organizations

As noted earlier, a century ago, most people lived in small groups of family, friends, and neighbors. Today, our lives revolve more and more around **formal organizations,** *large secondary groups organized to achieve their goals efficiently.* Formal organizations such as corporations and government agencies differ from small primary groups in their impersonality and their formally planned atmosphere.

When you think about it, organizing more than 300 million members of U.S. society is truly remarkable, whether it involves paving roads, collecting taxes, schooling children, or delivering the mail. To carry out most of these tasks, we rely on large formal organizations.

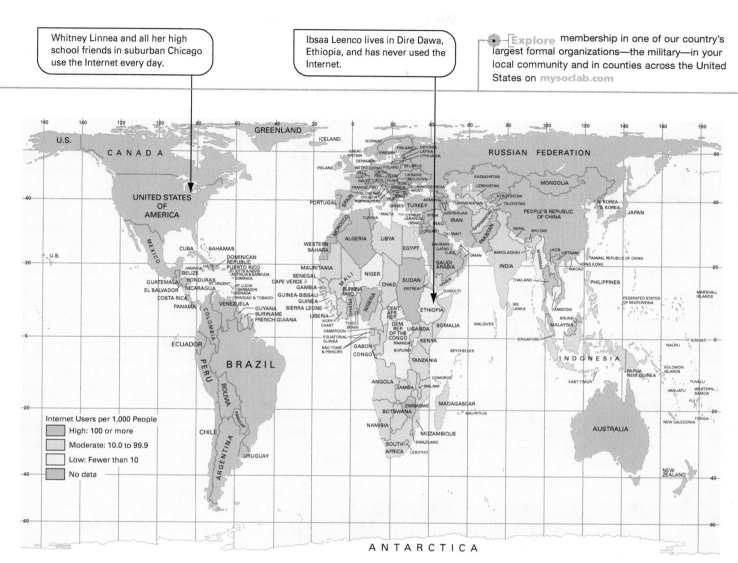

Whitney Linnea and all her high school friends in suburban Chicago use the Internet every day.

Ibsaa Leenco lives in Dire Dawa, Ethiopia, and has never used the Internet.

Explore membership in one of our country's largest formal organizations—the military—in your local community and in counties across the United States on mysoclab.com

Internet Users per 1,000 People

High: 100 or more

Moderate: 10.0 to 99.9

Low: Fewer than 10

No data

Window on the World

GLOBAL MAP 1   Internet Users in Global Perspective

This map shows how the Information Revolution has affected countries around the world. In most high-income nations, at least one-third of the population uses the Internet. By contrast, only a small share of people in low-income nations does so. What effect does this pattern have on people's access to information? What does this mean for the future in terms of global inequality?

Source: International Telecommunication Union (2009).

Types of Formal Organizations

Amitai Etzioni (1975) identified three types of formal organizations, distinguished by the reasons people participate in them: utilitarian organizations, normative organizations, and coercive organizations.

Utilitarian Organizations

Just about everyone who works for income belongs to a *utilitarian organization,* one that pays people for their efforts. Becoming part of a utilitarian organization—a business, government agency, or school system, for example—is usually a matter of individual choice, although most people must join one or another such organization to make a living. Explore on mysoclab.com

Normative Organizations

People join *normative organizations* not for income but to pursue some goal they think is morally worthwhile. Sometimes called *voluntary associations,* these include community service groups (such as Amnesty International, the PTA, the League of Women Voters, and the Red Cross), political parties, and religious organizations. In global perspective, people in the United States and in other high-income countries are the most likely to join voluntary associations. A recent study found that 72 percent of first-year college students in the United States said they had participated in some organized volunteer activity within the past year (Pryor et al., 2009; see also Curtis, Baer, & Grabb, 2001; Schofer & Fourcade-Gourinchas, 2001).

Coercive Organizations

Coercive organizations have involuntary memberships. People are forced to join these organizations as a form of punishment (prisons) or treatment (some psychiatric hospitals). Coercive organizations have special physical features, such as locked doors and barred windows, and are supervised by security personnel. They isolate people (whom they label "inmates" or "patients") for a period of time in order to radically change their attitudes and behavior. Recall the power of a total institution to change a person's sense of self.

It is possible for a single formal organization to fall into *all* of these categories from the point of view of different individuals. For example, a mental hospital serves as a coercive organization for a patient, a utilitarian organization for a psychiatrist, and a normative organization for a hospital volunteer.

Chris Haston\NBCU Photo Bank

Weber described the operation of the ideal bureaucracy as rational and highly efficient. In real life, actual large organizations often operate very differently from Weber's model, as can be seen on the television show *The Office*.

Origins of Formal Organizations

Formal organizations date back thousands of years. Elites who controlled early empires relied on government officials to collect taxes, undertake military campaigns, and build monumental structures, from the Great Wall of China to the pyramids of Egypt.

However, early organizations had two limitations. First, they lacked the technology to travel over large distances, to communicate quickly, and to gather and store information. Second, the preindustrial societies they were trying to rule had traditional cultures. **Tradition,** according to the German sociologist Max Weber, consists of *values and beliefs passed from generation to generation.* Tradition makes a society conservative, Weber explained, because it limits an organization's efficiency and ability to change.

By contrast, Weber described the modern worldview as **rationality,** *a way of thinking that emphasizes deliberate, matter-of-fact calculation of the most efficient way to accomplish a particular task.* A rational worldview pays little attention to the past and is open to any changes that might get the job done better or more quickly.

The rise of the "organizational society" rests on what Weber called the **rationalization of society,** *the historical change from tradition to rationality as the main type of human thought.* Modern society, he claimed, becomes "disenchanted" as sentimental ties give way to a rational focus on science, complex technology, and the organizational structure called bureaucracy.

Characteristics of Bureaucracy

Bureaucracy is *an organizational model rationally designed to perform tasks efficiently.* Bureaucratic officials regularly create and revise policy to increase efficiency. To appreciate the power and scope of bureaucratic organization, consider that any one of almost 400 million phones in the United States can connect you within seconds to any other phone in a home, a business, an automobile, or even a hiker's backpack on a remote trail in the Rocky Mountains. Such instant communication is beyond the imagination of people who lived in the ancient world.

Our telephone system depends on technology such as electricity, fiber optics, and computers. But the system could not exist without the organizational capacity to keep track of every telephone call—recording which phone called which other phone, when, and for how long—and presenting all this information to more than 200 million telephone users in the form of a monthly bill (Federal Communications Commission, 2008; CTIA, 2009).

● Seeing Sociology
in Everyday Life

Give an example of each of the factors listed here in the
operation of your college or university bureaucracy.

○ Making the Grade

The six traits listed here defined, for Weber, the *ideal*
bureaucracy. This means that in its pure form, bureaucracy has
all these traits. Actual organizations, of course, may differ in
some way from the ideal.

SUMMING UP

Small Groups and Formal Organizations

	Small Groups	Formal Organizations
Activities	Much the same for all members	Distinct and highly specialized
Hierarchy	Often informal or nonexistent	Clearly defined, corresponding to offices
Norms	General norms, informally applied	Clearly defined rules and regulations
Membership criteria	Variable; often based on personal affection or kinship	Technical competence to carry out assigned tasks
Relationships	Variable and typically primary	Typically secondary, with selective primary ties
Communications	Typically casual and face to face	Typically formal and in writing
Focus	Person-oriented	Task-oriented

What specific traits promote organizational efficiency? Max Weber (1978, orig. 1921) identified six key elements of the ideal bureaucratic organization:

1. **Specialization.** Our ancestors spent most of their time looking for food and finding shelter. Bureaucracy, by contrast, assigns individuals highly specialized jobs.

2. **Hierarchy of offices.** Bureaucracies arrange workers in a vertical ranking. Each person is thus supervised by someone "higher up" in the organization while in turn supervising others in lower positions. Usually, with few people at the top and many at the bottom, bureaucratic organizations take the form of a pyramid.

3. **Rules and regulations.** Rationally enacted rules and regulations guide a bureaucracy's operation. Ideally, a bureaucracy seeks to operate in a completely predictable way.

4. **Technical competence.** Bureaucratic officials have the technical competence to carry out their duties. Bureaucracies typically hire new members according to set standards and then monitor their performance. Such impersonal evaluation contrasts with the ancient custom of favoring relatives, whatever their talents, over strangers.

5. **Impersonality.** Bureaucracy puts rules ahead of personal whim so that both clients and workers are all treated in the same way. From this impersonal approach comes the commonplace image of the "faceless bureaucrat."

6. **Formal, written communications.** It is often said that the heart of bureaucracy is not people but paperwork. Rather than casual, face-to-face talk, bureaucracy depends on formal, written memos and reports, which accumulate in vast files.

Bureaucratic organization promotes efficiency by carefully hiring workers and limiting the unpredictable effects of personal taste and opinion. The Summing Up table reviews the differences between small social groups and large formal organizations.

Organizational Environment

All organizations exist in the larger world. How well any organization performs depends not only on its own goals and policies but also on the **organizational environment,** *factors outside an organization that affect its operation.* These factors include technology, economic and political trends, current events, the available workforce, and other organizations.

Modern organizations are shaped by *technology,* including copiers, telephones, and computer equipment. Computers give employees access to more information and people than ever before. At the same time, computer technology allows managers to closely monitor the activities of workers (Markoff, 1991).

Economic and political trends affect organizations. All organizations are helped or hurt by periodic economic growth or recession. Most industries also face competition from abroad as well as changes in laws—such as new environmental standards—at home.

○ Making the Grade

Just because an organization is efficient doesn't mean that people enjoy being part of it or that it is actually good for people. Weber feared the opposite: The more rational and bureaucratic society became, the less it would advance human well-being.

● Seeing Sociology
in Everyday Life

Do you think FEMA or other large government organizations are inherently inefficient, or do you think their leaders sometimes make bad decisions? Explain your answer.

Current events can have significant effects even on organizations that are far away. Events such as the rise in energy prices that followed the 2005 hurricanes that devastated the Gulf states, the 2006 elections that transferred leadership in Congress from Republicans to Democrats, and the 2008 elections that handed control of both the White House and Congress to the Democrats affected the operation of both government and business organizations.

Population patterns also affect organizations. The average age, typical level of education, social diversity, and size of a local community determine the available workforce and sometimes the market for an organization's products or services.

Other organizations also contribute to the organizational environment. To be competitive, a hospital must be responsive to the insurance industry and to organizations representing doctors, nurses, and other health care workers. It must also be aware of the medical equipment, health care procedures, and prices available at nearby facilities.

The Informal Side of Bureaucracy

Weber's ideal bureaucracy deliberately regulates every activity. In real-life organizations, however, human beings are creative (and stubborn) enough to resist bureaucratic regulation. Informality may amount to cutting corners on the job at times, but it can also provide the flexibility needed for an organization to adapt and be successful.

In part, informality comes from the personalities of organizational leaders. Studies of U.S. corporations document that the qualities and quirks of individuals—including personal charisma, interpersonal skills, and the ability to recognize problems—can have a great effect on organizational performance (Halberstam, 1986; Baron, Hannan, & Burton, 1999).

Authoritarian, democratic, and laissez-faire types of leadership (described earlier in this chapter) reflect individual personality as much as any organizational plan. Then, too, in the "real world" of organizations, leaders sometimes seek to benefit personally through abuse of organizational power. Many of the corporate leaders of banks and insurance companies that collapsed during the financial meltdown of 2008 walked off with multimillion-dollar "golden parachutes." More commonly, leaders take credit for the efforts of the people who work for them. For example, the responsibilities—and authority—of many secretaries are far greater than their official job titles and salaries suggest.

Communication offers another example of organizational informality. Memos and other written documents are the formal way to spread information through the organization. Typically, however, people create informal networks, or "grapevines," that spread information quickly, if not always accurately. Grapevines, using word of mouth and e-mail, are particularly important to rank-and-file workers because higher-ups often try to keep important information from them.

The spread of e-mail has "flattened" organizations somewhat, allowing even the lowest-ranking employee to bypass immediate superiors to communicate directly with the organization's leader or all fellow employees at once. Some organizations consider such "open channel" communication unwelcome and limit the use of e-mail. Leaders may also seek to protect themselves from a flood of messages each day. Microsoft Corporation (whose founder, Bill Gates, has an "unlisted" address that helps him limit his e-mail to hundreds of messages each day) has developed screens that filter out all messages except those from approved people (Gwynne & Dickerson, 1997).

Using new information technology together with age-old human ingenuity, members of formal organizations often find ways to personalize their work and surroundings. Such efforts suggest that we should take a closer look at some of the problems of bureaucracy.

Problems of Bureaucracy

We rely on bureaucracy to manage everyday life efficiently, but many people are uneasy about large organizations gaining too much influence. Bureaucracy can dehumanize and manipulate us, and some say it poses a threat to political democracy. These dangers are discussed in the following sections.

Bureaucratic Alienation

Max Weber held up bureaucracy as a model of productivity. Yet Weber was keenly aware of bureaucracy's potential to *dehumanize* the people it is supposed to serve. The impersonality that fosters efficiency also keeps officials and clients from responding to each other's unique personal needs. Typically, officials treat each client impersonally as a standard "case." Sometimes the tendency toward dehumanization goes too far, as in 2008 when the U.S. Army accidentally sent letters to family members of soldiers killed in Iraq and Afghanistan, addressing the recipients as "John Doe" ("Army Apologizes," 2009).

Formal organizations create *alienation,* according to Weber, by reducing the human being to "a small cog in a ceaselessly moving mechanism" (1978:988, orig. 1921). Although formal organizations are designed to benefit humanity, Weber feared that people might well end up serving formal organizations.

Bureaucratic Inefficiency and Ritualism

On Labor Day 2005, as people in New Orleans and other coastal areas were battling to survive in the wake of Hurricane Katrina, 600 firefighters from around the country assembled in a hotel meeting room in Atlanta awaiting deployment. Officials of the Federal Emergency Management Agency (FEMA) explained to the crowd that they were first going to be given a lecture on "equal opportunity, sexual harassment, and customer service." Then, the official continued, they would

bureaucratic ritualism a focus on rules and regulations to the point of undermining an organization's goals

bureaucratic inertia the tendency of bureaucratic organizations to perpetuate themselves

oligarchy the rule of the many by the few

scientific management the application of scientific principles to the operation of a business or other large organization

each be given a stack of FEMA pamphlets with the agency's phone number to distribute to people in the devastated areas. A firefighter stood up and shouted, "This is ridiculous. Our fire departments and mayors sent us down here to save lives, and you've got us doing *this?*" The FEMA official thundered back, "You are now employees of FEMA, and you will follow orders and do what you are told" ("Places," 2005:39).

Finally, new technology has greatly expanded networking in today's world, especially among younger people who typically make use of Facebook and other social networking Web sites. Once in cyberspace, however, information we post may end up being read by almost anyone, which can cause some serious problems. The Seeing Sociology in the News article on the next two pages takes a closer look.

People sometimes describe inefficiency by saying that an organization has too much "red tape," meaning that important work does not get done. The term "red tape" is derived from the ribbon used by slow-working eighteenth-century English administrators to wrap official parcels and records (Shipley, 1985).

To Robert Merton (1968), red tape amounts to a new twist on the familiar concept of group conformity. He coined the term **bureaucratic ritualism** to describe *focusing on rules and regulations to the point of undermining an organization's goals.* In short, rules and regulations should be a means to an end, not an end in themselves that takes the focus away from the organization's stated goals. After the terrorist attacks of September 11, 2001, the U.S. Postal Service continued to help deliver mail addressed to Osama bin Laden to a post office in Afghanistan, despite the objections of the FBI. It took an act of Congress to change the policy (Bedard, 2002).

Bureaucratic Inertia

If bureaucrats sometimes have little reason to work very hard, they have every reason to protect their jobs. Thus officials typically work to keep their organization going even when its goal has been realized. As Max Weber put it, "Once fully established, bureaucracy is among the social structures which are hardest to destroy" (1978:987, orig. 1921).

Bureaucratic inertia refers to *the tendency of bureaucratic organizations to perpetuate themselves.* Formal organizations tend to take on a life of their own beyond their formal objectives. For example, the U.S. Department of Agriculture still has offices in nearly every county in all fifty states, even though only about one county in seven has any working farms. Usually, an organization manages to stay in business by redefining its goals; for example, the Agriculture Department now performs a broad range of work not directly related to farming, including nutritional and environmental research.

George Tooker's painting *Government Bureau* is a powerful statement about the human costs of bureaucracy. The artist paints members of the public in a drab sameness—reduced from human beings to mere "cases" to be disposed of as quickly as possible. Set apart from others by their positions, officials are "faceless bureaucrats" concerned more with numbers than with providing genuine assistance (notice that the artist places the fingers of the officials on calculators).

George Tooker, *Government Bureau*, 1956. Egg tempera on gesso panel, 19⅝ × 29⅝ inches. The Metropolitan Museum of Art, George A. Hearn Fund, 1956 (56.78). Photograph courtesy of The Metropolitan Museum of Art/Art Resource, NY.

Oligarchy

Early in the twentieth century, Robert Michels (1876–1936) pointed out the link between bureaucracy and political **oligarchy,** *the rule of the many by the few* (1949, orig. 1911). According to what Michels called the "iron law of oligarchy," the pyramid shape of bureaucracy places a few leaders in charge of the resources of the entire organization.

Weber believed that a strict hierarchy of responsibility resulted in high organizational efficiency. But Michels countered that hierarchy also weakens democracy because officials can and often do use their access to information, resources, and the media to promote their own personal interests.

Furthermore, bureaucracy helps distance officials from the public, as in the case of the corporate president or public official who is "unavailable for comment" to the local press or the national president who withholds documents from Congress claiming "executive privilege." Oligarchy, then, thrives in the hierarchical structure of bureaucracy and reduces the accountability of leaders to the people (Tolson, 1995).

Political competition, term limits, a system of checks and balances, and the law prevent the U.S. government from becoming an out-and-out oligarchy. Even so, in U.S. political races, candidates who have the

ABC News

Professor Suspended After Joke About Killing Students on Facebook

BY DALIA FAHMY
March 3, 2010

The list of Facebook faux-pas just grew longer.

Gloria Gadsden, a sociology professor at East Stroudsburg University in Pennsylvania, says she was suspended last week after updating her Facebook status with complaints about work that alluded to violence.

In January, she wrote: "Does anyone know where I can find a very discreet hitman? Yes, it's been that kind of day." Then in February: "had a good day today. DIDN'T want to kill even one student.:-). Now Friday was a different story."

Gadsden says she posted the comments in jest, on a profile she thought could only be seen by friends and family. She says officials were notified of the posts by a student—even though she says she had no students in her "friend" list.

"I was just having a bad day, and I was venting to family and friends," says Gadsden, who says she didn't realize her comments could be read by the

public after Facebook relaxed its privacy standards in December. "My friends and family knew I was being facetious. They knew I wasn't targeting anyone."

Nevertheless, university officials were unhappy about the allusions to violence in the posts, she says, and in a meeting with her even mentioned the recent shooting spree by a disgruntled biologist at the University Alabama-Huntsville.

"Given the climate of security concerns in academia, the university has an obligation to take all threats seriously and act accordingly," Marilyn Wells, ESU's interim provost and vice president for academic affairs, told *The Chronicle of Higher Education* last week. Wells and other university officials did not return calls from ABC News seeking comment.

Workers have been getting in trouble often over their online vents. Not only do employers want to control their online image as closely as they can, but they are also vulnerable, like anybody else, to hurt pride.

"When you badmouth your boss and the boss is hearing, whether you're doing it online or at the coffee maker, the boss isn't going to be happy," says Jonathan Ezor, assistant professor of law and technology at Touro Law Center in Huntington, New York. "The fact that it's online makes it more easily findable and have a broader potential impact."

The comments that provoke employers into action usually contain obscenities or exaggerations that could hurt relations with customers.

Last year, for example, Dan Leone, a stadium worker for the Philadelphia Eagles, was fired after he reacted with an online obscenity to news that one of the Eagles' star players was leaving to join the Denver Broncos.

"Dan is [deleted] devastated about Dawkins signing with Denver. Dam Eagles R Retarted," was the comment that cost Leone his job.

Although he later apologized and tried to get his job back, his employer wouldn't budge. . . .

In the U.K., Virgin Atlantic Airlines fired thirteen cabin crew members after they made fun of

---

visibility, power, and money that come with already being in office enjoy a significant advantage. In recent congressional elections, as few as 6 percent of congressional officeholders running for reelection were defeated by their challengers (Center for Responsive Politics, 2009).

The Evolution of Formal Organizations

The problems of bureaucracy—especially the alienation it produces and its tendency toward oligarchy—stem from two organizational traits: hierarchy and rigidity. To Weber, bureaucracy is a top-down system: Rules and regulations made at the top guide every part of people's work down the chain of command. A century ago in the United States, Weber's ideas took hold in an organizational model called *scientific management*. We take a look at this model and then examine three challenges over the course of the twentieth century that gradually have led to a new model: the *flexible organization*.

Scientific Management

Frederick Winslow Taylor (1911) had a simple message: Most businesses in the United States were sadly inefficient. Managers had little idea of how to increase their business's output, and workers relied on the same tired skills of earlier generations. To increase efficiency, Taylor explained, business should apply the principles of modern

science. **Scientific management,** then, is *the application of scientific principles to the operation of a business or other large organization.*

Scientific management involves three steps. First, managers carefully observe the job performed by each worker, identifying all the operations involved and measuring the time needed for each. Second, managers analyze their data, trying to discover ways for workers to perform each job more efficiently. For example, managers might decide to give workers different tools or to reposition various work operations within the factory. Third, management provides guidance and incentives for workers to do their jobs more efficiently. If a factory worker moves 20 tons of pig iron in one day, for example, management would show the worker how to do the job more efficiently and then provide higher wages as the worker's productivity rises. Taylor concluded that if scientific principles were applied to all the steps of the production process, companies would become more profitable, workers would earn higher wages, and consumers would pay lower prices.

A century ago, the auto pioneer Henry Ford put it this way: "Save ten steps a day for each of 12,000 employees, and you will have saved fifty miles of wasted motion and misspent energy" (Allen & Hyman, 1999:209). In the early 1900s, the Ford Motor Company and many other businesses followed Taylor's lead and experienced dramatic improvements in efficiency.

The successful application of scientific management suggested that decision-making power in the workplace should rest with the owners and executives, who paid little attention to the ideas of their workers. As the decades passed, however, formal organizations faced passengers in their postings and quipped about defective engines.

The discount airline, owned by Sir Richard Branson, told *The Guardian* at the time that the postings were "totally inappropriate" and "brought the company into disrepute."

Social media mavens can even get in trouble before they've been hired. Remember the case of the Cisco fatty that went viral last year?

One Twitter user posted an update last year saying "Cisco just offered me a job! Now I have to weigh the utility of a fatty paycheck against the daily commute to San Jose and hating the work."

A Cisco employee responded, "Who is the hiring manager? I'm sure they would love to know that you will hate the work. We here at Cisco are versed in the Web."

Needless to say, the applicant did not end up working at Cisco.

Several Web sites, such as JobVent.com, have sprung up in recent years to make it easier for employees to vent their job frustrations online.

There's even a website called IhateDell.net that allows employees (and customers) to air their complaints about the computer maker.

In some cases, online postings by disgruntled employees can seriously damage a company's bottom line. Just ask Domino's Pizza.

Domino's sales dropped last year after an employee posed for five YouTube videos. In one, he stuffed cheese up his nose and put it into a sandwich. In another, he sneezed into a cheese steak sandwich.

Once the poser and the photographer—also a Domino's employee—were identified, they were fired and sued by Dominos.

In this case, the transgression seemed very clear. But employees often complain that their online posts are only used as excuses to fire them.

Gadsden, the professor from East Stroudsburg, says that university officials have been discriminating against her ever since she wrote an essay in *The Chronicle of Higher Education* saying universities don't do enough to retain minority faculty. . . .

"Their reaction (to the posts) was exaggerated," says Gadsden, noting that she was not given a warning or a chance to correct her actions before she was suspended.

WHAT DO YOU THINK?

1. Do you have a Facebook page? If so, whom do you allow to view it? Could something like what happened to Professor Gadsden or others mentioned in this article happen to you?

2. Is "badmouthing" your boss online more serious than verbal gossip among coworkers? Why or why not?

3. Do you think the university was justified in suspending Professor Gadsden? What would you have done to resolve this case?

"Professor Suspended After Joke About Killing Students on Facebook" by Dalia Fahmy. Copyright © 2010 ABC News Internet Ventures. Source: http://abcnews.go.com/Business/PersonalFinance/facebook-firings-employees-online-vents-twitter-postings-cost/story?id=9986796

important challenges involving race and gender, rising competition from abroad, and the changing nature of work itself. We now take a brief look at each of these challenges and how they prompted organizations to change.

The First Challenge: Race and Gender

In the 1960s, critics claimed that big businesses and other organizations engaged in unfair hiring practices. Rather than hiring on the basis of competence as Weber had proposed, they routinely excluded women and other minorities, especially from positions of power. Hiring on the basis of competence is partly a matter of fairness; it is also a matter of enlarging an organization's talent pool to promote efficiency.

Patterns of Privilege and Exclusion

In the early twenty-first century, as shown in Figure 3, non-Hispanic white men in the United States—33 percent of the working-age population—still held 63 percent of senior-level management jobs. Non-Hispanic white women also made up 33 percent of the population, but they held just 24 percent of executive positions (U.S. Equal Employment Opportunity Commission, 2009). The members of other minorities lagged further behind.

Rosabeth Moss Kanter (1977; Kanter & Stein, 1979) points out that excluding women and minorities from the workplace ignores the talents of more than half the population. Furthermore, underrepresented people in an organization often feel like socially isolated out-groups: uncomfortably visible, taken less seriously, and with fewer chances for promotion. Sometimes what passes for "merit" or good work in an organization is simply being of the right social category (Castilla, 2008).

Opening up an organization so that change and advancement happen more often, Kanter claims, improves everyone's on-the-job performance by motivating employees to become "fast-trackers" who work harder and are more committed to the company. By contrast, an organization with many dead-end jobs turns workers into less productive "zombies" who are never asked for their opinion on anything. An open organization also encourages leaders to seek out the ideas of all employees, which usually improves decision making.

The "Female Advantage"

Some organizational researchers argue that women bring special management skills that strengthen an organization. According to Deborah Tannen (1994), women have a greater "information focus" and more readily ask questions in order to understand an issue. Men, by contrast, have an "image focus" that makes them wonder how asking questions in a particular situation will affect their reputation.

In another study of women executives, Sally Helgesen (1990) found three other gender-linked patterns. First, women place greater value on communication skills and share information more than men do. Second, women are more flexible leaders who typically give their employees greater freedom. Third, compared to men, women tend to emphasize the interconnectedness of all organizational

● Seeing Sociology
in Everyday Life

Think of the jobs people in your family do—are they industrial jobs (making things) or postindustrial jobs (processing information)?

Diversity Snapshot

> Compared to their percentage of the total population, white men are overrepresented in senior management positions.

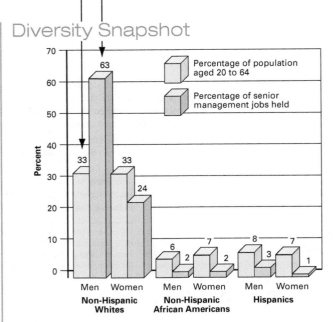

FIGURE 3   **U.S. Managers in Private Industry by Race, Sex, and Ethnicity, 2007**

White men are more likely than their population size suggests to be senior managers in private industry. The opposite is true for white women and other minorities. What factors do you think may account for this pattern?

Sources: U.S. Census Bureau (2009) and U.S. Equal Employment Opportunity Commission (2009).

industry, as well as companies making electronics, cameras, and many other products, has drawn attention to the "Japanese work organization." How has so small a country been able to challenge the world's economic powerhouse?

Japanese organizations reflect that nation's strong collective spirit. In contrast to the U.S. emphasis on rugged individualism, the Japanese value cooperation. In effect, formal organizations in Japan are more like large primary groups. A generation ago, William Ouchi (1981) highlighted differences between formal organizations in Japan and in the United States. First, Japanese companies hired new workers in groups, giving everyone the same salary and responsibilities. Second, many Japanese companies hired workers for life, fostering a strong sense of loyalty. Third, with the idea that employees would spend their entire careers there, many Japanese organizations trained workers in all phases of their operations. Fourth, although Japanese corporate leaders took ultimate responsibility for their organizations' performance, they involved workers in "quality circles" to discuss decisions that affected them. Fifth, Japanese companies played a large role in the lives of workers, providing home mortgages, sponsoring recreational activities, and scheduling social events. Together, such policies encouraged much more loyalty among members of Japanese organizations than was the case in their U.S. counterparts.

Not everything has worked out well for Japanese corporations. Around 1990, the Japanese economy entered a downward trend that has persisted for two decades. During this downturn, many Japanese companies changed their policies, no longer offering workers jobs for life or many of the other benefits noted by Ouchi. Japanese society is also aging—with a large share of the population over age sixty-five and not working—and this pattern is likely to slow economic growth in the future.

For the widely admired Toyota corporation, 2010 turned out to be a year of trouble. Having expanded its operations to become the world's largest auto company, Toyota was forced to announce recalls of millions of its vehicles due to mechanical problems, suggesting that one consequence of its rapid growth was the loss of some of the company's focus on what had been the key to its success all along—quality (Saporito, 2010).

operations. These patterns, which Helgesen dubbed the *female advantage,* help make companies more flexible and democratic.

In sum, one challenge to conventional bureaucracy is to become more open and flexible in order to take advantage of the experience, ideas, and creativity of everybody, regardless of race or gender. The result goes right to the bottom line: greater profits.

The Second Challenge: The Japanese Work Organization

In 1980, the corporate world in the United States was shaken to discover that the most popular automobile model sold in this country was not a Chevrolet, Ford, or Plymouth but the Honda Accord, made in Japan. And the trend continued: In 2008, the Japanese corporation Toyota passed General Motors to become the largest carmaker in the world (Fowler, 2008). Ironically, as late as the 1950s, the label "Made in Japan" generally indicated that a product was cheap and poorly made. But times have changed. The success of the Japanese auto

The Third Challenge: The Changing Nature of Work

Beyond rising global competition and the need to provide equal opportunity for all, pressure to modify conventional work organizations is also coming from changes in the nature of work itself. Over the past few decades, the economy of the United States has moved from industrial to postindustrial production. Rather than working in factories using heavy machinery to make *things,* more people today are using computers and other electronic technology to create or

● Seeing Sociology
in Everyday Life

Have you ever had a "dead-end" job? A job that demanded
creativity? Which would you prefer and why?

○ Making the Grade

As you read the discussion that follows, be sure you understand and
remember the four principles of McDonaldization.

process *information*. A postindustrial society, then, is characterized by information-based organizations.

Frederick Taylor developed his concept of scientific management at a time when most jobs involved tasks that, though often backbreaking, were routine. Workers shoveled coal, poured liquid iron into molds, welded body panels to automobiles on an assembly line, or shot hot rivets into steel girders to build skyscrapers. In addition, a large part of the U.S. labor force in Taylor's day was made up of immigrants, most of whom had little schooling and many of whom knew little English. The routine nature of industrial jobs, coupled with the limited skills of the labor force, led Taylor to treat work as a series of fixed tasks set down by management and followed by employees.

Many of today's information age jobs are very different: The work of designers, artists, consultants, writers, editors, composers, programmers, business owners, and others now demands creativity and imagination. What does this mean for formal organizations? Here are several ways in which today's organizations differ from those of a century ago:

1. **Creative freedom.** As one Hewlett-Packard executive put it, "From their first day of work here, people are given important responsibilities and are encouraged to grow" (Brooks, 2000:128). Today's organizations treat employees with information age skills as a vital resource. Executives can set production goals but cannot dictate how to accomplish tasks that require imagination and discovery. This gives highly skilled workers *creative freedom,* which means they are subject to less day-to-day supervision as long as they generate good results in the long run.

2. **Competitive work teams.** Many organizations allow several groups of employees to work on a problem and offer the greatest rewards to the group that comes up with the best solution. Competitive work teams—a strategy first used by Japanese organizations—draw out the creative contributions of everyone and at the same time reduce the alienation often found in conventional organizations (Maddox, 1994; Yeatts, 1994).

3. **A flatter organization.** By spreading responsibility for creative problem solving throughout the workforce, organizations take on a flatter shape. That is, the pyramid shape of conventional bureaucracy is replaced by an organizational form with fewer levels in the chain of command, as shown in Figure 4.

4. **Greater flexibility.** The typical industrial age organization was a rigid structure guided from the top. Such organizations may accomplish a good deal of work, but they are not especially creative or able to respond quickly to changes in their larger environment. The ideal model in the information age is a *more open* and *flexible* organization that both generates new ideas and adapts quickly to the rapidly changing global marketplace.

nyul\Fotolia, LLC - Royalty Free

During the last fifty years in the United States, women have moved into management positions throughout the corporate world. While some men initially opposed women's presence in the executive office, it is now clear that women bring particular strengths to the job, including leadership flexibility and communication skills. Thus, some analysts speak of women offering a "female advantage."

What does this all mean for organizations? As David Brooks puts it, "The machine is no longer held up as the standard that healthy organizations should emulate. Now, it's the ecosystem" (2000:128). Today's "smart" companies seek out intelligent, creative people (AOL calls its main buildings "Creative Centers") and nurture the growth of their talents.

Keep in mind, however, that many of today's jobs do not involve creative work at all. More correctly, the postindustrial economy has created two very different types of work: high-skill creative work and low-skill service work. Work in the fast-food industry, for example, is routine and highly supervised and thus has much more in common with factory work of a century ago than with the creative teamwork typical of today's information organizations. Therefore, at the same time that some organizations have taken on a flatter, more flexible form, others continue to use a rigid chain of command.

The "McDonaldization" of Society

As noted in the opening to this chapter, McDonald's has enjoyed enormous success, now operating more than 32,000 restaurants in the United States and around the world. Japan has more than 3,700

Is your college or university a top-down bureaucracy or a flatter, more flexible organization? How might you find out?

●─Read "The McDonaldization of Society" by George Ritzer on **mysoclab.com**

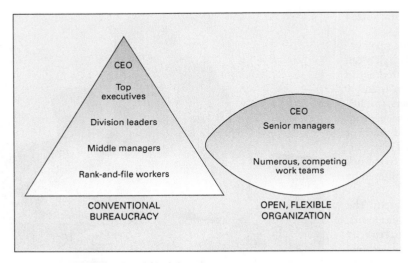

FIGURE 4   Two Organizational Models

The conventional model of bureaucratic organizations has a pyramid shape, with a clear chain of command. Orders flow from the top down, and reports of performance flow from the bottom up. Such organizations have extensive rules and regulations, and their workers have highly specialized jobs. More open and flexible organizations have a flatter shape, more like a football. With fewer levels in the hierarchy, responsibility for generating ideas and making decisions is shared throughout the organization. Many workers do their jobs in teams and have a broad knowledge of the entire organization's operation.

Golden Arches, and the world's largest McDonald's is found in China's capital, Beijing. ●─Read on **mysoclab.com**

McDonald's is far more than a restaurant chain; it is a symbol of U.S. culture. Not only do people around the world associate McDonald's with the United States, but here at home, one poll found that 98 percent of schoolchildren could identify Ronald McDonald, making him as well known as Santa Claus.

Even more important, the organizational principles that underlie McDonald's are coming to dominate our entire society. Our culture is becoming "McDonaldized,"[1] a clever way of saying that we model many aspects of life on the approach taken by the restaurant chain: Parents buy toys at worldwide chain stores all carrying identical merchandise; we drop in at a convenient shop for a ten-minute drive-through oil change; face-to-face communication is being replaced more and more with electronic methods such as voice mail,

e-mail, and instant messaging; more vacations take the form of resorts and tour packages; television packages the news in the form of ten-second sound bites; college admissions officers size up applicants they have never met by glancing at their GPAs and SAT scores; and professors assign ghostwritten textbooks[2] and evaluate students using tests mass-produced for them by publishing companies.

Can you tell what all these developments have in common?

Four Principles

According to George Ritzer (1993), the McDonaldization of society involves four basic organizational principles:

1. **Efficiency.** Ray Kroc, the marketing genius behind the expansion of McDonald's, set out to serve a hamburger, French fries, and a milkshake to a customer in fifty seconds. Today, one of the company's most popular items is the Egg McMuffin, an entire breakfast packaged into a single sandwich. In the restaurant, customers pick up their meals at a counter, dispose of their own trash, and stack their own trays as they walk out the door or, better still, drive away from the pickup window taking whatever mess they make with them. Such efficiency is now central to our way of life. We tend to think that anything done quickly is, for that reason alone, good.

2. **Predictability.** An efficient organization wants to make everything it does as predictable as possible. McDonald's prepares all food using set formulas. Company policies guide the performance of every job.

3. **Uniformity.** The first McDonald's operating manual declared the weight of a regular raw hamburger to be 1.6 ounces, its size to be 3.875 inches across, and its fat content to be 19 percent. A slice of cheese weighs exactly half an ounce, and French fries are cut precisely 9/32 inch thick.

   Think about how many of the objects we see every day around the home, the workplace, and the campus are designed and mass-produced uniformly according to a standard plan. Not just our environment but our everyday life experiences—

---

[1]The term "McDonaldization" was coined by Jim Hightower (1975); much of this discussion is based on the work of George Ritzer (1993, 1998, 2000) and Eric Schlosser (2002).

[2]A number of popular sociology textbooks were not written by the person whose name appears on the cover. This book is not one of them. Even the test bank that accompanies this text was written by the author.

Seeing Sociology in Everyday Life

Can you point to examples of McDonaldization beyond those noted below? What are they?

Go to the Multimedia Library at **mysoclab.com** to hear George Ritzer explain "The McDonaldization of Society"

© CatherineKarnow / CORBIS All Rights Reserved

David Levenson\Alamy Images

The best of today's information age jobs—including working at Google, the popular search engine Web site—allow people lots of personal freedom as long as they produce good ideas. At the same time, many other jobs, such as working the counter at McDonald's, involve the same routines and strict supervision found in factories a century ago.

from traveling the nation's interstate highways to sitting at home viewing national TV shows—are more standardized than ever before.

Almost anywhere in the world, a person can walk into a McDonald's restaurant and buy the same sandwiches, drinks, and desserts prepared in the same way.[3] Uniformity results from a highly rational system that specifies every action and leaves nothing to chance.

4. **Control.** The most unreliable element in the McDonald's system is human beings. After all, people have their good and bad days, and they sometimes let their minds wander or decide to do something a different way. To minimize the unpredictable human element, McDonald's has automated its equipment to cook food at a fixed temperature for a set length of time. Even the cash registers at McDonald's are keyed to pictures of the

menu items so that ringing up a customer's order is as simple as possible.

Similarly, automatic teller machines are replacing banks, highly automated bakeries produce bread while people stand back and watch, and chickens and eggs (or is it eggs and chickens?) emerge from automated hatcheries. In supermarkets, laser scanners at self-checkouts are phasing out human checkers. Much of our shopping now occurs in malls, where everything from temperature and humidity to the kinds of stores and products sold are subject to continuous control and supervision (Ide & Cordell, 1994). ● Go to **mysoclab.com**

Can Rationality Be Irrational?

There is no doubt about the popularity or efficiency of McDonald's. But there is another side to the story.

Max Weber was alarmed at the increasing rationalization of the world, fearing that formal organizations would cage our imaginations and crush the human spirit. As he saw it, rational systems are efficient but dehumanizing. McDonaldization bears him out. Each of the principles we have just discussed limits human creativity, choice, and freedom. Echoing Weber, Ritzer reaches the conclusion that "the ultimate irrationality of McDonaldization is that people could lose control over the system and it would come to control us" (1993:145). Perhaps even McDonald's understands the limits of

---

[3]As McDonald's has "gone global," a few products have been added or changed according to local tastes. For example, in Uruguay, customers enjoy the McHuevo (a hamburger with a poached egg on top); Norwegians can buy McLaks (grilled salmon sandwiches); the Dutch favor the Groenteburger (vegetable burger); in Thailand, McDonald's serves Samurai pork burgers; the Japanese can purchase a Chicken Tatsuta Sandwich (chicken seasoned with soy and ginger); Filipinos eat McSpaghetti (spaghetti with tomato sauce and bits of hot dog); and in India, where Hindus eat no beef, McDonald's sells a vegetarian Maharaja Mac (B. Sullivan, 1995).

⌐○ Making the Grade

The McDonaldization thesis is that rational organization is coming to define our way of life and this trend is in important ways harmful to our well-being.

⌐○ Making the Grade

The opposing trends are (1) expansion of flatter, more flexible organizations that value creativity and (2) the large number of routine service jobs that reflect the "McDonaldization of society."

CONTROVERSY & DEBATE

Computer Technology, Large Organizations, and the Assault on Privacy

JAKE: I'm doing MySpace. It's really cool.

DUNCAN: Why do you want to put your whole life out there for everyone to see?

JAKE: I'm famous, man!

DUNCAN: Famous? Ha! You're throwing away whatever privacy you have left.

Jake completes a page on MySpace.com, which includes his name and college, e-mail, photo, biography, and current personal interests. It can be accessed by billions of people around the world.

Late for a meeting with a new client, Sarah drives her car through a yellow light as it turns red at a main intersection. A computer linked to a pair of cameras notes the violation and takes one picture of her license plate and another of her sitting in the driver's seat. Seven days later, she receives a summons to appear in traffic court.

Julio looks through his mail and finds a letter from a Washington, D.C., data services company telling him that he is one of about 145,000

people whose name, address, Social Security number, and credit file have recently been sold to criminals in California posing as businesspeople. With this information, these crooks can obtain credit cards or take out loans in his name.

These are all cases showing that today's organizations—which know more about us than ever before and more than most of us even realize—pose a growing threat to personal privacy. Large organizations are necessary for today's society

Lillian Graeble

to operate. In some cases, organizations using information about us may actually be helpful. But cases of identity theft are on the rise, and personal privacy is on the decline.

In the past, small-town life gave people little privacy. But at least if people knew something about you, you were just as likely to know something about them. Today, unknown people "out there" can access information about each of us all the time without our learning about it.

In part, the loss of privacy is a result of more and more complex computer technology. Are you aware that every e-mail you send and every Web site you visit leaves a record in one or more computers? Most of these records can be retrieved by people you don't know, as well as by employers and other public officials.

Another part of today's loss of privacy reflects the number and size of formal organizations. As explained in this chapter, large organizations tend to treat people impersonally, and they have a huge appetite for information. Mix large organizations with ever more complex computer technology, and it is no wonder that

---

rationalization—the company has now expanded its offerings of more upscale foods, such as premium roasted coffee and salad selections that are more sophisticated, fresh, and healthful (Philadelphia, 2002).

The Future of Organizations: Opposing Trends

Early in the twentieth century, ever-larger organizations arose in the United States, most taking on the bureaucratic form described by Max Weber. In many respects, these organizations were like armies led by powerful generals who issued orders to their captains and lieu-

tenants. Ordinary soldiers, working in the factories, did what they were told.

With the emergence of the postindustrial economy after 1950, as well as rising competition from abroad, many organizations evolved toward the flatter, more flexible model that encourages communication and creativity. Such "intelligent organizations" (Pinchot & Pinchot, 1993; Brooks, 2000) have become more productive than ever. Just as important, for highly skilled people who enjoy creative freedom, these organizations create less of the alienation that so worried Weber.

But this is only half the story. Although the postindustrial economy created many highly skilled jobs, it created even more routine

● Seeing Sociology
in Everyday Life

Have large organizations reduced your privacy in ways you don't like?
Explain.

● Seeing Sociology
in Everyday Life

Are we giving away our own privacy by posting so much information
about ourselves on social networking sites such as Facebook?
Explain.

most people in the United States are concerned about who knows what about them and what people are doing with this information.

For decades, the level of personal privacy in the United States has been declining. Early in the twentieth century, when state agencies began issuing driver's licenses, for example, they generated files for every licensed driver. Today, officials can send this information at the touch of a button not only to the police but also to all sorts of other organizations. The Internal Revenue Service and the Social Security Administration, as well as government agencies that benefit veterans, students, the unemployed, and the poor, all collect mountains of personal information.

Business organizations now do much the same thing, and many of the choices we make end up in a company's database. Most of us use credit—the U.S. population now has more than 1 billion credit cards, an average of five per adult—but the companies that do "credit checks" collect and distribute information about us to almost anyone who asks, including criminals planning to steal our identity.

Then there are the small cameras found not only at traffic intersections but also in stores,

public buildings, and parking garages and across college campuses. The number of surveillance cameras that monitor our movements is rapidly increasing with each passing year. So-called security cameras may increase public safety in some ways—say, by discouraging a mugger or even a terrorist—at the cost of the little privacy we have left.

After the September 11, 2001, terrorist attacks, the federal government took steps (including the USA PATRIOT Act) to strengthen national security. Today, government officials more closely monitor not just who enters the country but the activities of all of us. Increased national security and privacy do not mix.

Some legal protections remain. Each of the fifty states has laws that give citizens the right to examine some records about themselves kept by employers, banks, and credit bureaus. The federal Privacy Act of 1974 also limits the exchange of personal information among government agencies and permits citizens to examine and correct most government files. In response to rising levels of identity theft, Congress is likely to pass more laws to regulate the sale of credit information. But so many organizations, private as well as public, now have

information about us—experts estimate that 90 percent of U.S. households are profiled in databases somewhere—that current laws simply cannot effectively address the privacy problem.

WHAT DO YOU THINK?

1. Do you believe that our concern about national security is destroying privacy? How can the loss of privacy threaten our security?

2. Do you use Internet sites such as http://www.myspace.com? Why do you think so many young people are eager to spread personal information in this way?

3. Have you checked your credit history recently? Do you know how to reduce the chances of having your identity stolen? (If not, one place to start is http://www.stopidentitytheft.org).

Sources: Robert Wright (1998), "Online Privacy" (2000), J. Rosen (2000), A. Hamilton (2001), Heymann (2002), O'Harrow (2005), and Bruxelles (2009).

service jobs, such as those offered by McDonald's. Fast-food companies now represent the largest pool of low-wage labor, aside from migrant workers, in the United States (Schlosser, 2002). Work of this kind, which Ritzer terms "McJobs," offers few of the benefits that today's highly skilled workers enjoy. On the contrary, the automated routines that define work in the fast-food industry, telemarketing, and similar fields are not very different from those that Frederick Taylor described a century ago.

Today, the organizational flexibility that gives better-off workers more freedom carries, for rank-and-file employees, the ever-present threat of "downsizing" (Sennett, 1998). Organizations facing global competition are eager to attract creative employees, but they are just

as eager to cut costs by eliminating as many routine jobs as possible. The net result is that some people are better off than ever while others worry about holding their jobs and struggle to make ends meet.

U.S. organizations remain the envy of the world for their productive efficiency. Indeed, there are few places on Earth where the mail arrives as quickly and dependably as it does in this country. But we should remember that the future is far brighter for some people than for others. In addition, as the Controversy & Debate box explains, formal organizations pose a mounting threat to our privacy, something to keep in mind as we envision our organizational future.

Seeing Sociology in Everyday Life

Groups and Organizations

To what extent is the concept of McDonaldization a part of our everyday lives?

This chapter explains that since the opening of the first McDonald's restaurant in 1948, the principles that underlie the fast-food industry—efficiency, predictability, uniformity, and control—have spread to many aspects of our everyday lives. Here is a chance to identify aspects of McDonaldization in several familiar routines. In each of the two photos on the facing page, can you identify specific elements of McDonaldization? That is, in what ways does the organizational pattern or the technology involved increase efficiency, predictability, uniformity, and control? In the photo below, what elements do you see that are clearly not McDonaldization? Why?

> **HINT** This process, which is described as the "McDonaldization of society," has made our lives easier in some ways, but it has also made our society ever more impersonal, gradually diminishing our range of human contact. Also, although this organizational pattern is intended to serve human needs, it may end up doing the opposite by forcing people to live according to the demands of machines. Max Weber feared that our future would be an overly rational world in which we all might lose much of our humanity.

Small, privately owned stores like this one were once the rule in the United States. But the number of "mom and pop" businesses is declining as "big box" discount stores expand. Why are small stores disappearing? What social qualities of these stores are we losing in the process?

Don Smetzer Photographer

Automated teller machines (ATMs) became common in the United States in the early 1970s. A customer with an electronic identification card can complete certain banking operations (such as withdrawing cash) without having to deal with a human bank teller. What makes the ATM one example of McDonaldization? Do you enjoy using ATMs? Why or why not?

At checkout counters in many supermarkets and large discount stores, the customer lifts each product through a laser scanner linked to a computer in order to identify what the product is and what it costs. The customer then inserts a credit or debit card to pay for the purchase and proceeds to bag the items.

Applying SOCIOLOGY in Everyday Life

1. Have colleges and universities been affected by the process called McDonaldization? Do large, anonymous lecture courses qualify as an example? Why? What other examples of McDonaldization can you identify on the college campus?

2. Visit any large public building with an elevator. Observe groups of people as they approach the elevator, and enter the elevator with them. Watch their behavior: What happens to conversations as the elevator doors close? Where do people fix their eyes? Can you explain these patterns?

3. Using campus publications or your school's Web page (and some assistance from an instructor), try to draw an organizational pyramid for your college or university. Show the key offices and how they supervise and report to one another.

Making the Grade

Groups and Organizations

Watch on mysoclab.com

What Are Social Groups?

SOCIAL GROUPS are two or more people who identify with and interact with one another.

A **PRIMARY GROUP** is small, personal, and lasting (examples include family and close friends).

A **SECONDARY GROUP** is large, impersonal, goal-oriented, and often of shorter duration (examples include a college class or a corporation).

See the Summing Up table.

Elements of Group Dynamics

GROUP LEADERSHIP

- *Instrumental leadership* focuses on completing tasks.
- *Expressive leadership* focuses on a group's well-being.
- *Authoritarian leadership* is a "take charge" style that demands obedience; *democratic leadership* includes everyone in decision making; *laissez-faire leadership* lets the group function mostly on its own.

GROUP CONFORMITY

- The Asch, Milgram, and Janis research shows that group members often seek agreement and may pressure one another toward conformity.
- Individuals use *reference groups*—including both *in-groups* and *out-groups*—to form attitudes and make evaluations.

GROUP SIZE and DIVERSITY

- Georg Simmel described the *dyad* as intense but unstable; the *triad*, he said, is more stable but can dissolve into a dyad by excluding one member.
- Peter Blau claimed that larger groups turn inward, socially diverse groups turn outward, and physically segregated groups turn inward.

NETWORKS are relational webs that link people with little common identity and limited interaction. Being "well connected" in networks is a valuable type of social capital.

social group two or more people who identify with and interact with one another

primary group a small social group whose members share personal and lasting relationships

secondary group a large and impersonal social group whose members pursue a specific goal or activity

instrumental leadership group leadership that focuses on the completion of tasks

expressive leadership group leadership that focuses on the group's well-being

groupthink the tendency of group members to conform, resulting in a narrow view of some issue

reference group a social group that serves as a point of reference in making evaluations and decisions

in-group a social group toward which a member feels respect and loyalty

out-group a social group toward which a person feels a sense of competition or opposition

dyad a social group with two members

triad a social group with three members

network a web of weak social ties

What Formal Organizations?

FORMAL ORGANIZATIONS are large secondary groups organized to achieve their goals efficiently.

UTILITARIAN ORGANIZATIONS pay people for their efforts (examples include businesses and government agencies).

NORMATIVE ORGANIZATIONS have goals people consider worthwhile (examples include voluntary associations such as the PTA).

COERCIVE ORGANIZATIONS are organizations people are forced to join (examples include prisons and mental hospitals).

formal organization a large secondary group organized to achieve its goals efficiently

tradition values and beliefs passed from generation to generation

rationality a way of thinking that emphasizes deliberate, matter-of-fact calculation of the most efficient way to accomplish a particular task

rationalization of society Weber's term for the historical change from tradition to rationality as the main type of human thought

Explore on mysoclab.com

What Are Formal Organizations? *(continued)*

All formal organizations operate in an **ORGANIZATIONAL ENVIRONMENT** that is influenced by
- technology
- political and economic trends
- current events
- population patterns
- other organizations

See the Summing Up table.

bureaucracy an organizational model rationally designed to perform tasks efficiently

organizational environment factors outside an organization that affect its operation

bureaucratic ritualism a focus on rules and regulations to the point of undermining an organization's goals

bureaucratic inertia the tendency of bureaucratic organizations to perpetuate themselves

oligarchy the rule of the many by the few

scientific management Frederick Taylor's term for the application of scientific principles to the operation of a business or other large organization

Modern Formal Organizations: Bureaucracy

BUREAUCRACY, which Max Weber saw as the dominant type of organization in modern societies, is based on
- specialization
- hierarchy of offices
- rules and regulations
- technical competence
- impersonality
- formal, written communication

PROBLEMS OF BUREAUCRACY include
- bureaucratic alienation
- bureaucratic inefficiency and ritualism
- bureaucratic inertia
- oligarchy

The Evolution of Formal Organizations

CONVENTIONAL BUREAUCRACY

MORE OPEN, FLEXIBLE ORGANIZATIONS

In the early 1900s, Frederick Taylor's **SCIENTIFIC MANAGEMENT** applied scientific principles to increase productivity.

In the 1960s, Rosabeth Moss Kanter proposed that opening up organizations for all employees, especially women and other minorities, increased organizational efficiency.

In the 1980s, global competition drew attention to the Japanese work organization's collective orientation.

The Changing Nature of Work

Recently, the rise of a postindustrial economy has created two very different types of work:
- highly skilled and creative work (examples include designers, consultants, programmers, and executives)
- low-skilled service work associated with the "McDonaldization" of society, based on efficiency, uniformity, and control (examples include jobs in fast-food restaurants and telemarketing)

 Read on mysoclab.com

Sample Test Questions

Multiple-Choice Questions

1. What name did Charles Horton Cooley give to a small social group whose members share personal and lasting relationships?
   a. expressive group
   b. in-group
   c. primary group
   d. secondary group

2. Which type of group leadership is concerned with getting the job done?
   a. laissez-faire leadership
   b. secondary group leadership
   c. expressive leadership
   d. instrumental leadership

3. The research done by Solomon Asch, in which subjects were asked to pick lines of the same length, showed that
   a. groups encourage their members to conform.
   b. most people are stubborn and refuse to change their minds.
   c. groups often generate conflict.
   d. group members rarely agree on everything.

4. Which of the following concepts refers to a social group that someone uses as a point of reference in making an evaluation or decision?
   a. out-group
   b. reference group
   c. in-group
   d. primary group

5. A network is correctly thought of as
   a. the most close-knit social group.
   b. a category of people with something in common.
   c. a social group in which most people know one another.
   d. a web of weak social ties.

6. From the point of view of a nurse, a hospital is a
   a. normative organization.
   b. coercive organization.
   c. utilitarian organization.
   d. All of the above are correct.

7. Bureaucracy is a type of social organization characterized by
   a. specialized jobs.
   b. offices arranged in a hierarchy.
   c. lots of rules and regulations.
   d. All of the above are correct.

8. According to Robert Michels, bureaucracy always means
   a. inefficiency.
   b. oligarchy.
   c. alienation.
   d. specialization.

9. Rosabeth Moss Kanter claims that large business organizations
   a. need to "open up" opportunity to encourage all workers to perform well.
   b. must have clear and stable rules to survive in a changing world.
   c. do well or badly depending on how talented the leader is.
   d. suffer if they do not adopt the latest technology.

10. The "McDonaldization of society" means that
    a. organizations can provide food for people more efficiently than families can.
    b. impersonal organizations concerned with efficiency, predictability, uniformity, and control are more and more common.
    c. it is possible for organizations to both achieve their goals and meet human needs.
    d. society today is one vast social network.

ANSWERS: 1(c); 2(d); 3(a); 4(b); 5(d); 6(c); 7(d); 8(b); 9(a); 10(b).

Essay Questions

1. How do primary groups differ from secondary groups? Give examples of each type of group in your own life.

2. According to Max Weber, what are the six traits that define bureaucracy? What is the advantage of this organizational form? What are several problems that often go along with it?

The McDonaldization of Society

GEORGE RITZER

According to George Ritzer, our society has become increasingly McDonaldized. That is, we constantly search for ways to maximize efficiency in diverse social settings. In this article, Ritzer explains how organizations like McDonald's have influenced other aspects of our social structure through their emphasis on rationality, efficiency, control, and predictability. As you read this article, think about the ways in which your own life has become McDonaldized.

McDonaldization implies a search for maximum efficiency in increasingly numerous and diverse social settings. *Efficiency* means choosing the optimum means to a given end. Let me clarify this definition. First, the truly optimum means to an end is rarely found. Rather, optimum in this definition implies the attempt to find and use the *best possible* means. . . .

In a McDonaldized society, people rarely search for the best means to an end on their own. Rather, they rely on the optimum means that have been previously discovered and institutionalized in a variety of social settings. Thus, the best means may be part of a technology, written into an organization's rules and regulations, or taught to employees during the process of occupational socialization. It would be inefficient if people always had to discover for themselves the optimum means to ends. . . .

❧ The Fast-Food Industry: We Do It All for Them

Although the fast-food restaurant did not create the yearning for efficiency, it has helped turn it into a nearly universal desire. Many sectors of society have had to change in order to operate in the efficient manner demanded by those accustomed to life in the fast lane of the fast-food restaurant. . . .

In the early 1950s, the dawn of the era of the fast-food restaurant, the major alternative to fast food was the home-cooked meal made mostly from ingredients previously purchased at various markets. . . .

But the home-cooked meal was, and still is, a relatively inefficient way to eat. It requires going to the market, preparing the ingredients, cooking the food, eating it, and cleaning up afterward. The restaurant has long been a more efficient alternative in terms of effort.

But restaurants can also be inefficient—it may take several hours to go to a restaurant, consume a meal, and then return home. The desire for more efficient restaurants led to the rise of some of the ancestors of the fast-food restaurants—diners, cafeterias, and early drive-through or drive-in restaurants. . . .

Above all else, Ray Kroc was impressed by the efficiency of the McDonald brothers' operation, as well as the enormous profit potential of such a system applied at a large number of sites. Here is how Kroc described his initial reactions to the McDonald's system:

> I was fascinated by the simplicity and effectiveness of the system.
>
> . . . each step in producing the limited menu was stripped down to its essence and accomplished with a minimum of effort. They sold hamburgers and cheeseburgers only. The burgers were . . . all fried the same way.[1]

. . .

Kroc and his associates experimented with each component of the hamburger to increase the efficiency of producing and serving it.

For example, they started with only partially sliced buns that arrived in cardboard boxes. The griddle workers had to spend time opening the boxes, separating the buns, slicing them in half, and discarding the leftover paper and cardboard. Eventually, they found that buns sliced completely in half could be used more efficiently. In addition, buns were made efficient by having them separated and shipped in reusable boxes. The meat patty received similar attention. For example, the paper between the patties had to have just the right amount of wax so that the patties would readily slide off the paper and onto the grill. Kroc made it clear that he aimed at greater efficiency:

> The purpose of all these refinements, and we never lost sight of it, was to make our griddle man's job easier to do quickly and well. And the other considerations of cost cutting, inventory control, and so forth were important to be sure, but they were secondary to the critical detail of what happened there at the smoking griddle. This was the vital passage of our *assembly-line,* and the product had to flow through it smoothly or the whole plant would falter.[2] [Italics added.)

. . .

Getting diners into and out of the fast-food restaurant has also been streamlined. As three observers put it, McDonald's has done "everything to speed the way from secretion to excretion."[3] Parking lots adjacent to the restaurant offer readily available parking spots. It's a short walk to the counter, and although there is sometimes a line, food is usually quickly ordered, obtained, and paid for. The highly limited menu makes the diner's choice easy in contrast to the many choices available in other restaurants. With the food obtained, it is but a few steps to a table and the beginning of the "dining experience." Because there is little inducement to linger, the diners generally gather the leftover paper, styrofoam, and plastic, discard them in a nearby trash receptacle, and get back in their cars to drive to the next (often McDonaldized) activity.

Not too many years ago, those in charge of fast-food restaurants discovered that the drive-through window made this whole process far more efficient. McDonald's opened its first drive-through in 1975 in Oklahoma City; within four years, almost half its restaurants had one. Instead of the "laborious" and "inefficient" process of parking the car, walking to the counter, waiting in line, ordering, paying, carrying the food to the table, eating, and disposing of the remnants, the drive-through window offered diners the option of driving to the window (perhaps waiting in a line of cars), ordering, paying, and driving off with the meal. You could eat while driving if you wanted to be even more efficient. The drive-through window is also efficient for the fast-food restaurant. As more and more people use the drive-through window, fewer parking spaces, tables, and employees are needed. Further, consumers take their debris with them as they drive away, thereby eliminating the need for additional trash receptacles and employees to empty those receptacles periodically.

· · ·

☺ Higher Education: *Just Fill in the Box*

In the educational system, specifically the university (now being dubbed "McUniversity"[4]), you can find many examples of the pressure for greater efficiency. One is the machine-graded, multiple-choice examination. In a much earlier era, students were examined individually by their professors. This may have been a good way to find out what students knew, but it was highly labor-intensive and inefficient. Later, the essay examination became very popular. While grading a set of essays was more efficient than giving individual oral examinations, it was still relatively inefficient and time-consuming. Enter the multiple-choice examination, the grading of which was a snap. In fact, graduate assistants could grade it, making it even more efficient for the professor. Now there are computer-graded examinations that maximize efficiency for both professors and graduate assistants. They even offer advantages to students, such as making it easier to study and limiting the effect of the subjective views of the grader on the grading process.

The multiple-choice examination still left the professor saddled with the inefficient task of composing the necessary sets of questions.

Furthermore, at least some of the questions had to be changed each semester because new students were likely to gain possession of old exams, The solution: Textbook companies provided professors with books (free of charge) full of multiple-choice questions to accompany textbooks required for use in large classes. However, the professor still had to retype the questions or have them retyped. Recently, publishers have begun to provide these sets of questions on computer disks. Now all the professor needs to do is select the desired questions and let the printer do the rest. With these great advances in efficiency, professors now can choose to have very little to do with the entire examination process, from question composition to grading.

Publishers have provided other services to make teaching more efficient for those professors who adopt their textbooks. With the adoption of a textbook, a professor may receive many materials with which to fill class hours—lecture outlines, computer simulations, discussion questions, videotapes, movies, even ideas for guest lecturers and student projects. Professors who choose to use all these devices need do little or nothing on their own for their classes. A highly efficient means of teaching, this approach frees up time for other much more valued activities (by professors, but not students) such as writing and research.

Finally, worth noting is the development of a relatively new type of "service" on college campuses. For a nominal fee, students are provided with lecture notes, from instructors, teaching assistants, and top-notch students, for their courses. No more inefficient note-taking, in fact, no more inefficient class attendance. Students are free to pursue more valuable activities such as poring over arcane journals in the graduate library or watching the "soaps."

• • •

Home Cooking (and Related Phenomena)

Given the efficiency of the fast-food restaurant, the home kitchen has had to grow more efficient or face total extinction. Had the kitchen not grown more efficient, a comedian could have envisioned a time when the kitchen would have been replaced by a large, comfortable telephone lounge used for calling Domino's for pizza delivery.

One key to the salvation of the kitchen is the microwave oven.[5] Far more efficient than conventional ovens for preparing a meal, the microwave has streamlined the process of cooking. Microwaves are usually faster than other ovens, and people can also prepare a wider array of foods in them. Perhaps most important, they spawned a number of microwavable foods (including soup, pizza, hamburgers, fried chicken, french fries, and popcorn) that permit the efficient preparation of the fare people usually find in fast-food restaurants. For example, one of the first microwavable foods produced by Hormel was an array of biscuit-based breakfast sandwiches "popularized in recent years by many of the fast-food chains," most notably McDonald's and its Egg McMuffin.[6] . . . In fact, many food companies now employ people who continually scout fast-food restaurants for new ideas. As one executive put it, "Instead of having a breakfast sandwich at McDonald's, you can pick one up from the freezer of your grocery store."[7] . . . Instead of getting into the car, driving to the restaurant, and returning home, people need only pop the desired foods in the microwave. . . .

Another reason efficiency in the kitchen has not damaged the fast-food business is that fast food offers many advantages over the "home-cooked" microwaved dinner. For one, people can have dinner out rather than just another meal at home. For another, as Stan Luxenberg has pointed out in *Roadside Empires,* McDonald's offers more than an efficient meal; it offers fun—brightly lit, colorful, and attractive settings, garish packaging, special inducements to children, giveaways, contests—in short, it offers a carnival-like atmosphere in which to buy and consume fast food.[8] Thus, faced with the choice of an efficient meal at home or one in a fast-food restaurant, many people will choose the latter.

• • •

The McDonaldization of food preparation and consumption has also reached the booming diet industry. Diet books promising all sorts of shortcuts to weight loss are often at the top of the best-seller lists. Losing weight is normally difficult and time-consuming, hence the lure of diet books that promise to make weight loss easier and quicker, that is, more efficient.

For those on a diet, and many people are on more or less perpetual diets, the preparation of low-calorie food has been streamlined. Instead of cooking diet foods from scratch, they may now purchase an array of prepared diet foods in frozen and/or microwavable form. For those who do not wish to go through the inefficient process of eating these diet meals, there are products even more streamlined such as diet shakes (Slim-Fast, for example) that can be "prepared" and consumed in a matter of seconds.

The issue of dieting points outside the home to the growth of diet centers such as Jenny Craig and Nutri/System. Nutri/System sells dieters, at substantial cost, prepackaged freeze-dried food. In what is close to the ultimate in streamlined cooking, all the dieter need do is add water. Freeze-dried foods are also efficient for Nutri/System, because they can be efficiently packaged, transported, and stored. Furthermore, the dieter's periodic visits to a Nutri/System center are efficiently organized. A counselor is allotted ten minutes with each client. During that brief time, the counselor takes the client's weight, blood pressure, and measurements, asks routine questions, fills out a chart, and devotes whatever time is left to "problem solving." If the session extends beyond the allotted ten minutes and other clients are waiting, the receptionist will buzz the counselor's room. Counselors learn their techniques at Nutri/System University where, after a week of training (no inefficient years of matriculation here), they earn certification and an NSU diploma.

Shopping

Shopping has also grown more efficient. The department store obviously is a more efficient place in which to shop than a series of specialty shops dispersed throughout the city or suburbs. The shopping mall increases efficiency by bringing a wide range of department stores and specialty shops under one roof. Kowinski describes the mall as "an extremely efficient and effective selling machine."[9] It is cost-efficient for retailers because it is the collection of shops and department stores ("mail synergy") that brings in throngs of people. And it is efficient for consumers because in one stop they can visit numerous shops, have lunch at a "food court" (likely populated by many fast-food chains), see a movie, have a drink, and go to an exercise or diet center.

The drive for shopping efficiency did not end with the malls. Seven-Eleven and its clones have become drive-up, if not drive-through, minimarkets. For those who need only a few items, it is far more efficient (albeit more costly) to pull up to a highly streamlined Seven-Eleven than to run to a supermarket. . . .

In recent years, catalogues (e.g., L.L. Bean, Lands' End) have become more popular. They enable people to shop from the comfort of their homes. Still more efficient, though it may lead to many hours in front of the TV, is home-television shopping. A range of products are paraded before viewers, who can purchase them simply by phoning in and conveniently charging their purchases. The latest advance in home shopping is the "scanfone," an at-home phone machine that includes "a pen-sized bar-code scanner, a credit card magnetic-strip reader, and a key pad." The customer merely "scans items from a bar-coded catalogue and also scans delivery dates and payment methods. The orders are then electronically relayed to the various stores, businesses, and banks involved."[10] Some mall operators fear that they will ultimately be put out of business because of the greater efficiency of shopping at home.

· · ·

Entertainment

With the advent of videotapes and video-rental stores, many people no longer deem it efficient to drive to their local theater to see a movie. Movies can now be viewed, often more than one at a sitting, in people's own dens. Those who wish even greater efficiency can buy one of the new television sets that enables viewers to see a movie while also watching a favorite TV show on an inset on the screen.

The largest video rental franchise in the United States, Blockbuster, predictably "considers itself the McDonald's of the video business."[11] . . . However, Blockbuster may already be in danger of replacement by even more efficient alternatives such as the pay-per-view movies offered by many cable companies. Instead of trekking to the video store, people just turn to the proper channel and phone the cable company. New small dishes allow people access to a wider range of video offerings. Now in the experimental stage, video-on-demand systems may some day allow people to order the movies available in video stores from the comfort of their homes. . . . Just as the video store replaced many movie theaters, video stores themselves may soon make way for even more efficient alternatives.

. . . Travel to exotic foreign locales has also grown more streamlined. The best example of this is the package tour. Take, for example, a thirty-day tour of Europe. To make it efficient, tourists visit only the major locales in Europe. Buses hurtle through cities, allowing tourists to glimpse the maximum number of sites in the time allowed. At particularly interesting or important sights, the bus may slow down or even stop to permit some picture taking. At the most important locales, a brief stopover is planned; there, a visitor can hurry through the site, take a few pictures, buy a souvenir, then hop back on the bus to head to the next attraction. The package tour can be seen as a mechanism that permits the efficient transport of people from one locale to another.

. . .

Dehumanization of Customers and Employees

. . . The fast-food restaurant offers its employees a dehumanizing work setting. Said Burger King workers, "A moron could learn this job, it's so easy" and "Any trained monkey could do this job."[12] Workers can use only a small portion of their skills and abilities. This is irrational from the organization's viewpoint, because it could obtain much more from its employees for the money (however negligible) it pays them. . . .

The minimal skill demands of the fast-food restaurant are also irrational from the employee's perspective. Besides not using all their skills, employees are not allowed to think and be creative on the job. This leads to a high level of resentment, job dissatisfaction, alienation, absenteeism, and turnover among those who work in fast-food restaurants.[13] In fact, the fast-food industry has the highest turnover rate—approximately 300% a year—of any industry in the United States. That means that the average fast-food worker lasts only about four months; the entire work force of the fast-food industry turns over approximately three times a year. . . .

The fast-food restaurant also dehumanizes the customer. By eating on a sort of assembly line, the diner is reduced to an automaton made to rush through a meal with little gratification derived from the dining experience or from the food itself. The best that can usually be said is that it is efficient and it is over quickly.

Some customers might even feel as if they are being fed like livestock in a highly rationalized manner. This point was made on TV a number of years ago in a *Saturday Night Live* skit, "Trough and Brew," a parody of a small fast-food chain called "Burger and Brew." In the skit, some young executives learn that a new fast-food restaurant called Trough and Brew has opened, and they decide to try it for lunch. When they enter the restaurant, bibs are tied around their necks. Then, they discover what resembles a pig trough filled with chili and periodically refilled by a waitress scooping new supplies from a bucket. The customers bend over, stick their heads into the trough, and lap up the chili as they move along the trough making high-level business decisions. Every so often they come up for air and lap some beer from the communal "brew basin." After they have finished their "meal," they pay their bills "by the head." Since their faces are smeared with chili, they are literally "hosed off" before they leave the restaurant. The young executives are last seen being herded out of the restaurant, which is being closed for a half-hour so that it can be "hosed down." *Saturday Night Live* was clearly ridiculing the fact that fast-food restaurants tend to treat their customers like lower animals.

Customers are also dehumanized by scripted interactions, and other efforts to make interactions uniform. "Uniformity is incompatible when human interactions are involved. Human interactions that are mass-produced may strike consumers as dehumanizing if the routinization is obvious or manipulative if it is not."[14] Dehumanization occurs when prefabricated interactions take the place of authentic human relationships.

· · ·

Another dehumanizing aspect of fast-food restaurants is that they minimize contact among human beings. For example, the nature of the fast-food restaurant makes the relationships between employees and customers fleeting at best. Because the average employee works part-time and stays only a few months, even the regular customer can rarely develop a personal relationship with him or her. All but gone are the days when one got to know well a waitress at a diner or the short order cook at a local greasy spoon. Few are the places where an employee knows who you are and knows what you are likely to order.

Contact between workers and customers is very short. It takes little time at the counter to order, receive the food, and pay for it. Both employees and customers are likely to feel rushed and to want to move on, customers to their dinner and employees to the next order. There is virtually no time for customer and counterperson to interact in such a context. This is even truer of the drive-through window, where thanks to the speedy service and the physical barriers, the server is even more distant.

These highly impersonal and anonymous relationships are heightened by the training of employees to interact in a staged, scripted, and limited manner with customers. Thus, the customers may feel that they are dealing with automatons rather than with fellow human beings. For their part, the customers are supposed to be, and often are, in a hurry, so they also have little to say to the McDonald's employee. Indeed, it could be argued that one of the reasons the fast-food restaurants succeed is that they are in time with our fast-paced and impersonal society. . . . People in the modern world want to get on with their business without unnecessary personal relationships. The fast-food restaurant gives them precisely what they want.

Not only the relationships between employee and customer, but other potential relationships are limited greatly. Because employees remain on the job for only a few months, satisfying personal relationships among employees are unlikely to develop. . . .

Relationships among customers are largely curtailed as well. Although some McDonald's ads would have people believe otherwise, gone for the most part are the days when people met in the diner or cafeteria for coffee or a meal and lingered to socialize. Fast-food restaurants clearly do not encourage such socializing. If nothing else, the chairs by design make people uncomfortable, so that they move on quickly. The drive-through windows completely eliminate the possibility of interaction with other customers.

• • •

Fast-food restaurants also tend to have negative effects on other human relationships. There is, for example, the effect on the family, especially the so-called "family meal." The fast-food restaurant is not conducive to a long, leisurely, conversation-filled dinnertime. Furthermore, as the children grow into their teens, the fast-food restaurant can lead to separate meals as the teens go at one time with their friends, and the parents go at another time. Of course, the drive-through window only serves to reduce further the possibility of a family meal. The family that gobbles its food while driving on to its next stop can hardly enjoy "quality time." Here is the way one journalist describes what is happening to the family meal:

> Do families who eat their suppers at the Colonel's, swinging on plastic seats, or however the restaurant is arranged, say grace before picking up a crispy brown chicken leg? Does dad ask junior what he did today as he remembers he forgot the piccalilli and trots through the crowds over to the counter to get some? Does mom find the atmosphere conducive to asking little Mildred about the problems she was having with

third conjugation French verbs, or would it matter since otherwise the family might have been at home chomping down precooked frozen food, warmed in the microwave oven and watching "Hollywood Squares"?[15]

There is much talk these days about the disintegration of the family, and the fast-food restaurant may well be a crucial contributor to that disintegration. In fact, as implied above, dinners at home may now not be much different from meals at the fast-food restaurant. Families tended to stop having lunch together by the 1940s and breakfast together by the 1950s. Today, the family dinner is following the same route. Even at home, the meal will probably not be what it once was. Following the fast-food model, people have ever more options to "graze," "refuel," nibble on this, or snack on that, rather than sit down at a formal meal. Also, because it may seem inefficient to do nothing but just eat, families are likely to watch television while they are eating. Furthermore, the din, to say nothing of the lure, of dinnertime TV programs such as *Wheel of Fortune* is likely to make it difficult for family members to interact with one another.

A key technology in the destruction of the family meal is the microwave oven and the vast array of microwavable foods it helped generate.[16] More than 70% of American households have a microwave oven. A *Wall Street Journal* poll indicated that Americans consider the microwave their favorite household product. In fact, the microwave in a McDonaldizing society is seen as an advance over the fast-food restaurant. Said one consumer researcher, "It has made even fast-food restaurants not seem fast because at home you don't have to wait in line." As a general rule, consumers demand meals that take no more than ten minutes to microwave, whereas in the past people were more often willing to spend a half hour or even an hour cooking dinner. This emphasis on speed has, of course, brought with it lower quality, but people do not seem to mind this loss: "We're just not as critical of food as we used to be."[17]

• • •

Homogenization

Another dehumanizing effect of the fast-food restaurant is that it has increased homogenization in the United States and, increasingly, throughout the world. This decline in diversity is manifest in the extension of the fast-food model to all sorts of ethnic foods. People are hard-pressed to find an authentically different meal in an ethnic fast-food chain. The food has been rationalized and compromised so that it is acceptable to the tastes of virtually all diners. Paradoxically, while fast-food restaurants have permitted far more people to experience ethnic food, the food that they eat has lost many of its distinguishing characteristics. The settings are also all modeled after McDonald's in one way or another.

The expansion of these franchises across the United States means that people find little difference between regions and between cities. Tourists find more familiarity and less diversity as they travel around the nation, and this is increasingly true on a global scale. Exotic settings are increasingly likely sites for American fast-food chains. The McDonald's and Kentucky Fried Chicken in Beijing are but two examples of this. . . . The spread of American and indigenous fast food throughout much of the world causes less and less diversity from one setting to another. The human craving for new and diverse experiences is being limited, if not progressively destroyed, by the spread of fast-food restaurants. The craving for diversity is being supplanted by the desire for uniformity and predictability.

• • •

◉ Conclusion

• • •

Although I have emphasized the irresistibility of McDonaldization, . . . my fondest hope is that I am wrong. . . . I hope that people can resist McDonaldization and create instead a more reasonable, more human world.

A few years ago, McDonald's was sued by the famous French chef, Paul Bocuse, for using his picture on a poster without his permission. Enraged, Bocuse said, "How can I be seen promoting this tasteless, boneless food in which everything is soft." Nevertheless, Bocuse seemed to acknowledge the inevitability of McDonaldization: "There's a need for this kind of thing . . . and trying to get rid of it seems to me to be as futile as trying to get rid of the prostitutes in the Bois de Bologne."[18] Lo and behold, two weeks later, it was announced that the Paris police had cracked down on prostitution in the Bois de Bologne. Said a police spokesperson, "There are none left." Thus, just as chef Bocuse was wrong about the prostitutes, perhaps I am wrong about the irresistibility of McDonaldization. Yet, before I grow overly optimistic, it should be noted that "everyone knows that the prostitutes will be back as soon as the operation is over. In the spring, police predict, there will be even more than before."[19] Similarly, it remains likely that no matter how intense the opposition, the future will bring with it more rather than less McDonaldization. Even if this proves to be the case, it is my hope that you will follow some of the advice outlined in this [article] for protesting and mitigating the worst effects of McDonaldization. Faced with Max Weber's iron cage and image of a future dominated by the polar night of icy darkness and hardness, I hope that if nothing else, you will consider the words of the poet Dylan Thomas: "Do not go gentle into that good night. . . . Rage, rage against the dying of the light."[20]

Endnotes

[1]Kroc, R. (1977). *Grinding it out.* New York: Berkeley Medallion Books, p. 8.

[2]Kroc, R. (1977). *Grinding it out.* New York: Berkeley Medallion Books, pp. 96–97.

[3]Kroker, A., Kroker, M., & Cook, D. (1989). *Panic encyclopedia: The definitive guide to the postmodern scene.* New York: St. Martin's Press, p. 119.

[4]Parker, M., & Jary, D. (1995). The McUniversity: Organization, management and academic subjectivity. *Organization, 2,* 1–19.

[5] "The microwave cooks up a new way of life. (1989, September 19). *Wall Street Journal,* p. B1; Microwavable foods—Industry's response to consumer demands for convenience. (1987). *Food Technology, 41,* 52–63.

[6] "Microwavable foods—Industry's response to consumer demands for convenience. *Food Technology, 41,* 54.

[7] Shapiro, E. (1991, October 14). A page from fast food's menu. *New York Times,* pp. D1, D3.

[8] Luxenberg, S. (1985). *Roadside empires: How the chains franchised America.* New York: Viking.

[9] Kowinski, W. S. (1985). *The malling of America: An inside look at the great consumer paradise.* New York: Morrow, p. 61.

[10] Swisher, K. (1992, April 16) Companies unveil "scanfone" shopping service. *Washington Post,* pp. B1, B15.

[11] Potts, M. (1991, December 9). Blockbuster struggle with merger script. *Washington Post/Washington Business,* p. 24; Shapiro, E. (1992, February 21). Market place: A mixed outlook for Blockbuster. *New York Times,* p. D6.

[12] Reiter, E. (1991). *Making fast food.* Montreal and Kingston: McGill-Queen's University Press, pp. 150, 167.

[13] Leidner disagrees with this, arguing that McDonald's "workers expressed relatively little dissatisfaction with the extreme routinization." See Leidner, R. (1993). *Fast food, fast talk: Service work and the routinization of everyday life.* Berkeley: University of California Press, p. 134. One could ask, however, whether this indicates a McDonaldizing society in which people, accustomed to the process, simply accept it as an inevitable part of their work.

[14] Leidner, R. (1993). *Fast food, fast talk: Service work and the routinization of everyday life.* Berkeley-University of California Press, p. 30.

[15] von Hoffman, N. (1978, November 23). The fast-disappearing family meal. *Washington Post,* p. C4.

[16] Visser, M. (1989, December). A meditation on the microwave. *Psychology Today,* pp. 38ff.

[17] "The microwave cooks up a new way of life. (1989, September 19). *Wall Street Journal,* p. B1.

[18]Cohen, R. (1992, February 18). Faux pas by McDonald's in Europe. *New York Times,* p. D1.

[19]Two quotes from Waxman, S. (1992, March 2). Paris's sex change operation. *Washington Post,* p. B1.

[20]Thomas, D. (1952). *The collected poems of Dylan Thomas.* "Do Not Go Gentle into That Good Night." New York: New Directions, p. 128.

☻ ☻ ☻

Questions

1. What is McDonaldization?

2. What are some negative outcomes of McDonaldization? What are some of the positive outcomes?

3. Is McDonaldization a social problem or does it cause social problems? Explain your response.

4. Describe some ways in which your life has become McDonaldized. What can you do to fight McDonaldization in your life?

5. Have you ever worked for McDonald's or another McDonaldized business? If so, does the behind-the-scenes reality compare with what the customer sees? How do your experiences compare with those described in the article?

The Empire of the Pigs

DONALD L. BARLETT AND JAMES B. STEELE

This article offers a graphic case study of the diverse costs of "corporate welfare"—incentives like subsidies, tax breaks, revenue bonds, and the like that noncorporate taxpayers fund. The authors maintain that some companies become expert at playing the "welfare game" to maximize their profits—with apparently little regard for the costs borne by the noncorporate community. As you read this article, consider the magnitude of these costs.

• • •

This is the story of how an extremely resourceful corporation plays the welfare game, maximizing the benefits to itself, often to the detriment of those who provide them. It's also a vivid reminder to cities and towns everywhere about the potential long-term liabilities they may one day face by spending public funds to get results that are best achieved by the free market.

Seaboard is a publicly owned company, but in fact it is the fiefdom of a reclusive Boston-area family (more on that later). A sort of mini-conglomerate, Seaboard has interests in hogs, strawberries, chickens, shrimp, salmon, flour, and wine. Its operations span four continents and nearly two dozen countries and range from cargo ocean liners to sugarcane. And like other profitable businesses, it collects subsidies—or, more accurately, corporate welfare—from local, state and federal governments. Indeed, officials trip over one another in the rush to extend taxpayer support to Seaboard—from the Federal Government's Overseas Private Investment Corp. (OPIC) in Washington to the Kansas state agency responsible for industrial

---

"The Empire of the Pigs," by Donald L. Barlett and James B. Steele, reprinted from *Time*, November 30, 1998, pp. 52–54, 57–58, 60, 62, 64.

development, to the utility authority in little Guymon, Okla. Wherever Seaboard is, there is a government throwing money at it. Money the company uses to build and equip plants, hire and train workers, export its products and expand overseas.

◉ This Little Piggy Skipped Town

For a close-up view of Seaboard, let's begin with Albert Lea. For most of this century, Wilson Foods operated that pork plant and was the town's largest employer. Wilson fell on hard times in the early 1980s, cut workers' average annual pay from $22,200 to $16,600 and eventually sold the plant to Farmstead Foods. In turn, that company went belly-up a few years later, after it lost its biggest customer—Wilson. Then, in December, 1990, just as workers were receiving the last of their unemployment checks, Seaboard appeared.

Once the company negotiated its sweetheart deal with the city, the Chamber of Commerce erected a billboard declaring, 35,000 FRIENDLY PEOPLE WELCOME SEABOARD CORP. At an appreciation luncheon, Rick Hofman, Seaboard's vice president of finance, observed that it is "really a pleasure to be associated with such a fine community and to have such a quality work force."

The more than $3 million Albert Lea handed out to help reopen the plant represented only the latest installment in corporate-welfare payouts. Because hog killing created serious pollution problems, Albert Lea earlier had kicked in $3.4 million to build a wastewater-treatment plant devoted mostly to servicing the pig factory. The hogs had your help as well: the Federal Government contributed $25.5 million, while the state of Minnesota gave $5.1 million. Total cost of the sewage plant: $34 million. The city also built new roads and water lines to the plant, built a parking lot and came up with $1 million to help erect a hog-slaughtering building.

• • •

Seaboard was unable to attract enough workers from Albert Lea to run the plant. Many former Farmstead employees had already left the area in search of work. More than 100 had retired. Still others declined to work for Seaboard wages—$4,500 a year less than the plant's 1983 wage and no vacation for the first year on the job.

Seaboard's solution: recruit Hispanic laborers from other areas of the U.S. as well as from Mexico and Central American countries like Guatemala. Soon the recently arrived immigrants began to stream into Albert Lea—with no money and no place to stay. It was a practice Seaboard would repeat in other towns, in other states.

It became common for several workers to share a room. Families couldn't afford local rents on a Seaboard wage. Eventually some went on welfare. In short, corporate welfare begot individual welfare.

Meantime, Seaboard failed to invest in upgrading its sewage-pretreatment facility. As a result, its waste began to overwhelm the city's municipal treatment plant. The city normally placed its treated sludge on soybean cropland, but by the second summer, city officials were in search of more land. As Sparks recalls, "We had so much sludge accumulation that . . . we had to go out in the middle of the summer, buy a crop (for $36,000) and plow it under because our storage capacity was exceeded."

Rather than overhaul the plant, Seaboard responded in the classic manner of corporate-welfare artists: it began quietly looking around for another town, another state. Alarmed, Albert Lea and Minnesota came up with an additional $12.5 million in incentives to keep the plant. But Seaboard had found a bigger patsy—Guymon (pop. 7,700) in Texas County, Okla. Guymon, the county, and the state put together an economic incentive package worth $21 million to entice Seaboard to the Oklahoma Panhandle, a section of the country where hogs and cattle far outnumber people.

Among the subsidies: Texas County borrowed $8 million to plow into the company up front. To pay off the loan, the county enacted a 1% sales tax. The state grated a $4 million, 10-year income tax credit with the understanding that it was "unlikely" the company would pay any income tax during those 10 years. The state spent $600,000 to train Seaboard's workers. The company received grants and low-interest loans to finance a waste-pre-treatment plant. (Remember the one in Albert Lea?) The company was excused from paying $2.9 million in real estate taxes.

As always, local and state officials were on hand when Seaboard announced in August 1992 that it would employ as many as 1,500 workers at its new pork-production facility. In time the plant will slaughter 4 million pigs a year. Oklahoma Governor David Walters declared the plant "a huge and much deserved economic boost to the entire Panhandle area, and to the state."

Meanwhile, back in Minnesota, Seaboard's local president was reassuring newspapers that the Albert Lea plant would remain open.

That was in August 1992. Seventeen months later, in January 1994, Seaboard announced that it would shutter its hog-slaughtering operations and lay off upwards of 600 employees. The company said it would keep about 300 workers to process and produce ready-to-buy meats like bacon, sausage and ham. (The number of employees eventually dropped to about 200, and Seaboard sold the business.)

It was not just Oklahoma's subsides that persuaded Seaboard to relocate. The Albert Lea work force was unionized; wages had risen to $19,000 a year—still $3,100 below their level in 1983, but too rich for Seaboard's blood. Guymon, by contrast, promised low-wage, nonunion labor. Also, Seaboard had decided it wanted to raise its own hogs for slaughter, not just buy them from farmers. Minnesota banned corporate hog farms. Oklahoma had had a similar ban but had repealed it before Seaboard came along.

When Seaboard moved on to Guymon, it left behind in Albert Lea the abandoned hog-slaughtering building, empty parking lots, a waste-treatment plant that now operates at only 50% of capacity and higher sewer bills to pay for it. And when Seaboard walked, the state had to come up with some $700,000 to retrain displaced workers or help them find new jobs.

"For 15 years, the community devoted the major portion of its federal and state legacy and a good share of local money to providing improvements to keep the slaughtering plant in our community (for

Seaboard and its predecessor)," says Sparks. "In retrospect," he says ruefully, "the money could have been better used."

❂ Ever Buy a Pig in a Poke?

In Oklahoma, it was starting to seem like deja vu all over again. The $21 million that state and local governments put up to bring Seaboard to the Panhandle was just the start. Guymon, like Albert Lea, couldn't supply the work force required by Seaboard. In time the company would need workers by the thousands. That's because the turnover rate in all processing plants runs close to 100% a year owing to the low wages. This slaughterhouse, one of the world's largest, will eventually kill an average of eight hogs a minute, 24 hours a day, 365 days a year—more than 4 million annually. So Seaboard repeated the Albert Lea hiring process—it attracted immigrant workers.

. . .

As was the case in Albert Lea, the freshly arrived immigrants had no place to stay, and the town that had never had a homeless shelter was forced to open one. Volunteers cleaned, repaired and painted a vacant motel. Unemployed individuals and families could stay up to one week at a cost of $10 a day, which included two meals. If they found work—largely at Seaboard—they could stay up to 90 days while they saved money for a permanent home.

Simultaneously, the state began training Seaboard workers even before the plant opened. Curriculums were provided in English, Spanish, Laotian and Vietnamese. In all, 3,300 Seaboard workers received training. The cost to taxpayers: $617,168.

Other costs began to pop up. By 1997 the Guymon schools bulged with new students. All grades exceeded the state-mandated teacher-pupil ratio. And enrollment is expected to jump one-third by the year 2000. Adding to the turmoil of overcrowding was the confusion about language. The district was compelled to add English-as-a-second-language classes. This year about 450 students, or 21%, were judged to have limited proficiency in English.

Some parents began to complain that their children were getting no education at all. But when the school district proposed $1.6 million in bond issues for new classrooms, equipment and buses, voters said no. The reason? A general anger directed at the huge hog farms. And a belief that Seaboard Corp. was not paying its way. Which, of course, it was not.

In 1997 the Oklahoma legislature agreed to spend $700 million on state roads and bridges. Of that figure, Guymon's and Texas County's share amounted to $37.3 million. That worked out to a per capita highway spending in Texas County of $2,200—or some 20 times what was earmarked for the rest of the state. Needless to say, most of the roadwork benefited Seaboard.

In addition, $47 million—a disproportionate amount—of the state's five-year capital-improvement program was set aside for Texas County for highway work to accommodate Seaboard truck convoys, which in time would haul 10,000 hogs a day into Guymon from all directions.

Then there was the local tax relief. For the 1996–97 fiscal year, Seaboard's Texas County tax bill totaled $1,118,000, according to John DeSpain, the county assessor. The state tax commission excused Seaboard from $700,000 of those taxes—on the grounds the new hog farms and slaughterhouse qualified as "manufacturing." The state, in turn, sent Texas County that sum from a special fund. In short, all other Oklahoma taxpayers picked up 63% of Seaboard's tax bill.

There's more: the company didn't even want to pay all the remaining $418,000, so it appealed. It won, and the state agreed to absorb an additional $193,000. In other words, the state paid 78% of Seaboard's real estate taxes.

As for the 1997–98 fiscal year, DeSpain said, Seaboard's tax bill increased to $1,580,000. The company was immediately excused from paying $1,090,000 of that—again, money that all other Oklahoma taxpayers must pay. Once more, Seaboard was dissatisfied and appealed. And again, the state consented to pick up $226,000 more. The bottom line: Seaboard was obliged to come up with just 17% of the taxes owed.

It should be noted that Seaboard did agree early on to contribute $175,000 to the Guymon schools each year—on the grounds that the old plant it replaced in 1992 had been taxed that amount. Even with that donation, its payments fall far short of what the company really owes. And it doesn't come close to providing the schools with the revenue needed to pay for Seaboard's presence in the community. One might think that would discourage other school districts from negotiating similar agreements. One would be wrong.

In December 1997 Seaboard promised to pay $125,000 to the Keyes schools in Cimarron County, which adjoins Texas County to the west. The money would allow the school system to replace the wiring and reopen a shuttered elementary school. In turn, Keyes agreed it would not oppose company plans to build a feed mill and 400 barns to house an additional 400,000 hogs.

Besides ballooning school costs. Keyes also may look forward to another set of rising statistics: crime. From 1991 to 1997 in Guymon, serious crimes went up 61%. Larcenies increased 50%, assaults jumped 96%, and auto theft shot up 200%. Rapes went from none to five. And for the first time, youth gangs appeared on Guymon streets. A resident says that "some students have expressed fear of even going to the restroom in the high school."

☻ Hog Heaven? Try Hog Hell

In a way, Guymon is fortunate that it has little available housing. If it did, the social costs it is paying for Seaboard's presence would have been worse. As it is, Seaboard workers often must settle in distant areas, like Liberal, Kans., another meat-packing center and magnet for immigrant workers. When Seaboard proposed establishing a hog farm in Seward County, where Liberal is the largest community, residents voted 3 to 1 to block construction. Nevertheless, Kansas state officials reportedly have assured Seaboard that the referendum is not binding.

The company already operates huge hog farms in five southwestern Kansas counties, where it accounts for more than one-quarter of the state's 1.5 million pig population. The pigs are raised in Kansas until they are ready for slaughter and are then trucked to the processing plant in Guymon. Kansas issued $9.6 million in industrial revenue bonds to help Seaboard develop the farms.

Actually, the term farm is a misnomer, for corporate hog farms bear no resemblance to traditional family farms. Instead, they are massive industrial operations. Call them pig factories.

In a long barn that houses about 1,000 animals, the hogs spend their days jammed next to one another, eating constantly until they grow from about 55 lbs. to 250 lbs. They stand on slatted floors so their wastes drop into a trough below that is flushed periodically into a nearby cesspit. The number of cesspits is exploding. From 1990 to 1998, the Oklahoma pig population soared 761%. Jumping from 230,000 to 1.98 million, with Seaboard accounting for about 80% of that number.

It is not pleasant living amid this. . . .

It's the ever present stench—the overpowering smell from Seaboards 40,000 hogs closely confined in 44 metal buildings, where exhaust fans continuously pump out tons of pungent ammonia, mixed with tons of grain dust and fecal matter, scented with the noxious odor of hydrogen sulfide (a poisonous gas produced by decaying manure that smells like rotten eggs), all combined with another blend of aromas wafting from five cesspits each 25 ft. deep and the size of a football field. They are, in effect, open-air sewage ponds, and 75 ft. below lies the Ogallala aquifer, which provides drinking and irrigation water for much of that part of the country.

Think of all that waste this way: imagine that you are sitting on the front porch of your farmhouse on the prairie, surrounded by four Washington Monuments, each filled to the top with pig manure. And then there are all the dead pigs lying about. By law, the carcasses are supposed to be deposited in Dumpsters with the lids tightly closed, and the contents disposed of daily. But with hundreds of thousands of hogs dying before their time each year. Seaboard often falls behind in disposing of them. Sometimes the overflow from Dumpsters is stacked nearby. Sometimes dead hogs are piled up beside barns, sometimes at the side of the road. And sometimes they lie about so long that the flesh rots away.

After issuing repeated warnings to Seaboard, the Oklahoma agriculture department fined the firm $157,500 in December 1997 for improper disposal. After an appeal, the company paid the state $88,200 for the infractions. In all, the Seaboard death toll reached 48 hogs an hour in 1997—420,000 for the year. And the carcasses are picked up only once a day—assuming the dead-pig truck is on schedule. Sometimes it isn't. Which is why at any given moment during the day there are hundreds of dead hogs lying about the fields of Texas County.

· · ·

To help staff its hog processing plant and farms, Seaboard has re-created the corporate model employed by the coal barons of the 1800s, whose workers lived in company-owned houses and shopped in company-owned stores.

In Guymon, Seaboard and local business leaders invested in an apartment complex and trailer parks to house the company's employees. Rent is automatically deducted from the paychecks of Seaboard workers. So, too, is the cost of meals that they eat at the plant. A two-bedroom apartment goes for $420 a month; for three bedrooms, $485. A Seaboard worker earns about $300 a week—before Social Security and income taxes are deducted.

· · ·

❧ Bringing Home the Bacon

Let us recount, for a moment, some of Seaboard's corporate welfare in the 1990s: Minnesota provided more than $3 million in economic incentives; Kentucky, $23 million; Kansas, $10 million; and Oklahoma, $100 million. The Federal Government's OPIC provided $25 million in insurance for business ventures abroad. As for the financial burdens imposed on other taxpayers by virtue of Seaboard's presence, no one knows the cost. It is in the tens of millions of dollar. And all this for jobs that pay little more than poverty-level wages.

All this welfare has helped propel Seaboard into the front ranks of American pork producers. As recently as 1989, the company did not own a single hog. This year it's the No. 5 producer in the country—and about to vault higher. Seaboard plans to build yet another processing plant, capable of slaughtering 4 million hogs a year, thereby doubling its output.

So who really profits from all of this? A secretive Boston family of millionaires.

Seaboard's stock is traded on the American Stock Exchange, and last week it closed at $387 a share. Some 75% of that stock is owned by another company, called Seaboard Flower Corp., and 95% of Seaboard Flour is owned by brothers H. Harry and Otto Bresky Jr., their sister Marjorie B. Shifman and family trusts. All told, the family's stock in Seaboard is worth $425 million.

And who are the Breskys? A Boston *Business Journal* article published in February 1993 described them this way: "The Bresky family could teach J. D. Salinger a thing or two about maintaining a low profile. . . . Try [to] find anyone in Boston who has even heard of the family, and you draw nothing but blanks. . . . The Breskys have never held memberships with local Chambers of Commerce or positions on the boards of local companies and nonprofit organizations."

• • •

Harry Bresky, president of both Seaboard Corp. and Seaboard Flour, presides over a work force of 12,000 employees, 10,200 of them in the U.S. Holdings include flour mills in Ecuador, Guyana, Haiti, Mozambique, Nigeria, Sierra Leone, and Democratic Republic of Congo; feed mills in Ecuador, Nigeria and Congo; 3,100 acres of shrimp ponds in Ecuador and Honduras; 37,000 acres of sugarcane, 4,200 acres of citrus and a sugar mill, all in Argentina; a winery in Bulgaria; other agricultural and business interests in Chile, Colombia, Costa Rica, Guatemala and Venezuela; electric-power-generating facilities in the Dominican Republic; shipping companies in Liberia; containerized cargo vessels running between Miami and Central and

South America; and, of course, the processing plant and hog farms in Oklahoma, Kansas, Texas and Colorado, along with poultry-processing plants, feed mills, hatcheries and a network of 700 contract chicken growers in Alabama, Georgia, Kentucky and Tennessee.

Harry Bresky, who earned just under $1 million in salary and bonus last year as Seaboard's top officer, didn't respond to TIME'S requests for an interview. But details of the business dealings of Seaboard and Bresky have emerged in a series of lawsuits filed over the years.

It all began in 1987, when Bresky fired Seaboard's vice president and chief financial officer, Donald Robohm, who had been with the company for more than a decade.

Robohm sued, charging "illegal and improper activity by Seaboard and other components of the Flour conglomerate, as directed by Bresky."

Robohm claimed the activities included "improper diversion of corporate opportunities from Seaboard," a public company, to Seaboard Flour, Bresky's private company. When Robohm refused to "cover up the conduct," he claimed, Bresky fired him for "not being 'a team player.'"

The lawsuit was settled and, according to court documents, both parties are prohibited from disclosing "information concerning the substance of the litigation and the substantive terms of its settlement."

Three years later, in 1990. Alan R. Kahn, a Wall Street investment broker and "Seaboard stockholder, filed a lawsuit in Delaware seeking an accounting of the profits earned by the Breskys through their intercompany dealings. Kahn alleged that the Breskys required Seaboard Corp. to enter into business deals with Seaboard Flour that generated "unlawful profits" for Seaboard Flour. In short, according to Kahn's allegations, the Breskys used their controlling positions in the two companies to move money from the public company to their private business.

Robohm was subpoenaed in the Kahn lawsuit, and he recited a litany of business dealings in which, he said, Bresky had interests in companies that profited from inflated contracts with Seaboard Corp.

According to his deposition, kickbacks were paid to officials in foreign governments; contracts were padded, with the excess money diverted to Swiss bank accounts; management fees were inflated; brokerage commissions ran 2 1/2 to five times the usual rate. And in the case of one Seaboard subsidiary, "there was a great deal of cash that was . . . unaccounted for."

• • •

The litigation dragged on for four years. Finally, in 1994, the lawsuit was settled when Seaboard Flour and the Breskys, without admitting "any liability or wrong-doing," agreed to pay $10.8 million to Seaboard Corp. For practical purposes, that meant the Breskys transferred money from the family-owned Seaboard Flour to the publicly traded but still family-controlled Seaboard Corp.

As for Harry Bresky, financial statements filed in the Kahn legal case show that in 1991 he reported a net worth of $84 million. That was back when Seaboard stock was less than half its present value. Like many millionaires, Bresky also enjoyed a comparatively low federal tax rate. On his 1990 U.S. income tax return, he reported adjusted gross income of $2.243 million and paid $503,000 in federal income and Social Security taxes. His effective overall tax rate worked out to 22.4%—just a few percentage points above the 16.8% rate paid by families earning $35,000 a year. Of course, Bresky had 64 times as much income.

From 1990 to 1997, Seaboard Corp. was the beneficiary of at least $150 million in economic incentives from federal, state and local governments to build and staff poultry- and hog-processing plants in the U.S.; insure its operations in foreign countries, and sell its products.

Local (and federal) taxpayers supplied the dollars not just for the outright corporate welfare, but also by picking up the costs of new classrooms and teachers, homelessness, increased crime, dwindling property values and an overall decline in the quality of life.

During those same years, the value of a share of Seaboard stock spiraled from $116 to $387, increasing the worth of the Bresky family holdings in the company from $125 million to $425 million.

Not bad work if you can get it. But you can't.

And that is the inequity of the entire, elaborate, jerry-built system of corporate welfare that infects and distorts the American economy. We are all left holding the bill.

◕ ◕ ◕

Questions

1. What is corporate welfare? Why is it provided?

2. Summarize what happened in Albert Lea, Minnesota.

3. Describe some of the costs of corporate welfare to workers, the community, the state, and the environment.

4. Given the histories of companies like Seaboard Corporation, why do so many communities try to attract such corporations?

5. Suppose there's a town meeting scheduled, at which participants will discuss the possibility of using incentives to persuade Seaboard Corporation to move its hog-farm operation into your community. Would you oppose or support this plan? Explain your response.

Deviance

From Chapter 7 of *Society: The Basics*, 11/e. John J. Macionis. Copyright © 2011 by Pearson Education. All rights reserved.

Deviance

- Why does every society have deviance?

- How does *who* and *what* are defined as deviant reflect social inequality?

- What effect has punishment had in reducing crime in the United States?

"I was like the guy lost in another dimension, a stranger in town, not knowing which way to go." With these words, Bruce Glover recalls the day he returned to his hometown of Detroit, Michigan, after being away for twenty-six years—a long stretch in a state prison. Now fifty-six years of age, Glover was a young man of thirty when he was arrested for running a call girl ring. Found guilty at trial, he was given a stiff jail sentence.

"My mother passed while I was gone," Glover continues, shaking his head. "I lost everything." On the day he walked out of prison, he realized just how true that statement was. He had nowhere to go and no way to get there. He had no valid identification, which he would need to find a place to live and a job. He had no money to buy the clothes he needed to go out and start looking. He turned to a prison official and asked for help. Only with the assistance of a state agency was he finally able to get some money and temporary housing (C. Jones, 2007).

©Santa Fabio

This chapter explores issues involving crime and criminals, asking not only how our criminal justice system handles offenders but also why societies develop standards of right and wrong in the first place. As you will see, the law is simply one part of a complex system of social control: Society teaches us all to conform, at least most of the time, to countless rules. We begin our investigation by defining several basic concepts.

What Is Deviance?

Deviance is *the recognized violation of cultural norms.* Norms guide virtually all human activities, so the concept of deviance is quite broad. One category of deviance is **crime,** *the violation of a society's formally enacted criminal law.* Even criminal deviance spans a wide range, from minor traffic violations to prostitution, sexual assault, and murder.

Most familiar examples of nonconformity are negative instances of rule breaking, such as stealing from a campus bookstore, assaulting a fellow student, or driving while intoxicated. But we also define especially righteous people—students who speak up too much in class or people who are overly enthusiastic about the latest electronic gadgets—as deviant, even if we give them a measure of respect. What all deviant actions or attitudes, whether negative or positive, have in common is some element of *difference* that causes us to think of another person as an "outsider" (H. S. Becker, 1966).

Not all deviance involves action or even choice. The very *existence* of some categories of people can be troublesome to others.

To the young, elderly people may seem hopelessly "out of touch," and to some whites, the mere presence of people of color may cause discomfort. Able-bodied people often view people with disabilities as an out-group, just as rich people may shun the poor for falling short of their high-class standards.

Social Control

All of us are subject to **social control,** *attempts by society to regulate people's thoughts and behavior.* Often this process is informal, as when parents praise or scold their children or when friends make fun of a classmate's choice of music. Cases of serious deviance, however, may bring action by the **criminal justice system,** *the organizations—police, courts, and prison officials—that respond to alleged violations of the law.*

How a society defines deviance, *who* is branded as deviant, and *what* people decide to do about deviance all have to do with the way a society is organized. Only gradually, however, have people come to understand that the roots of deviance are deep in society, as the chapter now explains.

The Biological Context

A century ago, most people understood—or more correctly, misunderstood—human behavior to be the result of biological instincts. Early interest in criminality therefore focused on biological

Deviance

deviance the recognized violation of cultural norms

crime the violation of a society's formally enacted criminal law

social control attempts by society to regulate people's thoughts and behavior

criminal justice system the organizations—police, courts, and prison officials—that respond to alleged violations of the law

causes. In 1876, Cesare Lombroso (1835–1909), an Italian physician who worked in prisons, theorized that criminals stand out physically, with low foreheads, prominent jaws and cheekbones, protruding ears, hairy bodies, and unusually long arms. All in all, Lombroso claimed that criminals look like our apelike ancestors.

Had Lombroso looked more carefully, he would have found the physical features he linked to criminality throughout the entire population. We now know that no physical traits distinguish criminals from noncriminals.

In the middle of the twentieth century, William Sheldon took a different approach, suggesting that body structure might predict criminality (Sheldon, Hartl, & McDermott, 1949). He cross-checked hundreds of young men for body type and criminal history and concluded that delinquency was most common among boys with muscular, athletic builds. Sheldon Glueck and Eleanor Glueck (1950) confirmed that conclusion but cautioned that a powerful build does not necessarily *cause* or even *predict* criminality. Parents, they suggested, tend to be somewhat distant from powerfully built sons, who in turn grow up to show less sensitivity toward others. In a self-fulfilling prophecy, people who expect muscular boys to be bullies may act in ways that bring about the aggressive behavior they expect.

Today, genetics research seeks possible links between biology and crime. In 2003, scientists at the University of Wisconsin reported results of a twenty-five-year study of crime among 400 boys. The researchers collected DNA samples from each boy and noted any history of trouble with the law. The researchers concluded that genetic factors (especially defective genes that, say, make too much of an enzyme) together with environmental factors (especially abuse early in life) were strong predictors of adult crime and violence. They noted, too, that these factors together were a better predictor of crime than either one alone (Lemonick, 2003; Pinker, 2003).

Deviance is always a matter of difference. Deviance emerges in everyday life as we encounter people whose appearance or behavior differs from what we consider "normal." Who is the "deviant" in this photograph? From whose point of view?

Melissa Moore\The Image Works

CRITICAL REVIEW Biological theories offer a limited explanation of crime. The best guess at present is that biological traits in combination with environmental factors explain some serious crime. Most of the actions we define as deviant are carried out by people who are physically quite normal.

In addition, because a biological approach looks at the individual, it offers no insight into how some kinds of behaviors come to be defined as deviant in the first place. Therefore, although there is much to learn about how human biology may affect behavior, research currently puts far greater emphasis on social influences.

CHECK YOUR LEARNING What does biological research add to our understanding of crime? What are the limitations of this approach?

Personality Factors

Like biological theories, psychological explanations of deviance focus on individual abnormality. Some personality traits are inherited, but most psychologists think personality is shaped primarily by social experience. Deviance, then, is viewed as the result of "unsuccessful" socialization.

Classic research by Walter Reckless and Simon Dinitz (1967) illustrates the psychological approach. Reckless and Dinitz began by asking teachers to categorize twelve-year-old male students as either likely or unlikely to get into trouble with the law. They then interviewed both the boys and their mothers to assess each boy's self-concept and how he related to others. Analyzing their results, the researchers found that the "good boys" displayed a strong conscience (what Freud called superego), could handle frustration, and identified

○ Making the Grade

Deviance, the violation of norms, is a broad concept. Crime, the violation of formally enacted law, is one type of deviance.

○ Making the Grade

The three arguments below explain why we cannot fully understand deviance only by looking at the deviant person. We need a broader, sociological perspective to examine society.

with cultural norms and values. The "bad boys," by contrast, had a weaker conscience, displayed little tolerance for frustration, and felt out of step with conventional culture.

As we might expect, the "good boys" went on to have fewer run-ins with the police than the "bad boys." Because all the boys lived in areas where delinquency was widespread, the investigators attributed staying out of trouble to a personality that controlled deviant impulses. Based on this conclusion, Reckless and Dinitz called their analysis *containment theory*.

○ **CRITICAL REVIEW** Psychologists have shown that personality patterns have some connection to deviance. Some serious criminals are psychopaths who do not feel guilt or shame, have no fear of punishment, and have little sympathy for the people they harm (Herpertz & Sass, 2000). However, as noted in the case of biological factors, most serious crimes are committed by people whose psychological profiles are normal.

Both biological and psychological research views deviance as a trait of individuals. The reason these approaches have limited value in explaining deviance is that wrongdoing has more to do with the organization of society. We now turn to a sociological approach, which explores where ideas of right and wrong come from, why people define some rule breakers but not others as deviant, and what role power plays in this process.

○ **CHECK YOUR LEARNING** Why do biological and psychological analyses not explain deviance very well?

Jose Azel\Aurora Photos, Inc.

Why is it that street-corner gambling like this is usually against the law but playing the same games in a fancy casino is not?

The Social Foundations of Deviance

Although we tend to view deviance as the free choice or personal failings of individuals, all behavior—deviance as well as conformity—is shaped by society. Three social foundations of deviance identified here will be detailed later in this chapter:

1. **Deviance varies according to cultural norms.** No thought or action is inherently deviant; it becomes deviant only in relation to particular norms. State law permits prostitution in rural areas of Nevada, although the practice is outlawed in the rest of the United States. Twelve states have gambling casinos, twenty-nine have casinos on Indian reservations, and four other states have casinos at racetracks. In all other states, casino gambling is illegal. Text-messaging while driving is legal in thirty-three states but against the law in seventeen others (six other states forbid the practice for young drivers). Until 2008, when a court struck down the law, only Florida legally banned gay men and lesbians from adopting a child (Ruggieri, 2008; American Gaming Association, 2009; National Conference of State Legislatures, 2010).

   Further, most cities and towns have at least one unique law. For example, Mobile, Alabama, outlaws the wearing of stiletto-heeled shoes; Pine Lawn, Missouri, bans saggy, "low-rider" pants; South Padre Island, Texas, bans the wearing of neckties; Mount Prospect, Illinois, has a law against keeping pigeons or bees; Topeka, Kansas, bans snowball fights; Hoover, South Dakota, does not allow fishing with a kerosene lantern; and Beverly Hills, California, regulates the number of tennis balls allowed on the court at one time (R. Steele, 2000; Wittenauer, 2007).

   Around the world, deviance is even more diverse. Albania outlaws any public display of religious faith, such as "crossing" oneself; Cuba bans citizens from owning personal computers; Vietnam can prosecute citizens for meeting with foreigners; Malaysia does not allow tight-fitting jeans for women; Saudi Arabia bans the sale of red flowers on Valentine's Day; Iran does not allow women to wear makeup and forbids the playing of rap music (Chopra, 2008).

2. **People become deviant as others define them that way.** Everyone violates cultural norms at one time or another. For example, have you ever walked around talking to yourself or "borrowed" a pen from your workplace? Whether such behavior defines us as mentally ill or criminal depends on how others perceive, define, and respond to it.

3. **Both norms and the way people define rule breaking involve social power.** The law, claimed Karl Marx, is

Deviance

○ Making the Grade

Notice that Durkheim considered deviance to be a natural and necessary part of all social organization.

○ Seeing Sociology in Everyday Life

Keeping in mind Durkheim's claim that society creates deviance to mark moral boundaries, can you suggest why we often define people only in terms of their deviance, for example, by calling someone an "addict" or a "thief"?

the means by which powerful people protect their interests. A homeless person who stands on a street corner speaking out against the government risks arrest for disturbing the peace; a mayoral candidate during an election campaign doing exactly the same thing gets police protection. In short, norms and how we apply them reflect social inequality.

The Functions of Deviance: Structural-Functional Analysis

The key insight of the structural-functional approach is that deviance is a necessary element of social organization. This point was made a century ago by Emile Durkheim.

Durkheim's Basic Insight

In his pioneering study of deviance, Emile Durkheim (1964a, orig. 1893; 1964b, orig. 1895) made the surprising statement that there is nothing abnormal about deviance. In fact, it performs four essential functions:

1. **Deviance affirms cultural values and norms.** As moral creatures, people must prefer some attitudes and behaviors to others. But any definition of virtue rests on an opposing idea of vice: There can be no good without evil and no justice without crime. Deviance is needed to define and support morality.

2. **Responding to deviance clarifies moral boundaries.** By defining some individuals as deviant, people draw a boundary between right and wrong. For example, a college marks the line between academic honesty and deviance by disciplining students who cheat on exams.

3. **Responding to deviance brings people together.** People typically react to serious deviance with shared outrage. In doing so, Durkheim explained, they reaffirm the moral ties that bind them. For example, after the September 11, 2001, terrorist attacks, people across the United States were joined by a common desire to protect the country and bring the perpetrators to justice.

4. **Deviance encourages social change.** Deviant people push a society's moral boundaries, suggesting alternatives to the status quo and encouraging change. Today's deviance, declared Durkheim, can become tomorrow's morality (1964b:71, orig. 1895). For example, rock-and-roll, condemned as immoral in the 1950s, became a mainstream, multibillion-dollar industry

Durkheim claimed that deviance is a necessary element of social organization, serving several important functions. After a man convicted of killing a child settled in their New Hampshire town, residents came together to affirm their community ties as well as their understanding of right and wrong. Has any event on your campus caused a similar reaction?

Jim Cole/AP Wide World Photos

just a few years later. In recent decades, hip-hop music has followed the same path toward respectability.

An Illustration: The Puritans of Massachusetts Bay

Kai Erikson's classic study of the Puritans of Massachusetts Bay brings Durkheim's theory to life. Erikson (2005b, orig. 1966) shows that even the Puritans, a disciplined and highly religious group, created deviance to clarify their moral boundaries. In fact, Durkheim might well have had the Puritans in mind when he wrote:

> Imagine a society of saints, a perfect cloister of exemplary individuals. Crimes, properly so called, will there be unknown; but faults which appear [insignificant] to the layman will create there the same scandal that the ordinary offense does in ordinary consciousness. . . . For the same reason, the perfect and upright man judges his smallest failings with a severity that the majority reserve for acts more truly in the nature of an offense. (1964b:68–69, orig. 1895)

Deviance is thus not a matter of a few "bad apples" but a necessary condition of "good" social living.

Deviance may be found in every society, but the *kind* of deviance people generate depends on the moral issues they seek to clarify. The Puritans, for example, experienced a number of "crime waves," including the well-known outbreak of witchcraft in 1692. With each response, the Puritans answered questions about the range of proper beliefs by celebrating some of their members and condemning others as deviant.

⌐○ Making the Grade

Merton's strain theory shows how people's opportunities (or lack of opportunities) to achieve cultural goals can encourage both deviance and conformity. In addition, what sociologists call people's "structure of opportunities" helps explain the type of deviance they engage in.

⌐○ Making the Grade

Study the definition of labeling theory, which is the key idea of the symbolic-interaction approach. Be sure you understand this statement: Deviance results not so much from what people do as from how others respond to what they do.

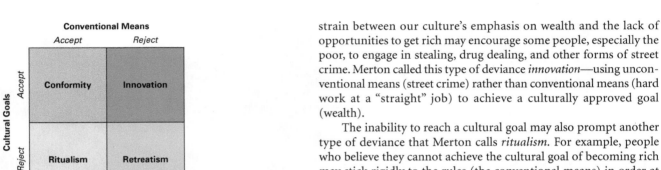

FIGURE 1   Merton's Strain Theory of Deviance

Combining a person's view of cultural goals and the conventional means to obtain them allowed Robert Merton to identify various types of deviance.

Source: Merton (1968).

Erikson discovered that although the offenses changed, the proportion of the population the Puritans defined as deviant remained steady over time. This stability, he concluded, confirms Durkheim's claim that society creates deviants to mark its changing moral boundaries. In other words, by constantly defining a small number of people as deviant, the Puritans maintained the moral shape of their society.

Merton's Strain Theory

Some deviance may be necessary for a society to function, but Robert Merton (1938, 1968) argued that too much deviance results from particular social arrangements. Specifically, the extent and kind of deviance depend on whether a society provides the *means* (such as schooling and job opportunities) to achieve cultural *goals* (such as financial success). Merton's strain theory of deviance is illustrated in Figure 1.

Conformity lies in pursuing cultural goals through approved means. Thus the U.S. "success story" is someone who gains wealth and prestige through talent, schooling, and hard work. But not everyone who wants conventional success has the opportunity to attain it. For example, people living in poverty may see little hope of becoming successful if they play by the rules. According to Merton, the

strain between our culture's emphasis on wealth and the lack of opportunities to get rich may encourage some people, especially the poor, to engage in stealing, drug dealing, and other forms of street crime. Merton called this type of deviance *innovation*—using unconventional means (street crime) rather than conventional means (hard work at a "straight" job) to achieve a culturally approved goal (wealth).

The inability to reach a cultural goal may also prompt another type of deviance that Merton calls *ritualism*. For example, people who believe they cannot achieve the cultural goal of becoming rich may stick rigidly to the rules (the conventional means) in order at least to feel respectable.

A third response to the inability to succeed is *retreatism*: rejecting both cultural goals and means so that one in effect "drops out." Some alcoholics, drug addicts, and street people are retreatists. The deviance of retreatists lies in their unconventional lifestyles and, perhaps more seriously, in what seems to be their willingness to live this way.

The fourth response to failure is *rebellion*. Like retreatists, rebels such as radical "survivalists" reject both the cultural definition of success and the conventional means of achieving it but go one step further by forming a counterculture supporting alternatives to the existing social order.

Deviant Subcultures

Richard Cloward and Lloyd Ohlin (1966) extended Merton's theory, proposing that crime results not simply from limited legitimate (legal) opportunity but also from readily accessible illegitimate (illegal) opportunity. In short, deviance or conformity depends on the *relative opportunity structure* that frames a person's life.

The life of Al Capone, a notorious gangster, illustrates Cloward and Ohlin's theory. As a son of poor immigrants, Capone faced barriers of poverty and ethnic prejudice, which lowered his odds of achieving success in conventional terms. Yet as a young man during the Prohibition era (the years between 1920 and 1933, when alcoholic beverages were banned in the United States), Capone found in his neighborhood people who could teach him how to sell alcohol illegally—a source of illegitimate opportunity. Where the structure of opportunity favors criminal activity, Cloward and Ohlin predict the development of *criminal subcultures,* such as Capone's criminal organization or today's inner-city street gangs.

But what happens when people are unable to find *any* opportunities, legal or illegal? Then deviance may take one of two forms. One is *conflict subcultures,* such as armed street gangs that regularly engage in violence, ignited by frustration and a desire for respect. Another possible outcome is the development of *retreatist subcultures,* in which deviants drop out and abuse alcohol or other drugs.

Albert Cohen (1971, orig. 1955) suggests that criminality is most common among lower-class youths because they have the least

Seeing Sociology in Everyday Life

An old saying goes, "Sticks and stones can break my bones, but names can never hurt me." What might labeling theory have to say about this claim?

labeling theory the idea that deviance and conformity result not so much from what people do as from how others respond to those actions

stigma a powerfully negative label that greatly changes a person's self-concept and social identity

medicalization of deviance the transformation of moral and legal deviance into a medical condition

opportunity to achieve success by conventional means. Neglected by society, they seek self-respect by creating a deviant subculture that defines as worthy the traits these youths do have. Being feared on the street may win few points with society as a whole, but it may satisfy a youth's desire to "be somebody" in a local neighborhood.

Walter Miller (1970, orig. 1958) adds that deviant subcultures are characterized by (1) *trouble,* arising from frequent conflict with teachers and police; (2) *toughness,* the value placed on physical size, strength, and agility, especially among males; (3) *smartness,* the ability to succeed on the streets, to outsmart or "con" others; (4) *a need for excitement,* the search for thrills, risk, or danger; (5) *a belief in fate,* a sense that people lack control over their own lives; and (6) *a desire for freedom,* often expressed as anger toward authority figures.

Finally, Elijah Anderson (1994, 2002; Kubrin, 2005) explains that in poor urban neighborhoods, most people manage to conform to conventional ("decent") values. Yet faced every day with neighborhood crime and violence, indifference or even hostility from police, and sometimes even neglect from their own parents, some young men decide to live by the "street code." To show that he can survive on the street, a young man displays "nerve," a willingness to stand up to any threat. Following this street code, the young man believes that even a violent death is better than being "dissed" (disrespected) by others. Some manage to escape the dangers, but the risk of ending up in jail—or worse—is very high for these young men, who have been pushed to the margins of our society.

CRITICAL REVIEW Durkheim made an important contribution by pointing out the functions of deviance. However, there is evidence that a community does not always come together in reaction to crime; sometimes fear of crime drives people to withdraw from public life (Liska & Warner, 1991; Warr & Ellison, 2000).

Merton's strain theory also has been criticized for explaining some kinds of deviance (stealing, for example) better than others (crimes of passion or mental illness). Furthermore, not everyone seeks success in conventional terms of wealth, as strain theory suggests.

The general argument of Cloward and Ohlin, Cohen, and Miller—that deviance reflects the opportunity structure of society—has been confirmed by later research (Allan & Steffensmeier, 1989; Uggen, 1999). However, these theories fall short by assuming that everyone shares the same cultural standards for judging right and wrong. If we define crime as including not just burglary and auto theft but also fraud and other crimes carried out by corporate executives and Wall Street tycoons, many more high-income people will be counted among criminals. There is evidence that people of all social backgrounds

Young people cut off from legitimate opportunity often form subcultures that many people view as deviant. Gang subcultures are one way young people gain the sense of belonging and respect denied to them by the larger culture.

have become more casual about breaking the rules, as the Seeing Sociology in Everyday Life box explains.

Finally, all structural-functional theories suggest that everyone who breaks the rules will be labeled deviant. However, becoming deviant is actually a highly complex process, as the next section explains.

CHECK YOUR LEARNING Why do you think many of the theories just discussed seem to say that crime is more common among people with lower social standing?

Deviant subcultures affect specific segments of the population. At the same time, as the economy rises and falls, the level of criminal activity typically goes up and down. Hard times, in short, tend to encourage widespread anxiety and a belief that we have to look out for ourselves any way we can. Seeing Sociology in the News on the next couple pages offers a recent chapter in this very old story.

Labeling Deviance: Symbolic-Interaction Analysis

The symbolic-interaction approach explains how people come to see deviance in everyday situations. From this point of view, definitions of deviance and conformity are surprisingly flexible.

Deviance

San Francisco Chronicle

Ex-Employees Turn to Cyber Crime after Layoffs

BY ALEJANDRO MARTINEZ-CABRERA
April 8, 2010

SAN FRANCISCO—When a slumping economy and historically high unemployment rates dropped the ax on the country's workforce and left the survivors wondering if—or when—they'd be next, law enforcers and security experts braced themselves for what they considered would be an almost inevitable rise in data breaches and high-tech crimes. And they were right.

National unemployment rates peaked in October at 10.1 percent and remained at 9.7 percent during the first two months of the year. Local law enforcers say the inability to find gainful employment has been a recurrent motivation behind new cases of identity theft and software piracy that drop on their desks almost daily.

"We're constantly coming across people who typically we wouldn't see and wouldn't engage in this criminal behavior if the economy was better. They see it as a way out," said Detective Sgt. Ken Taylor of California's Silicon Valley high-tech crimes task force Rapid Enforcement Allied Computer Team.

In one recent case under investigation, Taylor said, an unemployed San Mateo, California, woman in her twenties was detained with a large number of re-encoded credit cards in her possession. She said she was using them to buy food.

And a Fremont, California, man who had been recently laid off was arrested in February for selling pirated copies of a $2,500 Adobe design program for $150 on Craigslist. Task force members could look at cases of workers-turned-software-pirates all day every day, Taylor said.

According to cyber-security researchers, corporations across all industries have been dealing with a steadily growing number of internal data breaches since the financial meltdown.

A Verizon data-loss report noted that individuals with insider knowledge of organizations accounted for 20 percent of all breaches last year, and that number has been increasing as economic malaises drag on, said Chris Novak, managing principal of Verizon Business's Global Investigative Response Team.

Even though external attacks made up the bulk of the breaches, the report found that each internal incident compromised on average 100,000 individual pieces of sensitive information—at least 60,000 pieces more than external hacks.

Researchers say that anyone from top-level executives and IT personnel to low-level support employees can have access to data that can be sold illegally. A 2009 survey of almost 1,000 laid-off individuals found that 59 percent admitted keeping company data after leaving the business, according to the Ponemon Institute, a privacy research center in Traverse City, Michigan.

Labeling Theory

The central contribution of symbolic-interaction analysis is **labeling theory,** *the idea that deviance and conformity result not so much from what people do as from how others respond to those actions.* Labeling theory stresses the relativity of deviance, meaning that people may define the same behavior in any number of ways.

Consider these situations: A college student takes a sweater off the back of a roommate's chair and packs it for a weekend trip, a married woman at a convention in a distant city has sex with an old boyfriend, and a mayor gives a big city contract to a major campaign contributor. We might define the first situation as carelessness, borrowing, or theft. The consequences of the second situation depend largely on whether the woman's behavior becomes known back home. In the third situation, is the mayor choosing the best contractor or paying off a political debt? The social construction of reality is a highly variable process of detection, definition, and response.

Primary and Secondary Deviance

Edwin Lemert (1951, 1972) observed that some norm violations—say, skipping school or underage drinking—may provoke some reaction from others, but this process has little effect on a person's self-concept. Lemert calls such passing episodes *primary deviance.*

But what happens if people take notice of someone's deviance and really make something of it? After an audience has defined some action as primary deviance, the individual may begin to change, taking on a deviant identity by talking, acting, or dressing in a different way, rejecting the people who are critical, and repeatedly breaking the rules. Lemert (1951:77) calls this change of self-concept *secondary deviance.* He explains that "when a person begins to employ . . . deviant behavior as a means of defense, attack, or adjustment to the . . . problems created by societal reaction . . . , deviance [becomes] secondary." For example, say that people have begun describing a young man as an "alcohol abuser," which establishes primary deviance. These people may then exclude him from their friendship network. His response may be to become bitter toward them, start drinking even more, and seek the company of others who approve of his drinking. These actions mark the beginning of secondary deviance, a deeper deviant identity.

Stigma

Secondary deviance marks the start of what Erving Goffman (1963) called a *deviant career.* As people develop a deeper commitment to their deviant behavior, they typically acquire a **stigma,** *a powerfully negative label that greatly changes a person's self-concept and social identity.*

A stigma operates as a master status, overpowering other dimensions of identity so that a person is discredited in the minds of others and consequently becomes socially isolated. Often a person gains a stigma informally as others begin to see the individual in deviant terms. Sometimes, however, an entire community stigmatizes a person in a public way through what Harold Garfinkel (1956) calls a *degradation ceremony.* A criminal prosecution is one example, operating much like a high school graduation ceremony in reverse: A person stands before the community to be labeled in negative rather than positive terms.

In fact, data breach originators are "moving from being just the administrators and super-type users to your everyday users," Novak said.

"When data breaches are caused by administrators or super users, it's a big deal and the organization loses a great deal of information," he said. "When they come from average users, they're smaller pinpricks but can drag on longer and cost the company more in the long run."

Stolen data can range from employees' health care records or clients' credit card numbers to merger and acquisition plans, confidential agreements or valuable source code, said Rick Kam, president and co-founder of data breach prevention firm ID Experts.

Thieves can easily sell the information to cyber-criminal rings or use it as a bargaining chip to get a job with their former employer's competitors. According to the Ponemon Institute study, 67 percent of respondents said they would use "their former company's confidential, sensitive or proprietary information to leverage a new job."

"The issue of identity theft is all about opportunity," Kam said. "And our first instinct is to protect ourselves."

In one case handled by Kam's company six months ago, a disgruntled man went as far as trying to extort his former employer, a large health care provider, by threatening to release thousands of sensitive patient records that would have triggered an avalanche of lawsuits.

Those who remain employed but fear being the next to go can also grow alienated or resentful toward their companies and may be tempted to steal corporate data, said Kevin Rowney, director of breach response at Symantec.

"It's a common trend in economic history. Rising stress creates the circumstances that motivate people to go into financial fraud," Rowney said. "Employees in this economy feel it's every man for himself."

WHAT DO YOU THINK?

1. In what way does this article show that crime is not just a personal behavior but also a societal issue?

2. If anxiety and a sense that "it's every man for himself" breed crime, can you think of ways in which we can generate a stronger sense of community and collective responsibility? What would you suggest?

3. If you were a courtroom judge, would you be inclined to show leniency toward someone who engaged in cyber crime because the person was facing economic challenges? Why or why not?

"Ex-Employees Turn to Cyber Crime after Layoffs" by Alejandro Martinez-Cabrera, April 8, 2010, *San Francisco Chronicle*, is reprinted by permission of the publisher.

Retrospective and Projective Labeling

Once people stigmatize a person as deviant, they may engage in *retrospective labeling,* a reinterpretation of the person's past in light of some present deviance (Scheff, 1984). For example, after discovering that a priest has sexually molested a child, others rethink his past, perhaps offering comments such as "He always did want to be around young children." Retrospective labeling, which distorts a person's biography by being highly selective, typically deepens a deviant identity.

Similarly, people may engage in *projective labeling* of a stigmatized person, using a deviant identity to predict the person's future actions. Regarding the priest, people might say, "He's going to keep at it until he's caught." The more people in someone's social world think such things and act accordingly, the more these definitions affect the individual's self-concept, and the greater the chance that the predictions will come true.

Labeling Difference as Deviance

Is a homeless man who refuses to allow police to take him to a city shelter on a cold night simply trying to live independently, or is he "crazy"? People have a tendency to treat behavior that irritates or threatens them not simply as "different" but as deviance or even mental illness.

The psychiatrist Thomas Szasz (1961, 1970, 2003, 2004) claims that people are too quick to apply the label of mental illness to conditions that simply amount to differences we don't like. The only way to avoid this troubling practice, Szasz concludes, is to stop using the idea of mental illness entirely. The world is full of people whose differences in thought or action may irritate us, but such differences are not grounds for defining someone as mentally ill. Such labeling, Szasz says, simply enforces conformity to the standards of people powerful enough to impose their will on others.

Most mental health professionals reject the idea that mental illness does not exist. But they agree that it is important to think carefully about how we define "difference." First, people who are mentally ill are no more to blame for their condition than people who suffer from cancer or some other physical problem. Therefore, having a mental or physical illness is no grounds for a person being labeled "deviant." Second, people (especially those without the medical knowledge to diagnose mental illness) should avoid applying such labels just to make others conform to their own standards of behavior.

The Medicalization of Deviance

Labeling theory, particularly the ideas of Szasz and Goffman, helps explain an important shift in the way our society understands deviance. Over the past fifty years, the growing influence of psychiatry and medicine has led to the **medicalization of deviance,** *the transformation of moral and legal deviance into a medical condition.*

Medicalization amounts to swapping one set of labels for another. In moral terms, we judge people or their behavior as either "bad" or "good." However, the scientific objectivity of medicine passes no moral judgment, instead using clinical diagnoses such as "sick" or "well."

● Seeing Sociology in Everyday Life

Explain in your own words sociologist Howard Becker's (1966) statement that deviance is nothing more than behavior that people define as deviant.

SEEING SOCIOLOGY IN EVERYDAY LIFE

Deviant Subculture: Has It Become OK to Break the Rules?

ASTRID: Simon! You're downloading that music illegally. You'll get us both into trouble!

SIMON: Look, everyone cheats. Rich CEOs cheat in business. Ordinary people cheat on their taxes. Politicians lie. What else is new?

ASTRID: So it's OK to steal? Is that what you really believe?

SIMON: I'm not saying it's OK. I'm just saying everyone does it. . . .

It's been a couple of bad years for the idea of playing by the rules. First we learn that the executives of not just one but many U.S. corporations are guilty of fraud and outright stealing on a scale that most of us cannot even imagine. More recently, we realize that the Wall Street leaders running the U.S. economy not only did a pretty bad job of it but paid themselves tens of millions of dollars for doing so. And of course, even the Catholic church, which we hold up as a model of moral behavior, is still trying to recover from the charges that hundreds of priests have sexually abused parishioners (most of them under the age of consent) for decades while church officials covered up the crimes.

There have been plenty of theories offered about what is causing this widespread wrongdoing. Some suggest that the pressure to win—by whatever means necessary—in the highly competitive world of business and politics can be overwhelming. As one analyst put it, "You can get away with your embezzlements and your lies, but you can never get away with *failing*."

Such thinking helps explain the wrongdoing among many CEOs in the corporate world and the conviction of several members of Congress for ethics violations, but it offers little insight into the problem of abusive priests. In some ways at least, wrongdoing seems to have

Do you consider cheating in school wrong? Would you turn in someone you saw cheating? Why or why not?

become a way of life for just about everybody. For example, the Internal Revenue Service reports that Simon is right—millions of U.S. taxpayers cheat on their taxes, failing to pay an estimated $345 billion each year. The music industry claims that it has lost billions of dollars to illegal piracy of recordings, a practice especially common among young people. Perhaps most disturbing of all, surveys of students in high school, college, and also graduate school show that about half say that they cheated on a test at least once during the past year (Gallup, 2004; Morin, 2006).

Emile Durkheim viewed society as a moral system, built on a set of rules about what people should and should not do. Years earlier, another French thinker named Blaise Pascal made the opposite claim that "cheating is the foundation of society." Today, which of the two statements is closer to the truth?

WHAT DO YOU THINK?

1. In your opinion, how widespread is wrongdoing in U.S. society today?

2. Do you think the people who break the rules usually think that their actions are wrong? Why or why not?

3. What do you think are the reasons for the apparent increase in dishonesty?

Sources: Based on "Our Cheating Hearts" (2002) and Bono (2006).

To illustrate this idea, until the mid-twentieth century, most people viewed alcoholics as morally weak people easily tempted by the pleasure of drink. Gradually, however, medical specialists redefined alcoholism so that most people now consider it a disease, leading us to define alcoholics as "sick" rather than "bad." In the same way, obesity, drug addiction, child abuse, sexual promiscuity, and other behaviors that used to be strictly moral matters are widely defined today as illnesses for which people need help rather than punishment.

The Difference Labels Make

Whether we define deviance as a moral or a medical issue has three consequences. First, it affects *who responds* to deviance. An offense against common morality typically brings a reaction from members of the community or the police. A medical label, however, places the situation under the control of clinical specialists, including counselors, psychiatrists, and physicians.

A second issue is *how people respond* to deviance. A moral approach defines deviants as offenders subject to punishment. Medically, however,

Deviance

○— Making the Grade

Deviance can be defined as either a moral or a medical issue.
Be sure you understand the three key differences between
defining deviance one way or the other.

○— Seeing Sociology
in Everyday Life

Context guides how we define someone's action. For example, Amy
Bishop shot and killed her brother in 1986; back then, her action
was ruled accidental. In light of this recent shooting, authorities
reopened the earlier case and indicted Bishop.

they are patients who need treatment. Punishment is designed to fit the crime, but treatment programs are tailored to the patient and may involve any therapy that a specialist thinks might prevent future illness.

Third, and most important, the two labels differ on the issue of *the competence of the deviant person.* From a moral standpoint, whether we are right or wrong, at least we are responsible for our own behavior. Once we are defined as sick, however, we are seen as unable to control (or if "mentally ill," even to understand) our actions. People who are labeled incompetent are subject to treatment, often against their will. For this reason alone, defining deviance in medical terms should be done with extreme caution.

Sutherland's Differential Association Theory

Learning any social pattern, whether conventional or deviant, is a process that takes place in groups. According to Edwin Sutherland (1940), a person's tendency toward conformity or deviance depends on the amount of contact with others who encourage or reject conventional behavior. This is Sutherland's theory of *differential association.*

A number of studies confirm the idea that young people are more likely to engage in delinquent behavior if they believe that members of their peer group encourage such activity (Akers et al., 1979; Miller & Matthews, 2001). One recent investigation focused on sexual activity among eighth-grade students. Two strong predictors of such behavior in young girls were having a boyfriend who encouraged sexual relations and having girlfriends they believed would approve of such activity. Similarly, boys were encouraged to become sexually active by friends who rewarded them with high status in the peer group (Little & Rankin, 2001).

Hirschi's Control Theory

The sociologist Travis Hirschi (1969; Gottfredson & Hirschi, 1995) developed *control theory,* which states that social control depends on people's anticipating the consequences of their behavior. Hirschi assumes that everyone finds at least some deviance tempting. But the thought of a ruined career keeps most people from breaking the rules; for some, just imagining the reactions of family and friends is enough. On the other hand, people who think that they have little to lose from deviance are likely to become rule breakers.

Specifically, Hirschi links conformity to four different types of social control:

1. **Attachment.** Strong social attachments encourage conformity. Weak family, peer, and school relationships leave people freer to engage in deviance.

2. **Opportunity.** The greater a person's access to legitimate opportunity, the greater the advantages of conformity. By contrast,

In 2010, Amy Bishop, a biology professor with a Harvard Ph.D., was denied tenure by her colleagues at the University of Alabama Huntsville. Soon after that, she took a gun to a campus faculty meeting and killed three colleagues, wounding three others. What effect does the social standing of the offender have in our assessment of her as "crazy" or "sick" as opposed to simply "evil"?

someone with little confidence in future success is more likely to drift toward deviance.

3. **Involvement.** Extensive involvement in legitimate activities—such as holding a job, going to school, or playing sports—inhibits deviance (Langbein & Bess, 2002). By contrast, people who simply "hang out" waiting for something to happen have the time and energy to engage in deviant activity.

4. **Belief.** Strong beliefs in conventional morality and respect for authority figures restrain tendencies toward deviance. By contrast, people with a weak conscience (and who are left unsupervised) are more open to temptation (Stack, Wasserman, & Kern, 2004).

Hirschi's analysis calls to mind our earlier discussions of the causes of deviant behavior. Here again, a person's relative social privilege and family and community environment affect the risk of deviant behavior (Hope, Grasmick, & Pointon, 2003).

● Seeing Sociology
  in Everyday Life

Why do you think that politicians and other well-known
people who get into trouble with the law often claim they
have a problem with alcohol or other drugs and check into
"rehab"?

○ Making the Grade

Students often have difficulty clearly defining secondary
deviance and distinguishing it from primary deviance.
Carefully review these concepts.

[Photographer]/Stone/Getty Images

All social groups teach their members skills and attitudes that encourage
certain behavior. In recent years, discussion on college campuses has
focused on the dangers of binge drinking, which results in several dozen
deaths each year among young people in the United States. How much of
a problem is binge drinking on your campus?

○ **CRITICAL REVIEW** The various symbolic-interaction
theories all see deviance as a process. Labeling theory links
deviance not to action but to the *reaction* of others. Thus some
people are defined as deviant but others who think or behave in
the same way are not. The concepts of secondary deviance,
deviant career, and stigma show how being labeled deviant can
become a lasting self-concept.

Yet labeling theory has several limitations. First, because it
takes a highly relative view of deviance, labeling theory ignores
the fact that some kinds of behavior—such as murder—are condemned just about everywhere. Therefore, labeling theory is most
usefully applied to less serious issues, such as sexual promiscuity or mental illness. Second, research on the consequences
of deviant labeling does not clearly show whether deviant labeling produces further deviance or discourages it (Smith & Gartin,

1989; Sherman & Smith, 1992). Third, not everyone resists being
labeled as deviant; some people actively seek it (Vold & Bernard,
1986). For example, people engage in civil disobedience and
willingly subject themselves to arrest in order to call attention to
social injustice.

Sociologists consider Sutherland's differential association
theory and Hirschi's control theory important contributions to
our understanding of deviance. But why do society's norms and
laws define certain kinds of activities as deviant in the first place?
This important question is addressed by social-conflict analysis, the focus of the next section.

○ **CHECK YOUR LEARNING** Clearly define primary
deviance, secondary deviance, deviant career, and stigma.

Deviance and Inequality: Social-Conflict Analysis

The social-conflict approach links deviance to social inequality. That
is, who or what is labeled "deviant" depends on which categories of
people hold power in a society.

Deviance and Power

Alexander Liazos (1972) points out that the people we tend to define
as deviants—the ones we dismiss as "nuts" and "sluts"—are typically
not those who are bad or harmful as much as they are *powerless*. Bag
ladies and unemployed men on street corners, not corporate polluters
or international arms dealers, carry the stigma of deviance.

Social-conflict theory explains this pattern in three ways. First,
all norms—especially the laws of any society—generally reflect the
interests of the rich and powerful. People who threaten the wealthy
are likely to be labeled deviant, whether it's by taking people's property ("common thieves") or advocating a more egalitarian society
("political radicals"). Karl Marx, a major architect of the social-
conflict approach, argued that the law and all social institutions
support the interests of the rich. Or as Richard Quinney puts it,
"Capitalist justice is by the capitalist class, for the capitalist class, and
against the working class" (1977:3).

Second, even if their behavior is called into question, the powerful have the resources to resist deviant labels. The majority of the corporate executives who were involved in the corporate scandals of
recent years were not arrested, and only a small number ever went to
jail.

Third, the widespread belief that norms and laws are "just" and
"good" masks their political character. For this reason, although we
may condemn the unequal application of the law, most of us give
little thought to whether the laws themselves are really fair or not.

white-collar crime crime committed by people of high social position in the course of their occupations

corporate crime the illegal actions of a corporation or people acting on its behalf

organized crime a business supplying illegal goods or services

Deviance and Capitalism

In the Marxist tradition, Steven Spitzer (1980) argues that deviant labels are applied to people who interfere with the operation of capitalism. First, because capitalism is based on private control of property, people who threaten the property of others—especially the poor who steal from the rich—are prime candidates for being labeled deviant. Conversely, the rich who take advantage of the poor are less likely to be labeled deviant. For example, landlords who charge poor tenants high rents and evict those who cannot pay are not considered criminals; they are simply "doing business."

Second, because capitalism depends on productive labor, people who cannot or will not work risk being labeled deviant. Many members of our society think people who are out of work, even through no fault of their own, are somehow deviant.

Third, because the operation of the capitalist system depends on respect for authority figures, people who resist authority are likely to be labeled deviant. Examples are children who skip school or talk back to parents or teachers and adults who do not cooperate with employers or police.

Fourth, anyone who directly challenges the capitalist status quo is likely to be defined as deviant. Such has been the case with labor organizers, radical environmentalists, civil rights and antiwar activists, and feminists.

On the other side of the coin, society positively labels whatever supports the operation of capitalism. For example, winning athletes enjoy celebrity status because they make money and express the values of individual achievement and competition, both vital to capitalism. Also, Spitzer notes, we condemn using drugs of escape (marijuana, psychedelics, heroin, and crack) as deviant but promote drugs (such as alcohol and caffeine) that encourage adjustment to the status quo.

The capitalist system also tries to control people who don't fit into the system. The elderly, people with mental or physical disabilities, and Robert Merton's "retreatists" (people addicted to alcohol or other drugs) represent a "costly yet relatively harmless burden" to society. Such people, claims Spitzer, are subject to control by social welfare agencies. But people who openly challenge the capitalist system, including the inner-city "underclass" and revolutionaries—Merton's "innovators" and "rebels"—are controlled by the criminal justice system and, if necessary, military forces such as police SWAT teams and the National Guard.

Note that both the social welfare and criminal justice systems blame individuals, not the system, for social problems. Welfare recipients are considered unworthy freeloaders, poor people who rage at their plight are labeled rioters, anyone who actively challenges the government is branded a radical or a communist, and those who attempt to gain illegally what they will never get legally are rounded up as common criminals.

White-Collar Crime

In a sign of things to come, a Wall Street stockbroker named Michael Milken made headlines in 1987 when he was jailed for business fraud. Milken attracted attention because not since the days of Al Capone had anyone made so much money in one year: $550 million—about $1.5 million a day (Swartz, 1989).

Milken engaged in **white-collar crime**, defined by Edwin Sutherland in 1940 as *crime committed by people of high social position in the course of their occupations.* White-collar crime does not involve violence and rarely brings police with guns drawn to the scene. Rather, white-collar criminals use their powerful offices illegally to enrich themselves or others, often causing significant public harm in the process. For this reason, sociologists sometimes call white-collar offenses "crime in the suites" as opposed to "crime in the streets."

The most common white-collar crimes are bank embezzlement, business fraud, bribery, and violating antitrust laws that

Perhaps no one better symbolized the greed that drove the Wall Street meltdown of 2008 than Bernard Madoff, who swindled thousands of people and organizations out of some $50 billion. In 2009, after pleading guilty to eleven felony counts, Madoff was sentenced to 150 years in prison. Do you think white-collar offenders are treated fairly by our criminal justice system? Why or why not?

Christine Cornell/Agence France Presse/Getty Images

Seeing Sociology in Everyday Life

Imagine police holding a street gang, but not its individual members, responsible for an outbreak of violence. This is what happens in the case of corporate crime. What does this fact suggest about the link between crime and power?

Making the Grade

White-collar crime and corporate crime are similar concepts, and there is not always a clear line separating the two. White-collar criminals are *individuals* of high social position who commit crimes while doing their jobs. Corporate crime occurs when a *company* acts in violation of the law.

require businesses to be competitive. Sutherland (1940) explains that such white-collar offenses typically end up in a civil hearing rather than a criminal courtroom. *Civil law* regulates business dealings between private parties; *criminal law* defines a person's moral responsibilities to society. In practice, someone who loses a civil case pays for damage or injury but is not labeled a criminal. Furthermore, corporate officials are protected by the fact that most charges of white-collar crime target the organization rather than individuals.

In the rare cases that white-collar criminals are charged and convicted, they usually escape punishment. A government study found that those convicted of fraud and punished with a fine ended up paying less than 10 percent of what they owed; most managed to hide or transfer their assets to avoid paying up. Among white-collar criminals convicted of embezzlement, only about half ever served a day in jail. One accounting found that just 57 percent of the embezzlers convicted in the U.S. federal courts served prison sentences; the rest were put on probation or issued a fine (U.S. Bureau of Justice Statistics, 2010). As some analysts see it, until courts impose more prison terms, we should expect white-collar crime to remain widespread (Shover & Hochstetler, 2006).

Corporate Crime

Sometimes whole companies, not just individuals, break the law. **Corporate crime** consists of *the illegal actions of a corporation or people acting on its behalf.*

Corporate crime ranges from knowingly selling faulty or dangerous products to deliberately polluting the environment (Derber, 2004). The collapse of a number of corporations in recent years, linked to criminal conduct on the part of company officials, has cost tens of thousands of people their jobs and their pensions.

In addition, companies often violate safety regulations, resulting in injury or death. Between 2006 and 2010, more than 125 people died in underground coal mines in the United States, in many cases amid allegations of safety violations. We might also wonder whether any "safe" mines really exist in light of the fact that hundreds more people died from "black lung" disease resulting from years of inhaling coal dust. The death toll for all job-related hazards in the United States runs into the thousands, and more than 1 million people are injured on the job seriously enough to require time away from work (Jafari, 2008; U.S. Census Bureau, 2009; Mine Safety and Health Administration, 2009).

Organized Crime

Organized crime is *a business supplying illegal goods or services.* Sometimes crime organizations force people to do business with them, as when a gang extorts money from shopkeepers for "protection."

In most cases, however, organized crime involves selling illegal goods and services—often sex, drugs, or gambling—to willing buyers.

Organized crime has flourished in the United States for more than a century. The scope of its operations expanded among immigrants who found that this society was not willing to share its opportunities with them. Thus some ambitious minorities (such as Al Capone, mentioned earlier) made their own success, especially during Prohibition, when the government banned the production and sale of alcohol.

The Italian Mafia is a well-known example of organized crime. But other criminal organizations involve African Americans, Chinese, Colombians, Cubans, Haitians, Nigerians, and Russians, as well as others of almost every racial and ethnic category. Organized crime today involves a wide range of activities, from selling illegal drugs to prostitution to credit card fraud and selling false identification papers to illegal immigrants (Valdez, 1997; Federal Bureau of Investigation, 2008).

CRITICAL REVIEW According to social-conflict theory, a capitalist society's inequality in wealth and power shapes its laws and how they are applied. The criminal justice and social welfare systems thus act as political agents, controlling categories of people who are a threat to the capitalist system.

Like other approaches to deviance, social-conflict theory has its critics. First, this approach implies that laws and other cultural norms are created directly by the rich and powerful. At the very least, this is an oversimplification because the law also protects workers, consumers, and the environment, sometimes opposing the interests of corporations and the rich.

Second, social-conflict analysis argues that criminality springs up only to the extent that a society treats its members unequally. However, as Durkheim noted, deviance exists in all societies, whatever the economic system and their degree of inequality.

The various sociological explanations for crime and other types of deviance are summarized in the Applying Theory table.

CHECK YOUR LEARNING Define white-collar crime, corporate crime, and organized crime.

Deviance, Race, and Gender

What people consider deviant reflects the relative power and privilege of different categories of people. The following sections offer two examples: how racial and ethnic hostility motivates hate crimes and how gender is linked to deviance.

hate crime a criminal act against a person or a person's property by an offender motivated by racial or other bias

● APPLYING THEORY ●

Deviance

	Structural-Functional Approach	Symbolic-Interaction Approach	Social-Conflict Approach
What is the level of analysis?	Macro-level	Micro-level	Macro-level
What is deviance? What part does it play in society?	Deviance is a basic part of social organization. By defining deviance, society sets its moral boundaries.	Deviance is part of socially constructed reality that emerges in interaction. Deviance comes into being as individuals label something deviant.	Deviance results from social inequality. Norms, including laws, reflect the interests of powerful members of society.
What is important about deviance?	Deviance is universal: It exists in all societies.	Deviance is variable: Any act or person may or may not be labeled deviant.	Deviance is political: People with little power are at high risk of being labeled deviant.

Hate Crimes

A **hate crime** is *a criminal act against a person or a person's property by an offender motivated by racial or other bias.* A hate crime may express hostility toward someone based on race, religion, ancestry, sexual orientation, or physical disability. The federal government recorded 7,783 hate crimes in 2008 (U.S. Department of Justice, 2009).

In 1998, people across the country were stunned by the brutal killing of Matthew Shepard, a gay student at the University of Wyoming, by two men filled with hatred toward homosexuals. But such crimes are far from isolated cases. The National Coalition of Anti-Violence Programs reports that 40 percent of lesbians and gay men in the United States say that they have been the victims of hate violence in their adult lifetimes, and about 90 percent of such people report experiencing verbal abuse. People who contend with multiple stigmas, such as gay men of color, are especially likely to be victimized (Dang & Vianney, 2007; National Coalition of Anti-Violence Programs, 2010). Yet hate crimes can happen to anyone: In 2008, more than one of every six hate crimes based on race targeted white people (Federal Bureau of Investigation, 2009).

By 2009, forty-five states and the federal government had enacted legislation that raises penalties for crimes motivated by hatred. Supporters are gratified, but opponents charge that such laws, which increase the penalty for a crime based on the attitudes of the offender, amount to punishing "politically incorrect" thoughts. The Thinking About Diversity box on the next page takes a closer look at the issue of hate crime laws.

The Feminist Perspective: Deviance and Gender

Virtually every society in the world tries to control the behavior of women more than men. Historically, our own society has centered women's lives around the home. In the United States even today, women's opportunities in the workplace, in politics, in athletics, and in the military are more limited than men's. In some other parts of the world, the constraints on women are greater still. In Saudi Arabia, women cannot vote or legally operate motor vehicles; in Iran, women who expose their hair or wear makeup in public can be whipped; and not long ago, a Nigerian court convicted a divorced woman of bearing a child out of wedlock and sentenced her to death by stoning; her life was later spared out of concern for her child (Eboh, 2002).

Gender also figures into the theories about deviance noted earlier. For example, Robert Merton's strain theory defines cultural goals in terms of financial success. Traditionally at least, this goal has had more to do with the lives of men, because women have been socialized to define success in terms of relationships, particularly marriage and motherhood (E. B. Leonard, 1982). A more woman-focused theory might recognize the "strain" that results from the cultural ideal of equality clashing with the reality of gender-based inequality.

According to labeling theory, gender influences how we define deviance because people commonly use different standards to judge the behavior of females and males. Further, because society puts men

Deviance

Seeing Sociology
in Everyday Life

Why do you think that women are much less likely than men
to be arrested for a serious crime?

crimes against the person (violent crimes) crimes that direct violence or the threat of violence against others

crimes against property (property crimes) crimes that involve theft of money or property belonging to others

victimless crimes violations of law in which there are no obvious victims

---

THINKING ABOUT DIVERSITY: RACE, CLASS, & GENDER

Hate Crime Laws: Do They Punish Actions or Attitudes?

On a cool October evening, Todd Mitchell, an African American teenager, was standing with some friends in front of their apartment complex in Kenosha, Wisconsin. They had just seen the film *Mississippi Burning* and were fuming over a scene that showed a white man beating a young black boy as he knelt in prayer.

"Do you feel hyped up to move on some white people?" asked Mitchell. Minutes later, they saw a young white boy walking toward them on the other side of the street. Mitchell commanded, "There goes a white boy. Go get him!" The group swarmed around the youngster, beating him bloody and leaving him on the ground in a coma. The attackers took the boy's tennis shoes as a trophy.

Police soon arrested the boys and charged them with the beating. Todd Mitchell went to trial as the ringleader, and the jury found him guilty of aggravated battery *motivated by racial hatred*. Instead of receiving the usual two-year prison sentence, Mitchell was sent to jail for four years.

As this case illustrates, hate crime laws punish a crime more severely if the offender is motivated by bias against some category of people. Supporters make three arguments in favor of hate crime legislation. First, the offender's intentions are always important in weighing criminal responsibility, so considering hatred as an intention is nothing new. Second, victims of hate crimes typically suffer more serious injuries than victims of crimes with other motives. Third, a crime moti-

vated by racial or other bias is more harmful because it can inflame an entire community more than a crime carried out, say, for money.

Critics counter that while some hate crime cases involve hard-core racism, most are impul-

Do you think this example of vandalism should be prosecuted as a hate crime? In other words, should the punishment be more severe than if the spray painting were just "normal" graffiti? Why or why not?

sive acts by young people. Even more important, critics maintain, hate crime laws are a threat to First Amendment guarantees of free speech. Hate crime laws allow courts to sentence offenders not just for their actions but also for their attitudes. As the Harvard University law professor Alan Dershowitz cautions, "As much as I hate bigotry, I fear much more the Court attempting to control the minds of citizens." In short, according to critics, hate crime laws open the door to punishing beliefs rather than behavior.

In 1993, the U.S. Supreme Court upheld the sentence handed down to Todd Mitchell. In a unanimous decision, the justices reaffirmed that the government should not punish an individual's beliefs. But, they reasoned, a belief is no longer protected when it becomes the motive for a crime.

WHAT DO YOU THINK?

1. Do you think crimes motivated by hate are more harmful than those motivated by, say, greed? Why or why not?

2. Do you think minorities such as African Americans should be subject to the same hate crime laws as white people? Why or why not?

3. On balance, do you favor or oppose hate crime laws? Why?

Sources: Terry (1993), A. Sullivan (2002), and Hartocollis (2007).

---

in positions of power over women, men often escape direct responsibility for actions that victimize women. In the past, at least, men who sexually harassed or assaulted women were labeled only mildly deviant and sometimes escaped punishment entirely.

By contrast, women who are victimized may have to convince others—even members of a jury—that they are not to blame for their own sexual harassment or assault. Research confirms an important truth: Whether people define a situation as deviant—and, if they do, who in the situation is defined as deviant—depends on the sex of both the audience and the actors (King & Clayson, 1988).

Finally, despite its focus on inequality, much social-conflict analysis does not address the issue of gender. If economic disadvantage is a primary cause of crime, as conflict theory suggests, why do women (whose economic position is much worse than men's) commit far *fewer* crimes than men?

Crime

Crime is the violation of criminal laws enacted by a locality, a state, or the federal government. All crimes are composed of two distinct

Sam Pearson, who lives in Renville County, North Dakota, rarely locks his doors when he leaves the house.

Serge Shuman, who lives in Mecklenburg County, North Carolina, knows many people who have been victims of crime and avoids going out at night.

Explore the share of the population in prison in your local community and in counties across the United States on mysoclab.com

Seeing Ourselves

NATIONAL MAP 1

The Risk of Violent Crime across the United States

This map shows the risk of becoming a victim of violent crime. In general, the risk is highest in low-income, rural counties that have a large population of men between the ages of fifteen and twenty-four. After reading this section of the text, see whether you can explain this pattern.

Explore on mysoclab.com

Source: CAP Index (2009).

Risk of Violent Crime
- Above average
- Average
- Below average

---

elements: the *act* itself (or in some cases, a failure to do what the law requires) and *criminal intent* (in legal terminology, *mens rea,* or "guilty mind"). Intent is a matter of degree, ranging from willful conduct to negligence. Someone who is negligent does not set out deliberately to hurt anyone but acts (or fails to act) in a way that results in harm. Prosecutors weigh the degree of intent in determining whether, for example, to charge someone with first-degree murder, second-degree murder, or negligent manslaughter. Alternatively, they may consider a killing justifiable, as in self-defense.

Types of Crime

In the United States, the Federal Bureau of Investigation (FBI) gathers information on criminal offenses and regularly reports the results in a publication called *Crime in the United States.* Two major types of crime make up the FBI "crime index."

Crimes against the person, also referred to as *violent crimes,* are *crimes that direct violence or the threat of violence against others.* Violent crimes include murder and manslaughter (legally defined as "the willful killing of one human being by another"), aggravated assault ("an unlawful attack by one person on another for the purpose of inflicting severe or aggravated bodily injury"), forcible rape ("the carnal knowledge of a female forcibly and against her will"), and robbery ("taking or attempting to take anything of value from the care, custody, or control of a person or persons, by force or threat of force or violence and/or putting the victim in fear"). National Map 1 shows the risk of violent crime for all the counties in the United States.

Crimes against property, also referred to as *property crimes,* are *crimes that involve theft of money or property belonging to others.* Property crimes include burglary ("the unlawful entry of a structure to commit a [serious crime] or a theft"), larceny-theft ("the unlawful

taking, carrying, leading, or riding away of property from the possession of another"), motor vehicle theft ("the theft or attempted theft of a motor vehicle"), and arson ("any willful or malicious burning or attempt to burn the personal property of another").

A third category of offenses, not included in major crime indexes, is **victimless crimes,** *violations of law in which there are no obvious victims.* Also called *crimes without complaint,* they include illegal drug use, prostitution, and gambling. The term "victimless crime" is misleading, however. How victimless is a crime when young drug users embark on a life of crime to support their drug habit? What about a pregnant woman who, by smoking crack, permanently harms her baby? Or a gambler who loses the money needed to support himself and his family? Perhaps it is more correct to say that people who commit such crimes are both offenders and victims.

Because public views of victimless crime vary greatly, laws differ from place to place. Although gambling and prostitution are legal in only limited areas, both activities are common across the country.

Criminal Statistics

Statistics gathered by the FBI show crime rates rising from 1960 to 1990 and then declining after that. Even so, police count more than 11 million serious crimes each year. Figure 2 shows the trends for various serious crimes over the past four decades.

Always read crime statistics with caution, however, because they include only crimes known to the police. Almost all murders are reported, but other assaults—especially between people who know one another—often are not. Police records include an even smaller proportion of property crimes, especially when the losses are small.

Researchers check official crime statistics by conducting *victimization surveys,* in which they ask a representative sample of

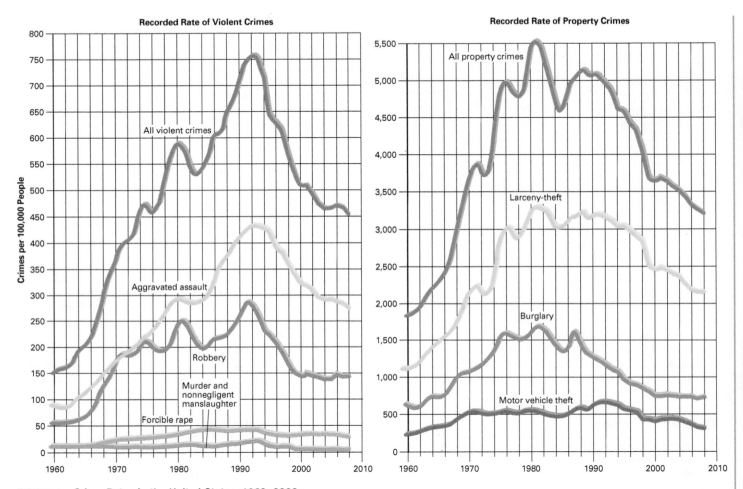

FIGURE 2   Crime Rates in the United States, 1960–2008

The graphs show the rates for various violent crimes and property crimes during recent decades. Since about 1990,
the trend has been downward.

Source: Federal Bureau of Investigation (2009).

people about their experiences with crime. Victimization surveys
carried out in 2008 showed that the actual number of serious crimes
was more than twice as high as police reports indicate (Rand, 2009).

The Street Criminal: A Profile

Using various government crime reports, we can draw a general
description of the categories of people most likely to be arrested for
crimes.

Gender

Although each sex makes up roughly half the population, police col-
lared males in 65.2 percent of all property crime arrests in 2008; the
other 34.8 percent of arrests involved women. In other words, men are
arrested almost twice as often as women for property crimes. In the
case of violent crimes, the difference is even greater, with 81.7 percent
of arrests involving males and just 18.3 percent females (more than
a four-to-one ratio).

Deviance

Go to the Multimedia Library at mysoclab.com to watch the ABC *20/20* video "Justice and Privilege"

Read "Race and Class in the Criminal Justice System" by David Cole on mysoclab.com

It may be that law enforcement officials are reluctant to define women as criminals. In global perspective, the greatest gender difference in crime rates occurs in societies that most severely limit the opportunities of women. In the United States, the difference in arrest rates for women and men has been narrowing, which probably indicates increasing gender equality in our society. Between 1999 and 2008, there was a 11.6 percent *increase* in arrests of women and a 3.1 percent *drop* in arrests of men (Federal Bureau of Investigation, 2009).

Age

Official crime rates rise sharply during adolescence, peak in the late teens, and fall as people get older. People between the ages of fifteen and twenty-four represent just 14 percent of the U.S. population, but in 2008, they accounted for 41.5 percent of all arrests for violent crimes and 48.3 percent of arrests for property crimes.

Social Class

The FBI does not assess the social class of arrested persons, so no statistical data of the kind given for age and gender are available. But research has long indicated that street crime is more widespread among people of lower social position (Thornberry & Farnsworth, 1982; Wolfgang, Thornberry, & Figlio, 1987).

Yet the connection between class and crime is more complicated than it appears on the surface. For one thing, many people see the poor as less worthy than the rich, whose wealth and power confer "respectability" (Tittle, Villemez, & Smith, 1978; Elias, 1986). And although crime—especially violent crime—is a serious problem in the poorest inner-city communities of the United States, most of these crimes are committed by a few hard-core offenders. The majority of people in inner-city neighborhoods have no criminal record at all (Wolfgang, Figlio, & Sellin, 1972; Elliott & Ageton, 1980; Harries, 1990).

The connection between social standing and criminality also depends on the type of crime. If we expand our definition of crime beyond street offenses to include white-collar crime, the "common criminal" suddenly looks much more affluent and may live in a $100 million home. ● Go to mysoclab.com

Race and Ethnicity

Both race and ethnicity are strongly linked to crime rates, although the reasons are many and complex. Official statistics indicate that 69.2 percent of arrests for index crimes in 2008 involved white people. However, arrests of African Americans are higher in proportion to their share of the general population. African Americans make up 12.8 percent of the population of the United States but account for 30.1 percent of the arrests for property crimes (versus 67.4 percent for whites) and 39.4 percent of arrests for violent crimes (versus 58.3 percent for whites) (Federal Bureau of Investigation, 2009).

"You look like this sketch of someone who's thinking about committing a crime."

There are several reasons for the disproportionate number of arrests among African Americans. First, in the United States, race is closely linked to social standing, which, as already explained, affects the likelihood of engaging in street crimes. Many poor people living in the midst of wealth come to see society as unjust and therefore are more likely to turn to crime to get their share (Blau & Blau, 1982; E. Anderson, 1994; Martinez, 1996).

Second, black and white family patterns differ: Seventy-two percent of non-Hispanic black children (compared with 28 percent of non-Hispanic white children) are born to single mothers. There are two risks associated with single parenting: Children get less supervision, and they are at greater risk of living in poverty. With more than one-third of African American children growing up in poor families (compared with one in nine white children), no one should be surprised at proportionately higher crime rates for African Americans (Courtwright, 1996; Jacobs & Helms, 1996; Hamilton, Martin, and Ventura, 2009; U.S. Census Bureau, 2009).

Third, prejudice prompts white police to arrest black people more readily and leads citizens to report African Americans more willingly, so people of color are overly criminalized (Chiricos, McEntire, & Gertz, 2001; Quillian & Pager, 2001; Demuth & Steffensmeier, 2004). Read on mysoclab.com

Fourth, remember that the official crime index does not include arrests for offenses ranging from drunk driving to white-collar violations. This omission contributes to the view of the typical criminal

Making the Grade

Remember that the profile of a criminal depends on the type of crime. Street crime involves a larger share of lower-income people; corporate crime involves mostly high-income people. With regard to race, most street crime is committed by whites.

Seeing Sociology in Everyday Life

Do you think stricter gun control laws would lower the level of deadly violence in the United States? Why or why not?

as a person of color. If we broaden our definition of crime to include drunk driving, business fraud, embezzlement, stock swindles, and cheating on income tax returns, the proportion of white criminals rises dramatically.

Keep in mind, too, that categories of people with high arrest rates are also at higher risk of being victims of crime. In the United States, for example, African Americans are six times as likely to die as a result of homicide as white people (Rogers et al., 2001; Heron et al., 2009).

Finally, some categories of the population have unusually low rates of arrest. People of Asian descent, who account for 4.5 percent of the population, figure in only 1.1 percent of all arrests. Asian Americans enjoy higher than average educational achievement and income. Also, Asian American culture emphasizes family solidarity and discipline, both of which keep criminality down.

Crime in Global Perspective

By world standards, the U.S. crime rate is high. Although recent crime trends are downward, there were 16,272 murders in this country in 2008, which amounts to one every half hour around the clock. In large cities such as New York, never does a week go by without someone being killed.

The rate of violent crime (but not property crime) in the United States is several times higher than in Europe. The contrast is even greater between our country and the nations of Asia, including India and Japan, where violent and property crime rates are among the lowest in the world.

Elliott Currie (1985) suggests that crime arises from our culture's emphasis on individual economic success, often at the expense of strong families and neighborhoods. The United States also has extraordinary cultural diversity—a result of centuries of immigration—that can lead to conflict. In addition, economic inequality is higher in this country than in most other high-income nations. Our society's relatively weak social fabric, combined with considerable frustration among the poor, increases the level of criminal behavior.

Another factor contributing to violence in the United States is extensive private ownership of guns. About two-thirds of murder victims in the United States die from shootings. The U.S. rate of handgun homicides is about five times higher than in Canada, a country that strictly limits handgun ownership (Federal Bureau of Investigation, 2009; Statistics Canada, 2009).

Surveys show that about one-third of U.S. households have at least one gun. In fact, there are more guns (about 283 million) than adults in this country, and 40 percent of these weapons are handguns, which are commonly used in violent crimes. In large part, gun ownership reflects people's fear of crime, yet easy availability of guns in this country makes crime more deadly (Brady Campaign, 2008; NORC, 2009).

Supporters of gun control claim that restricting gun ownership would reduce the number of murders in the United States. For example, the number of murders each year in Canada, where the law prevents most people from owning guns, is about the same as the number of murders in just the cities of New York and Newark in this country. But as critics of gun control point out, laws regulating gun ownership do not keep guns out of the hands of criminals, who almost always obtain guns illegally. They also claim that gun control is no magic bullet in the war on crime: The number of people in the United States killed each year by knives alone is three times the number of Canadians killed by weapons of all kinds (J. D. Wright, 1995; Munroe, 2007; Federal Bureau of Investigation, 2009; Statistics Canada, 2009).

By the end of 2008, gun sales to private citizens were up sharply, reflecting the fears on the part of many gun owners that the Obama administration would act to curtail gun ownership. Changes in the law may or may not occur in the next few years, but debate over the consequences of widespread gun ownership will continue (Potter, 2008).

December 24–25, traveling through Peru. In Lima, Peru's capital city, the concern with crime is obvious. Almost every house is fortified with gates, barbed wire, or broken glass embedded in cement at the top of a wall. Private security forces are everywhere in the rich areas along the coast, where we find the embassies, expensive hotels, and the international airport.

The picture is very different as we pass through small villages high in the Andes to the east. The same families have lived in these communities for generations, and people know one another. No gates or fences here. And we've seen only one police car all afternoon.

Crime rates are high in some of the largest cities of the world, such as Manila, Philippines, and São Paulo, Brazil, which have rapid population growth and millions of desperately poor people. Outside of big cities, however, the traditional character of low-income societies and their strong family structure allow local communities to control crime informally.

Some types of crime have always been multinational, such as terrorism, espionage, and arms dealing. But today, the globalization we are experiencing on many fronts also extends to crime. A case in point is the illegal drug trade. In part, the problem of illegal drugs in the United States is a *demand* issue. That is, the demand for cocaine and other drugs in this country is high, with high rates of addiction and many young people who are willing to risk arrest or even violent death for a chance to get rich in the drug trade. But the *supply* side of the issue is just as important. In the South American nation of Colombia, at least 20 percent of the people depend on cocaine production

Deviance

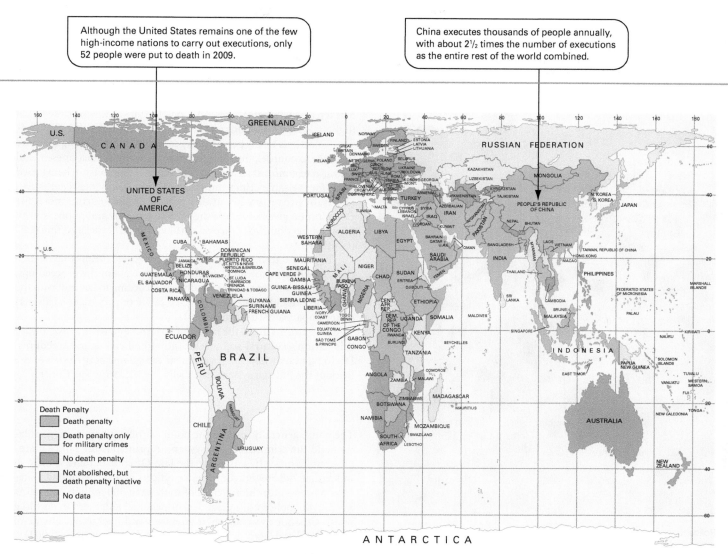

Although the United States remains one of the few high-income nations to carry out executions, only 52 people were put to death in 2009.

China executes thousands of people annually, with about 2½ times the number of executions as the entire rest of the world combined.

Death Penalty

- Death penalty
- Death penalty only for military crimes
- No death penalty
- Not abolished, but death penalty inactive
- No data

Window on the World

GLOBAL MAP 1   **Capital Punishment in Global Perspective**

The map identifies fifty-eight countries in which the law allows the death penalty for ordinary crimes; in nine more, the death penalty is reserved for exceptional crimes under military law or during times of war. The death penalty does not exist in ninety-five countries; in thirty-five more, although the death penalty remains in law, no execution has taken place in more than ten years. Compare rich and poor nations: What general pattern do you see? In what way are the United States and Japan exceptions to this pattern?

Source: Amnesty International (2010a).

for their livelihood. Not only is cocaine Colombia's most profitable export, but it outsells all other exports combined, including coffee. Clearly, then, drug dealing and many other crimes are closely related to social conditions both in this country and elsewhere.

Different countries have different strategies for dealing with crime. The use of capital punishment (the death penalty) is one

example. According to Amnesty International (2010b), five nations account for 93 percent of the world's executions carried out by governments. Global Map 1 shows which countries currently use capital punishment. The global trend is toward abolishing the death penalty: Amnesty International (2010a) reports that since 1985, more than sixty nations have ended this practice.

Due process—the idea that the criminal justice system should operate under the rule of law—guides the actions of police, court officials, and corrections officers.

plea bargaining a legal negotiation in which a prosecutor reduces a charge in exchange for a defendant's guilty plea

Kayte M. Deioma/PhotoEdit Inc.

Police must be allowed discretion if they are to handle effectively the many different situations they face every day. At the same time, it is important that the police treat people fairly. Here we see a police officer deciding whether or not to charge a young woman with driving while intoxicated. What factors do you think enter into this decision?

The U.S. Criminal Justice System

The criminal justice system is a society's formal response to crime. We shall briefly examine the key elements of the U.S. criminal justice system: police, the courts, and the system of punishment and corrections. First, however, we must understand an important principle that underlies the entire system, the idea of due process.

Due Process

Due process is a simple but very important idea: The criminal justice system must operate according to law. Criminal law is grounded in the first ten amendments to the U.S. Constitution—known as the Bill of Rights—adopted by Congress in 1791. The Constitution offers various protections to any person charged with a crime. Among these are the right to counsel, the right to refuse to testify against oneself, and the right to confront all accusers, as well as freedom from being tried twice for the same crime and freedom from being "deprived of life, liberty, or property without due process of law." Furthermore, the Constitution gives all people the right to a speedy and public trial by jury and freedom from excessive bail and from "cruel and unusual" punishment.

In general terms, the concept of due process means that anyone charged with a crime must receive (1) fair notice of the proceedings, (2) a hearing on the charges conducted according to law and with the ability to present a defense, and (3) a judge or jury that weighs evidence impartially (Inciardi, 2000).

Due process limits the power of government, with an eye toward this nation's cultural support of individual rights and freedoms. Deciding exactly how far government can go makes up much of the work of the judicial system, especially the U.S. Supreme Court.

Police

The police generally serve as the point of contact between a population and the criminal justice system. In principle, the police maintain public order by enforcing the law. Of course, there is only so much that 708,569 full-time police officers across the United States can do to monitor the activities of more than 300 million people. As a result, the police use a great deal of personal judgment in deciding which situations warrant their attention and how to handle them. Police also face danger on a daily basis. In most years, more than 100 U.S. police officers are killed in the line of duty.

Given these facts, how do police officers carry out their duties? In a study of police behavior in five cities, Douglas Smith and Christy Visher (1981; D. A. Smith, 1987) concluded that because they must act swiftly, police quickly size up situations in terms of six factors. First, the more serious they think the situation is, the more likely they are to make an arrest. Second, police take account of the victim's wishes in deciding whether or not to make an arrest. Third, the odds of arrest go up the more uncooperative a suspect is. Fourth, police are more likely to take into custody someone they have arrested before, presumably because this suggests guilt. Fifth, the presence of bystanders increases the chances of arrest. According to Smith and Visher, the presence of observers prompts police to take stronger control of a situation, if only to move the encounter from the street (the suspect's turf) to the police department (where law officers have the edge). Sixth, all else being equal, police are more likely to arrest people of color than to arrest whites, perceiving people of African or Latino descent as either more dangerous or more likely to be guilty.

Four Justifications for Punishment

retribution an act of moral vengeance by which society makes the offender suffer as much as the suffering caused by the crime

deterrence the attempt to discourage criminality through the use of punishment

rehabilitation a program for reforming the offender to prevent later offenses

societal protection rendering an offender incapable of further offenses temporarily through imprisonment or permanently by execution

Courts

After arrest, a court determines a suspect's guilt or innocence. In principle, U.S. courts rely on an adversarial process involving attorneys—one representing the defendant and another the state—in the presence of a judge who monitors legal procedures.

In practice, however, about 90 percent of criminal cases are resolved before court appearance through **plea bargaining,** *a legal negotiation in which a prosecutor reduces a charge in exchange for a defendant's guilty plea.* For example, the state may offer a defendant charged with burglary a lesser charge, perhaps possession of burglary tools, in exchange for a guilty plea.

Plea bargaining is widespread because it spares the system the time and expense of trials. A trial is usually unnecessary if there is little disagreement as to the facts of the case. Moreover, because of the high number of cases entering the system, prosecutors could not possibly bring every case to trial even if they wanted to. By quickly resolving most of their work, then, the courts can devote their resources to the most important cases.

But plea bargaining pressures defendants (who are presumed innocent) to plead guilty. A person can exercise the right to a trial, but only at the risk of receiving a more severe sentence if found guilty. Furthermore, low-income defendants must often rely on a public defender—typically an overworked and underpaid attorney who may devote little time to even the most serious cases (Novak, 1999). Plea bargaining may be efficient, but it undercuts both the adversarial process and the rights of defendants.

Punishment

In 2009, a man with a long criminal record who was out on bail on charges of raping a child walked into a coffee shop in Parkland, Washington, and shot and killed four uniformed police officers as they were doing "paperwork" on their laptops. Two days later, a massive manhunt ended when the man was killed in a confrontation with another police officer (MSNBC, 2009).

Such cases force us to wonder about the reasons that drive some people to deadly violence and also to ask how a society should respond to such acts. In the case of the Parkland shootings, the crime was resolved through gunfire. But typically, of course, a suspect is apprehended and put on trial. If found guilty, the next step is punishment.

What does a society gain through the punishment of wrongdoers? Scholars answer with four basic reasons, which are described in the following sections: retribution, deterrence, rehabilitation, and societal protection.

Many of our most popular television shows, including *The Good Wife*, show dedicated and skillful people moving our judicial system forward. We like to think that the court system carefully weighs the guilt and innocence of every person accused of a crime. As explained below, however, only 10 percent of criminal cases are actually resolved through a formal trial.

Retribution

The oldest justification for punishment is to satisfy a society's need for **retribution,** *an act of moral vengeance by which society makes the offender suffer as much as the suffering caused by the crime.* Retribution rests on the view that society exists in a moral balance. When criminality upsets this balance, punishment in equal measure restores the moral order, as suggested in the ancient code calling for "an eye for an eye, a tooth for a tooth."

In the Middle Ages, most people viewed crime as sin—an offense against God as well as society—that required a harsh response. Although critics point out that retribution does little to reform the offender, many people today still consider vengeance reason enough for punishment.

Deterrence

A second justification for punishment is **deterrence,** *the attempt to discourage criminality through the use of punishment.* Deterrence is based on the eighteenth-century Enlightenment idea that as calculating and rational creatures, humans will not break the law if they think that the pain of the punishment will outweigh the pleasure of the crime.

Deterrence emerged as a reform measure in response to harsh punishments based on retribution. Why put someone to death for stealing if theft can be discouraged by a prison sentence? As the concept of deterrence gained acceptance in industrial societies, execution

─○ Making the Grade

Carefully review the Summing Up table below to ensure that
you understand the four justifications for punishment.

Go to the Multimedia Library at **mysoclab.com**
to watch the ABC *Primetime* video "Juvenile
Corrections"

SUMMING UP

Four Justifications for Punishment

Retribution	The oldest justification for punishment.
	Punishment is society's revenge for a moral wrong.
	In principle, punishment should be equal in severity to the crime itself.
Deterrence	An early modern approach.
	Crime is considered social disruption, which society acts to control.
	People are viewed as rational and self-interested; deterrence works because the pain of punishment outweighs the pleasure of crime.
Rehabilitation	A modern strategy linked to the development of social sciences.
	Crime and other deviance are viewed as the result of social problems (such as poverty) or personal problems (such as mental illness).
	Social conditions are improved; treatment is tailored to the offender's condition.
Societal protection	A modern approach easier to carry out than rehabilitation.
	Even if society is unable or unwilling to rehabilitate offenders or reform social conditions, people are protected by the imprisonment or execution of the offender.

and physical mutilation of criminals were replaced by milder forms
of punishment such as imprisonment.

Punishment may deter crime in two ways. *Specific deterrence*
convinces an individual offender that crime does not pay. Through
general deterrence, punishing one person serves as an example to
others.

Rehabilitation

The third justification for punishment, **rehabilitation,** is *a program
for reforming the offender to prevent later offenses.* Rehabilitation arose
along with the social sciences in the nineteenth century. Since then,
sociologists have claimed that crime and other deviance spring from
a social environment marked by poverty or lack of parental supervision. Logically, then, if offenders learn to be deviant, they can also learn
to obey the rules; the key is controlling the environment. *Reformatories*
or *houses of correction* provided a controlled setting where people could
learn proper behavior.

Like deterrence, rehabilitation motivates the offender to conform. In contrast to deterrence and retribution, which simply make
the offender suffer, rehabilitation encourages constructive improvement. Unlike retribution, which demands that the punishment fit
the crime, rehabilitation tailors treatment to each offender. Thus
identical crimes would prompt similar acts of retribution but different rehabilitation programs. ○ Go to **mysoclab.com**

Societal Protection

A final justification for punishment is **societal protection,** *rendering
an offender incapable of further offenses temporarily through imprisonment or permanently by execution.* Like deterrence, societal protection is a rational approach to punishment intended to protect society
from crime.

In 2010, some 2.4 million people were in prison in the United
States. Although the crime rate has gone down since 1980, the number of offenders locked up has increased nearly fivefold. This rise in
the prison population reflects both tougher public attitudes toward
crime and an increasing number of arrests for drug-related crimes. As
a result, the United States now imprisons a larger share of its population than any other country in the world (Pew Center on the States,
2008; Sentencing Project, 2008; U.S. Bureau of Justice Statistics, 2010).

─○ **CRITICAL REVIEW**   The Summing Up table reviews the
four justifications for punishment. However, an accurate assessment of the consequences of punishment is no simple task.

The value of retribution lies in Durkheim's claim that punishing the deviant person increases society's moral awareness.
For this reason, punishment was traditionally a public event.
Although the last public execution in this country took place in
Kentucky more than seventy years ago, today's mass media
ensure public awareness of executions carried out inside prison
walls (Kittrie, 1971).

Deviance

● Seeing Sociology
in Everyday Life

Although there has been little change in public support for the death penalty as recorded in surveys, the long-term trend is toward fewer executions. Can you suggest reasons for this pattern?

Does punishment deter crime? Despite our extensive use of punishment, our society has a high rate of **criminal recidivism**, *later offenses by people previously convicted of crimes.* A government study reported that two-thirds of state prison inmates released from jail in 1994 were rearrested for a serious crime within three years. Other research tells us that about three-fourths of state prisoners have been incarcerated before (DeFina & Arvanites, 2002; Langan & Levin, 2002). So does punishment really deter crime? Fewer than one-half of all crimes are known to police, and of these, only about one in five results in an arrest. Most crimes, therefore, go unpunished, leading us to conclude, perhaps, that the old saying "crime doesn't pay" may not be entirely true.

Prisons provide short-term societal protection by keeping offenders off the streets, but they do little to reshape attitudes or behavior in the long term (Carlson, 1976; R. A. Wright, 1994). Perhaps rehabilitation is an unrealistic expectation, because according to Sutherland's theory of differential association, locking up criminals together for years probably strengthens criminal attitudes and skills. Imprisonment also breaks whatever social ties inmates may have in the outside world, which, following Hirschi's control theory, makes inmates likely to commit more crimes upon release.

○ CHECK YOUR LEARNING What are society's four justifications for punishment? Does sending offenders to prison accomplish each of them? How?

The Death Penalty

Perhaps the most controversial issue involving punishment is the death penalty. From 1993 through 2009, more than 3,500 people were sentenced to death in U.S. courts; 1,000 executions were carried out. In thirty-six states, the law allows the state to execute offenders convicted of very serious crimes such as first-degree murder. But while a majority of states do permit capital punishment, only a few states are likely to carry out executions. Across the United States, half of the 3,207 people on death row at the end of 2008 were in just four states: California, Texas, Florida, and Pennsylvania (U.S. Bureau of Justice Statistics, 2010).

Opponents of capital punishment point to research suggesting that the death penalty has limited value as a crime deterrent. Countries such as Canada, where the death penalty has been abolished, have not seen a rise in the number of murders. Critics also point out that the United States is the only Western, high-income nation that routinely executes offenders. As public concern about the death penalty has increased, the use of capital punishment declined from as many as ninety-eight executions in 1999 to thirty-seven in 2008 but rising again in 2009 to fifty-two.

To increase the power of punishment to deter crime, capital punishment was long carried out in public. Here is a photograph from the last public execution in the United States, with twenty-two-year-old Rainey Bethea standing on the scaffold moments from death in Owensboro, Kentucky, on August 16, 1937. Children as well as adults were in the crowd. Now that the mass media report the story of executions across the country, states carry out capital punishment behind closed doors.

Public opinion surveys reveal that the share of U.S. adults who claim to support the death penalty as a punishment for murder remains high (62 percent) and has been fairly stable over time (NORC, 2009:214). College students hold about the same attitudes as everyone else, with about two-thirds of first-year students expressing support for the death penalty (Pryor et al., 2008).

But judges, criminal prosecutors, and members of trial juries are less and less likely to call for the death penalty. One reason is that because the crime rate has come down in recent years, the public now has less fear of crime and is less interested in applying the most severe punishment.

A second reason is public concern that the death penalty may be applied unjustly. The analysis of DNA evidence—a recent advance—from old crime scenes has shown that many people were wrongly convicted of a crime. Across the country, between 1975 and 2010, at least 137 people who had been sentenced to death were released from death row after new DNA evidence demonstrated their innocence. Such findings were one reason that in 2000, the governor of Illinois stated that he could no longer support the death penalty, leading him to commute the death sentences of every person on that state's death row (S. Levine, 2003; Death Penalty Information Center, 2010).

Deviance

○ Making the Grade

"Community-based corrections" refers to ways of dealing with offenders without sending them to prison.

A third reason for the decline in the use of the death penalty is that more states now permit judges and juries to sentence serious offenders to life in prison without the possibility of parole. Such punishment offers to protect society from dangerous criminals who can be "put away" forever without requiring an execution.

Fourth and finally, many states now shy away from capital punishment because of the high cost of prosecuting capital cases. Death penalty cases require more legal work and demand superior defense lawyers, often at public expense. In addition, such cases commonly include testimony by various paid "experts," including physicians and psychiatrists, which also runs up the costs of trial. Then there is the cost of many appeals that almost always follow a conviction leading to the sentence of death. When all these factors are put together, the cost of a death penalty case typically exceeds the cost of sending an offender to prison for life. So it is easy to see why states often choose not to seek the death penalty. One accounting, for example, reveals that the state of New Jersey has been spending more than $10 million a year prosecuting death penalty cases that have yet to result in a single execution (Thomas & Brant, 2007).

Organizations opposed to the death penalty are challenging this punishment in court. In 2008, for example, the U.S. Supreme Court upheld the use of lethal injection against the charge that this procedure amounts to cruel and unusual punishment, which would be unconstitutional. There is no indication at present that the United States will end the use of the death penalty. But the trend is away from this type of punishment.

Community-Based Corrections

Prison is at the center of our system of corrections. Prisons keep convicted criminals off the streets. The thought of prison probably deters many people from committing serious crime. But the evidence suggests that locking people up does little to rehabilitate most offenders. Further, prisons are expensive, costing more than $25,000 per year to support each inmate, in addition to the high cost of building the facilities.

A recent alternative to prison that has been adopted by many cities and states across the country is **community-based corrections,** *correctional programs operating within society at large rather than behind prison walls.* Community-based corrections have three main advantages: They reduce costs, they reduce overcrowding in prisons, and they allow for supervision of convicts while eliminating the hardships of prison life and the stigma that accompanies going to jail. In general, the idea of community-based corrections is not so much to punish as to reform; such programs are therefore usually offered to individuals who have committed less serious offenses and who appear to be good prospects for avoiding future criminal violations (Inciardi, 2000).

Probation

One form of community-based corrections is *probation,* a policy of permitting a convicted offender to remain in the community under conditions imposed by a court, including regular supervision. Courts may require that a probationer receive counseling, attend a drug treatment program, hold a job, avoid associating with "known criminals," or anything else a judge thinks is appropriate. Typically, a probationer must check in with an officer of the court (the probation officer) on a regular schedule to make sure the guidelines are being followed. Should the probationer fail to live up to the conditions set by the court or commit a new offense, the court may revoke probation and send the offender to jail.

Shock Probation

A related strategy is *shock probation,* a policy by which a judge orders a convicted offender to prison for a short time and then suspends the remainder of the sentence in favor of probation. Shock probation is thus a mix of prison and probation that is intended to impress on the offender the seriousness of the situation while still withholding full-scale imprisonment. In some cases, shock probation takes place in a special "boot camp" facility where offenders might spend up to three months in a military-style setting intended to teach discipline and respect for authority (Cole & Smith, 2002).

Parole

Parole is a policy of releasing inmates from prison to serve the remainder of their sentences in the local community under the supervision of a parole officer. Although courts may sometimes sentence an offender to prison without the possibility of parole, most other inmates become eligible for parole after serving a certain portion of their sentence. At this time, a parole board evaluates the risks and benefits of an inmate's early release from prison. If parole is granted, the parole board then monitors the offender's conduct until the sentence is completed. Should the offender not comply with the conditions of parole or be arrested for another crime, the board can revoke parole, returning the offender to prison to complete the original sentence.

○ **CRITICAL REVIEW** Evaluations of probation and parole have been mixed. There is little question that community-based programs are much less expensive than conventional imprisonment; they also free up room in prisons for people who commit more serious crimes. Yet research suggests that although probation and shock probation do seem to work for some people, they do not significantly reduce criminal recidivism. Similarly, parole is useful to prison officials as a means to encourage good behavior among prison inmates who hope for early release. Yet levels of crime among those released on parole are so high that

CONTROVERSY & DEBATE

Violent Crime Is Down—but Why?

DUANE: I'm a criminal justice major, and I want to be a police officer. Crime is a huge problem in America, and police are what keeps the crime rate low.

SANDY: I'm a sociology major. As for combating crime, I'm not sure it's quite that simple....

During the 1980s, crime rates shot upward. Just about everyone lived in fear of violent crime, and in many larger cities, the numbers of people killed and wounded made whole neighborhoods seem like war zones. There seemed to be no solution to the problem.

Yet in the 1990s, serious crime rates began to fall so that in recent years they have returned to levels not seen in more than a generation. Why? Researchers point to several reasons:

1. **A reduction in the youth population.** It was noted earlier that young people (particularly males) are responsible for much violent crime. Between 1990 and 2000, the share of the population aged fifteen to twenty-four dropped by about 5 percent (in part because of the legalization of abortion in 1973).

2. **Changes in policing.** Much of the drop in crime (like the earlier rise in crime) has taken place in large cities. In New York City, the number of murders fell from 2,245 in 1990 to 475 in 2009, the lowest figure since the city started keeping reliable records in 1963. Part of the reason for the decline is that the city adopted a policy of *community policing,* which means that police are concerned not just with making arrests but with preventing crime. Officers get to know the areas they patrol and frequently stop

young men for jaywalking or other minor infractions so they can check them for concealed weapons (the word is out that you can be arrested for carrying a gun). In addition, there are more police at work in large cities. For example, Los Angeles added more than 2,000 police in the 1990s, and it, too, saw its violent crime rate fall during that period.

3. **More prisoners.** Between 1985 and 2009, the number of inmates in U.S. prisons soared from 750,000 to 2.4 million. The main reason for this increase is tough new laws that demand prison time for many crimes, especially drug offenses. As one analyst put it, "When you lock up an extra million people, it's got to have some effect on the crime rate" (Franklin Zimring, quoted in Witkin, 1998:31).

4. **A better economy.** The U.S. economy boomed during the 1990s. With unemployment down, more people were working, reducing the likelihood that some would turn to

A. Ramey/PhotoEdit Inc.

One reason that crime has gone down is that there are more than 2 million people incarcerated in this country. This has caused severe overcrowding of facilities such as this Maricopa County, Arizona, prison.

crime out of economic desperation. The logic here is simple: More jobs, fewer crimes. By the same token, the recent economic downturn has slowed the downward crime trend.

5. **The declining drug trade.** Many analysts think that the most important factor in reducing rates of violent crime is the decline of crack cocaine. Crack came on the scene around 1985, and violence spread, especially in the inner cities, as young people—facing few legitimate job opportunities and increasingly armed with guns—became part of a booming drug trade.

By the early 1990s, however, the popularity of crack had begun to fall as people saw the damage the drug was causing to entire communities. This realization, coupled with steady economic improvement and stiffer sentences for drug offenses, helped bring about the turnaround in violent crime.

The current picture looks better relative to what it was a decade or two ago. But one researcher cautions, "It looks better, but only because the early 1990s were so bad. So let's not fool ourselves into thinking everything is resolved. It's not."

WHAT DO YOU THINK?

1. Do you support the policy of community policing? Why or why not?

2. What do you see as the pros and cons of building more prisons?

3. Of all the factors mentioned here, which do you think is the most important in crime control? Which is least important? Why?

Sources: Winship & Berrien (1999), Donahue & Levitt (2000), Rosenfeld (2002), Liptak (2008), and C. Mitchell (2008).

a number of states have ended their parole programs entirely (Inciardi, 2000).

Such evaluations point to a sobering truth: By itself, the criminal justice system cannot eliminate crime. As the Controversy & Debate box explains, although police, courts, and pris-

ons do affect crime rates, crime and other deviance are not just the acts of "bad people" but reflect the operation of society itself.

○ **CHECK YOUR LEARNING** What are three types of community-based corrections? What are their advantages?

Seeing Sociology in Everyday Life

Deviance

Why do most of us—at least most of the time—obey the rules?

As this chapter explains, every society is a system of social control that encourages conformity to certain norms and discourages deviance or norm breaking. One way society does this is through the construction of heroes and villains. Heroes, of course, are people we are supposed to look up to and use as role models. Villains are people whom we look down on and reject their example. Organizations of all types create heroes that serve as guides to everyday behavior. In each case below, who is being made into a hero? Why? What are the values or behaviors that we are encouraged to copy in our own lives?

HINT A society without heroes and villains would be one in which no one cared how people think or act. Societies create heroes as role models that are supposed to inspire us to be more like them. Societies create heroes by emphasizing one aspect of someone's life and ignoring lots of other things. For example, Babe Ruth was a great ball player, but his private life was sometimes less than inspiring. Perhaps this is why the Catholic church never considers anyone a candidate for sainthood until after—usually long after—the person has died.

Charlie Campbell/The Star-Democrat/AP Wide World Photos

Colleges and universities create heroes in various ways. Here we see the president of Washington College (Maryland) awarding the Sophie Kerr Prize at a recent graduation ceremony. This prize, which included a check for more than $50,000, recognized English major Claire Tompkins's ability to write outstanding short stories. What is heroic in this case? What does graduating with honors or Latin praise (*cum laude* and so on) define as heroic? What about villains—how do colleges and universities create them, too?

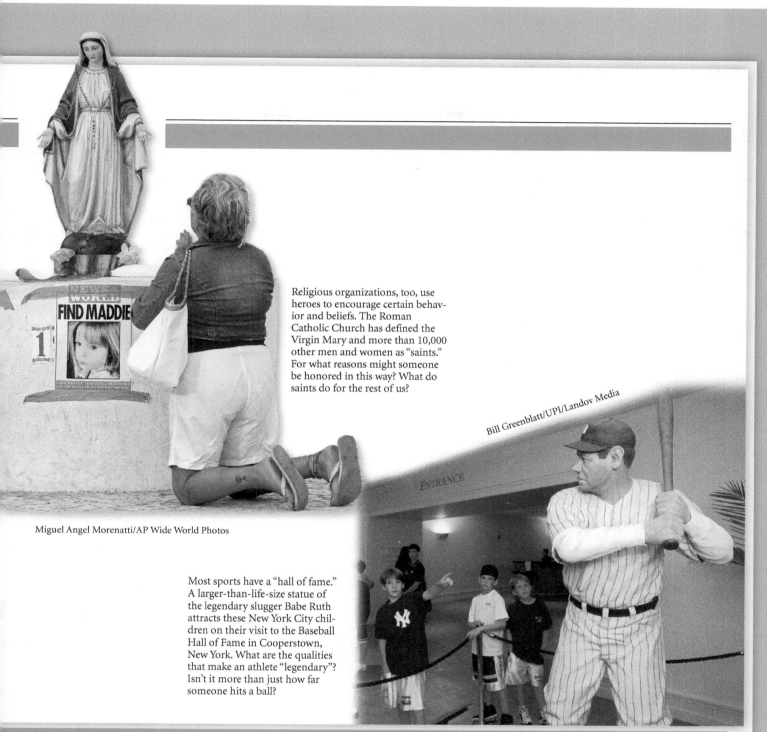

Religious organizations, too, use heroes to encourage certain behavior and beliefs. The Roman Catholic Church has defined the Virgin Mary and more than 10,000 other men and women as "saints." For what reasons might someone be honored in this way? What do saints do for the rest of us?

Bill Greenblatt/UPI/Landov Media

Miguel Angel Morenatti/AP Wide World Photos

Most sports have a "hall of fame." A larger-than-life-size statue of the legendary slugger Babe Ruth attracts these New York City children on their visit to the Baseball Hall of Fame in Cooperstown, New York. What are the qualities that make an athlete "legendary"? Isn't it more than just how far someone hits a ball?

Applying SOCIOLOGY in Everyday Life

1. Do athletic teams, fraternities and sororities, and even people in a college classroom create heroes and villains? Explain how and why.

2. Identity theft is a new type of crime that victimizes as many as 10 million people each year in the United States. Research this phenomenon, and explain how this offense differs from property crime that takes place "on the street." (Consider differences in the crime, the offenders, and the victims.)

3. Watch an episode of a real-action police show such as *Cops*. Based on what you see, how would you profile the people who commit crimes?

Making the Grade

Deviance

What Is Deviance?

DEVIANCE refers to norm violations ranging from minor infractions, such as bad manners, to major infractions, such as serious violence.

deviance the recognized violation of cultural norms

crime the violation of a society's formally enacted criminal law

social control attempts by society to regulate people's thoughts and behavior

criminal justice system the organizations—police, courts, and prison officials—that respond to alleged violations of the law

Theories of Deviance

BIOLOGICAL THEORIES
- focus on individual abnormality
- explain human behavior as the result of biological instincts

Lombroso claimed criminals have apelike physical traits; later research links criminal behavior to certain body types and genetics.

PSYCHOLOGICAL THEORIES
- focus on individual abnormality
- see deviance as the result of "unsuccessful socialization"

Reckless and Dinitz's *containment theory* links delinquency to weak conscience.

✓ *Biological and psychological theories provide a limited understanding of crime and other deviance because most violations are carried out by people who are normal.*

SOCIOLOGICAL THEORIES view all behavior—deviant as well as conforming—as products of society. Sociologists point out that
- what is deviant varies from place to place according to cultural norms
- behavior and individuals become deviant as others define them that way
- what and who a society defines as deviant reflect who has social power and who does not

Theoretical Analysis of Deviance

The Functions of Deviance: Structural-Functional Analysis

Durkheim claimed that deviance is a normal element of society that
- affirms cultural norms and values
- clarifies moral boundaries
- brings people together
- encourages social change

Merton's **strain theory** explains deviance in terms of a society's cultural goals and the means available to achieve them.

Deviant subcultures are discussed by Cloward and Ohlin, Cohen, Miller, and Anderson.

labeling theory the idea that deviance and conformity result not so much from what people do as from how others respond to those actions

stigma a powerfully negative label that greatly changes a person's self-concept and social identity

medicalization of deviance the transformation of moral and legal deviance into a medical condition

white-collar crime crime committed by people of high social position in the course of their occupations

corporate crime the illegal actions of a corporation or people acting on its behalf

organized crime a business supplying illegal goods or services

hate crime a criminal act against a person or a person's property by an offender motivated by racial or other bias

Labeling Theory: Symbolic-Interaction Analysis

Labeling theory claims that deviance depends less on what someone does than on how others react to that behavior. If people respond to primary deviance by stigmatizing a person, secondary deviance and a deviant career may result.

The **medicalization of deviance** is the transformation of moral and legal deviance into a medical condition. In practice, this means a change in labels, replacing "good" and "bad" with "sick" and "well."

Sutherland's **differential association theory** links deviance to how much others encourage or discourage such behavior.

Hirschi's **control theory** states that imagining the possible consequences of deviance often discourages such behavior. People who are well integrated into society are less likely to engage in deviant behavior.

See the Applying Theory table.

Deviance and Inequality: Social-Conflict Analysis

Based on Karl Marx's ideas, social-conflict theory holds that laws and other norms operate to protect the interests of powerful members of any society.

- **White-collar offenses** are committed by people of high social position as part of their jobs. Sutherland claimed such offenses are rarely prosecuted and are most likely to end up in civil rather than criminal court.
- **Corporate crime** refers to illegal actions by a corporation or people acting on its behalf. Although corporate crimes cause considerable public harm, most cases of corporate crime go unpunished.
- **Organized crime** has a long history in the United States, especially among categories of people with few legitimate opportunities.

Deviance, Race, and Gender

- What people consider deviant reflects the relative power and privilege of different categories of people.
- **Hate crimes** are crimes motivated by racial or other bias; they target people with disadvantages based on race, gender, or sexual orientation.
- In the United States and elsewhere, societies control the behavior of women more closely than that of men.

What Is Crime?

CRIME is the violation of criminal laws enacted by local, state, or federal governments. There are two major categories of serious crime:

- crimes against the person (violent crime), including murder, aggravated assault, forcible rape, and robbery
- crimes against property (property crime), including burglary, larceny-theft, auto theft, and arson

Explore on mysoclab.com

PATTERNS OF CRIME IN THE UNITED STATES

- Official statistics show that arrest rates peak in late adolescence and drop steadily with advancing age.
- About 65% of people arrested for property crimes and 82% of people arrested for violent crimes are male.
- Street crime is more common among people of lower social position. Including white-collar and corporate crime makes class differences in criminality smaller.
- More whites than African Americans are arrested for street crimes. However, more African Americans are arrested than whites in relation to their population size. Asian Americans have a lower-than-average rate of arrest.
- By world standards, the U.S. crime rate is high.

crimes against the person crimes that direct violence or the threat of violence against others; also known as *violent crimes*

crimes against property crimes that involve theft of money or property belonging to others; also known as *property crimes*

victimless crimes violations of law in which there are no obvious victims

Read on mysoclab.com

The U.S. Criminal Justice System

Police

The police maintain public order by enforcing the law.

- Police use personal discretion in deciding whether and how to handle a situation.
- Research suggests that police are more likely to make an arrest if the offense is serious, if bystanders are present, or if the suspect is African American or Latino.

Courts

Courts rely on an adversarial process in which attorneys—one representing the defendant and one representing the state—present their cases in the presence of a judge who monitors legal procedures.

- In practice, U.S. courts resolve most cases through plea bargaining. Though efficient, this method puts less powerful people at a disadvantage.

Punishment

There are four justifications for punishment:

- retribution
- deterrence
- rehabilitation
- societal protection

See the *Summing Up* table.

The **death penalty** remains controversial in the United States, the only high-income Western nation that routinely executes serious offenders. The long-term trend is toward fewer executions.

Community-based corrections include probation and parole. These programs lower the cost of supervising people convicted of crimes and reduce prison overcrowding but have not been shown to reduce recidivism.

plea bargaining a legal negotiation in which a prosecutor reduces a charge in exchange for a defendant's guilty plea

retribution an act of moral vengeance by which society makes the offender suffer as much as the suffering caused by the crime

deterrence the attempt to discourage criminality through the use of punishment

rehabilitation a program for reforming the offender to prevent later offenses

societal protection rendering an offender incapable of further offenses temporarily through imprisonment or permanently by execution

criminal recidivism later offenses by people previously convicted of crimes

community-based corrections correctional programs operating within society at large rather than behind prison walls

Sample Test Questions

Multiple-Choice Questions

1. Crime is a special type of deviance that
   a. refers to violations of formally enacted criminal law.
   b. always involves punishment.
   c. refers to the violation of any societal norms.
   d. causes the greatest harm to society.

2. Emile Durkheim explains that deviance is
   a. defined by the rich and used against the poor.
   b. harmful not just to victims but to society as a whole.
   c. often at odds with public morality.
   d. found in every society because it has useful consequences.

3. Using Robert Merton's strain theory, a person selling illegal drugs for a living would fall into which of the following categories?
   a. conformist
   b. innovator
   c. retreatist
   d. ritualist

4. Labeling theory states that deviance
   a. is a normal part of social life.
   b. always changes an offender's social identity.
   c. arises not from what people do as much as from how others respond to the action.
   d. All of the above are correct.

5. When Jake's friends began calling him a "dope-head," he left the group and spent more time smoking marijuana. He also began hanging out with others who used drugs, and by the end of the term, he had dropped out of college. Edwin Lemert would say this situation illustrates
   a. a case of primary deviance.
   b. the onset of secondary deviance.
   c. the formation of a deviant subculture.
   d. the beginning of retreatism.

6. A social-conflict analysis links deviance to
   a. who does and does not have power in the society.
   b. a society's moral values.
   c. how often the behavior occurs.
   d. how harmful the behavior is.

7. Stealing a laptop computer from the study lounge in your college dorm is an example of which of the following criminal offenses?
   a. a burglary
   b. motor vehicle theft
   c. robbery
   d. larceny-theft

8. The FBI's criminal statistics used in this chapter reflect
   a. all crimes that occur.
   b. offenses known to the police.
   c. offenses that result in an arrest.
   d. offenses that result in a criminal conviction.

9. Most people arrested for violent crime in the United States are
   a. white.
   b. African American.
   c. Hispanic.
   d. Asian.

10. Which of the following is the oldest justification for punishing an offender?
   a. deterrence
   b. societal protection
   c. retribution
   d. rehabilitation

ANSWERS: 1(a); 2(d); 3(b); 4(c); 5(b); 6(a); 7(d); 8(b); 9(a); 10(c).

Essay Questions

1. How does a sociological view of deviance differ from the common-sense notion that bad people do bad things?

2. How is social power linked to the creation of crime or other types of deviance? In your response, consider social class and race. Does gender also fit this pattern? Explain.

Ford vs. Firestone

KEITH NAUGHTON AND MARK HOSENBALL

This article discusses a recent example of corporate crime—in this case, crime that has cost human lives as well as dollars. The crime in question stemmed from a manufacturing defect in some of the tires made by Firestone. The tread on these tires has a tendency to separate and cause drivers to lose control of their vehicles. Despite this defect, Firestone continued to produce and sell these tires to Ford. Moreover, even though Ford received hundreds of claims for defective tires from consumers, the company continued to install them on its popular Explorer sports utility vehicle. For families of the victims who died or suffered injuries, the key questions are: When did these corporations know that the tires were defective, and why didn't they do something about it earlier?

. . .

Top executives from Ford Motor Co. and Bridgestone/Firestone were summoned before congressional panels last week to explain their role in a crisis that has mushroomed into a legal, public-relations and regulatory nightmare that threatens to consume both companies. With the possibility of criminal charges added to the mix, the simmering tensions between the long-time partners have burst into open hostilities. The two companies are engaged in bitter finger-pointing over who is responsible for the tire problems and why they didn't come to light sooner. Each is now mounting its own defense, a dynamic that gives joy to the personal-injury lawyers who have already hit the companies with more than 60 lawsuits. NEWSWEEK has

"Ford vs. Firestone," by Keith Naughton and Mark Hosenball, reprinted from *Newsweek*, September 18, 2000, pp. 26–33.

learned that Ford chairman William Clay Ford, Jr. is likely to take to the airwaves in a PR blitz designed to rebuild Ford's tarnished image.

Crisis-management experts aren't likely to write flattering case studies about how each company has responded so far. Before the congressional panel, Bridgestone's chief executive, Masatoshi Ono, said he accepted "full and personal responsibility" for the recall of 6.5 million ATX and Wilderness tires, found mostly on Ford Explorers. But he added that his company could not find a design defect that was causing tread to peel away at high speeds, and Firestone executives continued to blame much of the problem on consumers for improperly maintaining their tires. In his testimony, Ford's chief executive, Jacques Nasser, defiantly pointed a finger at Firestone, saying his company didn't know there was a defect with the tires "until we virtually pried the claims data from Firestone's hands and analyzed it" in July. Both companies agreed on one point, however: they said they didn't realize the scope of the lethal tire troubles until just before they issued a recall on Aug. 9.

But questions are mounting about just how much each company knew—and when it knew it. NEWSWEEK has obtained documents that show Firestone was chronicling a pattern of tire failures for the last three years, while Ford was also getting an early warning about safety problems from its own warranty data. And an internal Ford memo shows suspicions between the business partners about the safety record of the tires.

For their part, lawmakers have rejected the companies' claims of ignorance about the lethal problem. "That's rubbish," snapped New Mexico Rep. Heather Wilson. "You knew a long time ago." By the weekend, lawmakers were proposing new legislation to hold companies criminally responsible for covering up product defects, and Attorney General Janet Reno is considering an investigation into how Ford and Firestone handled the issue. This week Sen. John McCain will call Nasser and Ono back to Capitol Hill to explain again why they didn't act sooner to fix tires that began failing at an unusually high rate at least four years ago. Analysts say Firestone's very future in the United States is in question. For Ford the crisis threatens its crown jewel, the Explorer, which accounts for 25 percent of its annual profits.

That's why the Ford chairman is about to emerge from the shadows to defend his besieged company. Given his amiable and effective persona, observers have been asking, "Where's Bill?" In an interview with NEWSWEEK, Ford would not discuss his plans to take on more public involvement in the crisis but acknowledged that Ford's reputation has "really taken a heck of a hit. There's nothing more important to me than our company's reputation, because at the end of the day, that's my name on the building," he said. "That's why going through this is personally so painful." He said he remains frustrated that the cause of the tire defect has not been found and believes that uncertainty is fueling the crisis. And while he is convinced that the problem is with Firestone's tires and not the auto-maker's Explorer, Ford said his company is still examining how it handled the problem. "I can't tell you with 100 percent certainty that we did everything right," he said. "But I can promise this: we'll be open and honest, and if we uncover something we'll speak up."

At a Ford board meeting this week, the scion will present his directors with a plan to increase his public role in the crisis. Ford, who is the great-grandson of both Henry Ford and Harvey Firestone, is likely to appear in television ads that extol the Ford family heritage and promise that his company will always stand by consumers.

Better PR, however, won't blunt the escalating threat to the company. Congressional investigators say they are following a paper trail that shows both companies knew far earlier than they are publicly admitting that something was terribly wrong with the 15-inch tires outfitted on Explorers. Firestone's own financial analyses of damage and injury claims against the company document a pattern of problems at least as early as 1997. NEWSWEEK has learned that congressional investigators have three Firestone reports, from 1998, 1999 and 2000, that show unusually high rates of failures and tread peeling from ATX II tires, one of the types involved in the recall. In the 1999 report, obtained by NEWSWEEK, those recalled tires represented the majority of the company's tire claims in 1998 and 1997, even though that model accounted for less than 10 percent of Firestones total production. What's more, the 1999 report indicates that more than half the "seperation [*sic*]" claims Firestone received came from tires produced at its Decatur, Ill., factory. The tire-maker has contended it discovered only in July that the Decatur plant was the primary source of the problem, which led to a recall of the tires days later.

But the report's financial analysis of accident claims going back three years shows that the company had long been compiling and analyzing data on tires that shredded and where they were made. When asked at the congressional hearings last week about a similar report, dated Jan. 19, 2000, Firestone executive vice president Gary Crigger said that the data were compiled to assess only the company's financial liability. They were not shared, he said, with the company's safety engineers.

Congressional investigators also believe Ford ignored trends in its own warranty data indicating that it had a tire problem on its Explorer. Even though Ford doesn't warranty tires—that's Firestone's responsibility—the auto-maker received "hundreds" of claims for defective tires between 1991 and 2000, say congressional sources who have reviewed Ford's warranty data. Among those incidents are 148 claims for tread separation, the sources say. A Ford spokesman said any tire complaints the auto-maker received from consumers were "anecdotal" and turned over to Firestone for investigation. And Firestone repeatedly said there was no problem with the tires, Ford officials say.

One thing is undisputed: the blowouts, deaths and lawsuits began nearly a decade ago, shortly after the Explorer first hit the road. As sales soared for the wildly popular Explorer, reports of tire problems began to grow. But the accidents—and consumer complaints flowing into Firestone—began rapidly escalating in 1996. Plaintiffs' attorneys contend that the accidents began mounting then because highway speed limits increased to 70 miles per hour, exposing the tires' design flaws. "Even the junkiest tires stay together when the speed limit is low." says Ocala, Fla., lawyer Bruce Kaster, who has been involved in hundreds of tire lawsuits. Kaster insists that Ford "started the whole chain of events" by giving improper specifications to its tire supplier. Kaster and other plaintiffs' attorneys accuse Ford of lowering the tire pressure on the Explorer to prevent an unstable vehicle from flipping over. Ford officials call that tire-pressure allegation a "red herring" and point to accident data showing that the Explorer rolls over 26 percent less than other SUVs. They also say similar Goodyear tires on Explorers didn't have problems.

By 1998 Ford began receiving reports of Firestone tread separations on Explorers in Saudi Arabia. Ford took the complaints to Firestone, but had little faith that its tire supplier was owning up to problems. "Is it possible that Firestone is not telling us the whole story to protect them from a recall or lawsuit?" wrote Ford executive Glenn R. Drake in a Jan. 28,1999, e-mail obtained by NEWSWEEK. He urged Ford to launch an internal investigation "for our own peace of mind." But Ford didn't investigate the problem because it didn't have enough information from Firestone, Ford officials say.

As tire-shredding problems began to spread to other hot countries, like Venezuela, Firestone insisted its consumers were to blame for improperly caring for their tires. When Firestone refused to recall the tires, Ford began to replace them in August 1999 on nearly 50,000 vehicles in 16 foreign countries. But Ford didn't tell U.S. authorities about its overseas tire recall until federal safety regulators opened an investigation into Firestone tires in May, when consumer complaints jumped following media reports of Firestone tire failures. Facing accusations of a cover-up, Nasser pledged in the hearings last week that from now on, Ford would immediately reveal all foreign recalls to U.S. regulators. But Nasser was not contrite. He made his strongest accusations yet against Firestone. And he detailed how Ford had to ask Firestone five times this summer to turn over claims data that would finally illuminate the problem.

Firestone, wary of being openly hostile toward its biggest customer, is subtle in its criticism of Ford. In his apology, Ono talked of "families who have lost loved ones in these terrible rollover accidents." That's a jab at the high-riding Ford Explorer's propensity to flip over in an accident.

The tense relations between the companies put Ford's chairman in an unusual and uncomfortable position. Firestone has been supplying tires to Ford since 1906. Chairman Bill Ford's mother, Martha, is a Firestone heiress whose father was chief executive of Firestone. Even as the relationship has deteriorated, Ford needs Firestone for replacement tires. Despite Firestone's problems, the company remains confident it can work through the crisis. "We've been through tough times before and come back," says Firestone vice president Christine Karbowiak. "We'll do it this time."

Safety advocates are calling for a much wider recall, and federal regulators did issue a warning on an additional 1.4 million Firestone tires on Sept. 1. But for now Firestone is sticking with its original recall of 15-inch ATX, ATX II and Wilderness AT tires made at the Decatur plant. While fears are spreading about all Firestone tires, even Ford acknowledges that its longtime supplier still makes "world class" tires. And for now Ford still intends to offer Firestone tires on a redesigned Explorer coming next year, although it will also offer consumers a choice of ordering Michelin tires. Both Ford and Firestone report their sales have held up well during the crisis.

But the families of the victims are not in a forgiving mood. To them, no apology or excuse will ever make up for the fact that the companies could have warned consumers earlier. "If they would have told people, maybe they wouldn't have made as much money, but it would have saved dozens of lives," says Sara Romero, 12, who survived an Explorer rollover in Florida last December that killed her 37-year-old mother. "My mom didn't have to die. They could have told us." Now Ford and Firestone can tell it to a judge. The Romero family plans to file a wrongful-death lawsuit this week.

Questions

1. What behaviors on the part of officials at Ford and Firestone suggest that they knowingly acted in a negligent or criminal fashion?

2. When did Ford and Firestone realize that something might be wrong with the tires used on Explorers? Why didn't they do something about it at that time?

3. Both Ford and Firestone have made claims to divert liability to others. Describe these claims and explain who made them.

4. Go to the library and look up recent developments in the Ford vs. Firestone case. What has happened since this article was published (in September 2000)?

Thoughts on Class, Race, and Prison

ALAN BERKMAN AND TIM BLUNK

Two political activists wrote this selection while serving time in prison. In this piece, they attempt to portray prison from the perspective of the white, middle-class male. As you read, ask yourself whether this portrayal matches the ones that you usually see in the popular press. Also, think about how the authors' construction of their experiences might differ if they were poor or members of a minority group.

Having been locked up as political prisoners for the past five years, we have found a lot in several recent articles which was familiar and thought provoking. Certain descriptions of ping-ponging from jail to jail could be a log of some of our own trips conducted by the Bureau of Prisons (BoP), and we can verify accounts of how prisoners typically support one another. Perhaps most importantly, we strongly agree with the view—best expressed in an article by Sam Day published in the October 13, 1989 issue of *Isthmus*—that the threat of prison should not deter political activists from acting. We are concerned, though, that in so vividly portraying his own experience and utilizing it to demystify prison life, he may have played into some common misrepresentations of life in U.S. prisons.

First, a word about our own experiences. We've each spent time in prison for a variety of politically motivated acts. One of us (Alan Berkman) spent two years in a number of county jails in the Philadelphia area. The other (Tim Blunk) spent a year in New York's

"Thoughts on Class, Race, and Prison," by Alan Berkman and Tim Blunk, reprinted from *Cages of Steel: The Politics of Imprisonment in the United States,* edited by Ward Churchill, and J.J. Vanderwell, 1992, Maisonnueve Press. pp. 190–193.

Riker's Island. We've both been in a number of federal prisons, including the BoP's most repressive facility at Marion, Illinois. For the past 18 months, we've been together in the equivalent of a county jail in Washington, D.C. where we and four women activists face federal charges of resisting U.S. war crimes through "violent and illegal means" (we call this the Resistance Conspiracy Case). Tim is presently serving a 58 year sentence; Alan, 12 years. Having spent considerable time in the whole range of penal institutions, from county jails where most prisoners are pre-trial to Marion, where the average sentence is 40 years, we've been struck by how directly prisons reflect the social and economic realities of society as a whole.

We live in a country where large numbers of people, particularly young Afro-American, Latino and Native American women and men, have been written off by society. Government leaders look at the human devastation caused by their policies and declare war on the victims (the "war on drugs"). The racism and malignant neglect that permeate the schools, the labor market, the welfare system and social services of the Third World and poor white neighborhoods of our cities bear their inevitable fruit in the prisons. In prison, though, even the usual facade of "fairness" and "justice" by which such inequity is usually accompanied is dropped.

There are almost a million people in U.S. jails, state and federal prisons. More than 90% of these prisoners are in county jails and state prisons. D.C. jail, for example, is filled to capacity with poor, mis-educated, profoundly alienated young Afro-American men and women. It's a warehouse. There are no programs, no contact visiting, no privacy, and most importantly, no justice.

Particularly for political activists who are white and middle class, prison can be one of the few places where we look at America from the bottom up. We can understand poverty differently when we live with young people who've never had $20 in their pocket and who are constantly bombarded with the Gucci ads, the BMWs on *Miami Vice,* and the idea of free trips to Rio on *The Price is Right.* In a consumer society, if you've got nothing, you're considered to be nothing, and the frustration of this reality leads people into crime and drugs. You can see the deadness and despair in the eyes of too many of the people around you as they realize the American Dream is not for them now, and probably wasn't from the day they were born into the ghetto, the barrio or the reservation. And you'll get a feeling in your gut about the rage racism and poverty generate in the hearts of the oppressed. In fact, if you allow yourself, you'll learn quite a lot about the feelings that accompany that word, "oppressed."

What we've come to understand ever more deeply from our experience as prisoners is that the essence of oppression lies in dehumanization and disrespect. Being oppressed isn't just being a bit poorer or having a rougher life than your oppressor; it means being treated as if you're less of a human being than they are. For instance, we've consistently experienced the fact that you can be getting along okay with the guards and prison officials when they suddenly do something which is not only totally outrageous, but often a complete violation of their own supposed rule structure. You call them on it, and their response is to look at you—*through* you would be more accurate—as if you just weren't there. It doesn't matter a bit whether you're right or wrong. They deny that you have the right even to hold an opinion on the matter. It cuts at the very core of your sense of humanity and self-worth. It is infuriating and degrading.

Self-worth. Dignity. Self-respect. These are the feelings prison consciously or unconsciously is designed to destroy. These are the same feelings that racism and economic inequality in society work to destroy in the poor and people of color. This is why we believe Sam and others err when they reduce prison life to "three hots [meals] and a cot" and other minor indignities. It's like reducing chattel slavery to hard work, bad pay and poor living conditions. It leaves out the truth of the human dimension of oppression. And it leaves out the human reaction to prison conditions: rebellion. Prison "riots" are fundamentally slave rebellions.

Over the past few weeks, there have been one major and two minor prison uprisings in the Pennsylvania prison system. At Camp Hill, where prisoners destroyed much of the prison, the precipitating event seems trivial: the prison cancelled the semi-annual family day picnics where prisoners' relatives can bring home-cooked food and eat with their loved ones out on the yard. What's the big deal about two afternoons per year? Well, at one level, when you don't have much, even a *little* more deprivation hurts rather badly, especially when that deprivation concerns those precious bits of time you can spend with those closest to you and when you manage to feel most fully human. At a deeper level, the arbitrariness of the prison officials' decision in Pennsylvania gave the prisoners a clear message that they had nothing at all coming to them: *everything* is a "privilege," *nothing* is a right. The oppressor giveth, the oppressor taketh away. The oppressed have nothing to say in the matter, one way or the other. The oppressed—the prisoner in this instance—is a cipher, a statistic, nothing more than an animal whose basic needs of calories, shelter and waste disposal must (usually) be met. No more.

The "senseless violence" of burning buildings and smashing equipment which marked the Camp Hill rebellion—and which has marked prison uprisings from Attica to Atlanta, New Mexico, Los Angeles, and elsewhere—is, perhaps paradoxically, the most basic assertion of human dignity and self respect. "We do have a say," the prisoners are insisting. "We will exercise our rights as human beings one way or another, either as reasonable human beings in a reasonable situation, or this way if you insist the situation remain unreasonable. But either way you can ultimately do nothing to provide our demonstration of the fact that we *are people*." It is a very human response to a very inhuman situation, the same impulse which led to the great ghetto uprisings of Watts, Detroit and Newark during the 1960s, and which has led to similar phenomena in places like Miami during the 1980s.

Political activists who come to jail and are able to keep their eyes and hearts open will learn an enormous amount, both about themselves and about the world they live in. How do we deal with our own race/class biases to build principled relationships with those we live with? If we're white, how do we respond when the Aryan Brotherhood tells us they'll kick our ass if we eat with Afro-American, Latino or American Indian prisoners in the *de facto* segregated mess hall? How do we struggle against the pervasive and intense sexism in men's prisons? How do we remain caring and giving people without allowing ourselves to be taken advantage of and disrespected? How do we decide when to directly confront the power of the officials, and when not to? When do we get involved in other people's beefs, whether among prisoners or between prisoners and guards?

There's a lot to learn in prison, although it's certainly not the only, or even necessarily the best, place to learn it. Whatever else may be said, time spent behind bars—no more or less than any other sort of time—need never be "wasted." We agree with Sam and others when they say that fear of prison should never be paralyzing. While locked up, you'll more than likely get in shape, have the opportunity to read many of the books you always meant to plow through but never managed to get around to, learn to write letters which say more than just "howdy-do." Most importantly, you'll finally have the chance to identify with the oppressed on a gut level which is typically absent from the life experiences of most Euro-Americans. You'll come to understand power relationships in a new and far more meaningful way. And we're willing to bet that you'll come out more committed than ever to the need for fundamental social change.

☻　☻　☻

Questions

1. According to Berkman and Blunk, how are prisons designed to destroy one's humanity, dignity, and self-respect?

2. What did Berkman and Blunk "learn" in prison?

3. The authors are white and middle class. How might this identity have affected their experiences while in prison?

4. How might the authors' experiences have differed if they were poor or members of particular minority groups? What about if they were women?

Social Stratification

Social Stratification

- What is social stratification?

- Why does social inequality exist?

- How do social classes in the United States differ from one another?

Watch the *Core Concepts in Sociology* video "Social Class in the United States: Fact or Fiction?" on **mysoclab.com**

This chapter introduces the central concept of social stratification, which is important because our social standing affects almost everything about our lives. While making comparisons to other societies, the chapter surveys social stratification in the United States, identifying important measures of inequality and describing the U.S. class system.

Interfoto/Alamy

On April 10, 1912, the ocean liner *Titanic* slipped away from the docks of Southampton, England, on its first voyage across the North Atlantic to New York. A proud symbol of the new industrial age, the towering ship carried 2,300 men, women, and children, some of them enjoying more luxury than most travelers today could imagine. Many poor immigrants crowded the lower decks, journeying to what they hoped would be a better life in the United States.

Two days out, the crew received reports of icebergs in the area but paid little notice. Then, near midnight, as the ship steamed swiftly westward, a stunned lookout reported a massive shape rising out of the dark ocean directly ahead. Moments later, the *Titanic* collided with a huge iceberg, as tall as the ship itself, that split open its side as if the grand vessel were a giant tin can.

Seawater flooded into the vessel's lower levels, pulling the ship down by the bow. Within twenty-five minutes of impact, people were rushing for the lifeboats. By 2:00 A.M., the bow was completely submerged, and the stern rose high above the water. Clinging to the deck, quietly observed by those in lifeboats, hundreds of helpless passengers and crew solemnly passed their final minutes before the ship disappeared into the frigid Atlantic (W. Lord, 1976).

The tragic loss of more than 1,600 lives made news around the world. Looking back on this terrible event with a sociological eye, we see that some categories of passengers had much better odds of survival than others. In keeping with that era's traditional ideas about gender, women and children boarded the lifeboats first, with the result that 80 percent of those who died were men. Class was also a factor in who survived and who did not. More than 60 percent of the passengers traveling on first-class tickets were saved because they were on the upper decks, where warnings were sounded first and lifeboats were accessible. Only 36 percent of the second-class passengers survived, and of the third-class passengers on the lower decks, only 24 percent escaped drowning. On board the *Titanic,* class meant more than the quality of accommodations; it was a matter of life or death.

The fate of the passengers on the *Titanic* dramatically illustrates how social inequality affects the way people live—and sometimes whether they live at all. This chapter explores the important concept of social stratification and examines social inequality in the United States.

What Is Social Stratification?

Every society is marked by inequality, with some people having more money, schooling, health, and power than others. **Social stratification,** defined as *a system by which a society ranks categories of people in a hierarchy,* is based on four important principles:

1. **Social stratification is a trait of society, not simply a reflection of individual differences.** Many of us think of social standing in terms of personal talent and effort, and as a result, we often exaggerate the extent to which we control our own fate. Did a higher percentage of the first-class passengers on the *Titanic* survive because they were better swimmers than second- and third-class passengers? No. They did better because of their privileged position on the ship. Similarly, children born into wealthy families are more likely than children born into poverty to enjoy good health, do well in school, succeed in a career, and live a long life. Neither the rich nor the poor are responsible for creating social stratification, yet this system shapes the lives of us all.

2. **Social stratification carries over from generation to generation.** We have only to look at how parents pass their social position on to their children to understand that stratification is a trait of societies rather than individuals. Some individuals, especially in industrial societies, do experience **social mobility,** *a change in position within the social hierarchy.* Social mobility may be upward or downward. We celebrate the achievements of rare individuals such as Christina Aguilera and Michael Jordan, who rose from modest beginnings to fame and fortune. Some people also move downward in the social hierarchy because of business setbacks, unemployment, or illness. More often people move *horizontally;* they switch one job for another

at about the same social level. The social standing of most people remains much the same over their lifetime.

3. **Social stratification is universal but variable.** Social stratification is found everywhere. Yet *what* is unequal and *how* unequal it is vary from one society to another. In some societies, inequality is mostly a matter of prestige; in others, wealth or power is the key element of difference. In addition, some societies contain more inequality than others.

4. **Social stratification involves not just inequality but beliefs as well.** Any system of inequality not only gives some people more than others but also defines these arrangements as fair. Like the *what* of social inequality, the explanations of *why* people should be unequal differ from society to society.

William Albert Allard/National Geographic Image Collection

In rural India, the traditional caste system still shapes people's lives. This girl is a member of the "untouchables," a category below the four basic castes. She and her family are clothes washers, people who clean material "polluted" by blood or human waste. Such work is defined as unclean for people of higher caste position.

Caste and Class Systems

When comparing societies in terms of inequality, sociologists distinguish between *closed systems,* which allow little change in social position, and *open systems,* which permit much more social mobility. Closed systems are called *caste systems,* and more open systems are called *class systems.*

The Caste System

A **caste system** is *social stratification based on ascription, or birth.* A pure caste system is closed because birth alone determines a person's entire future, with little or no social mobility based on individual effort. People live out their lives in the rigid categories into which they were born, without the possibility for change for the better or worse.

An Illustration: India

Many of the world's agrarian societies are caste systems. Although India's economy is growing rapidly, much of the population still lives in traditional villages, where the caste system is part of everyday life. The traditional Indian system includes four major castes (or *varnas,* from a Sanskrit word that means "color"): Brahmin, Kshatriya, Vaishya, and Sudra. On the local level, however, each of these is composed of hundreds of subcaste groups (*jatis*).

From birth, caste position determines the direction of a person's life. First, with the exception of farming, which is open to everyone, families in each caste perform one type of work, as priests, soldiers, barbers, leather workers, sweepers, and so on.

Second, a caste system demands that people marry others of the same ranking. If people were to have "mixed" marriages with members of other castes, what rank would their children hold? Sociologists call this pattern of marrying within a social category *endogamous* marriage (*endo-* stems from the Greek word for "within"). According to tradition—this practice is now rare and found only in remote rural areas—Indian parents select their children's marriage partners, often before the children reach their teens.

Third, caste guides everyday life by keeping people in the company of "their own kind." Norms reinforce this practice by teaching, for instance, that a "purer" person of a higher caste position is "polluted" by contact with someone of lower standing.

Fourth, caste systems rest on powerful cultural beliefs. Indian culture is built on the Hindu tradition that doing the caste's life work and accepting an arranged marriage are moral duties.

Caste and Agrarian Life

Caste systems are typical of agrarian societies because agriculture demands a lifelong routine of hard work. By teaching a sense of moral duty, a caste system ensures that people are disciplined for a lifetime of work and are willing to perform the same jobs as their parents.

caste system social stratification based on ascription, or birth

class system social stratification based on both birth and individual achievement

meritocracy social stratification based on personal merit

Thus the caste system has hung on in rural India more than seventy years after being formally outlawed. People living in the industrial cities of India have many more choices about work and marriage partners than people in rural areas.

Another country dominated by caste is South Africa, although the racial system of *apartheid* is no longer legal and now in decline. The Thinking Globally box takes a closer look.

The Class System

Because a modern economy must attract people to work in many occupations other than farming, it depends on developing people's talents in diverse fields. This process of schooling and specialization gives rise to a **class system,** *social stratification based on both birth and individual achievement.*

Class systems are more open than caste systems, so people who gain schooling and skills may experience social mobility. As a result, class distinctions become blurred, and even blood relatives may have different social standings. Categorizing people according to their color, sex, or social background comes to be seen as wrong in modern societies as all people gain political rights and, in principle, equal standing before the law. In addition, work is no longer fixed at birth but involves some personal choice. Greater individuality also translates into more personal freedom in the process of selecting a marital partner.

Meritocracy

The concept of **meritocracy** refers to *social stratification based on personal merit.* Because industrial societies need to develop a broad range of abilities beyond farming, stratification is based not just on the accident of birth but also on *merit* (from a Latin word meaning "earned"), which includes a person's knowledge, abilities, and effort. A rough measure of merit is the importance of a person's job and how well it is done. To increase meritocracy, industrial societies expand equality of opportunity and teach people to expect unequal rewards based on individual performance.

In a pure meritocracy, which has never existed, social position would depend entirely on a person's ability and effort. Such a system would have ongoing social mobility, blurring social categories as individuals continuously move up or down in the system, depending on their latest performance.

Caste societies define merit in different terms, emphasizing loyalty to the system—that is, dutifully performing whatever job comes with the social position a person has at birth. Because they assign jobs before anyone can know anything about a person's talents or interests, caste systems waste human potential. On the other hand, because caste systems clearly assign everyone a "place" in society and a specific type of work, they are very orderly. A need for some amount of order is the reason that even industrial and postindustrial societies keep some elements of caste—such as letting wealth pass from generation to generation—rather than becoming complete meritocracies. A pure meritocracy, with individuals moving up and down the social ranking all the time, would pull apart families and other social groupings. After all, economic performance is not everything: Would we want to evaluate our family members solely on how successful they are in their jobs outside of the home? Probably not. Class systems in industrial societies move toward meritocracy to promote productivity and efficiency; but at the same time, they keep caste elements, such as family, to maintain order and social unity.

Status Consistency

Status consistency is *the degree of uniformity in a person's social standing across various dimensions of social inequality.* A caste system has little social mobility and high status consistency, so the typical person has the same relative standing with regard to wealth, power, and prestige as everyone else in the same caste. However, the greater mobility of class systems produces less status consistency. In the United States, most college professors with advanced degrees enjoy high social prestige but earn only modest incomes. Low status consistency means that it is much harder to define people's social position. Therefore, *classes* are much harder to define than *castes.*

Caste and Class: The United Kingdom

The mix of meritocracy and caste in class systems is well illustrated by the United Kingdom (Great Britain—composed of England, Wales, and Scotland—and Northern Ireland), an industrial nation with a long agrarian history.

Aristocratic England

In the Middle Ages, England had a system of aristocracy that resembled a caste. The aristocracy included the leading members of the church, who were thought to speak with the authority of God. Some clergy were local priests, who were not members of the aristocracy and who lived simple lives. But the highest church officials lived in palaces and presided over an organization that owned much land, which was the major source of wealth. Church leaders, who were typically referred to as the *first estate* in France and other European countries, also had a great deal of power to shape the political events of the day.

The rest of the aristocracy, which in France and other European countries was called the *second estate,* was a hereditary nobility that made up barely 5 percent of the population. The royal family—the king and queen at the top of the power structure—as well as lesser nobles (including several hundred families headed by men titled as dukes, earls, and barons) together owned most of the nation's land. Most of the men and women within the aristocracy were wealthy due to their land, and they had many servants for their homes as well as ordinary farmers to work their fields. With all their work done for

How much of your social position is due to merit (personal ability and effort), and how much is due to caste (passed on from your parents)?

status consistency the degree of uniformity in a person's social standing across various dimensions of social inequality

THINKING GLOBALLY

Race as Caste: A Report from South Africa

JEROME: I've been reading about racial caste in South Africa. I'm glad that's over.

REGGIE: But racial inequality is far from over. . . .

At the southern tip of the African continent lies South Africa, a country about the size of Alaska with a population of about 50 million. For 300 years, the native Africans who lived there were ruled by white people, first by the Dutch traders and farmers who settled there in the mid-seventeenth century and then by the British, who colonized the area early in the nineteenth century. By the early 1900s, the British had taken over the entire country, naming it the Union of South Africa.

In 1961, the nation declared its independence from Britain, calling itself the Republic of South Africa, but freedom for the black majority was still decades away. To ensure their political control over the black population, whites instituted the policy of *apartheid,* or racial separation. Apartheid, written into law in 1948, denied blacks national citizenship, ownership of land, and any voice in the nation's government. As a lower caste, blacks received little schooling and performed menial, low-paying jobs. White people with even average wealth had at least one black household servant.

The members of the white minority claimed that apartheid protected their cultural traditions from the influence of people they considered inferior. When blacks resisted apartheid, whites used brutal military repression to maintain their power. Even so, steady resistance— especially from younger blacks, who demanded a political voice and economic

opportunity—gradually forced the country to change. Criticism from other industrial nations added to the pressure. By the mid-1980s, the tide began to turn as the South African government granted limited political rights to people of mixed race and Asian ancestry. Next came the right of all people to form labor unions, to enter occupations once limited to whites, and to own property. Officials also repealed apartheid laws that separated the races in public places.

The pace of change increased in 1990 with the release from prison of Nelson Mandela, who led the fight against apartheid. In 1994, the first national election open to all races made Mandela president, ending centuries of white minority rule.

Despite this dramatic political change, social stratification in South Africa is still based on race. Even with the right to own property, one-fourth of black South Africans have no work, and half the population lives below the poverty line. The worst

off are some 7 million *ukuhleleleka,* which means "marginal people" in the Xhosa language. Soweto-by-the-Sea may sound like a summer getaway, but it is a shantytown, home to hundreds of thousands of people crammed into shacks made of packing cases, corrugated metal, cardboard, and other discarded materials. Recent years have seen some signs of prosperity. But for most families, there is no electricity for lights or refrigeration. Without plumbing, the majority of people use buckets to haul sewage. The community's women line up to take a turn at various water taps that each serves more than 1,000 people. Jobs are hard to come by, and those who do find work are lucky to earn $250 a month.

South Africa's current president, Jacob Zuma, who was elected in 2009, leads a nation still crippled by its history of racial caste. Tourism is up and holds the promise of an economic boom in years to come, but the country can break from the past only by providing real opportunity to all its people.

WHAT DO YOU THINK?

1. How has race been a form of caste in South Africa?

2. Although apartheid is no longer law, why does racial inequality continue to shape South African society?

3. Does race operate as an element of caste in the United States? Explain your answer.

Sources: Mabry & Masland (1999), Murphy (2002), and Perry (2009).

Tomasz Tomaszewski/National Geographic Image Collection

them by others, members of the aristocracy had no occupation and thought that engaging in any work for income was beneath them. They used their time to develop skills in horseback riding and warfare and to cultivate refined tastes in art, music, and literature.

To prevent their vast landholdings from being divided by heirs when they died, aristocrats devised the law of *primogeniture* (from the Latin meaning "firstborn"), which required that all property pass to

the oldest son or other male relation. Younger sons had to find other means of support. Some of these men became leaders in the church, where they would live as well as they were used to, and helped tie together the church and the state by having members of the same families running both. Other younger sons within the aristocracy became military officers or judges or took up other professions considered honorable for gentlemen. In an age when no woman

Social Stratification

Seeing Sociology
in Everyday Life

Are there any aristocratic elements of U.S. society? What are they?

Seeing Sociology
in Everyday Life

What do the distinctive accents in the speech of people in poor rural areas or poor inner cities in the United States say about their social history?

Getty Images/De Agostini Editore Picture Library

One of the major events of the twentieth century was the socialist revolution in Russia, which led to the creation of the Soviet Union. Following the ideas of Karl Marx, the popular uprising overthrew a feudal aristocracy, as depicted in the 1920 painting *Bolshevik* by Boris Mikhailovich Kustodiev.

could inherit her father's property and few women had the opportunity to earn a living on their own, a noble daughter depended for her security on marrying well.

Below the high clergy and the rest of the aristocracy, the vast majority of men and women were called *commoners* or, in France and other European countries, the *third estate*. Most commoners were serfs working land owned by nobles or the church. Unlike members of the aristocracy, most commoners had little schooling and were illiterate.

As the Industrial Revolution expanded England's economy, some commoners living in cities made enough money to challenge the nobility. More emphasis on meritocracy, the growing importance of money, and the expansion of schooling and legal rights eventually blurred the differences between aristocrats and commoners and gave rise to a class system.

Perhaps it is a sign of the times that these days, traditional titles are put up for sale by aristocrats who need money. In 1996, for example, Earl Spencer—the brother of Princess Diana—sold one of his titles, Lord of Wimbledon, to raise the $300,000 he needed to redo the plumbing in one of his large homes (McKee, 1996).

The United Kingdom Today

The United Kingdom has a class system today, but caste elements of the past are still evident. A small number of British families still

hold considerable inherited wealth and enjoy high prestige, schooling at excellent universities, and substantial political influence. A traditional monarch, Queen Elizabeth II, is the United Kingdom's head of state, and Parliament's House of Lords is composed of "peers," about half of whom are of noble birth. However, control of government has passed to the House of Commons, where the prime minister and other ministers typically reach their positions by achievement—winning an election—rather than by birth.

Lower in the class hierarchy, roughly one-fourth of the British people fall into the middle class. Some earn comfortable incomes from professions and businesses and are likely to have investments in the form of stocks and bonds. Below the middle class, perhaps half of all Britons consider themselves "working-class," earning modest incomes through manual labor. The remaining one-fourth of the British people make up the lower class, the poor who lack steady work or who work full time but are paid too little to live comfortably. Most lower-class Britons live in the nation's northern and western regions, which have been plagued by closings of mines and factories.

The British mix of caste elements and meritocracy has produced a highly stratified society with some opportunity to move upward or downward, much the same as exists in the United States (Long & Ferrie, 2007). Historically, British society has been somewhat more castelike than is the case in the United States, a fact reflected in the importance attached to linguistic accent. Distinctive patterns of speech develop when people are set off from one another over several generations. People in the United States treat accent as a clue to where a person lives or grew up (we can easily identify a midwestern "twang" or a southern "drawl"). In the United Kingdom, however, accent is more a mark of social class (upper-class people speak "the King's English," but most people speak "like commoners"). So different are these two accents that the British seem to be, as the saying goes, "a single people divided by a common language."

Classless Societies? The Former Soviet Union

Nowhere in the world do we find a society without some degree of social inequality. Yet some nations have claimed to be classless.

The Russian Revolution

The Union of Soviet Socialist Republics (USSR), which rivaled the United States as a military superpower in the mid- to late twentieth century, was born out of a revolution in Russia in 1917. The Russian Revolution ended the feudal estate system ruled by a hereditary

Social Stratification

Seeing Sociology in Everyday Life

As an example of structural social mobility, an expanding U.S. economy pushed the total wealth of U.S. households from $8 trillion in 1960 to about $50 trillion by 2000 (in constant dollars).

nobility and transferred most farms, factories, and other productive property from private ownership to state control. Following the lead of Karl Marx, who believed that private ownership of property was the source of social stratification, Soviet leaders boasted of becoming a classless society.

Critics, however, pointed out that based on their jobs, the Soviet people were actually stratified into four unequal categories. At the top were high government officials, known as *apparatchiks.* Next came the Soviet intelligentsia, including lower government officials, college professors, scientists, physicians, and engineers. Below them were manual workers and, at the lowest level, the rural peasantry.

In reality, the Soviet Union was not classless at all, and political power was concentrated in only a small percentage of the population. But putting factories, farms, colleges, and hospitals under state control did create greater economic equality (although with sharp differences in power) than in capitalist societies such as the United States.

The Modern Russian Federation

In 1985, Mikhail Gorbachev came to power with a new economic program known as *perestroika* ("restructuring"). Gorbachev saw that although the Soviet system had significantly reduced economic inequality, overall living standards lagged far behind those of other industrial nations. Gorbachev tried to generate economic growth by reducing the centralized control of the economy, which had proved to be inefficient.

Gorbachev's economic reforms turned into one of the most dramatic social movements in history. People throughout Eastern Europe blamed their poverty and lack of basic freedoms on the repressive ruling class of Communist party officials. Beginning in 1989, people throughout Eastern Europe toppled their socialist governments, and in 1991, the Soviet Union itself collapsed, with its largest republic remaking itself as the Russian Federation.

The Soviet Union's story shows that social inequality involves more than economic resources. Soviet society may not have had the extremes of wealth and poverty found in the United Kingdom and the United States. But an elite class existed all the same, based on political power rather than wealth.

What about social mobility in so-called classless societies? In the twentieth century, there was as much upward social mobility in the Soviet Union as in the United Kingdom or the United States. Rapidly expanding industry and government drew many poor rural peasants into factories and offices. This trend illustrates what sociologists call **structural social mobility,** *a shift in the social position of large numbers of people due more to changes in society itself than to individual efforts.*

November 24, Odessa, Ukraine. The first snow of our voyage flies over the decks as our ship docks at Odessa, the former Soviet Union's southern port on the Black Sea. Not far from the dock, we gaze up at the Potemkin Steps, the steep stairway up to the city, where the first shots of the Russian Revolution rang out. It has been six years since our last visit, and much has changed; indeed, the Soviet Union itself has collapsed. Has life improved? For some people, certainly. There are now chic boutiques in which well-dressed shoppers buy fine wines, designer clothes, and imported perfumes. Outside, shiny new Volvos, Mercedeses, and even a few Cadillacs stand out against the small Ladas from the "old days." But for most people, life seems much worse. Flea markets line the curbs as families sell their home furnishings. When meat sells for $4 a pound and the average person earns about $30 a month, people become desperate. Even the city has to save money by turning off streetlights after 8:00 P.M. The spirits of most people seem as dim as Odessa's streets.

During the 1990s, structural social mobility in the Russian Federation turned downward as that country experienced something similar to the Great Depression of the 1930s in the United States. One indicator is that the average life span for men dropped by eight years and for women by two years. Many factors contributed to this decline, including Russia's poor health care system, but the Russian people clearly have suffered in the turbulent period of economic change that began in 1991 (Bohlen, 1998; Gerber & Hout, 1998; Mason, 2004).

The hope was that in the long run, closing inefficient state industries would improve the nation's economic performance. The economy has expanded, but living standards have fallen and millions of Russians face hard times. The few people who made huge fortunes have seen much of their new wealth vanish in the recent recession. This fact, along with more government control over the Russian economy, has caused economic inequality to decline. At the same time, however, many people wonder what a return to a more socialist society will mean for their living standards and political freedoms (Zuckerman, 2006; Wendle, 2009).

China: Emerging Social Classes

Sweeping political and economic change has affected not just the Russian Federation but also the People's Republic of China. After the Communist revolution in 1949, the state took control of all farms, factories, and other productive property. Communist party leader Mao Zedong declared all work to be equally important, so officially, social classes no longer existed.

Seeing Sociology
in Everyday Life

A statement like "People get what they deserve" is an example of ideology that supports our market-based economy. Can you think of other common examples of ideology?

ideology cultural beliefs that justify particular social arrangements, including patterns of inequality

Davis-Moore thesis the functional analysis claiming that social stratification has beneficial consequences for the operation of society

By allowing a market economy to expand, especially in the coastal regions, China has experienced remarkable economic growth. The gambling industry in Macao now rivals that of Las Vegas.

The new program greatly reduced economic inequality. But as in the Soviet Union, social differences remained. The country was ruled by a political elite with enormous power and considerable privilege; below them were managers of large factories and skilled professionals; next came industrial workers; at the bottom were rural peasants, who were not even allowed to leave their villages to migrate to cities.

Further economic change came in 1978, when Mao died and Deng Xiaoping became China's leader. The state gradually loosened its hold on the economy, allowing a new class of business owners to emerge. Communist party leaders remain in control of the country, and some have prospered as they have joined the ranks of the small but wealthy elite who control new, privately run industries. China's economy has experienced rapid growth, and the nation has now moved into the middle-income category. Much of this new prosperity has been concentrated in coastal areas where living standards have soared far above those in China's rural interior.

Since the late 1990s, the booming cities along China's coast have become home to many thousands of people made rich by the expanding economy. In addition, these cities have attracted more than 100 million young migrants from rural areas in search of better jobs and a better life. Many more have wanted to move to the booming cities, but the government still restricts movement, which has the effect of slowing upward social mobility. For those who have been able to move, the jobs that are available are generally better than the work that people knew before. But many of these new jobs are dangerous, and most pay wages that barely meet the higher costs of living in the city, so the majority of the migrants remain poor. To make matters worse, the weakening global economy has caused many Chinese factories to lay off workers or even to shut down. As a result, beginning in 2008, some people began to migrate from cities back to the countryside—a case of downward social mobility (Atlas, 2007; Wu & Treiman, 2007; Chang, 2008; Powell, 2008).

A new category in China's social hierarchy consists of the *hai gui*, a term derived from words meaning "returned from overseas" or "sea turtles." The ranks of the "sea turtles" are increasing by tens of thousands each year as young men and women return from educations in other countries, in many cases from college and university campuses in the United States. These young people, most of whom were from privileged families to begin with, typically return to China to find many opportunities and soon become very influential (Liu & Hewitt, 2008).

In China, a new class system is emerging, a mix of the old political hierarchy and a new business hierarchy. Economic inequality in China has increased as members of the new business elite have become millionaires and even billionaires; as Figure 1 shows, it is now as great as in the United States. With so much change in China, patterns of social stratification are likely to remain in flux for some time to come (Bian, 2002; Kuhn, 2007).

Ideology: The Power behind Stratification

How do societies persist without sharing their resources more equally? The highly stratified British aristocracy lasted for centuries, and for 2,000 years people in India accepted the idea that they should be privileged or poor based on the accident of birth.

A major reason that social hierarchies endure is **ideology,** *cultural beliefs that justify particular social arrangements, including patterns of inequality.* A belief—for example, the idea that the rich are smart and the poor are lazy—is ideological to the extent that it supports inequality by defining it as fair.

Social Stratification

Making the Grade

The Davis-Moore thesis does not endorse any level or type of social stratification. It simply states that societies devise some system of unequal rewards to enhance efficient productivity.

Plato and Marx on Ideology

According to the ancient Greek philosopher Plato (427–347 B.C.E.), every culture considers some type of inequality fair. Although Karl Marx understood this, he was far more critical of inequality than Plato. Marx criticized capitalist societies for defending wealth and power in the hands of a few as a "law of the marketplace." Capitalist law, he continued, defines the right to own property, which encourages money to remain within the same families from one generation to the next. In short, Marx concluded, culture and institutions combine to support a society's elite, which is why established hierarchies last such a long time.

Historical Patterns of Ideology

Ideology changes along with a society's economy and technology. Because agrarian societies depend on most of their people performing a lifetime of labor, they develop caste systems that make carrying out the duties of a person's social position or "station" a moral responsibility. With the rise of industrial capitalism, an ideology of meritocracy arises, defining wealth and power as prizes to be won by the individuals who perform the best. This change means that the poor—often given charity under feudalism—are looked down on as personally undeserving. This harsh view is linked to the ideas of Herbert Spencer, as explained in the Thinking About Diversity box.

History shows how difficult it is to change social stratification. However, challenges to the status quo always arise. Traditional ideas about "a woman's place," for example, have given way to economic opportunity for women in societies today. The continuing progress toward racial equality in South Africa is another case of widespread rejection of the ideology of apartheid.

The Functions of Social Stratification

Why does social stratification exist at all? According to the structural-functional approach, social stratification plays a vital part in the operation of society. This argument was presented many years ago by Kingsley Davis and Wilbert Moore (1945).

The Davis-Moore Thesis

The **Davis-Moore thesis** states that *social stratification has beneficial consequences for the operation of a society.* How else, ask Davis and Moore, can we explain the fact that some form of social stratification has been found in every society?

Davis and Moore note that modern societies have hundreds of occupational positions of varying importance. Certain jobs—say, washing cars or answering a telephone—are fairly easy and can be

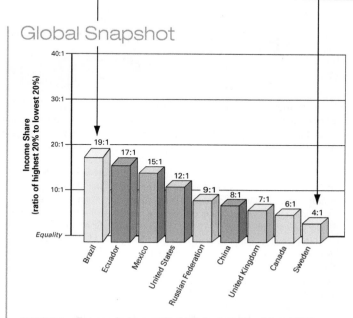

Driving to work in São Paulo, Brazil, Fabio Campos passes both gated mansions of the very rich and rundown shacks of the very poor.

On her way to work in Stockholm, Sweden, Sylvia Arnbjörg passes through mostly middle-class neighborhoods.

Global Snapshot

FIGURE 1   Economic Inequality in Selected Countries, 2008

Many low- and middle-income countries have greater economic inequality than the United States. But this country has more economic inequality than most high-income nations.

These data are the most recent available, representing income share for various years between 1998 and 2008.

Sources: U.S. Census Bureau (2009) and World Bank (2010).

performed by almost anyone. Other jobs—such as designing a new generation of computers or transplanting human organs—are very difficult and demand the scarce talents of people with extensive and expensive training.

Therefore, Davis and Moore explain, the greater the functional importance of a position, the more rewards a society attaches to it. This strategy promotes productivity and efficiency because rewarding important work with income, prestige, power, or leisure encourages people to do these things and to work better, longer, and harder. In short, unequal rewards (which is what social stratification is) benefit society as a whole.

Davis and Moore claim that any society could be egalitarian, but only to the extent that people are willing to let *anyone* perform *any* job. Equality also demands that someone who performs a job poorly be rewarded just as much as someone who performs the job well. Such a system clearly offers little incentive for people to try their best, reducing the society's productive efficiency.

The Davis-Moore thesis suggests the reason stratification exists; it does not state precisely what rewards a society should give to any

○ Making the Grade

Stratification systems produce ideas and beliefs that define their operation as just. In short, stratification involves not just who has what but also beliefs about justice—why people should have what they have.

○ Seeing Sociology
in Everyday Life

Following Davis and Moore's thinking, why do professors give grades from A to F? What would happen if they gave every student the same grade? Explain.

THINKING ABOUT DIVERSITY: RACE, CLASS, & GENDER

The Meaning of Class: Is Getting Rich "the Survival of the Fittest"?

JAKE: "My dad is amazing. He's really smart!"
FRANK: "You mean he's rich. He owns I don't know how many businesses."
JAKE: "Do you think people get rich without being smart?"

It's a question we all wonder about. How much is our social position a matter of intelligence? What about hard work? Being born to the "right family"? Even "dumb luck"?

More than in most societies, in the United States we link social standing to personal abilities including intelligence. This idea goes back a long time. We have all heard the words "the survival of the fittest," which describes our society as a competitive jungle in which the "best" survive and the rest fall behind. The phrase was coined by one of sociology's pioneers, Herbert Spencer (1820–1903), whose ideas about social inequality are still widespread today.

Spencer, who lived in England, eagerly followed the work of the natural scientist Charles Darwin (1809–1882). Darwin's theory of biological evolution held that a species changes phys-

ically over many generations as it adapts to the natural environment. Spencer incorrectly applied Darwin's theory to the operation of society, which does not operate according to biological principles. In Spencer's distorted view, society became the "jungle," with the "fittest" people rising to wealth and the "failures" sinking into miserable poverty.

As wrong as they were, it is no surprise that Spencer's views were popular among the rising U.S. industrialists of the day. John D. Rockefeller (1839–1937), who made a vast fortune building the oil industry, recited Spencer's "social gospel" to young children in Sunday school. As Rockefeller saw it, the growth of giant corporations—and the astounding wealth of their owners—was merely the result of the survival of the fittest, a basic fact of nature. Neither Spencer nor Rockefeller had much sympathy for the poor, seeing poverty as evidence of individuals' failing to measure up in a competitive world. Spencer opposed social welfare programs because he thought they penalized society's "best" people (through taxes) and

rewarded its "worst" members (through welfare benefits). By incorrectly using Darwin's theory, the rich could turn their backs on everyone else, assuming that inequality was inevitable and somehow "natural."

Today, sociologists point out that our society is far from a meritocracy, as Spencer claimed. And it is not the case that companies or individuals who generate lots of money necessarily benefit society. The people who made hundreds of millions of dollars selling subprime mortgages in recent years certainly ended up hurting just about everyone. But Spencer's view that the "fittest" rise to the top remains widespread in our very unequal and individualistic culture.

WHAT DO YOU THINK?

1. How much do you think inequality in our society can correctly be described as "the survival of the fittest"? Why?

2. Why do you think Spencer's ideas are still popular in the United States today?

3. Is how much you earn a good measure of your importance to society? Why or why not?

occupational position or how unequal rewards should be. It merely points out that positions a society considers crucial must offer enough rewards to draw talented people away from less important work.

○ **CRITICAL REVIEW** Although the Davis-Moore thesis is an important contribution to understanding social stratification, it has provoked criticism. Melvin Tumin (1953) wondered, first of all, how we assess the importance of a particular occupation. Perhaps the high rewards our society gives to physicians result partly from deliberate efforts by medical schools to limit the supply of physicians and thereby increase the demand for their services.

Furthermore, do rewards actually reflect the contribution someone makes to society? With income of about $275 million per year, Oprah Winfrey earns more in one day than the president of the United States earns all year. Would anyone argue that hosting a talk show is more important than leading a country? And what about members of the U.S. military serving in Iraq or Afghanistan? Although they face the daily risk of combat, a new

private first class in the United States Army earned a base salary of $20,500 in 2010 (Defense Finance and Accounting Service, 2010). And what about the heads of the big Wall Street financial firms that collapsed in 2008? It seems reasonable to conclude that these corporate leaders made some bad decisions, yet their salaries were astronomical. Even after finishing its worst year ever, with losses of $27 billion, Merrill Lynch paid bonuses of more than $1 million to each of more than 700 employees (Fox, 2009). The top people in the financial industry made out even better. In 2007, James Dimon, head of JPMorganChase, had earnings of more than $55 million; the same year, Lloyd Blankfein, head of Goldman Sachs, made more than $70 million—an amount it would take a typical U.S. Army private more than 3,000 years to earn. Do corporate executives deserve such megasalaries for their contributions to society?

Second, Tumin claimed that Davis and Moore ignore how the caste elements of social stratification can *prevent* the development of individual talent. Born to privilege, rich children have

capitalists people who own and operate factories and other businesses in pursuit of profits

proletarians people who sell their labor for wages

alienation the experience of isolation and misery resulting from powerlessness

● Seeing Sociology
in Everyday Life

Have you ever had a job that caused you to experience the alienation that concerned Karl Marx? Explain.

opportunities to develop their abilities, which is something many gifted poor children never have.

Third, living in a society that places so much importance on money, we tend to overestimate the importance of high-paying work; how do stockbrokers or people who trade international currencies really contribute to society? For the same reason, it is difficult for us to see the importance of work not oriented toward making money, such as parenting, creative writing, playing in a symphony, or just being a good friend to someone in need (Packard, 2002).

Finally, by suggesting that social stratification benefits all of society, the Davis-Moore thesis ignores how social inequality promotes conflict and can even provoke revolution. This criticism leads to the social-conflict approach, which provides a very different explanation for social inequality.

○ **CHECK YOUR LEARNING**   State the Davis-Moore thesis in your own words. What are Tumin's criticisms of this thesis?

Stratification and Conflict

Social-conflict analysis argues that rather than benefiting society as a whole, social stratification benefits some people and disadvantages others. This analysis draws heavily on the ideas of Karl Marx, with contributions from Max Weber.

Karl Marx: Class Conflict

As Marx saw it, the Industrial Revolution promised humanity a society free from want. Yet during Marx's lifetime, the capitalist economy had done little to improve the lives of most people. Marx set out to explain a glaring contradiction: how, in a society so rich, so many could be so poor.

In Marx's view, social stratification is rooted in people's relationship to the means of production. People either own productive property (such as factories and businesses) or sell their labor to others. In feudal Europe, the aristocracy and the church owned the productive land; the peasants toiled as farmers. Under industrial capitalism, the aristocracy was replaced by **capitalists** (sometimes called the *bourgeoisie*, a French word meaning "town dwellers"), *people who own and*

Oprah Winfey consistently earns more than $200 million a year and enjoys fame to match her fortune. Guided by the Davis-Moore thesis, why would societies reward some people so much more than others? How would Karl Marx answer this question differently?

Kevin Winter\Getty Images Inc.

Social Stratification

operate factories and other businesses in pursuit of profits. Peasants became the **proletarians,** *people who sell their labor for wages.* Capitalists and proletarians have opposing interests and are separated by a vast gulf of wealth and power, making class conflict inevitable.

Marx lived during the nineteenth century, a time when a small number of industrialists in the United States were amassing great fortunes. Andrew Carnegie, J. P. Morgan, and John Jacob Astor (one of the few rich passengers to drown on the *Titanic*) lived in fabulous mansions that were filled with priceless works of art and staffed by dozens of servants. Even by today's standards, their incomes were staggering. For example, Carnegie earned more than $20 million in 1900 (roughly $530 million in today's dollars), when the average worker earned roughly $500 a year (Baltzell, 1964; Williamson, 2010).

In time, Marx believed, the working majority would overthrow the capitalists once and for all. Capitalism would bring about its own downfall, Marx reasoned, because it makes workers poorer and poorer and gives them little control over what they make or how they make it. Under capitalism, work produces only **alienation,** *the experience of isolation and misery resulting from powerlessness.*

To replace capitalism, Marx imagined a *socialist* system that would meet the needs of all rather than just the needs of the elite few: "The proletarians have nothing to lose but their chains. They have a world to win" (Marx & Engels, 1972:362, orig. 1848).

○ **CRITICAL REVIEW**   Marx has had enormous influence on sociological thinking. But his revolutionary ideas, calling for the overthrow of capitalist society, also make his work highly controversial.

One of the strongest criticisms of the Marxist approach is that it ignores a central idea of the Davis-Moore thesis: that a system of unequal rewards is needed to place people in the right jobs and to motivate people to work hard. Marx separated reward from performance; his egalitarian ideal was based on the principle "from each according to ability, to each according to need" (Marx & Engels, 1972:388, orig. 1848). However, failure to reward individual performance may be precisely what caused the low productivity of the former Soviet Union and other socialist economies around the world. Defenders respond to such criticism by asking why we assume that humanity is inherently selfish rather than social; individual rewards are not the only way to motivate people to perform their social roles (M. S. Clark, 1991).

A second problem is that the revolutionary change Marx predicted has failed to happen, at least in advanced capitalist societies. The next section explains why.

blue-collar occupations lower-prestige jobs that involve mostly manual labor

white-collar occupations higher-prestige jobs that involve mostly mental activity

CHECK YOUR LEARNING   How does Marx's view of social stratification differ from the Davis-Moore thesis?

Why No Marxist Revolution?

Despite Marx's prediction, capitalism is still thriving. Why have industrial workers not overthrown capitalism? Ralf Dahrendorf (1959) suggested four reasons:

1. **Fragmentation of the capitalist class.**   Today, tens of millions of stockholders, rather than single families, own most large companies. Day-to-day corporate operations are in the hands of a large class of managers, who may or may not be major stockholders. With stock so widely held—about 50 percent of U.S. households own stocks—more and more people have a direct stake in the capitalist system (U.S. Census Bureau, 2010).

2. **A higher standard of living.**   A century ago, most U.S. workers were in factories or on farms in **blue-collar occupations**, *lower-prestige jobs that involve mostly manual labor.* Today, most workers are in **white-collar occupations**, *higher-prestige jobs that involve mostly mental activity.* These jobs are in sales,

customer support, management, and other service fields. Most of today's white-collar workers do not think of themselves as an "industrial proletariat." Just as important, the average income in the United States rose almost tenfold over the course of the twentieth century, even allowing for inflation, and the number of hours in the workweek decreased. Most workers today are far better off than workers were a century ago, an example of structural social mobility. One result of this rising standard of living is that more people support the status quo.

3. **More worker organizations.**   Workers today have the right to form labor unions that make demands of management, backed by threats of work slowdowns and strikes. As a result, labor disputes are settled without threatening the capitalist system.

4. **Greater legal protections.**   Over the past century, new laws made the workplace safer, and unemployment insurance, disability protection, and Social Security now provide workers with greater financial security.

A Counterpoint

These developments suggest that our society has smoothed many of capitalism's rough edges. Yet many observers claim that Marx's analysis of capitalism is still largely valid (Domhoff, 1983; Stephens, 1986; Boswell & Dixon, 1993; Hout, Brooks, & Manza, 1993). First, wealth remains highly concentrated, with 35 percent of all privately owned property in the hands of 1 percent of the U.S. population (Keister, 2000; Wolff, 2009). Second, many of today's white-collar jobs offer no more income, security, or satisfaction than factory work did a century ago. Third, many benefits enjoyed by today's workers came about through the class conflict Marx described; workers still struggle to hold on to what they have; and in recent years, many workers have actually lost pensions and other benefits. Fourth, although workers have gained legal protections, ordinary people still face disadvantages that the law cannot overcome. Therefore, social-conflict theorists conclude, even without a socialist revolution in the United States, Marx was still mostly right about capitalism.

Max Weber: Class, Status, and Power

Max Weber agreed with Karl Marx that social stratification causes social conflict, but he viewed Marx's two-class model as too simple. Instead, he viewed social stratification as involving three distinct dimensions of inequality.

The first dimension, economic inequality—the issue so important to Marx—Weber called *class* position.

Rich Pedroncelli/AP Wide World Photos

Back in the Great Depression of the 1930's, "tent cities" that were home to desperately poor people could be found in much of the United States. The depression came to an end, but poverty persisted. The recent recession sparked a resurgence of tent cities, including this one in Fresno, California. How would structural-functional analysis explain such poverty? What about the social-conflict approach?

Social Stratification

socioeconomic status (SES) a composite ranking based on various dimensions of social inequality

● APPLYING THEORY ●

Social Stratification

	Structural-Functional Approach	Social-Conflict Approach	Symbolic-Interaction Approach
What is the level of analysis?	Macro-level	Macro-level	Micro-level
What is social stratification?	Stratification is a system of unequal rewards that benefits society as a whole.	Stratification is a division of a society's resources that benefits some people and harms others.	Stratification is a factor that guides people's interactions in everyday life.
What is the reason for our social position?	Social position reflects personal talents and abilities in a competitive economy.	Social position reflects the way society divides resources.	The products we consume all say something about social position.
Are unequal rewards fair?	Yes. Unequal rewards boost economic production by encouraging people to work harder and try new ideas. Linking greater rewards to more important work is widely accepted.	No. Unequal rewards only serve to divide society, creating "haves" and "have-nots." There is widespread opposition to social inequality.	Maybe. People may or may not define inequality as fair. People may view their social position as a measure of self-worth, justifying inequality in terms of personal differences.

Weber did not think of classes as well-defined categories but as a continuum ranging from high to low. Weber's second dimension is *status,* or social prestige, and the third is *power.*

Weber's Socioeconomic Status Hierarchy

Marx viewed prestige and power as simple reflections of economic position and did not treat them as distinct dimensions of inequality. But Weber noted that status consistency in modern societies is often quite low: A local government official might exercise great power yet have little wealth or social prestige.

Weber, then, characterizes stratification in industrial societies as a multidimensional ranking rather than a hierarchy of clearly defined classes. In line with Weber's thinking, sociologists use the term **socioeconomic status (SES)** to refer to *a composite ranking based on various dimensions of social inequality.*

Inequality in History

Weber observed that each of his three dimensions of social inequality stands out at a different time in the history of human societies. Status or social prestige is the main dimension of difference in agrarian societies, taking the form of honor. Members of these societies gain prestige by conforming to cultural norms that apply to their particular rank.

Industrialization and the development of capitalism eliminate traditional rankings based on birth but create striking financial inequality. Thus in an industrial society, the crucial difference between people is the economic dimension of class.

Over time, industrial societies witness the growth of a bureaucratic state. Bigger government and the spread of all types of other organizations make power more important in the stratification system. Especially in socialist societies, where government regulates many aspects of life, high-ranking officials become the new ruling elite.

This historical analysis points to a final difference between Weber and Marx. Marx thought societies could eliminate social stratification by abolishing private ownership of productive property. Weber doubted that overthrowing capitalism would significantly lessen social stratification. It might reduce economic differences, he reasoned, but socialism would increase inequality by expanding government and concentrating power in the hands of a political elite. The popular uprisings against socialist bureaucracies in Eastern Europe and the former Soviet Union show that discontent can be generated by socialist political elites and thus support Weber's position.

conspicuous consumption buying and using products because of the "statement" they make about social position

SEEING SOCIOLOGY IN EVERYDAY LIFE

When Class Gets Personal: Picking (with) Your Friends

The sound of banjo music drifted across the field late one summer afternoon. I laid my brush down, climbed over the fence I had been painting, and walked toward the sound of the music to see what was going on. That's how I met my neighbor Max, a retired factory worker who lived just up the road. Max was a pretty good "picker," and within an hour, I was back on his porch with my guitar. I called Howard, a friend who teaches at the college, and he showed up a little while later, six-string in hand. The three of us jammed for a couple of hours, smiling all the while.

The next morning, I was mowing the grass in front of the house when Max came walking down the road. I turned off the lawnmower as he came down the driveway. "Hi, Max," I said. "Thanks for having us over last night. I really had fun."

"Don't mention it," Max responded. Then he shook his head a little and added, "Ya know, I

was thinkin' after you guys left. I mean, it was really somethin' how you guys looked like you

Getty Images, Inc.

were having a great time. With somebody like me!"

"Well, yeah," I replied, not sure what he meant. "You sure played better than we did."

Max looked down at the ground, embarrassed by the compliment. Then he added, "What I mean is that you guys were having a good time with somebody like *me*. You're both professors, right? *Doctors*, even . . ."

WHAT DO YOU THINK?

1. Why do you think Max felt that two college teachers would not enjoy spending time with him?

2. How does his reaction suggest that people take social position personally?

3. Can you think of a similar experience you have had with someone of a different social position?

CRITICAL REVIEW Weber's multidimensional view of social stratification greatly influenced sociologists and made the concept of socioeconomic status hierarchy popular. But critics (particularly those who favor Marx's ideas) argue that although social class boundaries may have blurred, industrial and postindustrial nations still show striking patterns of social inequality.

As will be explained shortly, economic inequality has increased recently in the United States. Although some people favor Weber's multidimensional hierarchy, others think, in light of this trend, that Marx's view of the rich versus the poor is closer to the truth.

CHECK YOUR LEARNING What are Weber's three dimensions of social inequality? According to Weber, which of them would you expect to be most important in the United States? Why?

Stratification and Interaction

Because social stratification has to do with the way an entire society is organized, sociologists (Marx and Weber included) typically treat it as a macro-level issue. But a micro-level analysis of social stratification is also important because people's social standing affects their

everyday interactions. The Applying Theory table on the previous page summarizes the contributions of three theoretical approaches to social stratification.

In most communities, people interact primarily with others of about the same social standing. This pattern begins with the fact that due to social stratification, people tend to live with others like themselves. In larger public spaces, such as a large shopping mall, we often see couples or groups made up of individuals whose appearance and shopping habits are similar. At the same time, people with very different social standing commonly keep their distance from one another. Well-dressed people walking down the street on their way to an expensive restaurant, for example, might move across the sidewalk or even cross the street to avoid getting close to others they think are homeless people. The Seeing Sociology in Everyday Life box gives another example of how differences in social class position can affect interaction.

Finally, just about everyone realizes that the way we dress, the car we drive (or the bus we ride), and even the food and drink we order at the campus snack bar say something about our budget and personal tastes. Sociologists use the term **conspicuous consumption** to refer to *buying and using products because of the "statement" they make about social position.* Ignoring the water fountain in favor of paying for bottled water tells people that you have extra money to spend. And

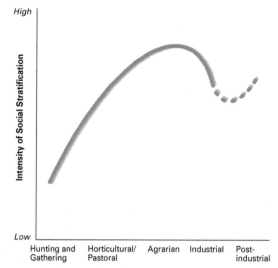

● Seeing Sociology
in Everyday Life

Have you recently had an everyday life experience that brought
home the importance of social stratification in our society?
Explain.

● Seeing Sociology
in Everyday Life

Can you identify aspects of everyday life that seem to suggest
that economic inequality is increasing? Explain.

no one needs a $100,000 automobile to get around, of course, but driving up in such a vehicle says "I have arrived" in more ways than one.

○ **CRITICAL REVIEW** A micro-level analysis of social stratification helps us see patterns of social inequality in our everyday lives. At the same time, the limitation of this approach is that it has little to say about how and why broad patterns of social inequality exist, which was the focus of the structural-functional and social-conflict approaches.

○ **CHECK YOUR LEARNING** Point to several ways in which social stratification shapes the way people of different social positions behave in the course of a typical day.

Stratification and Technology: A Global Perspective

We can weave together a number of observations made in this chapter by considering the relationship between a society's technology and its type of social stratification. This analysis draws on Gerhard Lenski's model of sociocultural evolution.

Hunting and Gathering Societies

With simple technology, hunters and gatherers produce only what is necessary for day-to-day living. Some people may produce more than others, but the group's survival depends on all sharing what they have. Thus no categories of people are better off than others.

Horticultural, Pastoral, and Agrarian Societies

As technological advances create a surplus, social inequality increases. In horticultural and pastoral societies, a small elite controls most of the surplus. Larger-scale agriculture is more productive still, and striking inequality—as great as at any time in history—places the nobility in an almost godlike position over the masses.

Industrial Societies

Industrialization pushes inequality downward. Prompted by the need to develop people's talents, meritocracy takes hold and weakens the power of traditional elites. Industrial productivity also raises the living standards of the historically poor majority. Specialized work demands schooling for all, sharply reducing illiteracy. A literate population demands a greater voice in political decision making, reducing social inequality and lessening men's domination of women.

Over time, even wealth becomes somewhat less concentrated (contradicting Marx's prediction). In the 1920s, the richest 1 percent of U.S. families owned about 40 percent of all wealth, a figure that fell

FIGURE 2 **Social Stratification and Technological Development: The Kuznets Curve**

The Kuznets curve shows that greater technological sophistication generally is accompanied by more pronounced social stratification. The trend reverses itself as industrial societies relax rigid, castelike distinctions in favor of greater opportunity and equality under the law. Political rights are more widely extended, and there is even some leveling of economic differences. However, the emergence of postindustrial society has brought an upturn in economic inequality, as indicated by the broken line added by the author.

Sources: Drawn by the author based on Kuznets (1955) and Lenski (1966).

to 30 percent by the 1980s as taxes—with higher tax rates for people with higher incomes—paid for new government programs benefiting the poor (Williamson & Lindert, 1980; Beeghley, 1989; U.S. House of Representatives, 1991). Such trends help explain why Marxist revolutions occurred in *agrarian* societies, such as Russia (1917), Cuba (1959), and Nicaragua (1979), where social inequality is most pronounced, rather than in *industrial* societies as Marx predicted. However, wealth inequality turned upward again after 1990 and is once again about the same as it was in the 1920s (Keister, 2000; Wolff, 2009). With the goal of reducing this trend, the Obama administration has expressed its intention to raise federal income tax rates on high-income individuals.

The Kuznets Curve

In human history, then, technological advances first increase but then moderate the intensity of social stratification. Greater inequality is functional for agrarian societies, but industrial societies benefit from

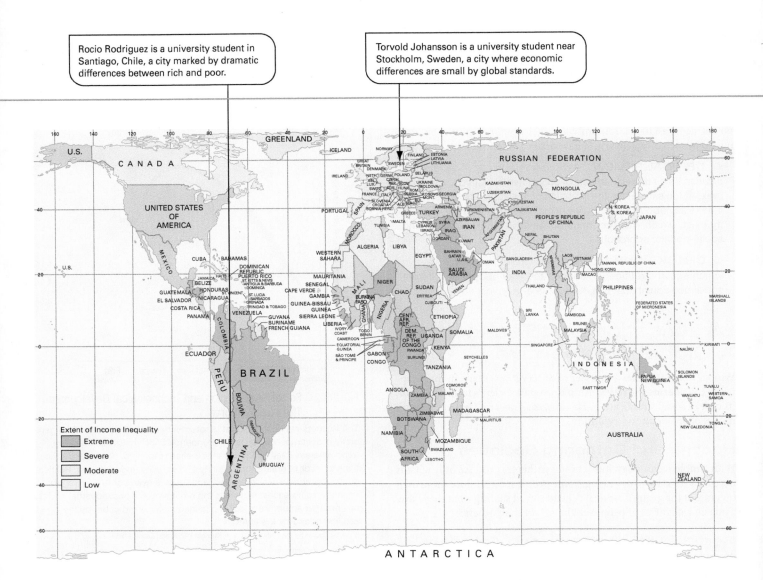

Rocio Rodriguez is a university student in Santiago, Chile, a city marked by dramatic differences between rich and poor.

Torvold Johansson is a university student near Stockholm, Sweden, a city where economic differences are small by global standards.

Extent of Income Inequality
- Extreme
- Severe
- Moderate
- Low

Window on the World

GLOBAL MAP 1   Income Inequality in Global Perspective

Societies throughout the world differ in the rigidity and extent of their social stratification and their overall standard of living. This map highlights income inequality. Generally speaking, the United States stands out among high-income nations, such as Great Britain, Sweden, Japan, and Australia, as having greater income inequality. The less economically developed countries of Latin America and Africa, including Colombia, Brazil, and the Central African Republic, as well as much of the Arab world, exhibit the most pronounced inequality of income. Is this pattern consistent with the Kuznets curve?

Source: Based on Gini coefficients obtained from World Bank (2008) and Central Intelligence Agency (2009).

a more equal system. This historical trend, recognized by the Nobel Prize–winning economist Simon Kuznets (1955, 1966), is illustrated by the Kuznets curve, shown in Figure 2.

Social inequality around the world generally supports the Kuznets curve. Global Map 1 shows that high-income nations that have passed through the industrial era (including the United States, Canada, and the nations of Western Europe) have somewhat less income inequality than nations in which a larger share of the labor force remains in farming (as is common in Latin America and Africa). At the same time, it is important to remember that income inequality reflects not just technological development but also a society's political and economic priorities. Income inequality in the

Social Stratification

Making the Grade

Notice in the two pie-charts below that wealth is
more unequally distributed than income.

income earnings from work or investments

wealth the total value of money and other assets, minus
outstanding debts

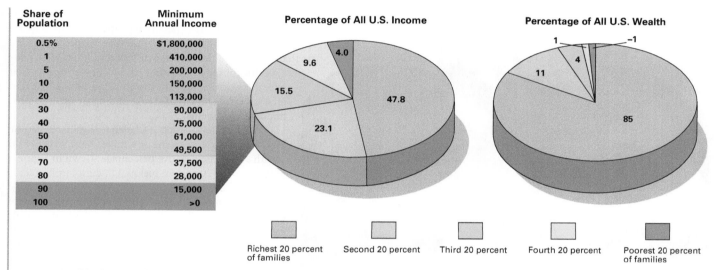

Share of Population	Minimum Annual Income
0.5%	$1,800,000
1	410,000
5	200,000
10	150,000
20	113,000
30	90,000
40	75,000
50	61,000
60	49,500
70	37,500
80	28,000
90	15,000
100	>0

Percentage of All U.S. Income

4.0
9.6
15.5
23.1
47.8

Percentage of All U.S. Wealth

1   −1
4
11
85

Richest 20 percent of families   Second 20 percent   Third 20 percent   Fourth 20 percent   Poorest 20 percent of families

FIGURE 3   **Distribution of Income and Wealth in the United States**

Income, and especially wealth, is divided unequally in U.S. society.

Sources: Income data from U.S. Census Bureau (2009); wealth data based on Bucks et al. (2009), Wolff (2009), and author estimates.

United States may have declined during much of the last century,
but this country still has more economic inequality than Canada,
countries throughout Europe, and Japan.

Another criticism of the Kuznets curve is that it was developed
by comparing societies at different levels of economic development
(using what sociologists call "cross-sectional data"). Such data do
not tell us about the future of any one society. In the United States,
recent trends showing increases in economic inequality suggest that
the Kuznets curve may require serious revision—represented by the
broken line in Figure 2. The fact that U.S. society is now experiencing greater economic inequality suggests that the long-term trend
may differ from what Kuznets projected half a century ago.

Inequality in the United States

The United States differs from most European nations and Japan in
never having had a titled nobility. With the significant exception of our
racial history, we have never known a caste system that rigidly ranks
categories of people.

Even so, U.S. society is highly stratified. Not only do the rich
have most of the money, but they also receive the most schooling,
enjoy the best health, and consume the most goods and services.
Such privilege contrasts sharply with the poverty of millions of
women and men who worry about paying next month's rent or a

doctor's bill when a child becomes ill. Many people think of the
United States as a "middle-class society" in which people are more or
less alike. But is this really the case?

Income, Wealth, and Power

One important dimension of economic inequality is **income**, *earnings
from work or investments.* The Census Bureau reports that the median
U.S. family income in 2008 was $61,521. The pie chart in the middle
of Figure 3 shows the distribution of income among all U.S. families.[1]
The richest 20 percent of families (earning at least $113,000 annu-
ally, with a mean of about $190,000) received 47.8 percent of all
income, and the bottom 20 percent (earning less than $28,000, with
a mean of about $16,000) received only 4.0 percent.

The table at the left in Figure 3 takes a closer look at income distribution. In 2008, the highest-paid 5 percent of U.S. families earned

---

[1]The Census Bureau reports both mean and median incomes for families ("two or
more persons related by blood, marriage, or adoption") and households ("two or more
persons sharing a living unit"). In 2008, mean family income was $79,634, higher than
median family income ($61,521) because high-income families pull up the mean but
not the median. For households, these figures are somewhat lower—a mean of
$68,424 and a median of $50,303—because families average 3.15 people and households average 2.57.

● Seeing Sociology
in Everyday Life

Why do you think so many people view the United States as a
middle-class society in which most people have more or less
equal social standing?

● Seeing Sociology
in Everyday Life

People of all social classes have the same right to vote. But
can you think of ways in which the rich have more power to
shape U.S. society than the rest of us?

Hill Street Studios/Getty Images, Inc. - Blend Images

Members of our society tend to think of social class in terms of income and wealth, as if
to say "I am what I own." For this reason, conspicuous consumption—buying and
displaying various goods partly with an eye toward gaining social standing in the eyes of
others—is a common pattern. How have you engaged in conspicuous consumption?

of homes, cars, investments, insurance policies, retirement pensions,
furniture, clothing, and all other personal property, minus a home
mortgage and other debts. The wealth of average people is not only
less than that of the rich but also different in kind. Most people's wealth centers on a home and a car—property that
generates no income—but the greater wealth of the rich
is mostly in the form of stocks and other income-pro-
ducing investments.

When financial assets are balanced against debts, the
lowest-ranking 40 percent of families have virtually no
wealth at all. The negative percentage shown in Figure 3
for the poorest 20 percent means that these families actually live in debt.

In the United States, wealth is an important source
of power. The small proportion of families that controls
most of the country's wealth also has the ability to shape
the agenda of the entire society. Some sociologists argue
that such concentrated wealth weakens democracy
because the political system primarily serves the interests
of the super-rich.

Occupational Prestige

In addition to generating income, work is also an important source of prestige. We commonly evaluate each other according
to the kind of work we do, giving greater respect to those who do
what we consider to be more important work and less to others with
more modest jobs.

Sociologists measure the relative social prestige of various occupations (NORC, 2009). Table 1 shows that people give high prestige
to occupations, such as medicine, law, and engineering, that require
extensive training and generate high income. By contrast, less prestigious work—as a waitress or janitor, for example—not only pays
less but requires less ability and schooling. Occupational prestige
rankings are much the same in all high-income nations (Lin & Xie,
1988).

In any society, high-prestige occupations go to privileged categories of people. In Table 1, for example, the highest-ranking occupations are dominated by men. We have to go more than a dozen
jobs down the list to find "registered nurse" and "secondary school
teacher," careers chosen mostly by women. Similarly, many of the
lowest-prestige jobs are commonly performed by people of color.

Schooling

Industrial societies have expanded opportunities for schooling, but
some people still receive much more than others. In 2009, although
almost 87 percent of women and men aged twenty-five and older had

at least $200,000 (averaging almost $327,000), or 20.5 percent of all
income, more than the total earnings of the lowest-paid 40 percent.
At the very top of the pyramid, the richest 0.5 percent earned at least
$1.8 million. In short, while a small number of people earn very high
incomes, the majority make do with far less.

Income is only one part of a person's or family's **wealth,** *the total
value of money and other assets, minus outstanding debts.* Wealth—
including stocks, bonds, and real estate—is distributed even more
unequally than income.

The pie chart at the right in Figure 3 shows the approximate distribution of wealth in the United States. The richest 20 percent of U.S.
families own roughly 85 percent of the country's entire wealth. High
up in this privileged category are the top 5 percent of families, the
"very rich," who own 62 percent of all private property. Richer still,
with wealth into the tens of millions of dollars, are the 1 percent of
families that qualify as "super-rich" and possess about 35 percent of the
nation's privately held resources (Keister, 2000; Keister & Moller, 2000;
Bucks et al., 2009; Wolff, 2009). At the top of the wealth pyramid, the
ten richest individuals in our society have a combined net worth of
more than $225 billion (Miller & Greenberg, 2009). This amount
equals the total property of nearly 2 million average families, enough
people to fill the cities of Chicago, Houston, and San Francisco.

The wealth of the average U.S. family is currently about
$120,300 (Bucks et al., 2009). Family wealth reflects the total value

Social Stratification

Seeing Sociology
in Everyday Life

Identify the jobs in Table 1 that have traditionally been
performed by people of color. What pattern do you discover?

Seeing Sociology
in Everyday Life

Reading down from the top of Table 1, how far do you
have to go before you see a job in which most workers would
be women?

Table 1   The Relative Social Prestige of Selected Occupations in the United States

White-Collar Occupations	Prestige Score	Blue-Collar Occupations	White-Collar Occupations	Prestige Score	Blue-Collar Occupations
Physician	86		Funeral director	49	
Lawyer	75		Real estate agent	49	
College/university professor	74		Bookkeeper	47	
Architect	73			47	Machinist
Chemist	73			47	Mail carrier
Physicist/astronomer	73		Musician/composer	47	
Aerospace engineer	72			46	Secretary
Dentist	72		Photographer	45	
Member of the clergy	69		Bank teller	43	
Psychologist	69			42	Tailor
Pharmacist	68			42	Welder
Optometrist	67			40	Farmer
Registered nurse	66			40	Telephone operator
Secondary school teacher	66			39	Carpenter
Accountant	65			36	Bricklayer/stonemason
Athlete	65			36	Child care worker
Electrical engineer	64		File clerk	36	
Elementary school teacher	64			36	Hairdresser
Economist	63			35	Baker
Veterinarian	62			34	Bulldozer operator
Airplane pilot	61			31	Auto body repairer
Computer programmer	61		Retail apparel salesperson	30	
Sociologist	61			30	Truck driver
Editor/reporter	60		Cashier	29	
	60	Police officer		28	Elevator operator
Actor	58			28	Garbage collector
Radio/TV announcer	55			28	Taxi driver
Librarian	54			28	Waiter/waitress
	53	Aircraft mechanic		27	Bellhop
	53	Firefighter		25	Bartender
Dental hygienist	52			23	Farm laborer
Painter/sculptor	52			23	Household laborer
Social worker	52			22	Door-to-door salesperson
	51	Electrician		22	Janitor
Computer operator	50			09	Shoe shiner

Source: Adapted from *General Social Surveys, 1972–2008: Cumulative Codebook* (Chicago: National Opinion Research Center, 2009), pp. 2310–2317.

○ Making the Grade

Notice in the section below how ancestry, race and ethnicity, and gender can operate as caste elements.

○ Seeing Sociology
in Everyday Life

To what extent is gender still an element of caste? That is, as you look around you, do women seem to have the same opportunities and privileges as men?

completed high school, just 29 percent of women and 30 percent of men were college graduates (U.S. Census Bureau, 2010).

Schooling affects both occupation and income because most (but not all) of the better-paying, white-collar jobs listed in Table 1 require a college degree or other advanced study. Most blue-collar jobs, which bring lower income and less prestige, require less schooling.

Ancestry, Race, and Gender

A class system rewards individual talent and effort. But nothing affects social standing as much as birth into a particular family, which has a strong bearing on future schooling, occupation, and income. Research suggests that more than one-third of our country's richest people—those with hundreds of millions of dollars in wealth—derived their fortunes mostly from inheritance (Miller & Newcomb, 2005; Harford, 2007). Inherited poverty shapes the future of tens of millions of others.

Also closely linked to social position in the United States is race. White people have a higher overall occupational standing than African Americans and also receive more schooling. The median African American family income was $39,879 in 2008, just 57 percent of the $70,070 earned by non-Hispanic white families. This difference in income makes a real difference in people's lives. For example, non-Hispanic white families are more likely to own their homes (75 percent do) than black families (47 percent) (U.S. Census Bureau, 2009).

Some of the racial difference in income results from the larger proportion of single-parent families among African Americans. Comparing only families that include a married couple, African American families earned 80 percent as much as non-Hispanic white families.

Over time, this income difference builds into a huge wealth gap (Altonji, Doraszelski, & Segal, 2000). A survey of families by the government's Federal Reserve found that median wealth for minority families, including African Americans, Hispanics, and Asian Americans ($27,800), is just 16 percent of the median ($170,400) for non-Hispanic white families (Bucks et al., 2009).

Social ranking involves ethnicity as well. Historically, people of English ancestry have enjoyed the most wealth and wielded the greatest power in U.S. society. The Latino population—the largest U.S. racial or ethnic minority—has long been disadvantaged. In 2008, the median income among Hispanic families was $40,500, which is 58 percent of the median income for non-Hispanic white families.

Of course, both men and women are found in families at every social level. Yet on average, women have less income, wealth, and occupational prestige than men. Among single-parent families, those headed by a woman are more than twice as likely to be poor as those headed by a man.

Social Classes in the United States

As noted earlier, rankings in a caste system are rigid and obvious to all. Defining the social categories in a more fluid class system, however, is not so easy. Followers of Karl Marx see two major social classes: capitalists and proletarians. Other sociologists find as many as six classes (Warner & Lunt, 1941) or even seven (Coleman & Rainwater, 1978). Still others side with Max Weber, believing that people form not clear-cut classes but a multidimensional status hierarchy.

Defining classes in the United States is difficult because of the relatively low level of status consistency. Especially toward the middle of the hierarchy, people's social position on one dimension may not be the same as their standing on another. For example, a government official may have the power to administer a multimillion-dollar budget yet earn only a modest personal income. Similarly, many members of the clergy enjoy ample prestige but only moderate power and low pay. Or consider the casino poker player who wins little respect but makes a lot of money.

Finally, the social mobility characteristic of class systems—again, most pronounced near the middle—means that social position may change during a person's lifetime, further blurring class boundaries. With these issues in mind, we can examine four general rankings: the upper class, the middle class, the working class, and the lower class.

The Upper Class

Families in the upper class—the top 5 percent of the U.S. population—earn at least $200,000, and some earn ten times that much or more. As a general rule, the more a family's income comes from inherited wealth in the form of stocks and bonds, real estate, and other investments, the stronger a family's claim to being upper-class.

In 2009, *Forbes* magazine profiled the richest 400 people in the United States who were worth at least $950 million (and as much as $50 billion) (Miller & Greenberg, 2009). These people form the core of the upper class or Karl Marx's "capitalists"—the owners of the means of production and thus of most of the nation's private wealth. Many of these people spend much of their time managing their own wealth. Many upper-class people with smaller fortunes are business owners, top executives in large corporations, or senior government officials. Historically, the upper class has been composed of white Anglo-Saxon Protestants, but this is less true today (Pyle & Koch, 2001).

┌─○ Making the Grade

Pay attention to a key difference between the small number of "upper-uppers," who are almost always born (or occasionally marry) into "old money," and the much larger number of "lower-uppers," who move upward socially as they earn lots of "new money."

┌─● Seeing Sociology
    in Everyday Life

When you think about the "American dream," you imagine rising to which part of the upper class? Explain your answer.

Thinkstock

H. Mark Weidman/Alamy Images

People often distinguish between the "new rich" and families with "old money." Men and women who suddenly begin to earn high incomes tend to spend their money on status symbols because they enjoy the new thrill of high-roller living and they want others to know of their success. Those who grow up surrounded by wealth, by contrast, are used to a privileged way of life and are more quiet about it. Thus the conspicuous consumption of the lower-upper class (*left*) can differ dramatically from the more private pursuits and understatement of the upper-upper class (*right*).

Upper-Uppers

The *upper-upper class,* sometimes called "blue bloods" or simply "society," includes less than 1 percent of the U.S. population (Baltzell, 1995). Membership is almost always the result of birth, as suggested by the old remark that the easiest way to become an upper-upper is to be born one. Most of these families possess enormous wealth that is primarily inherited. For this reason, members of the upper-upper class are said to have "old money."

Set apart by their wealth, upper-uppers live in exclusive neighborhoods such as Beacon Hill in Boston, the Rittenhouse Square section of Philadelphia, the Gold Coast of Chicago, and Nob Hill in San Francisco. Their children typically attend private schools with others of similar background and complete their formal education at high-prestige colleges and universities. In the historical pattern of European aristocrats, they study liberal arts rather than vocational skills.

Women of the upper-upper class often do volunteer work for charitable organizations. Such activities serve a dual purpose: They help the larger community, and they build networks that broaden this elite's power (Ostrander, 1980, 1984).

Lower-Uppers

Most upper-class people actually fall into the *lower-upper class.* And lower-uppers include some of the richest people in the world. The

queen of England is in the upper-upper class based not only on her fortune of $450 million but on her family tree. J. K. Rowling, author of the Harry Potter books, is easily worth twice as much—more than $1 billion—but this self-made woman (who was once on welfare) stands at the top of the lower-upper class. The major difference, in other words, is that members of the lower-upper class are the "working rich" who get their money mostly by earning it rather than inheritance. These "new rich" families—who make up 3 to 4 percent of the U.S. population—generally live in large homes in expensive neighborhoods, own vacation homes near the water or in the mountains, and send their children to private schools and good colleges. Yet most do not gain entry into the clubs and associations of "old money" families.

The Middle Class

Made up of 40 to 45 percent of the U.S. population, the large middle class has a tremendous influence on our culture. Television and movies usually show middle-class people, and most commercial advertising is directed at these average consumers. The middle class contains far more ethnic and racial diversity than the upper class.

Upper-Middles

People near the top of this category are called the *upper-middle class,* based on their above-average income in the range of $113,000 to

● Seeing Sociology
  in Everyday Life

What low-wage jobs have you held? Assess those
experiences in light of the box below.

Go to the Multimedia Library at **mysoclab.com**
to view the ABC *20/20* video "Poverty in
Camden, New Jersey"

SEEING SOCIOLOGY IN EVERYDAY LIFE

Nickel and Dimed: On (Not) Getting By in America

All of us know people who work at low-wage jobs as waitresses at diners, clerks at drive-throughs, or sales associates at discount stores such as Walmart. We see such people just about every day. Many of us actually *are* such people. In the United States, "common sense" tells us that the jobs people have and the amount of money they make reflect their personal abilities as well as their willingness to work hard.

Barbara Ehrenreich (2001) had her doubts. To find out what the world of low-wage work is really like, the successful journalist and author decided to leave her comfortable upper-middle-class life to live and work in the world of low-wage jobs. She began in Key West, Florida, taking a job as a waitress for $2.43 an hour plus tips. Right away, she found out she had to work much harder than she ever imagined. By the end of a shift, she was exhausted, but after sharing tips with the kitchen staff, she averaged less than $6.00 an hour. This was barely above the national minimum wage at the time and provided just enough income to pay the rent on her tiny apartment, buy food, and cover other basic expenses. She had to hope that she didn't get sick, because the job did not provide health insurance and

she couldn't afford to pay for a visit to a doctor's office.

After working for more than a year at a number of other low-wage jobs, including cleaning motels in Maine and working on the floor of a Walmart in Minnesota, she had rejected quite a bit of "common sense." First, she now knew that tens of millions of people with low-wage jobs work very hard every day. If you don't think so, Ehrenreich says, take on one of these jobs for yourself. Second, these jobs require not only hard work (imagine thoroughly cleaning three motel rooms every hour all day long) but also special skills and real intelligence (try waiting on ten tables in a restaurant at the same time and keeping everybody happy). She found that the people she worked with were, on aver-

PhotoEdit, Inc./ Jeff Greenberg

age, just as smart, clever, and funny as others she knew who wrote books for a living or taught at a college.

Why, then, do we think of low-wage workers as lazy or as having less ability? It surprised Ehrenreich to learn that many low-wage workers felt this way about themselves. In a society that teaches us to believe that personal ability is everything, we learn to size people up by their job. Ehrenreich discovered that many low-wage workers, subject to constant supervision, random drug tests, and other rigid rules that usually come with such jobs, end up feeling unworthy, even to the point of not trying for anything better. Such beliefs, she concludes, help support a society of extreme inequality in which some people live very well because of the low wages paid to the rest.

WHAT DO YOU THINK?

1. Have you ever held a low-wage job? If so, would you say you worked hard? What was your pay? Were there any benefits?

2. Ehrenreich claims that most well-off people in the United States are dependent on low-wage workers. What does she mean by this?

3. How much of a chance do most people with jobs at Wendy's or Walmart have to enroll in college and to work toward a different career? Explain.

$200,000 a year. Such income allows upper-middle-class families to live in a comfortable house in a fairly expensive area, own several nice automobiles, and build investments. Two-thirds of upper-middle-class children graduate from college, and postgraduate degrees are common. Many go on to high-prestige occupations as physicians, engineers, lawyers, accountants, and business executives. Lacking the power of the richest people to influence national or international events, upper-middles often play an important role in local political affairs.

Average-Middles

The rest of the middle class falls close to the center of the U.S. class structure. *Average-middles* typically work at less prestigious white-collar occupations as bank branch managers or high school teachers

or in highly skilled blue-collar jobs such as electrical work and carpentry. Family income falls between $49,000 and $113,000 a year, which is roughly the national average.[2]

Middle-class people generally build up a small amount of wealth over the course of their working lives, mostly in the form of a house and a retirement account. Most average-middle-class men and women are likely to be high school graduates, but the odds are just fifty-fifty that they will complete a college degree, usually at a less expensive, state-supported school.

---

[2]In some parts of the United States where the cost of living is very high (say, San Francisco), a family might need as much as $150,000 in annual income to reach the middle class.

Seeing Sociology in Everyday Life

If you wanted to assess someone's social class position and could ask only one question, what would it be? Explain your decision.

Go to the Multimedia Library at mysoclab.com to view author John Macionis responding to the question "What Difference Does Class Make?"

The Working Class

About one-third of the population falls within the working class (sometimes called the *lower-middle class*). In Marxist terms, the working class forms the core of the industrial proletariat. The blue-collar jobs held by members of the working class yield a family income of between $28,000 and $49,000 a year, somewhat below the national average. Working-class families have little or no wealth and are vulnerable to financial problems caused by unemployment or illness.

Many working-class jobs provide little personal satisfaction—requiring discipline but rarely imagination—and subject workers to continual supervision. These jobs also offer fewer benefits, such as medical insurance and pension plans. About two-thirds of working-class families own their homes, usually in lower-cost neighborhoods. College becomes a reality for only about one-third of working-class children.

The Lower Class

The remaining 20 percent of the population make up the lower class. Low income makes their lives insecure and difficult. In 2008, the federal government classified 40 million people (13.2 percent of the population) as poor. Millions more—called the "working poor"—are slightly better off, holding low-prestige jobs that provide little satisfaction and minimal income. Barely half manage to complete high school, and only one in four ever reaches college. In the Seeing Sociology in Everyday Life box, one sociologist describes the experience of trying to survive day-to-day doing low-wage work.

Society segregates the lower class, especially when the poor are racial or ethnic minorities. About 45 percent of lower-class families own their own home, typically in the least desirable neighborhoods. Although poor neighborhoods are often found in inner cities, lower-class families also live in rural areas, especially across the South.

⬤ Go to mysoclab.com

The Difference Class Makes

Social stratification affects nearly every dimension of our lives. In the following sections, we will briefly examine some of the ways social standing is linked to our health, values, politics, and family life.

⬤ Go to mysoclab.com

Health

Health is closely related to social standing. Children born into poor families are three times more likely to die from disease, neglect, accidents, or violence during their first year of life than children born into privileged families. Among adults, people with above-average incomes are almost twice as likely as low-income people to describe their health as excellent. In addition, on average, richer people live five years longer because they eat more nutritious food, live in safer and less stressful environments, and receive better medical care (Congressional Budget Office, 2008; Pleis & Lucas, 2009).

Values and Attitudes

Some values and attitudes vary from class to class. The "old rich" have an unusually strong sense of family history because their position is based on wealth passed down from generation to generation. Secure in their birthright privileges, upper-uppers also favor understated manners and tastes; many "new rich" people engage in conspicuous consumption, using homes, cars, and even airplanes as status symbols to make a statement about their social position.

Affluent people with greater education and financial security are also more tolerant of controversial behavior such as homosexuality. Working-class people, who grow up in an atmosphere of greater supervision and discipline and are less likely to attend college, tend to be less tolerant (Lareau, 2002; NORC, 2007).

Russell Lee\CORBIS- NY

Compared to high-income people, low-income people are half as likely to report good health and, on average, live about five fewer years. The toll of low income—played out in inadequate nutrition, little medical care, and high stress—is easy to see on the faces of the poor, who look old before their time.

○ Making the Grade

Be sure you understand how social class position involves not only money but also "cultural capital."

○ Seeing Sociology in Everyday Life

After reading the box below, think about times when you have felt out of place in some setting based on your social class position. Why did you feel this way? How do such feelings show that we often understand class differences in terms of personal worthiness?

THINKING ABOUT DIVERSITY: RACE, CLASS, & GENDER

The Power of Class: A Low-Income Student Asks, "Am I as Good as You?"

Marcella grew up without the privileges that most other students on the campus of this private, liberal arts college take for granted. During her senior year, she and I talked at length about her college experiences and why social class presented a huge challenge to her. Marcella is not her real name; she wishes to remain anonymous. I have summarized what she has said about her college life in the story that follows.

> When I came here, I entered a new world. I found myself in a strange and dangerous place. All around me were people with habits and ideas I did not understand. A thousand times, I thought to myself, I hope all of you will realize that there are other worlds out there and that I am from one of them. Will you accept me?
>
> I am a child of poverty, a young woman raised in a world of want and violence. I am now on the campus of an elite college. I may have a new identity as a college student. But my old life

is still going on in my head. I have not been able to change how I think of myself.

Do you want to find out more about me? Learn more about the power of social class to shape how we feel about ourselves? Here is what I want to say to you.

When I was growing up, I envied most of you. You lived in a middle-class bubble, a world that held you, protected you, and com-

Penny Tweedie/Stone/Getty Images

forted you. Not me. While your parents were discussing current events, planning family trips, and looking out for you, my father and mother were screaming at each other. I will never be able to forget summer nights when I lay in my bed, sticky with sweat, biting my fingernails as a telephone crashed against the wall that separated my room from theirs. My father was drunk and out of control; my mother ducked just in time.

Your fathers and mothers work in office buildings. They have good jobs, as doctors, lawyers, and architects; they are corporate managers; they run small businesses. Your mothers and fathers are people who matter. My mom takes the bus to a hospital where she works for $10 an hour cleaning up after people. She spends her shift doing what she is told. My dad? Who knows. He was a deadbeat, a drunk, a drug addict. I don't know if he still is or not. I haven't heard from him in eight years.

You grew up in a neighborhood and probably lived for many years in one

Social class has a great deal to do with an individual's self-concept. People with higher social standing experience more confidence in everyday interaction for the simple reason that others tend to view them as having greater importance. The Thinking About Diversity box describes the challenges faced by one young woman from a poor family attending a college where most students are from elite families.

Politics

Do political attitudes follow class lines? The answer is yes, but the pattern is complex. A desire to protect wealth prompts well-off people to take a more conservative approach to *economic* issues, favoring, for example, lower taxes. But on *social* matters such as abortion and gay rights, highly educated, more affluent people are more liberal. People of lower social standing, by contrast, tend to be economic liberals, favoring government social programs that benefit

them, but typically hold more conservative views on social issues (NORC, 2007).

A clearer pattern emerges when it comes to political involvement. Higher-income people, who are better served by the system, are more likely to vote and to join political organizations than people with low incomes. In presidential elections, more than three-fourths of adults with family incomes of at least $75,000 vote, compared to about half of adults with family incomes below $30,000 (Samuelson, 2003; U.S. Census Bureau, 2009).

Family and Gender

Social class also shapes family life. Generally, lower-class families are somewhat larger than middle-class families because of earlier marriage and less use of birth control. Another family pattern is that working-class parents encourage children to conform to conventional norms and respect authority figures. Parents of higher social standing

● Seeing Sociology
  in Everyday Life

An interesting mini-project is to ask your parents
(and also ask yourself) about changes in your family's
social position over the last several generations. What
factors are linked to these changes?

○ Making the Grade

Remember that social mobility has many forms—
including upward and downward—and also takes
place over one generation (intragenerational mobility)
or several generations (intergenerational mobility).

house. My family lived in low-cost rental housing. We moved a lot. When there was no money for rent, we packed up our stuff and moved to a new place. It seemed like we were always running away from something.

You grew up with books, with trips to the library, with parents who read to you. You learned how to speak well and have an impressive vocabulary. I never heard a bedtime story, and I had maybe one inspiring teacher. Most of what I know I had to learn on my own. Maybe that's why I always feel like I am trying to catch up to you.

You know how to use forks, knives, and spoons the right way. You know how to eat Chinese food and what to order at a Thai restaurant. You have favorite Italian dishes. You know how to order wine. You know about German beers, Danish cheeses, and French sauces. Me? I grew up having Thanksgiving dinner on paper plates, eating turkey served by social service volunteers. When you ask me to go with you to some

special restaurant, I make some excuse and stay home. I can't afford it. I am afraid you will find out how little I know about things you take for granted.

How did I ever get to this college? I remember one of my teachers telling me that I "have promise." The college admission office accepted me. But I am not sure why. I was given a scholarship that covers most of my tuition. That solved one big problem, and now I am here. But sometimes I am not sure I will stay. I have to study more than many of you to learn things you already know. I have to work two part-time jobs to make the money I needed to buy a used computer, clothes, and the occasional pizza at the corner place where many of you spend so much time.

It's amazing to me that I am here. I realize how lucky I am. But now that I am here, I realize that the road is so much longer than I thought it would be. Getting to this college was only part of the journey. The scholarship was only part of the answer. The biggest

challenge for me is what goes on every day—the thousands of ways in which you live a life that I still don't really understand, the thousands of things that I won't know or that I will do wrong that will blow my cover, and show me up for the fraud I am.

WHAT DO YOU THINK?

1. How does this story show that social class involves much more than how much money a person has?

2. Why does Marcella worry that other people will think she is a "fraud"? If you could speak to her about this fear, what would you say?

3. Have you ever had similar feelings about being less important than—or better than—someone else based on social class position? Explain.

pass on a different "cultural capital" to their children, teaching them to express their individuality and imagination more freely (Kohn, 1977; McLeod, 1995; Lareau, 2002).

The more money a family has, the more opportunities parents have to develop their children's talents and abilities. An affluent family earning more than $98,470 a year will spend $483,750 raising a child born in 2008 to the age of eighteen. Middle-class people, with an average income of about $75,000 a year, will spend $291,570, and a lower-class family earning less than $56,870 will spend $210,340 (Lino & Carlson, 2009). Privilege leads to privilege as family life reproduces the class structure in each generation.

Class also shapes our world of relationships. In a classic study of married life, Elizabeth Bott (1971, orig. 1957) found that most working-class couples divide their responsibilities according to traditional gender roles; middle-class couples, by contrast, are more egalitarian, sharing more activities and expressing greater intimacy. More recently, Karen Walker (1995) discovered that working-class

friendships typically serve as sources of material assistance; middle-class friendships are likely to involve shared interests and leisure pursuits.

Social Mobility

Ours is a dynamic society marked by quite a bit of social movement. Earning a college degree, landing a higher-paying job, or marrying someone who has a good income contributes to *upward social mobility;* dropping out of school, losing a job, or becoming divorced (especially for women) may result in *downward social mobility.*

Over the long term, though, social mobility is not so much a matter of individual changes as changes in society itself. In the first half of the twentieth century, for example, industrialization expanded the U.S. economy, pushing up living standards. Even people who were not good swimmers rode the rising tide of prosperity. More

intragenerational social mobility a change in social position occurring during a person's lifetime

intergenerational social mobility upward or downward social mobility of children in relation to their parents

○ Making the Grade

The changes in median family income shown below in Figure 4 are examples of structural social mobility.

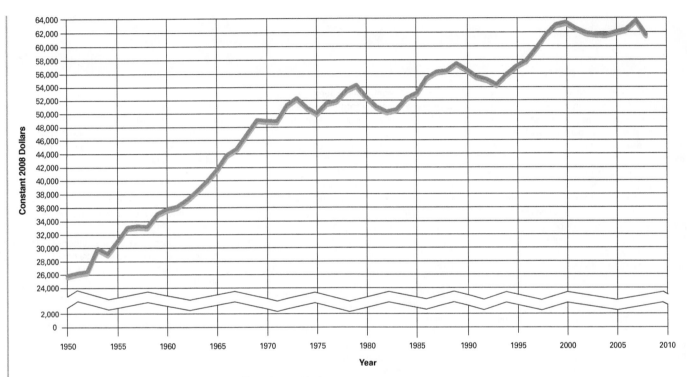

FIGURE 4 Median Annual Income, U.S. Families, 1950–2008

Average U.S. family income grew rapidly between 1950 and 1970. Since then, however, the increase has been smaller.

Source: U.S. Census Bureau (2009).

recently, the "outsourcing" of jobs and the closing of U.S. factories and other business operations has brought downward structural social mobility, dealing economic setbacks to many people. The economic downturn that hit hard in 2008 and 2009 reduced the income and economic opportunities of millions of people.

Sociologists distinguish between shorter- and longer-term changes in social position. **Intragenerational social mobility** is *a change in social position occurring during a person's lifetime* (*intra* is Latin for "within"). **Intergenerational social mobility,** *upward or downward social mobility of children in relation to their parents,* is important because it reveals long-term changes in society that affect everyone (*inter* is Latin for "between").

Myth versus Reality

In few societies do people think about "getting ahead" as much as in the United States. Moving up, after all, is the American dream. But is there as much social mobility in our country as we like to think?

One recent study of intergenerational mobility shows that about 32 percent of U.S. men had the same type of work as their fathers, 37 percent were upwardly mobile (for example, a son born to a father with a blue-collar job ends up doing white-collar work), and 32 percent were downwardly mobile (for example, the father has a white-collar job and the son does blue-collar work). Among women, 46 percent were upwardly mobile, 28 percent were downwardly mobile, and 27 percent showed no change compared to their fathers (Beller & Hout, 2006).

Horizontal social mobility—changing jobs at the same class level—is even more common. Overall, about 80 percent of children show some type of social mobility in relation to their parents (Hout, 1998; Beller & Hout, 2006).

Research points to four general conclusions about social mobility in the United States:

1. **Social mobility over the course of the past century has been fairly high.** A high level of mobility is what we would expect in an industrial class system.

Social Stratification

2. **Within a single generation, social mobility is usually small.** Most young families increase their income over time as they gain education and skills. A typical family headed by a thirty-year-old earned about $59,000 in 2008; a typical family headed by a fifty-year-old earned $77,000 (U.S. Census Bureau, 2009). Yet only a few people move from "rags to riches" (the way J. K. Rowling did) or lose a lot of money (a number of rock stars who made it big had little money left a few years later). Most social mobility involves small movement within one class level rather than large movement between classes.

3. **The long-term trend in social mobility has been upward.** Industrialization, which greatly expanded the U.S. economy, and the growth of white-collar work over the course of the twentieth century have raised living standards.

4. **Social mobility since the 1970s has been uneven.** Real income (adjusted for inflation) rose during the twentieth century until the 1970s. Since then, as shown in Figure 4, real income has risen and fallen, with overall smaller gains than was the case before 1970. Most recently, the economic recession that began in 2007 resulted in downward social mobility for many U.S. families. But general historical trends do not show the experiences of different categories of people, as the next section explains.

Mobility by Income Level

Figure 5 shows how U.S. families at different income levels made out between 1980 and 2008. Well-to-do families (the highest 20 percent, but not all the same families over the entire period) saw their incomes jump 55 percent, from an average $122,519 in 1980 to $190,400 in 2008. People in the middle of the population also had gains, but more modest ones. The lowest-income 20 percent actually lost ground, making an average of $43 less in 2008 than in 1980 (adjusted for inflation).

For families at the top of the income scale (the highest 5 percent), recent decades have brought a windfall. These families, with average income of almost $175,000 in 1980, were making $326,928 in 2008—nearly twice as much as they had made in 1980 (U.S. Census Bureau, 2009).

Mobility: Race, Ethnicity, and Gender

White people in the United States have always been in a more privileged position than people of African or Hispanic descent. Through the economic expansion of the 1980s and 1990s, more African Americans entered the ranks of the wealthy. But overall, the real income of African Americans has changed little in three decades. African American family income as a percentage of white family income has

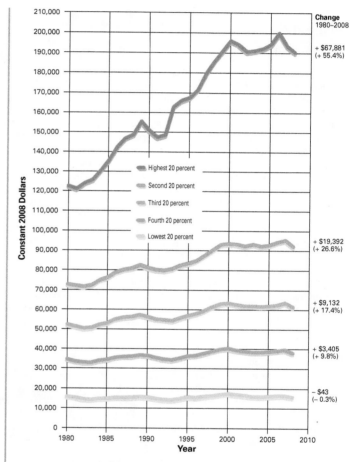

FIGURE 5 **Mean Annual Income, U.S. Families, 1980–2008 (in 2008 dollars, adjusted for inflation)**

The gap between high-income and low-income families is wider today than it was in 1980.

Source: U.S. Census Bureau (2009).

fallen slightly to 57 percent in 2008 from 61 percent in 1975. Compared with white families, Latino families lost ground between 1975 (when their average income was 66 percent of that of white families) and 2008 (when it had slipped to 58 percent) (Pomer, 1986; U.S. Census Bureau, 2009).

Feminists point out that historically, women have had less chance for upward mobility than men because most working women hold clerical jobs (such as secretary) and service positions (such as food server) that offer few opportunities for advancement.

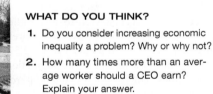

SEEING SOCIOLOGY IN EVERYDAY LIFE — As CEOs Get Richer, the Great Mansions Return

I grew up in Elkins Park, Pennsylvania, an older Philadelphia suburb that is a mostly middle-class community, although like most of suburbia, some neighborhoods boast bigger houses than others. What made Elkins Park special was that a century ago, a handful of great mansions were built by early Philadelphia industrialists. Back then, all there was to the town was these great "estates," separated by fields and meadows. By about 1940, however, most of this land had been split off into lots for the homes of newer middle-class suburbanites. The great mansions suddenly seemed out of place, with heirs disagreeing over who should live there and how to pay the rising property taxes. As a result, many of the great mansions were sold, the buildings taken down, and the land subdivided.

In the 1960s, when I was a teenager, a short bike ride could take me past the Breyer estate (built by the founder of the ice-cream company, now the township police building), the Curtis estate (built by a magazine publisher and transformed into a community park), and the Wanamaker estate (built by the founder of a large Philadelphia department store, now the site of high-rise apartments). Probably the grandest of them all was the Wiedner estate, modeled after a French chateau, complete with doorknobs and window pulls covered in gold; it now stands empty.

In their day, these structures were not just home to a family and many servants; they were also monuments to a time when the rich were, well, *really* rich. By contrast, the community that emerged on the grounds once owned by these rich families is middle-class, with modest homes on small lots.

But did the so-called Gilded Age of great wealth disappear forever? No. By the 1980s, a new wave of great mansions was being built in the United States. Take the architect Thierry Despont, who designs huge houses for the super-rich. One of Despont's "smaller" homes might be 20,000 square feet (about ten times the size of the average U.S. house), and they go all the way up to 60,000 square feet (as big as any of the Elkins Park mansions built a century ago and almost the size of the White House). These megahomes have

Indianapolis Star, Charlie Nye\AP Wide World Photos

kitchens as large as college classrooms, exercise rooms, indoor swimming pools, and even indoor tennis courts (Krugman, 2002).

Megahouses are being built by newly rich chief executive officers (CEOs) of large corporations. Although CEOs have always made more money than most people, recent years have seen executive compensation soar. Between 1970 and 2008, the average U.S. family saw only a modest increase in income (about 26 percent after inflation is taken into account). During the same period, the average compensation for the 100 highest-paid CEOs skyrocketed from $1.3 million (about 40 times the earnings of an average worker at that time) to $29.7 million (equal to 494 times the compensation of today's average worker). Richer still, the twenty highest-earning investment fund managers in 2008 (a terrible year for the stock market) had, on average, $465 million *each* in income, earning more in ten minutes than an average worker made all year (Story, 2009; Corporate Library, 2010; U.S. Census Bureau, 2010).

WHAT DO YOU THINK?

1. Do you consider increasing economic inequality a problem? Why or why not?

2. How many times more than an average worker should a CEO earn? Explain your answer.

3. Does very high CEO pay help or hurt stockholders? What about the general public? Explain your reasoning.

Over time, however, the earnings gap between women and men has been narrowing. Women working full time in 1980 earned 60 percent as much as men working full time; by 2008, women were earning 77 percent as much (U.S. Census Bureau, 2009).

Mobility and Marriage

Research points to the conclusion that marriage has an important effect on social standing. In a study of women and men in their for-ties, Jay Zagorsky (2006) found that people who marry and stay married accumulate about twice as much wealth as people who remain single or who divorce. Reasons for this difference include the fact that couples who live together typically enjoy double incomes and also pay only half the bills they would have if they were single and living in separate households.

It is also likely that compared to single people, married men and women work harder in their jobs and save more money. Why? Primarily because they are working not just for themselves but to

Seeing Sociology
in Everyday Life

In your opinion, how significantly has the recent economic
downturn affected people's optimism about their ability to
realize the "American dream"?

relative poverty the lack of resources of some people in
relation to those who have more

absolute poverty a lack of resources that is life-threatening

feminization of poverty the trend of women
making up an increasing proportion of the poor

support children and spouses who are counting on them (Popenoe, 2006).

Just as marriage pushes social standing upward, divorce usually makes social position go down. Couples who divorce take on the costs of supporting two households, which leaves them with less money for savings or other investment. After divorce, women are hurt more than men because typically the man earns more. Many women who divorce lose not only most of their income but also benefits such as health care and insurance coverage (Weitzman, 1996).

The American Dream: Still a Reality?

The expectation of upward social mobility is deeply rooted in U.S. culture. Through much of our history, the economy has grown steadily, raising living standards. Today, at least for some people, the American dream is alive and well. In 2008, fully 26 percent of U.S. families earned $100,000 or more, compared with just 7 percent back in 1967 (in dollars controlled for inflation). There are now at least 7 million millionaires in the United States, five times the number a decade ago (Rank & Hirschl, 2001; L. Eisenberg, 2007; U.S. Census Bureau, 2009; Wolff, 2009).

Yet not all indicators are so positive. Note these disturbing trends:

1. **For many workers, earnings have stalled.** The annual income of a fifty-year-old man working full time climbed by 65 percent between 1958 and 1974 (from $29,345 to $48,367 in constant 2008 dollars). Between 1974 and 2008, however, this worker's income fell by 6 percent to $45,540, even as the number of hours worked increased and the cost of necessities such as housing, education, gasoline, and medical care went way up (Russell, 1995a; U.S. Census Bureau, 2009).

2. **More jobs offer little income.** The expanding global economy has moved many industrial jobs overseas, reducing the availability of high-paying factory work here in the United States. At the same time, the expansion of our service economy means more of today's jobs—in fast-food restaurants or large discount stores—offer relatively low wages.

3. **Young people are remaining at home.** Currently, more than half of young people aged eighteen to twenty-four, unable to support a household, are still living with their parents. Since 1975, the average age at first marriage has moved upward four years (to 25.9 years for women and 28.1 years for men).

Over the past generation, more people have become rich, and the rich have become richer; as the Seeing Sociology in Everyday Life box explains, the highest-paid corporate executives have

enjoyed a runaway rise in their earnings. But at the same time, the increasing share of low-paying jobs has brought downward mobility for millions of families, feeding the fear that the chance to enjoy a middle-class lifestyle is slipping away. As a glance back at Figure 4 shows, although median family income doubled between 1950 and 1973, it has grown by only 18 percent since then (U.S. Census Bureau, 2009).

For years, the mass media have presented the American Dream as alive and well in "reality" shows such as *American Idol*, which is based on the idea that talent and effort can make anyone rich and famous. More recently, as Seeing Sociology in the News on the next two pages explains, television shows are presenting a more pessimistic view of people's chances to get ahead.

The Global Economy and the U.S. Class Structure

Underlying the shifts in U.S. class structure over recent decades is global economic change. Much of the industrial production that gave U.S. workers high-paying jobs a generation ago has been moved overseas, where wages are cheaper. With less industry at home, the United States now serves as a vast consumer market for industrial goods such as cars, stereos, cameras, and computers made in China, Japan, South Korea, and elsewhere.

High-paying jobs in manufacturing, held by 28 percent of U.S. workers in 1960, support fewer than 10 percent of workers today. In their place, the economy offers service work, which pays far less. Traditionally high-paying corporations such as USX (formerly United States Steel) now employ fewer people than the expanding McDonald's chain, and fast-food clerks make only a fraction of what steelworkers earn.

The global reorganization of work has not been bad news for everyone. The global economy is driving upward social mobility for educated people who specialize in law, finance, marketing, and computer technology. Even allowing for the downturn in 2008 and 2009, the global economic expansion also helped push up the stock market more than tenfold between 1980 and 2010, reaping profits for families with money to invest.

But the same trend has hurt many average workers, who have lost their factory jobs and now perform low-wage service work. In addition, many companies (General Motors and Ford are recent examples) have downsized—cutting the ranks of their workforce—in an attempt to stay competitive in world markets. As a result, although more than 50 percent of all married-couple families today contain two or more people in the labor force—more than twice the share in 1950—many families are working harder than ever before simply to hold on to what they have (A. L. Nelson, 1998; Sennett, 1998; U.S. Census Bureau, 2009).

The New York Times

Waking Up from American Dreams

By ANAND GIRIDHARADAS
February 13, 2010

The recent Super Bowl triumph of the New Orleans Saints fits the traditional narrative of limitless American possibility: a long-shot victory by a written-off team from a fate-battered city. But for the 38.6 million Americans who kept their televisions on after the game to watch the new reality show *Undercover Boss*, a different narrative was on offer, with a darker portrait of the extant American Dream.

American Idol–style contests have dominated reality television in the United States in recent years, with the Horatio Alger–style story line that anyone with talent and pluck can rise. *Undercover Boss* was built very differently, for a nation that is day by day growing more skeptical of that story line and more susceptible to other, less hopeful narratives.

Each week, the show dispatches a top executive at a leading American company to labor anonymously among his rank-and-file workers. It plays not on the traditional American fantasy that you,

too, can begin in the mailroom and become C.E.O. Instead, as the viewer comments online suggest, the show taps into a feeling that many Americans once considered un-American: pleasure in seeing the high and mighty humbled.

In the first episode, Larry O'Donnell, the president of Waste Management . . . is stunned to discover working-class realities. He is shocked that workers must punch in after lunch and lose two minutes of pay for every minute they are late. He encounters a worker with chronic kidney problems who must keep working. . . .

This being American television, there is, of course, a narrative twist. Mr. O'Donnell returns to his real life, shaken by his excursion among the people.

He summons his new working-class friends to headquarters one by one to disclose his identity. But it is revealing of present American realities that he makes no effort to change the system overall. . . . Rather, he throws them scraps—changing the lunch-tardiness policy, switching a working mother he met from an hourly to a salaried position. . . .

The Horatio Alger narrative maintains its hold in the United States. A Gallup/*USA Today* poll last year found that three-quarters of Americans still believe that if you work hard and follow the rules, you can achieve the American Dream.

But a large number of people also tell pollsters that it is becoming harder to get ahead, that tension is rising between rich and poor, that the rich are rich because of connections and fortunate birth. And for this writer, who recently returned to America after six years in India, it is hard to ignore a quiet turning in the culture . . . toward ideas more familiar in feudal places: that class is a fate, not a situation; that the contest is rigged against the underdog.

In India, a suffix enforces such stratification. It is "-wallah," and can be added to a service to denote the kind of person who provides it, generation after generation. A dhobiwallah is an inevitable launderer, a chaiwallah an inevitable server of tea. At times, it feels as if America, too, is becoming a Wallah Society.

Two sociologists, Greggor Mattson and Claude Fischer . . . recently concluded in the *Annual*

Poverty in the United States

Social stratification creates both "haves" and "have-nots." All systems of social inequality create poverty, or at least **relative poverty,** *the lack of resources of some people in relation to those who have more.* A more serious but preventable problem is **absolute poverty,** *a lack of resources that is life-threatening.*

About 1.4 billion human beings around the world—one person in five—are at risk of absolute poverty. Even in the affluent United States, families go hungry, sleep in parked cars or on the streets, and suffer from poor health simply because they are poor.

The Extent of Poverty

In 2008, the government classified 39.8 million men, women, and children—13.2 percent of the U.S. population—as poor. This count of relative poverty refers to families with income below an official poverty line, which, for a family of four, was set that year at $22,025. The poverty line is about three times what the government estimates a family will spend for food. But the income of the average poor family was just 59 percent of this amount. This means that the typical poor family had to get by on less than $13,000 in 2008 (U.S. Census Bureau, 2009).

Who Are the Poor?

Although no single description fits all poor people, poverty is greater among certain categories of our population. Where these categories overlap, the problem is especially serious.

Age

A generation ago, the elderly were the category of the population at greatest risk for poverty. But thanks to better retirement programs offered today by private employers and the government, the poverty rate for people over age sixty-five fell from 30 percent in 1967 to 9.7 percent—well below the national average—in 2008. Looking at it from another angle, about 9.2 percent (3.7 million) of the poor are elderly.

Today the burden of poverty falls most heavily on children and young adults. In 2008, some 19 percent of people under age eighteen (14.1 million children) and 18.4 percent of people ages eighteen to twenty-four (5.3 million young adults) were poor. Put another way, 49 percent of the U.S. poor are young people under the age of twenty-five.

Race and Ethnicity

Seventy percent of all poor people are white (including some who also describe themselves as Hispanic); 24 percent are African

Review of Sociology that class, among the least-discussed fault lines, has become the most salient— even more salient than race. . . . Increasingly, they write, rich and poor Americans live in separate, impermeable worlds: one of relatively plentiful salaried jobs [and] vibrant neighborhoods . . . and another that sees those things, and the larger dream, receding.

The shift can be sensed in American restaurants. What once distinguished them from restaurants elsewhere was an idea of classlessness: that the person with the grease-stained notepad and aching feet could, with luck and effort, become the person at the table; that there was no essential difference between them.

But the archetypal American waiter today is no longer the eager-eyed college student, paying his way through school, hatching big plans. Waiting tables is increasingly a profession, as in France, with older, brusquer servers whose vision of the world is tinged with resentment.

There is a quiet but unmistakable defensiveness in their voices, which ask in every interaction, "What, you think you're better than me?". . .

Humor can be more revealing than seriousness, and fiction more revealing than truth. So a good place to watch this turning in American ideas is *30 Rock*, the hit television show. . . .

Jack Donaghy, played by Alec Baldwin, is a suave, arrogant, heavily bonused television executive who lives in a world of private jets, secret restaurants, and [custom-made] suits. If earlier New York comedies like *Seinfeld* and *Friends* airbrushed class, giving everyone nice apartments regardless of occupation, *30 Rock* depicts a Goldman Sachsed America where the rich and not-rich spin in different orbits.

Alexis de Toqueville once marveled at an America where servants were "equals of their masters." . . . Yet in Jack Donaghy's America the classes have so diverged as to be physically distinct. When Mr. Donaghy crashes a younger colleague's high-school reunion and blends right in, he explains it thus: "Rich 50 is middle-class 38."

In another episode, in an echo of recent economic history, Mr. Donaghy convinces Kenneth . . . to surrender his life savings of $4,000 to be invested on his behalf. . . .

"Next stop: homeownership," Mr. Donaghy mocks. "I'm just kidding. The middle class is dying. You'll be renting forever."

Moments later, Kenneth learns that the stock has collapsed. All his money is lost.

WHAT DO YOU THINK?

1. Do you think reality shows like *American Idol* realistically portray people's ability to rise in the class system based on talent and hard work?

2. How realistic is the portrayal of our class system in *30 Rock*, which presents the rich and poor as living in different and disconnected worlds?

3. Do you feel that, if you work hard and follow the rules, you can achieve the American Dream? Explain your personal views on this question.

American (also including some who say they are also Hispanic). But in relation to their overall numbers, African Americans are about three times as likely as whites to be poor. In 2008, some 24.7 percent of African Americans (9.4 million people) lived in poverty, compared with 23.2 percent of Hispanics (11 million), 11.8 percent of Asian Americans (1.6 million), and 8.6 percent of non-Hispanic whites (17 million). The poverty gap between whites and minorities has changed little since 1975.

People of color have especially high rates of child poverty. Among African American children, 34.7 percent are poor; the comparable figures are 30.6 percent among Hispanic children and 10.6 percent among non-Hispanic white children (U.S. Census Bureau, 2009).

Gender and Family Patterns

Of all poor people age eighteen or older, 59 percent are women and 41 percent are men. This difference reflects the fact that women who head households are at high risk of poverty. Of all poor families, 48 percent are headed by women with no husband present, and just 8 percent are headed by single men.

The United States has experienced a **feminization of poverty**, which is defined as *the trend of women making up an increasing proportion of the poor*. In 1960, only 25 percent of all poor households were headed by women; the majority of poor families had both wives and husbands in the home. By 2008, however, the proportion of poor families headed by single women had nearly doubled to 48 percent.

The feminization of poverty is one result of a larger trend: the rapidly increasing number of households at all class levels headed by single women. This trend, coupled with the fact that households headed by women are at high risk of poverty, helps explain why women and their children now make up an increasing share of the U.S. poor.

Urban and Rural Poverty

In the United States, the greatest concentration of poverty is found in central cities, where the 2008 poverty rate stood at 17.7 percent. The poverty rate in suburbs is 9.8 percent. Thus the poverty rate for urban areas as a whole is 12.9 percent, lower than the 15.1 percent found in rural areas. National Map 1 shows that most of the counties with the highest poverty rate in the United States are rural.

Explaining Poverty

The richest nation on Earth contains tens of millions of poor people, a fact that raises serious questions. It is true, as some analysts remind us, that most poor people in the United States are far better off than

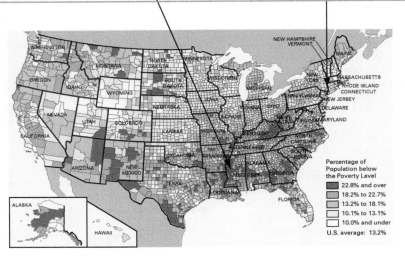

Anna Mae Peters lives in Nitta Yuma, Mississippi. Almost everyone she knows lives below the government's poverty line.

Julie Garland lives in Greenwich, Connecticut, where people have very high income and there is little evidence of poverty.

Explore the percentage of people living in poverty in your local community and in counties across the United States on mysoclab.com

Seeing Ourselves

NATIONAL MAP 1

Poverty across the United States

This map shows that the poorest counties in the United States—where the poverty rate is more than twice the national average—are in Appalachia, spread across the Deep South, along the border with Mexico, near the Four Corners region of the Southwest, and in the Dakotas. Can you suggest some reasons for this pattern?

Explore on mysoclab.com

Source: U.S. Census Bureau (2009).

Percentage of Population below the Poverty Level
- 22.8% and over
- 18.2% to 22.7%
- 13.2% to 18.1%
- 10.1% to 13.1%
- 10.0% and under

U.S. average: 13.2%

---

the poor in other countries: 34 percent of U.S. poor families own a home, 70 percent own a car, and only about 19 percent say they often go without food (U.S. Census Bureau, 2009). But there is little doubt that poverty harms the overall well-being of millions of people in this country.

Why is there poverty in the first place? We will examine two opposing explanations that lead to a lively and important political debate.

One View: Blame the Poor

One view holds that *the poor are primarily responsible for their own poverty.* Throughout the nation's history, people have placed a high cultural value on self-reliance, convinced that a person's social standing is mostly a matter of individual talent and effort. According to this view, society offers plenty of opportunities to anyone who is able and willing to take advantage of them, and the poor are people who cannot or will not work due to a lack of skills, schooling, or motivation.

In his study of Latin American cities, the anthropologist Oscar Lewis (1961) concluded that the poor become trapped in a *culture of poverty,* a lower-class subculture that can destroy people's ambition to improve their lives. Socialized in poor families, children become resigned to their situation, producing a self-perpetuating cycle of poverty.

In 1996, hoping to free people from what some saw as a culture of poverty in the United States, Congress changed the welfare system, which had provided a federal guarantee of financial assistance to poor people since 1935. The federal government continues to send money to the states to distribute to needy people, but benefits now carry strict limits—in most cases, no more than two years at a stretch and a total of five years altogether if a person moves in and out of the welfare system. The stated purpose of this reform was to force people to be self-supporting and move them away from dependency on government.

Another View: Blame Society

A different position, argued by the sociologist William Julius Wilson (1996a, 1996b; see also Mouw, 2000), holds that *society is primarily responsible for poverty.* Wilson points to the loss of jobs in our inner cities as the primary cause of poverty, claiming that there is simply not enough work to support families. Wilson sees any apparent lack of trying on the part of the poor as a result of little opportunity rather than as a cause of poverty. From Wilson's point of view, Lewis's analysis amounts to *blaming the victim,* that is, saying that victims are responsible for their own suffering (W. Ryan, 1976). To combat poverty and reduce the need for welfare, Wilson argues, the government should fund jobs and provide affordable child care for low-income mothers and fathers.

CRITICAL REVIEW The U.S. public is evenly divided over whether government or people themselves should take responsibility for reducing poverty (NORC, 2009:403). Government statistics show that 53 percent of the heads of poor families did not work at all during 2008, and an additional 31 percent worked only part time (U.S. Census Bureau, 2009). Such facts seem to support the "blame the poor" position because a major cause of poverty is not holding a job.

But the reasons that people do not work are more in step with the "blame society" position. Middle-class women may be able to combine working and child rearing, but this is much harder for poor

---

Social Stratification

Read "The Compassion Gap in American Poverty Policy" by Fred Block et al. on mysoclab.com

Seeing Sociology in Everyday Life

Our society has been more generous with the "worthy" poor (such as elderly people) than with the "unworthy" poor (such as able-bodied people who, we assume, should take care of themselves). Why do you think we have not done more to reduce poverty among children, who surely fall into the "worthy" category?

women who cannot afford child care, and few employers provide child care programs. As William Julius Wilson explains, many people are jobless not because they are avoiding work but because there are not enough jobs to go around. In short, the most effective way to reduce poverty is to ensure a greater supply of jobs as well as child care for parents who work (W. J. Wilson, 1996a; Pease & Martin, 1997; Duncan, 1999; Bainbridge, Meyers, & Waldfogel, 2003). Read on mysoclab.com

CHECK YOUR LEARNING Explain the view that the poor should take responsibility for poverty and the view that society is responsible for poverty. Which is closer to your own view?

The Working Poor

Not all poor people are jobless, and the *working poor* command the sympathy and support of people on both sides of the poverty debate. In 2008, some 16 percent of heads of poor families (1.3 million women and men) worked at least fifty weeks of the year and yet could not escape poverty. Another 31 percent of these heads of families (2.5 million people) remained poor despite having part-time employment. Put differently, 3.2 percent of heads of families who work full time earn so little that they remain poor (U.S. Census Bureau, 2009). Since July 2009, the the federal minimum wage has been $7.25 per hour. But at this level, working is no guarantee of escaping poverty—even earning $8.00 per hour, a full-time worker cannot lift an urban family of four above the poverty line.

Individual ability and personal initiative do play a part in shaping social position. However, the weight of sociological evidence points toward society, not individual character traits, as the primary source of poverty, because more and more available jobs offer only low wages. In addition, the poor are *categories* of people—female heads of families, people of color, people in inner-city neighborhoods isolated from the larger society—who face special barriers and limited opportunities.

The Controversy & Debate box takes a closer look at the current welfare debate. Understanding this important social issue can help us decide how our society should respond to the problem of poverty, as well as the problem of homelessness discussed next.

Homelessness

Each year, the government's Department of Housing and Urban Development conducts a national survey of cities and towns to find out how many people in the United States are homeless. The 2008

Henry Ossawa Tanner (1859-1937) *The Thankful Poor.* Private Collection. Art Resource, NY.

The African American artist Henry Ossawa Tanner captured the humility and humanity of impoverished people in his painting *The Thankful Poor*. This insight is important in a society that tends to define poor people as morally unworthy and deserving of their bitter plight.

Henry Ossawa Tanner (1859–1937), *The Thankful Poor*. Private collection. Art Resource, New York.

survey found about 664,414 people living in shelters, in transitional housing, and on the street on a single night in January. But, the government estimates, a much larger number—approximately 1.6 million people—are homeless for at least some time during the course of the year (U.S. Department of Housing and Urban Development, 2009). As with earlier estimates of the homeless population, critics claimed that the HUD estimate undercounted the homeless, who may well have numbered several million people. Some estimates suggest that as many as 3 million people are homeless for at least one night in a given year. In addition, they add, evidence suggests that the number of homeless people in the United States is increasing (L. Kaufman, 2004; National Coalition for the Homeless, 2009).

The familiar stereotypes of homeless people—men sleeping in doorways and women pushing rickety shopping carts containing everything they own—have been replaced by the "new homeless": people thrown out of work because of plant closings, women who take their children and leave home to escape domestic violence, women and men forced out of apartments by rent increases, and

Go to the Multimedia Library at mysoclab.com
to listen to the NPR report "A Few Small Steps
to Homelessness"

Seeing Sociology
in Everyday Life

Do you think people in the United States consider
homelessness to be a serious problem? Why or why not?

CONTROVERSY & DEBATE

The Welfare Dilemma

MARCO: *(rushing in through the door)* Sorry I'm late. I stopped at the store and got stuck behind some welfare mother in the checkout lane.

SERGEI: *(looking back with a confused grin)* Exactly what does a person on welfare look like?

What is *your* image of a welfare recipient? If you are like many people in the United States, you might think of a middle-aged African American woman. But you would be wrong. In truth, the typical person receiving welfare in this country is a child who is white.

There is a lot of confusion about welfare. There is also disagreement about whether this type of assistance is a good or bad idea. In 1996, Congress debated the issue and enacted a new law that ended the federal government's role in providing income assistance to poor households. In place of this federal program, new state-run programs now offer limited help to the poor, but they require people who receive aid to get job training or find work—or have their benefits cut off.

To understand how we got to where we are, let's begin by explaining what, exactly, welfare is. The term "welfare" refers to an assortment of policies and programs designed to improve the well-being of some low-income people. Until the welfare reform of 1996, most people used the term to refer to just one part of the overall system: Aid for Families with Dependent Children (AFDC), a federal program of monthly financial support for parents (mostly single women) to care for themselves and their children. In 1996, about 5 million households in the United States received AFDC for at least some part of the year.

David Urbina/PhotoEdit Inc.

Is society responsible for poverty or are individuals themselves to blame? When it comes to homeless families, most people think society should do more.

Conservatives opposed AFDC, claiming that rather than reducing child poverty, AFDC made the problem worse, in two ways. First, they claimed that AFDC weakened families, because for years after the program began, it paid benefits to poor mothers only if no husband lived in the home. As a result, the government was actually providing an economic incentive to women to have children outside of marriage, and they blame it for the rapid rise of out-of-wedlock births among poor people. To conservatives, marriage is one key to reducing poverty: Only about one in twenty married-couple families are poor; more than nine in ten AFDC families were headed by an unmarried woman.

Second, conservatives believe that welfare encourages poor people to become dependent on government handouts, the main reason that eight out of ten poor heads of households did not have full-time jobs. Furthermore, only 5 percent of single mothers receiving AFDC worked full time, compared to more than half of nonpoor single mothers. Conservatives say that welfare gradually moved well beyond its original purpose of short-term help to nonworking women with children (say, after

others unable to meet mortgage or rent payments because of low wages or no work at all. Today, no stereotype paints a complete picture of the homeless.

The large majority of homeless people report that they do not work, although about 20 percent have at least a part-time job (U.S. Conference of Mayors, 2007). Working or not, all homeless people have one thing in common: poverty. For that reason, the explanations of poverty just presented also apply to homelessness. Some people blame the *personal traits* of the homeless. More than one-third of homeless people are substance abusers, and one-fourth are mentally ill. More broadly, a fraction of 1 percent of our population, for one reason or another, seems unable to cope with our complex and highly competitive society (U.S. Department of Housing and Urban Development, 2009). ◯ Go to mysoclab.com

Others see homelessness resulting from *societal factors,* including low wages and a lack of affordable housing (Kozol, 1988; Bohannan, 1991; L. Kaufman, 2004). Supporters of this position point out that about one-third of the homeless consist of families, and children are the fastest-growing category of the homeless.

No one disputes that a large proportion of homeless people are personally impaired to some degree, but cause and effect are difficult to untangle. Long-term structural changes in the U.S. economy, cutbacks in social service budgets, and the recent economic downturn have all contributed to the problem of homelessness.

● Seeing Sociology
in Everyday Life

Do you see evidence of homelessness in your community?
Has the problem become worse during the recent economic
recession?

● Seeing Sociology
in Everyday Life

What are the arguments typically made by Democratic and
Republican politicians on the issue of poverty?

divorce or death of a husband) and gradually became a way of life. Once trapped in dependency, poor women would raise children who were themselves likely to be poor as adults.

Liberals have a different view. Why, they ask, do people object to government money going to poor mothers and children when most "welfare" actually goes to richer people? The cost of AFDC was as high as $25 billion annually—no small sum, to be sure, but much less than the $516 billion in annual Social Security benefits Uncle Sam provides to more than 40 million of our senior citizens, most of whom are not poor. And it is just a small fraction of the more than $1 trillion "bailout money" Congress voted in 2008 and 2009 to assist the struggling financial industry.

Liberals insist that most poor families who turn to public assistance are truly needy. Most of the people who are helped in this way are children. And they don't get very much. The typical household receives only about $500 per month in assistance, hardly enough to attract people to a life of welfare dependency. Even adding some additional money in the form of food stamps, households assisted by welfare still struggle well below the poverty line everywhere in the country. Therefore, liberals see

public assistance as a "Band-Aid approach" to the serious social problems of too few jobs and too much income inequality in the United States. As for the charge that public assistance weakens families, liberals agree that the share of families with one parent has gone up, but they see single parenting as a broad trend found at all class levels in many countries.

Back in 1996, the conservative arguments carried the day, ending the AFDC program. Our society's individualistic culture has always encouraged us to blame people themselves (rather than society) for poverty, which becomes a sign not of need but of laziness and personal failure (Inglehart et al., 2000). This view of the poor is probably the biggest reason that led Congress to replace the federal AFDC program with state-run programs called Temporary Assistance for Needy Families (TANF), requiring poor adults to get job training and limiting income assistance to two consecutive years with a lifetime limit of five years.

By 2008, the new TANF policy had cut the number of households receiving income assistance by more than half. This means that many single parents who were once on welfare have taken jobs or are receiving job training. With this mind, conservatives who

supported welfare reform see the new program as a huge success. The welfare rolls have been cut, and more people have moved from receiving a check to working to support themselves. But liberals claim that the reform is far from successful. They point out that many of the people who are now working earn so little pay that they are hardly better off than before. In other words, the reform has greatly reduced the number of people receiving welfare, but it has done little to reduce the extent of poverty.

WHAT DO YOU THINK?

1. How does our cultural emphasis on self-reliance help explain the controversy surrounding public assistance? Why do people not criticize benefits (such as home mortgage deductions) for people who are better off?

2. Do you approve of the time limits on benefits built into the TANF program? Why or why not?

3. Why do you think the welfare reforms have done little to reduce poverty?

Sources: Lichter & Crowley (2002), Lichter & Jayakody (2002), Von Drehle (2008), and U.S. Census Bureau (2009).

Class, Welfare, Politics, and Values

We have reviewed many facts about social inequality. In the end, however, our opinions about wealth and poverty depend not just on facts but also on our politics and values. As we might expect, the idea that social standing reflects personal merit is popular among well-off people; the opposing idea, that government should spread wealth more equally, finds favor among those who are less well off (NORC, 2009).

In the United States, our cultural emphasis on individual responsibility encourages us to see successful people as personally worthy and to view poor people as personally falling short. Such attitudes go a long way toward explaining why our society spends much more than

other high-income nations on education (to promote opportunity) but much less on public assistance programs (which directly support the poor).

Most members of our society are willing to accept a high level of income inequality, and many hold a harsh view of the poor. To the extent that we define poor people as undeserving, we look on public assistance programs as at best a waste of money and at worst a substitute for personal initiative.

Finally, the drama of social stratification extends far beyond the borders of the United States. The most striking social inequality is found not by looking inside one country but by comparing living standards in various parts of the world.

Seeing Sociology in Everyday Life

Social Stratification

How do we understand inequality in our society?

This chapter sketches the class structure of the United States and also explains how factors such as race are linked to social standing. You already know, for example, that the rate of poverty is three times higher for African Americans than for whites, and you have also learned that the typical black family earns just 57 percent as much as the typical (non-Hispanic) white family. But rich people—here, we'll define "rich" as a family earning more than $75,000 a year—come in all colors. Here's a chance to test your sociological thinking by answering several questions about how race affects being rich. Look at each of the statements below: Does the statement reflect reality or is it a myth?

1. In the United States, all rich people are white. *Reality or myth?*

2. Rich white families are actually richer than rich African American families. *Reality or myth?*

3. People in rich black families don't work as hard as members of rich white families. *Reality or myth?*

4. When you are rich, color doesn't matter. *Reality or myth?*

David De Lossy/Photodisc/Getty Images

1. *Of course, this is a myth.* But when it comes to being rich, race does matter: About 23 percent of African American families are affluent (for Hispanic families, 22 percent), compared to about 46 percent of non-Hispanic white families.

2. *Reality.* Rich white, non-Hispanic families have a mean (average) income more than $200,000 per year. Rich African American families average about $130,000 per year.

3. *Myth.* On average, rich black families are more likely to rely on multiple incomes (that is, they have more people working) than their white counterparts. In addition, rich white families receive more unearned income—income from investments—than rich African American families.

4. *Myth.* Rich African Americans still face social barriers based on their race, just as rich whites benefit from the privileges linked to their color.

Ronnie Kaufman/CORBIS- NY

Applying SOCIOLOGY in Everyday Life

1. Identify three ways in which social stratification is evident in the everyday lives of students on your campus. In each case, explain exactly what is unequal and what difference it makes. Do you think individual talent or family background is more important in creating these social differences?

2. Sit down with parents, grandparents, or other relatives, and assess the social position of your family over the last three generations. Has social mobility taken place? How much? Why?

3. During an evening of television viewing, assess the social class level of the characters you see on various shows. In each case, explain why you assign someone a particular social position. Do you find many clearly upper-class people? Middle-class people? Working-class people? Poor people? Describe the patterns you find.

Making the Grade

Social Stratification

⊙—[Watch on mysoclab.com

What Is Social Stratification?

SOCIAL STRATIFICATION is a system by which a society ranks categories of people in a hierarchy, so that some people have more money, power, and prestige than others.
Social stratification

- is a trait of society, not simply a reflection of individual differences
- carries over from one generation to the next
- is supported by a system of cultural beliefs that defines certain kinds of inequality as just
- takes two general forms: caste systems and class systems

social stratification a system by which a society ranks categories of people in a hierarchy

social mobility a change in position within the social hierarchy

caste system social stratification based on ascription, or birth

class system social stratification based on both birth and individual achievement

meritocracy social stratification based on personal merit

status consistency the degree of uniformity in a person's social standing across various dimensions of social inequality

structural social mobility a shift in the social position of large numbers of people due more to changes in society itself than to individual efforts

ideology cultural beliefs that justify particular social arrangements, including patterns of inequality

CASTE SYSTEMS

- are based on birth (ascription)
- permit little or no social mobility
- shape a person's entire life, including occupation and marriage
- are common in traditional, agrarian societies

CLASS SYSTEMS

- are based on both birth (ascription) and **meritocracy** (individual achievement)
- permit some social mobility
- are common in modern industrial and postindustrial societies

Theoretical Analysis of Social Stratification

The **STRUCTURAL-FUNCTIONAL APPROACH** points to ways social stratification helps society operate.

- The **Davis-Moore thesis** states that social stratification is universal because of its functional consequences.
- In caste systems, people are rewarded for performing the duties of their position at birth.
- In class systems, unequal rewards attract the ablest people to the most important jobs and encourage effort.

The **SOCIAL-CONFLICT APPROACH** claims that stratification divides societies into classes, benefiting some categories of people at the expense of others and causing social conflict.

- Karl Marx claimed that capitalism places economic production under the ownership of capitalists, who exploit the proletarians who sell their labor for wages.
- Max Weber identified three distinct dimensions of social stratification: economic class, social status or prestige, and power. Conflict exists between people at various positions on a multidimensional hierarchy of **socioeconomic status (SES)**.

Davis-Moore thesis the functional analysis claiming that social stratification has beneficial consequences for the operation of society

capitalists people who own and operate factories and other businesses in pursuit of profits

proletarians people who sell their labor for wages

alienation the experience of isolation and misery resulting from powerlessness

blue-collar occupations lower-prestige jobs that involve mostly manual labor

white-collar occupations higher-prestige jobs that involve mostly mental activity

socioeconomic status (SES) a composite ranking based on various dimensions of social inequality

conspicuous consumption buying and using products because of the "statement" they make about social position

The **SYMBOLIC-INTERACTION APPROACH**, a micro-level analysis, explains that we size people up by looking for clues to their social standing. **Conspicuous consumption** refers to buying and displaying products that make a "statement" about one's position in the social class system. Most people tend to socialize with others whose social standing is similar to their own.

See the *Applying Theory* table.

Social Stratification and Technology: A Global Perspective

Hunting and Gathering → Horticultural and Pastoral → Agrarian ⟶ Industrial ⟶ Postindustrial

- Gerhard Lenski explains that advancing technology initially increases social stratification, which is most intense in agrarian societies.

- Industrialization reverses the trend, reducing social stratification.

- In postindustrial societies, social stratification again increases.

See the *Kuznets curve* (Figure 2).

Inequality in the United States

SOCIAL STRATIFICATION involves many dimensions:

- *Income*: Earnings from work and investments are unequal, with the richest 20% of families earning twelve times as much as the poorest 20% of families.
- *Wealth*: The total value of all assets minus debts, wealth is distributed more unequally than income, with the richest 20% of families holding 85% of all wealth.
- *Power*: Income and wealth are important sources of power.
- *Prestige*: Work generates not only income but also prestige. White-collar jobs generally offer more income and prestige than blue-collar jobs. Many lower-prestige jobs are performed by women and people of color.
- *Family ancestry*, *race and ethnicity*, and *gender* all affect social standing.

income earnings from work or investments

wealth the total value of money and other assets, minus outstanding debts

Social Classes in the United States

$200,000

$200,000

$61,000

$61,000

$28,000

$28,000

UPPER CLASS—5% of the population. Most members of the upper-upper class, or "old rich," inherited their wealth; the lower-upper class, or "new rich," work at high-paying jobs.

MIDDLE CLASS—40 to 45% of the population. People in the upper-middle class have significant wealth; average-middles have less prestige and do white-collar work, and most attend college.

WORKING CLASS—30 to 35% of the population. People in the lower-middle class do blue-collar work; only about one-third of children attend college.

LOWER CLASS—20% of the population. Most people in the lower class lack financial security due to low income; many live below the poverty line; half do not complete high school.

intragenerational social mobility a change in social position occurring during a person's lifetime

intergenerational social mobility upward or downward social mobility of children in relation to their parents

- People with higher social standing generally have better health, hold certain values and political attitudes, and pass on advantages in the form of "cultural capital" to their children.
- Social mobility is common in the United States, as it is in other high-income countries, but typically only small changes occur from one generation to the next.
- Due to the expansion of the global economy, the richest families now earn more than ever; families near the bottom of the class system have seen only small increases.

Poverty in the United States

POVERTY PROFILE

- The government classifies 40 million people— 13.2% of the population—as poor.
- About 49% of the poor are young people under age 24.
- About 70% of the poor are white, but in relation to their population, African Americans and Hispanics are more likely to be poor.
- The "feminization of poverty" means that more poor families are headed by women.
- About 47% of the heads of poor families are among the "working poor" who work at least part time but do not earn enough to lift a family of four above the poverty line.
- Estimates place the number of people who are homeless at some time over the course of a year at between 1.6 and 3 million.

EXPLANATIONS OF POVERTY

- Blame individuals: The culture of poverty thesis states that poverty is caused by shortcomings in the poor themselves (Oscar Lewis).
- Blame society: Poverty is caused by society's unequal distribution of wealth and lack of good jobs (William Julius Wilson).

relative poverty the lack of resources of some people in relation to those who have more

absolute poverty a lack of resources that is life-threatening

feminization of poverty the trend of women making up an increasing proportion of the poor

●─ Read on mysoclab.com

◉─ Explore on mysoclab.com

Sample Test Questions

Multiple-Choice Questions

1. *Social stratification* refers to
   a. job specialization in modern societies.
   b. ranking categories of people in a hierarchy.
   c. the fact that some people work harder than others.
   d. inequality of personal talent and individual effort.

2. A caste system is social stratification
   a. based on individual achievement.
   b. based on merit.
   c. based on birth.
   d. in which just two categories of people are unequal.

3. Sonja has two advanced degrees, an average salary, and is working at a low-prestige job. Which concept best describes her situation?
   a. low status consistency
   b. horizontal social mobility
   c. upward social mobility
   d. high status consistency

4. According to the Davis-Moore thesis,
   a. equality is functional or useful for society.
   b. the more inequality a society has, the more productive it is.
   c. more important jobs must offer enough rewards to draw talent from less important work.
   d. societies with more meritocracy are less productive than those with caste systems.

5. Karl Marx claimed that society "reproduces the class structure." By this he meant that
   a. society benefits from inequality.
   b. class differences are passed on from one generation to the next.
   c. class differences are the same everywhere in the world.
   d. a classless society is impossible.

6. Max Weber claimed that social stratification is based on
   a. economic class.
   b. social status or prestige.
   c. power.
   d. All of the above are correct.

7. The wealthiest 20 percent of people in the United States own about how much of the country's privately owned wealth?
   a. 35 percent
   b. 55 percent
   c. 85 percent
   d. 95 percent

8. Which of the following jobs is an example of high-prestige work?
   a. telephone operator
   b. college professor
   c. child care worker
   d. cashier

9. Which of the following is another term for the working class?
   a. upper-middle class
   b. average-middle class
   c. lower class
   d. lower-middle class

10. Which quintile (20 percent) of the U.S. population has seen the greatest change in income over the last generation?
    a. the top quintile
    b. the middle quintile
    c. the lowest quintile
    d. All quintiles have seen the same change.

11. Change in social position during a person's own lifetime is called
    a. intergenerational social mobility.
    b. intragenerational social mobility.
    c. structural social mobility.
    d. horizontal social mobility.

12. Which age category of the U.S. population has the highest poverty rate?
    a. young people under the age of eighteen
    b. adults in their thirties
    c. middle-aged people in their forties
    d. seniors over age sixty-five

ANSWERS: 1(b); 2(c); 3(a); 4(c); 5(b); 6(d); 7(c); 8(b); 9(d); 10(a); 11(b); 12(a).

Essay Questions

1. Explain why social stratification is a creation of society and not just a reflection of individual differences.

2. How do caste and class systems differ? How are they the same? Why does industrialization introduce a measure of meritocracy into social stratification?

3. What is the extent of poverty in the United States? Who are the poor in terms of age, race and ethnicity, and gender?

The Growing Wealth Gap

HOLLY SKLAR
CHUCK COLLINS
BETSY LEONDAR-WRIGHT

Is the gap between the very few rich and the many, many poor increasing? The authors of this article argue that it is. Where is the gap most pronounced? The authors argue that the gap is apparent in a number of places and they offer specific examples such as less net worth for the average American household, greater debt, increases in food pantry visits, employed homeless people, and a greater number of people at risk to retire among countless others. All, however, is not lost. They conclude the article with some realistic strategies for narrowing the gap using social policy.

The booming economy has been a bust for millions of Americans. Most households have lower inflation-adjusted net worth now than they did in 1983, when the Dow was still at 1,000.

The top 1 percent of households have soared while most Americans have been working harder to stay in place, if they have not fallen further behind. Since the 1970s, the top 1 percent of households have doubled their share of the national wealth to 40 percent. The top 1 percent of households have more wealth than the entire bottom 95 percent. Financial wealth is even more concentrated. The top 1 percent of households have nearly half of all financial wealth (net worth minus net equity in owner-occupied housing), says economist Edward Wolff of New York University. Wealth is further concentrated at the top of the top 1 percent. The richest 0.5 percent of households have 42 percent of the financial wealth.

The total net worth of the median American household just about matches the projected sticker price of Ford's new supersized sports utility vehicle, the Excursion. Adjusting for inflation, the net worth of the household in the middle (the median household) fell from $54,600 in 1989 to $49,900 in 1997. Median financial wealth fell from $13,000 in 1989 to $11,700 in 1997.

The percentage of households with zero or negative net worth (greater debts than assets) increased from 15.5 percent in 1983 to 18.5 percent in 1995—nearly one out of five households. That's nearly double the rate in 1962 when the comparable figure was 9.8 percent—one out of ten households. The net worth of the poorest fifth of households averaged –$5,600 in 1997. That's down from –$3,000 in 1983.

Many households are deeper in debt. Debt as a percentage of personal income rose from 58 percent in 1973 to 76 percent in 1989 to an estimated 85 percent in 1997.

The growth in household debt has helped keep the economy growing despite wage stagnation at home and economic turmoil abroad—at a significant cost to many families and the nation's long-term economic health. "The unsustainable growth in debt," says John Schmitt of the Economic Policy Institute, "undermines the stability of the recovery and threatens to magnify the impact of any downturn." A rise in interest rates "could put some newly-indebted households over the edge. Even a mild increase in unemployment could produce a substantial rise in bad debts, private bankruptcies, and mortgage foreclosures."

The stock market boom has sent the fortunes of some Americans soaring while leaving many others in the dust. At a 15 percent annual return—big by historical standards—investments double about every five years. The recent stock market has done much better than that.

From 1983 to 1998, the Standard & Poor's 500 Index (S&P 500), a much broader gauge of the stock market than the Dow, grew a cumulative 1,336 percent with dividends reinvested. If you had put $10,000 in the stock market in 1983, you could have more than $143,000 today. Unfortunately, most Americans didn't have the $10,000 to invest then, and they don't have it today. A million dollars invested by a wealthy American in S&P 500 index stocks in 1983 would have ballooned to $14.4 million by the end of 1998.

Between 1983 and 1995, the S&P 500 delivered a huge cumulative return of 582 percent (with dividends reinvested). At the same time, the median household net worth dropped 11 percent and the bottom 40 percent lost an incredible 80 percent. The top 1 percent, meanwhile, gained 17 percent.

Between 1995 and 1998, S&P 500 stocks had an annualized return of 30 percent. Most of it went to the top 10 percent of households.

Four out of ten households now own stock directly and indirectly, but most still don't own much. Almost 90 percent of the value of all stocks and mutual funds owned by households is in the hands of the top 10 percent. According to Edward Wolff, an estimated 42 percent of the benefits of the increase in the stock market between 1989 and 1997 went to the richest 1 percent alone. The bottom 80 percent of households split 11 percent of the gains.

◉ The Wage Gap

Nine years into the longest peacetime expansion in U.S. history, average workers are still earning less, adjusting for inflation, than they did when Richard Nixon was president. Despite long-overdue wage growth since 1996, hourly wages for average workers in 1998 were still 6.2 percent below 1973, adjusting for inflation; weekly wages were 12 percent lower than in 1973. Nonfarm business productivity grew nearly 33 percent in the same period, according to the Economic Policy Institute.

What if wages had kept rising with productivity? What if they were 33 percent higher in 1998 than they were in 1973? The average hourly wage in 1998 would have been $18.10, rather than $12.77. That's a difference of $5.33 an hour—more than $11,000 for a full-time, year-round worker. The 30 cents workers gained in their hourly wages between 1997 and 1998 pales by comparison.

The pace of recent wage growth has already slowed despite tight labor markets in many parts of the country. The cumulative wages lost since 1973 will never be recovered—much less their lost investment potential.

The minimum wage has become a poverty wage. It was 19 percent lower in 1998 at $5.15 than it was in 1979, when it was worth $6.39, adjusted for inflation. The minimum wage used to bring a family of three, with a full-time worker, above the official poverty line. Now it doesn't bring a full-time worker with one child above the official poverty line.

Many Americans can't make ends meet today, much less build assets for the future. A recent study by the Urban Institute, *Snapshots of America's Families*, found that many families with incomes up to 200 percent of the federal poverty level—which they call lower-income families—had trouble supporting themselves and their families. Nearly three in ten lower-income families were unable to pay the mortgage, rent or utility bills at some point in the prior year. Nearly half of lower-income families reported worrying about or having difficulty affording food.

Low-income workers are turning increasingly to food banks and homeless shelters, which cannot keep up with the rising demand. In its 1998 survey of 30 major cities, the U.S. Conference of Mayors found that requests for emergency shelter by homeless families had risen 15 percent during the past year; 30 percent of the requests went unmet. The mayors also found that more than one-fifth of the urban homeless were employed. The mayors found that requests for emergency food increased an average of 14 percent during the past year. One out of five requests for food assistance went unmet.

A survey by Second Harvest, the nation's largest private network of food charities, found that nearly 40 percent of the households who received Second Harvest food in 1997 had at least one employed person. Recent visitors to a Greenwich, Connecticut food bank included "a cook from a local French restaurant, a construction worker, housekeepers from nearby estates who made the minimum wage, $5.15 an hour, and a woman who cared for the children of housekeepers" (*New York Times,* February 26, 1999).

According to the Washington-based Wider Opportunities for Women and the Boston-based Women's Educational and Industrial Union, the self-sufficiency standard (the level of income necessary to meet all basic needs, including taxes) for an adult and preschooler in high-cost Boston is $32,279— nearly twice the official poverty line for a family of four. In lower-cost Berkshire County, Massachusetts it's $24,678. No wonder many low-income workers—including growing numbers of former welfare recipients—can't make ends meet. Recent studies of former recipients and those combining work and welfare have found they typically earn between $8,000 and $10,800 annually. Most do not receive paid vacation, sick leave, or health benefits from their employers.

Retired people's incomes have long been said to rest on a "three-legged stool" of Social Security (and Medicare), private savings, and employer pensions. The stool is wobbling for some retirees and collapsing for others, as savings decline and pension coverage deteriorates.

Fewer than half of all workers (47 percent) were covered by pensions in 1996—down from 51 percent in 1979. To make matters worse, there has been a shift away from traditional "defined benefit" pension plans, which guarantee workers fixed retirement payments based on pre-retirement wages and years of service, toward "defined contribution" plans, such as 401(k)s, that take a chunk out of workers' paychecks and saddle employees with all the investment risk. According to the Economic Policy Institute, defined contribution plans accounted for 42 percent of all pension plans in 1997, up from 13 percent in 1975.

Lower-wage workers are far less likely than high-wage workers to be covered by any employer-sponsored retirement plan, further exacerbating the wealth gap. Only 16 percent of the lowest wage workers (the bottom fifth by income) were covered by employer-provided pension plans in 1996, versus 73 percent of workers in the top fifth. In addition to placing the investment risk on employees, defined contribution plans require employee contributions in order to receive company matching contributions, if offered. Many low-wage workers faced with the dilemma of choosing between feeding and housing their family today and saving for retirement in the future, do not participate in defined contribution plans even when given the option.

◉ Home $weet Home

As the Children's Defense Fund observes, "Homeownership has long been a central part of the American dream. It is also a major source of financial security and stability for young families, and an essential means of accumulating the equity that has enabled countless families later to borrow money in order to stave off a crisis, send a child to college, or help start a family business."

Fueled by low mortgage interest rates, the U.S. homeownership rate hit a record 66 percent in 1998, but for people under age 55, the rates were actually lower in 1998 than in 1982.

The biggest government support for home-ownership comes in the form of the tax deduction for mortgage interest on owner-occupied first and second homes. Unfortunately, much of the tax write-off goes to higher-income families. The more you can already afford to spend, the more the government subsidizes you. As the *New York Times* reports (January 10, 1999), for each dollar in tax savings from the mortgage-interest deduction "going to the average taxpayer making $200,000 or more, the average taxpayer in all lower income groups combined saves just 6 cents."

For the fiscal year ending September 30, 1999, the mortgage deduction will add up to about $53.7 billion. That's $23 billion more than total 1998 federal spending by the Department of Housing and Urban Development (under $31 billion). The mortgage deduction costs 23 times as much as the credit for low-income housing investment ($2.3 billion).

While tax subsidies for affluent homeowners remained high, federal funding for low-income housing was cut by 80 percent from 1978 to 1991, adjusting for inflation. Not surprisingly, shortages of affordable housing have increased greatly.

◉ The Racial Wealth Gap

While the racial income gap is terribly wide, the racial wealth gap is even worse. According to Edward Wolff, the median black household had a net worth of just $7,400 in 1995—about 12 percent of the $61,000 in median wealth for whites. Median black financial wealth (net worth minus home equity) was just $200—a mere 1 percent of the $18,000 in median financial wealth for whites. In the same year, nearly one out of three black households had zero or negative net worth, twice the rate among whites.

Hispanic households have even less wealth than blacks. The median Hispanic household had a net worth of only $5,000 in 1995—just 8 percent of whites. Median financial wealth was actually zero.

Because of employment, housing, insurance, and other discrimination, black and Latino families are far less likely than whites to own the homes in which they live. In 1995, the homeownership rate was 47 percent for blacks and 44 percent for Hispanics, about two-thirds the rate for white households (69 percent).

In 1999, the *Kansas City Star* analyzed mortgage applications taken by more than 500 area banks and mortgage companies from 1992 to 1997. As reported by Ted Sickinger, a former commercial loan officer, "lenders still reject minority mortgage applicants far more frequently than they do whites. Even high-income minorities are rejected more frequently than whites with lower incomes."

Moreover, "most loans made in minority neighborhoods refinance existing debt and are made by companies that often charge higher interest rates and fees. In white neighborhoods, by contrast, most loans are made at market rates and go to buy homes—the kind of lending that helps borrowers build wealth." Unlike the overt redlining of the past, the *Kansas City Star* found "discrimination with a smile."

Melvin Oliver and Thomas Shapiro analyzed the asset gap in their book, Black Wealth/White Wealth. Even if differences in income, occupation, education, and other factors are removed from the equation, a difference of $43,143 in average net worth remained in 1988. They call it "the costs of being black." For married couples, the difference was greater: $46,294. Housing discrimination is a major factor. Inheritance is another. White parents generally have far greater resources to pay for their children's college education, help them with their first home purchase, and bequeath them assets at death.

As Oliver and Shapiro observe, "Wealth signifies the command over financial resources that a family has accumulated over its lifetime along with those resources that have been inherited across generations."

Inequality is a matter of life and death—and not just for the poor. In the words of the University of Washington International Health Program and Health Alliance International, "the greater the income differences within populations (whether of whole countries or of cities or larger administrative areas within countries), the worse their health. This helps explain why the United States, the richest and most powerful country in the world (spending more than any other on health care), ranks below 25th in the league of countries ordered by life expectancy. Income differences between rich and poor are bigger in the United States than in any other developed nation."

A July 1998 report in the *American Journal of Public Health* found that higher income inequality is associated with increased mortality at all per capita income levels. "Given the mortality burden associated with income inequality," the report concludes, "business, private, and public sector initiatives to reduce economic inequalities should be a high priority."

◉ Closing the Wealth Gap

Increased inequality is not the result of natural phenomena like sun spots or shifting winds. It is the result of over two decades of public policies and private corporate practices that have benefitted asset owners at the expense of wage earners.

Where are we headed? "The Atlanta-based Affluent Market Institute predicts that by 2005 America's millionaires will control 60 percent of the nation's purchasing dollars," notes Jeff Gates in *The Ownership Solution*.

"Money makes money," said Adam Smith, author of *The Wealth of Nations*, long ago. Immediate steps are needed to enable low- and moderate-income families to earn, save, and invest more money, and build asset security. Here are some of the recommendations we offer in *Shifting Fortunes* to narrow the wealth gap.

KidSave Accounts Act. Legislation advanced by Senator Robert Kerrey (D-NE) with bipartisan support would guarantee every American child $1,000 at birth, plus $500 a year for children ages one to five, to be invested until retirement. Through compound returns over time, the account would grow substantially, provide a significant supplement to Social Security and other retirement funds, and enable many more Americans to leave inheritances to their children. That would strengthen opportunities and asset-building across generations. At an 8.5 percent return, for example, $1,000 set aside at birth would be worth $250,000 at age 65; the additional $2,500 set aside in the child's first five years would be worth $470,000.

Broadening Employee Ownership. While the overall trend in wealth growth has been toward concentration, a significant exception is among employee owners. As of 1997, more than 8 percent of total corporate equity was owned by non-management employees, up from less than 2 percent in 1987. This ownership takes the forms of Employee Stock Ownership Plans (ESOPs), profit-sharing plans, widely granted stock options, and other forms of broad ownership. In 1997, average employee owners had about $35,000 in corporate equity above what they were able to save from their paychecks.

In *The Ownership Solution,* Jeff Gates urges us to look beyond wage and job policies to expand the ownership stake that workers and their communities have in private enterprise. There are a range of public policies that could promote broader ownership and reward companies that share the wealth with employees, consumers and other stakeholders. These include encouraging employee ownership through government purchasing, licensing rights, public pension plan investments, loans and loan guarantee programs, and so on.

Individual Development Accounts (IDAs). IDAs are like individual retirement accounts, but are targeted to low- and moderate-income households to assist them in asset accumulation. Participants in IDAs may have their contributions matched by public or private dollars. A number of private charities have financed pilot IDA programs through community-based organizations. A generous federally funded matching IDA program would provide significant opportunities for asset-poor households to build wealth. Participants could withdraw funds from IDAs in order to purchase a home, finance a small business or invest in education or job-training. Even small amounts of money can make a substantial difference in whether or not individuals get on the asset-building train.

Living Wages and Full Employment. People would obviously have greater ability to save if their wages were higher. Low real wages have pushed a growing number of families into debt. Decent wages would enable families to save money, purchase assets, and plan for the future. Wage remedies include higher state and federal minimum wages and the passage of living wage ordinances. Protecting the right of employees to organize and join unions also greatly increases their wage earning potential. Laws prohibiting employment discrimination on the basis of race, gender, and so on should be strongly enforced.

Of course, you can't earn wages if you can't find a job. Government policies should promote full employment and assure jobs for every American who needs one.

Expand Earned Income Credit and Raise No-Tax Threshold. Progressive tax policies can enable families to keep more money in their pockets. These include an expanded earned income credit, an increased personal exemption, and a higher no-tax threshold.

Income Equity Act. Taxpayers presently subsidize excessive corporate executive salaries. Rep. Martin Sabo (D-MN) has introduced legislation to cap the tax deductibility of all salaries and bonuses at 25 times the lowest-paid worker in a firm. It would provide an incentive to increase salaries at the bottom. In the 105th Congress, there were over 60 cosponsors for this bipartisan legislation.

Taxing Capital Gains Like Wages. The tax burden is being shifted off of large asset owners and onto wage earners. The Social Security payroll tax has taken an increasingly bigger bite out of the paychecks of most wage earners, especially low- and middle-wage earners since income subject to Social Security tax is capped (the cap is now $72,600). Meanwhile, taxes on capital gains have been reduced substantially. Because of the 1997 Taxpayer Relief Act, which gave relief to the rich by reducing the tax rate on long-term capital gains from 28 percent to 20 percent, many workers now pay a higher tax rate on income from wages than wealthy investors pay on realized capital gains. A fair tax system would not favor income from assets over income from wages.

The wealth gap poses serious consequences for our economy, our communities, and our democracy. It's time to reduce the wealth gap and strengthen national prosperity.

◉ ◉ ◉

Questions

1. Describe the reality of the stock market for the average American investor.

2. Review the article for information related to employment. Isolate and construct a picture of employment in the United States. What strategies do the authors offer to empower the American worker? What other things might be done to improve the plight of the average American worker?

3. Describe what the authors mean by, "the costs of being black." What are the costs?

4. Examine the recommendations for narrowing the income gap. Debate which one appears to be the most realistic and immediate.

5. Review the recommendations for how to help low and moderate income families to earn, save, invest more money, and build security for themselves and their families. Explain which of these plans would make the biggest difference in people's lives.

Gender Stratification

From Chapter 10 of *Society: The Basics*, 11/e. John J. Macionis. Copyright © 2011 by Pearson Education. All rights reserved.

Gender Stratification

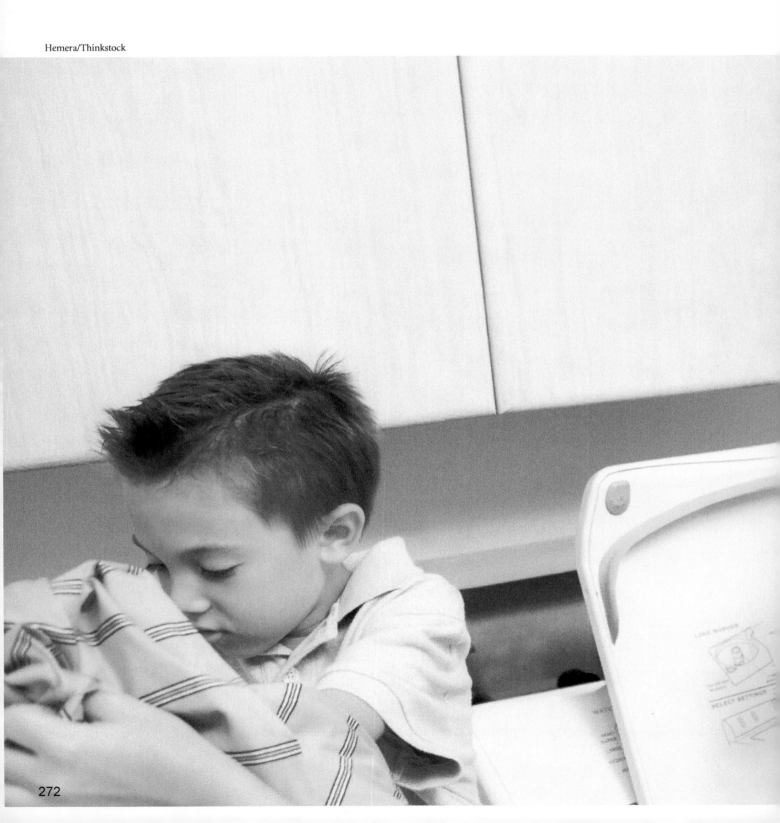

- How is gender a creation of society?

- What differences does gender make in people's lives?

- Why is gender an important dimension of social stratification?

Watch the *Core Concepts in Sociology* video "Similarities and Differences between Men and Women" on **mysoclab.com**

This chapter examines gender—the meaning societies attach to being female or male—and explains why gender is an important dimension of social stratification.

CORBIS- NY

At first we traveled quite alone . . . but before we had gone many miles, we came on other wagon-loads of women, bound in the same direction. As we reached different cross-roads, we saw wagons coming from every part of the country and, long before we reached Seneca Falls, we were a procession.

So wrote Charlotte Woodward in her journal as she made her way in a horse-drawn wagon along the rutted dirt roads leading to Seneca Falls, a small town in upstate New York. The year was 1848, a time when slavery was legal in much of the United States and the social standing of all women, regardless of color, was far below that of men. Back then, in much of the country, women could not own property, keep their own wages if they were married, draft a will, file lawsuits in a court (including lawsuits seeking custody of their own children), or attend college, and husbands were widely viewed as having unquestioned authority over their wives and children.

Some 300 women gathered at Wesleyan Chapel in Seneca Falls to challenge this second-class citizenship. They listened as their leader, Elizabeth Cady Stanton, called for expanding women's rights and opportunities, including the right to vote. At that time, most people considered such a proposal absurd and outrageous. Even many of those attending the conference were shocked by the idea: Stanton's husband, Henry, rode out of town in protest (Gurnett, 1998).

Much has changed since the Seneca Falls convention, and many of Stanton's proposals are now accepted as matters of basic fairness. But as this chapter explains, women and men still lead different lives in the United States and elsewhere in the world; in most respects, men are still in charge. This chapter explores the importance of gender and explains that gender, like class position, is a major dimension of social stratification.

Gender and Inequality

Biological differences divide the human population into categories of female and male. **Gender** refers to *the personal traits and social positions that members of a society attach to being female or male.* Gender, then, is a dimension of social organization, shaping how we interact with others and even how we think about ourselves. More important, gender also involves *hierarchy,* placing men and women in different positions in terms of power, wealth, and other resources. This is why sociologists speak of **gender stratification,** *the unequal distribution of wealth, power, and privilege between men and women.* In short, gender affects the opportunities and constraints we face throughout our lives.

Male-Female Differences

Many people think there is something "natural" about gender distinctions because biology does make one sex different from the other. But we must be careful not to think of social differences in biological terms. In 1848, for example, women were denied the vote because many people assumed that women did not have enough intelligence or interest in politics. Such attitudes had nothing to do with biology; they reflected the *cultural patterns* of that time and place.

Another example is athletic performance. In 1925, most people—both women and men—believed that the best women runners could never compete with men in a marathon. Today, as Figure 1 shows, the gender gap has greatly narrowed, and the best women runners routinely post better times than the fastest men of decades past. Here again, most of the differences between men and women turn out to be socially created.

Differences in physical ability between the sexes do exist. On average, males are 10 percent taller than women, 20 percent heavier, and 30 percent stronger, especially in the upper body (Ehrenreich, 1999). On the other hand, women outperform men in the ultimate

Gender Stratification

game of life itself: Life expectancy for men is 75.1 years, and women can expect to live 80.2 years (Heron et al., 2009).

In adolescence, males do a bit better on the mathematics and reading portions of the SAT, while females show stronger writing skills, differences that reflect both biology and socialization (Lewin, 2008; College Board, 2009). However, research does not point to any overall differences in intelligence between males and females.

Biologically, then, men and women differ in limited ways, with neither one naturally superior. But culture can define the two sexes differently, as the global study of gender described in the next section shows.

Gender in Global Perspective

The best way to see how gender is based in culture is by comparing one society to another. Three important studies highlight just how different "masculine" and "feminine" can be.

The Israeli Kibbutz

In Israel, collective Jewish settlements are called *kibbutzim.* The *kibbutz* (the singular form of the word) has been an important setting for gender research because gender equality is one of its stated goals; men and women share in both work and decision making.

In recent decades, kibbutzim have become less collective and thus less distinctive organizations. But for much of their history, both sexes shared most everyday jobs. Many men joined women in taking care of children, and women joined men in repairing buildings and providing armed security. Both sexes made everyday decisions for the group. Girls and boys were raised in the same way; in many cases, young children were raised together in dormitories away from parents. Women and men in the kibbutzim achieved remarkable (although not complete) social equality, evidence that culture defines what is feminine and what is masculine.

Margaret Mead's Research

The anthropologist Margaret Mead carried out groundbreaking research on gender. If gender is based in the biological differences between men and women, she reasoned, people everywhere should define "feminine" and "masculine" in the same way; if gender is cultural, these concepts should vary.

Mead (1963, orig. 1935) studied three societies in New Guinea. In the mountainous home of the Arapesh, Mead observed men and women with remarkably similar attitudes and behavior. Both sexes, she reported, were cooperative and sensitive to others—in short, what our culture would label "feminine."

Moving south, Mead studied the Mundugumor, whose head-hunting and cannibalism stood in striking contrast to the gentle ways of the Arapesh. In this culture, both sexes were typically selfish and aggressive, traits we define as "masculine."

The women's movement of the 1960s encouraged women to show their true abilities.

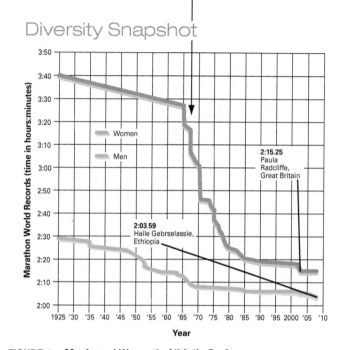

Diversity Snapshot

FIGURE 1 Men's and Women's Athletic Performance

Do men naturally outperform women in athletic competition? The answer is not obvious. Early in the twentieth century, men outpaced women by more than an hour in marathon races. But as opportunities for women in athletics have increased, women have been closing the performance gap. Only eleven minutes separate the current world marathon records for women (set in 2003) and for men (set in 2008).

Source: Marathonguide.com (2010).

Finally, traveling west to the Tchambuli, Mead discovered a culture that, like our own, defined females and males differently. But, Mead reported, the Tchambuli *reversed* many of our ideas of gender: Females were dominant and rational, and males were submissive, emotional, and nurturing toward children. Based on her observations, Mead concluded that culture is the key to gender distinctions because what one society defines as masculine another may see as feminine.

Some critics view Mead's findings as "too neat," as if she saw in these societies just the patterns she was looking for. Deborah Gewertz (1981) challenged what she called Mead's "reversal hypothesis," pointing out that Tchambuli males are really the more aggressive sex. Gewertz explains that Mead visited the Tchambuli (who themselves spell their name Chambri) during the 1930s, after they had lost much of their property in tribal wars, and observed men rebuilding their homes, a temporary role for Chambri men.

Do you think female and male athletes should compete on the same teams? Why or why not? Do you think men and women see this issue differently?

matriarchy a form of social organization in which females dominate males

patriarchy a form of social organization in which males dominate females

sexism the belief that one sex is innately superior to the other

George Murdock's Research

In a broader study of more than 200 preindustrial societies, George Murdock (1937) found some global agreement on which tasks are feminine and which masculine. Hunting and warfare, Murdock observed, generally fall to men, and home-centered tasks such as cooking and child care tend to be women's work. With their simple technology, preindustrial societies apparently assign roles reflecting men's and women's physical characteristics. With their greater size and strength, men hunt game and protect the group; because women bear children, they do most of the work in the home.

Beyond this general pattern, Murdock found much variety. Consider agriculture: Women did the farming in about the same number of societies as men; in most societies, the two sexes divided this work. When it came to many other tasks, from building shelters to tattooing the body, Murdock found that preindustrial societies were as likely to turn to one sex as the other.

CRITICAL REVIEW Global comparisons show that overall, societies do not consistently define tasks as feminine or masculine. With industrialization, the importance of muscle power declines, further reducing gender differences (Nolan & Lenski, 2007). In sum, gender is too variable to be a simple expression of biology; what it means to be female and male is mostly a creation of society.

CHECK YOUR LEARNING By comparing many cultures, what do we learn about the origin of gender differences?

Patriarchy and Sexism

Conceptions of gender vary, and there is evidence of societies in which women have greater power than men. One example is the Musuo, a very small society in southwestern China's Yunnan province, in which women control most property, select their sexual partners, and make most decisions about everyday life. The Musuo appear to be a case of **matriarchy** ("rule by mothers"), *a form of social organization in which females dominate males,* which has only rarely been documented in human history.

The pattern found almost everywhere in the world is **patriarchy** ("rule by fathers"), *a form of social organization in which males dominate females.* Global Map 1 shows the great variation in the relative power and privilege of women that exists from country to country. According to the United Nations' gender development index, Australia, Iceland, and Norway give women the highest social standing; by contrast, women in the Central African Republic, Sierra Leone, Mali, Afghanistan, and Niger have the lowest social standing compared with men. Of the world's 194 nations, the United States was ranked nineteenth in terms of gender equality (United Nations Development Programme, 2009).

The justification for patriarchy is **sexism,** *the belief that one sex is innately superior to the other.* Sexism is not just a matter of individual attitudes; it is built into the institutions of our society. *Institutional sexism* is found throughout the economy, with women highly concentrated in low-paying jobs. Similarly, the legal system has long excused violence against women, especially on the part of boyfriends, husbands, and fathers.

The Costs of Sexism

Sexism limits the talents and the ambitions of the half of the human population who are women. Although men benefit in some respects from sexism, their privilege comes at a high price. Masculinity in our culture encourages men to engage in many high-risk behaviors: using tobacco and alcohol, playing dangerous sports, and even driving recklessly. As Marilyn French (1985) argues, patriarchy drives men to relentlessly seek control, not only of women but also of themselves and their world. Thus masculinity is linked not only to accidents but also to suicide, violence, and stress-related diseases. The *Type A personality*—marked by chronic impatience, driving ambition, com-

Suzanne Porter\Alamy Images

In every society, people assume that certain jobs, patterns of behavior, and ways of dressing are "naturally" feminine while others are just as obviously masculine. But in global perspective, we see remarkable variety in such social definitions. These men, Wodaabe pastoral nomads who live in the African nation of Niger, are proud to engage in a display of beauty most people in our society would consider feminine.

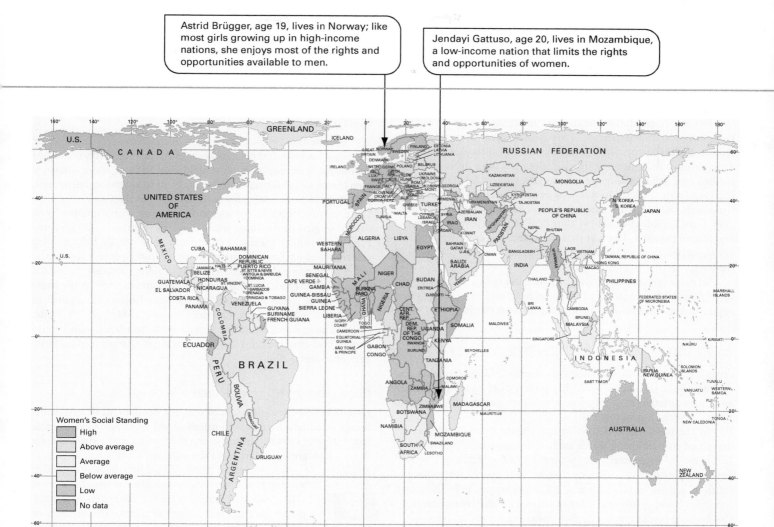

Astrid Brügger, age 19, lives in Norway; like most girls growing up in high-income nations, she enjoys most of the rights and opportunities available to men.

Jendayi Gattuso, age 20, lives in Mozambique, a low-income nation that limits the rights and opportunities of women.

Window on the World

GLOBAL MAP 1 **Women's Power in Global Perspective**

Women's social standing in relation to men's varies around the world. In general, women live better in rich countries than in poor countries. Even so, some nations stand out: In Australia, Iceland, and Norway women come closest to social equality with men.

Source: United Nations Development Programme (2009).

petiveness, and free-floating hostility—is one cause of heart disease and an almost perfect match with the behavior our culture considers masculine (Ehrenreich, 1983).

Finally, as men seek control over others, they lose opportunities for intimacy and trust. As one analyst put it, competition is supposed to "separate the men from the boys." In practice, however, it separates men from men and everyone else (Raphael, 1988).

Must Patriarchy Go On?

In preindustrial societies, women have little control over pregnancy and childbirth, which limits the scope of their lives. In those same societies, men's greater height and physical strength are valued resources that give them power. But industrialization, including birth control technology, increases people's choices about how to live. In societies like our own, biological differences offer little justification for patriarchy.

Gender Stratification

● Seeing Sociology
in Everyday Life

Did you grow up in a home in which females and males had different jobs and responsibilities? How did this experience affect your view of gender?

gender roles (also known as **sex roles**) attitudes and activities that a society links to each sex

But males are dominant in the United States and elsewhere. Does this mean that patriarchy is inevitable? Some researchers claim that biological factors such as differences in hormones and slight differences in brain structure "wire" the sexes with different motivations and behaviors—especially aggressiveness in males—making patriarchy difficult or perhaps even impossible to change (S. Goldberg, 1974; Rossi, 1985; Popenoe, 1993b; Udry, 2000). However, most sociologists believe that gender is socially constructed and *can* be changed. The fact that no society has completely eliminated patriarchy does not mean that we must remain prisoners of the past.

To understand why patriarchy continues today, we next examine how gender is rooted and reproduced in society, a process that begins in childhood and continues throughout our lives.

Gender and Socialization

From birth until death, gender shapes human feelings, thoughts, and actions. Children quickly learn that their society considers females and males different kinds of people; by about age three, they begin to think of themselves in these terms.

In the past, many people in the United States traditionally described women using terms such as "emotional," "passive," and "cooperative." By contrast, men were described as "rational," "active," and "competitive." It is curious that we were taught for so long to think of gender in terms of one sex being opposite to the other, especially because women and men have so much in common and also because research suggests that most people develop personalities that are a mix of feminine and masculine traits (Bem, 1993).

Just as gender affects how we think of ourselves, so it teaches us how to behave. **Gender roles** (also known as **sex roles**) are *attitudes and activities that a society links to each sex.* A culture that defines males as ambitious and competitive encourages them to seek out positions of leadership and play team sports. To the extent that females are defined as deferential and emotional, they are expected to be supportive helpers and quick to show their feelings.

Sex is a biological distinction that develops prior to birth. Gender is the meaning that a society attaches to being female or male. Gender differences are a matter of power, because what is defined as masculine typically has more importance than what is defined as feminine. Infants begin to learn the importance of gender by the way parents treat them. Do you think this child is a girl or a boy? Why?

Gender and the Family

The first question people usually ask about a newborn—"Is it a boy or a girl?"—has great importance because the answer involves not just sex but the likely direction of the child's life. In fact, gender is at work even before a child is born, because especially in lower-income nations, parents hope their firstborn will be a boy rather than a girl.

Soon after birth, family members welcome infants into the "pink world" of girls or the "blue world" of boys (Bernard, 1981). People even send gender messages in the way they handle infants. One researcher at an English university presented an infant dressed as either a boy or a girl to a number of women; her subjects handled the "female" child tenderly, with frequent hugs and caresses, while treating the "male" child more aggressively, often lifting him up high in the air or bouncing him on a knee (Bonner, 1984; Tavris & Wade, 2001). The lesson is clear: The female world revolves around cooperation and emotion, and the male world puts a premium on independence and action.

Gender and the Peer Group

About the time they enter school, children begin to move outside the family and make friends with others of the same age. Considerable research points to the fact that young children tend to form single-sex play groups (Martin & Fabes, 2001).

Peer groups teach additional lessons about gender. After spending a year watching children at play, Janet Lever (1978) concluded that boys favor team sports with complex rules and clear objectives such as scoring runs or making touchdowns. Such games nearly always have winners and losers, reinforcing masculine traits of aggression and control.

Girls, too, play team sports. But, Lever explains, girls also play hopscotch, jump rope, or simply talk, sing, or dance. These activities have few rules, and rarely is victory the ultimate goal. Instead of teaching girls to be competitive, Lever explains, female peer groups promote the interpersonal skills of communication and cooperation, presumably the basis for girls' future roles as wives and mothers.

The games we play offer important lessons for our later lives. Lever's observations recall Carol Gilligan's gender-based theory of moral reasoning. Boys, Gilligan (1982) claims, reason according to abstract principles. For them, "rightness" amounts to

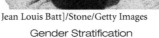

Jean Louis Batt]/Stone/Getty Images

Gender Stratification

● Seeing Sociology
in Everyday Life

Consider the statements "He fathered the child" and "She
mothered the child." How do you think gender shapes the
meaning of parenting?

● Seeing Sociology
in Everyday Life

What is your declared or likely major? Based on the classes
you have taken, what share of students in this major are
female and what share are male? Does this pattern agree
with those described here?

In our society, the mass media have enormous influence on our attitudes and behavior, and what we see shapes our views of gender. In the 2009 film *Twilight*, we see a strong, "take charge" male playing against a more passive female. Do you think the mass media create these gender patterns? Or it is more correct to say that they reproduce them? Is there another option?

Newscom

banking services, industrial companies, and alcoholic beverages. The authoritative voiceover—the voice that describes a product on television and radio—is almost always male (D. M. Davis, 1993).

A careful study of gender in advertising reveals that men usually appear taller than women, implying male superiority. Women, by contrast, are more frequently presented lying down (on sofas and beds) or, like children, seated on the floor. Men's facial expressions and behavior give off an air of competence and imply dominance; women often appear childlike, submissive, and sexual. Men focus on the products being advertised, and women often focus on the men (Goffman, 1979; Cortese, 1999).

Finally, advertising perpetuates what Naomi Wolf (1990) calls the "beauty myth." The Seeing Sociology in Everyday Life box on the next page takes a closer look at how this myth affects both women and men.

"playing by the rules." By contrast, girls consider morality a matter of responsibility to others.

Gender and Schooling

Gender shapes our interests and beliefs about our own abilities, guiding areas of study and, eventually, career choices (Correll, 2001). In high school, more girls than boys learn secretarial skills and take vocational classes such as cosmetology and food services. Classes in woodworking and auto mechanics attract mostly young men.

Women have now become a majority (57 percent) of the students on college campuses across the United States. As their numbers have increased, women have become well represented in many fields of study that once excluded them, including mathematics, chemistry, and biology. But men still predominate in many fields, including engineering, physics, and philosophy, and women cluster in the fine arts (including music, dance, and drama) as well as the social sciences (including anthropology and sociology). Newer areas of study are also gender-typed: More men than women take computer science, and courses in gender studies enroll mostly women.

Gender and the Mass Media

Since television captured the public imagination in the early 1950s, white males have held center stage; racial and ethnic minorities were all but absent from television until the early 1970s. And when both sexes appeared on camera, men generally played the brilliant detectives, fearless explorers, and skilled surgeons. Women played the less capable characters, often unnecessary except for the sexual interest they added to the story.

Historically, advertisements have shown women in the home, cheerfully using cleaning products, serving food, trying out appliances, and modeling clothes. Men predominate in ads for cars, travel,

Gender and Social Stratification

Gender involves more than how people think and act. It is also about how society is organized, how our lives are affected by social hierarchy. The reality of gender stratification can be seen in just about every aspect of our everyday lives. We look, first, to the world of working women and men.

Working Women and Men

In 1900, just one-fifth of women were in the U.S. labor force. Today, this figure has tripled, to 60 percent, and 75 percent of these working women work full time. The once common view that earning income is a man's role no longer holds true.

Factors that have contributed to change in the U.S. labor force include the decline of farming, the growth of cities, shrinking family size, and a rising divorce rate. The United States, along with most other nations of the world, considers women working for income the rule rather than the exception. Women make up almost half the U.S. paid labor force, and more than half of U.S. married couples depend on two incomes.

In the past, many younger women in the labor force were childless. But today, 60 percent of married women with children under age six are in the labor force, as are 74 percent of married women with children between six and seventeen years of age. For widowed, divorced, or separated women with children, the comparable figures are 64 percent of women with younger children and 76 percent of women with older children (U.S. Department of Labor, 2009).

Gender Stratification

Read "Maid to Order: The Politics of Other Women's Work" by Barbara Ehrenreich on mysoclab.com

● Seeing Sociology in Everyday Life

Do you think women on your campus are overly concerned with looking thin? Explain.

SEEING SOCIOLOGY IN EVERYDAY LIFE — The Beauty Myth

BETH: "I can't eat lunch. I need to be sure I can get into that black dress for tonight."

SARAH: "Maybe eating is more important than looking good for Tom."

BETH: "That's easy for you to say. You're a size 2 and Jake adores you!"

The Duchess of Windsor once remarked, "A woman can never be too rich or too thin." The first half of her observation might apply to men as well, but certainly not the second. After all, the vast majority of ads placed by the $10-billion-a-year U.S. cosmetics industry and the $35-billion diet industry target women.

According to Naomi Wolf (1990), certain cultural patterns create a "beauty myth" that is damaging to women. The beauty myth arises, first, because society teaches women to measure their worth in terms of physical appearance. Yet the standards of beauty embodied by the *Playboy* centerfold or the 100-pound New York fashion model are out of reach for most women.

The way society teaches women to prize relationships with men, whom they presumably attract with their beauty, also contributes to the beauty myth. Striving for beauty not only drives women to be extremely disciplined but also forces them to be highly attentive and responsive to men. In short, beauty-minded women try to please men and avoid challenging male power.

Belief in the beauty myth is one reason so many young women are focused on body image,

AP Wide World Photos

One way our culture supports the beauty myth is through beauty pageants for women; over the years, contestants have become thinner and thinner.

particularly being as thin as possible, often to the point of endangering their health. During the past several decades, the share of young women who develop an eating disorder such as anorexia nervosa (dieting to the point of starvation) or bulimia (binge eating followed by vomiting) has risen dramatically.

The beauty myth affects males as well: Men are told repeatedly that they should want to possess beautiful women. Such ideas about beauty reduce women to objects and motivate men to think of women as if they were dolls rather than human beings.

There can be little doubt that the idea of beauty is important in everyday life. According to Wolf, the question is whether beauty is about how we look or how we act.

WHAT DO YOU THINK?

1. Is there a "money myth" that states that people's income is a reflection of their worth? Does it apply more to one sex than to the other?

2. Can you see a connection between the beauty myth and the rise of eating disorders among young women in the United States?

3. Among people with physical disabilities, do you think that issues of "looking different" are more serious for women or for men? Why?

Gender and Occupations

Although women are closing the gap with men as far as working for income is concerned, the work done by the two sexes remains very different. The U.S. Department of Labor (2009) reports a high concentration of women in two types of jobs. Administrative support work draws 24 percent of working women, most of whom are secretaries or other office workers. These are called "pink-collar jobs" because 75 percent are filled by women. Another 16 percent of employed women perform service work. Most of these jobs are in the food service industries, child care, and health care. ▢ ● Read on mysoclab.com

Table 1 shows the ten occupations with the highest concentrations of women. These jobs tend to be at the low end of the pay scale,

with limited opportunities for advancement and with men as supervisors (U.S. Department of Labor, 2009).

Men dominate most other job categories, including the building trades, where 99 percent of brickmasons, stonemasons, and heavy-equipment mechanics are men. Likewise, men make up 87 percent of architects and engineers, 85 percent of police officers, 70 percent of physicians and surgeons, 66 percent of lawyers, and 57 percent of corporate managers. According to a recent survey, just 15 of the *Fortune* 500 companies in the United States have a woman as their chief executive officer, and just 15 percent of the seats on corporate boards of directors are held by women. In 2009, the highest-paid woman CEO in the United States had the same total compensation

As you look at Table 1, think about which jobs have a high concentration of men (some are noted in the text). How do they differ from the "feminine" jobs in Table 1?

Go to the Multimedia Library at mysoclab.com to listen to the NPR report "Women's Pay Disparity a Growing Campaign Issue"

as the ninth-highest-paid male CEO. Increasing the leadership role of women in the business world is not just a matter of fairness; research into the earnings of this country's 500 largest corporations showed that the companies with more women on the board also are the most profitable (Dickler, 2007; Graybow, 2007; Loomis, 2007; U.S. Department of Labor, 2009; Catalyst, 2010; *Fortune*, 2010).

Gender stratification in everyday life is easy to see: Female nurses assist male physicians, female secretaries serve male executives, and female flight attendants are under the command of male airline pilots. In any field, the greater a job's income and prestige, the more likely it is to be held by a man. For example, women represent 98 percent of kindergarten teachers, 81 percent of elementary and middle school teachers, 56 percent of secondary school educators, 46 percent of professors in colleges and universities, and 23 percent of college and university presidents (Chronicle of Higher Education, 2007; U.S. Department of Labor, 2009).

How are women kept out of certain jobs? By defining some kinds of work as "men's work," society defines women as less competent than men. In a study of coal mining in southern West Virginia, Suzanne Tallichet (2000) found that most men considered it "unnatural" for women to work in the mines. Women who did so were defined as deviant and subject to labeling as "sexually loose" or as lesbians. Such labeling made these women outcasts, presented a challenge to holding the job, and made advancement all but impossible.

In the corporate world, too, the higher in the company we look, the fewer women we find. You hardly ever hear anyone say out loud that women don't belong at the top levels of a company. But many people seem to feel this way, which can prevent women from being promoted. Sociologists describe this barrier as a *glass ceiling* that is not easy to see but blocks women's careers all the same (Benokraitis & Feagin, 1995).

One challenge to male domination in the workplace comes from women who are entrepreneurs. In 2008, there were more than 10 million woman-owned businesses in the United States, double the number of a decade ago; they employed more than 13 million people and generated $2 trillion in sales. By starting their own businesses, women have shown that they can make opportunities for themselves apart from large, male-dominated companies (Center for Women's Business Research, 2009).

Of course, gender stratification shapes the workforce not only in the United States but in other nations as well. Seeing Sociology in the News on next page provides a close look at Japan, a nation where, traditionally, patriarchy has been very strong, but where evidence of change is now beginning to appear.

Gender, Income, and Wealth

In 2008, the median earnings for women working full time were $35,903, and men working full time earned $46,566. This means that

Table 1 Jobs with the Highest Concentrations of Women, 2008

Occupation	Number of Women Employed	Percentage in Occupation Who Are Women
1. Speech-language pathologist	133,000	98.1
2. Dental hygienist	143,000	97.7
3. Preschool or kindergarten teacher	685,000	97.6
4. Dental assistant	263,000	96.3
5. Secretary or administrative assistant	3,296,000	96.1
6. Occupational therapist	87,000	95.9
7. Child care worker	1,314,000	95.6
8. Medical records and health information technician	98,000	95.0
9. Receptionist or information clerk	1,413,000	93.6
10. Licensed practical nurse	566,000	93.3

Source: U.S. Department of Labor (2009).

for every dollar earned by men, women earned about 77 cents. These earnings differences are greatest among older workers because older working women typically have less education and less seniority than older working men. Earnings differences are smaller among younger workers because younger men and women tend to have similar schooling and work experience.

Among full-time workers of all ages, 26 percent of women earned less than $25,000 in 2008, compared with 16 percent of comparable men. At the upper end of the income scale, men were more than twice as likely as women (22.2 percent versus 10.1 percent) to earn more than $75,000 (U.S. Census Bureau, 2009).

The main reason women earn less is the *type* of work they do: largely clerical and service jobs. In effect, jobs and gender interact. People still perceive jobs with less clout as "women's work," just as people devalue certain work simply because it is performed by women (England, Hermsen, & Cotter, 2000; Cohen & Huffman, 2003).

In recent decades, supporters of gender equality have proposed a policy of "comparable worth," paying people not according to the historical double standard but according to the level of skill and responsibility involved in the work. Several nations, including Great Britain and Australia, have adopted comparable worth policies, but these policies have found limited acceptance in the United States. As a result, women in this country lose as much as $1 billion in income annually. ● Go to mysoclab.com

A second cause of gender-based income inequality has to do with society's view of the family. Both men and women have children, of course, but our culture gives more of the responsibility of parenting to women. Pregnancy and raising small children keep many younger women out of the labor force at a time when their

CNN.com

Women on Board: Breaking the "Bamboo Ceiling"

By KYUNG LAH
April 22, 2010

TOKYO—Change a few circumstances in her life and Sakie Fukushima says she would have been a housewife. She was raised to be a good Japanese wife and homemaker, after all. That's what was expected of women of her generation—to sit behind their men, make their bentos, iron their shirts and watch them rise to lead Japan's economy.

Life did not go as Fukushima expected.

Sixty-year-old Fukushima is one of Japan's most powerful executives, sitting on the board of both U.S. and Japanese-based multinational companies. The fact that she is a female in one of the most male-dominated business cultures is a stunning backstory in one woman's remarkable ascent through the so-called "bamboo ceiling." Bamboo bends, and unlike glass, never breaks. But Fukushima managed to crack through, by working for a U.S. company.

"I was lucky to be in a place where the hard work was appreciated," said Fukushima, of her corporate beginnings at Korn-Ferry International. The American company saw her sales output, the highest in the Asia-Pacific region, as the reason for promotion.

An American mentor and her supportive husband urged Fukushima to push beyond her Japanese cultural expectations.

"If I was to work for a Japanese company, a large Japanese company, I don't think I would have come this far."

The World Economic Forum's Global Gender Gap Index ranks Japan 101 out of 134 countries. Part of the reason for the low ranking is that just 1.4 percent of Japanese executives are women.

What that has meant for women in the workplace is they are pushed to traditionally female roles: secretary and store clerk. It is a dismal reality for the world's second-largest economy, said Beth Brooke, Ernst and Young's Global vice chairwoman and a *Forbes* Magazine 100 most powerful woman.

"Japan is a very homogeneous society. So on the spectrum of diversity, not just gender, it is more difficult to embrace diversity because it's not a terribly diverse culture to begin with."

Ironically, Brooke believes the global economic slowdown and Japan's aging population is a chance to rediscover the people underutilized in the workforce.

"I think we have an opportunity to change the conversation here. Whether you're a country or a company, you need growth. Japan has an enormous opportunity, frankly, to see the opportunity to spark innovation through a gender lens of diversity. I think gender diversity is a big part of the solution."

Fukushima agreed, as she celebrates her recent appointment to the Bridgestone Corporation board. She is the first female to be elected to the Japanese company's boardroom.

"Experimenting is the best way to say it," said Fukushima, describing Japan's corporate senti-

ment toward women. "They know they have to have diversity but they don't know how to do it and how to use it effectively. As a result of increasing competition outside of Japan from China and Korea, the Japanese business community has realized it has to change. They can't rely on the past successful model of the 1970s and '80s. They will have to increase diversity, change the way of doing business in order to compete."

Fukushima's new colleague, Bridgestone Americas, Inc. CEO and President Gary Garfield, said he is encouraged that his company in Japan is catching up to other global companies.

He calls having a female on the board a no-brainer. His advice to Japanese companies: "Just branch out and do it. They'll be stronger for it. I think they'll be better companies for it."

WHAT DO YOU THINK?

1. What does the article say about why Japan has such strong gender stratification?

2. Are there reasons to think that Japan's future will be different from its past? What are they?

3. Does the "glass ceiling" in the United States differ from the "bamboo ceiling" in Japan? If so, how?

"Women on Board: Breaking the 'Bamboo Ceiling'" by Kyung Lah is reprinted by permission. Source: CNN.com, April 22, 2010.

male peers are making significant career advancements. When women workers return to the labor force, they have less job experience and seniority than their male counterparts (Stier, 1996; Waldfogel, 1997).

In addition, women who choose to have children may be unable or unwilling to take on fast-paced jobs that tie up their evenings and weekends. To avoid role strain, they may take jobs that offer shorter commuting distances, more flexible hours, and employer-provided child care services. Women pursuing both a career and a family are torn between their dual responsibilities in ways that men are not. One study found that almost half of women in competitive jobs took time off to have children, compared to about 12 percent of men (Hewlett & Luce, 2005). Role conflict is also experienced by women on campus, where one study concluded that young female professors with at least one child were at least 20 percent less likely to have tenure than comparable men in the same field (Shea, 2002).

The two factors noted so far—type of work and family responsibilities—account for about two-thirds of the earnings difference between women and men. A third factor—discrimination against women—accounts for most of the remainder (Fuller & Schoenberger, 1991). Because overt discrimination is illegal, it is practiced in subtle ways. Women on their way up the corporate ladder often run into the glass ceiling described earlier; company officials may deny its existence, but it effectively prevents many women from rising above middle management.

For all these reasons, women earn less than men in all major occupational categories. Even so, many people think that women own most of the country's wealth, perhaps because women typically outlive men. Government statistics tell a different story: Fifty-seven percent of people with $1.5 million or more in assets are men, although widows are highly represented in this elite club (Johnson & Raub, 2006; Internal Revenue Service, 2008). Just 10 percent of the people

Gender Stratification

● Seeing Sociology
  in Everyday Life

How is gender related to doing housework in your current
home or in the home in which you grew up?

identified by *Forbes* magazine as the richest people in the United States
in 2009 were women (Miller & Greenberg, 2009).

Housework: Women's "Second Shift"

In the United States, housework has always presented a cultural contradiction: We claim that it is essential for family life, but people get
little reward for doing it (Bernard, 1981). Here, as around the world,
taking care of the home and children has been considered "women's
work." As women have entered the labor force, the amount of housework women do has gone down, but the *share* done by women has
stayed the same. Figure 2 shows that overall, women average 15.2
hours of housework per week, compared with 9.0 hours for men. As
the figure shows, women in all categories do significantly more housework than men (Bureau of Labor Statistics, 2010).

Men do support the idea of women entering the paid labor force,
and most count on the money women earn. But many men resist
taking on an equal share of household duties (Heath & Bourne, 1995;
Harpster & Monk-Turner, 1998; Stratton, 2001).

Gender and Education

In the past, our society considered schooling more necessary for men,
who worked outside the home. But times have changed. By 1980, women
earned a majority of all associate and bachelor's degrees; in 2008, their
share was 59 percent (National Center for Education Statistics, 2010).

College doors have opened wider to women in recent decades,
and differences in men's and women's majors are becoming smaller.
In 1970, for example, women accounted for just 17 percent of bachelor's degrees in the natural sciences, computer science, and engineering; by 2008, the proportion had doubled to 34 percent.

In 1992, for the first time, women earned a majority of post-
graduate degrees, which are often a springboard to high-prestige
jobs. In all areas of study in 2008, women earned 61 percent of all
master's degrees and 50 percent of all doctorates (including 61 percent of all Ph.D. degrees in sociology). Women have also broken into
many graduate fields that used to be almost all male. For example, in
1970, only a few hundred women received a master's of business
administration (M.B.A.) degree, compared to more than 69,000 in
2008 (45 percent of all such degrees) (National Center for Education Statistics, 2010).

Despite this progress, men still predominate in some professional fields. In 2008, men received 53 percent of law degrees (LL.B.
and J.D.), 51 percent of medical degrees (M.D.), and 56 percent
of dental degrees (D.D.S. and D.M.D.) (National Center for Education Statistics, 2010). Our society still defines high-paying professions (and the drive and competitiveness needed to succeed in
them) as masculine. But the share of women in all these profes-

On average, women spend considerably
more time doing housework than men.

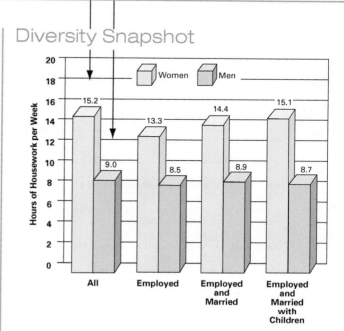

Diversity Snapshot

FIGURE 2   **Housework: Who Does How Much?**

Regardless of employment or family status, women do more housework
than men. What effect do you think the added burden of housework
has on women's ability to advance in the workplace?

Source: Bureau of Labor Statistics (2010).

sions has risen and is now close to half. When will parity be
reached? Probably not in the next few years. For example, the
American Bar Association (2010) reports that in 2009, men still
accounted for 53 percent of law school students across the United
States.

Gender and Politics

A century ago, almost no women held elected office in the United
States. In fact, women were legally barred from voting in national
elections until the passage of the Nineteenth Amendment to the Constitution in 1920. However, a few women were candidates for political office even before they could vote. The Equal Rights party
supported Victoria Woodhull for the U.S. presidency in 1872; perhaps it was a sign of the times that she spent election day in a New
York City jail. Table 2 identifies milestones in women's gradual movement into U.S. political life.

Today, thousands of women serve as mayors of cities and towns
across the United States, and tens of thousands more hold responsi-

Sweden, Norway, Finland, and Denmark have laws that require at least 25 percent of candidates for elected office to be women. Do you think the United States should enact such a law? Why or why not?

minority any category of people distinguished by physical or cultural difference that a society sets apart and subordinates

intersection theory analysis of the interplay of race, class, and gender, often resulting in multiple dimensions of disadvantage

Table 2	Significant Firsts for Women in U.S. Politics
1869	Law allows women to vote in Wyoming Territory.
1872	First woman to run for the presidency (Victoria Woodhull) represents the Equal Rights party.
1917	First woman elected to the House of Representatives (Jeannette Rankin of Montana).
1924	First women elected state governors (Nellie Taylor Ross of Wyoming and Miriam "Ma" Ferguson of Texas); both followed their husbands into office. First woman to have her name placed in nomination for the vice presidency at the convention of a major political party (Lena Jones Springs, a Democrat).
1931	First woman to serve in the Senate (Hattie Caraway of Arkansas); completed the term of her husband upon his death and won reelection in 1932.
1932	First woman appointed to the presidential cabinet (Frances Perkins, secretary of labor in the cabinet of President Franklin D. Roosevelt).
1964	First woman to have her name placed in nomination for the presidency at the convention of a major political party (Margaret Chase Smith, a Republican).
1972	First African American woman to have her name placed in nomination for the presidency at the convention of a major political party (Shirley Chisholm, a Democrat).
1981	First woman appointed to the U.S. Supreme Court (Sandra Day O'Connor).
1984	First woman to be successfully nominated for the vice presidency (Geraldine Ferraro, a Democrat).
1988	First woman chief executive to be elected to a consecutive third term (Madeleine Kunin, governor of Vermont).
1992	Political "Year of the Woman" yields record number of women in the Senate (six) and the House (forty-eight), as well as first African American woman to win election to U.S. Senate (Carol Moseley-Braun of Illinois), first state (California) to be served by two women senators (Barbara Boxer and Dianne Feinstein), and first woman of Puerto Rican descent elected to the House (Nydia Velazquez of New York).
1996	First woman appointed secretary of state (Madeleine Albright).
2000	First former First Lady to win elected political office (Hillary Rodham Clinton, senator from New York).
2001	First woman to serve as national security adviser (Condoleezza Rice); first Asian American woman to serve in a presidential cabinet (Elaine Chao).
2005	First African American woman appointed secretary of state (Condoleezza Rice).
2007	First woman elected as Speaker of the House (Nancy Pelosi). Record number of women in the Senate (sixteen) and the House (seventy).
2008	For the first time, women make up a majority of a state legislature (New Hampshire).
2009	Record number of women in the Senate (seventeen) and the House (seventy-three).

ble administrative jobs in the federal government. At the state level, 24 percent of state legislators in 2009 were women (up from just 5 percent in 1971). National Map 1 shows where in the United States women have made the greatest political gains.

Change is coming more slowly at the highest levels of power, although a majority of U.S. adults claim they would support a qual-

ified woman for any office, including the presidency. In 2008, Hillary Clinton came close to gaining the presidential nomination of the Democratic party, losing out to Barack Obama, who became the nation's first African American president. In 2009, 6 of the 50 state governors were women (12 percent), and in Congress, women held 73 of the 435 seats in the House of Representatives (17 percent) and 17 of the 100 seats in the Senate (17 percent) (Center for American Women and Politics, 2009a).

Women make up half of Earth's population, but they hold just 19 percent of seats in the world's 187 parliamentary governments. Although this represents a rise from the 3 percent of seats they held fifty years ago, only in sixteen countries, among them Sweden and Norway, do women represent more than one-third of the members of parliament (Paxton, Hughes, & Green, 2006; Inter-Parliamentary Union, 2009).

Gender and the Military

Since colonial times, women have served in the U.S. armed forces. Yet in 1940, at the outset of World War II, just 2 percent of armed forces personnel were women. In the fall of 2009, women represented 14 percent of all deployed U.S. troops as well as people serving in all capacities in the armed forces.

Clearly, women make up a growing share of the U.S. military, and almost all military assignments are now open to both women and men. But law prevents women from engaging in offensive warfare. Even so, the line between troop support and outright combat is easily crossed, as women serving in Iraq have learned. In fact, between May 2003 and January 2010, the war in Iraq claimed the lives of 103 female soldiers.

The debate on women's role in the military has been going on for centuries. Some people object to opening doors in this way, claiming that women lack the physical strength of men. Others reply that military women are better educated and score higher on intelligence tests than military men. But the heart of the issue is our society's deeply held view of women as *nurturers*—people who give life and help others—which clashes with the image of women trained to kill.

Whatever our views of women and men, the reality is that military women are in harm's way. In part, this fact reflects the strains of a military short of personnel. In addition, the type of insurgency that surrounds our troops in Iraq and Afghanistan can bring violent combat to any soldier at any time. Finally, our modern warfare technology blurs the distinction between combat and noncombat personnel. A combat pilot can fire missiles at a target miles away; by contrast, nonfighting medical evacuation teams must travel directly into the line of fire (Segal & Hansen, 1992; Wilcox, 1992; Kaminer, 1997; McGirk, 2006).

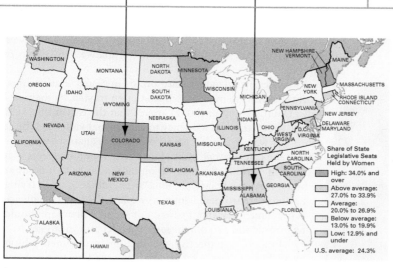

In general, the western states have a higher percentage of legislators who are women than the southern states.

Share of State Legislative Seats Held by Women

- High: 34.0% and over
- Above average: 27.0% to 33.9%
- Average: 20.0% to 26.9%
- Below average: 13.0% to 19.9%
- Low: 12.9% and under

U.S. average: 24.3%

Explore the percentage of women in management, business, and finance in your local community and in counties across the United States on mysoclab.com

Seeing Ourselves

NATIONAL MAP 1

Women in State Government across the United States

Although women make up half of U.S. adults, just 24 percent of the seats in state legislatures are held by women. Look at the state-by-state variations in the map. In which regions of the country have women gained the greatest political power? What do you think accounts for this pattern?

Explore on mysoclab.com

Source: Center for American Women and Politics (2009b).

Are Women a Minority?

A **minority** is *any category of people distinguished by physical or cultural difference that a society sets apart and subordinates.* Given the clear economic disadvantage of being a woman in our society, it seems reasonable to say that women are a minority in the United States even though they outnumber men.[1]

Even so, most white women do not think of themselves in this way (Lengermann & Wallace, 1985). This is partly because, unlike racial minorities (including African Americans) and ethnic minorities (say, Hispanics), white women are well represented at all levels of the class structure, including the very top.

Bear in mind, however, that at every class level, women typically have less income, wealth, education, and power than men. Patriarchy makes women depend on men—first their fathers and later their husbands—for their social standing (Bernard, 1981).

Minority Women: Intersection Theory

If women are defined as a minority, what about minority women? Are they doubly handicapped? This question lies at the heart of **intersection theory,** *analysis of the interplay of race, class, and gender, which often results in multiple dimensions of disadvantage.* Research shows that disadvantages linked to race and gender often combine to produce especially low social standing for some people (Ovadia, 2001).

Income data confirm this theory. Looking first at race and ethnicity, the median income in 2008 for African American women working full time was $31,525, which is 84 percent as much as the $37,610 earned by non-Hispanic white women; Hispanic women earned $26,997—just 72 percent as much as their white counterparts. Looking at gender, African American women earned 84 percent as much as African American men, and Hispanic women earned 87 percent as much as Hispanic men.

Combining these disadvantages, African American women earned 61 percent as much as non-Hispanic white men, and Hispanic women earned 53 percent as much (U.S. Census Bureau, 2009). These differences reflect minority women's lower positions in the occupational and educational hierarchies. These data confirm that although gender has a powerful effect on our lives, it does not operate alone. Class position, race and ethnicity, gender, and sexual orientation form a multilayered system that provides disadvantages for some and privileges for others (Saint Jean & Feagin, 1998).

Violence against Women

In the nineteenth century, men claimed the right to rule their households, even to the point of using physical discipline against their wives, and a great deal of "manly" violence is still directed against women. A government report estimates that 364,000 aggravated assaults against women occur annually. To this number can be added 164,000 rapes or sexual assaults and perhaps 1.5 million simple assaults (U.S. Bureau of Justice Statistics, 2009).

Gender violence is also an issue on college and university campuses. According to research carried out by the U.S. Department

---

[1]Sociologists use the term "minority" instead of "minority group" because, as explained in "Groups and Organizations" women make up a *category*, not a group. People in a category share a status or identity but generally do not know one another or interact.

Making the Grade

Feminists argue that rape is not about sex but about power. It is this claim that makes sexual violence against women not just a crime but a matter of gender stratification.

sexual harassment comments, gestures, or physical contacts of a sexual nature that are deliberate, repeated, and unwelcome

Michael Newman\PhotoEdit Inc.

The basic insight of intersection theory is that various dimensions of social stratification—including race and gender—can add up to great disadvantages for some categories of people. Just as African Americans earn less than whites, women earn less than men. Thus African American women confront a "double disadvantage," earning just 61 cents for every dollar earned by non-Hispanic white men. How would you explain the fact that some categories of people are much more likely to end up in low-paying jobs like this one?

of Justice, in a given academic year, about 3 percent of female college students become victims of rape (either attempted or completed). Projecting these figures over a typical five-year college career, about 20 percent of college women experience rape. In 90 percent of all campus cases, the victim knew the offender, and most of the assaults took place in the woman's living quarters (Karjane, Fisher, & Cullen, 2005).

Off campus as well, most gender-linked violence occurs where men and women interact most: in the home. Richard Gelles (cited in Roesch, 1984) argues that with the exception of the police and the military, the family is the most violent organization in the United States, and it is women who suffer most of the injuries. The risk of violence is especially great for low-income women living in families that face a great deal of stress; low-income women also have fewer options to get out of a dangerous home (Smolowe, 1994; Frias & Angel, 2007).

Violence toward women also occurs in casual relationships. Most rapes involve men known, and often trusted, by their victims. Dianne Herman (2001) argues that the extent of sexual abuse shows that the tendency toward sexual violence is built into our way of life. All forms of violence against women—from the catcalls that intimidate women on city streets to a pinch in a crowded subway to physical assaults that occur at home—express what she calls a "rape culture" of men trying to dominate women. Feminists explain that sexual violence is fundamentally about *power,* not sex, and therefore should be understood as a dimension of gender stratification.

In global perspective, violence against women is built into other cultures in many different ways. One case in point is the practice of female genital mutilation, a painful and often dangerous surgical procedure that is performed in more than two dozen countries and is also known to occur in the United States, as shown in Global Map 2. The Thinking About Diversity box on the page after next describes an instance of female genital mutilation that took place in California and asks whether this practice, which some people defend as promoting "morality," amounts to a case of violence against women.

Violence against Men

If our way of life encourages violence against women, it may encourage even more violence against men. In more than 80 percent of cases in which a police officer makes an arrest for a violent crime, including murder, robbery, and assault, the offender is a male. In addition, 54 percent of all victims of violent crime are also men (Federal Bureau of Investigation, 2009; U.S. Bureau of Justice Statistics, 2009).

Our culture tends to define masculinity in terms of aggression and violence. "Real men" work and play hard, speed on the highways, and let nothing stand in their way. A higher crime rate is one result. But even when no laws are broken, men's lives involve more stress and isolation than women's lives, which is one reason that the suicide rate for men is four times higher than for women (Heron et al., 2009). In addition, as noted earlier, men live, on average, about five fewer years than women.

Violence is not simply a matter of choices made by individuals. It is built into our very way of life, with resulting harm to both men and women. In short, the way any culture constructs gender plays an important part in how violent or peaceful that society will be.

Gender Stratification

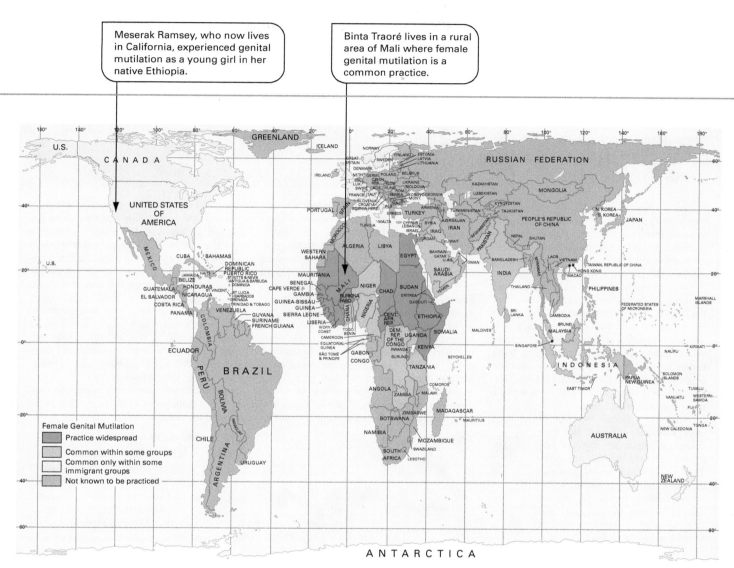

Meserak Ramsey, who now lives in California, experienced genital mutilation as a young girl in her native Ethiopia.

Binta Traoré lives in a rural area of Mali where female genital mutilation is a common practice.

Window on the World

GLOBAL MAP 2 **Female Genital Mutilation in Global Perspective**

Female genital mutilation is known to be performed in at least twenty-eight countries around the world. Across Africa, the practice is common and affects a majority of girls in the eastern African nations of Sudan, Ethiopia, and Somalia. In several Asian nations, including India, the practice is limited to a few ethnic minorities. In the United States, Canada, several European nations, and Australia, there are reports of the practice among some immigrants.

Sources: Seager (2003), World Health Organization (2006), and UNICEF (2009).

Sexual Harassment

Sexual harassment refers to *comments, gestures, or physical contacts of a sexual nature that are deliberate, repeated, and unwelcome.* During the 1990s, sexual harassment became an issue of national importance that rewrote the rules for workplace interaction between women and men.

Most (but not all) victims of sexual harassment are women. The reason is that, first, our culture encourages men to be sexually assertive and to see women in sexual terms. As a result, social interaction between men and women in the workplace, on campus, and elsewhere can easily take on sexual overtones. Second, most people in positions of power—including business executives, doctors, bureau chiefs, assembly line supervisors, professors, and military

○ Seeing Sociology
in Everyday Life

Have you ever experienced sexual harassment on the job? What about on the campus? What are the options for people who experience this problem?

○ Making the Grade

Pornography is an issue that provokes opposition from both conservatives (on moral grounds) and liberals and feminists (on inequality grounds); the two political positions agree on their opposition to pornography, but for different reasons.

THINKING ABOUT DIVERSITY: RACE, CLASS, & GENDER

Female Genital Mutilation: Violence in the Name of Morality

Meserak Ramsey, a woman born in Ethiopia and now working as a nurse in California, paid a visit to an old friend's home. Soon after arriving, she noticed her friend's eighteen-month-old daughter huddled in the corner of a room in obvious distress. "What's wrong with her?" she asked.

Ramsey was shocked when the woman said her daughter had recently had a clitoridectomy, the surgical removal of the clitoris. This type of female genital mutilation—performed by a midwife, a tribal practitioner, or a doctor and typically without anesthesia—is common in Nigeria, Sierra Leone, Senegal, Sudan, Ethiopia, Somalia, and Egypt and is known to be practiced in certain cultural groups in other nations around the world. It is illegal in the United States.

Among members of highly patriarchal societies, husbands demand that their wives be virgins at marriage and remain sexually faithful thereafter. The point of female genital mutilation is to eliminate sexual feeling, which, people assume, makes the girl less likely to violate sexual norms and thus be more desirable to men. In about one-fifth of all cases, an even more severe procedure, called infibulation, is performed, in which the entire external genital area is removed and the surfaces are stitched together, leaving only a small hole for urination and menstruation. Before marriage, a husband has the right to open the wound and ensure himself of his bride's virginity.

How many women have undergone female genital mutilation? Worldwide, estimates place the number at more than 100 million (World Health Organization, 2010). In the United States, hundreds or even thousands of such procedures are performed every year. In most cases, immigrant mothers and grandmothers who have themselves been mutilated insist that young girls in their family follow their example. Indeed, many immigrant women demand the procedure *because* their daughters now live in the United States, where sexual mores are more lax. "I don't have to worry about her now," the girl's mother explained to Meserak Ramsey. "She'll be a good girl."

Medically, the consequences of female genital mutilation include more than loss of sexual pleasure. Pain is intense and can last for

years. There is also the danger of infection, infertility, and even death. Ramsey knows the anguish all too well: She herself underwent genital mutilation as a young girl. She is one of the lucky ones who has had few medical problems since. But the extent of her suffering is suggested by this story: She invited a young U.S. couple to stay at her home. Late at night, she heard the woman's cries and burst into their room to investigate, only to learn that the couple was making love and the woman had just had an orgasm. "I didn't understand," Ramsey recalls. "I thought that there must be something wrong with American girls. But now I know that there is something wrong with me." Or with a system that inflicts such injury in the name of traditional morality.

WHAT DO YOU THINK?

1. Is female genital mutilation a medical procedure or a means of social control? Explain your answer.

2. Can you think of other examples of physical mutilation imposed on women? What are they?

3. What do you think should be done about the practice of female genital mutilation in places where it is widespread? Do you think respect for human rights should override respect for cultural differences in this case?

Kuenzig/laif\Aurora Photos, Inc.

These young women have just undergone female genital mutilation. What do you think should be done about this practice?

Sources: Crossette (1995) and Boyle, Songora, & Foss (2001).

officers—are men who oversee the work of women. Surveys carried out in widely different work settings show that about 5 percent of women claim that they have been harassed on the job in the last year and about half of women say they receive unwanted sexual attention (NORC, 2009).

Sexual harassment is sometimes obvious and direct: A supervisor may ask for sexual favors from an employee and make threats if the advances are refused. Courts have declared that such *quid pro quo* sexual harassment (the Latin phrase means "one thing in return for another") is a violation of civil rights.

More often, however, the problem of unwelcome sexual attention is a matter of subtle behavior—sexual teasing, off-color jokes, comments about someone's looks—that may or may not be intended to harass anyone. But based on the *effect* standard, which

Seeing Sociology
in Everyday Life

The Internet has made pornography more accessible; do
you think it has become more socially acceptable as well?
Why or why not?

Making the Grade

Functional analysis essentially claims that gender
differences were functional in the past but, due to
changes in technology, these differences are much less
functional now.

is favored by many feminists, such actions add up to creating a *hostile environment* for women in the workplace. Incidents of this kind are far more complex because they involve different perceptions of the same behavior. For example, a man may think that repeatedly complimenting a co-worker on her appearance is simply being friendly. The co-worker, on the other hand, may believe the man is thinking of her in sexual terms and is not taking her work seriously, an attitude that could harm her job performance and prospects for advancement.

Pornography

Pornography is defined as sexually explicit material that causes sexual arousal. However, people take different views of exactly what is or is not pornographic; the law gives local communities the power to define whether sexually explicit material violates "community standards of decency" and lacks "any redeeming social value."

Traditionally, people have raised concerns about pornography as a *moral* issue. But pornography also plays a part in gender stratification. From this point of view, pornography is really a *power* issue because most pornography dehumanizes women, treating them as the playthings of men.

In addition, there is widespread concern that pornography encourages violence against women by portraying them as weak and undeserving of respect. Men show contempt for women defined in this way by striking out against them. Surveys show that about half of U.S. adults think that pornography encourages people to commit rape (NORC, 2009:341).

Like sexual harassment, pornography raises complex and sometimes conflicting concerns. Despite the fact that some material may offend just about everyone, many people defend the rights of free speech and artistic expression. Nevertheless, pressure to restrict pornography has increased in recent decades, reflecting both the long-standing concern that pornography weakens morality and the more recent concern that it is demeaning and threatening to women.

Theoretical Analysis of Gender

Why does gender exist in all known societies? Sociology's macro-level approaches—the structural-functional and social-conflict approaches—address the central place of gender in social organization. In addition, the symbolic-interaction approach helps us see the importance of gender in everyday life. The Applying Theory table on the next page summarizes the important insights offered by each of these approaches.

Sven Hagolani/Zefa\Corbis RF

In recent decades, our society has recognized sexual harassment as an important problem. As a result, at least officially, unwelcome sexual attention is no longer tolerated in the workplace. To what extent do you think sexual comments, off-color jokes, and unnecessary touching still take place on the job?

Structural-Functional Analysis

The structural-functional approach views society as a complex system of many separate but integrated parts. From this point of view, gender serves as a means to organize social life.

The earliest hunting and gathering societies had little power over biology. Lacking effective birth control, women could do little to prevent pregnancy, and the responsibilities of child care kept them close to home. At the same time, men's greater strength made them better suited for warfare and hunting. Over the centuries, this sex-based division of labor became institutionalized and largely taken for granted (Lengermann & Wallace, 1985; Freedman, 2002).

Industrial technology opens up a much greater range of cultural possibilities. With human muscle power no longer the main energy source, the physical strength of men becomes less important. In addition, the ability to control reproduction gives women greater choices about how to live. Modern societies relax traditional gender roles as the societies become more meritocratic because rigid roles waste an enormous amount of human talent. Yet change comes slowly because gender is deeply rooted in culture.

Talcott Parsons: Gender and Complementarity

As Talcott Parsons (1942, 1951, 1954) observed, gender helps integrate society, at least in its traditional form. Gender forms a

Making the Grade

Carefully review the Applying Theory table below
to be sure that you understand the three theoretical
approaches to gender.

Seeing Sociology
in Everyday Life

Based on your observations, do you think women
make more eye contact than men do? What other
gender-related patterns have you noticed?

● APPLYING THEORY ●

Gender

	Structural-Functional Approach	Symbolic-Interaction Approach	Social-Conflict Approach
What is the level of analysis?	Macro-level	Micro-level	Macro-level
What does gender mean?	Parsons described gender in terms of two complementary patterns of behavior: masculine and feminine.	Numerous sociologists have shown that gender is part of the reality that guides social interaction in everyday situations.	Engels described gender in terms of the power of one sex over the other.
Is gender helpful or harmful?	Helpful. Gender gives men and women distinctive roles and responsibilities that help society operate smoothly. Gender builds social unity as men and women come together to form families.	Hard to say; gender is both helpful and harmful. In everyday life, gender is one of the factors that helps us relate to one another. At the same time, gender shapes human behavior, placing men in control of social situations. Men tend to initiate most interactions, while women typically act in a more deferential manner.	Harmful. Gender limits people's personal development. Gender divides society by giving power to men to control the lives of women. Capitalism makes patriarchy stronger.

complementary set of roles that links women and men into family units and gives each sex responsibility for carrying out important tasks. Women take the lead in managing the day-to-day life of the household and raising children. Men connect the family to the larger world as they participate in the labor force.

Thus gender plays an important part in socialization. Society teaches boys—presumably destined for the labor force—to be rational, self-assured, and competitive. Parsons called this complex of traits *instrumental* qualities. To prepare girls for child rearing, socialization stresses *expressive* qualities, such as emotional responsiveness and sensitivity to others.

Society encourages gender conformity by instilling in men and women a fear that straying too far from accepted standards of masculinity or femininity will cause rejection by the opposite sex. In simple terms, women learn to reject nonmasculine men as sexually unattractive, and men learn to reject unfeminine women. In sum, gender integrates society both structurally (in terms of what we do) and morally (in terms of what we believe).

CRITICAL REVIEW Influential in the 1950s, this approach has lost much of its standing today. First, structural-functionalism assumes a singular vision of society that is not shared by everyone. For example, historically, many women have worked outside the home because of economic necessity, a fact

not reflected in Parsons's conventional, middle-class view of social life. Second, Parsons's analysis ignores the personal strains and social costs of rigid gender roles. Third, in the eyes of those seeking sexual equality, Parsons's gender "complementarity" amounts to little more than women submitting to male domination.

CHECK YOUR LEARNING In Parsons's analysis, what functions does gender perform for society?

Symbolic-Interaction Analysis

The symbolic-interaction approach takes a micro-level view of society, focusing on face-to-face interaction in everyday life. Gender affects everyday interaction in a number of ways.

Gender and Everyday Life

If you watch women and men interacting, you will probably notice that women typically engage in more eye contact than men do. Why? Holding eye contact is a way of encouraging the conversation to continue; in addition, looking directly at someone clearly shows the other person that you are paying attention.

This pattern is an example of sex roles, defined earlier as the way a society defines how women and men should think and behave. To

Gender Stratification

○ Making the Grade

The structural-functional approach is a more "horizontal" view of gender that emphasizes complementarity. The social-conflict approach is a more "vertical" view of gender that emphasizes inequality. The symbolic-interaction approach is the micro-level look at gender in everyday life.

○ Making the Grade

Remember that, despite their differences, both the structural-functional and social-conflict approaches understand gender at the macro-level of analysis. The symbolic-interaction approach is a micro-level look at gender at the level of individual experience.

understand such patterns, consider the fact that people with more power tend to take charge of social encounters. When men and women engage one another, as they do in families and in the workplace, it is men who typically initiate the interaction. That is, men speak first, set the topics of discussion, and control the outcomes. With less power, women are expected to be more *deferential,* meaning that they show respect for others of higher social position. In many cases, this means that women (just like children or others with less power) spend more time being silent and also encouraging men (or others with more power) not just with eye contact but by smiling or nodding in agreement. As a technique to control a conversation, men often interrupt others, just as they typically feel less need to ask the opinions of other people, especially those with less power (Tannen, 1990, 1994; Henley, Hamilton, & Thorne, 1992; Ridgeway & Smith-Lovin, 1999).

○ **CRITICAL REVIEW** The strength of the symbolic-interaction approach is helping us see how gender plays a part in shaping almost all our everyday experiences. Because our society defines men (and everything that is defined as masculine) as having more value than women (and what is defined as feminine), just about every familiar social encounter is "gendered," so that men and women interact in distinctive and unequal ways.

The symbolic-interaction approach suggests that individuals socially construct the reality they experience as they interact every day, using gender as one element of their personal "performances." Gender can be a useful guide to how we behave. Yet gender, as a structural dimension of society, is beyond the immediate control of any of us as individuals and also gives some people power over others. Therefore, patterns of everyday social interaction reflect our society's gender stratification. Everyday interaction also helps reinforce this inequality. For example, to the extent that fathers take the lead in family discussions, the entire family learns to expect men to "display leadership" and "show their wisdom"; to the extent that mothers let them take the lead, the family learns to expect women to be deferential to men.

A limitation of the symbolic-interaction approach is that by focusing on situational social experience, it says little about the broad patterns of inequality that set the rules for our everyday lives. To understand the roots of gender stratification, we have to "look up" to see more closely how society makes men and women unequal. We will do this using the social-conflict approach.

○ **CHECK YOUR LEARNING** Point to several ways that gender shapes the everyday face-to-face interactions of individuals.

FPG\Getty Images Inc. - Hulton Archive Photos

In the 1950s, Talcott Parsons proposed that sociologists interpret gender as a matter of *differences.* As he saw it, masculine men and feminine women formed strong families and made for an orderly society. In recent decades, however, social-conflict theory has reinterpreted gender as a matter of *inequality.* From this point of view, U.S. society places men in a position of dominance over women.

Social-Conflict Analysis

From a social-conflict point of view, gender involves differences not just in behavior but in power as well. Consider the striking similarity between the way traditional ideas about gender benefit men and the way oppression of racial and ethnic minorities benefits white people. Conventional ideas about gender do not make society operate smoothly; on the contrary, they create division and tension, with men seeking to protect their privileges as women challenge the status quo.

The social-conflict approach draws heavily on the ideas of Karl Marx. Yet as far as gender is concerned, Marx was a product of his times, and his writings focused almost entirely on men. However, his friend and collaborator Friedrich Engels did develop a theory of gender stratification.

Friedrich Engels: Gender and Class

Looking back through history, Engels saw that in hunting and gathering societies, the activities of women and men, though different, had equal importance. A successful hunt brought men great prestige, but the vegetation gathered by women provided most of a group's food supply. As technological advances led to a productive surplus,

Seeing Sociology in Everyday Life

Based on your personal experiences, to what extent would you agree or disagree with the statement that we would be better off if the concept of gender were eliminated? Explain.

feminism support of social equality for women and men, in opposition to patriarchy and sexism

social equality and communal sharing gave way to private property and ultimately a class hierarchy. At this point, men gained significant power over women. With surplus wealth to pass on to heirs, upper-class men needed to be sure that their sons were their own, which led them to control the sexuality of women. The desire to control property brought about monogamous marriage and the family. Women were taught to remain virgins until marriage, to remain faithful to their husbands thereafter, and to build their lives around bearing and raising one man's children.

According to Engels (1902, orig. 1884), capitalism makes male domination even stronger. First, capitalism creates more wealth, which gives greater power to men as income earners and owners of property. Second, an expanding capitalist economy depends on turning people, especially women, into consumers who seek personal fulfillment by buying and using products. Third, society assigns women the task of maintaining the home to free men to work in factories. The double exploitation of capitalism, as Engels saw it, lies in paying low wages for male labor and paying women no wages at all.

CRITICAL REVIEW Social-conflict analysis is strongly critical of conventional ideas about gender, claiming that society would be better off if we minimized or even did away with this dimension of social structure. That is, this approach regards conventional families, which traditionalists claim are personally and socially positive, as a social evil. A problem with social-conflict analysis, then, is that it minimizes the extent to which women and men live together cooperatively and often happily in families. A second problem lies in the assertion that capitalism is the basis of gender stratification. In fact, agrarian societies are typically more patriarchal than industrial-capitalist societies. Although socialist nations, including the People's Republic of China and the former Soviet Union, did move women into the labor force, by and large they provided

NASCAR racing has always been a masculine world. But Danica Patrick has made a name for herself as an outstanding driver. At the same time, she has made much of her income from trading on her good looks, including the 2009 *Sports Illustrated* swimsuit edition. Are men as likely to do the same? Why or why not?

John Bazemore\AP Wide World Photos

Gender Stratification

women with very low pay in sex-segregated jobs (Rosendahl, 1997; Haney, 2002).

CHECK YOUR LEARNING According to Engels, how does gender support social inequality in a capitalist class system?

Feminism

Feminism is *support of social equality for women and men, in opposition to patriarchy and sexism.* The first wave of feminism in the United States began in the 1840s as women opposed to slavery, including Elizabeth Cady Stanton and Lucretia Mott, drew parallels between the oppression of African Americans and the oppression of women. Their main objective was obtaining the right to vote, which was finally achieved in 1920. But other disadvantages persisted, causing a second wave of feminism to arise in the 1960s that continues today.

Basic Feminist Ideas

Feminism views the everyday lives of women and men through the lens of gender. How we think of ourselves (gender identity), how we act (gender roles), and our social standing as women or men (gender stratification) are all rooted in the operation of society.

Although feminists disagree about many things, most support five general principles:

1. **Working to increase equality.** Feminist thinking is political; it relates ideas to action. Feminism is critical of the status quo, pushing for change toward social equality for women and men.

2. **Expanding human choice.** Feminists argue that cultural ideas about gender divide the full range of human qualities into two opposing and limiting spheres: the female world of emotion and cooperation and the male world of rationality and competition. As an alternative, feminists propose a "reintegration of humanity" by which all individuals develop all human traits (French, 1985).

3. **Eliminating gender stratification.** Feminism opposes laws and cultural norms that limit the education, income, and job opportunities of women. For this reason, feminists have long supported passage of the Equal Rights Amendment

● Seeing Sociology
 in Everyday Life

On your campus, do men's organizations (such as fraternities
and athletic teams) enjoy any special privileges? What about
women's organizations?

(ERA) to the U.S. Constitution, which states, in its entirety,
"Equality of rights under the law shall not be denied or
abridged by the United States or any State on account of sex."
The ERA was first proposed in Congress in 1923. Although it
has widespread support, it has yet to become law.

4. **Ending sexual violence.** Today's women's movement seeks to
eliminate sexual violence. Feminists argue that patriarchy distorts relationships between women and men, encouraging violence against women in the form of rape, domestic abuse, sexual
harassment, and pornography (A. Dworkin, 1987; Freedman,
2002).

5. **Promoting sexual freedom.** Finally, feminism advocates
women's control over their sexuality and reproduction. Feminists support the free availability of birth control information.
As Figure 3 shows, about two-thirds of married U.S. women of
childbearing age use contraception; the use of contraceptives
is far less common in many lower-income nations. Most feminists also support a woman's right to choose whether to have
children or to end a pregnancy, rather than allowing men—
husbands, physicians, and legislators—to control their reproduction. Many feminists also support gay people's efforts to
end prejudice and discrimination in a largely heterosexual culture (Ferree & Hess, 1995; Armstrong, 2002).

Types of Feminism

Although feminists agree on the importance of gender equality, they
disagree on how to achieve it: through liberal feminism, socialist feminism, or radical feminism (Stacey, 1983; L. Vogel, 1983; Ferree &
Hess, 1995; Armstrong, 2002; Freedman, 2002). The Applying Theory
table on next page highlights key arguments made by each type of
feminist thinking.

Liberal Feminism

Liberal feminism is rooted in classic liberal thinking that individuals
should be free to develop their own talents and pursue their own
interests. Liberal feminists accept the basic organization of our society but seek to expand the rights and opportunities of women; they
look to passage of the Equal Rights Amendment as an important step
to achieving this goal. Liberal feminists also support reproductive
freedom for all women. They respect the family as a social institution
but seek changes in society, including more widely available maternity
and paternity leave and child care for parents who work.

Given their beliefs in the rights of individuals, liberal feminists
think that women should advance according to their individual efforts
and merit, rather than by working collectively for change. Both women
and men, through personal achievement, are capable of improving
their lives, as long as society removes legal and cultural barriers.

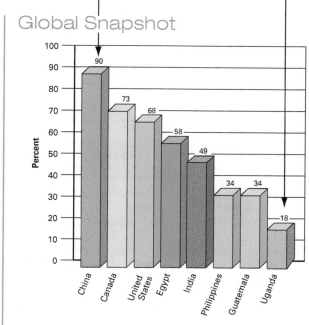

Achen Eke, age 24 and mother of
three, lives in Uganda, where most
women do not have access to
contraception.

Chen-chi Bai, age 31 and the mother
of one boy, lives in China, where
contraception is encouraged and
widely practiced.

Global Snapshot

**FIGURE 3 Use of Contraception by Married Women
of Childbearing Age**

In the United States, most married women of childbearing age use contraception. In many lower-income countries, however, most women do
not have the opportunity to make this choice.

Source: Population Reference Bureau (2009).

Socialist Feminism

Socialist feminism evolved from the ideas of Karl Marx and Friedrich
Engels. From this point of view, capitalism increases patriarchy by concentrating wealth and power in the hands of a small number of men.
Socialist feminists do not think the reforms supported by liberal feminists go far enough. They believe that the family form fostered by capitalism must change in order to replace "domestic slavery" with some
collective means of carrying out housework and child care. Replacing
the traditional family can come about only through a socialist revolution that creates a state-centered economy to meet the needs of all.

Radical Feminism

Like socialist feminism, *radical feminism* finds liberal feminism inadequate. Radical feminists believe that patriarchy is so firmly
entrenched that even a socialist revolution would not end it. Instead,
reaching the goal of gender equality means that society must eliminate gender itself.

○ Making the Grade

Feminism is one type of social-conflict approach to understanding gender.

○ Making the Grade

The three types of feminism all agree on the importance of gender and the need to make women and men more socially equal. They disagree on the way to do that, with liberal feminism involving the least societal change and radical feminism involving the most.

● APPLYING THEORY ●

Feminism

	Liberal Feminism	Socialist Feminism	Radical Feminism
Does it accept the basic order of society?	Yes. Liberal feminism seeks change only to ensure equality of opportunity.	No. Socialist feminism supports an end to social classes and to family gender roles that encourage "domestic slavery."	No. Radical feminism supports an end to the family system.
How do women improve their social standing?	Individually, according to personal ability and effort.	Collectively, through socialist revolution.	Collectively, by working to eliminate gender itself.

One possible way to achieve this goal is to use the new reproductive technology that has been developed by scientists in recent decades. This technology has the ability to separate women's bodies from the process of childbearing. With an end to motherhood, radical feminists reason, society could leave behind the entire family system, liberating women, men, and children from the oppression of family, gender, and sex itself (A. Dworkin, 1987). Radical feminism seeks an egalitarian and gender-free society, a revolution much more sweeping than that sought by Marx.

Opposition to Feminism

Because feminism calls for significant change, it has always been controversial. But today, just 20 percent of U.S. adults say they oppose feminism, a share that has declined over time (NORC, 2009). Figure 4 shows a similar downward trend in opposition to feminism among college students after 1970. Note, however, that little change has occurred in recent years and that more men than women express antifeminist attitudes.

Feminism provokes criticism and resistance from both men and women who hold conventional ideas about gender. Some men oppose sexual equality for the same reasons that many white people have historically opposed social equality for people of color: They do not want to give up their privileges. Other men and women, including those who are neither rich nor powerful, distrust a social movement (especially its radical expressions) that attacks the traditional family and rejects patterns that have guided male-female relations for centuries.

Men who have been socialized to value strength and dominance may feel uneasy about feminist ideals of men as gentle and warm (Doyle, 1983). Similarly, some women whose lives center on their husbands and children may think that feminism does not value the social roles that give meaning to their lives. In general, opposition to feminism is greatest among women who have the least education and those who do not work outside the home (Marshall, 1985; Ferree & Hess, 1995).

Race and ethnicity play some part in shaping people's attitudes toward feminism. In general, African Americans (especially African American women) express the greatest support of feminist goals, followed by whites, with Hispanic Americans holding somewhat more traditional attitudes when it comes to gender (Kane, 2000).

Resistance to feminism is also found within academic circles. Some sociologists charge that feminism ignores a growing body of evidence that men and women do think and act in somewhat different ways, which may make complete gender equality impossible. Furthermore, say critics, with its drive to increase women's presence in the workplace, feminism undervalues the crucial and unique contribution women make to the development of children, especially in

⌐● Seeing Sociology
      in Everyday Life

Do you think women should get ahead primarily through
individual effort or by collective action? Explain.

⌐● Seeing Sociology
      in Everyday Life

Looking at the figure below, why do you think that,
over the years, more male students than female
students have opposed feminism?

the first years of life (Baydar & Brooks-Gunn, 1991; Popenoe, 1993b; Gibbs, 2001).

Finally, there is the question of *how* women should go about improving their social standing. A large majority of adults in the United States think that women should have equal rights, but 70 percent also say that women should advance individually, according to their training and abilities; only 10 percent favor women's rights groups or collective action (NORC, 2007:430).

For these reasons, most opposition to feminism is directed toward its socialist and radical forms, while support for liberal feminism is widespread. In addition, we are seeing an unmistakable trend toward gender equality. In 1977, 65 percent of all adults endorsed the statement "It is much better for everyone involved if the man is the achiever outside the home and the woman takes care of the home and family." By 2008, the share supporting this statement had dropped to 36 percent (NORC, 2009:360).

Gender: Looking Ahead

Predictions about the future are no more than educated guesses. Just as economists disagree about the likely inflation rate a year from now, sociologists can offer only general observations about the likely future of gender and society.

Change so far has been remarkable. A century ago, women were second-class citizens, without access to many jobs, barred from public office, and with no right to vote. Although women remain socially disadvantaged, the movement toward equality has surged ahead. Two-thirds of people entering the workforce in the 1990s were women, and in 2000, for the first time, a majority of families had both husband and wife in the paid labor force. Today's economy depends a great deal on the earnings of women. In addition, as recent research shows, 22 percent of married men in the United States have wives who earn more than they do (Fry & Cohn, 2010).

Many factors have contributed to this transformation. Perhaps most important, industrialization and advances in computer technology have shifted the nature of work from physically demanding tasks that favored male strength to jobs that require thought and imagination. This change

Student Snapshot

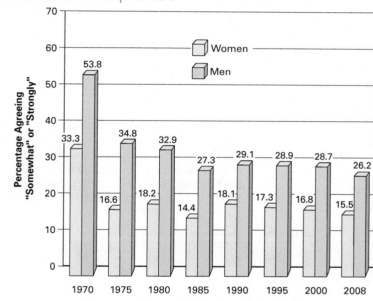

Statement: "The activities of married women are best confined to the home and family."

FIGURE 4   **Opposition to Feminism among First-Year College Students, 1970–2008**

The share of college students expressing antifeminist views declined after 1970. Men are still more likely than women to hold such attitudes.

Sources: Astin et al. (2002) and Pryor et al. (2009).

puts women and men on an even footing. Also, because birth control technology has given us greater control over reproduction, women's lives are less constrained by unwanted pregnancies.

Many women and men have deliberately pursued social equality. For example, sexual harassment complaints in the workplace are taken much more seriously today than they were a generation ago. As more women assume positions of power in the corporate and political worlds, social changes in the twenty-first century may be as great as those that have already taken place.

Seeing Sociology in Everyday Life

Can you spot "gender messages" in the world around you?

As this chapter makes clear, gender is one of the basic organizing principles of everyday life. Most of the places we go and most of the activities we engage in as part of our daily routines are "gendered," meaning that they are defined as either more masculine or more feminine. Understanding this fact, corporations keep gender in mind when they market products to the public. Take a look at the ads below. In each case, can you explain how gender is at work in selling these products?

> **HINT** Looking for "gender messages" in ads is a process that involves several levels of analysis. Start on the surface, by noting everything obvious in the ad, including the setting, the background, and especially the people. Then notice how the people are shown—what they are doing, how they are situated, their facial expressions, how they are dressed, and how they appear to relate to each other. Finally, state what you think is the message of the ad, based on both the ad itself and also what you know about the surrounding society.

Image courtesy of The Advertising Archives

There are a lot of gender dynamics going on in this ad. What do you see?

Generally, our society defines cosmetics as feminine because most cosmetics are marketed toward women. How and why is this ad different?

What gender messages do you see in this ad?

Image courtesy of The Advertising Archives

Applying SOCIOLOGY in Everyday Life

1. Look through some recent magazines, and select three advertisements that involve gender. In each case, provide analysis of how gender is used in the ad.

2. Watch several hours of children's television programming on a Saturday morning. Notice the advertising, which mostly sells toys and breakfast cereal. Keep track of what share of toys are "gendered," that is, aimed at one sex or the other. What traits do you associate with toys intended for boys and those intended for girls?

3. Do some research on the history of women's issues in your state. When was the first woman sent to Congress? What laws once existed that restricted the work women could do? Do any such laws exist today? Did your state support the passage of the Equal Rights Amendment or not? What share of political officials today are women?

Making the Grade

Gender Stratification

◉┤Watch on mysoclab.com

Gender and Inequality

GENDER refers to the meaning a culture attaches to being female or male.

- Evidence that gender is rooted in culture includes global comparisons by Margaret Mead and others showing how societies define what is feminine and masculine in various ways.
- Gender is not only about difference: Because societies give more power and other resources to men than to women, gender is an important dimension of social stratification. **Sexism** is built into the operation of social institutions.
- Although some degree of **patriarchy** is found almost everywhere, it varies throughout history and from society to society.

gender the personal traits and social positions that members of a society attach to being female or male

gender stratification the unequal distribution of wealth, power, and privilege between men and women

matriarchy a form of social organization in which females dominate males

patriarchy a form of social organization in which males dominate females

sexism the belief that one sex is innately superior to the other

Gender and Socialization

Through the socialization process, gender becomes part of our personalities (**gender identity**) and our actions (**gender roles**). All the major agents of socialization—family, peer groups, schools, and the mass media—reinforce cultural definitions of what is feminine and masculine.

gender roles (sex roles) attitudes and activities that a society links to each sex

Gender and Social Stratification

Gender stratification shapes **THE WORKPLACE**:

- A majority of women are now in the paid labor force, but 40% hold clerical or service jobs.
- Comparing full-time U.S. workers, women earn 77% as much as men.
- This gender difference in earnings results from differences in jobs, differences in family responsibilities, and discrimination.

Gender stratification shapes **FAMILY LIFE**:

- Most unpaid housework is performed by women, whether or not they hold jobs outside the home.
- Pregnancy and raising small children keep many women out of the labor force at a time when their male peers are making important carreer gains.

Gender stratification shapes **EDUCATION**:

- Women now earn 59% of all associate's and bachelor's degrees.
- Women make up 47% of law school students and are an increasing share of graduates in professions traditionally dominated by men, including medicine and business administration.

minority any category of people distinguished by physical or cultural difference that a society sets apart and subordinates

intersection theory analysis of the interplay of race, class, and gender, often resulting in multiple dimensions of disadvantage

sexual harassment comments, gestures, or physical contacts of a sexual nature that are deliberate, repeated, and unwelcome

▣┤Read on mysoclab.com

Gender stratification shapes **POLITICS**:

- Until a century ago, almost no women held elected office in the United States.
- In recent decades, the number of women in politics has increased significantly.
- Even so, the vast majority of elected officials, especially at the national level, are men.
- Women make up only about 14% of U.S. military personnel.

INTERSECTION THEORY investigates the intersection of race, class, and gender, factors that combine to cause special disadvantages to some categories of people.

- Women of color encounter greater social disadvantages than white women and earn much less than white men.
- Because all women have a distinctive social identity and are disadvantaged, they are a minority, although most white women do not think of themselves this way.

VIOLENCE AGAINST WOMEN AND MEN is a widespread problem that is linked to how a society defines gender. Related issues include

- **sexual harassment**, which mostly victimizes women because our culture encourages men to be assertive and to see women in sexual terms.
- **pornography**, which portrays women as sexual objects. Many see pornography as a moral issue; because pornography dehumanizes women, it is also a power issue.

◉┤Explore on mysoclab.com

Theoretical Analysis of Gender

The STRUCTURAL-FUNCTIONAL APPROACH suggests that

- in preindustrial societies, distinctive roles for males and females reflect biological differences between the sexes.
- in industrial societies, marked gender inequality becomes dysfunctional and gradually decreases.

Talcott Parsons described gender differences in terms of complementary roles that promote the social integration of families and society as a whole.

The SYMBOLIC-INTERACTION APPROACH suggests that

- individuals use gender as one element of their personal performances as they socially construct reality through everyday interactions.
- gender plays a part in shaping almost all our everyday experiences.

Because our society defines men as having more value than women, the sex roles that define how women and men should behave place men in control of social situations; women play a more deferential role.

The SOCIAL-CONFLICT APPROACH suggests that

- gender is an important dimension of social inequality and social conflict.
- gender inequality benefits men and disadvantages women.

Friedrich Engels tied gender stratification to the rise of private property and a class hierarchy. Marriage and the family are strategies by which men control their property through control of the sexuality of women. Capitalism exploits everyone by paying men low wages and assigning women the task of maintaining the home.

 See the Applying Theory table.

Feminism

FEMINISM

- endorses the social equality of women and men and opposes patriarchy and sexism.
- seeks to eliminate violence against women.
- advocates giving women control over their reproduction.

There are three types of feminism:

- Liberal feminism seeks equal opportunity for both sexes within the existing society.
- Socialist feminism claims that gender equality will come about by replacing capitalism with socialism.
- Radical feminism seeks to eliminate the concept of gender itself and to create an egalitarian and gender-free society.

Today, only 20% of U.S. adults say they oppose feminism. Most opposition is directed toward socialist and radical feminism. Support for liberal feminism is widespread.

feminism support of social equality for women and men, in opposition to patriarchy and sexism

See the Applying Theory table.

Sample Test Questions

Multiple-Choice Questions

1. Gender is not just a matter of personal traits but also a matter of differences in
   a. power.
   b. wealth.
   c. prestige.
   d. All of the above are correct.

2. The anthropologist Margaret Mead studied gender in three societies in New Guinea and found that
   a. all societies define femininity in much the same way.
   b. all societies define masculinity in much the same way.
   c. what is feminine in one society may be masculine in another.
   d. the meaning of gender is changing everywhere toward greater equality.

3. For all of us raised in U.S. society, gender shapes our
   a. feelings.
   b. thoughts.
   c. actions.
   d. All of the above are correct.

4. There is a "beauty myth" in U.S. society that encourages
   a. women to believe that their personal importance depends on their looks.
   b. beautiful women to think they do not need men.
   c. men to improve their physical appearance in order to attract women.
   d. women to disregard beauty in favor of personal achievement.

5. In the United States, what share of women work for income?
   a. 80 percent
   b. 60 percent
   c. 40 percent
   d. 20 percent

6. In the U.S. labor force,
   a. men and women have the same types of jobs.
   b. men and women earn the same pay.
   c. women are still concentrated in several types of jobs.
   d. a majority of working women hold "pink-collar" jobs.

7. For which of the following categories of people in the United States is it true that women do more housework than men?
   a. people who work for income
   b. people who are married
   c. people who have children
   d. All of the above are correct.

8. In the United States, women in the labor force working full time earn how much for every dollar earned by men working full time?
   a. 77 cents
   b. 87 cents
   c. 91 cents
   d. 97 cents

9. Before the 2010 elections, women held about what percentage of seats in Congress?
   a. 7 percent
   b. 17 percent
   c. 37 percent
   d. 57 percent

10. The Equal Rights Amendment, which would expand the rights and opportunities of women, reflects which of the following types of feminism?
    a. socialist feminism
    b. liberal feminism
    c. radical feminism
    d. All of the above are correct.

ANSWERS: 1(d); 2(c); 3(d); 4(a); 5(b); 6(c); 7(d); 8(a); 9(b); 10(b).

Essay Questions

1. How do the concepts "sex" and "gender" differ? Why is the chapter called "Gender Stratification" rather than "Sex Stratification?"

2. Why is gender correctly considered a dimension of social stratification? How does gender intersect other dimensions of inequality, such as class, race, and ethnicity?

America's Divorce Problem

STEVEN L. NOCK, JAMES D. WRIGHT, AND LAURA SANCHEZ

In an attempt to address high divorce rates, Louisiana passed the nation's first covenant marriage bill in 1997, and Arizona soon followed. As well-intentioned as the legislators in these states may have been, the authors of this article argue that covenant marriage is a simplistic solution for a complex problem; it cannot and does not address all of the social factors that may cause a couple to divorce. They describe how covenant marriage differs from traditional marriage, review how the option of no-fault divorce increased divorce rates, and present the perspectives of progressives, religious leaders, feminists, and traditionalists on covenant marriage.

On August 15, 1997, Louisiana made an historic change in its domestic relations laws by enacting the nation's first "covenant marriage" bill. Following Louisiana's lead, Arizona enacted similar legislation in May 1998 and other covenant marriage (CM) bills are now under consideration in at least twenty additional states. . . . Here we consider just what covenant marriage is and why it is a concept whose time appears to have come. We also take up and respond to the most common objections or reservations that people have expressed about it

"America's Divorce Problem," by Steven L. Nock, James D. Wright, and Laura Sanchez, reprinted from *Society*, vol. 36, no. 4, 1999, pp. 43–52.

◉ What is "Covenant Marriage?"

Couples wishing to marry in Louisiana are now required to choose between two marriage regimes: the standard marriage with virtually unrestricted access to no-fault divorce or a covenant marriage designed to be somewhat harder both to enter and to exit. The covenant option specifically acknowledges that marriage is a lifelong commitment and differs from conventional marriage in a number of additional ways:

- Covenant marriage requires premarital counseling. Counseling must include discussions of the seriousness of marriage, the life-long commitment being made by the couple to their marriage, the obligation to seek marital counseling if problems arise later in the marriage, and the exclusive grounds for divorce or legal separation in a covenant marriage. Couples must sign an affidavit acknowledging their commitment and prove that they have received counseling on these issues.

- Likewise, divorce from a covenant marriage requires the couple to have sought marriage counseling and to have made a good-faith effort to resolve their differences.

- Although a no-fault divorce is still possible for covenant marriages, the new law requires that the couple live separate and apart for two years (vs. six months under the current marriage regime) or be legally separated for eighteen months.

- Dissolving a covenant marriage in less than two years requires one person to prove fault on the part of the other. Acceptable "faults" are the traditional ones: felony conviction, abuse, abandonment, or adultery. Irreconcilable differences, general incompatibility, irretrievable breakdown of the marriage, or "we just don't get along any more" are not acceptable grounds for divorce, so if these are the problem, then you have to wait the full two years.

- Newly marrying couples must choose either the covenant or the standard regime. It is not true that the law requires new marriages to be covenants or abolishes the standard regime (a point about which there has been some confusion).

- And finally, the law allows currently married couples to convert (or as proponents prefer, "upgrade") to covenants.

(The Arizona law differs in some details but is essentially the same as the Louisiana law, and the same is true of CM bills now under consideration in other states.)

Hailed by some as *the* solution to America's divorce problem and denounced by others as a huge step backwards, covenant marriage will prove to be neither. Or such in any case is our working hypothesis after the first year in a long-term effort to evaluate these emergent covenant marriage regimes. On the positive side, the transparent intent of the law is to make marriage a more enduring commitment. . . . The law is also clearly intended to promote a more sober consideration of the commitments and obligations that marriage entails. These, we believe, are undeniably good things. On the negative side, we are quick to acknowledge that familial well-being is threatened by any number of large-scale social, economic, and political forces, that marriages go sour for many reasons, only a few of which can be anticipated in advance, and thus that a couple who has consummated a covenant rather than standard marriage has, in reality, done relatively little to stave off the forces that will buffet them in the years ahead.

◉ Why Some People Like the Idea . . .

Since the 1970s, all states have had virtually unrestricted no-fault divorces available to any married person who wanted one. The only restriction in most cases is a waiting period that can be as short as a few months and is rarely more than a year. The no-fault revolution, successful everywhere, was motivated by a belief that the former marriage regime trapped many women and children in difficult, abusive, or otherwise unsatisfactory marriages. Shifting cultural values about divorce, remarriage, and related issues were also contributing factors. Divorce rates, of course, had been going up prior to the no-fault movement and continued to go up thereafter, in the last decade, they have finally begun to come down. The effects of no-fault divorce on overall divorce rates are still debated among specialists, with a rough consensus that no-fault divorce produced a short-run increase in divorce rates, but that the long-term increase was probably the result of other factors.

No-fault divorce is itself a controversial concept. Among many feminists and other progressive thinkers, the old marriage regime was a prison that trapped women in lousy relationships. No-fault divorce makes it much easier to terminate these relationships, thereby increasing women's options, and is therefore unambiguously good. By the same logic, anything that would seem to decrease women's options or make divorce more difficult to attain (such as CM) is unambiguously bad. Among pro-family advocates and other traditionalists and social conservatives, on the other hand, no-fault divorce is seen as having created a "divorce culture" where traditional values of love, fidelity, commitment, and obligation are no longer respected. By making divorce so easy to obtain, the no-fault regime has ruined the lives of countless people, many of them children who are emotionally traumatized by divorce, and many others women whose financial well-being is ruined when their marriages fall apart. For many traditionalists, no-fault divorce has been the root of much evil and is unambiguously bad; CM attempts to stem the no-fault tide and is therefore to be encouraged and promoted.

The covenant marriage "movement". . . and the larger anti-divorce movement of which it is a part, stem from widespread dissatisfaction with the current social and legal landscape of marriage and divorce and a concern that no-fault divorce laws have come to threaten the institution of marriage itself. Politically, then, covenant marriage is motivated by the same concerns that brought us the "Defense of Marriage" Act and our current national obsession with so-called family values. Many contend, with some evidence, that the no-fault regime has fostered a model of marriage as a contract with the state acting as the neutral enforcer of the bargains struck by self-interested parties. This, it is said, often leaves women vulnerable, harms the interests of children, and undermines the general social welfare; at the very least, it is destructive of values of caring and commitment that produce stability in families. Others argue that no-fault divorce has transformed marriage into an illusory contract that provides no remedy for the breach of marriage vows. In this view, easy no-fault divorce encourages (or at minimum fails to discourage) opportunistic behavior by husbands and threatens the marital investments of wives.

Whatever the pathways of cause and effect, divorce rates in the United States are generally high and most research in the past decade suggests that our previously casual attitude about divorce and its consequences for people, particularly children, was myopic. It seems obvious that there is something akin to a "divorce culture" in the United States today and that, in many cases, the effects of this culture are more deleterious than beneficial. This view is clearly shared by many state legislators who are now trying through covenant marriage laws and other methods to resurrect notions of fault in marital dissolution, to create rules for marital termination that protect the interests of wives and children, and to recover a world in which marriage is a privileged and respected status. . . .

Many people fail to appreciate that CM as enacted in Louisiana and Arizona changes the terms of all marriages in a unique way. In no other state must marrying couples decide which system of laws will govern their marriages. By forcing couples to decide between covenant or conventional marriage, the law introduces an element of contractual negotiation about the terms of the marriage relationship. At minimum, this requires couples to contemplate and discuss their own chances for a divorce and to express their understandings about the meaning of marriage.

· · ·

In many respects, or so it seems to us, covenant marriage simply adds to the marriage vows a clause that affirms, ". . . and we really mean it!" What objection could possibly be mounted to anything that helps couples take their marriages more seriously if that is, indeed, what they have freely chosen to do? Or that might assist them in keeping their marriages together some years in the future?

☻ . . . And Others Hate It

The fact is, covenant marriage has been publicly opposed by progressives, feminists, traditionalists, and religious leaders, although for very different reasons in each case. . . . Herewith, an overview of the emergent terms of the CM debate:

One thing leads to another. If it accomplishes nothing else, CM creates two distinct kinds of marriage governed by separate legal restrictions and requires couples to choose between them. Well, if there can be two systems of marriage rather than only one, then why not three? Or four? Or dozens? Some fear, not without justification, that covenant marriage takes a treacherous first step towards a plurality of marital regimes and that the next steps might be legal recognition of such things as gay marriages, or trial marriages, or marriages of convenience, or even polygamy and God knows what else. Once we have started down this path, where will it end?

. . .

Covenant marriage arose in Louisiana (and pretty much everywhere else) as an issue of the religious right and as part of the national "defense of marriage" movement. The "defense of marriage" movement (and the ensuing 1996 "Defense of Marriage" Act) was in turn a reaction to a suit brought by gay couples against the state of Hawaii alleging discrimination because they were not allowed to marry. As this case made its way to the Supreme Court, many states came to realize that an unfavorable decision could effectively legalize gay marriage everywhere, and so state after state rushed to enact legislation that would survive Court scrutiny, outlaw gay marriage, and free the state from having to recognize gay marriages performed elsewhere. The Congress solidified these separate state efforts with the

1996 Act affirming that marriage is between "one man and one woman"—what amounts to a national prohibition against gay marriage. In Louisiana and Arizona, part of the "defense of marriage" effort was a covenant marriage bill—which, by admitting free choice into the marital contract, might pave the way (or so many fear) for a wild proliferation of marital regimes, including gay marriage itself!

Not everyone is opposed to a plurality of marital regimes; indeed, a persuasive argument can be made that the law should grant consenting adults pretty wide latitude in defining their intimate relationships to one another and in coming to legally acknowledged understandings between themselves about the sharing of property, debts, and domestic chores, about childbearing and child-rearing, and about the agreed-upon terms through which their relationship can be dissolved. The issue would be neither here nor there to that immense majority of married people in this country who arrange their lives in broad accord with a rather simple and traditional model of matrimony.

On the other hand, there are also persuasive arguments against a proliferation of marital regimes, and if the "one thing" of covenant marriage did lead to "another" thing or two, there would be some cause for concern. Warts and all, a conventional monogamous heterosexual marital union is an institutionalized feature of this and nearly all other societies. Broad consensus exists about what it means to be a wife, a husband, a married father or mother. These institutionalized roles are embedded in our cultural understanding of things and allow us to make realistic assumptions about individual and family life.

• • •

Shared understandings of social roles, role relationships, and associated behavioral expectations are the glue that holds societies together and we should therefore be cautious about fundamental redefinitions of these most basic adult roles.

Marriage and divorce are not the government's business. A participant in one of several focus groups we have convened to talk about covenant marriage expressed her misgivings thusly: "I don't think big government should step in. I don't like the thought of government [being] involved in these issues." . . .

The idea that things like marriage and divorce are not the proper business of governments was a surprisingly common theme in nearly all of our focus groups. Because of the religious origins and symbolism of covenant marriage, many were concerned that the new law violated the doctrine of the separation of church and state. The reality, of course, is that federal, state and local governments require people to obtain licenses and have blood tests before they can get married, grant authority to perform marriages, say who can marry and who cannot, establish minimum ages at which persons can marry without parental consent, set waiting periods for divorce, specify the terms of divorce, adjudicate disputes among divorcing couples about the distribution of their common property, award custody of children, place children in foster care, define appropriate sexual partners and sexual acts, and otherwise find ways—for better or for worse—to regulate practically every aspect of our intimate relations with others. Has government no right to do any of this?

Moreover, while the objection to state involvement in marriage was a common theme in our focus groups, not one person objected to (or even found fault with) the state's involvement in the consequences of divorce. Though the state is viewed as having no legitimate interest in fostering stronger marriages, it is apparently viewed as responsible for picking up the pieces when marriages fail—an evident contradiction. Since the state must pay for much of the individual and aggregate costs of welfare, diminished educational attainments, higher rates of out-of-wedlock births, and other problems that are clearly among the consequences of divorce, the state has a very legitimate interest in minimizing these costs. Indeed, one wonders why there was so little concern about the public expenditures associated with divorce throughout the recent debate over "reforming" welfare. One obvious way to 'reform' welfare would be to strengthen marriages.

A couple of decades ago, governments everywhere relaxed the standards for divorce and removed proof of fault as a condition for divorce. In this fashion, governments took away a divorce regime that attempted to keep marriages together, even bad marriages, and gave couples a no-fault regime where marriages were and are very easy to dissolve. Can it now be legitimately said that government has no right to allow marrying couples to freely deprive themselves of the presumed "benefits" of the no-fault system if they want to?

The benefits of counseling, both before and after marriage, are overstated. To the extent that CM is an effort to make marriages stronger (and not just harder to get out of), it is through the mandatory counseling provisions, and people on all sides of the debate express doubts about the likely efficacy of these provisions. One of our focus groups, this involving about a dozen members of the Louisiana chapter of the National Organization of Women (NOW), hit this theme with particular force: "You know, the knee-jerk reaction is [that] counseling is a good thing. Well, counseling with whom?" The group expressed particularly skeptical opinions about the counseling that couples might receive from priests, ministers, rabbis, and other religious leaders. One participant characterized this form of counseling as "Indoctrination 101." Much of the concern was that religious-based counselors would simply tell women, "you should quit your job and serve your husband, like it says in the Bible." Or urge that all marriages, even profoundly destructive and abusive ones, should be preserved no matter the cost.

There is nothing in the Louisiana law (or in Arizona's) to protect couples from bad counseling or to establish minimum standards of training or performance for counselors, whether lay or religious, so the concern with the quality of the required counseling experience is certainly legitimate. On the other hand, one need not be an enthusiast for the counseling profession to acknowledge that young couples might profit from an extended discussion of marriage, commitment, and fidelity with a concerned adult sometime prior to the wedding. Amatai Etzioni has noted that about 20 percent of those who receive premarital counseling decide not to marry their would-be spouse, so it is clear that at least some people derive value from the experience (*New York Times*, August 13, 1997). . . . Granted, premarital counseling will not prevent all bad marriages from occurring and post-marital counseling will not solve every problem that arises in a marriage, but the conclusion that there is no value at all to be derived from the counseling process seems harsh. Probably, the value lies less in the advice couples are given than in the process of confronting and discussing the possibility that the marriage will not last, the seriousness of each partner's commitment to the other, the expectations each brings to the marriage. Frank and sober reflection on these points can hardly be a bad thing.

At the same time, the counseling requirements raise important questions about training, licensure, and certification of counselors. The Louisiana law allows any priest, minister, rabbi, clerk of the Religious Society of Friends, any clergyman of any religious sect, or lay marriage counselors to offer the required premarital and marital counseling. If Louisiana (or any other state) is going to require counseling for whatever reason, there is presumably some obligation for the state to set appropriate standards for training and continuing professional education, to issue licenses, and to provide some assurance that minimum quality standards will be upheld. And what of the covenant couple who wishes to divorce but who cannot afford the required counseling? Must the state make counseling available to all, regardless of their ability to pay?

Covenant marriage won't work because people will always find a way to get divorced if they want to. The "full faith and credit" clause of the Constitution requires that marriages entered legally in one state be recognized as legal in others (so long as they do not violate state law). The same is true of divorce. Indeed, prior to the institution of no-fault divorce, there was a small industry in towns like Las Vegas and Reno that depended entirely on the fact that divorces granted in Nevada were recognized as legal divorces everywhere else. So while a covenant couple married in Louisiana will have a harder-than-average time divorcing in Louisiana, there's nothing to stop them from driving to Mississippi or flying to Nevada to dissolve their marriage and thereby to subvert the "fault" provisions of their covenant marriage.

. . .

We have no quarrel with the conclusion that couples intent on dissolving their marriages will always find ways to do so. But would the original marital covenant give the aggrieved party, usually but not always the wife, grounds for a civil suit to recover damages resulting from the breach of the marital contract? Could the jilted spouse sue for recovery of the marital investment, most of all once the fault of the other spouse had been alleged and proven? It will be some years before we know for certain the answers to these questions—but it will be a brave soul indeed who decides to be the first to find out. Even if covenant marriage does not prevent or even postpone many divorces, it may well provide the victims with awesome new legal weaponry by which to extract revenge. The potential deterrent effects of this on male opportunism, sexual antics and adventures, and related peccadilloes probably should not be dismissed out of hand.

Covenant marriage is a return to the "bad old days" where women and children were often trapped in unsatisfactory marriages (or worse). Marriage can be and often is a prison for women and covenant marriage just puts more guards in the towers. Contemporary feminism has developed in part as a reaction against traditionally-defined female roles, familial roles hardly to be excepted. No-fault divorce and the more general relaxation of traditional expectations about what women could and could not do was a hard-won and significant victory for the feminist cause and the rights won in that struggle are not to be lightly surrendered. In some variants of the feminist world view, efforts to strengthen marriage or prevent divorce are looked upon with misgivings because women tend to suffer when marriages are "strong." . . . Leaving women no way to escape from an abusive spouse is a particularly pressing concern.

Many who argue against covenant marriage on these grounds seem not to appreciate the provisions of the Louisiana law that allow immediate dissolution of covenant marriages in the face of a felony conviction, adultery, abandonment, or abuse. Contrary to a common misconception, the two-year waiting period (or 18 month separation requirement) does not apply in these cases. On the other hand, if a couple wishes to dissolve their covenant marriage simply because they have decided they are no longer compatible, that too is allowed, but they have to wait the full two years (living separate and apart for two years satisfies the law's definition of abandonment).

The feminist rejoinder is that proving fault can be difficult, especially in cases involving domestic violence. Yes, judges can terminate covenant marriages if abuse can be proven. But will they? And will they do so in time? Allegations of fault may stimulate further attacks and more brutality; long waiting periods extend the woman's time at risk. . . .

On the other hand, it is hard to see how no-fault divorce protects women in this matter any more than a fault regime would, or how a covenant marriage protects them any less. Sooner or later in the process of terminating an abusive relationship, the wife has to "reveal her plans" and incur whatever risk the revelation entails. Otherwise, there is nothing the police, courts, or counselors can do. Any effort to persuade an abusive husband to stop it, or rather, any effort that goes beyond mere pleading, involves calling the abuse to the attention of someone with the authority or wherewithal to intervene. Nothing about covenant marriage per se changes the legal situation or interactional dynamics between abusers and the abused.

Some women in abusive relationships find a way to get out of them and in these cases, divorce is, fundamentally, a liberation. And some women make significant personal and economic sacrifices in the course of their marriages, particularly in the early years, only to watch the marriage dissolve as hubby goes lusting after his secretary or the Avon lady or the neighbor's wife (or husband), and in these cases, divorce is, just as fundamentally, a complete disaster. It is not obvious which of these constitutes the larger threat to the well-being of women as a whole. It is certainly likely that as many women (or more) will derive advantage from covenant marriages by the deterrent to male abandonment and sexual escapades as will be "trapped" in abusive marriages by the marginally tougher divorce provisions.

. . .

It is now conceded by almost all experts that, on average, women suffer more from divorce than men. In the majority of cases, men are better off financially, and women worse off, after divorce than before. In fact, about a third of all divorces result in the woman spending some time below the poverty line. In these all-too-common cases, women will gain more than they lose if divorces are harder to get.

Covenant marriage denigrates conventional marriage. The Catholic Church has expressed reservations about covenant marriage, in part because in the eyes of the Church, all marriages are covenants between a man, a woman, and God. Creating a separate legal status for covenant marriages therefore implies that standard marriages are inferior—"marriage lite," a barely passable imitation of the real thing. (The Catholic Church also objects to the premarital counseling provision because it requires a discussion of divorce, which the Church also does not recognize.)

By defining one category of marriages as "better" than another (and "better" can mean almost anything in this context—more romantic, more stable, more religious, more committed, more traditional), the covenant marriage option also opens up the possibility that couples will be coerced by parents, churches and even one another into accepting the covenant option ("real" marriage) when, in fact, they would prefer not to. A news release from the American Civil Liberties Union (dated August 18, 1997) makes the point: "The 'option' of a covenant marriage could constitute a form of emotional blackmail in which a reluctant man or woman is pressured into the contract and later regrets it."

In one important sense, this concern is not only well-taken but is pretty much the entire point of covenant marriage. Many people these days have a pretty casual attitude towards marriage and divorce, and it was certainly in the minds of Louisiana state legislators that covenant marriage might cause people to take these things more seriously and, indeed, restore marriage to a privileged, not to say honored, status in society. It is also true that marriage itself is frequently used as "emotional blackmail" through which men and women are sometimes pressured into doing things they'd rather not. Just how is covenant marriage any different?

Civil libertarians have expressed deep concerns about religious coercion to enter covenant marriages. Katha Pollitt, a columnist for *The Nation*, expressed an on-air fear in a recent *Nightline* feature on the Louisiana CM law that "there will be a lot of psychological pressure on some people and more than psychological pressure, I think there'll be real religious pressure. In fact, some Louisiana churches are already saying we will only marry you if you sign a covenant contract."

The experience to date suggests that this concern, while valid, has been overstated. Pollitt's "some Louisiana churches" is in fact a single Presbyterian congregation in Baton Rouge that has announced that all its future marriages will be covenants. Several other churches—perhaps a few dozen of them—have also begun to promote covenant marriage by either sponsoring congregation-wide "upgrades" (several thousand couples converted to covenant marriage in mass ceremonies on a single Sunday: Valentine's Day, 1998) or urging couples about to be married to consider the covenant option (statewide, there were about 750 "new" covenant marriages through the end of 1998). And while other churches may well follow these leads, even to the point of requiring covenant marriages, the much-feared stampede of churches begging, requiring, or otherwise coercing a flood of covenant marriages out of a recalcitrant flock has simply not materialized, nor is it likely to. As we have already suggested, many aspects of covenant marriage remain controversial even within the context of traditional Christian beliefs.

Through the first six months of the new covenant marriage regime, very few couples exercised the covenant option. In the past six months or so, between 2.5 percent and 3.0 percent of "new" marriages have been covenant marriages. This figure might rise somewhat in the coming years as more people learn about the option, but to the extent that young couples are being told that the option exists, the vast majority prove to be uninterested and it is very unlikely that CM will ever comprise more than five or so percent of the total. So if there is any real "coercion" going on out there, it is definitely not very effective.

Divorce is not the problem but rather a symptom of the problem. Progressive and feminist critics of CM are nearly unanimous in their belief that bad marriages are the real problem and that no-fault divorce is therefore the solution, since the no-fault regime makes bad marriages easier to dissolve. These critics correctly see the CM "movement" as part of a larger "anti-divorce movement" which in turn can be indifferent to the often-exorbitant costs of bad marriages. None of these critics allege that divorce is a positive or enjoyable experience for anyone. To the contrary, divorce is recognized as emotionally traumatic and often financially devastating. But bad marriages are also intensely traumatic, often more traumatic than the process of discontinuing them. Barbara Ehrenreich writing in *Time* magazine (April 8, 1996) reminds us that "just as there are bad marriages, there are [also] good divorces in which both parents maintain their financial and emotional responsibility for the kids." Indeed, the negative consequences of divorce are themselves routinely overstated. From Ehrenreich: "The alleged psyche-scarring effects of divorce have been grossly exaggerated." And from Katha Pollitt: "There is no study that shows that children do worse in divorce than they do in a really dysfunctional home." According to these critics, the covenant marriage movement errs in its assumption that divorce is always bad and that all marriages deserve to be kept together no matter the cost; the other side of the coin is that the law really doesn't do anything to make marriages better, just harder to terminate.

· · ·

Nearly everyone concedes that divorce is, in the typical case, emotionally hurtful and often financially disastrous. No credible study shows otherwise and no party to the dispute over CM disagrees. Likewise, no one in their right mind would assert that all marriages should be held together at all costs, no matter what. We have already emphasized more than once that the law explicitly acknowledges that some marriages are destructive and require immediate termination; the law also provides the legal machinery by which to terminate them.

But enough evidence has now accumulated on the down-side of divorce to force recognition that divorce, like marriage, is not something to be taken lightly or entered into without serious reflection and discussion. Through the pre-marital counseling provision, covenant marriage is meant to force couples to take their marriages more seriously; the post-marital counseling provision, the restricted grounds for fault divorces, and the extended waiting period for no-fault divorces are all meant to get couples to take their divorces more seriously as well. The symbolism of a "covenant marriage" is altogether too religious and traditional for the tastes of many, but it is hard to quarrel with the substance of what the law intends to accomplish.

One might also ask, if divorce is only a "symptom" of bad marriages, then what are bad marriages a symptom of? Family specialists know that there is no one factor, or even a relatively small set of factors, that can adequately account for the break-up of marriages. Many marriages in the contemporary era go bad for economic reasons; here it is worth emphasizing that the young people of today comprise the first generation in history that cannot simply assume they will end up better off economically than their parents. Young adults, especially minority adults in the inner cities, have lost a third of their earning capacity in the last decade; poverty rates in the 1980s and 1990s have been generally higher than anything witnessed in this country since the onset of the War on Poverty in 1964. Crime, drugs, violence and disease threaten families; inadequate schools threaten families; industrial relocation threatens families; the dismantling of the welfare state threatens families. As we have already said, the viability of marriage and family life is under assault from any number of large-scale forces, very few of which can be influenced by the legal terms under which couples choose to marry. And if state legislators believe that passing a covenant marriage law adequately addresses even a few of these large-scale forces, they are seriously deluded.

Covenant marriage reinforces traditional gender roles and is an effort to make (or keep) women subservient to men. Many people seem to object to covenant marriage more on symbolic than substantive grounds. The very concept of a covenant marriage, as Terry O'Neill has observed, is an "endorsement of the belief that marriage symbolically represents Christ's covenant with the church." For the contemporary secular humanist, any reference or even allusion to religion or religiosity is anathema, and CM certainly has its religious connotations. It is also not wrong to suggest that in Louisiana (and for that matter, everywhere else), covenant marriage is a creation of the religious right and is motivated in most cases by deep, nearly fanatical desires to resurrect traditional family values, most certainly including the idea that men should be the heads of their households and women should be deferential and subservient towards them. Some therefore feel that covenant marriage is really little more than a misguided effort to put the force of law behind Biblical pronouncements about women's "proper role" in marriage.

But one must guard against confusing the reasons why the covenant marriage law was passed with the effects it is likely to have, or mistaking the symbolism of the concept for its substance. Covenant marriage may well seem to be both "too religious" and "too chauvinistic," but we have read the Louisiana law front to back several times, and it contains nothing that would deny covenant marriages to atheists who wanted them or that would prevent a covenant couple from forging a completely egalitarian or otherwise "unconventional" relationship. Nothing about the law dictates how covenant couples must arrange their private affairs inside the framework of their marriage.

• • •

The practical effect of covenant marriage ultimately has nothing to do with religion or traditional male and female roles. It has everything to do with giving people more choices. In the present case, the choice being offered is between a standard marriage that is readily terminated through the applicable no-fault regime and a covenant marriage that is more difficult both to enter and to exit. CM says in practical effect that no one other than couples themselves can decide which form of marriage is best for them. Thus, the law begins to change marriage from a status to a free contract between adults. . . .

As is perhaps obvious, a great deal that is presently being said and written about covenant marriage is misguided. But that certainly does not mean that there are no interesting issues or questions raised by the emergence and probable diffusion of covenant marriage regimes.

. . .

The big question is whether covenant marriages will prove to differ from standard marriages in their stability, duration, or overall health, net of the effects of selection factors. Do they produce fewer divorces? Happier marriages? More well-adjusted children? Are the spouses in covenant marriage less likely to cheat on one another? Is there less physical, verbal and emotional abuse in covenant marriages than standard ones? Are family relations more functional? More democratic? Or do covenant marriages promote highly traditional patterns of familial interaction, where wives are subordinate to husbands and children are "seen but not heard"? What will become of the covenant in the out-years, when marriages start to fail and the adult partners are looking for a way out? Argumentation by enthusiasts and skeptics cannot substitute for valid evidence reliably gathered.

. . .

   ◉   ◉   ◉

Questions

1. What is covenant marriage? How does it differ from conventional marriage?

2. What is no-fault divorce? How has it affected the divorce rate?

3. Outline the various perspectives on covenant marriage. Which one was the most persuasive? Why?

4. Why do the authors argue that covenant marriage is not the solution to the divorce problem? Is their argument persuasive? Why or why not?

5. Where do you stand on the issue of covenant marriage? Explain your position.

Race and Ethnicity

From Chapter 11 of *Society: The Basics*, 11/e. John J. Macionis. Copyright © 2011 by Pearson Education. All rights reserved.

Race and Ethnicity

- What are race and ethnicity, and how are they created by society?

- Why does the United States have so much racial and ethnic diversity?

- How are race and ethnicity important dimensions of social inequality today?

Watch the *Core Concepts in Sociology* video "Racial Stereotypes and Discrimination" on mysoclab.com

This chapter explains how race and ethnicity are created by society. Both race and ethnicity are not only matters of difference but also dimensions of social inequality.

On a cool November morning in New York City, an instructor in a sociology class at Bronx Community College is leading a small-group discussion of race and ethnicity. He explains that the meaning of both concepts is far less clear than most people think. Then he asks, "How do you describe yourself?"

Eva Rodriguez leans forward in her chair and is quick to respond. "Who am I? Or should I say *what* am I? This is hard for me to answer. Most people think of race as black and white. But it's not. I have both black and white ancestry in me, but you know what? I don't think of myself in that way. I don't think of myself in terms of race at all. It would be better to call me Puerto Rican or Hispanic. Personally, I prefer the term 'Latina.' Calling myself Latina says I have mixed racial heritage, and that's what I am. I wish more people understood that race is not clear-cut."

This chapter examines the meaning of race and ethnicity. There are now millions of people in the United States who, like Eva Rodriguez, do not think of themselves in terms of a single category but as having a mix of ancestry.

The Social Meaning of Race and Ethnicity

As the story that opened this chapter suggests, people often confuse "race" and "ethnicity." For this reason, we begin with some basic definitions.

Race

A **race** is *a socially constructed category of people who share biologically transmitted traits that members of a society consider important.* People may classify one another racially on the basis of physical characteristics such as skin color, facial features, hair texture, and body shape.

Racial diversity appeared among our human ancestors as the result of living in different geographic regions of the world. In regions of intense heat, people developed darker skin (from the natural pigment melanin), which offers protection from the sun; in moderate climates, people developed lighter skin. Such traits are literally only skin deep because human beings the world over are members of a single biological species.

The striking variety of racial traits found today is also the product of migration; genetic characteristics once common to a single place are now found in many lands. Especially pronounced is the racial mix in the Middle East (that is, western Asia), historically a crossroads of migration. Greater racial uniformity characterizes more isolated peoples such as the island-dwelling Japanese. But every population has some genetic mixture, and increasing contact ensures even more racial blending of physical characteristics in the future.

Although we often think of race in terms of biological elements, race is a socially constructed concept. It is true that human beings differ in any number of ways involving physical traits, but a "race" comes into being only when the members of a society decide that some particular physical trait (such as skin color or eye shape) actually *matters*.

Because race is a matter of social definitions, it is a highly variable concept. For example, the members of U.S. society consider racial differences more important than people of many other countries. We also tend to "see" three racial categories—typically, black, white, and Asian—while other societies identify many more categories. People in Brazil, for instance, distinguish between *branca* (white), *parda* (brown), *morena* (brunette), *mulata* (mulatto), *preta* (black), and *amarela* (yellow) (Inciardi, Surratt, & Telles, 2000).

In addition, race may be defined differently by various categories of people within a society. In the United States, for example, research shows that white people "see" black people as having darker skin color than black people do (Hill, 2002).

The meaning and importance of race not only differ from place to place but also change over time. Back in 1900, for example, it was common in the United States to consider people of Irish, Italian, or Jewish ancestry as "nonwhite." By 1950, however, this was no longer the case, and such people today are considered part of the "white" category (Loveman, 1999; Brodkin, 2007).

Race and Ethnicity

Researchers have found that biracial and multiracial people choose different racial identities in different settings, depending on whom they are with (Harris & Sim, 2002). Have you ever experienced such a "racial shift"? Explain.

David Young-Wolff\PhotoEdit Inc.

David Young-Wolff\PhotoEdit Inc.

Owen Franken\CORBIS- NY

Charles O'Rear\CORBIS- NY

Paul W. Liebhardt

Buddy Mays\Alamy Images

The range of biological variation in human beings is far greater than any system of racial classification allows. This fact is made obvious by trying to place all of the people pictured here into simple racial categories.

Today, the Census Bureau allows people to describe themselves using more than one racial category (offering six single-race options and fifty-seven multiracial options). Our society officially recognizes a wide range of multiracial people (U.S. Census Bureau, 2008).

Racial Types

Scientists invented the concept of race more than a century ago as they tried to organize the world's physical diversity into three racial types. They called people with relatively light skin and fine hair *Caucasoid,* people with darker skin and coarse hair *Negroid,* and people with yellow or brown skin and distinctive folds on the eyelids *Mongoloid.*

Sociologists consider such terms misleading at best and harmful at worst. For one thing, no society contains biologically "pure" people. The skin color of people we might call "Caucasoid" (or "Indo-European," "Caucasian," or more commonly, "white") ranges from very light (typical in Scandinavia) to very dark (in southern India). The same variation exists among so-called "Negroids" ("Africans" or, more commonly, "black" people) and "Mongoloids" ("Asians"). In fact, many "white" people (say, in southern India) actually have darker skin than many "black" people (the Aborigines of Australia).

Overall, the three racial categories differ in just 6 percent of their genes, and there is actually more genetic variation *within* each category than *between* categories. This means that two people in the European nation of Sweden, randomly selected, are likely to have at least as much genetic difference as a Swede and a person in the African nation of Senegal (Harris & Sim, 2002; American Sociological Association, 2003; California Newsreel, 2003).

So just how important is race? From a biological point of view, knowing people's racial category allows us to predict almost nothing about them. Why, then, do societies make so much of race? Such categories allow societies to rank people in a hierarchy, giving some people more money, power, and prestige than others and allowing some people to feel that they are inherently "better" than others.

Because race may matter so much, societies sometimes construct racial categories in extreme ways. Throughout much of the twentieth century, for example, many southern states labeled as "colored" anyone with as little as one thirty-second African ancestry (that is, one African American great-great-great-grandparent). Today, the law allows parents to declare the race of a child (or not) as they wish. Even so, most members of our society are still very sensitive to people's racial backgrounds.

Race and Ethnicity

minority any category of people distinguished by physical or cultural
difference that a society sets apart and subordinates

Table 1 Racial and Ethnic Categories
in the United States, 2008

Racial or Ethnic Classification*	Approximate U.S. Population	Share of Total Population
Hispanic descent	**46,943,613**	**15.4%**
Mexican	30,783,559	10.1
Puerto Rican	4,216,533	1.4
Cuban	1,617,010	0.5
Other Hispanic	10,371,511	3.4
African descent	**39,058,834**	**12.8**
Nigerian	266,204	0.1
Ethiopian	165,747	0.1
Somalian	82,716	<
Other African	38,544,167	12.6
Native American descent	**2,443,422**	**0.8**
American Indian	1,993,316	0.7
Alaska Native	101,365	<
Other Native American	348,741	0.1
Asian or Pacific Island descent	**14,111,185**	**4.6**
Chinese	3,077,783	1.0
Asian Indian	2,495,998	0.8
Filipino	2,425,697	0.8
Vietnamese	1,431,980	0.5
Korean	1,344,267	0.4
Japanese	710,063	0.2
Cambodian	186,068	0.1
Other Asian or Pacific Islander	2,439,329	0.8
West Indian descent	**2,560,348**	**0.8**
Arab descent	**1,573,530**	**0.5**
Non-Hispanic European descent	**199,491,458**	**65.6**
German	50,272,200	16.5
Irish	36,278,332	11.9
English	27,517,339	9.0
Italian	17,749,037	5.8
Polish	9,887,099	3.3
French	9,446,927	3.1
Scottish	5,827,046	1.9
Dutch	4,928,917	1.6
Norwegian	4,643,339	1.5
Other Non-Hispanic European	32,941,222	10.8
Two or more races	**7,013,872**	**2.3**

*People of Hispanic descent may be of any race. Many people also identify with more than
one ethnic category. Therefore, figures total more than 100 percent.*
< indicates less than 0.1 percent.

Source: U.S. Census Bureau (2009).

A Trend toward Mixture

Over many generations and throughout the Americas, genetic traits
from around the world have become mixed. Many "black" people
have a significant Caucasoid ancestry, just as many "white" people
have some Negroid genes. Whatever people may think, race is not a
black-and-white issue.

Today, people are more willing to define themselves as multiracial. On the U.S. Census Bureau's American Community Survey
(2009), more than 7 million people described themselves by checking two or more racial categories. The number of interracial births
in the United States has been increasing. In 2008, some 4 percent of
children under the age of five were multiracial, compared to less than
1 percent of people age sixty-five and older.

Ethnicity

Ethnicity is *a shared cultural heritage.* People define themselves—or
others—as members of an *ethnic category* based on common ancestors, language, and religion that give them a distinctive social identity.
The United States is a multiethnic society that favors the English language; even so, almost 56 million people (20 percent of the U.S.
population over the age of five) speak Spanish, Italian, German,
French, Chinese dialects, or some other language in their homes. In
California, more than 40 percent of the population does so (U.S.
Census Bureau, 2009).

With regard to religion, the United States is a predominantly
Protestant nation, but most people of Spanish, Italian, and Polish
ancestry are Roman Catholic, and many others of Greek, Ukrainian,
and Russian descent belong to the Eastern Orthodox Church. More
than 6 million Jewish Americans have ancestral ties to various nations
around the world. The population of Muslim men and women is
increasing and is variously estimated at between 2 and 3 million (Pew
Research Center, 2007b).

Like the reality of race, the meaning of ethnicity is socially constructed, becoming important only because society defines it that way.
For example, U.S. society defines people of Spanish descent as "Latin,"
even though Italy probably has a more "Latin" culture than Spain.
People of Italian descent are viewed not as Latin but as "European"
and thus less "different" (Camara, 2000; Brodkin, 2007). Like racial
differences, the importance of ethnic differences can change over time.
A century ago, Catholics and Jews were considered "different" in the
predominantly Protestant United States. This is much less true today.

Keep in mind that race is constructed from *biological* traits and
ethnicity is constructed from *cultural* traits. Of course, the two may
go hand in hand. For example, Japanese Americans have distinctive
physical traits and, for those who maintain a traditional way of life,
a distinctive culture as well. Table 1 provides the most recent data on
the racial and ethnic diversity of the United States.

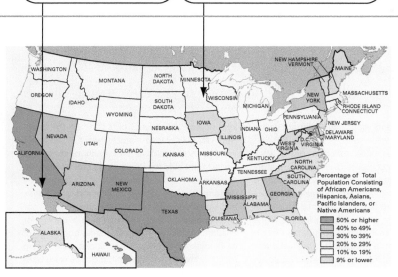

Marcos Chapa attends college in San Diego and lives in a community where most people are in some minority category.

Marianne Blumquist attends a community college in a small town an hour west of Minneapolis, where there are few racial or ethnic minorities.

Explore the percentage of foreign-born people in your local community and in counties across the United States on mysoclab.com

Seeing Ourselves

NATIONAL MAP 1

Where the Minority Majority Already Exists

In 2008, minorities were a majority in four states—Hawaii, California, New Mexico, and Texas—as well as the District of Columbia. At the other extreme, Vermont and Maine have the lowest share of racial and ethnic minorities (about 5 percent each). Why are states with high minority populations located in the South and Southwest?

Explore on mysoclab.com

Source: U.S. Census Bureau (2009).

Percentage of Total Population Consisting of African Americans, Hispanics, Asians, Pacific Islanders, or Native Americans

- 50% or higher
- 40% to 49%
- 30% to 39%
- 20% to 29%
- 10% to 19%
- 9% or lower

On an individual level, people either play up or play down their ethnicity, depending on whether they want to fit in or stand apart from the surrounding society: Immigrants may drop their cultural traditions over time or, like many people of Native American descent in recent years, try to revive their heritage. For most people, ethnicity is a more complex issue than race because they identify with several ethnic backgrounds. The golf star Tiger Woods, for example, describes himself as one-eighth American Indian, one-fourth Thai, one-fourth Chinese, one-eighth white, and one-fourth black (J. E. White, 1997).

Minorities

March 3, Dallas, Texas. Spending a day or two in just about any hotel in a major U.S. city presents a lesson in contrasts: The majority of the guests checking in and out are white; the majority of the employees who carry the luggage, serve the food, and clean the rooms are racial or ethnic minorities.

A **minority** is *any category of people distinguished by physical or cultural difference that a society sets apart and subordinates.* Minority standing can be based on race, ethnicity, or both. As shown in Table 1, white people of non-Hispanic background (65.6 percent of the total) are still a majority of the U.S. population. But the share of minorities is increasing. Today, minorities are a majority in four states (California, New Mexico, Texas, and Hawaii) and in half of the country's 100 largest cities. By about 2042, minorities are likely to form a majority of the U.S. population (Mather & Pollard, 2008). National Map 1 shows where a minority majority already exists.

Minorities have two important characteristics. First, society imposes on them a *distinct identity,* which may be based on physical or cultural traits. Second, minorities experience *subordination.* As this chapter shows, U.S. minorities typically have lower income, lower occupational prestige, and limited schooling. Class, race, and ethnicity, as well as gender, are overlapping and reinforcing dimensions of social stratification. The Thinking About Diversity box describes the struggles of recent Latin American immigrants to the United States.

Of course, not all members of a particular minority category are disadvantaged. For example, some Latinos are quite wealthy, certain Chinese Americans are celebrated business leaders, and African Americans are among our nation's political leaders. But even job success rarely allows individuals to escape their minority standing. Race or ethnicity often serves as a *master status* that overshadows personal accomplishments.

Minorities usually make up a small proportion of a society's population, but that is not always the case. Black South Africans are disadvantaged even though they are a numerical majority in their country. In the United States, women make up slightly more than half the population but are still struggling for the opportunities and privileges enjoyed by men.

Prejudice and Stereotypes

November 19, Jerusalem, Israel. We are driving along the edge of this historical city, a holy place to Jews, Christians, and Muslims, when Razi, our taxi driver, spots a small group of Falasha—Ethiopian Jews—on a street corner. "Those people over there," he begins, "they are different.

prejudice a rigid and unfair generalization about an entire category of people

stereotype a simplified description applied to every person in some category

racism the belief that one racial category is innately superior or inferior to another

THINKING ABOUT DIVERSITY: RACE, CLASS, & GENDER

Hard Work: The Immigrant Life in the United States

Early in the morning, it is already hot in Houston as a line of pickup trucks snakes slowly into a dusty yard, where 200 laborers have been gathered since dawn, hoping for a day's work. The driver of the first truck opens his window and tells the foreman that he is looking for a crew to spread boiling tar on a roof. Abdonel Cespedes, the foreman, turns to the crowd, and after a few minutes, three workers step forward and climb into the back of the truck. The next driver is looking for two experienced housepainters. The scene is repeated over and over as men and a few women leave to dig ditches, spread cement, hang drywall, open clogged septic tanks, or crawl under houses to poison rats.

As each driver pulls into the yard, the foreman asks, "How much?" Most of the people in the trucks offer $5 an hour. Cespedes automatically responds, "$7.25; the going rate is $7.25 for an hour's hard work." Sometimes he convinces people to pay that much, but usually not. The workers, who come from Mexico, El Salvador, and Guatemala, know that dozens of them will end up with no work at all this day. Most accept $5 or $6 an hour because they know that when the day is over, $50 is better than nothing.

Labor markets like this one are common in large cities, especially across the southwestern United States. The surge in immigration in recent years has brought millions of people to this country in

search of work, and most have little schooling and speak little English.

Manuel Barrera has taken a day's work moving the entire contents of a store to a storage site. He arrives at the boarded-up building and gazes at the mountains of heavy furniture that he must carry out to a moving van, drive across town, and then carry again. He sighs when he realizes how hot it is outside and that it is even hotter inside the building. He will have no break for lunch. No one says anything about toilets. Barrera shakes his head. "I will do this

These immigrants gather on a New York City street corner every morning hoping to be hired for construction work that pays about $60 a day with no benefits.

kind of work because it puts food on the table. But I did not foresee it would turn out like this."

The hard truth is that immigrants to the United States do the jobs that no one else wants. At the bottom level of the national economy, they perform low-skill jobs in restaurants and hotels and on construction crews, and they work in private homes cooking, cleaning, and caring for children. Across the United States, about half of all housekeepers, household cooks, tailors, and restaurant waiters in the United States were born abroad. Few immigrants make much more than the minimum wage ($7.25 in 2009), and rarely do immigrant workers receive any health or pension benefits. Many well-off families take the labor of immigrants as much for granted as they do their air-conditioned cars and comfortable homes.

WHAT DO YOU THINK?

1. In what ways do you or members of your family depend on the low-paid labor of immigrants?

2. Do you favor allowing the 12 million immigrants who entered this country illegally to earn citizenship? What should be done?

3. Should the U.S. government act to reduce the number of immigrants entering the country in the future? Why or why not?

Sources: Based on Booth (1998), Tumulty (2006), and U.S. Department of Labor (2008).

Joe Raedle\Getty Images Inc.

> *They don't drive cars. They don't want to improve themselves. Even when our country offers them schooling, they don't take it." He shakes his head at the Ethiopians and drives on.*

Prejudice is *a rigid and unfair generalization about an entire category of people.* Prejudice is unfair because *all* people in some category are described as the same, based on little or no direct evidence. Prejudice may target people of a particular social class, sex, sexual orientation, age, political affiliation, race, or ethnicity.

Prejudices are *prejudgments* that can be either positive or negative. Our positive prejudices exaggerate the virtues of people like ourselves, and our negative prejudices condemn those who are different from us. Negative prejudice can be expressed as anything from mild dislike to outright hostility. Because such attitudes are rooted in culture, everyone has at least some prejudice.

Prejudice often takes the form of a **stereotype** (*stereo* is derived from a Greek word meaning "solid"), which is *a simplified description applied to every person in some category.* Many white people hold

Go to the Multimedia Library at **mysoclab.com** to watch the ABC News *20/20* video "Colorism"

Seeing Sociology in Everyday Life

Do you think students on your campus have become more accepting of social diversity? Explain why or why not.

stereotypical views of minorities. Stereotyping is especially harmful to minorities in the workplace. If company officials see minority workers only in terms of a stereotype, they will make assumptions about their abilities, steer them toward certain jobs, and limit their access to better opportunities (R. L. Kaufman, 2002).

Minorities, too, stereotype whites and also other minorities (T. W. Smith, 1996; Cummings & Lambert, 1997). Surveys show, for example, that more African Americans than whites express the belief that Asians engage in unfair business practices and that more Asians than whites criticize Hispanics for having too many children (Perlmutter, 2002).

Measuring Prejudice: The Social Distance Scale

One measure of prejudice is *social distance,* how closely people are willing to interact with members of some category. In the 1920s, Emory Bogardus developed the *social distance scale* shown in Figure 1. Bogardus (1925) asked students at colleges and universities in the United States how closely they were willing to interact with people in thirty racial and ethnic categories. People express the greatest social distance (most negative prejudice) by declaring that some category of people should be barred from the country entirely (point 7 in the figure); at the other extreme, people express the least social distance (most social acceptance) by saying they would accept a member of some category into their family through marriage (point 1).

Bogardus (1925, 1967; Owen, Elsner, & McFaul, 1977) found that people felt much more social distance from some categories than from others. In general, students in his surveys expressed the most social distance from Hispanics, African Americans, Asians, and Turks by indicating that they would accept such people as co-workers but not as neighbors, close friends, or family members. People expressed the least social distance from those from northern and western Europe, including English and Scottish people, and also Canadians, indicating that they were willing to include them in their families by marriage. ⬤ Go to **mysoclab.com**

What patterns of social distance do we find among college students today? A recent study using the same social distance scale[1] reported three major findings (Parrillo & Donoghue, 2005):

1. **Student opinion shows a trend toward greater social acceptance.** Today's students express less social distance from all minorities than students did decades ago. Figure 1 shows that the mean (average) score on the social distance scale declined from 2.14 in 1925 to 1.93 in 1977 and to 1.44 in 2001. Respondents (81 percent of whom were white) showed notably greater acceptance of African Americans, a category of people that moved up from near the bottom in 1925 to the top one-third in 2001.

2. **People see less difference between various minorities.** The earliest studies found the difference between the highest- and lowest-ranked minorities (the range of averages) equal to almost three points on the scale. As the figure shows, the most recent research produced a range of averages of less than one point, indicating that today's students tend to see fewer differences between various categories of people.

3. **The terrorist attacks of September 11, 2001, may have reduced social acceptance of Arabs and Muslims.** The most recent study was conducted just a few weeks after September 11, 2001. Perhaps the fact that the nineteen men who attacked the World Trade Center and the Pentagon were Arabs and Muslims is part of the reason that students ranked these categories last on the social distance scale. However, not a single student gave Arabs or Muslims a 7, indicating that they should be barred from the country. On the contrary, the 2001 mean scores (1.94 for Arabs and 1.88 for Muslims) show higher social acceptance than students in 1977 expressed toward eighteen of the thirty categories of people studied.

Racism

A powerful and harmful form of prejudice, **racism** is *the belief that one racial category is innately superior or inferior to another.* Racism has existed throughout world

David Young-Wolff\PhotoEdit Inc.

Recent research measuring student attitudes confirms the trend of declining prejudice toward all racial and ethnic categories. On your campus, does race or ethnicity guide people's choice in romantic attachments? Do some racial and ethnic categories mix more often than others? Explain your answer.

[1]Parrillo and Donoghue dropped seven of the categories used by Bogardus (Armenians, Czechs, Finns, Norwegians, Scots, Swedes, and Turks), claiming that they were no longer visible minorities. He added nine new categories (Africans, Arabs, Cubans, Dominicans, Haitians, Jamaicans, Muslims, Puerto Ricans, and Vietnamese), claiming that these are visible minorities today. This change probably encouraged higher social distance scores, making the trend toward decreasing social distance all the more significant.

○ Making the Grade

On the social distance scale, the higher the number, the greater the social distance, meaning more negative prejudice.

○ Making the Grade

The text presents four theories of prejudice. Check your understanding of each by completing this sentence: "This theory explains that prejudice is caused by . . ."

Student Snapshot

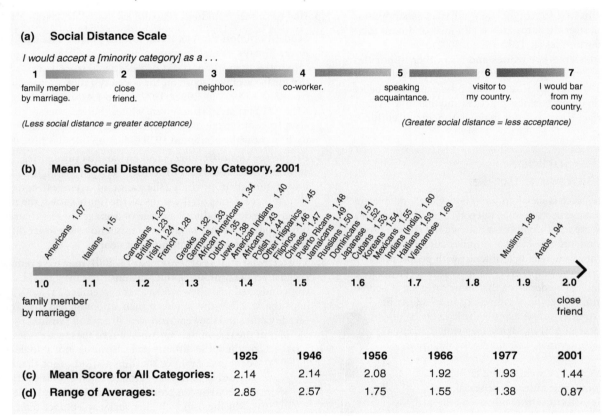

(a) **Social Distance Scale**

I would accept a [minority category] as a . . .

1	2	3	4	5	6	7
family member by marriage.	close friend.	neighbor.	co-worker.	speaking acquaintance.	visitor to my country.	I would bar from my country.

(Less social distance = greater acceptance)   *(Greater social distance = less acceptance)*

(b) **Mean Social Distance Score by Category, 2001**

Americans 1.07, Italians 1.15, Canadians 1.20, British 1.23, Irish 1.24, French 1.28, Greeks 1.32, Germans 1.33, African Americans 1.34, Dutch 1.35, Jews 1.38, American Indians 1.40, Polish 1.43, Other Hispanics 1.44, Filipinos 1.46, Chinese 1.47, Puerto Ricans 1.48, Jamaicans 1.49, Russians 1.50, Dominicans 1.51, Japanese 1.52, Cubans 1.53, Koreans 1.54, Mexicans 1.55, Indians (India) 1.60, Haitians 1.63, Vietnamese 1.69, Muslims 1.88, Arabs 1.94

1.0	1.1	1.2	1.3	1.4	1.5	1.6	1.7	1.8	1.9	2.0

family member by marriage   close friend

	1925	**1946**	**1956**	**1966**	**1977**	**2001**
(c) **Mean Score for All Categories:**	2.14	2.14	2.08	1.92	1.93	1.44
(d) **Range of Averages:**	2.85	2.57	1.75	1.55	1.38	0.87

FIGURE 1 **Bogardus Social Distance Research**

The social distance scale is a good way to measure prejudice. Part (a) illustrates the complete social distance scale, from least social distance at the far left to greatest social distance at the far right. Part (b) shows the mean (average) social distance score received by each category of people in 2001. Part (c) presents the overall mean score (the average of the scores received by all racial and ethnic categories) in specific years. These scores have fallen from 2.14 in 1925 to 1.44 in 2001, showing that students express less social distance from minorities today than they did in the past. Part (d) shows the range of averages, the difference between the highest and lowest scores in given years (in 2001, for instance, it was 0.87, the difference between the high score of 1.94 for Arabs and the low score of 1.07 for Americans). This figure has also become smaller since 1925, indicating that today's students tend to see fewer differences between various categories of people.

Source: Parrillo & Donoghue (2005).

history. Despite their many achievements, the ancient Greeks, the peoples of India, and the Chinese all considered people unlike themselves inferior.

Racism has also been widespread throughout the history of the United States, where ideas about racial inferiority supported slavery.

Today, overt racism in this country has decreased because more people believe in evaluating others, in the words of Martin Luther King Jr., "not by the color of their skin but by the content of their character."

Even so, racism remains a serious social problem, as some people still argue that certain racial and ethnic categories are smarter than

Go to the Multimedia Library at **mysoclab.com** to listen to the NPR report "Race and Intelligence: Politicizing the Findings"

scapegoat a person or category of people, typically with little power, whom people unfairly blame for their own troubles

SEEING SOCIOLOGY IN EVERYDAY LIFE

Does Race Affect Intelligence?

As we go through an average day, we encounter people of various racial and ethnic categories. We also deal with people who are very intelligent as well as those whose abilities are more modest. But is there a connection between race or ethnicity and intelligence?

Common stereotypes say that Asian Americans are smarter than white people and that the typical white person is more intelligent than the average African American. Throughout the history of the United States, many people have assumed that some categories of people are smarter than others. Just as important, people have used this thinking to justify the privileges of the allegedly superior category and even to bar supposedly inferior people from entering this country.

So what do we know about intelligence? Scientists know that people, as individuals, differ in mental abilities. The distribution of human intelligence forms a "bell curve," as shown in the figure. A person's *intelligence quotient* (IQ) is calculated as the person's mental age in years, as measured by a test, divided by the person's actual age in years, with the result multiplied by 100. An eight-year-old who performs like a ten-year-old has an IQ of $10 \div 8 = 1.25 \times 100 = 125$. Average performance is defined as an IQ of 100.

In a controversial study of intelligence and social inequality, Richard Herrnstein and Charles Murray (1994) claim that race is related to measures of intelligence. More specifically, they say that the average IQ for people of European ancestry is 100, for people of East Asian ancestry is 103, and for people of African ancestry is 90.

Such assertions go against our democratic and egalitarian beliefs that no racial type is naturally better than another. Because these findings can increase prejudice, critics argue that intelligence tests are not valid and even that the concept of intelligence has little real meaning.

Most social scientists believe that IQ tests do measure something important that we think of as intelligence, and they agree that *individuals* vary in intellectual aptitude. But they reject the idea that any *category* of people, on average, is naturally smarter than any other. So how do we explain the overall differences in IQ scores by race?

Thomas Sowell (1994, 1995) explains that most of this difference results not from biology but from environment. In some skillful sociological detective work, Sowell traced IQ scores for various racial and ethnic categories throughout the twentieth century. He found that on average, early-twentieth-century immigrants from European nations such as Poland, Lithuania, Italy, and Greece, as well as from Asian countries including China and Japan, scored 10 to 15 points below the U.S. average. But by the end of the twentieth century, people in these same categories had IQ scores that were average or above average. Among Italian Americans, for example, average IQ jumped almost 10 points; among Polish and Chinese Americans, the increase was almost 20 points.

Because genetic changes occur over thousands of years and most people in these categories marry others like themselves, biological factors cannot explain such a rapid rise in IQ scores. The only reasonable explanation is

changing cultural patterns. The descendants of early immigrants improved their intellectual performance as their standard of living rose and their opportunity for schooling increased.

Sowell found that much the same was true of African Americans. Historically, the average IQ score of African Americans living in the North has been about 10 points higher than the average score of those living in the South. Among the descendants of African Americans who migrated from the South to the North after 1940, IQ scores went up, just as they did for descendants of European and Asian immigrants. Thus environmental factors appear to be critical in explaining differences in IQ among various categories of people.

According to Sowell, these test score differences tell us that *cultural patterns matter*. Asians who score high on tests are no smarter than other people, but they have been raised to value learning and pursue excellence. For their part, African Americans are no less intelligent than anyone else, but they carry a legacy of disadvantage that can undermine self-confidence and discourage achievement. ● Go to **mysoclab.com**

WHAT DO YOU THINK?

1. If IQ scores reflect people's environment, are they valid measures of intelligence? Could they be harmful?

2. According to Thomas Sowell, why do some racial and ethnic categories show dramatic short-term gains in average IQ scores?

3. Do you think parents and schools influence a child's IQ score? If so, how?

others. The Seeing Sociology in Everyday Life box explains that these commonsense stereotypes fail to recognize that racial differences in mental abilities result from environment rather than from biology.

Theories of Prejudice

Where does prejudice come from? Social scientists provide several answers to this vexing question, focusing on frustration, personality, culture, and social conflict.

Scapegoat Theory

Scapegoat theory holds that prejudice springs from frustration among people who are themselves disadvantaged (Dollard et al., 1939). Take the case of a white woman who is frustrated by her low-paying job in a textile factory. Directing her hostility at the powerful factory owners carries the obvious risk of being fired; therefore, she may blame her low pay on the presence of minority co-workers. Her prejudice does not improve her situation, but it is a relatively safe way to express

The New York Times

In Job Hunt, College Degree Can't Close Racial Gap

By MICHAEL LUO
December 1, 2009

Johnny R. Williams, 30, would appear to be an unlikely person to have to fret about the impact of race on his job search, with companies like JPMorgan Chase and an M.B.A. from the University of Chicago on his résumé.

But after graduating from business school last year and not having much success garnering interviews, he decided to retool his résumé, scrubbing it of any details that might tip off his skin color. His membership, for instance, in the African American business students association? Deleted.

"If they're going to X me," Mr. Williams said, "I'd like to at least get in the door first."

Similarly, Barry Jabbar Sykes, 37, who has a degree in mathematics from Morehouse College, a historically black college in Atlanta, now uses Barry J. Sykes in his continuing search for an information technology position, even though he has gone by Jabbar his whole life.

"Barry sounds like I could be from Ireland," he said.

That race remains a serious obstacle in the job market for African Americans, even those with degrees from respected colleges, may seem to some people a jarring contrast to decades of progress by blacks, culminating in President Obama's election.

But there is ample evidence that racial inequities remain when it comes to employment. Black joblessness has long far outstripped that of whites. And strikingly, the disparity . . . has been even more pronounced for those with college degrees, compared with those without. Education, it seems, does not level the playing field—in fact, it appears to have made it more uneven. . . .

The unemployment rate for black male college graduates 25 and older in 2009 has been nearly twice that of white male college graduates—8.4 percent compared with 4.4 percent.

Various academic studies have confirmed that black job seekers have a harder time than whites. A study published several years ago in *The American Economic Review* titled "Are Emily and Greg More Employable than Lakisha and Jamal?" found that applicants with black-sounding names received 50 percent fewer callbacks than those with white-sounding names.

A more recent study, published this year in *The Journal of Labor Economics* found white, Asian, and Hispanic managers tended to hire more whites and fewer blacks than black managers did.

The discrimination is rarely overt, according to interviews with more than two dozen college-educated black job seekers around the country. . . . Instead, those interviewed told subtler stories, referring to surprised looks and offhand comments, interviews that fell apart almost as soon as they began, and the sudden loss of interest from companies after meetings. . . .

Mr. Williams recently applied to a Dallas money management firm that had posted a position with top business schools. The hiring manager had seemed ecstatic to hear from him, telling him they had trouble getting people from prestigious business schools to move to the area. . . . .

But when Mr. Williams later met two men from the firm for lunch, he said they appeared stunned when he strolled up to introduce himself.

---

anger, and it may give her the comforting feeling that at least she is superior to someone.

A **scapegoat,** then, is *a person or category of people, typically with little power, whom other people unfairly blame for their own troubles.* Because they have little power and thus are usually "safe targets," minorities often are used as scapegoats.

Authoritarian Personality Theory

Theodor Adorno and his colleagues (1950) considered extreme prejudice a personality trait of certain individuals. This conclusion is supported by research indicating that people who show strong prejudice toward one minority are usually intolerant of all minorities. These *authoritarian personalities* rigidly conform to conventional cultural values and see moral issues as clear-cut matters of right and wrong. According to Adorno, people who grow up developing authoritarian personalities also view society as naturally competitive, with "better" people (like themselves) dominating those who are weaker (all minorities).

Adorno and colleagues also found the opposite pattern to be true: People who express tolerance toward one minority are likely to be accepting of all. Such people tend to be more flexible in their moral judgments and treat all people as equals.

Adorno thought that people with little education and those raised by cold and demanding parents tend to develop authoritarian

personalities. Filled with anger and anxiety as children, they grow into hostile and aggressive adults who seek out scapegoats.

Culture Theory

A third theory claims that although extreme prejudice is found in certain people, some prejudice is found in everyone. Why? Because prejudice is part of the culture in which we all live and learn. The Bogardus social distance studies help prove the point. Bogardus found that students across the country had mostly the same attitudes toward specific racial and ethnic categories, feeling closer to some and more distant from others.

More evidence that prejudice is rooted in culture is the fact that minorities express the same attitudes as white people toward categories other than their own. Such patterns suggest that individuals hold prejudices because we live in a "culture of prejudice" that has taught us to view certain categories of people as "better" or "worse" than others.

Do we live a "culture of prejudice"? Seeing Sociology in the News explains that minority job-seekers, especially those with good training, have reason to think that the answer may be yes.

Conflict Theory

A fourth explanation proposes that prejudice is used as a tool by powerful people not only to justify privilege for themselves but also to

"Their eyes kind of hit the ceiling a bit," he said. "It was kind of quiet for about 45 seconds."

The company's interest in him quickly cooled, setting off the inevitable questions in his mind.

Discrimination in many cases may not even be intentional, some job seekers pointed out, but simply a matter of people gravitating toward similar people, casting about for the right "cultural fit," a buzzword often heard in corporate circles.

There is also the matter of how many jobs, especially higher-level ones, are never even posted and depend on word-of-mouth and informal networks, in many cases leaving blacks at a disadvantage. A recent study published in the academic journal *Social Problems* found that white males receive substantially more job leads for high-level supervisory positions than women and members of minorities.

Many interviewed, however, wrestled with "pulling the race card," groping between their cynicism and desire to avoid the stigma that blacks are too quick to claim victimhood. After all, many had gone to good schools and had accomplished résumés. Some had grown up in well-to-do settings, with parents who had raised them never to doubt how high they could climb. Moreover, there is President Obama, perhaps the ultimate embodiment of that belief.

Certainly, they conceded, there are times when their race can be beneficial, particularly with companies that have diversity programs. But many said they sensed that such opportunities had been cut back over the years ... Others speculated there was now more of a tendency to deem diversity unnecessary after Mr. Obama's triumph.

In fact, whether Mr. Obama's election has been good or bad for their job prospects is hotly debated. Several interviewed went so far as to say that they believed there was only so much progress that many in the country could take, and that there was now a backlash against blacks. ...

It is difficult to overstate the degree that they say race permeates nearly every aspect of their job searches, from how early they show up to interviews to the kinds of anecdotes they try to come up with. ...

Nearly all said they agonized over job applications that asked them whether they would like to identify their race. Most said they usually did not.

WHAT DO YOU THINK?

1. Based on the article, what evidence do you find of outright prejudice against people of color? What evidence do you find of subtle prejudice?

2. One might wonder if what seems to be racial prejudice is simply a bad job market for everyone. What do you find in the article that suggests that this is not the case?

3. Sometimes people don't intend to discriminate racially, but want to employ someone who is a "cultural fit." Explain this pattern. Have you ever experienced anything like this?

Adapted from the original article, "In Job Hunt, College Degree Can't Close Racial Gap," by Michael Luo, published in *The New York Times* on December 1, 2009. Copyright © by The New York Times Company. All rights reserved. Used by permission and protected by the Copyright Laws of the United States. The printing, copying, redistribution, or retransmission of the Material without express permission is prohibited.

oppress others. Anglos who look down on Latino immigrants in the Southwest, for example, can get away with paying the immigrants low wages for hard work. Similarly, all elites benefit when prejudice divides workers along racial and ethnic lines and discourages them from working together to advance their common interests (Geschwender, 1978; Olzak, 1989; Rothenberg, 2008).

According to another conflict-based argument, made by Shelby Steele (1990), minorities themselves encourage *race consciousness* (which is sometimes called "identity politics") in order to win greater power and privileges. Because of their historical disadvantage, minorities claim that they are victims entitled to special consideration based on their race. Although this strategy may bring short-term gains, Steele cautions that such thinking often sparks a backlash from whites or others who oppose "special treatment" on the basis of race or ethnicity.

Discrimination

Closely related to prejudice is **discrimination,** *unequal treatment of various categories of people.* Prejudice refers to *attitudes;* discrimination is a matter of *action.* Like prejudice, discrimination can be either positive (providing special advantages) or negative (creating obstacles) and ranges from subtle to extreme.

Institutional Prejudice and Discrimination

We typically think of prejudice and discrimination as the hateful ideas or actions of specific people. But Stokely Carmichael and Charles Hamilton (1967) point out that far greater harm results from **institutional prejudice and discrimination,** *bias built into the operation of society's institutions,* including schools, hospitals, law enforcement, and the workplace. For example, researchers have shown that banks reject home mortgage applications from minorities at a higher rate—or charge higher rates for the same mortgage—compared to white applicants, even when income and quality of neighborhood are held constant (Gotham, 1998; Blanton, 2007).

According to Carmichael and Hamilton, people are slow to condemn or even recognize institutional prejudice and discrimination because it often involves respected public officials and long-established traditions. A case in point is *Brown* v. *Board of Education of Topeka,* the 1954 Supreme Court decision that ended the legal segregation of U.S. schools. The principle of "separate but equal" schooling had been the law of the land, supporting racial inequality by allowing school segregation. Despite this change in the law, more than half a century later, most U.S. students still attend schools in which one race overwhelmingly predominates (KewalRamani et al., 2007). In 1991, the courts pointed out that neighborhood

◘┤Read "Use of Black English and Racial Discrimination in Urban Housing Markets" by Douglas S. Massey and Garvey Lundy on **mysoclab.com**

prejudice a rigid and unfair generalization about an entire category of people

discrimination unequal treatment of various categories of people

institutional prejudice and discrimination bias built into the operation of society's institutions

miscegenation biological reproduction by partners of different racial categories

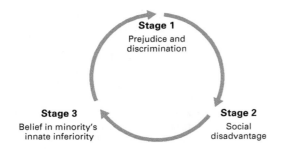

Stage 1
Prejudice and discrimination

Stage 3
Belief in minority's innate inferiority

Stage 2
Social disadvantage

Stage 1: Prejudice and discrimination begin, often as an expression of ethnocentrism or an attempt to justify economic exploitation.

Stage 2: As a result of prejudice and discrimination, a minority is socially disadvantaged, occupying a low position in the system of social stratification.

Stage 3: This social disadvantage is then interpreted not as the result of earlier prejudice and discrimination but as evidence that the minority is innately inferior, unleashing renewed prejudice and discrimination by which the cycle repeats itself.

FIGURE 2 **Prejudice and Discrimination: The Vicious Circle**
Prejudice and discrimination can form a vicious circle, perpetuating themselves.

schools will never provide equal education as long as our population is racially segregated, with most African Americans living in central cities and most white people and Asian Americans living in suburbs. ◘┤Read on **mysoclab.com**

Prejudice and Discrimination: The Vicious Circle

Prejudice and discrimination reinforce each other. The Thomas theorem offers a simple explanation of this fact: *Situations that are defined as real become real in their consequences* (Thomas & Thomas, 1928; Thomas, 1966:301, orig. 1931).

As Thomas recognized, stereotypes become real to people who believe them and sometimes even to those victimized by them. Prejudice on the part of white people toward people of color does not produce *innate* inferiority, but it can produce *social* inferiority, pushing minorities into low-paying jobs, inferior schools, and racially segregated housing. Then, as white people interpret that social disadvantage as evidence that minorities do not measure up, they unleash a new round of prejudice and discrimination, giving rise to a vicious circle in which each perpetuates the other, as shown in Figure 2.

Majority and Minority: Patterns of Interaction

Social scientists describe interaction between majority and minority members of a society in terms of four models: pluralism, assimilation, segregation, and genocide.

Pluralism

Pluralism is *a state in which people of all races and ethnicities are distinct but have equal social standing.* In other words, people who differ in appearance or social heritage all share resources roughly equally.

The United States is pluralistic to the extent that almost all categories of people have equal standing under the law. In addition, large cities contain countless "ethnic villages" where people proudly display the traditions of their immigrant ancestors. These include New York's Spanish Harlem, Little Italy, and Chinatown; Philadelphia's Italian "South Philly"; Chicago's "Little Saigon"; and Latino East Los Angeles. New York City alone supports hundreds of magazines, newspapers, and radio stations in more than ninety languages (Paul, 2001; Logan, Alba, & Zhang, 2002; New York Community Media Alliance, 2008).

But the United States is not truly pluralistic, for three reasons. First, although most people value their cultural heritage, few want to live exclusively with others exactly like themselves (NORC, 2009). Second, our tolerance for social diversity goes only so far. One reaction to the growing proportion of minorities in the United States is a social movement to make English the nation's official language. Third, as you will see later in this chapter, people of various colors and cultures do *not* have equal social standing.

Assimilation

Many people think of the United States as a "melting pot" in which different nationalities blend together. But rather than everyone "melting" into some new cultural pattern, most minorities have adopted the dominant culture established by the earliest settlers. Why? Because doing so is both the avenue to upward social mobility and a way to escape the prejudice and discrimination directed against more visible foreigners. Sociologists use the term **assimilation** to describe *the process by which minorities gradually adopt patterns of the dominant culture.* Assimilation involves changing styles of dress, values, religion, language, and friends.

The amount of assimilation varies by category. For example, in the United States, Canadians have "melted" more than Cubans, the Dutch more than Dominicans, Germans more than the Japanese. Multiculturalists oppose making assimilation a goal because it suggests that minorities are "the problem" and the ones who need to do all the changing.

Note that assimilation involves changes in ethnicity but not in race. For example, many descendants of Japanese immigrants have discarded their ethnic traditions but retain their racial identity. For racial traits to diminish over generations, **miscegenation,** or *biological reproduction by partners of different racial categories,* must occur. Although interracial marriage is becoming more common, it still amounts to only 7 percent of all U.S. marriages (U.S. Census Bureau, 2010).

Segregation

Segregation is *the physical and social separation of categories of people.* Sometimes minorities, especially religious orders such as the Amish, voluntarily segregate themselves. Usually, however, majorities segregate minorities by excluding them. Neighborhoods, schools, occupations, hospitals, and even cemeteries may be segregated. Pluralism encourages cultural distinctiveness without disadvantage; segregation enforces separation that harms a minority.

Racial segregation has a long history in the United States, beginning with slavery and evolving into racially separate housing, schooling, buses, and trains. Decisions such as the 1954 *Brown* case have reduced *de jure* (Latin, "by law") discrimination in the United States. However, *de facto* ("in fact") segregation continues in the form of countless neighborhoods that are home to people of a single race.

Despite some recent decline, segregation continues in the United States. For example, Livonia, Michigan, is 92 percent white, and neighboring Detroit is 83 percent African American. Kurt Metzger (2001) explains, "Livonia was pretty much created by white flight [from Detroit]." Research shows that across the country, whites (especially those with young children) continue to avoid neighborhoods where African Americans live (Emerson, Yancey, & Chai, 2001; Krysan, 2002). At the extreme, Douglas Massey and Nancy Denton (1989) documented the *hypersegregation* of poor African Americans in some inner cities. Hypersegregation means having little contact of any kind with people beyond the local community. Hypersegregation is the daily experience of about 20 percent of poor African Americans

and is a pattern found in about twenty-five large U.S. cities (Wilkes & Iceland, 2004).

Genocide

Genocide is *the systematic killing of one category of people by another.* This deadly form of racism and ethnocentrism violates nearly every recognized moral standard, yet it has occurred time and again in human history.

Genocide was common in the history of contact between Europeans and the original inhabitants of the Americas. From the sixteenth century on, the Spanish, Portuguese, English, French, and Dutch forcibly colonized vast empires. Although most native people died from diseases brought by Europeans, against which they had no natural defenses, many who opposed the colonizers were killed deliberately (Matthiessen, 1984; Sale, 1990).

Genocide also occurred in the twentieth century. Beginning in 1915, more than 1 million Armenians were killed by the Ottoman Empire. Likewise, unimaginable horror befell European Jews during Adolf Hitler's reign of terror. During the Holocaust that lasted from about 1935 to 1945, the Nazis murdered more than 6 million Jewish men, women, and children, along with gay people, Gypsies, and people with handicaps. The Soviet dictator Josef Stalin murdered on an even greater scale, killing some 30 million real and imagined enemies during decades of violent rule. Between 1975 and 1980, Pol Pot's Communist regime in Cambodia butchered all "capitalists," which included anyone able to speak a Western language. In all, some 2 million people (one-fourth of the population) perished in the Cambodian "killing fields."

Tragically, genocide continues in the modern world. Recent examples include Hutus killing Tutsis in the African nation of Rwanda, Serbs killing Bosnians in the Balkans of Eastern Europe, and the killing of hundreds of thousands of people in the Darfur region of Sudan.

These four patterns of minority-majority contact have all been played out in the United States. Although many people proudly point to patterns of pluralism and assimilation, it is also important to recognize the degree to which U.S. society has been built on segregation (of African Americans) and genocide (of Native Americans). The remainder of this chapter examines how these four patterns have shaped the past and present social standing of major racial and ethnic categories in the United States.

Should we expect people who come to the United States to change their language and other cultural patterns in order to "fit in," or should we expect them to hold onto their own traditions? Why?

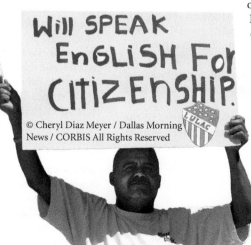

© Cheryl Diaz Meyer / Dallas Morning News / CORBIS All Rights Reserved

Race and Ethnicity

Seeing Sociology
in Everyday Life

In your city or town, are there minority neighborhoods? Which categories of people live there? To what degree is your community racially or ethnically segregated?

Making the Grade

As the maps on the facing page show, Native peoples were the original inhabitants of the Americas, and new immigrants pushed them farther west as the United States took form.

Western History Collections, University of Oklahoma Libraries. Phillips Collection 357

In an effort to force assimilation, the U.S. Bureau of Indian Affairs took American Indian children from their families and placed them in boarding schools like this one, Oklahoma's Riverside Indian School. There they were taught to speak English by non-Indian teachers with the goal of making them into "Americans."

Race and Ethnicity in the United States

Give me your tired, your poor,
Your huddled masses yearning to breathe free,
The wretched refuse of your teeming shore,
Send these, the homeless, tempest-tossed to me:
I lift my lamp beside the golden door.

These words by Emma Lazarus, inscribed on the base of the Statue of Liberty, express cultural ideals of human dignity, personal freedom, and economic opportunity. Indeed, the United States has provided more of the "good life" to more immigrants than any other nation. More than 1.5 million immigrants come to this country every year, and their ways of life create a social mosaic that is especially evident in large cities.

However, as a survey of racial and ethnic minorities in the United States will show, our country's golden door has opened more widely for some than for others. We turn to the history and current social standing of the major categories of the U.S. population.

Native Americans

The term "Native Americans" refers to the hundreds of societies—including Aleuts, Cherokee, Zuni, Sioux, Mohawk, Aztec, and Inca—who first settled the Western Hemisphere. Some 30,000 years before

Christopher Columbus landed in the Americas, migrating peoples crossed a land bridge from Asia to North America where the Bering Strait (off the coast of Alaska) lies today. Gradually, they spread throughout North and South America.

When the first Europeans arrived late in the fifteenth century, Native Americans numbered in the millions. But by 1900, after centuries of conflict and acts of genocide, the "vanishing Americans" numbered just 250,000 (Dobyns, 1966; Tyler, 1973). The land they controlled also shrank dramatically, as National Map 2 shows.

Columbus first referred to the Native Americans that he encountered as "Indians" because he mistakenly thought he had reached the coast of India. Columbus found the native people passive and peaceful, in stark contrast to the materialistic and competitive Europeans (Matthiessen, 1984; Sale, 1990). Yet Europeans justified the seizure of Native Americans' lands by calling them thieves and murderers (Josephy, 1982; Matthiessen, 1984; Sale, 1990).

After the Revolutionary War, the new U.S. government adopted a pluralistic approach to Native American societies and tried to gain more land through treaties. Payment for land was far from fair, however, and when Native Americans resisted surrendering their homelands, the U.S. government simply used its superior military power to evict them. By the early 1800s, few Native Americans remained east of the Mississippi River.

In 1871, the United States declared Native Americans wards of the government and adopted a strategy of forced assimilation. Relocated to specific territories designated as "reservations," Native Americans continued to lose their land and were on their way to losing their culture as well. Reservation life encouraged dependency on outsiders, replacing ancestral languages with English and traditional religion with Christianity. Officials took many children from their parents and handed them over to boarding schools, where they were resocialized as "Americans." Authorities gave local control of reservations to the few Native Americans who supported government policies, and they distributed reservation land, traditionally held collectively, as private property to individual families (Tyler, 1973).

Not until 1924 were Native Americans entitled to U.S. citizenship. After that, many migrated from the reservations, adopting mainstream cultural patterns and marrying non–Native Americans. Today, one-half of Native Americans consider themselves biracial or multiracial (U.S. Census Bureau, 2009), and many large cities now contain sizable Native American populations. However, as Table 2 shows, the income of Native Americans is far below the U.S. average, and relatively few Native Americans earn a college degree.[2]

From in-depth interviews with Native Americans in a western city, Joan Albon (1971) concluded that their low social standing was a result of cultural factors, including their noncompetitive view of life

┌─○ Making the Grade

People tend to think about race and ethnicity when they deal with categories of people whom they think of as "other." WASPs have race and ethnicity, too, of course, but U.S. society does not construct these into a minority identity.

┌─● Seeing Sociology in Everyday Life

In what ways does being a WASP (or simply being white) confer privilege on people?

Seeing Ourselves

NATIONAL MAP 2

Land Controlled by Native Americans, 1790 to Today

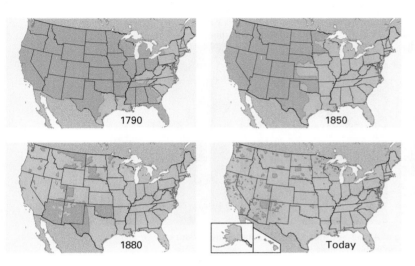

In 1790, Native Americans controlled three-fourths of the land (blue-shaded areas) that eventually became the United States. Today, Native Americans control 304 reservations, scattered across the United States, that account for just 2 percent of the country's land area. How would you characterize these locations?

Source: Published in *The New York Times* on March 18, 1998. Copyright © 1998 by The New York Times Company. All rights reserved. Used by permission and protected by the Copyright Laws of the United States. The printing, copying, redistribution, or retransmission of the Material without express written permission is prohibited.

and reluctance to pursue higher education. In addition, she noted, many Native Americans have dark skin, which makes them targets of prejudice and discrimination.

Members of the more than 200 American Indian nations in the United States today are reclaiming pride in their cultural heritage. Traditional cultural organizations report a surge in new membership applications, and many children can now speak native languages better than their parents. The legal right of Native Americans to govern their reservations has enabled some tribes to build profitable gaming casinos. But the wealth produced from gambling has enriched relatively few Native peoples, and most profits go to non-Indian investors (Bartlett & Steele, 2002). While some prosper, most Native Americans remain severely disadvantaged, with a profound sense of the injustice they have suffered at the hands of white people.

White Anglo-Saxon Protestants

White Anglo-Saxon Protestants (WASPs) were not the first people to inhabit the United States, but they soon dominated the nation after European settlement began. Most WASPs are of English ancestry, but this category also includes people from Scotland and Wales. With some 35 million people claiming English, Scottish, or Welsh ancestry, 12 percent of our society has some WASP background, and WASPs are found at all class levels (U.S. Census Bureau, 2009).

Many people associate WASPs with elite communities along the East and West Coasts. But the highest concentrations of WASPs are in Utah (because of migrations of Mormons with English ancestry), Appalachia, and northern New England (also due to historical patterns of immigration).

Looking back in time, WASP immigrants were highly skilled and motivated to achieve by what we now call the Protestant work ethic. Because of their numbers and power, WASPs were not subject to the prejudice and discrimination experienced by other categories of immigrants. In fact, the historical dominance of WASPs has led others to want to become more like them (K. W. Jones, 2001).

WASPs were never one single group; especially during colonial times, hostility separated English Anglicans from Scottish Presbyterians (Parrillo, 1994). But in the nineteenth century, most WASPs joined together to oppose the arrival of "undesirables" such as the Germans in the 1840s and Italians in the 1880s. Those who could afford it sheltered themselves in exclusive suburbs and restrictive clubs. Thus the 1880s—the decade when the Statue of Liberty first welcomed immigrants to the United States—also saw the

---

[2]In making comparisons of education and income, keep in mind that various categories of the U.S. population have different median ages. In 2008, the median age for all U.S. people was 36.8 years; for Native Americans, the figure was 31.2 years. Because people's schooling and income increase over time, this age difference accounts for some of the disparities shown in Table 2.

Table 2   The Social Standing of Native Americans, 2008

	Native Americans	Entire U.S. Population
Median family income	$43,190	$61,521
Percentage in poverty	24.2%	13.2%
Completion of four or more years of college (age 25 and over)	12.7%	29.5%

Source: U.S. Census Bureau (2009).

● Seeing Sociology
in Everyday Life

Do you think that Marian Anderson, who broke a "color line" in
1936 by being invited to the White House, would have imagined
our nation having an African American president?

● Seeing Sociology
in Everyday Life

In your opinion, how much change has there been in racial
prejudice and discrimination against African Americans during
your lifetime? Explain your position.

Photographs and Prints Division, Schomburg Center for
Research in Black Culture/The New York Public
Library/Astor, Lenox and Tilden Foundations

Courtesy of the Library of Congress

The efforts of these four women greatly advanced the social standing of African Americans in the United States. Pictured
from left to right: Sojourner Truth (1797–1883), born a slave, became an influential preacher and outspoken abolitionist
who was honored by President Lincoln at the White House. Harriet Tubman (1820–1913), after escaping from slavery
herself, masterminded the flight from bondage of hundreds of African American men and women via the "Underground
Railroad." Ida Wells-Barnett (1862–1931), born to slave parents, became a partner in a Memphis newspaper and served as
a tireless crusader against the terror of lynching. Marian Anderson (1897–1993), an exceptional singer whose early career
was restrained by racial prejudice, broke symbolic "color lines" by singing in the White House in 1936 and on the steps of
the Lincoln Memorial to a crowd of almost 100,000 people in 1939.

founding of the first country club with exclusively WASP members
(Baltzell, 1964).

By about 1950, however, WASP wealth and power had peaked, as
indicated by the 1960 election of John Fitzgerald Kennedy, the first
Irish Catholic president. Yet the WASP cultural legacy remains. English is this country's dominant language and Protestantism the majority religion. Our legal system also reflects its English origins. But the
historical dominance of WASPs is most evident in the widespread use
of the terms "race" and "ethnicity" to describe everyone but them.

African Americans

Africans accompanied European explorers to the New World in the
fifteenth century. But most accounts trace the beginning of black
history in the United States to 1619, when a Dutch trading ship
brought twenty Africans to Jamestown, Virginia. Many more ships
filled with African laborers followed. Whether these people arrived
as slaves or as indentured servants (who paid for their passage by
agreeing to work for a period of time), being of African descent on
these shores soon became virtually synonymous with being a slave. In
1661, Virginia enacted the first law in the new colonies recognizing
slavery (Sowell, 1981).

Slavery was the foundation of the southern colonies' plantation
system. White people ran plantations using slave labor, and until
1808, some were also slave traders. Traders—including North Americans, Africans, and Europeans—forcibly transported some 10 million Africans to various countries in the Americas, including 400,000
to the United States. On small sailing ships, hundreds of slaves were
chained for the several weeks it took to cross the Atlantic Ocean.
Filth and disease killed many and drove others to suicide. Overall,
perhaps half died en route (Franklin, 1967; Sowell, 1981).

The reward for surviving the miserable journey was a lifetime of
servitude. Although some slaves worked in cities at various trades,
most labored in the fields, often from daybreak until sunset and even
longer during the harvest. The law allowed owners to use whatever
disciplinary measures they deemed necessary to ensure that slaves
were obedient and hardworking. Even killing a slave rarely prompted
legal action. Owners also divided slave families at public auctions,
where human beings were bought and sold as property. Unschooled
and dependent on their owners for all their basic needs, slaves had
little control over their lives (Franklin, 1967; Sowell, 1981).

Some free people of color lived in both the North and the South,
laboring as small-scale farmers, skilled workers, and small business
owners. But the lives of most African Americans stood in glaring contradiction to the principles of freedom on which the United States
was founded. The Declaration of Independence states, "We hold these
Truths to be self-evident, that all Men are created equal, that they are
endowed by their Creator with certain unalienable Rights, that among
these are Life, Liberty, and the Pursuit of Happiness." However, most
white people did not apply these ideals to African Americans. In
the *Dred Scott* case in 1857, the U.S. Supreme Court addressed the

Race and Ethnicity

Go to the Multimedia Library at mysoclab.com to watch the Reverend Martin Luther King Jr. deliver his famous "I Have a Dream" speech

Jim Crow laws are a clear example of institutional discrimination.

question "Are slaves citizens?" by writing, "We think they are not, and that they are not included, and were not intended to be included, under the word 'citizens' in the Constitution, and can therefore claim none of the rights and privileges which that instrument provides for and secures for citizens of the United States" (quoted in Blaustein & Zangrando, 1968:160). Thus arose what the Swedish sociologist Gunnar Myrdal (1944) called the "American dilemma": a democratic society's denial of basic rights and freedoms to one category of people. People would speak of equality, in other words, but then fail to extend the same rights and freedoms to all categories of people. Many white people resolved this dilemma by defining black people as naturally inferior and therefore undeserving of equality (Leach, 2002).

In 1865, the Thirteenth Amendment to the Constitution outlawed slavery. Three years later, the Fourteenth Amendment reversed the *Dred Scott* ruling, granting citizenship to all people born in the United States. The Fifteenth Amendment, ratified in 1870, stated that neither race nor previous condition of servitude should deprive any (male) citizen of the right to vote. However, so-called *Jim Crow laws*—classic cases of institutionalized discrimination—segregated U.S. society into two racial castes. Especially in the South, white people beat and lynched black people (and some white people) who challenged the racial hierarchy.

The twentieth century brought dramatic changes for African Americans. After World War I, tens of thousands of women and men fled the rural South for jobs in northern factories. Although most did find economic opportunities, few escaped racial prejudice and discrimination, which placed them lower in the social hierarchy than white immigrants arriving from Europe.

In the 1950s, a national civil rights movement set the climate for a landmark judicial decision that outlawed segregated schools, and in the 1960s, legislation outlawed overt discrimination in employment and public accommodations. The Black Power movement in the 1960s and 1970s gave African Americans a renewed sense of pride and purpose. ⬤ Go to mysoclab.com

Despite these gains, people of African descent continue to occupy a lower social position in the United States, as shown in Table 3. The median income of African American families in 2008 ($39,879) was only 57 percent of non-Hispanic white family income ($70,070), a ratio that has changed little in thirty years.[3] Black families remain three times as likely as white families to be poor.

The number of African American families securely in the middle class rose by more than half between 1980 and 2008; 41 percent

---

[3]Here again, a median age difference (non-Hispanic whites, 41.1; blacks, 33.3) accounts for some of the income and educational disparities. More important is a higher proportion of one-parent families among blacks than whites. If we compare only married-couple families, African Americans (median income $61,509 in 2008) earned 80 percent as much as non-Hispanic whites ($77,356).

Table 3   The Social Standing of African Americans, 2008

	African Americans	Entire U.S. Population
Median family income	$39,879	$61,521
Percentage in poverty	24.7%	13.2%
Completion of four or more years of college (age 25 and over)	19.3%	29.5%

Source: U.S. Census Bureau (2009).

earn $50,000 or more each year. This means that the African American community is now economically diverse. Even so, a majority of African Americans are still working-class or poor. In recent years, many have seen earnings slip as urban factory jobs, vital to residents of central cities, have been lost to other countries where labor costs are lower. This is one reason that black unemployment is almost twice as high as white unemployment; among African American teenagers in many cities, the unemployment figure exceeds 40 percent (R. A. Smith, 2002; U.S. Department of Labor, 2010).

Since 1980, African Americans have made remarkable educational progress. The share of adults completing high school rose from half to 84 percent in 2008, nearly closing the gap between blacks and whites. Between 1980 and 2008, the share of African American adults with at least a college degree rose from 8 percent to more than 19 percent. But as Table 3 shows, African Americans are still well below the national average when it comes to completing four years of college.

The political clout of African Americans has greatly increased. As a result of both black migration to the cities and white flight to the suburbs, African Americans have gained greater political power in urban places, and many of this country's largest cities have had African American mayors. At the national level, the election of Barack Obama as this country's forty-fourth president—the first African American to hold this office—is a historic and hugely important event. It demonstrates that our society has moved beyond the assumption that race is a barrier to the highest office in the land (West, 2008). Yet in early 2010, African Americans accounted for just 39 members of the House of Representatives (9 percent of 435), one member (out of 100) in the Senate, and two state governors (National Governors Association, 2010; U.S. House of Representatives, 2010; U.S. Senate, 2010).

In sum, for nearly 400 years, people of African ancestry in the United States have struggled for social equality. As a nation, the United States has come far in this pursuit. Overt discrimination is now illegal, and research documents a long-term decline in prejudice against African Americans (Firebaugh & Davis, 1988; J. Q. Wilson, 1992; NORC, 2009).

Fifty years after the abolition of slavery, W. E. B. Du Bois (1913) pointed to the extent of black achievement but cautioned that racial

Table 4   The Social Standing of Asian Americans, 2008

	All Asian Americans	Chinese Americans	Japanese Americans	Asian Indian Americans	Filipino Americans	Korean Americans	Entire U.S. Population
Median family income	$73,578	$81,823	$83,762	$99,783	$87,069	$66,055	$61,521
Percentage in poverty	11.8%	11.9%	8.9%	7.8%	5.4%	13.4%	13.2%
Completion of four or more years of college (age 25 and over)	52.3%	52.1%	46.3%	70.1%	48.0%	49.8%	29.5%

Source: U.S. Census Bureau (2009).

caste remained strong in the United States. Almost a century later, this racial hierarchy persists.

Asian Americans

Although Asian Americans share some racial traits, enormous cultural diversity marks this category of people. In 2008, the total number of Asian Americans exceeded 13.5 million, or about 4.5 percent of the U.S. population. The largest category of Asian Americans is people of Chinese ancestry (3.1 million), followed by those of Asian Indian (2.5 million), Filipino (2.4 million), Vietnamese (1.5 million), Korean (1.3 million), and Japanese (710,000) descent. More than one-third of Asian Americans live in California.

Many young Asian Americans have commanded attention and respect as academic high achievers and are disproportionately represented at our country's best colleges and universities. Many of their elders have also made economic and social gains; most Asian Americans now live in middle-class suburbs. Yet despite (and sometimes because of) their achievements, Asian Americans are sometimes avoided or treated with hostility (Chua-Eoan, 2000; Lee & Marlay, 2007).

The achievement of some Asian Americans has given rise to a "model minority" stereotype that is misleading because it hides the differences in class standing found among their ranks. We will focus on the history and current standing of Chinese Americans and Japanese Americans—the longest-established Asian American minorities—and conclude with a brief look at the most recent arrivals.

Chinese Americans

Chinese immigration to the United States began in 1849 with the economic boom of California's Gold Rush. New towns and businesses sprang up overnight, and the demand for cheap labor attracted some 100,000 Chinese immigrants. Most Chinese workers were young, hardworking men willing to take low-status jobs that whites did not want. But the economy soured in the 1870s, and desperate whites began to compete with the Chinese for whatever work could be found. Suddenly, the hardworking Chinese were seen as a threat. Economic hard times led to prejudice and discrimination (Ling, 1971; Boswell, 1986).

Soon laws were passed barring Chinese people from many occupations, and public opinion turned strongly against the "Yellow Peril."

In 1882, the U.S. government passed the first of several laws limiting Chinese immigration. This action caused domestic hardship because in the United States, Chinese men outnumbered Chinese women by twenty to one. This sex imbalance drove the Chinese population down to only 60,000 by 1920. Because Chinese women already in the United States were in high demand, they soon lost much of their traditional submissiveness to men (Hsu, 1971; Lai, 1980; Sowell, 1981).

Responding to racial hostility, some Chinese moved east; many more sought the relative safety of urban Chinatowns. There Chinese traditions flourished, and kinship networks, called *clans*, offered financial assistance to individuals and represented the interests of all. At the same time, however, living in an all-Chinese community discouraged people from learning English, which limited their job opportunities (Wong, 1971).

A renewed need for labor during World War II prompted President Franklin Roosevelt to end the ban on Chinese immigration in 1943 and to extend the rights of citizenship to Chinese Americans born abroad. Many responded by moving out of Chinatowns and seeking cultural assimilation. In turn-of-the-century Honolulu, for example, 70 percent of the Chinese people lived in Chinatown; today, the figure is below 20 percent.

By 1950, many Chinese Americans had experienced upward social mobility. Today, people of Chinese ancestry are no longer limited to self-employment in laundries and restaurants; many hold high-prestige positions, especially in fields related to science and technology.

As shown in Table 4, the median family income of Chinese Americans in 2008 was $81,823, higher than the national average of $61,521. However, the higher income of all Asian Americans reflects a larger number of family members in the labor force.[4]

---

[4]Median age for all Asian Americans in 2008 was 35.8 years, somewhat below the national median of 36.8 and the non-Hispanic white median of 41.1. But specific categories vary widely in median age: Japanese, 45.4; Filipino, 38.9; Chinese, 38.3; Korean, 37.1; Asian Indian, 32.6; Cambodian, 30.9; Hmong, 20.6 (U.S. Census Bureau, 2009).

○ Seeing Sociology
in Everyday Life

On your campus, do students of any one race or ethnic category
tend to hang out together? Explain the patterns you see.

○ Seeing Sociology
in Everyday Life

Recent research on social distance indicates that most of
today's college students say they are more accepting of
African Americans than Asian Americans. Does this square
with your experiences? What about people in the country as
a whole—are they more accepting of Asian Americans or
African Americans? Why?

Chinese Americans also have an enviable record of educational achievement, standing significantly above the national average in college graduation.

Despite their success, many Chinese Americans still deal with subtle (and sometimes blatant) prejudice and discrimination. Such hostility is one reason that poverty among Chinese Americans stands near the national average. The problem of poverty is most common among those who remain in the socially isolated Chinatowns working in restaurants or other low-paying jobs, raising the question of whether racial and ethnic enclaves help their residents or exploit them (Portes & Jensen, 1989; Kinkead, 1992; Gilbertson & Gurak, 1993).

Japanese Americans

Japanese immigration to the United States began slowly in the 1860s, reaching only 3,000 by 1890. Most of these immigrants came to the Hawaiian Islands (annexed by the United States in 1898 and made a state in 1959) to take low-paying jobs. After 1900, as the number of Japanese immigrants to California increased (reaching 140,000 by 1915), white hostility increased (Takaki, 1998). In 1907, the United States signed an agreement with Japan limiting the entry of men—the chief economic threat—while allowing Japanese women to immigrate to ease the sex ratio imbalance. In the 1920s, state laws in California and dozens of other states mandated segregation and banned interracial marriage, virtually ending further Japanese immigration. Not until 1952 did the United States extend citizenship to foreign-born Japanese.

Japanese and Chinese immigrants differed in three important ways. First, there were fewer Japanese immigrants, so they escaped some of the hostility directed at the more numerous Chinese. Second, the Japanese knew much more about the United States than the Chinese did, which helped them assimilate (Sowell, 1981). Third, Japanese immigrants preferred rural farming to clustering in cities, which made them less visible. But many white people objected to Japanese ownership of farmland, so in 1913, California barred further purchases. Many foreign-born Japanese (called the *Issei*) responded by placing farmland in

On average, Asian Americans have income above the national median. At the same time, however, the poverty rate in many Asian American communities—including San Francisco's Chinatown—is well above average.

the names of their U.S.-born children (*Nisei*), who were constitutionally entitled to citizenship.

Japanese Americans faced their greatest crisis after Japan bombed the U.S. naval fleet at Pearl Harbor, Hawaii, on December 7, 1941. Rage was directed at the Japanese living in the United States. Some people feared that the Japanese here would spy for Japan or commit acts of sabotage. Within a year, President Franklin Roosevelt signed Executive Order 9066, an unprecedented action designed to ensure national security by detaining people of Japanese descent in military camps. Authorities soon relocated 120,000 people of Japanese descent (90 percent of all U.S. Japanese) to remote inland reservations (Sun, 1998; Ewers, 2008).

Concern about national security always rises in times of war, but Japanese internment was sharply criticized. First, it targeted an entire category of people, not one of whom was ever known to have committed a disloyal act. Second, roughly two-thirds of those imprisoned were *Nisei*, U.S. citizens by birth. Third, the United States was also at war with Germany and Italy, but no comparable action was taken against people of German or Italian ancestry.

Relocation meant selling homes, furnishings, and businesses on short notice for pennies on the dollar. As a result, almost the entire Japanese American population was economically devastated. Herded into military prisons, surrounded by barbed wire, and guarded by armed soldiers, families crowded into single rooms, often in buildings that had previously sheltered livestock. The internment ended in 1944 when the Supreme Court declared it unconstitutional, although the last camp did not close until March 1946 (after the war had ended). In 1988, Congress awarded $20,000 to each of the victims as token compensation for the hardships they endured.

After World War II, Japanese Americans staged a dramatic recovery. Having lost their traditional businesses, many entered new occupations, and driven by cultural values stressing the importance of education and hard work, Japanese Americans have enjoyed remarkable success. In 2006, the median income of Japanese American households was more than 35 percent above the national average, and the rate of poverty among Japanese Americans was well below the national figure.

Race and Ethnicity

○ Making the Grade

Compare the data in the various tables in this section
of the chapter to assure that you have learned the
social standing of each racial and ethnic category.

○ Seeing Sociology
in Everyday Life

Do you think Latinos are fairly represented in today's
television shows and films? Explain your position.

Table 5 The Social Standing of Hispanic Americans, 2008

	All Hispanics	Mexican Americans	Puerto Ricans	Cuban Americans	Entire U.S. Population
Median family income	$40,466	$41,538	$43,944	$51,290	$61,521
Percentage in poverty	23.2%	22.9%	24.0%	14.2%	13.2%
Completion of four or more years of college (age 25 and over)	13.2%	9.0%	15.8%	25.4%	29.5%

Source: U.S. Census Bureau (2009).

Upward social mobility has encouraged cultural assimilation and intermarriage. Younger Japanese Americans rarely live in residential enclaves, as many Chinese Americans still do, and most marry non-Japanese partners. In the process, many have abandoned their traditions, including the Japanese language. A large share of Japanese Americans, however, belong to ethnic associations as a way of maintaining their ethnic identity. Still, some appear to be caught between two worlds, no longer culturally Japanese yet, because of racial differences, not completely accepted in the larger society.

Recent Asian Immigrants

More recent immigrants from Asia include Filipinos, Indians, Koreans, Vietnamese, Guamanians, and Samoans. Overall, the Asian American population increased by 86 percent between 1990 and 2008 and currently accounts for more than one-third of all immigration to the United States (U.S. Department of Homeland Security, 2009).

The entrepreneurial spirit is strong among Asian immigrants. In part this reflects cultural patterns that stress achievement and self-reliance, but having one's own small business is also a strategy for dealing with societal prejudice and discrimination. Small business success is one reason that Asian American family income is above the national average, but it is also true that in many of these businesses, a number of family members work long hours.

Another factor that raises the family income of Asian Americans is a high level of schooling. As shown in Table 4, for all categories of Asian Americans, the share of adults with a four-year college degree is well above the national average. Among Asian Indian Americans, who have the highest educational achievement of all Asian Americans, more than two-thirds of all men and women over the age of twenty-five have completed college, a proportion that is more than twice the national average. This remarkable educational achievement is one reason that Asian Indian Americans had a median family income of almost $100,000 in 2008, about 62 percent higher than the national average.

In sum, a survey of Asian Americans presents a complex picture. The Japanese come closest to having achieved social acceptance. But some surveys reveal greater prejudice against Asian Americans than against African Americans (Parrillo & Donoghue,

2005). Median income data suggest that many Asian Americans have prospered. But these numbers reflect the fact that many Asian Americans live in Hawaii, California, or New York, where incomes are high but so are living costs (Takaki, 1998). Then, too, many Asian Americans remain poor. One thing is clear—their high immigration rate means that people of Asian ancestry will play a central role in U.S. society in the decades to come.

Hispanic Americans/Latinos

In 2008, the number of Hispanics in the United States topped 46 million (15.4 percent of the U.S. population), surpassing the number of Asian Americans (13.6 million, or 4.5 percent of the U.S. population) and even African Americans (39 million, or 12.8 percent) and making Hispanics the largest racial or ethnic minority. However, keep in mind that few who fall in this category describe themselves as "Hispanic" or "Latino." Like Asian Americans, Hispanics are really a cluster of distinct populations, each of which identifies with a particular ancestral nation (Marín & Marín, 1991). About two out of three Hispanics (some 31 million) are Mexican Americans. Puerto Ricans are next in number (4.2 million), followed by Cuban Americans (1.6 million). Many other nations of Latin America are represented by smaller numbers.

Although the Hispanic population is increasing all over the country, most Hispanic Americans live in the Southwest. One of three Californians is Latino (in greater Los Angeles, almost half the people are Latino). National Map 3 shows the distribution of the Hispanic, African American, Asian American, and Arab American populations across the United States.

Median family income for all Hispanics—$40,466 in 2008—stands well below the national average.[5] As the following sections explain, however, some categories of Hispanics have fared better than others.

Mexican Americans

Some Mexican Americans are descendants of people who lived in a part of Mexico annexed by the United States after the Mexican

---

[5]The 2008 median age of the U.S. Hispanic population was 27.7 years, far below the non-Hispanic white median of 41.1 years. This difference accounts for some of the disparity in income and education.

American War (1846–48). However, most Mexican Americans are recent immigrants. Today, more immigrants come to the United States from Mexico than from any other country.

Like many other immigrants, many Mexican Americans have worked as low-wage laborers, on farms or elsewhere. Table 5 shows that the 2008 median family income for Mexican Americans was $41,538, about two-thirds the national average. Almost one-fourth of Mexican American families are poor—nearly twice the national average. Finally, despite gains since 1980, Mexican Americans still have a high dropout rate and receive much less schooling, on average, than the U.S. population as a whole.

Puerto Ricans

The island of Puerto Rico, like the Philippines, became a U.S. possession when Spain was defeated at the end of the Spanish-American War in 1898. In 1917, Congress passed the Jones Act, which made Puerto Ricans (but not Filipinos) U.S. citizens and made Puerto Rico a territory of the United States.

New York City is home to more than 750,000 Puerto Ricans. About one-third of this community is severely disadvantaged. Adjusting to cultural patterns on the U.S. mainland—including, for many, learning English—is one major challenge; also, Puerto Ricans with darker skin encounter prejudice and discrimination. As a result, more people now return to Puerto Rico each year than arrive: Between 1990 and 2008, the Puerto Rican population of New York actually fell by more than 100,000 (Navarro, 2000; U.S. Census Bureau, 2009).

This "revolving door" pattern limits assimilation. Two out of three Puerto Rican families in the United States speak Spanish at home. Speaking only Spanish maintains a strong ethnic identity but limits economic opportunity. Puerto Ricans also have a much higher rate of woman-headed households than other Hispanics, a pattern that puts families at greater risk of poverty (U.S. Census Bureau, 2009).

Table 5 shows that the 2008 median family income for Puerto Ricans was $43,944, or about 71 percent of the national average. Although long-term mainland residents have made economic gains, more recent immigrants from Puerto Rico struggle to find work. Overall, Puerto Ricans remain the most socially disadvantaged Hispanic minority.

Cuban Americans

In little more than a decade after the 1959 Marxist revolution led by Fidel Castro, 400,000 Cubans had fled to the United States. Most settled with other Cuban Americans in Miami. Many immigrants were highly educated business and professional people who wasted little time becoming as successful in the United States as they had been in their homeland.

Table 5 shows that the median family income for Cuban Americans in 2008 was $51,290, above that of other Hispanics but still well below the national average. The 1.6 million Cuban Americans living in the United States today have managed a delicate balancing act, achieving in the larger society while holding on to much of their traditional culture. Of all Hispanics, Cubans are the most likely to speak Spanish in their homes: more than eight out of ten families do so. However, cultural distinctiveness and living in highly visible communities such as Miami's Little Havana provoke hostility from some people.

Arab Americans

Arab Americans are another U.S. minority whose numbers are increasing. Like Hispanic Americans, these are people whose ancestors lived in a variety of countries. What is sometimes called "the Arab world" includes twenty-two nations and stretches across northern Africa, from Mauritania and Morocco on Africa's west coast to Egypt and Sudan on Africa's east coast, and extends into the Middle East (western Asia), including Iraq and Saudi Arabia. Not all the people who live in these nations are Arabs, however; for example, the Berber people in Morocco and the Kurds of Iraq are not Arabs.

Jim West\Alamy Images

In 2010, claiming the federal government is not securing our borders, Arizona officials enacted a new law making law enforcement officials more proactive in determining the immigrant status of people they have a lawful reason to engage. While popular in Arizona, the new law drew the fire of critics who saw the law as an attack on people of Hispanic descent.

● Seeing Sociology
  in Everyday Life

Look closely at the maps. Can you explain why various
categories of people tend to be concentrated in certain
regions of the United States?

○ Making the Grade

Remember that Hispanic Americans are the largest
racial/ethnic minority in the United States,
representing more than 15 percent of the nation's
population.

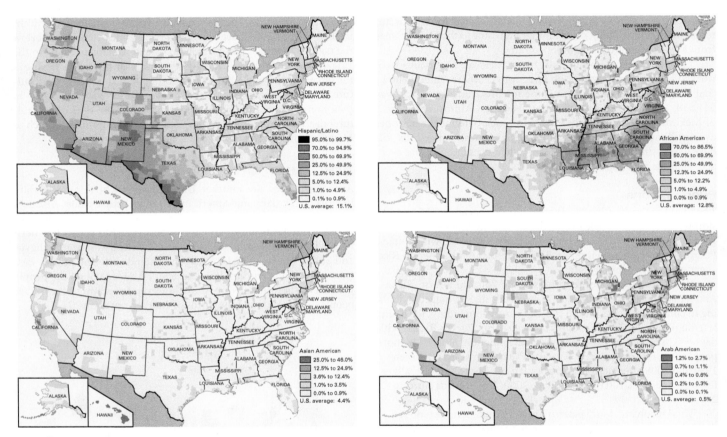

Seeing Ourselves

NATIONAL MAP 3

The Concentration of Hispanics or Latinos, African Americans, Asian Americans, and Arab Americans, by County

In 2008, people of Hispanic or Latino descent represented 15.4 percent of the U.S. population; 12.8 percent were African Americans,
4.6 percent Asian Americans, and 0.5 percent Arab Americans. These maps show the geographic distribution of these categories of
people in 2000. Comparing them, we see that the southern half of the United States is home to far more minorities than the northern half.
But do they all concentrate in the same areas? What patterns do the maps reveal?

Sources: U.S. Census Bureau (2001, 2009).

Arab cultures differ from society to society, but they share widespread use of the Arabic alphabet and language and have Islam as
their dominant religion. But keep in mind that "Arab" (an ethnic category) is not the same as "Muslim" (a follower of Islam). A majority
of the people living in most Arab countries are Muslims, but some
Arabs are Christians or followers of other religions. In addition, most
of the world's Muslims do not live in Africa or the Middle East and
are not Arabs.

Because many of the world's nations have large Arab populations, immigration to the United States has created a culturally
diverse population of Arab Americans. Some Arab Americans are
Muslims and some are not; some speak Arabic and some do not;
some maintain the traditions of their homeland and some do not. As
is the case with Hispanic Americans and Asian Americans, some are
recent immigrants and some have lived in this country for decades
or even for generations.

Race and Ethnicity

Seeing Sociology in Everyday Life

Do you know of any highly educated immigrants who worked as professionals in their birth nations and who are now performing working-class jobs here in the United States? Why might immigrants have to do this?

Seeing Sociology in Everyday Life

Do any members of your family consider themselves to be "white ethnics"? Do you? Explain.

As noted back in Table 1, the government gives the official number of Arab Americans as 1.6 million, but because people may not declare their ethnic background, it is likely that the actual number is at least twice as high.[6] The largest populations of Arab Americans have ancestral ties to Lebanon (32 percent of all Arab Americans), Egypt (12 percent), and Syria (10 percent). Most Arab Americans (69 percent) report ancestral ties to one nation, but 30 percent report ancestors in more than one nation, which may include both Arab and non-Arab countries (U.S. Census Bureau, 2009). National Map 3 shows that the Arab American population is distributed throughout the United States.

Included in the Arab American population are people of all social classes. Some are highly educated professionals who work as physicians, engineers, and educators; others are working-class people who perform various skilled jobs in factories or on construction sites; still others do service work in restaurants, hospitals, or other settings or work in small family businesses. As shown in Table 6, median family income for Arab Americans is above the national average ($70,073 compared to the national median of $61,521 in 2008), but Arab Americans have a higher than average poverty rate (16.1 percent, versus 13.2 percent for the population as a whole). Arab Americans are highly educated; 46 percent have a college degree, compared to 30 percent of the adult population as a whole (U.S. Census Bureau, 2009).

There are large, visible Arab American communities in a number of U.S. cities, including New York, Chicago, Los Angeles, Houston, and Dearborn (Michigan). Even so, Arab Americans may choose to downplay their ethnicity as a way to avoid prejudice and discrimination. The fact that many of the recent terrorist attacks against the United States and other nations have been carried out by Arabs has fueled a stereotype that links being Arab (or Muslim) with being a terrorist. This stereotype, like all stereotypes, is unfair because it blames an entire category of people for the actions of a few individuals. But it is probably the reason that the social distance research discussed earlier in this chapter shows students expressing more negative attitudes toward Arabs than toward any other racial or ethnic category. It also helps explain why Arab Americans have been targets of an increasing number of hate crimes and why many Arab Americans feel that they are subject to "ethnic profiling" by police officers and security personnel that threatens their privacy and civil liberties (Ali & Juarez, 2003; Ali, Lipper, & Mack, 2004; Hagopian, 2004).

Arab American communities can be found in many large cities on the East and West Coasts of the United States, but the heaviest concentrations are found across the upper Midwest. This mosque rises above the cornfields in a rural area near Toledo, Ohio.

Peter Yates|CORBIS- NY

White Ethnic Americans

The term "white ethnics" recognizes the ethnic heritage and social disadvantages of many white people. White ethnics are non-WASPs whose ancestors lived in Ireland, Poland, Germany, Italy, or other European countries. More than half of the U.S. population falls into one or more white ethnic categories.

High rates of emigration from Europe in the nineteenth century first brought Germans and Irish and then Italians and Jews to this country. Despite cultural differences, all shared the hope that the United States would offer greater political freedom and economic opportunity than their homelands. Most did live better in this country, but the belief that "the streets of America were paved with gold" turned out to be a far cry from reality. Many immigrants found only hard labor for low wages.

White ethnics also endured their share of prejudice and discrimination. Many employers shut their doors to new immigrants, posting signs such as "None need apply but Americans" (Handlin, 1941:67). In 1921, Congress enacted a quota system that greatly limited immigration, especially by southern and eastern Europeans, who

Table 6	The Social Standing of Arab Americans, 2008	
	Arab Americans	**Entire U.S. Population**
Median family income	$70,073	$61,521
Percentage in poverty	16.1%	13.2%
Completion of four or more years of college (age 25 and over)	45.5%	29.5%
Source: U.S. Census Bureau (2009).		

[6]The 2008 median age for Arab Americans was 30.6 years, below the national median of 36.8 years.

● Seeing Sociology
in Everyday Life

Do you know your school's policy on affirmative action?

● Seeing Sociology
in Everyday Life

Do you support affirmative action in college
admission for some or all minorities? Explain your
point of view.

CONTROVERSY & DEBATE

Affirmative Action: Solution or Problem?

STEPHANIE: I think Barbara Gruttner got, well, a raw deal. She should have been admitted.

GINA: Perhaps. But diversity is important. I believe in affirmative action.

MARCO: Maybe some people do get into college more easily. But that includes guys like me whose father went here.

Barbara Gruttner, who is white, claimed that she was the victim of racial discrimination and that the University of Michigan Law School unfairly denied her application for admission while admitting many less qualified African American applicants. The basis of her claim was the fact that Michigan, a state university, admitted just 9 percent of white students with her grade point average and law school aptitude test scores while admitting 100 percent of African American applicants with comparable scores.

In 2003, the U.S. Supreme Court heard Gruttner's complaint in a review of the admissions policies of both the law school and the undergraduate program at the University of Michigan. In a six-to-three decision, the Court ruled against Gruttner, claiming that the University of Michigan Law School could use a policy of affirmative action that takes account of the race of applicants in the interest of creating a socially diverse student body. At the same time, however, the

Court struck down the university's undergraduate admissions policy, which awarded points not only for grades and college board scores but also for being a member of an underrepresented minority. A point system of this kind, the Court ruled, is too close to the rigid quota systems rejected by the Court in the past.

Carl D. Walsh\Aurora Photos, Inc.

With this ruling, the Supreme Court continued to oppose quotalike systems while at the same time reaffirming the importance of racial diversity on campus. Thus colleges and universities can take account of race in order to increase the number of traditionally underrepresented students as long as race is treated as just one variable in a process that evaluates each applicant as an individual (Stout, 2003).

How did the controversial policy of affirmative action begin? The answer takes us back to the end of World War II, when the U.S. government funded higher education for veterans of all races. The so-called G.I. Bill held special promise for African Americans, most of whom needed financial assistance to enroll in college. By 1960, government funding helped 350,000 black men and women attend college.

There was just one problem: Even with advanced schooling, these individuals were not finding the kinds of jobs for which they were qualified. So the Kennedy administration devised a program of "affirmative action" to provide broader opportunities to qualified minorities. Businesses and universities were instructed to monitor hiring, promotion, and admissions policies to eliminate discrimination against minorities, even if unintended.

were likely to have darker skin and different cultural backgrounds than the dominant WASPs. This quota system continued until 1968.

In response to prejudice and discrimination, many white ethnics formed supportive residential enclaves. Some also gained footholds in businesses and trades: Italian Americans entered the construction industry, Irish Americans worked in construction and civil service jobs, Jews predominated in the garment industry, and many Greeks (like the Chinese) worked in the retail food business (W. M. Newman, 1973).

Many white ethnics still live in traditional working-class neighborhoods, although those who prospered have gradually assimilated. Most descendants of immigrants who labored in sweatshops and lived in crowded tenements now make enough money to lead comfortable lives. As a result, their ethnic heritage has become a source of pride.

Race and Ethnicity: Looking Ahead

The United States has been, and will remain, a land of immigrants. Immigration has brought striking cultural diversity and tales of hope, struggle, and success told in hundreds of languages.

Most immigrants arrived in a great wave that peaked about 1910. The next two generations brought economic gains and at least some assimilation. The government also extended citizenship to Native Americans (1924), foreign-born Filipinos (1942), Chinese Americans (1943), and Japanese Americans (1952).

Another wave of immigration began after World War II and swelled as the government relaxed immigration laws in the 1960s.

○ Seeing Sociology
in Everyday Life

Can you provide examples of xenophobia in our society today?

○ Making the Grade

Reading the box below, be sure you see that the policy of affirmative action has changed over time, largely as the result of court decisions.

Defenders of affirmative action see it, first, as a sensible response to our nation's racial and ethnic history, especially for African Americans, who suffered through two centuries of slavery and a century of segregation under Jim Crow laws. Throughout our history, they claim, being white gave people a big advantage. They see minority preference today as a step toward fair compensation for unfair majority preference in the past.

Second, given our racial history, many analysts doubt that the United States will ever become a color-blind society. They claim that because prejudice and discrimination are rooted deep in U.S. culture, simply claiming that we are color-blind does not mean that everyone will be treated fairly.

Third, supporters maintain that affirmative action has worked. Where would minorities be today if the government had not enacted this policy in the 1960s? Major employers, such as fire and police departments in large cities, began hiring minorities and women for the first time only because of affirmative action. This program has helped expand the African American middle class and increased racial diversity on college campuses and in the workplace.

Only about 10 percent of white people say they support racial preferences for African Americans. Even among African Americans themselves, just 46 percent support this policy

(NORC, 2009). Critics point out, first of all, that affirmative action was intended as a temporary remedy to ensure fair competition but soon became a system of "group preferences" and quotas—in short, a form of "reverse discrimination," favoring people not because of talent and effort but because of race, ethnicity, or sex.

Second, critics say, if racial preferences were wrong in the past, they are wrong now. Why should whites today, many of whom are far from privileged, be penalized for past discrimination that was in no way their fault? Our society has undone most of the institutional prejudice and discrimination of earlier times—doesn't the election of an African American president suggest that? Giving entire categories of people special treatment compromises standards of excellence and calls into question the real accomplishments of minorities.

A third argument against affirmative action is that it benefits those who need it least. Favoring minority-owned corporations or holding places in law school helps already privileged people. Affirmative action has done little for the African American underclass that needs the most help.

There are good arguments for and against affirmative action, and people who want our society to have more racial and ethnic equality fall on both sides of the debate. Voters in a num-

ber of states, including California, Washington, Michigan, and Nebraska, have passed ballot initiatives banning the use of affirmative action based on gender or race. In 2008, however, voters in Colorado voted down such a proposal. So the country remains divided on this issue. The disagreement is not whether people of all backgrounds should have equal opportunity but whether the current policy of affirmative action is part of the solution or part of the problem.

WHAT DO YOU THINK?

1. In view of the fact that society has historically favored males over females and whites over people of color, would you agree that white males have received more "affirmative action" than anyone? Why or why not?

2. Should affirmative action include only disadvantaged categories of minorities (say, African Americans and Native Americans) and exclude more affluent categories (such as Japanese Americans)? Why or why not?

3. Do you think the election of Barack Obama as the nation's first African American president suggests that affirmative action is no longer needed? Why or why not?

Sources: Bowen & Bok (1999), Kantrowitz & Wingert (2003), Flynn (2008), Leff (2008), and NORC (2009).

Today, about 1.5 million people come to the United States each year—about 1.1 million legally and another 400,000 illegally. This is almost twice the number that arrived during the "Great Immigration" a century ago (although newcomers now enter a country that has five times as many people). Most of today's immigrants come not from Europe but from Latin America and Asia, with Mexicans, Chinese, Indians, and Filipinos arriving in the largest numbers.

Many new arrivals face much the same prejudice and discrimination experienced by those who came before them. In 1994, California voters passed Proposition 187, which stated that illegal immigrants should be denied health care, social services, and public education; it was later overturned in federal court. More recently, voters there mandated that all children learn English in school. Some landowners in the

Southwest have taken up arms to discourage illegal immigrants crossing the border from Mexico. Even so, we continue to debate how to best deal with the more than 12 million illegal immigrants already here.

Even minorities who have been in the United States for generations feel the sting of prejudice and discrimination. Affirmative action, a policy meant to provide opportunities for racial and ethnic minorities, is also hotly debated, as the Controversy & Debate box describes.

Like those of earlier generations, today's immigrants hope to blend into U.S. society without completely giving up their traditional culture. Some still build racial and ethnic enclaves, so the Little Havanas and Koreatowns of today stand alongside the Little Italys and Chinatowns of the past. In addition, new arrivals carry the hope that racial and ethnic diversity can be a source of pride rather than a badge of inferiority.

Seeing Sociology in Everyday Life

Is our society becoming more accepting of racially and ethnically mixed couples and friendship groups?

As the social distance research presented in this chapter shows, today's college students express greater acceptance of social diversity. Look at the two corporate advertisements shown here. What evidence of greater acceptance do you see? In your opinion, does this evidence mean that our society has really changed? Why or why not?

Image courtesy of The Advertising Archives

Here's an ad from 1957, when the civil rights movement was just getting under way. Based on what you have read in this chapter, how does this reflect what U.S. society was like fifty years ago in terms of racial segregation?

> **HINT** On the face of it, today's ads suggest far greater racial and ethnic tolerance than was true in the 1950s, when we rarely saw images of people of different categories interacting with one another. The social distance research noted in this chapter also supports the idea that tolerance is increasing. Being more racially inclusive is also a smart business policy, in light of of the increasing economic resources of various minority categories of the U.S. population.

Especially in the case of advertising aimed at young people, racial and ethnic mixing has become the rule. How accurately does this image reflect everyday life? Do you think young people differ from older people in their degree of social tolerance? Explain.

Applying SOCIOLOGY in Everyday Life

1. Thinking about your own campus, can you point to ways in which race does not matter in students' lives? In what ways does race still matter? On balance, how important is race today?

2. Does your college or university take account of race and ethnicity in its admissions policies? Ask to speak with an admissions officer to see what you can learn about your school's use of race and ethnicity in admissions. Ask whether there is a "legacy" policy that favors children of parents who attended the school.

3. Give several of your friends or family members a quick quiz, asking them what share of the U.S. population is white, Hispanic, African American, and Asian. You will probably find that most white people exaggerate the size of the African American population (C. A. Gallagher, 2003). Why do you think this is so?

Making the Grade

Race and Ethnicity

👁 Watch on mysoclab.com

The Social Meaning of Race and Ethnicity

RACE refers to socially constructed categories based on biological traits a society defines as important.
- The meaning and importance of race vary from place to place and over time.
- Societies use racial categories to rank people in a hierarchy, giving some people more money, power, and prestige than others.
- In the past, scientists created three broad categories—Caucasoids, Mongoloids, and Negroids—but there are no biologically pure races.

ETHNICITY refers to socially constructed categories based on cultural traits a society defines as important.
- Ethnicity reflects common ancestors, language, and religion.
- The importance of ethnicity varies from place to place and over time.
- People choose to play up or play down their ethnicity.
- Societies may or may not set categories of people apart based on differences in ethnicity.

race a socially constructed category of people who share biologically transmitted traits that members of a society consider important

ethnicity a shared cultural heritage

minority any category of people distinguished by physical or cultural difference that a society sets apart and subordinates

Minorities are people of various racial and ethnic categories who are visually distinctive and disadvantaged by a society.

 Explore on mysoclab.com

Prejudice and Stereotypes

PREJUDICE is a rigid and unfair generalization about a category of people.
- The social distance scale is one measure of prejudice.
- One type of prejudice is the **STEREOTYPE,** a simplified description applied to every person in some category.
- **RACISM,** a very destructive type of prejudice, asserts that one race is innately superior or inferior to another.

There are four **THEORIES OF PREJUDICE:**
- **Scapegoat theory** claims that prejudice results from frustration among people who are disadvantaged.
- **Authoritarian personality theory** (Adorno) claims that prejudice is a personality trait of certain individuals, especially those with little education and those raised by cold and demanding parents.
- **Culture theory** (Bogardus) claims that prejudice is rooted in culture; we learn to feel greater social distance from some categories of people.
- **Conflict theory** claims that prejudice is a tool used by powerful people to divide and control the population.

prejudice a rigid and unfair generalization about an entire category of people

stereotype a simplified description applied to every person in some category

racism the belief that one racial category is innately superior or inferior to another

scapegoat a person or category of people, typically with little power, whom other people unfairly blame for their own troubles

Discrimination

DISCRIMINATION is treating various categories of people unequally.
- Prejudice refers to *attitudes*; discrimination involves *actions*.
- Institutional prejudice and discrimination is bias built into the operation of society's institutions, including schools, hospitals, the police, and the workplace.
- Prejudice and discrimination perpetuate themselves in a vicious circle, resulting in social disadvantage that fuels additional prejudice and discrimination.

discrimination unequal treatment of various categories of people

institutional prejudice and discrimination bias built into the operation of society's institutions

📖 Read on mysoclab.com

Majority and Minority: Patterns of Interaction

PLURALISM requires that racial and ethnic categories, although distinct, have roughly equal social standing.

- U.S. society is pluralistic in that all people in the United States, regardless of race or ethnicity, have equal standing under the law.
- U.S. society is not pluralistic in that all racial and ethnic categories do not have equal social standing.

ASSIMILATION is the process by which minorities gradually adopt the patterns of the dominant culture.

- Assimilation involves changes in dress, language, religion, values, and friends.
- Assimilation is a strategy to escape prejudice and discrimination and to achieve upward social mobility.
- Some categories of people have assimilated more than others.

pluralism a state in which people of all races and ethnicities are distinct but have equal social standing

assimilation the process by which minorities gradually adopt patterns of the dominant culture

miscegenation biological reproduction by partners of different racial categories

segregation the physical and social separation of categories of people

genocide the systematic killing of one category of people by another

SEGREGATION is the physical and social separation of categories of people.

- Although some segregation is voluntary (for example, the Amish), majorities usually segregate minorities by excluding them from neighborhoods, schools, and occupations.
- *De jure* segregation is segregation by law; *de facto* segregation describes settings that contain only people of one category.
- Hypersegregation means having little social contact with people beyond the local community.

GENOCIDE is the systematic killing of one category of people by another.

- Historical examples of genocide include the extermination of Jews by the Nazis and the killing of Western-leaning people in Cambodia by Pol Pot.
- Recent examples of genocide include Hutus killing Tutsis in the African nation of Rwanda, Serbs killing Bosnians in the Balkans of Eastern Europe, and the systematic killing in the Darfur region of Sudan.

Race and Ethnicity in the United States

NATIVE AMERICANS, the earliest human inhabitants of the Americas, have endured genocide, segregation, and forced assimilation. Today, the social standing of Native Americans is well below the national average.

WHITE ANGLO-SAXON PROTESTANTS (WASPs) were most of the original European settlers of the United States, and many continue to enjoy high social position today.

AFRICAN AMERICANS experienced two centuries of slavery. Emancipation in 1865 gave way to segregation by law (the so-called Jim Crow laws). In the 1950s and 1960s, a national civil rights movement resulted in legislation that outlawed segregated schools and overt discrimination in employment and public accommodations. Today, despite legal equality, African Americans are still disadvantaged.

ASIAN AMERICANS have suffered both racial and ethnic hostility. Although some prejudice and discrimination continue, both Chinese and Japanese Americans now have above-average income and schooling. Asian immigrants—especially Chinese, Indians, and Filipinos—now account for more than one-third of all immigration to the United States.

HISPANIC AMERICANS OR LATINOS, the largest U.S. minority, include manyethnicities sharing a Spanish heritage. Mexican Americans, the largest Hispanicminority, are concentrated in the Southwest and are the poorest Hispanic category. Cubans, concentrated in Miami, are the most affluent Hispanic category.

ARAB AMERICANS are a growing U.S. minority. Because they come to the United States from so many different nations, Arab Americans are a culturally diverse population, and they are represented in all social classes. They have been a target of prejudice and hate crimes in recent years as a result of a stereotype that links all Arab Americans with terrorism.

WHITE ETHNIC AMERICANS are non-WASPs whose ancestors emigrated from Europe in the nineteenth and twentieth centuries. In response to prejudice and discrimination, many white ethnics formed supportive residential enclaves.

Sample Test Questions

Multiple-Choice Questions

1. *Race* refers to _____ considered important in a society, and *ethnicity* refers to _____.
   a. biological traits; cultural traits
   b. cultural traits; biological traits
   c. our differences; what we all have in common
   d. what we all have in common; our differences

2. People of Hispanic descent make up what share of the U.S. population?
   a. 45.4 percent
   b. 35.4 percent
   c. 25.4 percent
   d. 15.4 percent

3. A minority is defined as a category of people who
   a. at one time were disadvantaged.
   b. are less than half of a society's population.
   c. are defined as different and are disadvantaged.
   d. are below average in terms of income.

4. In the United States, four states have a "minority majority." Which of the following states is *not* one of them?
   a. California
   b. Florida
   c. Texas
   d. New Mexico

5. Research using the Bogardus social distance scale shows that U.S. college students
   a. are less prejudiced than students fifty years ago.
   b. believe that Arabs and Muslims should be kept out of the country.
   c. have the strongest prejudice against African Americans.
   d. All of the above are correct.

6. *Prejudice* is a matter of _____, and *discrimination* is a matter of _____.
   a. biology; culture
   b. attitudes; behavior
   c. choice; social structure
   d. social structure; culture

7. The United States is not truly pluralistic today because
   a. part of our population lives in "ethnic enclaves."
   b. this country has a history of slavery.
   c. different racial and ethnic categories are unequal in social standing.
   d. All of the above are correct.

8. Which concept is illustrated by immigrants from Ecuador coming to the United States and learning to speak the English language?
   a. genocide
   b. segregation
   c. assimilation
   d. pluralism

9. When the first Europeans came to the Americas in the late 1400s, Native Americans
   a. followed shortly thereafter.
   b. had just migrated from Asia.
   c. came on ships with them from Europe.
   d. had inhabited this land for 30,000 years.

10. Which is the largest category of Asian Americans in the United States?
    a. Chinese Americans
    b. Japanese Americans
    c. Korean Americans
    d. Vietnamese Americans

ANSWERS: 1(a); 2(d); 3(c); 4(b); 5(a); 6(b); 7(c); 8(c); 9(d); 10(a).

Essay Questions

1. What is the difference between race and ethnicity? What does it mean to say that race and ethnicity are socially constructed?

2. What is a minority? Pointing to specific facts in this chapter, support the claim that African Americans and Arab Americans are both minorities in the United States.

Fighting like a Ballplayer: Basketball as a Strategy Against Social Disorganization

Scott N. Brooks

There are few paths to mainstream success that are clearly open to young black men. The most visibly successful African-American men are entertainers and professional athletes, but the odds of an average black man succeeding in one of these careers are slim. However, as Scott N. Brooks shows in this article, making it as a professional athlete isn't a necessary condition for basketball having a positive influence on young men's lives. Brooks demonstrates that being a basketball player can protect young African-American men from the lure of street-corner culture.

Many inner-city black neighborhoods in South Philadelphia are variations of the 'hood—places with high rates of poverty, violence, single-headed households, drug dealing, and premature death. Here and in similar urban American neighborhoods, people are indirectly monitored and supervised through physical boundaries, fraternal and compound policing,[1] and limited access to mainstream social services. These conditions are symptomatic of social disorganization. Children are raised under tenuous conditions where relationships and trust are strained early on and adult efforts must be

Reprinted from *Against the Wall: Poor, Young, Black, and Male (The City in the Twenty-First Century)* (2008), by permission of University of Pennsylvania Press.

combined. Parents and guardians seek to keep young males from the street, hoping that they will resist the allure of the corner—both a metaphor for street culture and a real place in the poorest communities—and avoid the inevitable violence, incarceration, or death that is associated with the street. In South Philadelphia, basketball is used to combat social disorganization and give young men some tools to counter the draw of the corner.

Elijah Anderson (1990) theorizes about the place of the black, poor, urban, young male in public. He describes what it means to be at this intersection: a young black man is stereotyped and has a negative history based upon the social position of his group; he is considered dangerous, criminal, and guilty. Black men's understanding of this presumption operates as part of their double consciousness; to be successful, they must understand that this stereotype operates and use it to inform them when dealing with others, black and non-black, in most public and formal institutional settings. This stereotype is a direct function of growing social disorganization: poor people who are increasingly impoverished and socially isolated offer displays of "ghetto-specific behavior" and get characterized as having a "culture of poverty." This viewpoint ignores the larger systemic and institutionalized framework of racism. Behavior is an adaptive response to the ongoing assault of macro- and microlevel processes, including cuts in federal, state, and city social spending, racialized policing, and historic and continuing segregation, that has adverse racial and class effects. The black poor get poorer and become more isolated from any possibility of geographic and economic mobility. Social organization at micro-levels can work to mitigate these effects, although with limited microlevel results.

In this context, basketball is a critically important activity. The sport is organized in many different ways that bring adults and youth together, and serious participation and integration into basketball activities build and bridge networks, providing additional resources and opportunities for young men. Young men are encouraged to maintain or regain positive senses of self through being given an opportunity to show that they can succeed at something positive and should not be presumed criminal, guilty, and inherently bad.

According to numerous articles, academic and journalistic, black men, particularly from the inner city, have an athleticized identity. This identity is not developed spontaneously through peer groups; it is passed down from older black men and propagated via media images and the racialization of such sports as basketball and football. Black youth are likely to learn about and develop an intense passion for sports at early ages and come to see athletic achievement as a significant measure of their masculinity and peer group status.[2] Athletic performance is a vehicle through which young black men may express their masculinity. Moreover, the importance of athletic achievement for perceptions of masculinity and status extends into adulthood, particularly for black men who earn high basketball status in their youth but work in blue-collar or low-level white-collar professions where their work rarely provides high occupational prestige or economic returns. For these men, basketball identity becomes their preferred "master status"; it represents the peak of their social career, at the same time that it highlights their skewed life course and low-status position in adulthood.

This chapter demonstrates the importance of basketball as an effective social organization of men, young men, and their families against social disorganization.[3] Basketball seen from this vantage point is not simply a "hoop dream"—young men's unrealistic hope and fixation on basketball and other athletic endeavors as a ticket out of the ghetto. Rather, basketball is an institution and way of life that enables young men to cope in the current context and reduces the social-psychological impact of being negatively stereotyped and marginalized. I learned about the significance of basketball in young men's lives while coaching young black men from impoverished communities in South Philadelphia through the Blade Rodgers League. Over a period of four years, I conducted formal and informal group and individual interviews and hung out with kids, tutoring them in school work, going on errands, and accompanying them to juvenile court. Participant observation on the basketball court and in players' neighborhoods and homes enabled me to understand the real difference their involvement in the sport and the social networks surrounding basketball made in their lives.[4]

◉ Avoiding the Corner by Being a Ballplayer

Many adult black men who are involved with youth basketball leagues and play at local parks and gyms are actively engaged in the lives of young men. Their presence is significant, as studies of black families and poor black inner-city communities often highlight the "disappearance" or absence of black male role models—fathers, uncles, and other males—from the households in which young men live.[5] Notably, the adult black men who are the backbone of organized basketball activities in Philadelphia act as role models and advisors to younger black men, both inside and outside basketball.[6]

The Blade Rodgers League was created primarily to give kids, especially young black males, a place to go to escape the draw of the corner and street activity. The league emphasizes respecting and listening to adults because adults are valuable resources. Kids who participate are taught to respect elders, especially those involved with the league. League coordinators and the founder remove kids from games and expel them from the league altogether for poor behavior during games and league events. Often, players as well as coaches are pulled aside and spoken to regarding their behavior toward referees, league staff, or one another. League officials speak regularly of basketball's usefulness, but acknowledge that young men need help from others to be successful.

The most important aspect of this league is its network of adult men who coach, referee, and serve various administrative and coordinating roles. Without the network, the explicit and implicit missions of the league would fail. The network is made up of older men who have all worked with kids. Most have been a part of the league for over twenty years. The rest are younger men who enjoy working with kids as a way to give back. Many work in the juvenile criminal justice system. The league's coordinator, T.D., is a retired probation officer; Chuck, the co-coordinator and one of the founders, worked as a nonteaching assistant in a local public school and as a drug counselor and therapist; another staff member is a retired police officer;

and others work in schools as security officers and non-teaching assistants. The network is tied together through basketball. It is a web of former "great" local ballplayers connected to the larger network of Philadelphia basketball, local college coaches, and professional coaches and players. These men are in a position not only to help some kids get a chance to play in college and even the professional ranks but also to teach young basketball hopefuls how to navigate the world beyond basketball and outside their communities.

I coached under Chuck, an "old head"—a term used by the kids in South Philly to describe older men, particularly those who mentor younger men. Chuck, now in his late sixties, has played and coached basketball for most of his life, and been a part of the Blade Rodgers League since its beginnings in 1968. He is called a youth advocate by some and praised by women and men, mothers and fathers, current and former players for his commitment to young people. Chuck loves basketball and claims that it saved his life, and he coaches young men to save as many as he can. Still, he is realistic about basketball and young men's possibilities. "Scott, for one of these kids to make it outta here, it's a miracle. Most of them end up on the corner." For adult men like Chuck and others who support young men who are not their own kin, the major reward is emotional, seeing someone succeed (generally measured by educational and occupational attainment) and having played a role in his success.

Basketball remains valuable and necessary in the eyes of Chuck and other men involved with youth basketball. It can have significant short-term and potential long-term benefits as an activity that kids want to do and that brings them to adults for help; kids regard it as worthwhile, rewarding, and effective in social and economic mobility. Being a basketball player is a positive identity and can possibly lead to a good life, free from drugs, incarceration, and violence. In many respects, being a basketball player or an athlete is deemed the opposite of being a thug and hanging on the corner, although some athletes do hang out on the street, run wild, and get into trouble. Players, coaches, and others believe that basketball players are largely distinguishable from other young men in their community because they devote themselves to trying to be the best basketball players they can be; this is how they gain status in their communities, and, hopefully, how they can achieve upward mobility.[7] In this way, basketball players have formed a group identity that is in direct opposition to other types of poor young black male peer groups. This positive valuation is justified by the activities associated with being an athlete. Playing ball seriously requires goal setting, discipline, and commitment and often leads to higher self-esteem and increasing social pressure to live up to idealized expectations. Thus basketball, as an institution, is a cultural force that socializes youth, reinforcing normative values and beliefs in democracy, fair play, and meritocracy.[8]

One evening after practice, I gave rides home to three high school players: Jermaine (fifteen years old), Ray (sixteen), and Darrell (fifteen). I asked them about some men, both older and younger, whom we saw standing on a corner. Our interaction illustrates what young men mean when they identify themselves with basketball players rather than with thugs (also called hustlers or drug dealers).

"Who are those guys on the corner?" I inquired.

"Drug dealers," Darrell responded without much thought.

"How do you know?" I questioned, wanting to know what he knew about these guys that clued him in to their being drug dealers as opposed to loafers, kids waiting for their parents to come home, or men who had just gotten off work.

"Everybody know," he said matter-of-factly.

"Do you *know* them?" I probed further.

"Yeah. I mean no. They know me, but I don't know them," he replied.

"I know them, Scott," Ray said. "Well, I don't *know* them, know them. But I know them. One of them used to go to our school."

Jermaine added, "Yeah, that Turk. But he don't go to school no more. He just hang out on the corner."

"How do *they* know *you*, then? They know you from school or the neighborhood . . . ?" I asked.

"Because we play ball," Darrell shot back.

"Just because you play ball they *know* you?" I asked with some disbelief.

"Yeah, 'cause they seen me play," Darrell said.

"They know us because we play ball and get girls, Scott," Jermaine added.

Darrell grew frustrated with my questioning and tried to summarize his point. "Basically, you either a thug or an athlete. And if you an athlete then you get respect, and girls like that. They [the thugs we saw] just wasting they lives."

In identifying different segments of the local population, Darrell, Jermaine, and Ray make it clear they are choosing to be part of a certain group. Each camp has its own characteristics and predicted behaviors. Thugs are young men who hang out on the corner and sell drugs, but ballplayers are respected and perceived as doing something positive, since playing well adds to their chances for upward mobility. A more immediate reward is that young women find athletes attractive.[9] Moreover, if a youth is perceived to have the potential to escape poverty through basketball, his social position is enhanced. Known basketball players are seen as "good" kids, and kids who hang out on the corner are not viewed as positively. For thugs, local "respect" is based on fear, not admiration, because they are considered "wastes" and negative influences or forces in the community.

One individual's experiences in high school illustrate how race, gender, and class scripted his interactions with civil authorities, yet his connection with basketball and the Blade Rodgers League staff were useful in his negotiating the juvenile justice system. Some adult men with whom he was connected indirectly through the league mentored and advised him, appealing to his basketball identity.

☙ Paul's Story

I met Paul at basketball practice. He did not really stand out, although he always seemed to be in a good mood. He smiled and laughed often, especially when other kids were being scolded and picked on. His ability did not set him apart either; he was an average basketball player, but gave a lot of effort. He was finishing his tenth grade year, which meant that he would be moving up to the advanced high school level of the Rodgers League. This was a big jump, because the eleventh and twelfth graders in the Rodgers League were the best players in the city and neighboring areas. Paul established himself early in league play as a leader; he was vocal on the court and knew how plays were to be run. A problem was that he was emotional and explosive, sometimes having too many words for referees. Referees often warned Chuck and me to calm Paul down.

Paul's childhood was fairly typical for a kid growing up in South Philly. His father had never been around. His mother, Tasha, married twice, though neither marriage was to Paul's father, and had three sons, all of whom had different fathers. According to Tasha, she and Paul's father had intended to get married, but he deserted her when she told him of the pregnancy. In his absence, Paul's "stepfathers" had been father figures. Tasha's first husband, the father of her oldest son, played a large role in Paul's life. Paul said he was the father he never had, even though Paul was the product of a relationship Tasha had after their divorce. Tasha and her second husband, Paul's actual step-father, separated when Paul was in middle school. Paul did not care much for him, and referred to him as "*his* dad," meaning his younger brother's dad.

Paul's brothers and his mother live in different places but remain close. Paul lives with Tasha and her boyfriend, "Mr. Larry," in a home that they rent a block south of Tasha's mother's home. Paul's older brother, Tommy, lives with the grandmother, and his younger brother, Andre, lives with his father. Andre comes "down" to stay with him and their mother on the weekends from Germantown, a neighborhood about ten miles north of South Philly. Paul sees Tommy throughout the week because of their proximity. They attend high school basketball and football games, go clothes shopping, and eat together regularly. Within this living arrangement, Paul has gotten used to a significant amount of freedom and self-management. Paul often cooks and shops for himself and abides by his own rules. In a real sense, Paul has already entered adulthood. No one acts as an authority disciplining him and making decisions for him. He interacts with his mother as though they are peers.

On one visit to Paul's home with Chuck, we took note of the interaction between Paul and his mother. After leaving, Chuck asked me, "You see how he talks to his mother? He don't have no respect for her. But when he wants some new sneaks or some grub [food] then it's all sweetness. But I don't blame the kids, I blame the parents. They let them get away with that shit. For a kid like Paul basketball may be his only hope. We might be the only adults that can speak to him, the only ones telling 'em right."

Chuck observed that Paul's condescension toward his mother during their interaction suggested that Paul felt equal or superior to his mother, perhaps smarter, while he remained her dependent. In Chuck's eyes this was out of order: a dependent child should act as a dependent and defer to a parent or guardian. More important, this stance highlighted Paul's sense of independence and manhood. He was much bigger than his mother, managed his own activities, and made his own decisions. But he was still a child who needed parental guidance; he needed to understand and respect authority as a means of growing up and becoming self-sufficient. Paul's situation is typical, but youthful independence often has grave implications in the context of urban poverty and social conditions in the community.

One day changed Paul's plans. Paul called me very late one Friday night. I asked him "what's up" and began to scold him about calling so late. He told me that he had been trying to get in touch with Chuck because his father, meaning his first stepfather, had been murdered a few days earlier and the funeral had been postponed to Saturday. I offered my condolences, told him I would let Chuck know about the change in the funeral date, and confirmed our next meeting for algebra tutoring.

The next morning I called Chuck to relay the message regarding the new time for the funeral. I told him about the late night call and he abruptly asked me if Paul was okay. I was a little confused. I explained that Paul had called to tell him and me about the new funeral time, but as I finished my thought, my voice trailed off; I couldn't believe that I had been so insensitive. Chuck jumped in, "I'm sorry to bring up the psychological stuff, Scott. But you know that's my thing." Chuck was right. It made no sense that Paul would call me to look for Chuck. He didn't really call to tell me about the funeral, he wanted to talk. I had missed the opportunity to be an emotional support for him.

I tried to reach Paul three times over the next two days, but either no one answered or Tasha or Mr. Larry told me that they would give him the message that I had called. Paul did not return my call. Tuesday afternoon came and I called, as I normally did, to make sure that we were still going to meet; he had stood me up once or twice, and I found that checking in reminded him and ensured that he would be home. This time Tasha answered the phone.

I called her by name, "Hey Tasha, it's Scott."

"Weren't you supposed to be meeting Paul today?"

"Yeah, that's why I'm calling."

"Well, you ain't gonna meet him today. It'll have to be tomorrow Thursday or some other time."

She spoke curtly and in a very stern tone. I was taken aback. I was not sure what to take from her tone, but it did not sound good. I wondered if I had done something. I asked her why.

"You never guess where he at."

"Where?"

"In jail."

Tasha told me that Paul had gotten into a fight with a school police officer and been charged with assault. She claimed she knew the policeman, he was a friend of the family, and she was confident that the charges would be dropped.

"But I ain't worried. Paul's a good kid, he ain't never had no trouble with the law. He probably be released later tonight."

I told her I was sorry to hear about all the trouble, but she reassured me that everything would be alright. She asked me how late Paul could call me, so that he could return my call, and she thanked me for agreeing to tutor Paul in algebra.

Paul called me a couple of days later. He was his usual upbeat self and sounded in pretty good spirits. I asked when he had got home and he told me that he got home that night I spoke with his mom. I asked him about what had happened at school.

Paul told me that he was leaving the lunchroom and heard someone call his name when he was outside. He turned to see another young man approaching him and talking "smack" or insulting him. The young man, it seemed, was "showing out" to a bunch of girls;

insulting Paul as a means to show that he was tough and unafraid of Paul despite his reputation for fighting. As the young man approached and continued to talk, he began taking off his coat. Paul did not wait for the young man to shed the coat; the movement to remove it triggered Paul's response. He saw this move as getting ready to fight, so he beat him to the punch. He hit him in the face, knocking him down, and then jumped on top of him, pounding him with his fists. After a number of blows, Paul got up and left the young man.

Paul began to walk toward the principal's office to face the inevitable when someone yelled, "Who was fighting?" Some girls pointed at Paul and yelled, "He was." Paul stood still as the school police officer ran toward him. The officer grabbed Paul's shirt with a punch. Paul was taken off guard and fought back until other officers came to help and Paul felt a barrage of hits and kicks to the face and body. Paul's girlfriend, Mia, tried to assist Paul and fought the officers. She got involved because of the excessive blows to his face, head, and body that the officer and back-up inflicted upon him. Paul felt that she had done the proper thing in "standing by her man." When the altercation was over, Paul and Mia were both charged with assault, Paul with 5 counts and Mia with 3. They both were given a court date for a month later and expelled from their school. The young man Paul fought, who had started the whole ordeal, had no charges brought against him because he did not fight the officers.

Paul was given two different court dates, a school disciplinary hearing regarding his educational future, and a civil case for assaulting a police officer. In the disciplinary hearing the judge would determine if he could return to Jackson Street High School or be reassigned. The judge ruled that Paul was not allowed to return to Street and was reassigned to Woodland, considered the worst and most dangerous school in the city. Upon hearing the ruling, Tasha said, she and Paul both broke down and cried. Both felt that Paul's actions were right and the officer was in the wrong. The policeman had hit him first and Paul responded by retaliating and protecting himself. The judge told Paul that on the street this reaction might have gotten him killed by regular police officers. He was probably right, but Tasha still felt that Paul had not been treated fairly.

Tasha believed this judge had made up his mind before they had even arrived. The judge claimed that Paul had a "history," a record of past troubles over his public school career. The judge recounted from some file that Paul had received four "pink notices" (detention slips) during the last three years and had been held back in the first grade. Tasha was amazed that the judge had used information about Paul's past to make a judgment about his present character. In her eyes, Paul was a "good" kid because he was not involved in drugs, had been an active athlete and steered clear of gangs, and had not been arrested before. But the judge's construction of Paul fit the common construction that Anderson (1990, 1999) calls the "black male in public." In this way, Paul was guilty as a function of his social position in relation to civil authorities. Paul's behavior was regarded as reflecting his antipathetic relationship to police and teachers, institutional authorities, and the wider white social system. He was inherently deviant and needed to be punished, controlled, and dominated by formal authorities because he was poor, young, black, and male.

The fate of many young men in Paul's neighborhood has been negatively determined by one event combined with their "past" and intersectional identity: being urban, poor, black, young, and male. This identity carries little or no social, economic, or political capital when confronted with formal civil authorities. No recourse or appeal can be made when a judge says a young man is of bad character and gives a judgment with possible adverse and life-changing consequences. Paul was expelled from the school that his mother, brother, and friends attended. He was reassigned to a school with a bad reputation where several probation officers had offices and worked full-time on site. This outcome was only half of Paul's problems; he still had to await his date in family court (where juvenile cases are heard) for assaulting the officer. Might he be incarcerated just months before he turned eighteen? Could they charge him as an adult?

At that critical juncture, Paul found out that his girlfriend, Mia, was pregnant. He was unsure not only about his education but also about his whole future. How would having a child affect his life? He had said before the pregnancy that he knew that Mia was "the one," his soulmate, and that he wanted to marry her after he went to college and got a good job. Becoming a parent would undoubtedly put a strain on these plans. Could he attend college and be a father? Would he marry her now? Could he still get the good job?

Paul's connections with the adult men in the basketball league meant that his story differs from that of other young black men in trouble with the formal authorities. Paul's association with the Blade Rodgers League had increased his social networks. He had me, Chuck, and others in his corner, to offer knowledge and support, and even to vouch for him to the officials wielding the power to shape his future.

I talked to Chuck about what had happened to Paul. He told me to have Paul come down to the league so we could come up with a game plan for how Paul might proceed in family court in front of a judge. Chuck believed we could help Paul because TD, the league coordinator and Chuck's longtime assistant coach, was a probation officer who worked at the courthouse. I went down to the league and met with Chuck and Paul before we spoke with TD. Chuck listened closely to Paul's story and instructed Paul to say as little as possible so that he could focus on what TD had to say. TD had often worked in this capacity, helping one of the league's guys, and had little tolerance for excuses.

We found TD after the day's games, and Chuck told TD that Paul needed his help. TD looked to Paul and asked, "What's up, man?" Paul explained that he had been in a fight and that he was in trouble for assaulting a school police officer. TD shook his head and started in: "What are you doing, man? You better than that. You a ballplayer. You not supposed to be getting into stuff like that." Paul tried to defend himself, and talked about the officer pushing him while hand-cuffing the other kid. Paul said that he told the officer not to touch him but the officer hit him in the face and then he fought back. Evidently, Paul did not understand what he had done wrong. When TD asked him why he fought back, Paul said that the officer wasn't supposed to put his hands on him. TD shook his head and told Paul that his attitude and disrespect for authority was the problem. Chuck tried to tell Paul not to say too much, "Just listen, man." TD asked if Paul had played for the school's team and Paul responded that he had not because he had broken his ankle.

Then TD asked Paul why he wasn't in school. Paul explained that the judge had told him to go to Woodland. TD asked him why that mattered: "If you trying to go to school, then you go to school. It don't matter where you at." Chuck stood up for Paul and tried to explain that Woodland was a bad school and gang territory. Paul said that he would just get into more trouble. TD replied that he needed to get rid of that "macho bullshit." He told Paul that as a basketball player he should have had social carte blanche in school.

TD was suggesting that there were benefits to being an athlete: if he had been on the ball team he might have been treated differently by the school and been able to avoid the fight. And at Woodland Paul might be able to avoid problems if he were involved with sports. Athletes generally are not brought into gang stuff, especially if they are promising athletes. Being part of a team implies that a youth has backup, the support of his teammates, who tend to be taller and bigger than others.

Wrapping up the conversation, Chuck told TD that Paul had a court date later that month. TD instructed Paul how to dress for court and speak with the public defender and judge. Last, TD reminded Paul that his attitude had gotten him into trouble. TD had an office in the same building as the courtroom and told Paul to visit his office before seeing the judge. Chuck told Paul to go to TD's office the next day between 10 and 11:30 A.M. to try to get TD to work on the judge before the date. After the meeting Chuck scolded Paul for trying to defend his behavior to TD, who, as a probation officer, understood the system and could possibly help him.

All this happened within the context of the league. I was the point person between Paul and the league's network, and in regular contact with Paul and Chuck. Then Paul, Chuck, and I arranged to meet at the league. Chuck listened to Paul's story and scolded him for being out of control. Still, he told Paul that we had a plan and explained what came next—talking to TD, what to expect from this meeting, and how Paul was to behave. TD then heard Paul's situation and questioned and reprimanded him before offering a solution and speculating on the outcome. Paul had resources because as a basketball player he had developed relationships with men who were in positions to help him, inform him of critical information: how to behave (yes sir, yes ma'am), how to dress for court, and what outcomes to expect. At the same time, Paul received feedback and admonishments from each of us. All this guidance lessened Paul and Tasha's worries.

The time finally came for Paul to go before the family court judge, Paul and Tasha had been down to court for his original trial date in December, but the proceeding was postponed until January. I was able to make the second "notice to appear." I entered the building, went to the security desk, checked in my cell phone, and signed a guest list, after checking the docket and finding which courtroom Paul was scheduled to be in. I went through the metal detector and followed the signs to courtrooms A and B. I entered an adjoining room where those being tried waited with friends and family.

There was a buzz of activity and talk as people waited their turn. The kids were quieter than their parents. They seemed nervous and unsure of their fate, having nothing to distract them from what was looming. One black woman, the mother of a child, said to an older black woman, who seemed to be the grandmother, "This is worse than waiting in the hospital." Many folks seemed to know each other. Paul recognized and spoke to a young woman who attended his school about her reason for being in court. She said that she was there for truancy because she had missed too much school. This young woman seemed almost cavalier; she smiled and laughed easily as though her impending case was of little consequence. Was she putting on a front?

Most of the action was the lawyers making deals. They were wheeling and dealing, moving between a courtroom, which was closed and seemed secretive, and the huge waiting room. Three lawyers, two women and a man, interacted and moved between the waiting room and courtroom. The women were public defenders serving the entirety of the room. Periodically they would go to the front of the room, identified by the direction in which half the chairs faced, and call names to meet their next client.

Each case was put into the queue and handled in pieces. The lone male district attorney (DA) fielded the multitude of cases on the docket. The system worked as an assembly line. First came the public defender's introduction to the client; followed by a brief negotiation with the DA. The public defender returned to the client to discuss the options and specifics of disposition and sentencing, and then checking with the client before making the final deal with the DA regarding how he or she wished to plead. The court proceeding before the judge seemed a mere formality; the cases were generally decided before the kids even saw the judge.

The young woman whom Paul had spoken with entered the courtroom and exited only ten minutes later. Her mother stood crying, her head down. When Paul went up to her to ask what happened, she said she was ordered to go to a group home. A young, pregnant white woman entered the courtroom before being brought out in cuffs. Her mother was distraught; the young woman was downcast, with tears staining her face. The mother's emotion filled the air and left a hush in the room. Prior to sentencing she had seemed so confident, meddling with her younger brothers and sisters and speaking loudly and boldly in her conversation. This was serious now. The room became thick with tension and fear. Waiting kids could no longer believe that this was play; something real was happening in the courtroom.

Tasha, Paul, Mia, and Mia's mother were clearly nervous, and their nervousness grew with each horrifying scene of a young person being sentenced. But Paul had me there, to speak with the public defender and clarify questions and answers, and more important, he had someone helping him on the inside. Paul had already gone to TD's office to remind him that the day had come. TD came into the courtroom periodically to check with the public defender and reassure all of us. After TD's third and final trip, he returned and told us that Paul was going to get six months' probation. He asked how old Paul was (just a month from his eighteenth birthday) and then optimistically said that he'd be fine because this offense would be on his juvenile record, which would not matter when he turned eighteen.

Inside the courtroom, the proceedings went quickly. The DA gave the brief story: Paul got into a fight in school and then resisted arrest, fighting the school officers and injuring the officer, who was present. The judge then looked toward Mia, and the DA added that Mia assaulted the officer, kicking him, while Paul was being restrained. The DA also informed the judge that an agreement had been made. The judge stopped reading the paperwork to address Paul and Mia.

Judge O'Malley was the fifty-something son of a retired Philadelphia judge, called an "a-hole" by one probation officer who said "he ain't nothing like his father. His father was real cool. He act like he got something to prove." O'Malley sat tall on the bench, as though a god, but leaned over and looked down at the "criminals" to give effect.

"This is why our schools are in the shape that they're in," Judge O'Malley said firmly. "It's because of students like you." He went on: "Young lady, it looks like you've been nothing but trouble." He perused some paperwork and continued: "Fights, disrespecting your teachers, and disobedience. How would you feel if someone kicked your father in the head?"[10] The judge shook his head disapprovingly and then told Paul and Mia that they were to take a drug test by giving a urine sample upstairs immediately. "Are you clean? I am not going to get these tests back and have them say that you're dirty, am I? Tell me now. Because if they come back positive for drugs, I'll hold you in contempt of court for lying and then you will be tried as an adult. You hear me, son?"

The judge's statements and questions reflected his tough love approach to sentencing young persons, and a general pessimism held toward young black women and men. He claimed that kids, and Paul and Mia as representatives, were the root of Philadelphia's educational woes. Of course, the judge was simply trying to make a point: kids have a role in the plight of public schooling. But this point is particularly meaningful when considering Paul's two court appearances. In the first hearing, Paul was said to have a troubled past that ran back ten years to first grade; in his second appearance, he was considered emblematic of what is wrong with the whole educational system. Paul was questioned about smoking weed and threatened with being tried as an adult if he had a positive urine test. An altercation with another youth at school had led to something much more serious with long-term implications. This escalation of an ordinary conflict into an event with major educational and legal consequences highlights the layered aspersion that comes with being black and male.

After the urine tests proved negative, Paul and Mia were given six months probation and 25 hours of community service. Paul, Tasha, and I were directed to the probation office to get the necessary paper-work for processing, including a community service record sheet. A black man in his mid-thirties named Randy greeted us and spoke to Paul with familiarity. "Paul. Man, what you doing in here?" Paul sheepishly responded that he had gotten into a fight. Tasha looked at the man quizzically, trying to place him.

"Aw, don't worry, Ma. This happens to many young bulls. Paul used to play ball for me. Yeah, and he used to come over and ride my [motorcycle] bikes. I'll have to tell Tony [another coach] I saw you." Randy tried to comfort Tasha. "Ma, he a good kid, he'll be all right. But I wouldn't have pleaded guilty. If it were my son, I'll tell you what I would have done. I would have pleaded innocent because probation and community service, that's the worst they could have given you. I would have held out for community service only. But it's all right. I got a guy who works at the school and he'll take care of him."

The dealings between the public defender and DA are efficient. Clients are given very few options for how they are to plead and esti-mates of their sentence connected with their options. Appealing for different representation, going to trial, or taking some other action that slows efficiency is not offered. Each defendant is assumed to be guilty; the cases are simply negotiations of what punishment will be given. Paul did not have the resources to retain his own attorney, nor did he, Tasha, or I understand the rules of the game. TD played into the game. In his eyes, Paul had clearly done wrong by assaulting an officer and needed to be taught a lesson that would stay with him only if he accepted responsibility and completed his community service while staying clean from criminal activity. New knowledge of alternatives came up after Paul serendipitously met with his former basketball coach, Randy, from the league. Seeing Randy and talking about past times lightened Paul's mood and even brought a smile and some laughs. Randy added to Paul's experience by giving him a shortcut to completing his service hours.

Then Randy looked at all of us. "Where you gonna do your community service?"

"I don't know," Paul said.

"You wanna put down Blade Rodgers?" Randy asked.

Paul said, "Yes."

"You could work in the league right away, do whatever they need you to do—sweep, keep score, know what I mean, and you could have it all finished before he [the probation officer] even contacts you. And I'll put you with my man [a probation officer Randy knew]. He already full, but I'll talk to him. He'll take care of you."

Meeting Randy was a fortunate but fortuitous event; there was no other probation officer in the office when we arrived. Randy affirmed Paul's goodness and spoke of his trouble as common. Treating a young black man getting in trouble as a normal situation is not a positive thing, but Randy's words lifted Paul's head, rather than shaming him. Ultimately, the presence of Chuck, TD, Randy, and me countered Paul's interactions with the judges and court system. Rather than having a history that he could not overcome and living under a cloud of suspicion, Paul was reminded of his basketball identity and supported with words, given encouragement and advice, and accompanied and spoken for.

❂ The End of Dreams

The whole ordeal represented an end of dreams for Paul and his mother. He had hoped to attend college and get a well-paying job, but this was contingent on playing sports. How else would Paul get to college? His grades were not good, but being a promising athlete might make teachers think of him differently, as an athlete, and if he were considered a high-caliber athlete he would be given information regarding college that he would most likely not otherwise get. Being expelled and sent to another school and having to give up high school sports ended Paul's dream of upward mobility via athletics. Tasha wanted Paul to do something to make her proud, and she felt that the local corner and street life were too alluring. She implored Paul to do something, to try harder in school if he wanted to go to college, or to join the military. "I would rather see my son die serving his country, than die on the street corner," Tasha declared.

After completing his GED in night school, Paul enlisted and remains active in military service. Paul visited Chuck and me at practice to let us know how he was doing. He felt connected to us because of our assistance, but also because he maintained a sense of himself as an athlete. This identity gave him an alternative perspective to interpret his experiences and consider options for his future. He felt accountable for his actions: fighting in school and resisting an officer, we had told him, was stupid and therefore his punishment was deserved. He made unusual decisions, relative to other young men in his community, by continuing school and joining the military in line with his positive identity. He did not have to see his life as over or unredeemable; he had committed himself to steering clear of the corner and street.

Basketball is important, not simply as a form of recreation or means to fame and riches, but as an institution where kids can gain a positive social identity as a basketball player and develop contacts with networks of "decent" men. The league was created as a response to community decline, the growing dearth of male role models, and limited opportunities for youth to learn and play basketball. With its explicit mission to help kids, the league is an organization of "decent" men who help young, poor, black men by being able to provide guidance, offer support, counter the pessimism surrounding young black male identity, and create shortcuts for navigating otherwise tricky and adversarial systems. While this assistance does not guarantee positive outcomes, Paul's case clearly demonstrates how resources have been organized and men have gathered to improve the lives of young men in the midst of the social disorganization found in poor urban and black communities.

However, basketball does not offer a cure for poverty and social marginality. As Harry Edwards (1969) has reminded us time and again, basketball leaves little room for luck, injury, or errors, and it develops few, if any, skills that can be transferred into other occupations. Rather, the organization of basketball demonstrates the importance of a perceived route toward upward mobility and self-esteem. Young black men see black men succeeding at various levels of basketball, in college and in the professional ranks; what it takes to succeed seems clear, and black men are supported in this endeavor. In what other occupational areas can this be said? To solve the structural problems of black education and employment, we need local and federal policies that not only link jobs to growing industries, as has been done in some welfare policy, but also create transparent processes, organizations, direct links to other to more practical activities and careers, and support networks to build confidence and self-worth for young urban poor black men and women.

Endnotes

[1] Fraternal and compound policing refer to a style of policing whereby police officers are typically assigned to areas whose residents share their racial-ethnic background—folks watching their own folks. This style of policing has predictable effects, increasing tensions within groups and limiting mobility for nonwhite police officers. This practice implicitly suggests that the best policing is done through cultural homogeneity rather than through training and objectivity, or "professional" policing. For more details, see J. Wilson 1968.

[2] Many scholars discuss athletic identity and consider how race, gender, and class play significant roles in young black men becoming athletes and using athletic achievement as a status marker; see, for example, Sailes 1998; Messner 1988. Elsewhere (Brooks 2004), I consider the ways in which athletic identity endures into black male adulthood as a sign of inequality, since athletic achievement typically occurs between the ages of fifteen and thirty and represents the social status peak of poor black men. This pattern is in direct contrast with the social status and financial peaks in the life course of middle-class whites, which occur about ten years later and are accompanied with much higher economic gains.

[3] At the same time, I recognize the obvious trope of the "endangered black male," which illustrates the continuing obsession with the black man as central to black politics, leadership, and family stability, while deemphasizing black women and implicitly suggesting that they are less important than men.

[4]Spradley 1980 was an extremely useful guide to recording, coding, and analyzing information gathered through participant observation.

[5]Previous research has measured the effects on children, particularly boys, of growing up without close adult male role models; young males from such backgrounds are more likely to be arrested for petty and serious crimes, join gangs and be drawn into the drug trade at young ages, and ultimately to be absent in the lives of their own children. While it is unclear whether men who are not kin can take the place of biological fathers, it is clear that father figures are important and can play a significant role in the outcomes of children in poverty, particularly if the father figure lives in the same household. See Furstenberg 1995; Furstenberg and Harris 1993. However, many researchers provide evidence and interpretations that contradict the idea that black adult men are absent or irresponsible, lacking the desire to work and support their families. See especially Liebow 1967; Anderson 1976; Duneier 1992; Young 2004.

[6]While studies on Midnight Basketball programs yield mixed results on basketball as an effective intervention in inner-city and violence-filled communities, many recreation programs lack the mentoring and rigorous involvement of positive male figures found in the league studied here. See Hartmann 2001, 2003.

[7]For a discussion of role engulfment among college basketball players, see Adler and Adler 1991.

[8]A critique of this positive view of basketball might be that young men are being taught to assimilate and conform to mainstream standards. But this is complicated. Young men look for opportunities to play, build a reputation, and be promoted. However, "black" sports are popular activities simply because black men are disproportionately represented and considered dominant. Therefore, involvement in basketball reinforces young black men's sense of black masculinity and difference from other men (particularly white men), while forcing them to conformity to mainstream white standards in some way.

[9]Some say the fixation poor black males have on sports is a waste of human potential. See Edwards 1969; Sailes 1996; Harris 1997; Hoberman 1997 for discussions of the dangerous effects of high athletic achievement on the black urban poor. Blumer (1958) theorizes how groups define themselves favorably when comparing themselves to one or more additional groups. In *Stigma* (1963), Goffman suggests that individuals

with stigma sometimes create their own groups, using different criteria, and raise the status of their stigma over the standards of the "normals." Whyte (1981) illustrates how this was done empirically. The "corner boys" ranked one another based on bowling ability, ease and ability to get along with young women, and fighting skills. A person's standing among the "college boys" was linked to performance in academic or intellectual endeavors in high school or college. Participation in high-brow cultural activities or potential for escaping their poor neighborhood was also taken into consideration.

[10]Young black women have the fastest growing rate of incarceration, a phenomenon that is undertheorized. Nikki Jones's work (2004) fills some of the void, illuminating how social environment and culture lead to young women having similar rationales for fighting. In this case, Mia protected Paul's back, in line with male gang behavior.

References

Adler, Patricia, and Peter Adler. 1991. *Backboards and Blackboards: College Athletes and Role Engulfment.* New York: Columbia University Press.

Anderson, Elijah. 1999. *The Code of the Street: Decency, Violence, and the Moral Life of the Inner City.* New York: W.W. Norton.

———. 1990. *Streetwise: Race, Class, and Change in an Urban Community.* Chicago: University of Chicago Press.

———. 1976. *A Place on the Corner.* Chicago: University of Chicago Press.

Blumer, Herbert, 1958. Race prejudice as a sense of group position. *Pacific Sociological Review* 1 (Spring): 3–6.

Brooks, Scott N. 2004. Putting the blessings on him: Vouching and basketball status work. In *Being Here and Being There: Fieldwork Encounters and Ethnographic Discoveries*, ed. Elijah Anderson, Scott N. Brooks, Raymond Gunn, and Nikki Jones. *Annals of the American Academy of Political and Social Science* 595 (September): 80–90.

Duneier, Mitchell, with photographs by Ovie Carter. 1992. *Slim's Table: Race, Respectability, and Masculinity.* Chicago: University of Chicago Press.

Edwards, Harry S. 1969. *The Revolt of the Black Athlete.* New York: Free Press.

Furstenberg, Frank. 1995. Fathering in the inner city. In *Fatherhood: Contemporary Theory, Research, and Social Policy*, ed. William Marsiglio, 119–47. Thousand Oaks, Calif.: Sage.

Furstenberg, Frank, and Kathleen M. Harris. 1993. When and why fathers matter. In *Young Unwed Fathers: Changing Roles and Emerging Policies*, ed. Robert I. Lerman and Theodora J. Ooms, 117–38. Philadelphia: Temple University Press.

Goffman, Erving. 1963. *Stigma: Notes on the Management of Spoiled Identity*. Englewood Cliffs, N.J.: Prentice-Hall.

Harris, Othello. 1997. The role of sport in the black community. *Sociological Focus* 30: 311–20.

Hartmann, Douglass. 2003. Theorizing sport as social intervention. *Quest* 55: 118–40.

———. 2001. Notes on Midnight Basketball and the cultural politics of recreation, race and at-risk urban youth. *Journal of Sport & Social Issues* 24 (November): 339–71.

Hoberman, John. 1997. *Darwin's Athletes: How Sport Has Damaged Black America and Preserved the Myth of Race*. New York: Houghton Mifflin.

Jones, Nikki, 2004. "It's not where you live, it's how you live": How young women negotiate conflict and violence in the inner city. In *Being Here and Being There: Fieldwork Encounters and Ethnographic Discoveries*, ed. Elijah Anderson, Scott N. Brooks, Raymond Gunn, and Nikki Jones. *Annals of the American Academy of Political and Social Science* 595 (September): 49–62.

Liebow, Elliott. 1967. *Tally's Corner: A Study of Negro Streetcorner Men*. Boston: Little, Brown.

Messner, Michael S. 1988. Masculinities and athletic careers. *Gender & Society* 3: 71–88.

Sailes, Gary A. 1998. *African Americans in Sport: Contemporary Themes*. Piscataway, N.J.: Transaction Publishers.

———. 1996. An examination of basketball performance orientations among African American males. *Journal of African American Men* 1 (4): 37–46.

———. 1987. A socio-economic explanation of black sports participation patterns. *Western Journal of Black Studies* 11: 164–67.

Spradley, James P. 1980. *Participant Observation*. New York: Holt, Rinehart, Winston.

Whyte, William Foote. 1981. *Street Corner Society: The Social Structure of an Italian Slum*. 3rd ed. Chicago: University of Chicago Press.

Wilson, James Q. 1968. *Varieties of Police Behavior: The Management of Law and Order in Eight Communities.* Cambridge, Mass.: Harvard University Press.

Wilson, William Julius. 1987. *The Truly Disadvantaged: The Inner City, the Underclass, and Public Policy.* Chicago: University of Chicago Press.

Young, Alford. 2004. *The Minds of Marginalized Black Men: Making Sense of Mobility, Opportunity, and Future Life Chances.* Princeton, N.J.: Princeton University Press.

☻ ☻ ☻

Questions

1. How does being a basketball player help young black men avoid the lure of street-corner culture?

2. Give specific examples from Paul's story that show how being a basketball player helps protect young black men from street-corner culture. How does Paul's story end? Did basketball protect him?

3. What are the pros and cons of using athletic pursuits to help young African-American men improve their lives?

4. Sketch out the role of older adult men as depicted in this article. Why do they get involved?

5. Use the findings from this research to formulate a proposal for a Saturday night basketball league for young African-American men in your community.

Problems in Education

PROBLEMS IN EDUCATION

Math can

be hard enough, but imagine the difficulty when a teacher is just one chapter ahead of the students.

It happens, and it happens more often to poor and minority students. Those children are about twice as likely to have math teachers who don't know their subject, according to a report by the Education Trust, a children's advocacy group.

Studies show the connection between teachers' knowledge and student achievement is particularly strong in math.

"Individual teachers matter a tremendous amount in how much students learn," said Ross Wiener, who oversees policy issues at the organization.

The report looked at teachers with neither an academic major nor certification in the subjects they teach. Among the findings, which were based on Education Department data:

- In high-poverty schools, two in five math classes have teachers without a college major or certification in math.
- In schools with a greater share of African American and Latino children, nearly one in three math classes is taught by such a teacher.

Math is important because it is considered a "gateway" course, one that leads to greater success in college and the workplace. Kids who finish Algebra II in high school are more likely to get bachelor's degrees. And people with bachelor's degrees earn substantially more than those with high school diplomas.

The teaching problem is most acute in the middle grades, 5–8, the report said. That's a crucial time for math, said Ruth Neild, a research scientist at Johns Hopkins University.

"This is a time when kids are making a really important transition from arithmetic to mathematics," Neild said. "It takes careful instruction, and if kids can't get that, and really get it, they're not going to succeed in math in high school."

Yet it can be tougher to find qualified teachers for middle schools, especially in low-income areas, said Neild, who studied the problem in Philadelphia public schools. She did not work on the Education Trust report.

Teachers should not be blamed for out-of-field teaching, the report said. It can happen anywhere there is a teacher shortage in a particular discipline. It can also happen where there is no shortage but where school administrators have planned poorly.

Congress tried to fix the problem in the sweeping 2002 No Child Left Behind Law. The law insisted that all teachers in core academic subjects be "highly qualified" by 2006.

But the most well-known aspect of No Child Left Behind is its requirement for annual state tests in reading and math, and the penalties it imposes on schools that fail to make progress.

The teacher requirement is less well-known, and also less onerous. States were allowed to come up with their own definitions of "highly qualified." As a result, most teachers in the U.S. today are deemed highly qualified.

When it comes to out-of-field teaching, state officials may be understating the problem, the report said.

Researchers compared two different sets of Education Department data, reports from state officials and a survey of teachers themselves. Teachers said out-of-field teaching happens far more often than states reported for highly qualified purposes.

Wiener, the Education Trust official, said teaching is the key to fulfilling the goal of No Child Left Behind — that every student will be able to read and do math on grade level by 2014.

"We cannot meet our goals for increasing student achievement unless and until we focus on improving teaching quality and the effectiveness of teachers in front of the classroom," Wiener said.[1]

---It's hard to imagine that in 21st-century America, the richest nation in the world, children in public schools are failing to learn basics such as reading and writing.

The federal government has tried allocating more money to education and reworking curricula, but still many children are not succeeding in the classroom. What is the recourse?

As Americans, most of us would agree that a free and public education is the right of every citizen. With this said, how can education be a social problem? In this chapter, we will discuss issues related to quality and access of education in the United States, as well as how these factors are linked to problems of race, social class, and gender.

get the topic: WHAT ARE THE SOCIAL PROBLEMS IN EDUCATION?

EDUCATION is the process by which people gain or develop knowledge.

HIDDEN CURRICULUM refers to lessons taught in schools that are unrelated to academic learning.

Education in Society

Over the years I've spent teaching in the classroom, I have experienced many different things: students making out in the back of the room, others answering cell phones in the middle of class, and of course those wanting to know if they "missed anything" on a day they were absent. All faculty have their favorite student horror story, and as a former student, I have my favorite faculty horror story too. But although these experiences take place in an academic setting, can they be considered "education?"

Education is the process by which people gain or develop knowledge. Throughout most of human history, education was informal, usually passing from elders to the next generation. Since the industrial revolution, education has become a more formal system by which society passes on its information and has been linked to economic advancement.

In this way, schools connect to the job system because they often train individuals for specific types of work. For example, to become a nurse, you have to go to nursing school. When you complete school,

you have the benefit of a high salary and a sure career path, and the community benefits from your medical knowledge. Other types of degrees are not as specific. For example, with a sociology degree, a person can do many different types of jobs, from working at a bank to analyzing social services. However, the key point is that the individual has achieved an educational milestone in reaching his or her degree.

Education levels vary slightly by gender. As you can see in the chart below, more women have some college experience but more men complete higher education degrees.

It's also worth noting that the status dropout rate—the percentage of 16- to 24-year olds who are not enrolled in school and do not have a high school credential, whether a diploma or GED—has declined severely over the last 30 years. In 1980, the percentage of dropouts in the United States was 14.1 percent. By 2007, it was down to 8.7 percent. This rate varies significantly by ethnicity. Hispanics have the highest dropout rate—21.4 percent in 2007—while blacks and whites have lower rates, at 8.4 and 5.3 percent, respectively.[2]

History of Education

HISTORY OF PUBLIC EDUCATION IN THE UNITED STATES

When colonists first arrived in the "New World" from England, they brought with them their form of education and educational institutions. Rich in tradition, these educational settings were frequently attended only by the elite. They provided classical education for religious purposes.

In 1647, Massachusetts was the first colony to require compulsory schooling, opening education to everyone. Most other colonies left education in the hands of parents or private organizations, which required individuals to pay their own tuition. After the Revolutionary War, the states began to form four key beliefs regarding education: It should be free to the user, publicly run, nonreligious, and universal (compulsory). In time, these schools expanded their focus. In addition to teaching students the basics of reading, writing, and arithmetic, they sought to teach new immigrant children to be "good citizens" and to develop proper morals.

During the era of westward expansion, American schools often took the form of one-room school houses, with one teacher presiding over children who varied greatly in age and ability. The one-room school presented problems. If, for example, your teacher was not good at math, your math education would be limited. In rural areas particularly, textbooks were nearly unheard of; rather, students would bring with them whatever books could

Educational Attainment of the Population 25 Years and Older, 2007		
Highest Educational Level Achieved	Male Students (%)	Female Students (%)
Less than High School	16.1	15.0
High School Graduate	30.1	30.2
Some College	25.6	28.1
Bachelor's Degree	17.6	17.2
Graduate or Professional Degree	10.7	9.6

Source: Data from the U.S. Census Bureau, *2007 American Community Survey*, Table SE:T22.

>>> **One-room schoolhouses** are a part of public school history. **Some contemporary Amish schools still make use of them today.**

Joe Sohm/Chromosohm/Stock Connection

be found in their homes and learn to read those. By today's standards, these early publicly funded schoolhouses provided the equivalent of an elementary education. It wasn't until the mid-1800s that secondary schools began appearing, and these were generally only attended by those seeking college entrance. High schools were not publically funded until the 1900s, and they still only educated a small percentage of the population. For example, when I was a child, I vividly remember my grandmother proudly telling me that she had completed the eighth grade, which at her time was as far as a girl was likely to go in school.[3]

Higher education did not look like it does today, either. Early on, college education and development was not much different from elementary education. For example, Harvard University was first and foremost a school to train ministers. Created in the 1600s, it primarily served the elite, and the recruitment of faculty there and elsewhere was based on the piety of the professors rather than their expertise. In early colleges, there were few faculty members and almost no specialized fields of study. Over time, this changed as faculty became more focused on specific disciplines.[4]

EDUCATION: SPREADING THE FIVE "MYTHS" THROUGHOUT SOCIETY

Education is no longer just about teaching the three Rs—reading, 'riting, and 'rithmetic. Education has expanded into a social movement, stemming from the ideas of building a nation and its ideology. In elementary school, did you start the day with the pledge of allegiance? If so, what did that teach—reading or patriotism? Scholars suggest that the U.S. educational system spreads five "myths" throughout society.[5]

1 **Myth of the individual.** This myth supports the belief that the primary unit in society is the individual—not the family, clan, or ethnic group. Therefore, it is up to the individual to learn in order to improve his or her place in society.

2 **Myth of the nation as a group of individuals.** In this myth, the nation is no longer the property of a king or some group of elites. Instead, individuals make up society and the nation. Therefore, by developing your skills and knowledge, you are bettering yourself and, by extension, the nation.

3 **Myth of progress.** This myth proposes that society's goal is to improve the status of both current and future residents. Thus, childhood education can support the idea that a nation is working toward self-improvement.

4 **Myth of socialization and life cycle continuity.** This myth supposes that childhood socialization leads to adult character. Therefore, if children are socialized properly, this will lead to good character that ultimately benefits the nation in the long run. Might the pledge of allegiance lead some to enter the military later in life?

5 **Myth of the state as the guardian of the nation.** This final myth encourages the belief that it is the state's job to raise good, loyal, and patriotic children who will become the next generation of good, loyal, and patriotic adults. In this way, socializing children is not the role of the family but the job of the nation.[5]

It's important to note that not all groups of people enter into the state education system, in part because they do not believe in these myths. For example, the Amish refuse to participate in state-sponsored education in order to keep their children socialized in their group. Instead, they established and continue to run their own schools.[6] Many friends of mine choose to homeschool their children out of a desire to keep the state out of their business. Is it a social problem for the state to raise our children? Is it good for the long-term health of the nation? Let's look at this further.

HIDDEN CURRICULUM IN SCHOOLS

Many schools have taken to fund-raising through their students. From lemonade stands on the front sidewalk to multi-thousand-dollar school-wide fund-raisers selling wrapping paper or pizzas, children learn the value of hard work and service to obtain a goal outside the school's curriculum. Whether you realize it or not, all of those fund-raising efforts *you* may have been involved in during your grammar and high school years taught you things about capitalism and goal-setting that really had nothing to do with reading, writing, or arithmetic.

The transfer of academic knowledge to the next generation is a primary goal, but schools also socialize students in what some call the "hidden curriculum." The term **hidden curriculum** refers to lessons taught in schools that are unrelated to academic learning. Schools teach students about citizenship when they have "mock" elections; through healthy competition and contests, they teach the use of

Jupiterimages/Creatas/Getty Images, Inc - Jupiter Images

 Fund-raisers teach the **hidden curriculum of capitalism.**

planning, goal-setting, training, and teamwork; they teach children to follow orders, routines, and other seemingly arbitrary regulations, which ultimately result in our following real laws that sometimes seem senseless. These all help make us a part of the community and thereby make the community run more smoothly.

The hidden curriculum also applies to how students socialize one another. Students take what they've learned in the hallways, playgrounds, and cafeterias at school and apply it to the outside world. One of the most important lessons we learn in school is how to get along with our peers. It helps us negotiate our way through life and has almost nothing to do with knowing how to read.[7]

EDUCATION THROUGHOUT THE WORLD

Every nation has some type of educational system; however, not all educational systems are equal. The amount of resources, funding, and worth placed on education varies, which in turn creates the social problem of inequality in global education. A country's socioeconomic status has a huge effect on its education system. Systems in developing countries often

Regional Literacy Rates for Adults (aged 15+), 2005–2007

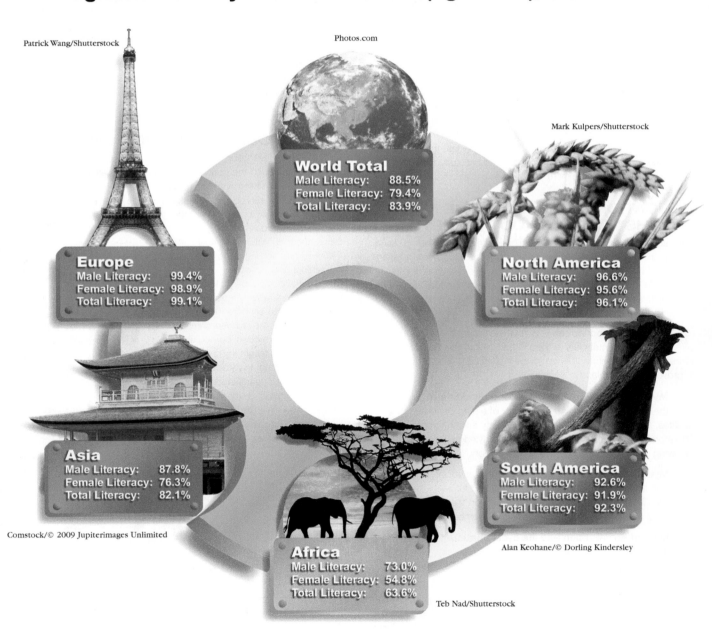

Patrick Wang/Shutterstock

Photos.com

Mark Kulpers/Shutterstock

World Total
Male Literacy: 88.5%
Female Literacy: 79.4%
Total Literacy: 83.9%

Europe
Male Literacy: 99.4%
Female Literacy: 98.9%
Total Literacy: 99.1%

North America
Male Literacy: 96.6%
Female Literacy: 95.6%
Total Literacy: 96.1%

Asia
Male Literacy: 87.8%
Female Literacy: 76.3%
Total Literacy: 82.1%

South America
Male Literacy: 92.6%
Female Literacy: 91.9%
Total Literacy: 92.3%

Africa
Male Literacy: 73.0%
Female Literacy: 54.8%
Total Literacy: 63.6%

Comstock/© 2009 Jupiterimages Unlimited

Alan Keohane/© Dorling Kindersley

Teb Nad/Shutterstock

Source: Data from United Nations Educational, Scientific, and Cultural Organization (UNESCO) Institute for Statistics.

College Participation vs. College Completion

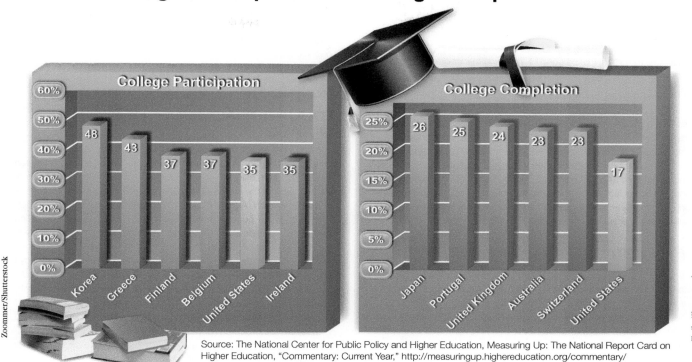

Source: The National Center for Public Policy and Higher Education, Measuring Up: The National Report Card on Higher Education, "Commentary: Current Year," http://measuringup.highereducation.org/commentary/introduction.cfm, Accessed August 7, 2009.

The United States ranks within the top five countries when it comes to college participation of young adults aged 18 to 24. **But the United States ranks much lower—** 16th of the 27 countries compared—**in terms of college completion.**[20]

fail to provide students with basic educational needs and struggle to sustain stable educational institutions. Paraguay, Sri Lanka, and the Philippines are all countries in which one in five students goes to a school with no running water.[8] How might such a situation affect their ability to learn?

In general, poorer nations often have low **literacy rates**, or low percentages of people in the population who can read and write. When you consider the lack of education in some nations, it becomes apparent why some countries seem mired in the same problems year after year. In Sierra Leone, for example, only 47 percent of men and 24 percent of women older than 15 are literate. This falls far below the world literacy rate of 88 percent of men and 79 percent of women.[9] These numbers also demonstrate another facet of social inequality of education throughout much of the world: Women and girls are rarely treated equal to their male counterparts. Note that the number of literate women is almost half the number of educated men in Sierra Leone. Likewise, as you can see in the literacy rates shown on the previous page, male literacy rates are higher than female literacy rates in every region of the world. You learned about gender stratification, and these data illustrate a social problem in patriarchal societies—that of unequal educational access. Knowledge is power, but women continue to be left out of the knowledge loop in many areas of the globe.

Education provides the ability for a nation to compete globally. You can see from the data that Europe and North America have the strongest literacy rates, and yet the literacy rate for Europe is almost 100 percent, while in North America, it is not nearly that high. This trend is consistent with another social problem in the U.S. education system.

For the last two decades, the United States has had no noticeable increase in college participation rates. Meanwhile, many nations have increased their college ranks and now surpass the United States.[10] Why might this be occurring? One reason may be a lack of funding for college. The United States ranks 57th in the world in educational spending as a percentage of gross domestic product.[11] This ranking is below nations like France, Norway, and the United Kingdom—all nations that have surpassed the United States in graduation rates.[12]

Let's look further at the issue of higher education. Of 27 countries measured, the United States ranks fifth in college participation, yet it is 16th in the number of degrees issued to college students.[13] In fact, the graduation rate for incoming freshmen in the United States is about 56 percent when measured over a six-year period.[14] High school graduation rates have also decreased, although those who do graduate are more likely to attend a two- or four-year college today than a few years ago. The social problems of low educational attainment can lead to long-term problems for a nation by limiting its potential for economic growth.[15]

A country's wealth plays a central role in education, so lack of funding and resources from a nation-state can weaken a system. Governments in sub-Saharan Africa spend only 2.4 percent of the world's public resources on education; however, many of them spend a higher percentage of their entire wealth on it than the United States does. For example, Sudan ranks 42nd in spending as a percentage of GDP, while the United States ranks 57th.[16]

PRESTIGE GAP is the divide between those who have the privilege of attending elite schools and obtaining success in the job market, and those who don't.

TEACHER EXPECTANCY EFFECT is the impact of a teacher's expectations on a student's performance.

GRADE INFLATION is the trend of assigning higher grades than previously assigned to students for completing the same work.

So, is educational spending a social problem? Clearly, the United States spends a lot of money, and yet as a percentage of our total wealth, we rank rather low. Furthermore, the facts indicate that we are losing ground to many nations in number of college degrees. However, between 1997 and 2007, the number of degrees issued by higher education U.S. institutions increased from 24 to 29 percent.[17] So, the number of degrees is increasing, just not as fast as in many European nations. But who exactly is receiving these degrees? Does one's race, gender, or socioeconomic status affect his or her educational attainment? You bet it does.

Problems with Higher Education

The cost of college can have a strong influence on educational attainment. In the United States, the government only pays for primary and secondary education. For higher education, people have to pay their own way—on average $6,595 a year for in-state tuition at a four-year university—which often deters low-income individuals from seeking advanced educations.[18] In other industrialized countries, education at all levels is free. For example, in Sweden, primary, secondary, and postsecondary schools are free of tuition, courtesy of the Swedish government and taxpayers. This allows all students who meet certain academic standards to attend any school regardless of economic status.[19]

In stark contrast is the quest for an Ivy-league education in the United States. It has become increasingly evident to students that in order to obtain one of society's top-paying jobs, they must first attend an Ivy-league school where they'll make the contacts and receive the education that employers require. This is not to say that state or non-Ivy schools prepare students any less vigorously for the rigors of the elite workforce. However, there is a general belief in the United States that by attending and succeeding in a prestigious school, your ticket will be written to whatever employment you so desire.[1]

Unfortunately, as these top-performing students are choosing to attend elite schools, they are creating what is known as the **prestige gap**.

Students who may be equally able to perform but unable to foot the bills of an elite education will be unable to compete in vying for jobs available in an ever-more-competitive market. When "great minds" are pooled together into certain schools, the give-and-take of classroom discussions in other schools may be less provocative. And it follows that excellent faculty will be sought to teach at elite universities, widening the prestige gap even further.[2]

Problems in Education
EDUCATIONAL DISCREPANCIES IN RACE

Hollywood movies such as *Dangerous Minds*, *Lean on Me*, and *Freedom Writers* focus on the efforts of students who are not expected to succeed because of their environment and socioeconomic status. For millions of students around the United States, though, this is more than a movie—it's a real-life trend. A 2007 U.S. Census survey revealed that 31.8 percent of the white population and 52.1 percent of the Asian population ages 25 and older have completed four years of college or more, whereas only 18.5 percent of African Americans and 12.7 percent of Hispanics showed similar attainment.[26] What accounts for this discrepancy? Consider that poor and undereducated people are segregated into inner-city schools. It is here that students are most likely to encounter teachers and administrators with very low expectations for student attainment and extremely limited resources. With the inequality between rich and poor, racial minorities from poor areas are being left behind by the education system. In this way, some suggest that society is locking them out of the competition for empowerment from the very beginning.[27]

TEACHER EXPECTANCY AND ATTAINMENT

Perhaps another part of the problem for racial minorities and poor children has to do with teacher expectation. This is referred to as the **teacher expectancy effect**—the impact of a teacher's expectations on a student's performance—and it doesn't just apply to poor and minority students.[28] The idea is that if a teacher expects that a student will love the class and do well, the student generally does. Of course, measuring teacher expectations is a difficult thing to do.

Some studies show that expectancies influence not only individual student performance, but also the performance of the entire school.[29]

▶▶ GO GL🌐BAL

The South Korean Educational System

Since the 1960s, education has become the most valuable resource to the South Korean people. Living in a country that lacks exportable natural resources, families have made educating their children the number-one priority.

The South Korean system enforces a national curriculum and spreads the resources much more equitably than the United States does. The South Koreans also allocate a greater amount of their national budget to educational spending.[23]

The country's commitment to education reaps rewards—93 percent of South Korean students graduate from high school, compared to 75 percent of U.S. students.[24]

To be sure, there are valid criticisms of the South Korean educational system: The conformist regimen and relentless workload requires the students to study for eight or more hours per day *outside* of school; the endless push to study and learn stifles creativity; classes average about 40 students; and there are few national universities to choose from, driving students to study abroad.[25]

Allyn & Bacon Royalty-Free Collection/Photodisc

<<< South Korean students attain lofty goals through **a work ethic that is unmatched worldwide.**

Top Ten Universities Worldwide

Rank	School	Tuition (in $)
1	Harvard University	37,012
2	Yale University	36,500
3	University of Cambridge	5,145*
4	University of Oxford	5,145*
5	California Institute of Technology	34,584
6	Imperial College London	5,145*
7	University College London	5,145*
8	University of Chicago	39,381
9	Massachusetts Institute of Technology	37,782
10	Columbia University	41,316

*converted from pounds

Photos.com

Sources: U.S. News & World Report, "National Universities Rankings," http://colleges.usnews.rankingsandreviews.com/best-colleges/national-universities-rankings, Acessed August 31, 2009; O'Leary, John, Nunzio Quacquarelli, and Martin Ince. *Top Universities Guide*. London: Quacquarelli Symonds Limited, 2009, http://www.topuniversities.com/top-universities-guide, Accessed August 31, 2009; "Universities," Guiardian.co.uk, http://www.guardian.co.uk/education/list/educationinstitution, Accessed August 31, 2009; Graeme Paton, "University tuition fees 'need to rise to £6,500,'" Telegraph.co.uk, March 16, 2009, http://www.telegraph.co.uk/education/universityeducation/5001170/University-tuition-fees-need-to-rise-to-6500.html, Accessed August 31, 2009.

∧
∧ Generally speaking, the more prestigious the school, the more it costs to attend in the
∧ United States. **In contrast, universities in the United Kingdom only charge up to $5,145 for an undergraduate education.**

Other studies suggest less obvious findings, which propose that teachers may indeed influence students' self-perception, but it is that perception that influences academic achievement.[30] Regardless, it seems obvious that teachers have great power to influence students, both positively and negatively. In inner-city schools where teacher turnover is often quite high, this becomes a significant problem.

ACADEMIC ACHIEVEMENT

There is an increase in the practice of grade inflation in American high schools and universities. **Grade inflation** is the trend of assigning higher grades than previously assigned to students for completing the same work. Students' grade point averages over the last 20 years have increased by roughly one third of a letter grade.[31] It is unlikely that student performance alone could have contributed to this trend.

Students have begun to see the default grade as an A. Professors nationwide are noticing a sense of entitlement from their students, which results in arrogant assumptions regarding a student's "right" to a superior grade for work that was just average.[32]

To combat this growing trend, universities have begun offering seminars integrated into introductory courses for freshmen. The seminars encourage students to think differently about their work and their lives, so that they can relearn what education truly is.[33]

think social problems: WHAT THINKING DRIVES EDUCATION IN SOCIETY?

> **HUMAN CAPITAL** is a person's combination of skills, knowledge, traits, and personal attributes.
>
> **CREDENTIALISM** is an emphasis on educational degrees as a prerequisite for advancement.

Theories Behind Education

There are several theories put forth by sociologists regarding what criteria students use when evaluating whether or not to attend college.

FUNCTIONALISM

Functionalists tend to look at how structures in a society work to support the society. Recall the literacy data shown earlier in the chapter. In general, when you look at regions of the world, the higher the literacy rate, the wealthier and more advanced that region. Why? Because education helps a student improve his or her **human capital**—a combination of skills, knowledge, traits, and personal attributes. Education also helps integrate the student into society by teaching him or her about the nation's history, government, and social norms. Finally, a public education provides parents a place to occupy their children, allowing adults to work and perform other needed tasks in society.[34]

Allyn & Bacon Royalty-Free Collection/Photodisc

>> Obtaining **a college degree is the first step in finding success** in the marketplace.

SYMBOLIC INTERACTIONISM

Having a degree opens doors for people. In the United States, many students choose to go to college because of the reality of **credentialism**—an emphasis on educational degrees as a prerequisite for advancement. In today's global economy, many of the "good jobs" are now service and white-collar jobs. In short, they require a college degree, but this was not always true. Neither of my parents had college degrees, but with hard work they held white-collar jobs in business management and accounting. This was attainable at the time because hard work, intelligence, and ability were enough to climb from a labor job to a white-collar job. Not anymore. Employers use education as a type of litmus test to determine who is and who is not qualified.[35]

CONFLICT THEORY

Have you ever noticed how the power structure of a school mimics the power structures of society? Samuel Bowles and Herbert Gintis (1976) believe that schools follow a capitalist structure. Administrators control teachers, teachers control students, and students control other students. This pecking order, in a sense, trains students to understand the hierarchy of capitalism. Just like workers who fear for their jobs and must provide labor to their bosses, students must respond to the whims of their teachers.[36]

Conflict theorists also point out the inequality built into the system as well. If education is the doorway to opportunity, then conflict theorists would be interested in how those opportunities are distributed in society. As we have already discussed, public education is not the same in all places; wealthy neighborhoods have better educational outcomes than poorer ones. Conflict theorists point to the problems of the inner cities and the lack of funding to combat such ills as part of the reason.

The hidden curriculum, on the other hand, serves to re-enforce an ideology of fairness and equality within the United States, the validity of which is certainly debatable. Patriotism, capitalism, and even democracy are all reinforced in schools today. Conflict theorists raise the question as to whether this is in students' best interests.

Throughout the world, governments spend more on education of the elite than they do on the education of the poor. This is particularly true in higher education, where there is a strong link between social class and the ability to attend college. If you attend a state college, you're receiving tax assistance to go to school. But even though this funding allows some of the less fortunate to get a degree, less-educated people from wealthier homes continue to dominate society.[37] Even in locations that have tried to create equity between rich neighborhoods and poor ones, the outcomes continue to favor those with the higher social class.[38]

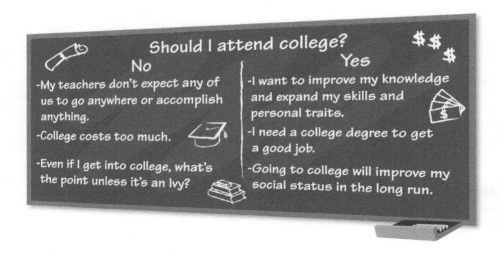

Should I attend college?

No
- My teachers don't expect any of us to go anywhere or accomplish anything.
- College costs too much.
- Even if I get into college, what's the point unless it's an Ivy?

Yes
- I want to improve my knowledge and expand my skills and personal traits.
- I need a college degree to get a good job.
- Going to college will improve my social status in the long run.

discover solutions to social problems:
WHAT CAN WE DO TO ENCOURAGE EDUCATIONAL EQUALITY?

No Child Left Behind

The *No Child Left Behind Act of 2001* (NCLB) is a bipartisan act of Congress that was proposed by President George W. Bush. Generally speaking, the NCLB Act requires states to test students in particular grades, with the results determining the state's eligibility to receive federal funds. Schools that fall behind run the risk of having their funding cut. Where possible, parents are given the choice to transfer their child to a better school. NCLB is designed to reform the way we view education with a four-pronged approach: stronger accountability, increased freedom for states and communities, expanded use of proven education methods, and increases in educational choices for parents.[39]

States measure progress in schools by testing every student in grades 3 through 8 in reading and math by administering annual tests.

Although this Act seems like a much-needed overhaul to make schools and states accountable for student achievement and dropout and illiteracy rates, some have seen it as one of the most controversial pieces of legislation in the history of federal educational policy-making.[40] What's the trouble?

Some sociologists believe that the gaps observed in the educational system are mistaken as educational malfunctions. We know that poor children often fail to receive the same quality of education as wealthier ones. We also know that test results tend to show a strong correlation between schools in poorer areas and schools that fail to achieve the standards of accountability.[41] Certainly, school structures can affect a child's ability to learn. Is it fair to set up national standards and apply them equally, regardless of the location, funding, and social setting? Sociologists tend to say no. Race, social class, and geographic location mean that a one-size-fits-all approach is unlikely to work well.[42]

Furthermore, NCLB expects parents to effectively negotiate the education system, which is problematic especially when parents are themselves not well educated. It seems dubious that the current system will work equally well for everyone, especially racial minorities, immigrants, and the poor.[43]

CHARTER SCHOOLS

Charter schools are nonsectarian public schools of choice that operate with freedom from many of the regulations that apply to traditional public schools. The name "charter school" may have originated in the 1970s when Ray Budde, an educator in New England, suggested that small groups of teachers be given charters (contracts) by their local school boards to explore new educational approaches in a smaller, less bureaucratic setting.[44] From there, this idea blossomed and spread, as various states enacted charter school laws, and President Clinton called for the creation of 3,000 new schools by 2002; President George W. Bush followed that up by dedicating $200 million to charter schools in 2002.

Win McNamee/CORBIS- NY

The No Child Left Behind Act has **changed the way schools are held accountable for helping students succeed.**

CHARTER SCHOOLS are nonsectarian public schools of choice that operate with freedom from many of the regulations that apply to traditional public schools.

The "charter" that establishes such a school is a performance contract detailing the school's mission, program, goals, number of students served, methods of assessment, and ways to measure success. Charters are typically granted for three to five years, after which the group who granted the charter will review the goals of the school and determine whether the contract should be renewed.

Charter schools are responsible for producing positive academic results and adhering to the charter contract. These schools are accountable to several groups: the sponsor who grants them, the parents who choose them, and the public that funds them.[45]

Charter schools remain much smaller in population than regular public schools, and they recruit students with demographic characteristics that are similar to the surrounding population in terms of socioeconomic status and race.[46]

One problem that has occurred in offering school choice is a phenomenon known as "white flight." Whites tend to flee an area and its schools as the level of non-white enrollment increases.[47] Research suggests that charter schools tend to segregate students by race, because white students enroll in them in higher percentages than racial minorities. In short, charter schools are creating a further segregated educational system. In the end, both race and parents influence who attends a charter school.[48]

Despite the drawbacks, charter schools have demonstrated an improved alternative to the mainstream public education. Charter schools can re-enroll dropout students, replace failing public schools, create parent/learning centers, and pilot innovative learning models.[49] Critics still wonder, however, whether charter schools will improve opportunities for academically or economically advantaged students if separation by choice continues to encourage isolation and segregation.[50]

The city of New Orleans has attempted a unique experiment with charter school education. After the devastation of Hurricane Katrina in 2005, some public schools were destroyed and many students were displaced. As the city started to rebuild itself, it set up an unprecedented number of charter schools. Now 53 percent of students are enrolled in charter schools, as opposed to just 2 percent before the hurricane.[51]

Some administrators have revamped the structures and curricula that were used at New Orleans public schools. The hope is that these charter schools will help improve the education system in New Orleans, which was in bad shape even before Katrina.[52] So far, the results are mixed. Some studies show that the new schools have improved education in the area, while others show no significant difference.[53] It will be interesting to see the outcome of the charter school chapter in New Orleans as well as in American educational history.

WRAP YOUR MIND AROUND THE THEORY

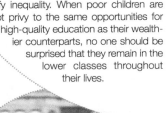

Functionalism holds that **education helps socialize young people into society.** How have **your experiences** with education **affected the way you interact with peers, professors, and authorities?**

FUNCTIONALISM

Functionalists believe that education fulfills several functions of society. It allows parents to work, knowing that their children are safe and learning. It also provides a place to socialize children into society. This strengthens the human capital of the student and provides a firm foundation for society to expand and prosper.

CONFLICT THEORY

Conflict theorists believe that education serves as a vehicle to keep the social classes separate. For example, higher education is generally most available to children from the upper classes, thereby guaranteeing that they will be able to gain high-paying jobs and maintain their positions in society. This can serve as a stratification tool to maintain and justify inequality. When poor children are not privy to the same opportunities for high-quality education as their wealthier counterparts, no one should be surprised that they remain in the lower classes throughout their lives.

HOW DOES EDUCATION AFFECT SOCIETY?

SYMBOLIC INTERACTIONISM

Symbolic theorists focus on labeling things. Credentials may or may not mean anything about your superiority over another candidate to do a particular job; however using a college degree as a prerequisite provides a social definition that can be useful to an employer and society. It opens doors to the college graduate and closes them to those without formal education.

Conflict theorists suggest that education maintains the separation of social classes. How do the **success and opportunities given to the upper class** contrast with the **inequalities suffered by lower classes?**

Interactionists believe that **a college degree is a social definition** that makes someone more likely to get hired for a job, even if that person is not necessarily more qualified. **How do disciplines such as medicine or physics widen the gap between people who have or have not pursued a formal education?**

Pro & Con

School Choice via Charters or Vouchers

There are determined and well-researched arguments flowing from both sides of the debate over school choice. What does each side have to say?

Pro

- Competition in anything breeds improvement.
- Choice offers a way out of a low-performing school for those interested.
- Choice supports educational innovation because it supports alternatives to the traditional school setting.
- School choice can match child and parent needs; both will be more involved and committed to the school.
- School choice can improve the idea of outcome-based education, whereby measurable outcomes become the standard of quality.

Con

- Schools of choice create inequities by taking the more desirable students and abandoning the weaker ones. This results in a two-tier system: the haves and the have-nots.
- Students in schools of choice have fewer opportunities to learn from students of different backgrounds.
- Accessing these schools requires motivated, informed parents, which not all students have.
- School choice changes the focus from education for the public good to education for the private good. Education is no longer being seen as providing "some common experiences in common settings." Will those without children in schools continue to support education in light of this change?

MAKE CONNECTIONS

Social Class, Race, and Gender Outcomes

As you have seen in this chapter, many factors play key roles in the attainment of an equitable and appropriate education. Simply based on family, geography, or gender, some students may not have a fighting chance to achieve the one thing that might free them from the bondage of biases—a worthwhile education.

In this chapter you've learned that students who live in poverty are often forgotten by the educational system. They are the lowest achievers from whom the least is expected, receiving the barest of educations with the fewest methods and resources. There have been some efforts to level the playing field for these students, including charter schools and the No Child Left Behind Act. Though not perfect, these programs attempt to remedy some of the egregious oversights regarding the students who so easily fall through the cracks of the educational system.

Gender influences the social problems a person experiences. Throughout the world there remain many women who are denied opportunities for education based solely on their gender.

Racial and ethnic inequality still exists in the United States. It is true that many racial groups are disproportionately poor, and that students in poverty-stricken neighborhoods receive a worse education because their schools receive the least tax benefits. Charter schools offer some families an alternative to public schools; however, that often does little more than segregate students further.

From Classroom to Community } High-Quality Schools and Faculty

My mom is an elementary school teacher, so it was natural for me to gravitate to an elementary school for a fall semester internship. I worked as a teacher's aide, helping out two days a week in Ms. Alvary's second-grade classroom. The students, although obviously poor, were so sweet and eager to be in the classroom. Many of them came from unstable homes and bad neighborhoods, and I often wondered if they preferred being at school because of this.

During my third week there, I began to take notice of Ms. Alvary's teaching style. Now, I know I was still a student myself, but I'd been in school a long time, and I knew something wasn't adding up. The teacher was disorganized and often let the students wander from learning station to learning station for an hour or more without instruction. Written assignments were almost never given, and lessons seemed mostly to consist of arts and crafts that the children could do independently. Although the kids were content to cut and color, they also seemed to know that something was missing.

I asked Ms. Alvary one day how she became a teacher. She told me that this was her first real teaching job and that she was hired two years ago out of an ESL program at the local community center. She said that the school was desperate to fill the position, and although she wasn't certified, she was—as she put it—"at the right place at the right time."

In this day and age, how can it be that an American public school could hire someone totally unqualified? It's no wonder that students aren't learning the basics of language or math.

How much worse will it get for my little second graders as they progress through the system, and who will speak out and help them? All through the fall, I tried to convince myself to approach the principal and speak to him about firing Ms. Alvary, or call the school board to complain about a poor hiring choice. But in the end, what good would it have done?

WHAT ARE THE SOCIAL PROBLEMS IN EDUCATION?

the five myths of education, the hidden curriculum, poor performance compared with global education attainment, inequality in race
and gender, grade inflation, and entitlement

Jupiterimages/Creatas/Getty
Images, Inc - Jupiter Images

WHAT THINKING DRIVES EDUCATION IN SOCIETY?

helping students who seek to improve their human capital and
credentials and who desire to hold an elite job, teaching the norms
and values of society, and maintaining the stratification of
inequality in the social classes

Allyn & Bacon Royalty-Free
Collection/Photodisc

WHAT CAN WE DO TO ENCOURAGE EDUCATIONAL
EQUALITY?

implement social policies such as the No Child Left Behind Act
and school choice via vouchers or charters

Win McNamee/CORBIS- NY

get the topic: WHAT ARE THE SOCIAL PROBLEMS IN EDUCATION?

Education in Society
History of Education

Problems with Higher Education
Problems in Education

Theories Behind Education
No Child Left Behind

Theory

FUNCTIONALISM

- education fulfills several functions of society
- education teaches dominant norms and values to better a society

SYMBOLIC INTERACTIONISM

- credentials such as a college degree provide opportunities for some
  and eliminate them for others

CONFLICT THEORY

- higher education is most available to students from the upper classes
- separation of social classes by the availability of education maintains
  and justifies inequality

Key Terms

education is the process by which people gain or develop knowledge.

hidden curriculum refers to lessons taught in schools that are unrelated to academic learning.

literacy rate is the percentage of people in a population who can read and write.

prestige gap is the divide between those who have the privilege of attending elite schools and

obtaining success in the job market, and those who don't.

teacher expectancy effect is the impact of a teacher's expectations on a student's performance.

grade inflation is the trend of assigning higher grades than previously assigned to students for completing the same work.

human capital is a person's combination of skills, knowledge, traits, and personal attributes.

credentialism is an emphasis on educational degrees as a prerequisite for advancement.

charter schools are nonsectarian public schools of choice that operate with freedom from many of the regulations that apply to traditional public schools.

Sample Test Questions

These multiple-choice questions are similar to those found in the test bank that accompanies this textbook.

1. What group of learners suffers *most* as a result of inequitable tax-receipt distribution to schools?
 a. females
 b. upper class
 c. lower class
 d. immigrants

2. Which of the following is a myth associated with education?
 a. The nation is the property of a group of elites.
 b. Childhood socialization leads to adult character.
 c. The family is the primary unit.
 d. Society's goal is to improve the morality of the nation.

3. Which is *not* an objective of the No Child Left Behind Act of 2001?
 a. Implementing stronger accountability will produce results.
 b. Schools will use proven educational methods.
 c. Parents will have more choices in where and how their children are educated.
 d. Greater restraints will be placed on states and communities.

4. Why might parents choose to send their child to a charter school?
 a. The child is in a low-performing school that shows no sign of improvement.
 b. Their family is transient.
 c. The larger class sizes promote lively debate.
 d. The oversight by the federal government will ensure successful learning.

5. An example of hidden curriculum is
 a. spelling bees.
 b. reciting the pledge of allegiance.
 c. field trips to art museums.
 d. cafeteria food choices.

ESSAY

1. What are your thoughts about the lack of certified math teachers in schools, particularly middle schools? Who is responsible, and how can it be remedied?

2. Describe the difficulties in attaining an education if you were a student in a high-poverty school. What would be the greatest obstacle?

3. Consider the pros and cons of the No Child Left Behind Act of 2001. Has this legislation helped or hindered education for the children it was written to include? How?

4. Why do some believe that society is locking racial minorities out of the competition for empowerment from the very beginning?

5. Given the trend that fewer American students are obtaining college degrees while other countries are increasing their numbers, discuss how the global economy will be affected, particularly the world status of the United States.

WHERE TO START YOUR RESEARCH PAPER

For U.S. Census facts and information, go to http://www.census.gov

To view educational statistics, go to http://nces.ed.gov http://www.uis.unesco.org

To learn more about grade inflation, go to http://www.gradeinflation.com/

For more information about No Child Left Behind, visit http://www.ed.gov/nclb/landing.jhtml

To learn more about charter schools, go to http://www.uscharterschools.org/pub/uscs_docs/index.htm

ANSWERS: 1. c; 2. b; 3. d; 4. a; 5. b

Remember to check www.thethinkspot.com for additional information, downloadable flashcards, and other helpful resources.

Endnotes

1. Libby Quaid, "Study: Math Teachers a Chapter Ahead of Students," *ABC News,* November 25, 2008, http://abcnews.go.com/US/wireStory?id=6329327.

2. U.S. Department of Education, National Center for Education Statistics, "Fast Facts," Accessed August 26, 2009, http://nces.ed.gov/FastFacts/display.asp?id=16.

3. Frank J. McVeigh and Loreen Wolfer, *Brief History of Social Problems: A Critical Thinking Approach*. Lanham, MD: University Press of America, 2004.

4. Harvey Kantor and Robert Lowe, "Reflections on history and quality education," *Educational Researcher*, 2004. 33(5): 6–10.

5. Francisco O. Ramirez and John Boli, "The Political Construction of Mass Schooling: European Origins and Worldwide Institutionalization," *Sociology of Education,* 1987. 60: 2–17.

6. John Andrew Hostetler, *Amish Society.* Baltimore: The Johns Hopkins University Press, 1993.

7. Annette Hemmings, "The 'Hidden' Corridor Curriculum," *High School Journal*, 2000. 83(2): 1–10.

8. UNESCO Institute for Statistics, "Under-privileged Children Also Disadvantaged in the Classroom," http://www.uis.unesco.org/ev.php?ID57200_201&ID25DO_TOPIC.

9. UNESCO Institute for Statistics, "Literacy Rates," Accessed August 12, 2008, http://stats.uis.unesco.org/unesco/TableViewer/document.aspx?ReportId5121&IF_Language5eng&B

R_Country 56940; The Central Intelligence Agency, "Sierra Leone," Accessed July 17, 2008, https://www.cia.gov/library/publications/the-world-factbook/print/ sl.html.

10. Organisation for Economic Co-operation and Development, "OECD Briefing Note for the United States," http://www.oecd.org/dataoecd/22/51/39317423.pdf.

11. The Central Intelligence Agency, "Country Comparison: Education Expenditures," Accessed August 26, 2009, https://www.cia.gov/library/publications/the-world-factbook/rankorder/2206rank.html.

12. The Central Intelligence Agency, "Country Comparison: Education Expenditures," Accessed July 17, 2008, https://www.cia.gov/library/publications/the-world-factbook/print/sl.html.

13. Ibid.

14. NCHEMS Information Center, "Graduation Rates," Accessed August 26, 2009, http://www.higheredinfo.org/dbrowser/?level=nation&mode=graph&state=0&submeasure=27.

15. Thomas J. Tierney, "How Is American Higher Education Measuring Up? An Outsider's Perspective," in *American Higher Education: How Does it Measure Up for the 21st Century?* San Jose, CA: The National Center for Public Policy and Higher Education, 2006.

16. The Central Intelligence Agency, "Country Comparison: Education Expenditures," Accessed August 26, 2009, https://www.cia.gov/library/publications/the-world-factbook/rankorder/2206rank.html.

17. Institute of Educational Sciences, "Digest of Education Statistics: 2007," Accessed June 29, 2009, http://nces.ed.gov/programs/digest/d07/.

18. College Board, "2008-2009 College Prices," Accessed June 30, 2009, http://www.collegeboard.com/student/pay/add-it-up/4494.html.

19. Estia in Sweden, "Higher Education," Accessed June 30, 2009, http://www.estia.educ.goteborg.se/sv-estia/edu/edu_sys5.html.

20. The National Center for Public Policy and Higher Education, Measuring Up: The National Report Card on Higher Education, "Commentary: Current Year," Accessed August 7, 2009, http://measuringup.highereducation.org/commentary/ introduction.cfm.

21. Philip J. Cook and Robert H. Frank, "The Economic Payoff of Attending an Ivy-League Institution," *The Chronicle of Higher Education,* January 5, 1996.

22. Ibid.

23. David A. Lynch, "USA Could Learn from South Korean Schools," *USA Today*, November 18, 2008, http://abcnews.go.com/Business/story?id=6293334&page=1.

24. Ibid.

25. Ibid.

26. U.S. Census Bureau, "Percent of People 25 Years and Over Who Have Completed High School or College, by Race, Hispanic Origin and Sex: Selected Years 1940 to 2007," Accessed June 30, 2009, http://www.census.gov/population/socdemo/education/cps2007/tabA-2.xls.

27. Jonathan Kozol, *Savage Inequalities: Children in America's Schools*. New York: Crown Publishers, 1992.

28. Robert Rosenthal and Lenore Jacobson, *Pygmalion in the Classroom.* New York: Holt, 1968.

29. Hussain Al-Fadhili and Madhu Singh, "Teachers' Expectancy and Efficacy as Correlates of School Achievement in Delta, Mississippi," *Journal of Personnel Evaluation in Education*, 2006. 19(1-2): 51-67.

30. Margaret R. Kuklinksy and Rhona S. Weinstein, "Classroom and Developmental Differences in a Path Model of Teacher Expectancy Effects," *Child Development*, 2001. 72(5): 1554-1579.

31. The National Center for Educational Statistics, "America's High School Graduates: Results from the 2005 NAEP High School Transcript Study," Accessed June 30, 2009, http://nces.ed.gov/nationsreportcard/pdf/studies/2007 467.pdf.

32. Max Roosevelt, "Student Expectations Seen as Causing Grade Disputes," *New York Times*, February 18, 2009, http://www.nytimes.com/2009/02/18/education/18college.html?_r=1&emc=eta1.

33. Ibid.

34. Philo Washburn, "The public school as an agency of political socialization," *Quarterly Journal of Ideology*, 1986. 10(2): 24-35.

35. Randall Collins, *The Credential Society.* New York: Academic Press, 1979; Randall Collins, "Functional and Conflict Theories of Educational Stratification," *American Sociological Review*, 1971. 36: 1002-1019.

36. Samuel Bowles and Herbert Gintis, *Schooling in capitalist America: educational reform and the contradictions of economic life*. New York: Basic Books, 1976.

37. Hilary Metcalf, "Increasing Inequality in Higher Education: The Role of Term-Time Working," *Oxford Review of Education*, 2003. 29(3): 315-329.

38. Pauline Lipman, "Making the Global City, Making Inequality: The Political Economy and Cultural Politics of Chicago School Policy," *American Educational Research Journal*, 2002. 39(2): 379-419.

39. United States Department of Education, "Why NCLB is important," Accessed July 1, 2009, http://www.ed.gov/nclb/overview/importance/list.jhtml?page=2&size=10&sort=date&desc= show.

40. David Karen, "No Child Left Behind? Sociology Ignored!" *Sociology of Education*, 2005. 78: 165-182.

41. Ibid.

42. Ibid.

43. Joyce L. Epstein, "Attainable Goals? The Spirit and Letter of the No Child Left Behind Act on Parental Involvement," *Sociology of Education*, 2005. 78(2): 179-182.

44. U.S. Charter Schools, "History," Accessed July 1, 2009, http://www.uscharterschools.org/pub/uscs_docs/o/history.htm.

45. U.S. Charter Schools, "Overview and Benefits," Accessed July 1, 2009, http://www.uscharterschools.org/pub/uscs_docs/o/index.htm.

46. Robert R. O'Reilly and Lynn Bosetti, "Charter Schools: The Search for Community," *Peabody Journal of Education*, 2000. 75(4): 19–36.

47. Linda A. Renzulli and Lorraine Evans, "School Choice, Charter Schools, and White Flight," *Social Problems*, 2005. 53(3): 398–418.

48. Ibid.

49. George F. Garcia and Mary Garcia, "Charter Schools— Another Top-Down Innovation," *Educational Researcher*, 1996. 25(8): 34–36.

50. Ibid.

51. Jay Mathews, "Charter Schools' Big Experiment," *The Washington Post*, June 9, 2008, http://www.washingtonpost.com/wp-dyn/content/article/2008/06/08/AR2008060802174.html.

52. Ibid.

53. Pamela N. Frazier-Anderson, "Public Schooling in Post-Hurricane Katrina New Orleans: Are Charter Schools the Solution or Part of the Problem?" *Journal of African American History*, 2008. 93(3): 410–429.

High Stakes are for Tomatoes

PETER SCHRAG

Many parents and educators believe that young people's math, English, science, and reading skills are woefully deficient. To counter that problem and to hold schools more accountable, many states have instituted competency examinations that students must pass in order to be promoted. Due to many complaints about unfairness, a backlash has emerged to halt the use of such tests. As you read this article, take a position on mandatory competency testing.

By now it's hardly news that as education has risen to the top of the national agenda, a great wave—some would say a frenzy—of school reform has focused on two related objectives: more-stringent academic standards and increasingly rigorous accountability for both students and schools.

In state after state, legislatures, governors, and state boards, supported by business leaders, have imposed tougher requirements in math, English, science, and other fields, together with new tests by which the performance of both students and schools is to be judged. In some places students have already been denied diplomas or held back in grade if they failed these tests. In some states funding for individual schools and for teachers' and principals' salaries—and in some, such as Virginia, the accreditation of schools—will depend on how well students do on the tests. More than half the states now require tests for student promotion or graduation.

But a backlash has begun.

"High Stakes are for Tomatoes," by Peter Schrag, reprinted from *The Atlantic Monthly*, vol. 286, no. 2, 2000, pp. 19–21.

- In Massachusetts this spring some 300 students, with the support of parents, teachers, and community activists, boycotted the Massachusetts Comprehensive Assessment System (MCAS) tests ("Be a hero, take a zero") and demanded that if students had good enough records or showed other evidence of achievement, they be allowed to graduate even if they hadn't passed the test. Last November, after a strong majority of students failed the test, the state board of education lowered the same for passing to the level that the state designates as "needs improvement."

- In Wisconsin last year the legislature, pressed by middle-class parents, refused to fund the exit examination that the state had approved just two years earlier. After an extended battle with Governor Tommy Thompson, who has been a national leader in the push for higher standards and greater accountability, a compromise was reached under which student achievement will be assessed on a variety of criteria. Failing the exam will not result in the automatic denial of a diploma.

- In Virginia this spring parents, teachers, and school administrators opposed to the state's Standards of Learning assessments, established in 1998, inspired a flurry of bills in the legislature that called for revising the tests or their status as unavoidable hurdles for promotion and graduation. One bill would also have required that each new member of the state board of education "take the eighth grade Standards of Learning assessments in English, mathematics, science, and social sciences" and that "the results of such assessments . . . be publicly reported." None of the bills passed, but there's little doubt that if the system isn't revised and the state's high failure rates don't decrease by 2004, when the first Virginia seniors may be denied diplomas, the political pressure will intensify. Meanwhile, some parents are talking about Massachusetts-style boycotts.

· · ·

The backlash, touching virtually every state that has instituted high-stakes testing, arises from a spectrum of complaints: that the focus on testing and obsessive test preparation, sometimes beginning in kindergarten, is killing innovative teaching and curricula and driving out good teachers; that (conversely) the standards on which the tests are based are too vague, or that students have not been taught the material on which the tests are based; that the tests are unfair to poor and minority students, or to others who lack test-taking skills; that the tests overstress young children, or that they are too long (in Massachusetts they can take thirteen to seventeen hours) or too tough or simply not good enough. In Massachusetts, according to students protesting MCAS, some students designated as needing improvement outscored half their peers on national standardized tests. "Testing season is upon us," says Mickey VanDerwerker, a leader of Parents Across Virginia United to Reform SOL, "and a lot of kids are so nervous they're throwing up." In Oakland, California, a protest organizer named Susan Harman is selling T-shirts proclaiming HIGH STAKES ARE FOR TOMATOES.

Some of the backlash comes from conservatives who a decade ago battled state-imposed programs that they regarded as anti-family exercises in political correctness. Although she has always thought of herself as a "bleeding-heart liberal," Mary O'Brien, a parent in Ohio who calls herself "an accidental activist" and is the leader of the statewide petition drive against the Ohio Proficiency Tests, complains that the state has no business trying to control local school curricula. In suburban Maryland this spring some parents kept their children out of school on test days, because they regard the Maryland School Performance and Assessment Program as a waste of time. They complain that it is used only to evaluate schools, not students—thereby objecting to almost precisely what parents in some other states are demanding. "It's more beneficial to have my child in his seat in the fifth grade practicing long division," one Maryland parent told a *Washington Post* reporter.

But many more of the protesters—parents, teachers, and school administrators—are education liberals: progressive followers of John Dewey, who believe that children should be allowed to discover things for themselves and not be constrained by "drill-and-kill" rote learning. They worry that the tests are stifling students and teachers. Most come from suburbs with good, even excellent, schools. Instead of the tests they want open-ended exercises—portfolios of essays, art and science projects, and other "authentic assessments"—that in their view more genuinely measure what a student really knows and can do. They have gotten strong reinforcement from, among others, FairTest, of Cambridge, Massachusetts, which opposes standardized testing; Senator Paul Wellstone, of Minnesota, who is sponsoring an anti-testing bill in Congress; Alfie Kohn, a prolific writer and polemicist who argues that the standards movement is a travesty that has "turned teachers into drill sergeants" in the traditionalist belief that "making people suffer always produces the best results"; and Gerald Bracey, an education researcher and a critic of the widespread belief that U.S. students are far behind their peers overseas, which has given impetus to the standards movement.

The anti-testing backlash is beginning to cohere as an integrated national effort. Earlier this year some 600 test critics attended a national conference on high-stakes testing, at Columbia University's Teachers College, to discuss effects, alternatives, and strategies: how to get the attention of legislators, what kinds of cases would be suited to civil-rights litigation, what assessments ensure accountability, how to achieve higher standards without high-stakes tests. Some on the left believe that the whole standards movement is a plot by conservatives to show up the public schools and thus set the stage for vouchers. All believe that poor and minority kids, who don't test well, are the principal victims of the tests and the standards movement. They contend (correctly) that almost no testing experts and none of the major testing companies endorse the notion of using just one test to determine promotion or graduation or, for that matter, the salaries of teachers and principals. But so far legislators and governors haven't paid much attention.

Among the most articulate critics of the tests are the boycotting students, who complain about narrowing opportunities and shrinking curricula. The most exciting ninth-grade course in his school, says Will Greene, a high school sophomore in Great Barrington,

Massachusetts, is a science-and-technology class with a lot of hands-on experimentation. In the 1998–1999 school year, when students could take the class without worrying about MCAS, eighty students enrolled; this past year enrollment fell to thirty. Greene says that students feel the course will not help them pass the test, and failing the test next year could mean they don't get a diploma. "At least create a test," wrote Alison Maurer, an eighth-grader in Cambridge, Massachusetts, "that doesn't limit what students learn, something that shows what we have learned, not what we haven't."

The movement is a long way from achieving critical mass. The two most prominent lawsuits brought to date—one in Texas, challenging the test as racially biased; the other in Louisiana, arguing that students hadn't had a chance to learn the material—have failed. The boycotts are still small, and polls, by Public Agenda and other organizations, continue to show that 72 percent of Americans—and 79 percent of parents—support tougher academic standards and oppose social promotion "even if [the outcome is] that significantly more students would be held back." Those numbers seem to reinforce the argument of Diane Ravitch, an education historian, an education official in the Bush Administration, and a strong supporter of standards, who has described the protesters as "crickets"—few in number, but making a disproportionate amount of noise. "There's tremendous support" for tests, Ravitch says, "among elected officials and in the business community." She may also be correct when she says that a great many of those who profess to oppose the high-stakes tests oppose all testing and all but the fuzziest standards. They are the same people, Ravitch argues, who in the end cheat kids by demanding too little and forever blaming children's inability to read or to do elementary math on the shortcomings of parents, neighborhoods, and the culture. Scrap the tests and we're back to the same neglect and indifference, particularly toward poor, marginal students, that we had before. Letting students who can't read, write, or do basic math graduate is doing no one a favor.

Yet even Ravitch is concerned about what she calls the "test obsession" and the backlash it could create if large numbers of students fail and the whole system unravels. The accountability structure in Virginia has been set up in such a way that even if the vast majority of students pass the tests, a large percentage of schools could fail the accompanying Standards of Accreditation. Under the SOA, any school in which more than 30 percent of students fail in 2007 will be subject to loss of accreditation. That, according to a study by the conservative Thomas Jefferson Institute for Public Policy, in Springfield, Virginia, is a formula that fosters public distrust of both the schools and the system. The study points out that because high-scoring students are concentrated in just a handful of districts, only 6.5 percent of Virginia schools met the SOA in 1999, when 35 percent of all Virginia students passed all the required SOL tests.

The Jefferson Institute study illustrates a wider set of problems underlying the new standards and tests. In an effort to look like the toughest guy on the block, some states have imposed standards that will be difficult if not impossible for many students and schools to meet. Members of the Virginia Board of Education are negotiating over allowing students to graduate without necessarily passing a standardized test. As noted, Massachusetts has already lowered the passing score on MCAS. A policy in Los Angeles to hold back all failing students has been modified. And merit-scholarship systems have been created in Michigan and California to keep top students from blowing off the test. The states that have had the least trouble with backlash are those, like Texas, that set standards low enough (and the Texas standards are far too low, in the view of some critics) that a large percentage of students can pass the tests.

It is, of course, in the public ambivalence about where the bar should be set that the larger uncertainty about the standards movement lies. Robert B. Schwartz, the president of Achieve, an organization created in 1996 by governors and business executives to defend the standards movement (at that time mostly against conservative attacks), recognizes that despite the polls, "not enough has been done to bring the public along." In most cases the tests and standards were imposed from the top down, with little input either from teachers—often regarded as the problem rather than the solution—or from parents (who in Arizona and California are not even allowed to see old test questions). What's needed now, Schwartz says, is to bolster public understanding and "capacity building," including professional development for teachers, to make the whole system work. "The good news," he told a reporter from *Education Week* in April, is that "states are not simply stopping with raising the bar, and shouting at kids and teachers to jump higher, but are moving to address the support question."

The question, as Schwartz knows, is whether resources—and particularly the quality of teaching in inner cities—will catch up with the demands on students. Since April, Schwartz has also acknowledged that as the day of reckoning approaches for millions of American students, the backlash will spread and intensify. "It's easy to assent in the abstract," he told me recently. "When it's my kid, it's something different." In the mid-1990s Delaware threw out a testing program because, in the words of Achieve, the legislature "had been unprepared for high rates of student failure."

In his state of education speech in February the U. S. Secretary of Education, Richard Riley, a strong advocate of accountability and standards, seemed to recognize the danger. "Setting high expectations," he said, "does not mean setting them so high that they are unreachable except for only a few. . . . If all of our efforts to raise standards get reduced to one test, we've gotten it wrong. If we force our teachers to teach only to the test, we will lose their creativity. . . . If we are so consumed with making sure students pass a multiple-choice test that we throw out the arts and civics then we will be going backwards instead of forward."

And yet the line between the political drive to be tough and indifference to standards in the name of creativity and diversity sometimes seems hard to draw. Diane Ravitch says that a person much missed in this debate is the late Albert Shanker, a longtime president of the American Federation of Teachers, who was relentless in his push for high standards for both students and teachers. But Shanker also pointed out that if only one standard for graduation exists, it will necessarily be low, because the political system can't support a high rate of failure. Shanker suggested two criteria: a basic competency level required of everyone, combined with honors diplomas, by whatever name, for students who do better and achieve more. The issue of the tradeoff between minimum competency and what is sometimes called "world-class standards" is rarely raised in any explicit manner, but it has bedeviled this debate since the beginning. As the standards requirements begin to take effect, and as more parents face the possibility that their children will not graduate, pressure to lower the bar or eliminate it entirely will almost certainly increase. Conversely, as more people come to understand that the "Texas miracle" and other celebrated successes are based on embarrassingly low benchmarks, those, too, will come under attack. The most logical outcome would be the Shanker solution. But in education politics, where ideology often reigns, logic is not always easy to come by.

Questions

1. What is high-stakes testing? Why have most states adopted some form of testing for promotion?

2. What are some of the criticisms of high-stakes testing? How valid are these criticisms?

3. Explain the Shanker solution to high-stakes testing. Do you think that this a reasonable resolution to the debate?

4. Write a letter to the editor in which you take a stand on high-stakes testing.

Homogeneous or Heterogeneous Grouping: The Tracking Debate

Maureen T. Hallinan, University of Notre Dame
Jeannie Oakes, University of California–Los Angeles

This essay is a rather frank exchange on the benefits and detriments of tracking in public schools. Maureen Hallinan discusses the theory behind this long-standing practice and the "supposed" benefits for students. Jeannie Oakes agrees that the concept may have been appropriate, but argues that the implementation of this organizational/pedagogical tool has inadvertently fostered inequality in the schools.

☻ Tracking: From Theory to Practice—Maureen T. Hallinan

The term *tracking* refers to the practice of assigning students to instructional groups on the basis of ability. Originally, secondary school students were assigned to academic, general, or vocational tracks, with the courses within those tracks designed to prepare students for postsecondary education or careers. More recently, these track categories have been replaced by course levels, with students typically being assigned to advanced, honors, regular, or basic courses. These course levels continue to be referred to as tracks, with the regular and higher-level courses loosely equivalent to the academic track and the basic and lower courses loosely equivalent to the general and vocational tracks. Most secondary and junior high or middle schools track students for English and mathematics, and many schools track for social studies, science, language, and other courses.

Tracking is an organizational practice whose aim is to facilitate instruction and to increase learning. The theory of tracking argues that tracking permits teachers to tailor instruction to the ability level of their students. A good fit between a student's ability and the level of instruction is believed to maximize the effectiveness and efficiency of the instructional process. Thus, tracking is meant to promote cognitive development; it is not designed to influence or modify students' social or emotional growth.

The practice of tracking is currently a topic of intense debate. The concern focuses on two issues pertaining to the effectiveness and equity of tracking. The first is whether tracking is more effective in promoting students' learning than are other methods of grouping. The second is whether all students benefit from tracking to the same degree.

The tracking debate is fed by conjunctures and assumptions about the way tracking operates and how it affects students. Among these beliefs are that track placement is determined primarily by academic criteria, that tracks are strictly homogeneous with respect to ability, that track assignments tend to be permanent, that tracking has a negative effect on the self-esteem of low-ability students, that low-ability students are difficult to teach because they are not highly motivated to learn, and that tracking limits the college options of low-track students.

Research on Tracking

A number of fairly rigorous empirical studies, including both surveys and case studies, have provided information about how students are assigned to tracks and about the effects of track levels on students' learning. . . . Empirical research supports the following conclusions about tracking.

Assignment to Tracks

1. In practice, the assignment of students to tracks is based not only on academic considerations, which would lead to strictly homogeneous groupings, but on nonacademic factors. Academic factors that influence track placement are grades, scores on standardized tests, teachers' and counselors' recommendations, prior track placement, and course prerequisites. Nonacademic considerations include course conflicts, cocurricular and extracurricular schedules, work demands, and teacher and curricular resources. A reliance on nonacademic factors increases the heterogeneity of ability groups and leads to overlapping ability distributions in adjacent tracks.

2. Schools vary in the constellation of factors on which they rely to assign students to tracks and in the weight they attach to each factor. . . .

3. Track assignments tend to be less permanent than is commonly believed. It is not uncommon for a student to change tracks during a school year and from one school year to the next. . . .

4. A greater proportion of minority and low-income students are assigned to the lower tracks. When academic achievement is controlled, the race-ethnicity and income effect on track assignment decreases, but does not disappear.

5. Higher social status is associated with placement in a higher track. . . .

Effects of Tracking

1. The quantity and quality of instruction increases with the level of the track. The curriculum and related instructional materials are more interesting and engaging in higher tracks. The amount of time spent on instruction, as opposed to administrative and disciplinary tasks, is greater in higher tracks. . . .

2. Students in high-ability tracks learn more and at a faster pace than do those in lower-ability tracks.

3. Tracking provides no advantage over heterogeneous grouping with respect to the achievement of students in the middle-ability range.

These conclusions indicate that tracking, as currently practiced, tends to be both inequitable and, at least for some students, ineffective. Tracking provides fewer learning opportunities for low-ability students than for those with higher ability. Since low ability is related to race, ethnicity, and socioeconomic status, tracking discriminates against students in these demographic categories. The disadvantages of tracking for low-ability students perpetuate the effects of background characteristics on achievement. Tracking also disadvantages lower-ability students by conveying on them lower social status. Differences among schools in the effectiveness and equity of tracking place additional constraints on access to learning opportunities for some students, usually those of lower ability.

In general, empirical research seems to provide the rationale for eliminating tracking as an organizational and pedagogical practice. However, the decision to detrack a school may be premature and unwarranted. To evaluate the effectiveness and equity of tracking in an effort to determine how it can be improved, rather than eliminated, it is necessary to examine its intended and unintended consequences.

Tracking as an Organizational Practice

. . . The intended purpose of tracking is to increase the effectiveness and efficiency of instruction. If tracking operated according to theory, students at all ability levels and from all backgrounds would learn more in tracked classes than in untracked ones. However, tracking produces unintended consequences that impede the attainment of its goal. Some of these consequences are inherent in the nature of tracking, whereas others are due to the failure of tracking practice to reflect tracking theory. These consequences make tracking less effective and less equitable than intended. . . .

Modifying Negative Consequences

(1) **Segregation.** One unintended negative consequence of tracking is the way it segregates students by race or ethnicity and socioeconomic status. Since academic achievement is related to students' background, minority and low-income students are disproportionately assigned to lower tracks. Even if the quality of instruction were the same across tracks, this segregating effect would concern educators and parents.

Although the segregation produced by tracking may be unavoidable, its negative effects can be countered by integrating students in their untracked classes and in other school activities. Ensuring that students spend a large part of their school day in integrated settings should lessen the negative effects of assignment to a small number of segregated classes. . . .

(2) **Low social status.** A second negative feature of tracking is its effects on students' social status. Tracking typically leads to a social hierarchy based on track level and academic performance. Students who are assigned to the lower tracks are apt to receive less respect

from their peers and to be assigned lower status in the academic hierarchy. Lower status can have negative consequences for learning by decreasing a student's motivation and effort. In addition, rewards typically are given to higher-track students, which could further discourage or alienate lower-track students.

To counter the negative social dynamics created by tracking, school authorities need to create structures and methods to support the social and emotional experiences of lower-track students. Restructuring the reward system to broaden the bases for social recognition and respect is one way to enhance the status of low-track students.

(3) Heterogeneous tracks. A third negative consequence of tracking results from the failure of authorities to create strictly homogeneous tracks. In practice, track levels are rarely as homogeneous as they could be. In most cases, the distribution of achievement in one track overlaps, to a surprising degree, with the distribution in adjacent tracks. Typically, students at the high end of the distribution in one track have higher achievement than do those at the low end of the distribution in the next higher track. . . . The failure of students to benefit from tracking may be due partly to the failure of schools to create homogeneous tracks.

Moreover, students develop cognitively at different rates. Even when a track structure is homogeneous at the beginning of a school year, students' different rates of growth introduce heterogeneity into the tracks during the school year. When students' track placements are permanent, either across a school year or for longer periods, allowance is not made for the heterogeneity that arises from these differential rates of growth. . . .

What is needed is a flexible tracking policy that allows for reassignments to preserve the homogeneity of tracks. . . .

. . .

(4) Slower achievement of students in low tracks. The most serious, unintended negative effect of tracking is the slower growth in achievement of students in low tracks. This effect is caused, in part, by instructional inadequacies in the lower tracks. Instruction in many low tracks can be characterized by uninteresting lessons and instructional materials, by teachers' low expectations and standards for their students' performance, by low standards or teachers' performance, and by a significant number of interruptions in instruction owing to disciplinary problems.

Educational authorities have the ability to modify each of these characteristics of instruction in lower tracks. Teachers can provide more interesting instructional materials without going beyond the students' level of comprehension. They also can alter their assumptions about the learning potential of low-ability students. . . . Teachers can raise their expectations and requirements for students' performance. Principals can devise reward systems that are aimed at improving teachers' instruction, and teachers can provide rewards that motivate students to study. The school can consistently and publicly acknowledge the accomplishments of students in all academic tracks. Principals and counselors can devise methods of dealing with disciplinary problems without infringing on the teachers' instructional time.

(5) Negative social psychological consequences. In addition, negative social psychological processes occur in lower tracks that further jeopardize learning for lower-ability students. . . . Students are likely to view their assignments to low tracks as evidence that teachers have a low regard for their academic abilities and as an indication that they cannot be successful in school and should not aspire to go to college. . . . Discouragement usually results in students' detachment from learning and often leads to disruptive behavior or withdrawal. This negative cycle tends to be self-perpetuating.

Change or intervention can occur at any point in the negative social psychological processes that interfere with learning. The principal and faculty of a school can make a determined effort to communicate a positive message about the meaning of different track levels. Teachers can increase the academic demands they place on lower-track students and challenge these students to achieve. They can offer students frequent opportunities to succeed and provide tangible and public rewards for success and improvement. . . . In short, educators can forestall or reverse the negative social psychological dynamics that often accompany placements in low tracks by fostering a more positive attitude about track placement and students' potential. . . .

A common reaction to these unintended negative consequences of tracking is to call for the abandonment of tracking as an educational practice. A more tempered response would be to improve the way tracking is practiced, so it better fits the ideal, and to counter students' negative cognitive, social psychological, or behavioral responses to being tracked. The negative effect of tracking on integration in schools can be reduced by a committed effort to eliminate racism in a school and by avoiding segregation in nontracked classes and other school activities.

Objective versus Subjective Criteria

The effectiveness and equity of tracking are also influenced by the way students are assigned to track levels. . . .

Assignments to tracks that are based strictly on objective, academic criteria, such as standardized test scores, academic grades, and prerequisites for courses, produce the most academically homogeneous groups. When more arbitrary criteria are applied, such as counselors' and teachers' recommendations, parents' and students' preferences, and schedule conflicts with other academic courses or with cocurricular and extracurricular activities, tracks tend to be more heterogeneous. . . .

• • •

Schools differ in the criteria on which they base their decisions on track placements. Some schools rely heavily on objective measures, others use indicators of a student's improvement. . . . Differences in criteria among schools represent one way that tracking can transmit unequal learning opportunities to students.

. . .

A . . . serious consequence of standardizing criteria for admission to tracks and of basing admission primarily on objective measures of achievement is related to the equity of tracking. Administrators avoid setting objective criteria because doing so results in the assignment of fewer minority students to the higher tracks and disproportionately more minority students to the lower tracks. Since most administrators deplore this segregative aspect of tracking, they tend to prefer less objective measures of ability. To resolve this dilemma, it is necessary to compromise between the two desired goals of effectiveness and equity. In addition, however, schools need to make systematic, concerted efforts to improve the performance of low-ability students, so these students can meet the criteria for admission to higher tracks.

Conclusion

Tracking clearly has many shortcomings. Some of them, such as its segregative aspect and its effects on students' social status, are difficult to eliminate. However, schools have a number of opportunities to reduce these negative effects of tracking by ensuring that non-tracked classes and other school activities are integrated and by expanding the bases of social status to include nonacademic talents.

Other shortcomings of tracking result not from the organizational technique itself, but from the way tracking is practiced in schools. Efforts to reform the practice should be directed toward improving the quantity and quality of instruction at all track levels, particularly the lower ones. . . . Schools also need to guard against lessening the motivation of lower-track students by providing support mechanisms and reward systems for all students, including those in the lower tracks.

Finally, to ensure that tracking works as intended, great care is needed in making initial track assignment and in permitting students to change tracks when their original placements are no longer appropriate. Improving the fit of track assignments is a complex task. It requires school authorities to choose criteria that are valid measures of students' abilities and that reduce the likelihood of inappropriate placements. In the design of a student's schedule, track placement must take priority over other scheduling considerations. . . .

In general many of the criticisms leveled against tracking can be avoided by improving, rather than eliminating, tracking. The compelling advantage of retaining tracking, at least in certain subjects, is that it facilitates instruction and learning. The many teachers who favor tracking have concluded, from pedagogical experience, that teaching heterogeneously grouped students without additional resources, such as teacher aides and supplementary material, is a formidable task. . . . If educators are willing to put serious efforts into creating a tracking system that attempts to maximize effectiveness and equity, the results should benefit students at all levels of ability.

⊛ More than Misapplied Technology: A Normative and Political Response to Hallinan on Tracking —Jeannie Oakes

After responding to tracking advocates' distortions of the research, I am gratified to see that Maureen Hallinan has the facts straight. But, then again, Hallinan cannot be said to be an advocate of tracking— or can she? As a critic of tracking, she offers a reasonable definition of tracking, correctly identifies its explicit purposes, rightly recounts the widespread assumptions about how tracking works and how it affects students, and accurately summarizes research findings on the way students are assigned to tracks and tracking's actual effects on learning. Hallinan concludes her review of the research, as most other scholars do, by saying that the evidence on tracking adds up to a rationale for eliminating the practice, particularly since lower ability is associated with race, ethnicity, and social-class status students at a considerable educational disadvantage. So far, so good.

At this point in Hallinan's essay, something odd happens. She offers conclusions and a rationale that are indistinguishable from the new generation of tracking *advocates*. Hallinan asserts that it is not only premature, but likely to be unwarranted, to consider "detracking" schools! Like supporters of tracking, few of whom argue that tracking is currently done well, she contends that "a more tempered response" to the overwhelmingly negative evidence is for schools to make tracking practice more consistent with tracking theory and to balance the inherently negative features of tracking with countervailing policies and practices.

I find the disjunction between Hallinan's review of the evidence and the implications she draws astonishing, Having spent the past three years studying 16 racially mixed secondary schools that have taken the tracking research seriously and responded with "detracking" reforms, my own conclusions depart dramatically from Hallinan's. . . .

Hallinan argues that tracking is essentially an organizational technique with intended and unintended consequences. Tracking's unintended consequences, she contends, are what impede tracking's intended goal of enabling students at all levels to learn more than they would in mixed-ability classes. Some of these unintended consequences are inherent in tracking, whereas others represent the failure of implementation—that is, schools do not properly enact tracking theory. This line of argument treats tracking itself as a disembodied practice, a technical matter that is far more a product of organizational structure than of the humans who enact it. . . .

In striking contrast, my work finds the structure of tracking to be embedded in cultural and political contexts, replete with good intentions, bad intentions, and messy human decision making. Consequently, I have come to believe that attempts to understand tracking apart from its normative and political content are sorely inadequate. For example, Hallinan characterizes the debate about tracking as a concern with issues of effectiveness and equity in relation to cognitive outcomes—learning. The folks who are working to detrack the schools I am studying would agree, but they also view tracking as being centrally unconcerned with students' life chances, including the transfer of social, economic, and political privilege, and racial and social-class discrimination.

Most educators cannot imagine tracking as a technical, neutral organizational practice that is unrelated to personal, societal, or vocational purposes. . . .

. . .

Asserting the good intentions of educators and the neutrality of tracking as an organizational technology, Hallinan softens the evidence about the disproportionately negative impact of tracking on low-income students and minority students. She argues that the racial and social-class segregation that occurs may be inevitable, given the unfortunate coincidence of "low ability" and low-income and minority status, but that the diminished outcome that accompany this segregation are unintended consequences. . . . Hallinan then contends that tracking's segregative effects can be counterbalanced by mixing students by race and social class in their untracked classes and by creating a nonracist school atmosphere. She claims that tracking's lamentable impact on students' social status—including low-track students' diminished motivation and effort—can be circumvented if schools alter their reward structures in ways that extend higher status to low-track students. . . .

Hallinan's ameliorative strategies are recognized by educators who are grappling with tracking's negative consequences as tried-and-false methods of the past. First, they see that few students miss the clear status message carried by racially identifiable tracking in high-status academic classes. Even if lower-status classes and extracurricular activities are more evenly mixed racially, students and adults in all but the most extraordinary schools have their stereotypes and prejudices reinforced by racially identifiable high- and low-track classes. . . . A school may become calmer around racial issues with human relations efforts, but it cannot embody egalitarianism or social justice without deeper changes in tracking structures and the norms and political relations these structures enact.

Nearly all educators are well aware that low-track students consistently have lower-quality opportunities to learn than do their peers in higher tracks. They also recognize that these differences are not appropriate modifications of curriculum and instruction to differences in the abilities of students in various groups, but that they take the form of gross inequalities in access to knowledge, instructional resources, and well-qualified teachers. Many educators have spent their careers trying to beef up the low-track curriculum, to adopt a more positive disposition toward the capacities of low-track students, and to alter the reward systems that work against these students. These educators would undoubtedly find insulting the suggestion that an "attitude adjustment" (Hallinan's phrase) would enable them to be persuasive in communicating a positive message about the meaning of different track levels and would effectively cancel out low-track students' accurate perceptions that schools have a low regard for their abilities and prospects for success in school.

In addition to salutary efforts to integrate students, to enhance low-track students' feelings of worth outside tracked classrooms, and to improve the low-track curriculum, Hallinan suggests that tracking could be vastly improved if educators more faithfully enacted tracking theory by making tracks more homogeneous. To accomplish this greater uniformity within tracks, she recommends two changes. First, schools should base track assignments on the most "objective" measures of ability and achievement. Second, schools should employ some flexible placement practices, such as frequent reassessments and reassignments to other tracks. . . .

Track assignments stem from more than the cognitive criteria and the structural constraints (such as scheduling conflicts and limited resources) that Hallinan lists. Although these factors are important, there is consistent evidence that background factors, including the discriminatory placement of minority students in low tracks, also come into play. Neither the negative impact of minority status nor discriminatory placement practices are obvious in analyses of large-scale survey data, particularly when the data are aggregated across school systems. . . .

Let me explain this a bit more. Senior high schools in low-income, high-minority communities are similar in structure to those in White and wealthy suburban areas. That is, in both types of communities the schools strive to be "comprehensive" and to offer both college preparatory and non-college preparatory programs and courses. Teachers and students in both settings have no difficulty pointing out which programs are designed for high-, average-, and low-ability students. However, such communities and schools are not so similar in how well students score on traditional measures of academic ability and achievement. Differences in the typical "ability" composition of schools (with students in White and wealthy schools scoring higher, on average) mean that many minority students of attending schools in predominantly minority communities demonstrate ability levels—as measured by test scores—-that would not be high enough to qualify them for academic tracks in whiter and wealthier communities. However, because their schools need to fill a requisite number of academic track "slots," some of these students are enrolled in the academic tracks at their schools. Consequently, when data about two such communities are aggregated, one finds a pattern of track placement that appears to give a slight advantage to African American students (after controlling for ability) of being assigned to academic tracks. This aggregation can mask considerable discrimination against minority students in high-track placements in both such systems.

When analyses of the relationship among race, ability, and placements within particular schools and school systems are performed, a different understanding results. For example, I recently analyzed the relationship between race and track placement (controlling for achievement) within schools in five medium-size city school systems with racially mixed student populations. In each of these schools and systems, I found clear evidence of discriminatory placements, with Whites and Asians considerably (and statistically significantly) more likely to be placed in academic classes than comparably achieving African American and Latino students. . . .

When one looks carefully at such systems, one finds that much of the heterogeneity within tracks come about precisely because powerful parents are able to secure high-track placements for their unqualified children. This represents a type of political pressure that is not likely to respond to appeals to fairness. When a status preference exists, savvy parents of high socioeconomic status (SES) will use their considerable political capital on behalf of their children. Lower SES and minority students, whose ascribed characteristics work against them in their initial track placements, tend to have families who are precluded from such political maneuvering by their ignorance of schools' frequent acquiescence to parental pressure or by their timidity about exercising such pressure. Parents of students who are currently in the higher tracks would surely resist the reassignment of their children to lower tracks with even greater vehemence than they resist the dismantling of the track system itself.

Within schools, factors related to students' race and social class shape educators' perceptions of appropriate class placements. Educators value being able to exercise their professional judgment to make exceptions to rigid tracking practices for students who "work hard but don't test well," for those whose parents promise to provide support with private tutoring, and so on. The fact that such students are disproportionately White and middle class will do little to persuade educators that such exceptions are not "fair."

In the end, Hallinan's suggestions simply beg the questions, arguing that schools can solve the inequities of tracking by solving the inequities of tracking—as if the norms, politics, and practices of schools are pieces of separate games to be played independently. My work has persuaded me that if inequalities of tracking are nothing other than the normative and political guises of tracking itself.

Hallinan argues that if tracking were fixed, it could benefit students at all ability levels. But, she also acknowledges that there is no empirical evidence that such benefits accrue. I can only speculate, based on years and years of discussion with advocates of tracking, why Hallinan resists "detracking" as a way to confront the problems of tracking. These reasons often include (1) a wish to circumvent comprehensive changes in other school regularities that schools must make when they move to heterogeneous ability grouping (such as changing staffing patterns, redistributing resources, reconceptualizing the curriculum and instruction, restructuring grading practices, and more), (2) a wish to avoid scrutiny of long-standing norms underlying schools' definition and evaluations of intelligence and learning (including such constructs as high-, average-, and low ability), and (3) a wish to avoid the often-nasty political contentiousness (not the least of which is the threat of "bright flight") that "detracking" reforms often bring. It may also be the case that Hallinan, like some other social scientists, believes that her role is simply to observe social phenomena without altering them and thus makes a highly conservative stance on reform.

I have come to believe, from studying educators as they struggle firsthand with detracking reforms (many with surprising success), that heterogeneity, in itself, may be the necessary lever to ensure that low-status students have access to a high-quality curriculum, teachers, and learning experiences—to say nothing of seats next to their advantaged White peers and the increased status that comes with them. Furthermore, although tracking places a *disproportionate* burden on low-income, minority children, the group that is *numerically* most affected by tracking are low- and middle-SES White children who are identified as something other than "high track." As long as students view themselves as "low," and they are concentrated in classes where teachers expect them to act as such, rich, multidimensional educational opportunities are unlikely to come their way.

Without a doubt, "detracking" is an extraordinary reform to undertake, and those in schools that are attempting it would be the first to agree. Yet, these educators believe, often with firsthand experience that is backed by a growing body of research, that they can teach all students well. Together. And, as dramatic as it may seem, they also believe that it is their professional and moral obligation to try.

◉ Further Thoughts on Tracking
—Maureen T. Hallinan

To have a meaningful discussion, it is necessary to define tracking and detracking. *Tracking,* or homogeneous grouping, is the organization of students for instruction, based on their ability and achievement. The practice is based on the belief that it promotes learning by providing a good fit between the level of instruction and students' learning needs. *Detracking,* or heterogeneous grouping, is the arrangement of students for instruction into groups that include students with a wide range of abilities. The rationale for detracking is the belief that cognitive diversity can be an effective teaching technique.

Both tracking and detracking, as Oakes notes, occur in a specific normative and political milieu. The school milieu can support the positive features of a school's organizational structure and promote learning, or it can undermine the pedagogical effectiveness of an organizational structure and obstruct learning. Typically, it is the school's climate and political and social agenda, not the practice of tracking or detracking, that accounts for a school's success or failure.

Most of the negative consequences of tracking can be attributed to a school environment that fails to provide the support needed to make tracking effective. Tracking itself is not designed to be a political tool, nor is it meant to influence the normative climate of a school. To assert that tracking is a failure because it is associated with a set of negative norms or a discriminatory political or social climate is a misplaced criticism. A tracked school's failure to provide students with equal opportunities to learn is not due to tracking, but to the absence of the school's commitment to equality. The negative impact of the segregation created by tracking is caused by the failure to embed tracking in an atmosphere that would counter this situation.

Remedying the deficiences of tracking requires moving the school and political fabric of the school. It may involve changing teacher's and students' attitudes and behaviors, altering the reward structure of the school, and reorganizing the curriculum. It also may require modifying teachers' philosophies of education and political persuasions. The resulting positive school climate will enable students to take advantage of the benefits of tracking to increase their academic achievement.

When Oakes and others advocate detracking, they usually imply more than heterogeneous grouping. Proponents of detracking describe schools that have an ideal social and political climate. They refer to the use of pedagogical techniques that support lower-ability students, a curriculum that is tailored to a child's learning needs, the employment of teacher aides to assist teachers, diverse curricular assignments and projects and an underlying respect for various manifestations of intelligence. These descriptions place heterogeneous grouping in a culture and political climate that is nondiscriminatory and that aims to accommodate the unique learning needs of each student. It is likely that this positive normative climate and support structure, rather than heterogeneous grouping, is responsible for the success of detracked schools. Homogeneous grouping may be equally effective in the same kind of environment, whereas heterogeneous grouping may be less successful than tracking in schools with a negative social climate.

The results of empirical research on their effects of ability and nonability groups on students' learning underscore the importance of separating a grouping practice from the government in which it is practiced to evaluate its effectiveness. . . . On average, students do equally well in grouped and ungrouped instructional arrangements. But in ability grouped schools, the high-ability students tend to learn more, and the low-ability students tend to learn less than in heterogeneously grouped schools. This consistent finding implies either that ability grouping is inherently detrimental to low-ability students (and advantageous to high-ability students) or that intervening factors modify the effects of ability grouping on students who differ in ability. Both survey and ethnographic data indicate the latter.

The intervening factors that researchers identify as reducing the effectiveness of tracking for low-ability students undoubtedly are reflections of a school's normative, social, and political climate. Consequently, it is likely that a school's context, rather than its grouping practices, should be the object of reform. Replacing tracking and detracking without changing the climate of the school is unlikely to improve students' learning. On the other hand, changing a school's climate may eliminate the need to abandon tracking. . . .

⊚ One More Thought
—Jeannie Oakes

Forty years ago this month, the Supreme Court ruled that school segregation was unconstitutional because separate is *inherently* unequal. It was clear to the Warren Court that in the 60 years since *Plessy*, school segregation had proved to be neither a neutral practice nor one that was separable from the negative racial norms and the discriminatory political context in which it was embedded. The Court recognized that the practice of racial separation was both a cause and an effect of a social climate of discrimination and inequality. By *definition*, racial segregation existed in communities that at least tolerated discrimination and inequality, and, in contrast, those communities that voluntarily initiated school desegregation were places committed to equal opportunity for all students. Thus, the Court did not rule that the harms of segregation could be remedied by changing philosophies or political persuasions. . . . The *Brown* ruling recognized that, although for convenience and analysis, sociologists may talk about structures, norms, and politics as components of society, these components are not distinct or separable.

Tracking is partly, but not only, about race. Whereas African American and Latino children disproportionately wind up in lower-track classes, most of the children who are disadvantaged by tracking are poor and working-class Whites. The segregation mechanism of tracking, at least ostensibly, is ability. However, like racial segregation, tracking builds inequalities into schools that both devalue and materially disadvantage those groups who are least able to defend themselves. Ability, like race, is a social construction that leads schools to define and treat children from powerless groups—Black, Brown, and White—as expendable. Thus, like racial segregation, tracking carries with it class-based damage that can neither be avoided nor compensated for. Tracking's supporters, much like opponents of the *Brown* ruling, argue otherwise, claiming that separate could be equally effective if school and classroom environments were good. They ask that institutionalized segregation by ability be left in place because the real culprits are attitudes, behaviors, reward structures, philosophies, political persuasions, culture, and normative climate. I find little to support their position, either in the empirical evidence or in principle.

☙ ☙ ☙

Questions

1. What is tracking? How is it defined?

2. What are the positive and negative effects of tracking?

3. What information is used to determine track assignment? How objective is this information? How subjective?

4. According to Oakes, why does Hallinan (and advocates of tracking in general) resist "detracking"? Do these reasons seem valid? Explain your response.

5. To what degree is tracking a discriminatory practice? Discuss this issue in relation to initial track placement as well as learning outcomes. Include the role of gender, race, ethnicity, and social class in your answer.

6. Recall your own schooling experiences, particularly in middle school and high school. Which of your classes were tracked? Which were not? Were your "tracked" classes more or less homogenous than your "detracked" classes? How flexible were your track assignments? (I.e., were you able to move up a track relatively easily during the school year? Between school years?) Given these answers, would your own schooling experiences support Hallinan's view or Oates' view?

Economics and Politics

Economics and Politics

- What is a social institution?

- How does change in the economy reshape society?

- Why do some critics say the United States is not really a democracy?

Watch the Core Concepts in Sociology video "Money and Politics" on **mysoclab.com**

Chapter Overview

This chapter explores the operation of the economy, a major social institution, and explains how changes in economic production have reshaped society. The chapter then examines politics, a second major social institution, with attention to the character and causes of war and terrorism.

Spencer Tirey\AP Wide World Photos

Here's a quick quiz about the U.S. economy. (Hint: All six questions have the same right answer.)

- Which business do 137 million people in the United States visit each week?
- Which business sells the products of more than 61,000 companies?
- Which U.S. company, on average, opens a new or remodeled store every day?
- Which U.S. company buys more than $18 billion worth of goods each year from China, which, if the company were a country, would be China's seventh largest trading partner?
- Which U.S. company created 33,000 new jobs domestically (and another 30,000 in other countries) in 2008?
- Which single company actually grew in size during the recent economic downturn?

The answer, of course, is Walmart, the global discount store chain founded by Sam Walton, who opened his first store in Arkansas in 1962. In 2009, Walmart announced revenues of $401 billion in annual sales through more than 4,000 stores in the United States and 3,615 stores in other countries from Brazil to China, making it the second-largest corporation in the nation.

But not everyone is pleased with the expansion of Walmart. Across the United States, many people have joined a social movement to keep Walmart out of their local communities, fearing the loss of local businesses and, in some cases, local culture. Critics claim that the merchandising giant pays low wages, keeps out unions, and sells many products made in sweatshops abroad. In 2010, a federal court ruled that a Walmart would go to trial to defend against claims by women of sex discrimination (Saporito, 2003; Walsh, 2007; A. Clark, 2010; Walmart, 2010).

This chapter explores the economy and the closely related institution of politics. A number of very large corporations, including Walmart, are at the center of the U.S. economy, raising questions about just how the economy operates, whose interests it ought to serve, and to what extent big business shapes the political life of the United States.

Economics and politics are **social institutions,** *major spheres of social life or societal subsystems organized to meet human needs.*

The Economy: Historical Overview

The **economy** is *the social institution that organizes a society's production, distribution, and consumption of goods and services.* The economy operates, for better or worse, in a generally predictable manner. *Goods* are commodities ranging from necessities (such as food, clothing, and shelter) to luxury items (such as cars, swimming pools, and yachts). *Services* are activities that benefit people (including the work of priests, physicians, teachers, and computer software specialists).

Three times in the past, technological revolutions reorganized the economy and, in the process, transformed social life.

The Agricultural Revolution

The earliest societies were made up of hunters and gatherers living off the land. In these technologically simple societies, there was no distinct economy; producing and consuming were part of family life.

Harnessing animals to plows around 5,000 years ago permitted the development of agriculture, which was fifty times more productive than hunting and gathering. The resulting surpluses meant that not everyone had to produce food, so many people took on other specialized work: making tools, raising animals, and building dwellings. Soon towns sprang up, linked by networks of traders dealing in food, animals, and other goods. These four factors—agricultural technology, specialized work, permanent settlements, and trade—made the economy a distinct social institution.

The Industrial Revolution

By the mid-eighteenth century, a second technological revolution was under way, starting in England and spreading to the United States

Seeing Sociology
in Everyday Life

Can you list several jobs in today's economy that represent industrial work and postindustrial work?

social institution a major sphere of social life or societal subsystem, organized to meet human needs

economy the social institution that organizes a society's production, distribution, and consumption of goods and services

postindustrial economy a productive system based on service work and high technology

and elsewhere. Industrialization changed the economy in five fundamental ways:

1. **New sources of energy.** Throughout history, "energy" had meant the muscle power of people or animals. Then, in 1765, the English inventor James Watt introduced the steam engine. A hundred times more powerful than animal muscles, early steam engines soon drove heavy machinery.

2. **Centralization of work in factories.** Steam-powered machinery moved work from homes to factories, centralized workplaces that housed the machines.

3. **Manufacturing and mass production.** Before the Industrial Revolution, most people grew or gathered raw materials such as grain, wood, or wool. In an industrial economy, the focus shifts so that most people turn raw materials into a wide range of finished products such as furniture and clothing.

4. **Specialization.** Centuries ago, people worked at home making products from start to finish. In the factory, a laborer repeats a single task over and over, making only a small contribution to the finished product.

5. **Wage labor.** Instead of working for themselves, factory workers became wage laborers working for strangers, who often cared less for them than for the machines they operated.

The Industrial Revolution gradually raised the standard of living as countless new products fueled an expanding marketplace. Yet the benefits of industrial technology were shared very unequally, especially at the beginning. Some factory owners made huge fortunes, while the majority of industrial workers lived close to poverty. Children, too, worked in factories or in coal mines for pennies a day. As time went on, workers formed labor unions to represent their interests collectively to factory owners. In the twentieth century, new laws banned child labor, set minimum wage levels, improved workplace safety, and extended schooling and political rights to a larger segment of the population.

The Information Revolution and Postindustrial Society

By about 1950, the nature of production was changing once again. The United States was creating a **postindustrial economy**, *a productive system based on service work and high technology.* Automated machinery (and later, robotics) reduced the role of human labor in factory production and expanded the ranks of clerical workers and managers. The postindustrial era is marked by a shift from industrial work to service work.

As societies industrialize, a smaller share of the labor force works in agriculture. In the United States, much of the agricultural work that remains is performed by immigrants from lower-income nations. These farm workers from Mexico travel throughout Florida during the tomato harvest.

Chris Thomaidis\Getty Images Inc. - Stone Allstock

Driving this economic change is a third technological breakthrough: the computer. Just as the Industrial Revolution did two-and-a-half centuries ago, the Information Revolution has introduced new kinds of products and new forms of communication and has changed the character of work. There have been three significant changes:

1. **From tangible products to ideas.** The industrial era was defined by the production of goods; in the postindustrial era, people work with symbols. Computer programmers, writers, financial analysts, advertising executives, architects, editors, and various types of consultants make up more of the labor force in the information age.

2. **From mechanical skills to literacy skills.** The Industrial Revolution required mechanical skills, but the Information Revolution requires literacy skills: speaking and writing well and, of course, knowing how to use a computer. People able to communicate effectively are likely to do well; people without these skills face fewer opportunities.

3. **From factories to almost anywhere.** Industrial technology drew workers to factories located near power sources, but computer technology allows people to work almost anywhere. Laptop and wireless computers and cell phones now turn the home, car, or even an airplane into a "virtual office." What this means for everyday life is that new information technology blurs the line between our lives at work and at home.

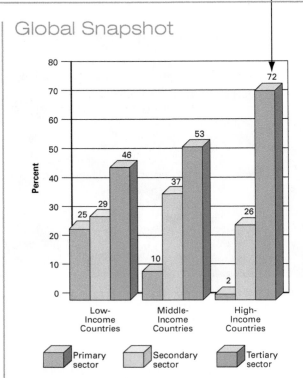

primary sector the part of the economy that draws raw materials from the natural environment

secondary sector the part of the economy that transforms raw materials into manufactured goods

tertiary sector the part of the economy that involves services rather than goods

global economy economic activity that crosses national borders

Global Snapshot

> In high-income nations such as the United States, almost three out of four jobs are in the tertiary or service sector of the economy.

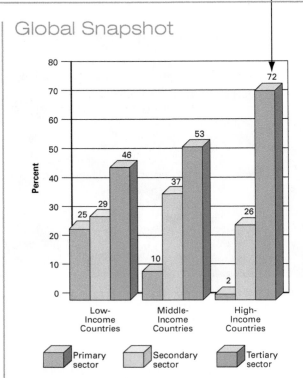

FIGURE 1 The Size of Economic Sectors, by National Income Level

As countries become richer, the primary sector becomes a smaller part of the economy and the tertiary or service sector becomes larger.

Source: Estimates based on World Bank (2009).

Sectors of the Economy

The three revolutions just described reflect a shifting balance among the three sectors of a society's economy. The **primary sector** is *the part of the economy that draws raw materials from the natural environment*. The primary sector—agriculture, raising animals, fishing, forestry, and mining—is largest in low-income nations. Figure 1 shows that 25 percent of the economic output of low-income countries is in the primary sector, compared with 10 percent of economic activity among middle-income nations and just 2 percent in high-income countries like the United States.

The **secondary sector** is *the part of the economy that transforms raw materials into manufactured goods*. This sector expands quickly as societies industrialize. It includes operations such as refining petroleum into gasoline and turning metals into tools and automobiles. The globalization of industry means that just about all the world's

countries have a significant share of workers employed in the secondary sector. Figure 1 shows that the secondary sector now accounts for a greater share of economic output in middle-income nations than it does in high-income countries.

The **tertiary sector** is *the part of the economy that involves services rather than goods*. The tertiary sector grows with industrialization, accounting for 46 percent of economic output in low-income countries, 53 percent in middle-income countries, and 72 percent in high-income countries. About 80 percent of the U.S. labor force is in service work, including secretarial and clerical jobs and work in food service, sales, law, health care, advertising, and teaching (U.S. Department of Labor, 2009).

The Global Economy

New information technology is drawing people around the world together and creating a **global economy,** *economic activity that crosses national borders*. The development of a global economy has five major consequences.

First, we see a global division of labor: Different regions of the world specialize in one sector of economic activity. As Global Map 1 shows, agriculture represents about half the total economic output of the world's poorest countries. Global Map 2 shows that most of the economic output of high-income countries, including the United States, is in the service sector. In short, the world's poorest nations specialize in producing raw materials, and the richest nations specialize in the production of services.

Second, an increasing number of products pass through more than one nation. Look no further than your morning coffee: The beans may have been grown in Colombia and transported to New Orleans on a freighter that was registered in Liberia, made in a shipyard in Japan using steel from Korea, and fueled by oil from Venezuela.

Third, national governments no longer control the economic activity that takes place within their borders. In fact, governments cannot even accurately regulate the value of their national currencies because dollars, euros, pounds sterling, and yen are traded around the clock in the financial markets of New York, London, and Tokyo.

A fourth consequence of the global economy is that a small number of businesses operating internationally now control a vast share of the world's economic activity. Using the latest available data, the 1,500 largest multinational companies account for half the world's economic output (DeCarlo, 2009; World Bank, 2010).

Fifth and finally, the globalization of the economy raises concerns about the rights and opportunities of workers. Critics of this trend claim that the United States is losing jobs—especially factory

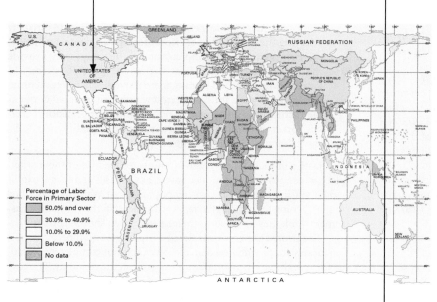

Sandra Johanson is a hygiene technician on a large corporate-owned farm in Kansas. She is one of the relatively few people in the United States working in agriculture.

Lily May Vale is an investment analyst in Sydney, Australia. Like most people in high-income nations, she works in the service sector.

Window on the World

GLOBAL MAP 1

Agricultural Employment in Global Perspective

The primary sector of the economy is largest in the nations that are least developed. In the poor countries of Africa and Asia, up to half of all workers are farmers. This picture is altogether different in the world's most economically developed countries—including the United States, Canada, Great Britain, and Australia—which have a mere 2 percent of their labor force in agriculture.

Source: Data from International Labour Organization (2010).

Percentage of Labor Force in Primary Sector
- 50.0% and over
- 30.0% to 49.9%
- 10.0% to 29.9%
- Below 10.0%
- No data

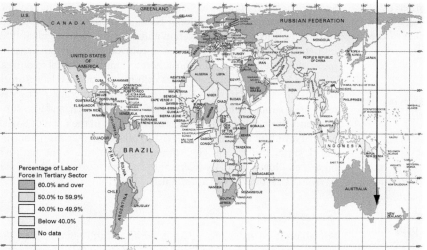

GLOBAL MAP 2

Service-Sector Employment in Global Perspective

The tertiary sector of the economy becomes larger as a nation's income level rises. In the United States, Canada, the countries of Western Europe, much of South America, Australia, and Japan, about two-thirds of the labor force performs service work.

Source: Data from International Labour Organization (2010).

Percentage of Labor Force in Tertiary Sector
- 60.0% and over
- 50.0% to 59.9%
- 40.0% to 49.9%
- Below 40.0%
- No data

jobs—to low-income nations. This means that workers here face lower wages and higher unemployment. At the same time, many workers abroad are paid extremely low wages. As a result, say critics, the global expansion of capitalism threatens the well-being of workers throughout the world.

The world is still divided into 194 politically distinct nations. But the rising level of international economic activity makes nationhood less significant than it was even a decade ago.

Economic Systems: Paths to Justice

October 20, Saigon, Vietnam. Sailing up the narrow Saigon River is an unsettling experience for anyone who came of age in the 1960s. People like me need to remember that Vietnam is a country, not a war, and that

Seeing Sociology in Everyday Life

Supporters of Walmart sometimes make the claim that this store has done a lot to reduce poverty in the United States by giving working people low prices for things they need. Do you agree with this view? Why or why not?

nearly forty years have passed since the last U.S. helicopter lifted off the rooftop of the U.S. embassy, ending our country's presence there.

Saigon is now a boomtown. Neon signs bathe the city's waterfront in color; hotels, bankrolled by Western corporations, push skyward from a dozen construction sites; taxi meters record fares in U.S. dollars, not Vietnamese dong; and Visa and American Express stickers decorate the doors of trendy restaurants and fashionable shops that cater to tourists from Japan, France, and the United States.

There is heavy irony here: After decades of fighting, millions of lives lost on both sides, and the victory of Communist forces, the Vietnamese are doing an about-face and turning toward capitalism. What we see today is what might well have happened had the U.S. forces won the war.

Every society's economic system makes a statement about justice by determining who is entitled to what. Two general economic models are capitalism and socialism. However, no nation anywhere in the world has an economy that is completely one or the other; rather, capitalism and socialism are two ends of a continuum along which all real-world economies can be located. We will look at each of these models in turn.

Capitalism

Capitalism is *an economic system in which natural resources and the means of producing goods and services are privately owned.* An ideal capitalist economy has three distinctive features:

1. **Private ownership of property.** In a capitalist economy, individuals can own almost anything. The more capitalist an economy is, the more private ownership there is of wealth-producing property such as factories, real estate, and natural resources.

2. **Pursuit of personal profit.** A capitalist society seeks to create profit and wealth. The profit motive is the reason people take new jobs, open new businesses, or try to improve products. Making money is considered the natural way of economic life. Just as important, the Scottish philosopher Adam Smith (1723–1790) claimed that as individuals pursue their self-interest, the entire society prospers (1937, orig. 1776).

3. **Competition and consumer choice.** A purely capitalist economy is a free-market system with no government interference (sometimes called a *laissez-faire economy,* from the French words meaning "leave it alone"). Adam Smith stated that a freely competitive economy regulates itself by the "invisible hand" of the law of supply and demand.

Consumers guide a market economy, Smith explained, by selecting the goods and services offering the greatest value. As producers compete for the customer's business, they provide the highest-quality goods at the lowest possible prices. In Smith's time-honored phrase, from narrow self-interest comes "the greatest good for the greatest number of people." Government control of an economy, on the other hand, distorts market forces by reducing the quantity and quality of goods, shortchanging consumers in the process.

Justice in a capitalist system amounts to freedom of the marketplace, where anyone can produce, invest, buy, and sell according to individual self-interest. The increasing popularity of Walmart, described in the opening to this chapter, reflects the fact that the company's customers think they get a lot for their money when shopping there.

The United States is considered a capitalist nation because most businesses are privately owned. However, it is not completely capitalist because the government plays a large role in the economy. The government owns and operates a number of businesses, including almost all of this country's schools, roads, parks, museums, the U.S. Postal Service, the Amtrak railroad system, and the entire U.S. military. The U.S. government also had a major hand in building the Internet. In addition, governments use taxation and other forms of regulation to influence what companies produce, to control the quality and cost of merchandise, and to motivate consumers to conserve natural resources.

The U.S. government also sets minimum wage levels, enforces workplace safety standards, regulates corporate mergers, provides farm price supports, taxes everyone on what they earn, and also supplements the income of a majority of its people in the form of Social Security, public assistance, student loans, and veterans' benefits. Local, state, and federal governments combined are the nation's biggest employer, with 17 percent of the nonfarm labor force on their payrolls (U.S. Bureau of Labor Statistics, 2010).

Socialism

Socialism is *an economic system in which natural resources and the means of producing goods and services are collectively owned.* In its ideal form, a socialist economy rejects each of the three characteristics of capitalism just described in favor of three opposite features:

1. **Collective ownership of property.** A socialist economy limits rights to private property, especially property used to generate income. Government controls such property and makes housing and other goods available to all, not just to the people with the most money.

2. **Pursuit of collective goals.** The individualistic pursuit of profit goes against the collective orientation of socialism. What

welfare capitalism an economic and political system that combines a mostly market-based economy with extensive social welfare programs

state capitalism an economic and political system in which companies are privately owned but cooperate closely with the government

Making the Grade

What do you see as advantages and disadvantages of capitalism and socialism?

Capitalism still thrives in Hong Kong (*left*), evident in streets choked with advertising and shoppers. Socialism is more the rule in China's capital, Beijing (*right*), a city dominated by government buildings rather than a downtown business district.

capitalism celebrates as the "entrepreneurial spirit," socialism condemns as greed; individuals are urged to work for the common good of all.

3. **Government control of the economy.** Socialism rejects capitalism's laissez-faire approach in favor of a *centrally controlled* or *command economy* operated by the government. Commercial advertising thus plays little role in socialist economies.

Justice in a socialist context means not competing to gain wealth but meeting everyone's basic needs in a roughly equal manner. From a socialist point of view, the common capitalist practice of giving workers as little in wages and benefits as possible to boost company earnings is unjust because it puts profits before people.

North Korea and more than two dozen other nations in Asia, Africa, and Latin America model their economies on socialism, placing almost all wealth-generating property under state control (Miller, Holmes, & Kim, 2010). The extent of world socialism declined during the 1990s as countries in Eastern Europe and the former Soviet Union geared their economies toward a market system. More recently, however, voters in Bolivia, Venezuela, Ecuador, and other nations in South America have elected leaders who are moving the national economies in a socialist direction.

Welfare Capitalism and State Capitalism

Most of the nations in Western Europe—especially Sweden, Denmark, and Italy—have market-based economies but also offer broad social welfare programs. Analysts call this third type of economic system **welfare capitalism,** *an economic and political system that combines a mostly market-based economy with extensive social welfare programs.*

Under welfare capitalism, a nation's government owns some of the largest industries and services, such as transportation, the mass media, and health care. In Sweden and Italy, about 12 percent of economic production is *nationalized,* under state control. Most industry is left in private hands, but all economic activity is subject to extensive government regulation. High taxation (aimed especially at the rich) funds a wide range of social welfare programs, including universal health care and child care, that benefit the entire population (Olsen, 1996; CQ Press, 2009).

Another alternative is **state capitalism,** *an economic and political system in which companies are privately owned but cooperate closely with the government.* State capitalism is the rule in the nations along the Pacific Rim. Japan, South Korea, and Singapore are all capitalist countries, but their governments work in partnership with large companies, supplying financial assistance and controlling foreign imports to help their businesses compete in world markets (Gerlach, 1992).

Relative Advantages of Capitalism and Socialism

Which economic system works best? Comparing economic models is difficult because all nations mix capitalism and socialism to varying degrees. In addition, nations differ in cultural attitudes toward work, access to natural resources, levels of technological development, and

○─ Making the Grade

Both capitalism and socialism have advantages and disadvantages. One general point on which most experts agree is that capitalism is more productive and socialism generates more social equality.

Seeing Sociology in Everyday Life

Do you think the United States is moving toward capitalism or socialism at the moment? Explain.

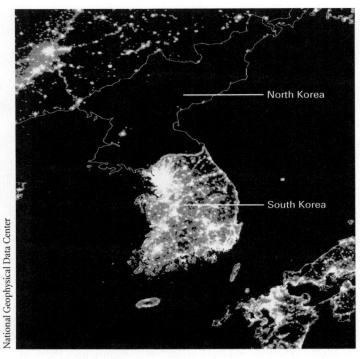

National Geophysical Data Center

Directly comparing the economic performance of capitalism and socialism is difficult because nations differ in many ways. But a satellite image of socialist North Korea and capitalist South Korea at night shows the dramatically different electrical output of the two nations, one indication of economic activity.

patterns of trade. Despite such complicating factors, some crude comparisons are revealing.

Economic Productivity

One key dimension of economic performance is productivity. A commonly used measure of economic output is *gross domestic product* (GDP), the total value of all goods and services produced within the nation's borders each year. Per capita (per-person) GDP allows us to compare the economic performance of nations of different population sizes.

The output of mostly capitalist countries in the late 1980s—before the end of socialist economies in the Soviet Union and Eastern Europe—varied somewhat but averaged about $13,500 per person. The comparable figure for the mostly socialist former Soviet Union and nations of Eastern Europe was about $5,000. This means that the capitalist countries outproduced the socialist nations by a ratio of 2.7 to 1 (United Nations Development Programme, 1990).

A recent comparison of socialist North Korea (per capita GDP of $1,800) and capitalist South Korea ($24,801) provides an even sharper contrast (United Nations Development Programme, 2009; Central Intelligence Agency, 2010).

Economic Equality

The distribution of resources within the population is another important measure of how well an economic system works. A comparative study of Europe in the mid-1970s, when that region was split between mostly capitalist and mostly socialist countries, compared the earnings of the richest 5 percent of the population and the poorest 5 percent (Wiles, 1977). Societies with mostly capitalist economies had an income ratio of about 10 to 1; the figure for socialist countries was 5 to 1. In other words, capitalist economies support a higher overall standard of living but with greater income inequality. Said another way, socialist economies create more economic equality but provide a lower overall living standard.

Personal Freedom

One additional consideration in evaluating capitalism and socialism is the personal freedom each system gives its people. Capitalism emphasizes the *freedom to pursue self-interest* and depends on the ability of producers and consumers to interact with little interference by the state. Socialism, by contrast, emphasizes *freedom from basic want*. The goal of equality requires the state to regulate the economy, which in turn limits personal choices and opportunities for citizens.

Can a single society offer both political freedom and economic equality? In the capitalist United States, our political system offers many personal freedoms, but the economy generates a lot of inequality, and freedom is not worth as much to a poor person as to a rich one. By contrast, North Korea or Cuba has considerable economic equality, but people cannot speak out or travel freely within or outside of the country. Perhaps the closest any countries have come to "having it all" is Denmark—the Thinking Globally box takes a closer look.

Changes in Socialist and Capitalist Countries

In 1989 and 1990, the nations of Eastern Europe, which had been seized by the former Soviet Union at the end of World War II, overthrew their socialist regimes. These nations—including the former German Democratic Republic (East Germany), the Czech Republic, Slovakia, Hungary, Romania, and Bulgaria—are all moving toward capitalist market systems after decades of state-controlled economies. At the end of 1991, the Soviet Union itself formally dissolved, and many of its former republics introduced some free-market principles into their economies. Within a decade, three-fourths of former Soviet

THINKING GLOBALLY

Want Equality and Freedom? Try Denmark

Denmark is a small nation in northwestern Europe with about 5.5 million people. This country is a good example of the economic and political system called welfare capitalism, in which a market economy is mixed with broad government programs that provide for the welfare of all Danish people.

Most Danes consider life in their country to be very good. There is a high standard of living—Denmark's per-person GDP is $36,130, which lags a bit behind the figure of $45,592 for the United States. But Denmark has only 60 percent as much income inequality as we have in this country. Its unemployment rate for 2009 was 6.4 percent, lower than the 9.3 percent in the United States.

Low inequality and low unemployment are largely the result of government regulation of the economy. Taxes in Denmark are the highest in the world, with most people paying about 40 percent of their income in taxes and those earning over about $70,000 paying more than 50 percent. That's in addition to a sales tax of 25 percent on everything people buy. These high taxes increase economic equality (by taking more taxes from the rich and giving more benefits to the poor), and they also allow the government to fund the social

welfare programs that provide benefits to everyone. For example, every Danish citizen is entitled to government-funded schooling and

To enable men and women to work for income, the government of Denmark grants paid child-care leave to both fathers and mothers.

government-funded health care, and each worker receives at least five weeks of paid vacation leave each year. People who lose their jobs receive about 90 percent of their prior income from the government for up to four years.

Many people—especially the Danes themselves—feel that Denmark offers an ideal mix of political freedom (Danes have extensive political rights and elect their leaders) and economic security (all citizens benefit from extensive government services and programs).

WHAT DO YOU THINK?

1. What evidence of less income inequality might you expect to see in Denmark if you were to visit that country?

2. Would you be willing to pay most of your income in taxes if the government provided you with benefits such as schooling and health care? Why or why not?

3. Do you think most people in the United States would like to have our society become more like Denmark? Why or why not?

Sources: Fox (2007), OECD (2009), and United Nations Development Programme (2009).

government enterprises were partly or entirely in private hands (Montaigne, 2001).

There were many reasons for these sweeping changes. First, the capitalist economies far outproduced their socialist counterparts. The socialist economies were successful in achieving economic equality, but living standards were low compared with those of Western Europe. Second, Soviet socialism was heavy-handed, rigidly controlling the media and restricting individual freedoms. In other words, socialism did away with *economic* elites, as Karl Marx predicted, but as Max Weber foresaw, socialism increased the power of *political* elites.

So far, the market reforms in Eastern Europe are proceeding unevenly. Some nations (Czech Republic, Slovakia, Poland, and the Baltic states of Latvia, Estonia, and Lithuania) are doing relatively well. But other countries (Romania, Bulgaria, and the Russian Federation) have been buffeted by price increases and falling living standards. Officials hope that expanding production will gradually bring

a turnaround. However, the introduction of a market economy has brought with it an increase in economic inequality (Ignatius, 2008; World Bank, 2008).

A number of countries, primarily in South America, have recently been heading in a more socialist direction. In 2005, the people of Bolivia elected Evo Morales, a former farmer, union leader, and activist, as their new president, over a wealthy business leader who was educated in the United States. This election placed Bolivia in a group of South American nations—including Ecuador, Venezuela, Brazil, Chile, and Uruguay—that are moving toward more socialist economies. The reasons for the shift toward socialism vary from country to country, but the common element is economic inequality. In Bolivia, for example, the economy has grown in recent decades, but most of the benefits have gone to a wealthy business elite. By contrast, more than half the country's people remain very poor (Howden, 2005).

● Seeing Sociology
  in Everyday Life

Have you or someone in your family ever been a member of a labor union? What advantages or disadvantages did union membership provide?

○ Go to the Multimedia Library at **mysoclab.com** to see author John Macionis describe the changing nature of work

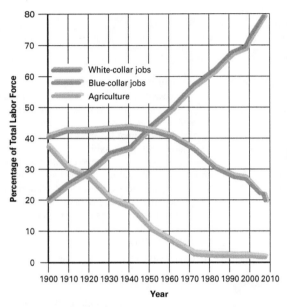

FIGURE 2   **The Changing Pattern of Work in the United States, 1900–2009**

Compared to a century ago, when the economy involved a larger share of factory and farm work, making a living in the United States now involves mostly white-collar service jobs.

Source: Estimates based on U.S. Department of Labor (2010).

Work in the Postindustrial U.S. Economy

Economic change is occurring not just in the socialist world but also in the United States. In 2009, a total of 138 million people in this country—58 percent of those aged sixteen and over—were working for income. A larger share of men (63 percent) than women (54 percent) had jobs, a gap that is holding steady over time. Among men, 57.3 percent of African Americans were employed, compared with 67.2 percent of whites, and 71.9 percent of Hispanics. Among women, 54.5 percent of African Americans were employed, compared with 55.9 percent of whites and 53.2 percent of Hispanics; 60.2 percent of Asian men and women were employed (U.S. Department of Labor, 2010).

The Changing Workplace

In 1900, roughly 40 percent of U.S. workers were farmers. In 2009, 1.6 percent were in agriculture. The family farm of yesterday has been replaced by *corporate agribusinesses*. Land is now more productive, but this change has caused painful adjustments across the country as a way of life is lost (Dudley, 2000). Figure 2 illustrates the shrinking role of the primary sector in the U.S. economy.

A century ago, industrialization swelled the ranks of blue-collar workers. By 1950, however, a white-collar revolution had moved most workers from factories into service occupations. By 2009, some 80 percent of the labor force worked in the service sector, and almost all new jobs were being created in this sector (U.S. Department of Labor, 2009).

Much service work—including sales, clerical positions, and work in hospitals and restaurants—pays much less than older factory jobs. This means that many jobs in the postindustrial era provide only a modest standard of living. Women and other minorities, as well as many young people just starting their working careers, are the most likely to have jobs doing low-paying service work (Kalleberg, Reskin, & Hudson, 2000; Greenhouse, 2006). ● Go to **mysoclab.com**

Labor Unions

The changing U.S. economy has seen a decline in *labor unions,* organizations that seek to improve wages and working conditions. During the Great Depression of the 1930s, union membership increased rapidly until it reached more than one-third of nonfarm workers by 1950. Union rolls peaked around 1970 at almost 25 million. Since then, membership has declined to about 12.3 percent of nonfarm workers, or some 15.3 million men and women. Looking more closely, 37.4 percent of government workers are members of unions, compared with just 7.2 percent of private (nongovernment) workers (Clawson & Clawson, 1999; U.S. Department of Labor, 2010).

The pattern of union decline holds in most other high-income countries, yet unions claim a far smaller share of workers in the United States than elsewhere. Union membership is around 18 percent in Japan, between 20 and 40 percent in much of Europe, and 29 percent in Canada, and it reaches a high of 71 percent in Sweden (Visser, 2006; OECD, 2010).

The widespread decline in union membership in the United States reflects the shrinking industrial sector of the economy. Newer service jobs—such as sales jobs at retailers like Walmart, described in the opening to this chapter—are unlikely to be unionized. Citing low wages and worker complaints, unions are trying to organize Walmart employees, so far without winning over a single store. The weak economy of the past few years has given unions a short-term boost. The Obama administration is supporting new laws that may make it easier for workers to form unions. But long-term gains probably depend on the ability of unions to adapt to the new global economy. Union members in the United States, used to seeing foreign workers as "the enemy," will have to build new international alliances (Rousseau, 2002; Dalmia, 2008; M. Allen, 2009).

Professions

All kinds of jobs today are called *professional;* there are professional tennis players, professional housecleaners, and even professional exterminators. As distinct from an *amateur* (from the Latin for "lover," meaning one who acts out of love for the activity itself), a professional performs some task to earn a living. But what exactly is a profession?

A **profession** is *a prestigious white-collar occupation that requires extensive formal education.* People performing this kind of work make a *profession,* or public declaration, of their willingness to work according to certain principles. Professions include the ministry, medicine, law, academia, and fields such as architecture, accountancy, and social work. An occupation is considered a profession to the extent that it demonstrates four basic characteristics (W. J. Goode, 1960; Ritzer & Walczak, 1990):

1. **Theoretical knowledge.** Professionals have a theoretical understanding of their field rather than mere technical training. Anyone can master first-aid skills, for example, but doctors have a theoretical understanding of human health. This means that although playing tennis, cleaning houses, and exterminating insects may be important, they do not really qualify as professions.

2. **Self-regulating practice.** The typical professional is self-employed, "in private practice" rather than working for a company. Professionals oversee their own work and observe a code of ethics.

3. **Authority over clients.** Because of their expertise, professionals are sought out by clients, who value their advice and follow their directions.

4. **Community orientation rather than self-interest.** The traditional professing of duty states an intention to serve the community rather than merely to seek income.

In almost all cases, professional work requires not just a college degree but a graduate degree. Not surprisingly, professions are well represented among the jobs beginning college students say they hope to get after graduation, as shown in Figure 3.

Many occupations that do not qualify as true professions nonetheless seek to *professionalize* their services. Claiming professional standing usually begins by renaming the work to suggest special, theoretical knowledge, moving the field away from its original, lesser reputation. Stockroom workers become "inventory supply managers," and exterminators are reborn as "insect control specialists."

Interested parties may also form a professional association that certifies their skills. The organization then licenses its members,

In a society such as ours, with so many different types of work, no one career attracts the interest of more than a small share of today's students.

Student Snapshot

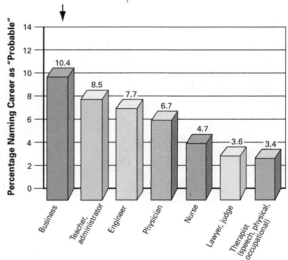

FIGURE 3 **The Careers Most Commonly Named as Probable by First-Year College Students, 2009**

Today's college students expect to enter careers that pay well and carry high prestige.

Source: Pryor et al. (2009).

writes a code of ethics, and emphasizes the work's importance in the community. To win public acceptance, a professional association may also establish schools or other training facilities and perhaps start a professional journal. Not all occupations try to claim professional status. Some *paraprofessionals,* including paralegals and medical technicians, have specialized skills but lack the extensive theoretical education required of full professionals.

Self-Employment

Self-employment—earning a living without being on the payroll of a large organization—was once common in the United States. About 80 percent of the labor force was self-employed in 1800, compared with just 7 percent of workers today (8.4 percent of men and 5.0 percent of women) (U.S. Department of Labor, 2010).

Lawyers, physicians, architects, and other professionals are well represented among the ranks of the self-employed in the United States. But most self-employed workers are small business owners, plumbers, farmers, carpenters, freelance writers and editors, artists, and long-distance truck drivers. In all, the self-employed are more likely to have blue-collar than white-collar jobs.

○ Seeing Sociology
in Everyday Life

Has the current recession affected you or members of your
family? Explain.

○

Go to the Multimedia Library at **mysoclab.com**
to view the video "Consequences of Poverty"

In the film *Up in the Air,* George Clooney plays the character Ryan Bingham, a
corporate "downsizer." In this role, Bingham travels around the country presiding over
layoffs and is paid by company executives who are too cowardly to fire people
themselves. In your opinion, what do companies owe their employees—just pay for
work performed, or is everyone entitled to broader job security?

Women own 28 percent of this nation's small businesses, and
the share is rising. The 6.5 million firms owned by U.S. women
employ almost 7 percent of the labor force and generate close to
$1 trillion in annual sales (U.S. Small Business Administration, 2006).

Unemployment and Underemployment

Every society has some level of unemployment. For one thing, few
young people entering the labor force find a job right away; workers
may leave their jobs to seek new work or to stay at home raising
children; others may be on strike or suffer from long-term illnesses;
and still others lack the skills to perform useful work.

But unemployment is not just an individual problem; it is also
caused by the economy. Jobs disappear as occupations become obsolete and companies change the way they operate. Since 1980, the 500
largest U.S. businesses eliminated more than 5 million jobs while
creating even more new ones.

Generally, companies downsize to become more competitive or
close down entirely in the face of foreign competition or economic
recession. During the recession that began in 2008 in the United
States, several million jobs were lost, with unemployment rising in
just about every part of the economy. Jobs have been lost not only by
blue-collar workers but also by white-collar workers who had typically
weathered downturns in the past (U.S. Department of Labor, 2010).

In 2008, just as the country was falling into recession,
7 million people over the age of sixteen were unemployed,
about 4.6 percent of the civilian labor force (U.S. Department of Labor, 2008b). But by the end of 2009, more than
15 million were unemployed, pushing the unemployment
rate to 10 percent. In some regions of the country, especially rural areas, unemployment rates are usually far
worse—about double the national average.

Figure 4 shows that unemployment among African
Americans (14.8 percent) is nearly twice the rate among
white people (8.5 percent). Among all categories of people,
unemployment is lower among whites than among African
Americans, although the gap between white and black
teenagers is especially large. For all categories of people, a
good way to reduce the risk of unemployment is to earn a
college degree: As the figure shows, the unemployment rate
for college graduates is around 4.5 percent—less than half
the national average.

Underemployment is also a problem for millions of
workers. In an era of corporate bankruptcy, the failure of
large banks, and downsizing by companies throughout the
U.S. economy, millions of workers—the lucky ones who
still have their jobs—have been left with lower salaries,
fewer benefits such as health insurance, and disappearing
pensions. Rising global competition, weaker worker organizations,
and economic recession have combined to allow many people to
keep their jobs only by agreeing to cutbacks in pay or to the loss of
other benefits (K. Clark, 2002; Gutierrez, 2007; McGeehan, 2009).

In addition, the government reports that more than 28 million people work part time, defined as less than thirty-five hours a week.
Although most say they are satisfied with this arrangement, at least one-
third claim that they want more work but cannot find it (U.S. Department of Labor, 2010). In all, as the country struggles to climb out of the
recent recession, it is likely that one in five workers is working less than
what is desired, is out of work and looking for a job, or is a "discouraged
worker" who has given up entirely. ○ **Go to mysoclab.com**

Workplace Diversity: Race
and Gender

In the past, white men were the mainstay of the U.S. labor force.
However, the nation's proportion of minorities is rising rapidly. The
African American population is increasing faster than the popula-
tion of non-Hispanic white people. The rate of increase in the Asian
American and Hispanic populations is even greater.

Such dramatic changes are likely to affect U.S. society in countless ways. Not only will more and more workers be women and

Can you think of advantages and disadvantages of being able to work almost anywhere? Do the benefits of the "anywhere office" outweigh the downsides?

The best strategy to reduce your risk of being without a job is to complete a college education.

minorities, but the workplace will have to develop programs and policies that meet the needs of a socially diverse workforce and also encourage everyone to work together effectively and respectfully. The Thinking About Diversity box on the next page takes a closer look at some of the issues involved in our changing workplace.

New Information Technology and Work

July 2, Ticonderoga, New York. The manager of the local hardware store scans the bar codes of a bagful of items. "The computer doesn't just total the costs," she explains. "It also keeps track of inventory, places orders with the warehouse, and decides which products to continue to sell and which to drop." "Sounds like what you used to do, Maureen," I respond with a smile. "Yep," she nods, with no smile at all.

Another workplace issue is the increasing role of computers and other new information technology. The Information Revolution is changing what people do in a number of ways (Rule & Brantley, 1992; Vallas & Beck, 1996):

1. **Computers are deskilling labor.** Just as industrial machines replaced the master craftsworkers of an earlier era, computers now threaten the skills of managers. More business operations are based not on executive decisions but on computer modeling. In other words, a machine decides whether to place an order, stock a dress in a certain size and color, or approve a loan application.

2. **Computers are making work more abstract.** Most industrial workers have a hands-on relationship with their product. Postindustrial workers use symbols to perform abstract tasks, such as making a company more profitable or making software more user-friendly.

3. **Computers limit workplace interaction.** Spending time at computer terminals, workers become isolated from one another.

4. **Computers increase employers' control of workers.** Computers allow supervisors to check employees' output continuously, whether they work at keyboard terminals or on assembly lines.

5. **Computers allow companies to relocate work.** Because computer technology allows information to flow almost anywhere instantly, the symbolic work in today's economy may not take place where we might think. We have all had the experience of calling a business (for instance, a hotel or bookstore) located in our own town only to find out that we are talking to a person at a computer workstation thousands of miles away. Computer

Diversity Snapshot

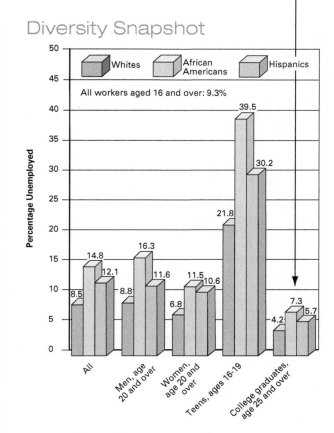

FIGURE 4 **Official U.S. Unemployment Rates for Various Categories of Adults, 2009**

Although college graduates have a low risk of unemployment, race is related to unemployment for all categories of people.

Source: U.S. Department of Labor (2010).

technology provides the means to outsource many jobs—especially service work—to other places where wages may be lower.

Perhaps in the wake of widespread failures on Wall Street, there will be a trend away from allowing computers to manage risk, putting responsibility for business decisions back in the hands of people (Kivant, 2008). Or perhaps both computers and people have flaws that will always prevent us from living in a perfect world. But the rapidly increasing reliance on computers in business reminds us that new technology is never socially neutral. It changes the relationships between people in the workplace, shapes the way we work, and often

○ Making the Grade

Corporation are one example of the formal organizations discussed in "Groups and Organizations."

THINKING ABOUT DIVERSITY: RACE, CLASS, & GENDER

Twenty-First-Century Diversity: Changes in the Workplace

An upward trend in the U.S. minority population is changing the workplace. As the figure shows, the number of non-Hispanic white men in the U.S. labor force will rise by less than 1 percent between 2010 and 2018, but the number of African American men will increase by 9 percent, the number of Hispanic men will increase by 25 percent, and the number of Asian men will increase by 22 percent.

Among non-Hispanic white women, the projected rise is less than 1 percent; among African American women, 10 percent; and among Asian women, 24 percent. Hispanic women will show the greatest gains, estimated at 30 percent.

Within a decade, non-Hispanic white men will represent 34 percent of all workers, and that figure will continue to drop. As a result, companies that welcome social diversity will tap the largest pool of talent and enjoy a competitive advantage leading to higher profits (Graybow, 2007; Toossi, 2007; Harford, 2008; U.S. Department of Labor, 2009).

Welcoming social diversity means, first, recruiting talented workers of both sexes and all racial and cultural backgrounds. But developing the potential of all employees requires meeting the needs of women and other minorities, which may not be the same as those of white men. For example, child care at the workplace is a big issue for working mothers with small children.

Second, businesses must develop effective ways to deal with tension that arises from social differences. They will have to work harder to ensure that workers are treated equally and respectfully, which means having zero tolerance for racial or sexual harassment.

Third, companies will have to rethink current promotion practices. At present, 72 percent of the directors of *Fortune* 100 companies are white men; 28 percent are women or other minorities (Executive Leadership Council, 2008).

In a survey of U.S. companies, the U.S. Equal Employment Opportunity Commission (2009) confirmed that non-Hispanic white men, who make up 33 percent of adults aged twenty-five to sixty-four, hold 53 percent of management jobs; the comparable figures are 34 and 29 percent, respectively, for non-Hispanic white women, 12 and 7 percent for non-Hispanic African Americans, and 14 and 6 percent for Hispanics.

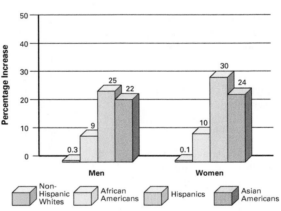

Projected Increase in the Number of People in the U.S. Labor Force, 2010–2018

Looking ahead, the share of minorities in the U.S. labor force will increase much faster than the share of white men and women.

Source: U.S. Department of Labor (2009).

WHAT DO YOU THINK?

1. What underlying factors are increasing the social diversity of the U.S. workplace?

2. In what specific ways do you think businesses should support minority workers?

3. In what other settings (such as schools) is social diversity becoming more important? Why?

---

alters the balance of power between employers and employees. Understandably, then, people welcome some aspects of the Information Revolution and oppose others.

Corporations

At the core of today's capitalist economy is the **corporation,** *an organization with a legal existence, including rights and liabilities, separate from that of its members.* Incorporating makes an organization a legal entity, able to enter into contracts and own property. Of the more than 30 million businesses in the United States, 6 million are incorporated (U.S. Census Bureau, 2009). Incorporating protects the wealth of owners from lawsuits that result from business debts or harm to consumers; it can also mean a lower tax rate on the company's profits.

Economic Concentration

Most U.S. corporations are small, with assets of less than $500,000, so it is the largest corporations that dominate our nation's economy. In 2006, the government listed 2,568 corporations with assets exceeding $2.5 billion, representing 80 percent of all corporate assets (Internal Revenue Service, 2009).

The largest U.S. corporation, measured in terms of sales, is Exxon Mobil, with 2009 revenue of more than $440 billion. This is more money than the combined tax revenues collected by forty-three states.

Seeing Sociology in Everyday Life

Have you ever had a job like that shown in the photo below? What were the advantages and disadvantages of such work?

Second in line is Walmart, with annual sales of more than $400 billion.

Conglomerates and Corporate Linkages

Economic concentration creates *conglomerates,* giant corporations composed of many smaller corporations. Conglomerates form as corporations enter new markets, spin off new companies, or merge with other companies. For example, PepsiCo is a conglomerate that includes Pepsi-Cola, Frito-Lay, Gatorade, Tropicana, and Quaker.

Many conglomerates are linked because they own each other's stock, the result being worldwide corporate alliances of staggering size. Until 2009, General Motors, for example, owned Opel (Germany), Vauxhall (Great Britain), Saab (Sweden), and a share of Daewoo (South Korea) and had partnerships with Suzuki and Toyota (Japan). Similarly, Ford owned Volvo (Sweden) and still maintains a small interest in Aston Martin (Great Britain) and Mazda (Japan).

Corporations are also linked through *interlocking directorates,* networks of people who serve as directors of many corporations (Weidenbaum, 1995; Kono et al., 1998). These boardroom connections provide access to valuable information about other companies' products and marketing strategies. While perfectly legal, such linkages encourage illegal activity, such as price fixing, as companies share information about their pricing policies.

Alamy Images

In today's corporate world, computers are changing the nature of work just as factories did more than a century ago. In what ways is computer-based work different from factory work? In what ways do you think it is very much the same?

Corporations: Are They Competitive?

According to the capitalist model, businesses operate independently in a competitive market. But in light of the extensive linkages that exist between them, it is obvious that large corporations do not operate independently. Also, a few large corporations dominate many markets, so they are not truly competitive.

Federal law forbids any company from establishing a **monopoly,** *domination of a market by a single producer,* because with no competition, such a company could simply charge whatever is wanted for its products. But **oligopoly,** *domination of a market by a few producers,* is both legal and common. Oligopoly arises because the huge investment needed to enter a major market, such as the auto industry, is beyond the reach of all but the biggest companies. In addition, true competition involves risk, which big business tries to avoid.

The federal government seeks to regulate corporations in order to protect the public interest. Yet as corporate scandals have shown—most recently, involving the housing mortgage business and the collapse of so many banks—regulation is often too little too late, resulting in harm to millions of people. The U.S. government is also the

corporate world's single biggest customer, and in 2008 and 2009, it stepped in to support many struggling corporations with multibillion-dollar bailout programs. Especially during tough economic times, the public tends to support a greater role for the government in the economy (Sachs, 2009).

Corporations and the Global Economy

Corporations have grown so large that they now account for most of the world's economic output. The biggest corporations are based in the United States, Japan, and Western Europe, but their marketplace is the entire world. Many large companies such as McDonald's and the chipmaker Intel earn most of their money outside the United States.

Global corporations know that poor countries contain most of the world's people and resources. In addition, labor costs there are attractively low: A manufacturing worker in Mexico, who earns about $2.88 an hour, labors for more than a week to earn about what a worker in Japan (who averages about $19.68 an hour) or the United States ($24.03 an hour) earns in a single day (U.S. Department of Labor, 2009).

The impact of multinational corporations on low-income countries is controversial. Modernization theorists claim that multinational corporations, by unleashing the great productivity of capitalism, raise living standards in poor nations, offering tax revenues, capital investment, new jobs, and advanced technology that together accelerate economic growth (Berger, 1986; Firebaugh & Beck, 1994; Firebaugh & Sandu, 1998).

CONTROVERSY & DEBATE

The Market: Does the "Invisible Hand" Look Out for Us or Pick Our Pockets?

The market or government planning? Governments rely on one or the other to determine the products and services companies will produce and what people will consume. So important is this question that the answer has much to do with how nations define themselves, choose their allies, and identify their enemies.

Historically, U.S. society has relied on the "invisible hand" of the market to make economic decisions. Market dynamics move prices up or down according to the supply of products and buyer demand. The market thus links the efforts of countless people, each of whom—to restate Adam Smith's insight—is motivated only by self-interest. Defenders of the market system—including the economists Milton Friedman and Rose Friedman (1980)—claim that a more or less freely operating market system is the key to this country's high standard of living.

But others point to the contributions government makes to the U.S. economy. First, government must step in to carry out tasks that no private company could do as well, such as defending the country against enemies abroad or terrorists at home. Government (in partnership with private companies) also plays a key role in building and maintaining public projects such as roads, utilities, schools, libraries, and museums.

The Friedmans counter that whatever the task, government usually ends up being very inefficient. They claim that for most people, the least satisfying goods and services available today—public schools, the postal service, and passenger railroad service—are government-operated. The products we enjoy most—household appliances, computers and other electronics, fashionable clothes—are products of the market. The Friedmans and other supporters of free markets believe that minimal state regulation serves the public interest best.

But supporters of government intervention in the economy make other arguments. First, they claim that the market has incentives to produce only what is profitable. Few private companies set out to meet the needs of poor people because by definition, poor people have little money to spend.

Second, the market has certain self-destructive tendencies that only the government can curb. In 1890, for example, the government passed the Sherman Antitrust Act to break up the monopolies that controlled the nation's oil and steel production. In the decades since then—and especially after President Franklin Roosevelt's New Deal of the 1930s—government has taken a strong regulatory role to control inflation (by setting interest rates), enhance the well-being of workers (by imposing workplace safety standards), and benefit consumers (by setting standards for product quality). Especially after the failure of the market to prevent a serious economic downturn in 2008, the public voiced support

for a larger government presence in the national economy.

Third, because the market magnifies social inequality, the government must step in on the side of social justice. Since capitalist economies concentrate income and wealth in the hands of a few, it is necessary for government to tax the rich at a higher rate to ensure that wealth reaches more of the population.

Does the market's "invisible hand" look out for us or pick our pockets? Although most people in the United States favor a free market, they also support government intervention that benefits the public. In recent years, public confidence in corporations has fallen, and confidence in the federal government has gone up. Government's job is not only to ensure national security but also to maintain economic stability. The Obama administration claims that the government needs to expand its efforts to put people to work by, for example, repairing the nation's roads and bridges as well as developing new sources of energy.

During the 1980s, support for the free market was strong; today, we see a swing back to support for a larger government role in the economy. In the decades to come, we should expect to see people in the United States, and also around the world, continuing to debate the best balance of market forces and government decision making.

WHAT DO YOU THINK?

1. Do you agree or disagree with the statement that "the government is best that governs least"? Why?

2. Do you think people support less government control of the economy in good times and more government control in bad times? Why or why not?

3. In what ways has the Obama administration expanded the role of government in the U.S. economy? What about the auto industry? The regulation of Wall Street?

Rob Colvin\Getty Images, Inc - Artville LLC

To what extent do you think government regulation of the economy is necessary?

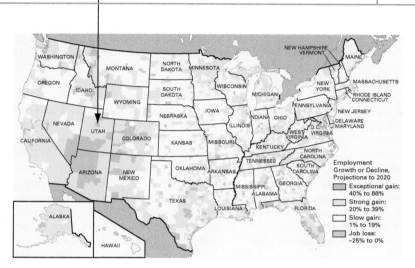

Leon Acosta, age 23 and just out of college, has relocated to Park City, Utah, where he has found a good job and lots of friends his own age.

Explore dominant industries in your local community and in counties across the United States on mysoclab.com

Seeing Ourselves

NATIONAL MAP 1

Where the Jobs Will Be: Projections to 2020

The economic prospects for people living in counties across the United States are not the same. Gains in jobs are projected to be strong for most areas in the Western states as well as for Florida; some areas in the East and the Midwest are also expected to gain jobs. But job growth will be slow at best in the midsection of the country, with a number of counties even projected to lose jobs in the years to come.

Explore on mysoclab.com

Source: Woods & Poole Economics, Washington, D.C. Copyright © 2007.

Employment
Growth or Decline,
Projections to 2020

- Exceptional gain: 40% to 88%
- Strong gain: 20% to 39%
- Slow gain: 1% to 19%
- Job loss: −25% to 0%

Dependency theorists respond that multinationals in fact make global inequality worse by blocking the development of local industries and by pushing poor countries to produce goods for export rather than food and other products for local people. From this standpoint, multinationals make poor nations increasingly dependent on rich nations (Wallerstein, 1979; Dixon & Boswell, 1996; Kentor, 1998).

In short, modernization theory praises the market as the key to progress and affluence for all the world's people. Dependency theory takes a different position, calling for replacing markets with government-based economic policies. The Controversy & Debate box takes a closer look at the issue of market versus government economies.

The Economy: Looking Ahead

Social institutions are a society's ways of meeting people's needs. But as we have seen, the U.S. economy only partly succeeds in this mission. As the years go by, our economy experiences alternating periods of expansion and recession. And in both good times and bad, our economy provides for some people much better than for others.

One important trend that underlies change in the economy is the Information Revolution. First, the share of the U.S. labor force engaged in manufacturing is less than half of what it was in 1960; service work, especially computer-related jobs, makes up the difference. For industrial workers, the postindustrial economy has brought unemployment and declining wages. Our society must face up to the challenge of providing millions of men and women with the language and computer skills they need to succeed in the modern economy. Yet in recent years, millions of people in "good" service jobs have found themselves out of work. In addition, there are regional differences in the economic outlook: National Map 1 shows which

regions are projected to gain jobs and which are expected to lose them by the year 2020.

A second transformation of recent years is the expansion of the global economy. Two centuries ago, the ups and downs people experienced reflected events and trends in their own town. One century ago, communities were economically linked so that one town's prosperity depended on producing goods demanded by people elsewhere in the country. Today, we have to look beyond the national economy because, for example, the historical rise in the cost of gasoline at our local gas station has as much to do with increasing demand for oil around the world, especially in India and China. As both producers and consumers, we are now subject to factors and forces that are both distant and unseen.

Finally, analysts around the world are rethinking conventional economic models. The global economy shows that socialism is less productive than capitalism, one important reason behind the collapse of socialist regimes in Eastern Europe and the Soviet Union. But capitalism has its own problems, including high levels of inequality and a steady stream of corporate scandal—two important reasons that the economy now operates with significant government regulation.

What will be the long-term effects of all these changes? Two conclusions seem certain. First, the economic future of the United States and other nations will be played out in a global arena. The new postindustrial economy in the United States has emerged as more industrial production has moved to other nations. Second, it is imperative that we address the urgent challenges of global inequality and population increase. Whether the world reduces or enlarges the gap between rich and poor societies may well steer our planet toward peace or war.

Politics: Historical Overview

There is a close link between economics and **politics** (also known as the "polity"), *the social institution that distributes power, sets a society's goals, and makes decisions.* Early in the twentieth century, Max Weber (1978, orig. 1921) defined **power** as *the ability to achieve desired ends despite resistance from others.* The use of power is the business of **government,** *a formal organization that directs the political life of a society.* Governments typically claim to help people, but at the same time, governments demand that people obey the rules. Yet, as Weber noted, most governments do not openly threaten their people. Most of the time, people respect (or at least accept) their society's political system.

No government, Weber explained, is likely to keep its power for very long if compliance comes only from the threat of brute force, because there could never be enough police to watch everyone—and who would watch the police? Every government therefore tries to make itself seem legitimate in the eyes of the public.

This brings us to the concept of **authority,** *power that people perceive as legitimate rather than coercive.* A society's source of authority depends on its economy. According to Weber, preindustrial societies rely on *traditional authority,* power legitimized by respect for long-established cultural patterns. Woven into a society's collective memory, traditional authority may seem almost sacred. Chinese emperors in centuries past were legitimized by tradition, as were the nobles in medieval Europe.

Traditional authority declines as societies industrialize. For example, royal families still exist in ten European nations, but the democratic cultures of countries such as the United Kingdom, Sweden, and Denmark have shifted power to commoners elected to office. Weber explained that the expansion of rational bureaucracy is the modern foundation of authority. *Rational-legal authority* (sometimes called *bureaucratic authority*) is power legitimized by rationally enacted law.

Traditional authority is tied to family; rational-legal authority flows from offices in governments. A traditional monarch passes power on to heirs; a modern president takes office and gives up power according to law.

Weber described one additional type of authority that has surfaced throughout history. *Charismatic authority* is power legitimized by

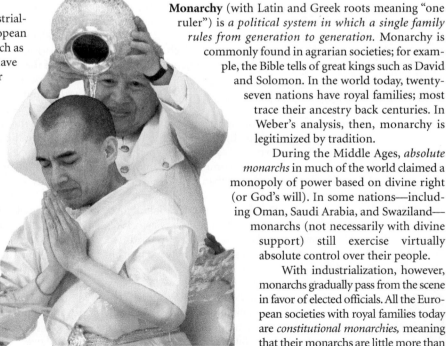

Monarchy is linked to both religion and family. In 2004, the coronation ceremony of Cambodia's first new king in fifty years, Norodom Sihamoni, included a religious ritual performed by his father.

Chor Sokunthea/Reuters\CORBIS- NY

the extraordinary personal qualities—the *charisma*—of a leader. Unlike its traditional and rational-legal counterparts, charismatic authority depends less on a person's ancestry or office and more on personality. Followers see in charismatic leaders some special, perhaps even divine, power. Examples of charismatic leaders include Jesus of Nazareth; Nazi Germany's Adolf Hitler; India's liberator, Mahatma Gandhi; and civil rights leader Martin Luther King Jr. All charismatic leaders aim to radically transform society, which explains why charismatics are almost always controversial and why few of them die of old age.

Because charismatic authority flows from a single individual, the leader's death creates a crisis. The survival of a charismatic movement, Weber explained, requires the **routinization of charisma:** *the transformation of charismatic authority into some combination of traditional and bureaucratic authority.* After the death of Jesus, for example, followers institutionalized his teachings in a church, built on tradition and bureaucracy. Routinized in this way, Christianity has lasted 2,000 years.

Politics in Global Perspective

The world's political systems differ in countless ways. Generally, however, they fall into four categories: monarchy, democracy, authoritarianism, and totalitarianism.

Monarchy

Monarchy (with Latin and Greek roots meaning "one ruler") is *a political system in which a single family rules from generation to generation.* Monarchy is commonly found in agrarian societies; for example, the Bible tells of great kings such as David and Solomon. In the world today, twenty-seven nations have royal families; most trace their ancestry back centuries. In Weber's analysis, then, monarchy is legitimized by tradition.

During the Middle Ages, *absolute monarchs* in much of the world claimed a monopoly of power based on divine right (or God's will). In some nations—including Oman, Saudi Arabia, and Swaziland—monarchs (not necessarily with divine support) still exercise virtually absolute control over their people.

With industrialization, however, monarchs gradually pass from the scene in favor of elected officials. All the European societies with royal families today are *constitutional monarchies,* meaning that their monarchs are little more than

Go to the Multimedia Library at mysoclab.com to view the ABC/*Nightline* video "Old-Fashioned Democracy"

symbolic heads of state; actual governing is the responsibility of elected officials, led by a prime minister and guided by a constitution. In these countries, nobility *reigns*, but elected officials actually *rule*.

Democracy

The historical trend throughout most of the world has been toward **democracy,** *a political system that gives power to the people as a whole.* Because it is unrealistic to expect all citizens to be involved in governing, our system is in fact a *representative democracy,* which puts authority in the hands of leaders who from time to time compete for office in elections.

Most high-income countries of the world, including those that still have royal families, claim to be democratic. Industrialization and democracy go together because both require a literate populace. Also, with industrialization, the traditional legitimization of power in a monarchy gives way to rational-legal authority. Thus democracy and rational-legal authority are linked just like monarchy and traditional authority.

But high-income countries such as the United States are not truly democratic, for two reasons. First, there is the problem of bureaucracy. The U.S. federal government has 2.7 million regular employees and several million more paid for by special funding. Add to this the 1.45 million uniformed service personnel and 64,000 legislative and judicial branch personnel—more than 4 million workers in all. Another 19.7 million people work in 89,500 local governments across the country. Most of the officials who run the government are never elected by anyone and do not have to answer directly to the people.

The second problem involves economic inequality: Rich people have far more political power than poor people. Most of our political leaders have been wealthy men and women, and in politics, "money talks." Given the even greater resources of billion-dollar corporations, how well does our "democratic" system listen to the voices of "average people"? ● Go to mysoclab.com

Still, democratic nations do provide many rights and freedoms. Global Map 3 on the next page shows one assessment of political freedom around the world. According to Freedom House, an organization that tracks political trends, eighty-nine of the world's nations (with 46 percent of the global population) were "free," respecting many civil liberties, in 2009. This represents a gain for democracy: Just eighty-five nations were free a decade earlier (Freedom House, 2010).

Authoritarianism

Some governments prevent their people from having any voice in politics. **Authoritarianism** is *a political system that denies the people participation in government.* An authoritarian government is indifferent to people's needs and offers them no voice in selecting leaders. The absolute monarchies in Saudi Arabia and Oman are authoritarian, as is the military junta in Ethiopia.

Totalitarianism

> **October 30, Beijing, China.** Several U.S. students are sitting around a computer in the lounge of a Chinese university dormitory. They are taking turns running Internet searches on keywords such as "democracy" and "Amnesty International." They soon realize that China's government filters the results of Internet searches, permitting only officially approved sites to appear. One Chinese student who

In early 2010, Google users placed flowers and candles outside the company's headquarters in Beijing after government leaders demanded that the Web giant accept state censorship. Rather than comply with government demands, Google chose to close down its operations within China, although they continued to operate in Hong Kong. If you were a company leader, would you support this principled action or would you agree to state censorship in order to gain access to the vast Chinese market?

Economics and Politics

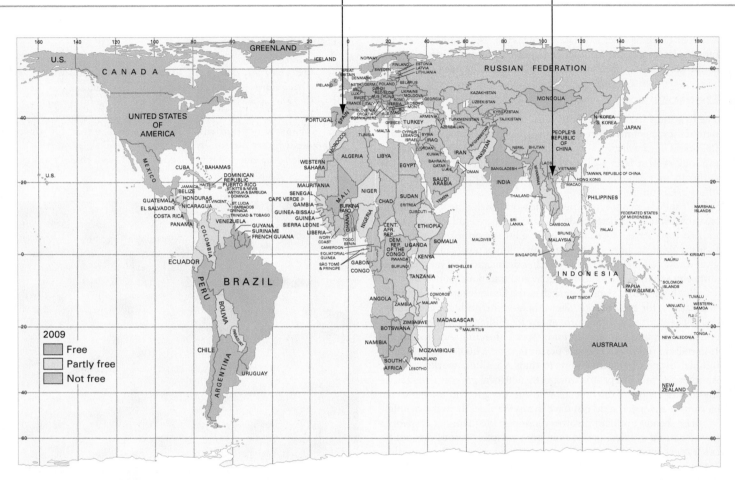

2009
- Free
- Partly free
- Not free

Window on the World

GLOBAL MAP 3   **Political Freedom in Global Perspective**

In 2009, a total of 89 of the world's 194 nations at that time, containing 46 percent of all people, were politically "free"; that is, they offered their citizens extensive political rights and civil liberties. Another 58 countries, which included 20 percent of the world's people, were "partly free," with more limited rights and liberties. The remaining 47 nations, home to 34 percent of humanity, fall into the category of "not free." In these countries, government sharply restricts individual initiative. While there have been some setbacks in recent years, between 1989 and 2009, democracy made significant gains, largely in Latin America and Eastern Europe. In Asia, India (containing 1.1 billion people) returned to the "free" category in 1999. In 2000, Mexico joined the ranks of nations considered "free" for the first time.

Source: Freedom House (2010).

is watching points out that things could be worse—in North Korea, she explains, most students have no access to computers at all.

The most intensely controlled political form is **totalitarianism,** *a highly centralized political system that extensively regulates people's lives.* Totalitarianism emerged in the twentieth century as governments gained the ability to rigidly control their populations.

The Vietnamese government closely monitors the activities of all its citizens. Similarly, the government of North Korea uses surveillance equipment and powerful computers to control its people by collecting and storing information about them.

Although some totalitarian governments claim to represent the will of the people, most seek to bend people to the will of the government.

As the term "totalitarian" implies, such governments have a *total* concentration of power, allowing no organized opposition. Denying the people the right to assemble and controlling access to information, these governments create an atmosphere of isolation and fear. In the former Soviet Union, for example, most citizens had no access to telephone directories, copiers, fax machines, or accurate city maps.

Socialization in totalitarian societies is highly political, seeking obedience and commitment to the system. In North Korea, one of the world's strictest totalitarian states, pictures of leaders and political messages are everywhere, reminding citizens that they owe total allegiance to the state. Government-controlled schools and mass media present only official versions of events.

Totalitarian governments span the political spectrum from fascist (including Nazi Germany) to communist (such as North Korea). In all cases, however, one party claims total control of the society and permits no opposition.

A Global Political System?

Is globalization changing politics in the same way that it is changing the economy? On one level, the answer is no. Although most of today's economic activity is international, the world remains divided into nation-states just as it has been for centuries. The United Nations (founded in 1945) was a small step toward global government, but its political role in world affairs has been limited.

On another level, however, politics has become a global process. For some analysts, multinational corporations represent a new political order because of their enormous power to shape events throughout the world. In other words, politics is dissolving into business as corporations grow larger than governments.

Also, the Information Revolution has moved national politics onto the world stage. With e-mail, text messaging, and cell phones everywhere, few countries can conduct their political affairs in complete privacy.

Finally, several thousand *nongovernmental organizations* (NGOs) seek to advance global issues, such as human rights (Amnesty International) and environmental protection (Greenpeace). NGOs will continue to play a key role in expanding the global political culture.

In sum, just as individual nations are losing control of their own economies, governments cannot fully manage the political events occurring within their borders.

Politics in the United States

After fighting a war against Great Britain to gain political independence, the United States replaced the British monarchy with a representative democracy. Our nation's political development reflects its cultural history as well as its capitalist economy.

U.S. Culture and the Rise of the Welfare State

The political culture of the United States can be summed up in one word: individualism. This emphasis is found in the Bill of Rights, which guarantees freedom from undue government interference. It was this individualism that the nineteenth-century poet and philosopher Ralph Waldo Emerson had in mind when he said, "The government that governs best is the government that governs least."

But most people stop short of Emerson's position, believing that government is necessary to defend the country, operate highway systems and schools, maintain law and order, and help people in need. To accomplish these things, the United States has developed a complex **welfare state**, *a system of government agencies and programs that provides benefits to the population.* Government benefits begin even before birth (through prenatal nutrition programs) and continue into old age (through Social Security and Medicare). Some programs are especially important to the poor, who are not well served by our capitalist economic system; but students, farmers, homeowners, small business operators, veterans, performing artists, and even executives of giant corporations get various subsidies and supports. In fact, a majority of U.S. adults looks to government for at least part of their income.

Today's welfare state is the result of a gradual increase in the size and scope of government. In 1789, when the presence of the federal government amounted to little more than a flag in most communities, the entire federal budget was a mere $4.5 million ($1.50 for every person in the nation). Since then, it has steadily risen, reaching $3.6 trillion in 2010 ($11,697 for every person in the country).

Similarly, when our nation was founded, one government employee served every 1,800 citizens. Today, about one in six people in the United States is a government employee—more than are engaged in manufacturing (U.S. Census Bureau, 2009; U.S. Bureau of Labor Statistics, 2010).

Despite this growth, the U.S. welfare state is still smaller than those of many other high-income nations. Figure 5 shows that government is larger in most of Europe, especially in Scandinavian countries such as Denmark and Sweden.

The Political Spectrum

Who supports a bigger welfare state? Who wants to cut it back? Answers to such questions reveal attitudes that form the *political spectrum,* which ranges from the extremely liberal on the left to the extremely conservative on the right. In the United States, about one-fourth of adults fall on the liberal or "left" side, and one-third say they are conservative, placing themselves on the political "right." The remaining 40 percent claim to be moderates, in the political "middle" (NORC, 2009:189).

Seeing Sociology
in Everyday Life

Where do you fall on the political spectrum? On social issues,
are you more liberal or more conservative? What about on
economic issues?

Global Snapshot

In Denmark, people look to government for a
much greater share of goods and services than
they do in the United States.

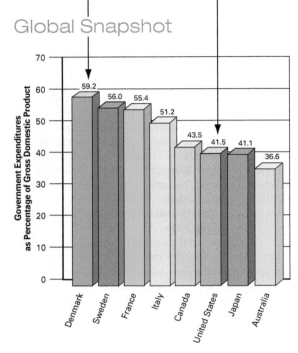

FIGURE 5 **The Size of Government, 2010**

Government activity accounts for a smaller share of economic output in
the United States than in other high-income countries.

Source: OECD (2010).

The political spectrum helps us understand the ways people think about the economy. *Economic issues* focus on economic inequality. On economic issues, liberals support extensive government regulation of the economy and a larger welfare state in order to reduce income inequality. Economic conservatives want to limit the hand of government in the economy and allow market forces more freedom.

The political spectrum can also be applied to *social issues,* which are moral questions about how people ought to live. Social issues include abortion, the death penalty, gay rights, and the treatment of minorities. Social liberals support equal rights and opportunities for all categories of people, view abortion as a matter of individual choice, and oppose the death penalty because it has been unfairly applied to minorities. The "family values" agenda of social conservatives supports traditional gender roles and opposes gay marriage, affirmative action, and other "special programs" for minorities. Social conservatives condemn abortion as morally wrong and support the death penalty as a just response to the most serious crimes.

Of the two major political parties in the United States, the Republican party is more conservative on both economic and social issues and the Democratic party is more liberal. But both parties favor big government when it advances their particular aims. During the 2008 presidential campaign, for example, Republican John McCain supported bigger government in the form of a stronger military; Democrat Barack Obama also favored enlarging government to expand the social "safety net" that would provide, for example, health care coverage for all.

Most people mix conservative and liberal attitudes. With wealth to protect, many higher-income people hold conservative views on economic issues. Yet their extensive schooling and secure social standing lead most to be social liberals. Lower-income people show the opposite pattern, with most being liberal on economic issues but supporting a socially conservative agenda (NORC, 2007; Ohlemacher, 2008). African Americans, both rich and poor, tend to be liberal (especially on economic issues) and for half a century have voted Democratic (95 percent cast ballots for the Democratic candidate, Barack Obama, in 2008). Historically, Latinos, Asian Americans, and Jews have also supported the Democratic party (Kohut, 2008).

Women tend to be somewhat more liberal than men. Among U.S. adults, more women lean toward the Democratic party, while more men vote for Republican candidates. In 2008, for example, 56 percent of women but just 49 percent of men voted for Barack Obama. Figure 6 shows how this pattern has changed over time among college students. Although there have been shifts in student attitudes—to the right in the 1970s and to the left beginning in the mid-1990s—college women have remained consistently more liberal than college men (Astin et al., 2002; Sax et al., 2003; NORC, 2007; Pryor et al., 2007).

Party Identification

Because many people hold mixed political attitudes, with liberal views on some issues and conservative stands on others, party identification in this country is weak. Surveys show that about 49 percent favor the Democratic party and about 33 percent the Republican party, yet just 19 percent claim to be "strong Democrats" and 10 percent to be "strong Republicans." About 16 percent say they are "independent" (NORC, 2009:179). This lack of strong party identification is one reason each of the two major parties gains or loses power from election to election. Democrats held the White House in 1996 and gained ground in Congress in 1996, 1998, and 2000. In 2002 and 2004, the tide turned as Republicans made gains in Congress and kept control of the White House. In 2006, the tide turned again, with Democrats gaining control of Congress and winning the White House in 2008. In special elections in 2009 and 2010, Republicans were picking up seats again.

Go to the Multimedia Library at
mysoclab.com to view the video
"Lobbying and Special Interest Groups"

Read "Is Congress Really for Sale?"
by Paul Burstein on **mysoclab.com**

Lower-income people have more pressing financial needs, and so they tend to focus on economic issues, such as job wages and benefits. Higher-income people, by conrast, provide support for many social issues, such as animal rights.

There is also a rural-urban divide in U.S. politics. People in urban areas typically vote Democratic, and those in rural areas vote Republican. National Map 2 shows the county-by-county results for the 2008 presidential election.

Special-Interest Groups

For years, a debate has raged across the United States about the private ownership of firearms. Organizations such as the Brady Campaign to Prevent Gun Violence support stricter gun-control laws; other organizations, including the National Rifle Association, strongly oppose such measures. Each is an example of a *special-interest group,* people organized to address some economic or social issue. Special-interest groups, which include associations of older adults, farmers, fireworks producers, and environmentalists, are strong in nations where political parties tend to be weak. Many special-interest groups employ *lobbyists* to support their political goals. Washington, D.C., is home to about 14,000 lobbyists (Center for Responsive Politics, 2010). Go to **mysoclab.com**

Political action committees (PACs) are formed by special-interest groups to raise and spend money in support of political aims. PACs channel most of their funds directly to candidates likely to support their interests. Since they were created in the 1970s, the number of PACs has grown rapidly to more than 5,200 (Federal Election Commission, 2009).

Because of the rising costs of campaigns, most candidates eagerly accept financial support from PACs. In the 2008 congressional elections, 27 percent of all campaign funding came from PACs, and senators who were seeking reelection received, on average, $2 million each in PAC contributions. Supporters maintain that PACs represent the interests of a vast assortment of businesses, unions, and church groups, thereby increasing political participation. Critics counter that organizations supplying cash to politicians expect to be treated favorably in return, so that in effect PACs try to buy political influence ("Abramoff Effect," 2006; Federal Election Commission, 2009). Read on **mysoclab.com**

In 2008, the candidates for the U.S. presidency spent more than $1 billion on their campaigns, and another $1.4 billion was spent by congressional candidates and people running for all other political offices. Does having the most money matter? The answer is yes: In 94 percent of the congressional races, the candidate with the most money ended up winning the election. Concerns about the power of money led to much discussion of campaign financing. In 2002, Congress passed a modest reform, limiting the amount of unregulated money that candidates can collect. Despite this change, both presidential races since then set new records for campaign spending (Center for Responsive Politics, 2009). And in 2010, the Supreme Court rejected limits on the election spending of corporations, unions, and other large organizations (Liptak, 2010).

● Seeing Sociology
   in Everyday Life

As Figure 6 suggests, college students have always been more
liberal than the population as a whole.
Why do you think that almost half of today's young people do not
vote? Have you registered to vote?

Go to the Multimedia Library at **mysoclab.com**
to view the video "Democracy: Those Who Don't
Participate"

Student Snapshot

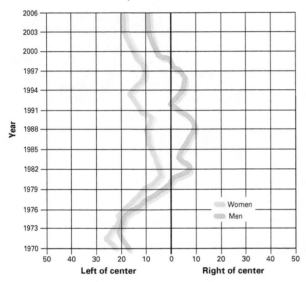

FIGURE 6   **Left-Right Political Identification of College
Students, 1970–2006**

Student attitudes moved to the right after 1970 and shifted left in the
late 1990s. College women tend to be more liberal than college men.

Sources: Astin et al. (2002), Sax et al. (2003), and Pryor et al. (2007).

Voter Apathy

A disturbing fact of U.S. political life is that many people in this country do not vote. In fact, U.S. citizens are less likely to vote today than
they were a century ago. In the 2000 presidential election, which was
decided by a few hundred votes, only half the registered voters went
to the polls. In 2008, participation rose to 63 percent, which was the
highest turnout since 1960. But this turnout is still lower than in
almost all other high-income countries (Center for the Study of the
American Electorate, 2009).

Who is and who is not likely to vote? Research shows that women
are slightly more likely than men to cast a ballot. People over sixty-
five are much more likely to vote than college-age adults (almost half
of whom have not even registered). Non-Hispanic whites are more
likely to vote (66 percent voted in 2008) than African Americans (65
percent in 2008, up from 56 percent in 2004) and Hispanics (50 percent). Generally speaking, people with a bigger stake in society—
homeowners, parents with children at home, people with extensive
schooling and good jobs—are more likely to vote. Income matters,
too: People earning more than $75,000 a year are much more likely

to vote (79 percent in 2008) than people earning less than $10,000 (49
percent) (U.S. Census Bureau, 2009).

Of course, we should expect some nonvoting because at any
given time, millions of people are sick or disabled; millions more are
away from home at college or elsewhere or have moved to a new
neighborhood and have forgotten to reregister. In addition, register-
ing and voting depend on the ability to read and write, which discourages the tens of millions of U.S. adults who have limited literacy
skills. Finally, people with physical disabilities that limit mobility
have a lower turnout than the general population (Schur & Kruse,
2000; Brians & Grofman, 2001).

Conservatives suggest that apathy amounts to *indifference* to
politics because most people are content with their lives. Liberals
and especially political radicals on the far left of the political spectrum counter that apathy reflects *alienation* from politics among
people who are so deeply dissatisfied with society that they doubt
that elections will make any real difference. The fact that candidates
such as Barack Obama have drawn so many new voters into the political process and the fact that the disadvantaged and powerless are
least likely to vote suggest that the liberal explanation for voter apathy is probably closer to the truth. ● Go to **mysoclab.com**

Should Convicted Criminals Vote?

Although the right to vote is at the very foundation of our country's
claim to being democratic, all states except Vermont and Maine have
laws that bar people in jail from voting. More than half the states bar
people convicted of serious crimes from voting while they are on probation or on parole. Eleven states ban voting even after people have
completed their sentences, subject to various appeals to restore voting rights. Overall, 5.3 million people (including 1.4 million African
American men) in the United States do not have the right to vote
(Sentencing Project, 2009).

Should government take away people's political rights as a punishment for criminal acts? The legislatures in most of our fifty states
have said yes. But critics point out that this practice may be politically motivated, because preventing convicted criminals from voting makes a difference in the way elections in this country turn out.
Convicted felons (who tend to be lower-income people) show better than a two-to-one preference for Democratic over Republican
candidates. Even allowing for expected voter apathy, one study concluded that if these laws had not been in force, Democrats would
have won more congressional races and in 2000 Al Gore would have
defeated George W. Bush for the presidency (Uggen & Manza, 2002).
In 2009, such political considerations led Congress to debate the
Democracy Restoration Act, which would establish a process to
restore voting rights for convicted criminals who have completed
their sentences.

Go to the Multimedia Library at mysoclab.com to view 2004 presidential election results in your local community. What similarities and differences in voting patterns across the country do you see between 2004 and 2008?

Seeing Ourselves

NATIONAL MAP 2

The Presidential Election, 2008: Popular Vote by County

Barack Obama won the 2008 presidential election with 53 percent of the total popular vote, but he received a majority of the vote in only about one-fourth of the nation's counties. Obama and other Democrats did well in more densely populated urban areas, while John McCain and other Republicans did well in less populated rural areas. Can you explain why rural areas are mostly Republican and urban areas mostly Democratic? What other social differences do you think distinguish the areas that voted Republican and Democratic? ● Go to mysoclab.com

Theoretical Analysis of Power in Society

Sociologists have long debated how power is spread throughout the U.S. population. Power is a very difficult topic to study because decision making is complex and often takes place behind closed doors. Despite this difficulty, researchers have developed three competing models of power in the United States.

The Pluralist Model: The People Rule

The **pluralist model,** closely linked to structural-functional theory, is *an analysis of politics that sees power as spread among many competing interest groups.* Pluralists claim, first, that politics is an arena of negotiation. No single organization can expect to achieve all of its goals. Organizations therefore operate as *veto groups,* realizing some goals but mostly keeping opponents from achieving all of theirs. The political process relies heavily on creating alliances and compromises among numerous interest groups so that policies gain wide support. In short, pluralists see power as spread widely throughout society, with all people having at least some voice in the political system (Dahl, 1961, 1982; Rothman & Black, 1998).

The Power-Elite Model: A Few People Rule

The **power-elite model,** based on social-conflict theory, is *an analysis of politics that sees power as concentrated among the rich.* The term "power elite" was coined by C. Wright Mills (1956), a social-conflict theorist who argued that the upper class holds most of society's wealth, prestige, and power.

Mills claimed that members of the power elite are in charge of the three major sectors of society: the economy, government, and the military. The power elite is made up of the "super-rich" (corporate executives and major stockholders); top officials in Washington, D.C. and state capitals; and the highest-ranking officers in the U.S. military.

Further, Mills explained that these elites move from one sector to another, building power as they go. Former Vice President Dick Cheney, for example, moved back and forth between powerful positions in the corporate world and the federal government. General Colin Powell moved from a top position in the U.S. military to become secretary of state. More broadly, when presidents fill cabinet posts, most of these powerful public officials are millionaires. This was true in the Bush administration and is probably the case for about half of those in the Obama administration.

Power-elite theorists say that the United States is not a democracy because our economic and political systems give a few people so much power that the average person's voice cannot be heard. They reject the pluralist idea that various centers of power serve as checks and balances on one another; according to the power-elite model, those at the top are powerful enough that they face no real opposition (Bartlett & Steele, 2000; Moore et al., 2002).

The Marxist Model: The System Is Biased

A third approach to understanding U.S. politics is the **Marxist political-economy model,** *an analysis that explains politics in terms of the operation of a society's economic system.* Like the power-elite model, the

Making the Grade

Generally, the pluralist model is close to sociology's structural-functional approach; the power-elite model is based on social-conflict theory, as is the Marxist political-economy model, which is more radical because it implies that changes in basic social institutions are needed to make the country truly democratic.

political revolution the overthrow of one political system in order to establish another

Marxist approach rejects the idea that the United States is a political democracy. But the power-elite model focuses on the enormous wealth and power of certain individuals; the Marxist model goes further and sees bias rooted in the nation's institutions, especially its economy. Karl Marx believed that a society's economic system (capitalist or socialist) shapes its political system. Therefore, power elites do not simply appear out of nowhere; they are creations of the capitalist economy.

From this point of view, reforming the political system—by, say, limiting the amount of money that rich people can contribute to political candidates—is unlikely to bring about true democracy. The problem does not lie in the people who exercise great power or the people who don't vote; the problem is the system itself—what Marxists call the "political economy of capitalism." In other words, as long as the United States has a predominantly capitalist economy, the majority of people will be shut out of politics, just as they are exploited in the workplace.

CRITICAL REVIEW The Applying Theory table summarizes the three models of the U.S. political system. Which model is most accurate? Over the years, research has shown support for each one. In the end, of course, how you think our political system ought to work is as much a matter of political values as it is of scientific fact.

Classic research by Nelson Polsby (1959) supports the pluralist model. Polsby studied the politics of New Haven, Connecticut, where he found that key decisions involving urban renewal, choosing political candidates, and running the city's schools were made by different groups. Polsby concluded that in New Haven, no one group—not even the upper class—ruled all the others.

Robert Lynd and Helen Lynd (1937) studied Muncie, Indiana (which they called "Middletown," to suggest that it was a typical city), and documented the fortune amassed by a single family, the Balls, from its business producing glass jars. Their findings support the power-elite position. The Lynds showed how the Ball family dominated the city's life, pointing to that family's name on a local bank,

One of the most significant political forces to develop in recent years is the "tea party" movement. Supporters claim that government has grown too big, too expensive, and now threatens the freedom of ordinary people. Do you see government as a "problem" the way many people on the right side of the political spectrum do? Or do you see it as the "solution" the way many people on the left side of the political spectrum do? Why?

university, hospital, and department store. In Muncie, according to the Lynds, the power elite boiled down to more or less a single family.

From the Marxist perspective, the point is not which individuals make decisions. Rather, as Alexander Liazos (1982:13) explains, "The basic tenets of capitalist society shape everyone's life: the inequalities of social classes and the importance of profits over people." As long as the basic institutions of society are organized to meet the needs of the few rather than the many, Liazos concludes, a democratic society is impossible.

Clearly, the political system in the United States gives almost everyone the right to participate in politics through elections. But as the power-elite and Marxist models point out, at the very least, the U.S. political system is far less democratic than most people think. Most citizens have the right to vote, but the major political parties and their candidates typically support only the positions that are acceptable to the most powerful segments of society and in tune with the operation of our capitalist economy.

Whatever the reasons, many people in the United States appear to be losing confidence in their leaders. Only about 60 percent of U.S. adults report having "some" or "a great deal" of confidence that members of Congress and other government officials will do what is best for the country (NORC, 2009:282–84).

CHECK YOUR LEARNING What is the main argument of the pluralist model of power? What about the power-elite model? The Marxist political-economy model?

Power beyond the Rules

Politics is always a matter of disagreement over a society's goals and the means to achieve them. A political system tries to settle controversy within a system of rules. But political activity sometimes breaks the rules or even tries to do away with the entire system.

Revolution

Political revolution is *the overthrow of one political system in order to establish another.* Revolution goes beyond *reform,* or change within a system, and even beyond a *coup d'état* (in French, literally, "blow to

Newscom

Economics and Politics

⌐○ Making the Grade

Use the Applying Theory table to review the three political models.

⌐○ Making the Grade

Revolution, in which one political system is replaced by another, involves far greater change than reform, which implies change within the present system.

● APPLYING THEORY ●

Politics

	Pluralist Model	Power-Elite Model	Marxist Political-Economy Model
Which theoretical approach is applied?	Structural-functional approach	Social-conflict approach	Social-conflict approach
How is power spread throughout society?	Power is spread widely so that all groups have some voice.	Power is concentrated in the hands of top business, political, and military leaders.	Power is directed by the operation of the capitalist economy.
Is the United States a democracy?	Yes. Power is spread widely enough to make the country a democracy.	No. Power is too concentrated for the country to be a democracy.	No. The capitalist economy sets political decision making, so the country is not a democracy.

the state"), as when one leader topples another. Revolution involves change in the type of system itself.

No political system is immune to revolution, nor does revolution produce any one type of government. Our own Revolutionary War (1775–76) replaced colonial rule by the British monarchy with a representative democracy. French revolutionaries in 1789 also overthrew a monarch, only to set the stage for the return of monarchy in the person of Napoleon. In 1917, the Russian Revolution replaced a monarchy with a socialist government built on the ideas of Karl Marx. In 1991, a second Russian revolution dismantled the socialist Soviet Union, and the nation was reborn as fifteen independent republics, the largest of which—known as the Russian Federation—has moved closer to a market system with a somewhat greater political voice for its people.

Despite their striking variety, revolutions share a number of traits (Tocqueville, 1955, orig. 1856; Skocpol, 1979; Tilly, 1986):

1. **Rising expectations.** Common sense suggests that revolution is more likely when people are severely deprived, but history shows that most revolutions occur when people's lives are improving. Rising expectations, rather than bitterness and despair, make revolution more likely.

2. **Unresponsive government.** Revolution becomes more likely when a government is unwilling to reform itself, especially when demands for change being made by powerful segments of society are ignored.

3. **Radical leadership by intellectuals.** The English philosopher Thomas Hobbes (1588–1679) claimed that intellectuals provide the justification for revolution and universities are often at the center of political change. Students played a key role in China's prodemocracy movement and in the uprisings in Eastern Europe.

4. **Establishing a new legitimacy.** Overthrowing a political system is not easy, but ensuring a revolution's long-term success is harder still. Some revolutionary movements are held together merely by hatred of the past regime and fall apart once new leaders are installed. Revolutionaries must also guard against counterrevolutionary drives led by overthrown leaders. This explains the speed and ruthlessness with which victorious revolutionaries typically dispose of former leaders.

Scientific research cannot declare that a revolution is good or bad. That judgment depends on the personal values of the citizenry, and the full consequences of such an upheaval become evident only after many years.

Terrorism

The terrorist attacks on the United States on September 11, 2001, involving four commercial airliners, killed nearly 3,000 innocent people (from sixty-eight nations), injured many thousands more, destroyed the twin towers of the World Trade Center in New York City, and seriously damaged the Pentagon in Washington, D.C. Not since the attack on Pearl Harbor at the outbreak of World War II had the United States suffered such a blow. This event was the most serious terrorist act ever recorded.

Kiefer Sutherland is special agent Jack Bauer in the popular television drama, *24.* In the show, Bauer works for the Los Angeles Counter Terrorism unit, and typically supports taking "any means necessary" to prevent terror attacks. Should the same standards that guide police work in criminal cases always apply to potential terrorist situations? Why or why not?

Third, democratic societies reject terrorism in principle, but they are especially vulnerable to terrorists because they give broad civil liberties to their people and have less extensive police networks. In contrast, totalitarian regimes make widespread use of state terrorism, but their vast police power gives individuals few opportunities for acts of terror against the government.

Fourth and finally, terrorism is always a matter of definition. Governments claim the right to maintain order, even by force, and may label opposition groups who use violence as "terrorists." Political differences may explain why one person's "terrorist" is another's "freedom fighter" (Jenkins, 2003).

Although hostage taking and outright killing provoke popular anger, taking action against terrorists is difficult. Most terrorist groups have no formal connection to any established state, so identifying the parties responsible may be all but impossible. In addition, a military response may risk confrontation with other governments. Yet as the terrorism expert Brian Jenkins warns, a failure to respond "encourages other terrorist groups, who begin to realize that this can be a pretty cheap way to wage war" (quoted in Whitaker, 1985:29).

War and Peace

Terrorism refers to *acts of violence or the threat of violence used as a political strategy by an individual or a group.* Like revolution, terrorism is a political act beyond the rules of established political systems. According to Paul Johnson (1981), terrorism has four distinguishing characteristics.

First, terrorists try to paint violence as a legitimate political tactic, despite the fact that such acts are condemned by virtually every nation. Terrorists also bypass (or are excluded from) established channels of political negotiation. Therefore, terrorism is a weak organization's strategy against a stronger enemy. In recent decades, terrorism has become commonplace in international politics. In 2008, there were 11,770 acts of terrorism worldwide, which claimed 15,765 lives (including the deaths of 33 U.S. citizens) and injured more than 34,000 people. Most of those killed were in Iraq, but major terrorist attacks took place in many nations, including Afghanistan, India, and Somalia (National Center for Counterterrorism, 2009).

Second, terrorism is used not just by groups but also by governments against their own people. *State terrorism* is the use of violence, generally without support of law, by government officials. State terrorism is lawful in some authoritarian and totalitarian states, which survive by creating widespread fear and intimidation. Saddam Hussein, for example, relied on secret police and state terror to protect his power in Iraq.

Perhaps the most critical political issue is **war,** *organized, armed conflict among the people of two or more nations, directed by their governments.* War is as old as humanity, but understanding it is crucial today because we now have weapons that can destroy the entire planet.

At almost any moment during the twentieth century, nations somewhere in the world were engaged in violent conflict. In its short history, the United States has participated in eleven major wars. From the Revolutionary War to our current engagement in Iraq and Afghanistan, more than 1.3 million U.S. men and women have been killed in armed conflicts, as shown in Figure 7, and many times that number have been injured. Thousands more have died in undeclared wars and limited military actions around the world.

The Causes of War

Wars occur so often that we might think that there is something natural about armed conflict. But there is no evidence that human beings must wage war under any particular circumstances. On the contrary, governments around the world usually have to force their people to go to war.

Like other forms of social behavior, warfare is a product of society that is more common in some places than in others. The Semai

Economics and Politics

of Malaysia, among the most peace-loving of the world's peoples, rarely resort to violence. In contrast, the Yąnomamö are quick to wage war.

If society holds the key to war or peace, under what circumstances do humans go to war? Quincy Wright (1987) cites five factors that promote war:

1. **Perceived threats.** Nations mobilize in response to a perceived threat to their people, territory, or culture. Leaders justified the U.S.-led military campaign against Iraq, for example, by stressing the threat that Saddam Hussein posed to neighboring countries and also to the United States.

2. **Social problems.** When internal problems cause widespread frustration at home, a nation's leaders may try to divert public attention by attacking an external "enemy" as a form of scapegoating. Although U.S. leaders defended the 2003 invasion of Iraq as a matter of national security, the start of the war effectively shifted the nation's attention away from the struggling national economy and boosted the popularity of then-President George W. Bush.

3. **Political objectives.** Poor nations, such as Vietnam, have used wars to end foreign domination. Powerful countries such as the United States may benefit from periodic shows of force to increase global political standing.

4. **Moral objectives.** Nations rarely claim that they are going to war to gain wealth and power. Instead, their leaders infuse military campaigns with moral urgency. By calling the 2003 invasion of Iraq "Operation Iraqi Freedom," U.S. leaders portrayed the mission as a morally justified war of liberation from an evil tyrant.

5. **The absence of alternatives.** A fifth factor promoting war is the lack of alternatives. Although the goal of the United Nations is to maintain international peace by finding alternatives to war, the organization has had limited success in preventing conflict between nations.

Social Class, Gender, and the Military

In World War II, three out of every four men in the United States in their late teens and twenties served in the military, either voluntarily or by being *drafted*—called to service. Only those who were ruled ineligible due to some physical or mental problem performed no military service. Today, by contrast, there is no draft, and fighting is done by a volunteer military. But not every member of our society is equally likely to volunteer.

One recent study concluded that the military has few young people who are rich and few who are very poor. Rather, working-class people look to the military for a job, to become eligible for money to go to college, or simply to get out of the small town where they grew up. In

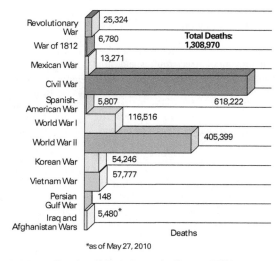

FIGURE 7 **Deaths of Americans in Eleven U.S. Wars**
Almost half of all U.S. deaths in war occurred during the Civil War (1861–65).
Sources: Compiled from various sources by Maris A. Vinovskis (1989) and the author.

addition, the largest number of volunteers comes from the South, where regional culture is more supportive of the military and where most military bases are located. As two analysts put it, "America's military seems to resemble the makeup of a two-year commuter or trade school outside Birmingham or Biloxi far more than that of a ghetto or barrio or four-year university in Boston" (Halbfinger & Holmes, 2003:1).

Throughout our nation's history, women have been a part of the U.S. military. In recent decades, however, women have taken on greater importance in the armed forces. For one thing, the share of women is on the rise, now standing at 15 percent of all military personnel. Just as important, although regulations continue to keep many military women out of harm's way, more women are now engaging in combat. Seeing Sociology in the News on the next two pages takes a closer look at the changes under way.

Is Terrorism a New Kind of War?

People speak of terrorism as a new kind of war. War has historically followed certain patterns: It is played out according to basic rules, the warring parties are known to each other, and the objectives of the warring parties—which generally involve control of territory—are clearly stated.

Terrorism breaks from these patterns. The identity of terrorist individuals and organizations may not be known, those involved

The New York Times

G.I. Jane Breaks the Combat Barrier

BY LIZETTE ALVAREZ
August 16, 2009

As the convoy rumbled up the road in Iraq, Specialist Veronica Alfaro was struck by the beauty of fireflies dancing in the night. Then she heard the unmistakable pinging of tracer rounds and, in a Baghdad moment, realized the insects were illuminated bullets.

She jumped from behind the wheel of her gun truck, grabbed her medical bag and sprinted fifty yards to a stalled civilian truck. On the way, bullets kicked up dust near her feet. She pulled the badly wounded driver to the ground and got to work.

Despite her best efforts, the driver died, but her heroism that January night last year earned Specialist Alfaro a Bronze Star for valor. . . .

"I did everything there," Ms. Alfaro, 25, said of her time in Iraq. "I gunned. I drove. I ran as a truck commander. And underneath it all, I was a medic."

Before 2001, America's military women had rarely seen ground combat. Their jobs kept them mostly away from enemy lines, as military policy dictates.

But the Afghanistan and Iraq wars, often fought in marketplaces and alleyways, have changed that. In both countries, women have repeatedly proved their mettle in combat. . . .

"Iraq has advanced the cause of full integration for women in the Army by leaps and bounds," said Peter R. Mansoor, a retired Army colonel. . . . "They have earned the confidence and respect of male colleagues."

Their success, widely known in the military, remains largely hidden from public view. In part, this is because their most challenging work is often the result of a quiet circumvention of military policy.

Women are barred from joining combat branches like the infantry, armor, Special Forces and most field artillery units and from doing support jobs while living with those smaller units. Women can lead some male troops into combat as officers, but they cannot serve with them in battle.

Yet, over and over, in Iraq and Afghanistan, Army commanders have resorted to bureaucratic trickery when they needed more soldiers for crucial jobs, like bomb disposal and intelligence. On paper, for instance, women have been "attached" to a combat unit rather than "assigned."

This quiet change has not come seamlessly— and it has altered military culture on the battlefield in ways large and small. Women need separate bunks and bathrooms. They face sexual discrimination and rape, and counselors and rape kits are now common in war zones. Commanders also confront a new reality: that soldiers have sex, and some will be evacuated because they are pregnant.

Nonetheless, as soldiers in the Iraq and Afghanistan wars, women have done nearly as much in battle as their male counterparts: patrolled streets with machine guns, served as gunners on vehicles, disposed of explosives, and driven trucks down bomb-ridden roads. They have proved indispensable in their ability to interact with and search Iraqi and Afghan women for

may deny their responsibility, and their goals may be unclear. The 2001 terrorist attacks against the United States were not attempts to defeat the nation militarily or to secure territory. They were carried out by people representing not a country but a cause, one not well understood in the United States. In short, they were expressions of anger and hate intended to create widespread fear.

Conventional warfare is symmetrical, with two nations sending armies into battle. By contrast, terrorism is a new kind of war: an asymmetrical conflict in which a small number of attackers use terror and their own willingness to die as a means to level the playing field against a much more powerful enemy. Although the terrorists may be ruthless, the nation under attack must use caution in its response to terrorism because little may be known about the identity and location of the parties responsible.

The Costs and Causes of Militarism

The cost of armed conflict extends far beyond battlefield casualties. Together, the world's nations spend more than $1.4 trillion annually for military-related purposes. Spending this much diverts resources from the desperate struggle for survival by hundreds of millions of poor people.

Defense is the U.S. government's second biggest expenditure (after Social Security), accounting for about 20 percent of all federal spending, which amounted to more than $700 billion in 2010. The United States has emerged as the world's single military superpower, accounting for about 42 percent of the world's military spending. Put another way, the United States spends nearly as much on the military as the rest of the world's nations combined (Stockholm International Peace Research Institute, 2009; U.S. Office of Management and Budget, 2010).

For decades, military spending went up because of the *arms race* between the United States and the former Soviet Union, which dropped out of the race after its collapse in 1991. But some analysts (who support power-elite theory) link high military spending to the domination of U.S. society by a **military-industrial complex,** *the close association of the federal government, the military, and defense industries.* The roots of militarism, then, lie not just in external threats but also in institutional structures here at home (Marullo, 1987; Barnes, 2002b).

A final reason for continuing militarism is regional conflict. In the 1990s, localized wars broke out in Bosnia, Chechnya, and Zambia and long-standing conflict continues between Israel and the Palestinians. Even limited wars have the potential to grow and involve other countries, including the United States. India and Pakistan— both nuclear powers—moved to the brink of war in 2002 and then pulled back. In 2003, the announcement by North Korea that it, too, had nuclear weapons raised tensions in Asia. Iran continues to pursue nuclear technology, raising fears that this nation may soon have an atomic bomb.

weapons, a job men cannot do for cultural reasons. The Marine Corps has created revolving units—"lionesses"—dedicated to just this task. . . .

[In some] cases, the rules were bent to get women into combat positions.

In 2004 and 2005, Michael A. Baumann, now a retired lieutenant colonel, commanded thirty enlisted women and six female officers as part of a unit patrolling in the Rashid district of Baghdad, an extremely dangerous area at the time.

On paper, he followed military policy. The women were technically assigned to a separate chemical company of the division. In reality, they were core members of his field artillery battalion. Mr. Baumann said the women trained and fought alongside his male soldiers. Everyone from Mr. Baumann's commanders to the commanding general knew their true function, he said. . . .

Brought up as an old-school Army warrior, Mr. Baumann said he had seriously doubted that women could physically handle infantry duties, citing the weight of the armor and the gear, the heat of Baghdad and the harshness of combat.

"I found out differently," said Mr. Baumann. . . . "Not only could they handle it, but in the same way as males. . . . I had full trust and confidence in their abilities." . . .

War is different today, they say. Technology has changed the way some of these jobs are done, making them more mechanized and less strength-dependent. Warfare in Iraq involves a lot more driving than walking.

What is more, not all combat jobs are the same. Handling field artillery or working in Bradleys [the Army's armored fighting vehicle], for example, are jobs more suited to some women than light infantry duties, which can require carrying heavy packs for miles. . . .

Any change to the policy would require Congressional approval, which lawmakers say is unlikely in the middle of two wars. But women in the military and their allies want their performance in combat to count for something. . . .

In Mr. Baumann's view, the reality on the ground long ago outpaced the debate.

"We have crossed that line in Iraq," he said. "Debate it all you want folks, but the military is going to do what the military needs to do. And they are needing to put women in combat."

WHAT DO YOU THINK?

1. Do you consider the work being done by Veronica Alfaro to be a step forward for women? Why or why not?

2. Looking at the wars in Iraq and Afghanistan, what factors have moved more U.S. women into combat?

3. Would you support a policy that allowed women to take all military assignments, including combat branches? Why or why not?

Nuclear Weapons

Despite the easing of superpower tensions, the world still contains more than 8,000 operational nuclear warheads, representing a destructive power of several tons of TNT for every person on the planet. If even a small fraction of this stockpile is used in war, life as we know it would end. Albert Einstein, whose genius contributed to the development of nuclear weapons, reflected, "The unleashed power of the atom has changed everything save our modes of thinking and we thus drift toward unparalleled catastrophe" ("Atomic Education," 1946). In short, nuclear weapons make full-scale war unthinkable in a world not yet capable of peace.

The United States, the Russian Federation, Great Britain, France, the People's Republic of China, Israel, India, Pakistan, and probably North Korea all have nuclear weapons. A few nations stopped the development of nuclear weapons—Argentina and Brazil halted work in 1990, and South Africa dismantled its arsenal in 1991. But by 2015, there could be ten new nations in the "nuclear club," and as many as fifty countries by 2025 (Grier, 2006). Such a trend makes any regional conflict very dangerous to the entire planet.

Mass Media and War

The 2003 U.S.-led invasion of Iraq was the first war in which television crews traveled with U.S. troops, reporting as the campaign unfolded. The mass media provided ongoing and detailed reports of events; cable television made available live coverage of the war twenty-four hours a day, seven days a week.

Media outlets "frame" the news according to their own politics. Those media outlets that were critical of the war—especially the Arab news channel Al-Jazeera—tended to report the slow pace of the conflict, the casualties to the U.S. and allied forces, and the deaths and injuries suffered by Iraqi civilians, all of which was information that would increase pressure to end the war. Media outlets that were supportive of the war—including most news organizations in the United States—tended to report the rapid pace of the war and the casualties to Iraqi forces and to downplay any harm to Iraqi civilians as minimal and unintended. In short, the power of the mass media to provide selective information to a worldwide audience means that television and other media may be almost as important to the outcome of a conflict as the military forces who are doing the actual fighting.

Pursuing Peace

How can the world reduce the dangers of war? Here are the most recent approaches to peace:

1. **Deterrence.** The logic of the arms race holds that security comes from a "balance of terror" between the superpowers. The principle of *mutual assured destruction* (MAD) means that a nation launching a first strike against another will face greater

● Seeing Sociology
in Everyday Life

Do you think the world is getting better at avoiding war? Explain.

● Making the Grade

Identify and explain the four approaches to peace discussed below.

Joe McNally, Life Magazine ©TimePix

One reason to pursue peace is the rising toll of death and mutilation caused by millions of land mines placed in the ground during wartime and left there afterward. Civilians—many of them children—maimed by land mines receive treatment in this Kabul, Afghanistan, clinic.

But disarmament has limitations. No nation wants to be weakened by eliminating its defenses. Successful diplomacy depends on everyone involved sharing responsibility for a common problem (Fisher & Ury, 1988). Although the United States and the Russian Federation continue to negotiate arms reduction agreements, the world now faces threats from other nations such as North Korea and Iran.

4. Resolving underlying conflict. In the end, reducing the dangers of war may depend on resolving underlying conflicts by promoting a more just world. Poverty, hunger, and illiteracy are all root causes of war. Perhaps the world needs to reconsider the wisdom of spending thousands of times as much money on militarism as we do on efforts to find peaceful solutions (Sivard, 1988; Kaplan & Schaffer, 2001).

retaliation. This deterrence policy kept the peace for almost fifty years during the Cold War. Yet it encouraged an enormous arms race and cannot control nuclear proliferation, which represents a growing threat to peace. Deterrence also does little to stop terrorism or to prevent wars that are started by a stronger nation (such as the United States) against a weaker foe (such as the Taliban government in Afghanistan or Saddam Hussein's Iraq).

2. **High-technology defense.** If technology created the weapons, perhaps it can also protect us from them; such is the claim of the *strategic defense initiative* (SDI). Under SDI, satellites and ground installations would destroy enemy missiles soon after they were launched. In a survey shortly after the 2001 terrorist attacks, two-thirds of U.S. adults supported SDI (Thompson & Waller, 2001; "Female Opinion," 2002). However, critics claim that the system, which they refer to as "Star Wars," would be, at best, a leaky umbrella. Others worry that building such a system will spark another massive arms race. In 2009, the Obama administration stated that as part of its Ballistic Missile Defense System, the United States was expanding land- and sea-based missile defense systems in the Persian Gulf but not in Eastern Europe.

3. **Diplomacy and disarmament.** Some analysts believe that the best road to peace is diplomacy rather than technology (Dedrick & Yinger, 1990). Teams of diplomats working together can increase security by reducing, rather than building, weapons stockpiles.

Politics: Looking Ahead

Just as economies are changing, so are political systems. Several problems and trends are likely to be important in the decades to come.

One troublesome problem in the United States is inconsistency between our democratic ideals and our low turnout at the polls. Perhaps, as conservative pluralist theorists say, many people do not bother to vote because they are content with their lives. On the other hand, the liberal power-elite theorists may be right when they say that people withdraw from a system that concentrates so much wealth and power in the hands of a few people. Or perhaps, as radical Marxist critics claim, people find that our political system offers little real choice, limiting options and policies to those that support our capitalist economy. In any case, the current high level of apathy and distrust in our nation's government reflect a widespread desire for political change.

A second issue is the global rethinking of political models. The Cold War between the United States and the Soviet Union encouraged people to think of politics in terms of two opposing models, capitalism and socialism. Today, however, people are more likely to consider a broader range of political systems that link government to the economy in various ways. Welfare capitalism, as found in Sweden and Denmark, or state capitalism, as found in South Korea and Japan, are just two possibilities. The Thinking Globally box takes a look at the debate over the chances for the emergence of democratic governments in the world's Islamic countries.

Third, we still face the danger of war in many parts of the world. Even as the United States and the Russian Federation dismantle

THINKING GLOBALLY

Islam and Freedom: A "Democracy Gap"?

One of the reasons given by the U.S. government for sending troops to Iraq was to encourage the spread of democracy in the Middle East, especially in countries with Islamic populations.

But does the Middle East really need democracy? Is democracy a goal that is sought—and equated with freedom—everywhere? The answer is not entirely clear because nations have unique political histories and "freedom" means different things in different cultural settings.

Political freedom is a basic element of all democracies. Freedom House, an organization that monitors political freedom around the world, tracks people's right to vote, to express ideas freely, and to move about without undue interference from government. It reports that the region of the world with the least political freedom stretches from Africa through the Middle East to Asia.

Many of the nations that Freedom House characterizes as "not free" have populations that are largely Islamic. According to the Pew Forum on Religion and Public Life in 2008, 50 of the world's 194 nations had an Islamic majority population. Just 9 of these countries had democratic governments (18 percent). Of the 144 nations without a majority Islamic population, 109 (76 percent) had democratic governments. In other words, countries without Islamic majorities are four times more likely to have democratic governments than countries with Islamic majorities. Freedom House concludes that countries with Islamic majority populations display a "democracy gap."

This relative lack of political democracy was found in all world regions that have Islamic-majority nations—in Africa, central Europe, the Middle East, and Asia. The pattern is especially strong among the sixteen Islamic-majority states in the Middle East and North Africa that are ethnically Arabic: Not one is an electoral democracy.

What explains this "democracy gap"? Freedom House points to four factors. First, Islamic-majority countries are typically less developed economically, with widespread poverty and limited schooling for their people. Second, these countries have cultural traditions that provide women with few economic, educational, or political opportunities. Third, while most countries limit the power of religious elites in government, and some (including the United States) even require a "separation of church and state," Islamic-majority nations support giving Islamic leaders political power. In two recent cases—Iran and Afghanistan under the Taliban—Islamic leaders have had formal control of government; in many more countries, religious leaders exert considerable influence on political outcomes.

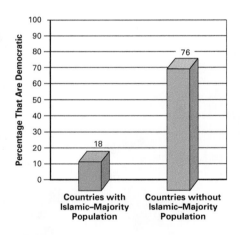

Democracy and Islam

Today, democratic government is much less common in countries with Islamic-majority populations. Fifty years ago, the same was true of countries with Catholic-majority populations.

Fourth and finally, the enormous wealth that comes from Middle Eastern oil plays a part in preventing democratic government. In Iraq, Saudi Arabia, Kuwait, Qatar, the United Arab Emirates, and other nations, this resource has provided astounding riches to a small number of families, money they can use to shore up their political control. In addition, oil wealth permits elites to build airports and other modern facilities without encouraging broader economic development that would raise the living standards of the majority.

For all these reasons, Freedom House concludes that the road to democracy for Islamic-majority nations is likely to be long. But today's patterns may not predict those of tomorrow. In 1950, very few Catholic-majority countries (mostly in Europe and Latin America) had democratic governments. Today, however, most of these nations are democratic. Note too that 40 percent of the world's Muslims—who live in Nigeria, Turkey, Bangladesh, India, Indonesia, and the United States—already live under democratic governments. But perhaps the best indicator that change is already under way is that by the end of 2009, Freedom House had added two more countries with Islamic majorities (Indonesia and Mali) to the list of "free" nations of the world.

WHAT DO YOU THINK?

1. Is the United States right or wrong in trying to bring about a democratic political system in Iraq? Explain your answer.

2. Do you expect to see greater democracy in Islamic-majority countries fifty years from now? Why or why not?

3. Can you point to several reasons that Muslims might object to the kind of political system we call "democracy"? Explain.

Sources: Karatnycky (2002), Pew Forum on Religion and Public Life (2008), and Freedom House (2010).

some warheads, vast stockpiles of nuclear weapons remain, and nuclear technology continues to spread around the world. In addition, new superpowers are likely to arise (the People's Republic of China and India are likely candidates), just as regional conflicts and terrorism are likely to continue. We can only hope (and vote!) for leaders who will work toward finding nonviolent solutions to the age-old problems that provoke war, thereby putting us on the road to world peace.

Seeing Sociology in Everyday Life

How important are you to the political process?

Historically, as this chapter explains, young people have been less likely than older people to take part in politics. But, as a study of the 2008 election suggests, that trend may be changing as evidence builds that young people intend to have their voices heard.

> **HINT** In the 2008 presidential campaign, thousands of young people served as volunteers for both major political candidates, telephoning voters or walking door to door in an effort to increase public interest, raise money, and get people to the polls on Election Day. Many celebrities—including musicians and members of the Hollywood entertainment scene—also spoke out in favor of a candidate, most of them favoring the Democratic Party. But most important of all is voting, and your vote counts as much as that of any celebrity. Are you registered to vote? Will you turn out next Election Day?

Thousands of young people volunteered to assist the 2008 presidential candidates in their campaigns. In what ways do you think young people helped their candidates simply by using the telephone?

Dr. Billy Ingram/WireImage\Getty Images Inc.

You don't need to be a campaign worker to make a difference. What is the easiest—and in the end, the most important—way to be a part of the political process?

William Thomas Cain\Getty Images Inc.

Tom Morello, guitarist for "Rage Against the Machine" and other bands, has made political activism a central part of his career as a musician, speaking for various left-of-center causes. Can you identify other celebrities who have tried to shape public opinion?

Paul Warner\AP Wide World Photos

Applying SOCIOLOGY in Everyday Life

1. The following Web site provides data on how people voted in the 2008 presidential election by gender, age, race, income, religion, and other variables: http://www.cnn.com/ELECTION/2008. Visit this site, and develop a profile of the typical Democratic voter and the typical Republican voter. Which variables best predict differences in voting preference?

2. Freedom House, an organization that studies civil rights and political liberty around the world, publishes an annual report, "Freedom in the World." Find a copy in the library, or examine global trends and the political profile of any country on the Web at http://www.freedomhouse.org.

3. Visit a discount store such as Walmart or Kmart and do a little "fieldwork" in an area of the store that interests you. Pick ten products and see where they are made. Do the results support the existence of a global economy?

Making the Grade

Economics and Politics

◉ Watch on mysoclab.com

The Economy: Historical Overview

The **ECONOMY** is the major social institution through which a society produces, distributes, and consumes goods and services.
- In technologically simple societies, economic activity is simply part of family life.
- The Agricultural Revolution (5,000 years ago) made the economy a distinct social institution based on agricultural technology, specialized work, permanent settlements, and trade.
- The Industrial Revolution (beginning around 1750) expanded the economy based on new sources of energy and specialized work in factories that turned raw materials into finished products.
- The postindustrial economy is based on a shift to service work and computer technology.

✓ Today's expanding global economy produces and consumes products and services with little regard for national borders. The world's 1,500 largest corporations account for half of the world's economic output.

PRIMARY SECTOR
- draws raw materials from the natural environment
- is of greatest importance (25% of the economy) in low-income nations

SECONDARY SECTOR
- transforms raw materials into manufactured goods
- is a significant share (26–37%) of the economy in low-, middle-, and high-income nations

TERTIARY SECTOR
- produces services rather than goods
- is the largest sector (46–72%) in low-, middle-, and high-income countries

social institution a major sphere of social life, or societal subsystem, organized to meet human needs

economy the social institution that organizes a society's production, distribution, and consumption of goods and services

postindustrial economy a productive system based on service work and computer technology

primary sector the part of the economy that draws raw materials from the natural environment

secondary sector the part of the economy that transforms raw materials into manufactured goods

tertiary sector the part of the economy that involves services rather than goods

global economy economic activity that crosses national borders

Economic Systems: Paths to Justice

CAPITALISM is based on private ownership of property and the pursuit of profit in a competitive marketplace. Capitalism results in
- greater productivity
- higher overall standard of living
- greater income inequality
- freedom to act according to self-interest

SOCIALISM is grounded in collective ownership of productive property through government control of the economy. Socialism results in
- less productivity
- lower overall standard of living
- less income inequality
- freedom from basic want

capitalism an economic system in which natural resources and the means of producing goods and services are privately owned

socialism an economic system in which natural resources and the means of producing goods and services are collectively owned

welfare capitalism an economic and political system that combines a mostly market-based economy with extensive social welfare programs

state capitalism an economic and political system in which companies are privately owned but cooperate closely with the government

Work in the Postindustrial U.S. Economy

JOBS
- Agricultural work represents about 1.5% of jobs.
- Blue-collar, industrial work has declined to 18.5% of jobs.
- White-collar, service work has increased to 80% of jobs.

SELF-EMPLOYMENT
- 7.7% of U.S. workers are self-employed.
- Many professionals fall into this category, but most self-employed people have blue-collar jobs.

UNEMPLOYMENT
- Unemployment has many causes, including the operation of the economy itself.
- In 2009, 10% of the country's labor force was unemployed.
- At highest risk for unemployment are young people and African Americans.

profession a prestigious white-collar occupation that requires extensive formal education

◉ Explore on mysoclab

Corporations

CORPORATIONS form the core of the U.S. economy.
- The largest corporations, which are conglomerates, account for most corporate assets and profits.
- Many large corporations operate as multinationals, producing and distributing products in nations around the world.

corporation an organization with a legal existence, including rights and liabilities, separate from that of its members

monopoly the domination of a market by a single producer

oligopoly the domination of a market by a few producers

Politics: Historical Overview

POLITICS is the major social institution by which a society distributes power and organizes decision making. Max Weber claimed that raw power is transformed into *legitimate authority* in three ways:

- Preindustrial societies rely on tradition to transform power into authority. Traditional authority is closely linked to kinship.
- As societies industrialize, tradition gives way to rationality. *Rational-legal authority* underlies the operation of bureaucratic offices as well as the law.
- At any time, however, some individuals transform power into authority through charisma. *Charismatic authority* is linked to extraordinary personal qualities (as found in Jesus of Nazareth, Adolf Hitler, and Mahatma Gandhi).

politics the social institution that distributes power, sets a society's goals, and makes decisions

power the ability to achieve desired ends despite resistance from others

government a formal organization that directs the political life of a society

authority power that people perceive as legitimate rather than coercive

routinization of charisma the transformation of charismatic authority into some combination of traditional and bureaucratic authority

Politics in Global Perspective

MONARCHY is common in agrarian societies; leadership is based on kinship.

DEMOCRACY is common in modern societies; leadership is linked to elective office.

AUTHORITARIANISM is any political system that denies the people participation in government.

TOTALITARIANISM concentrates all political power in one centralized leadership.

✓ *The world is divided into 194 politically independent nation-states. A political trend, however, is the growing wealth and power of multinational corporations. In an age of computers and other new information technology, governments can no longer control the flow of information across their borders.*

monarchy a political system in which a single family rules from generation to generation

democracy a political system that gives power to the people as a whole

authoritarianism a political system that denies the people participation in government

totalitarianism a highly centralized political system that extensively regulates people's lives

Politics in the United States

U.S. government has expanded over the past two centuries, although the *welfare state* in the United States is smaller than in most other high-income nations.

The *political spectrum*, from the liberal left to the conservative right, involves attitudes on both economic issues and social issues.

Special-interest groups advance the political aims of specific segments of the population.

Voter apathy runs high in the United States: Only 63% of eligible voters went to the polls in the 2008 presidential election.

welfare state a system of government agencies and programs that provides benefits to the population

Read on mysoclab.com

Theoretical Analysis of Power

The **PLURALIST MODEL** claims that political power is spread widely in the United States.

The **POWER-ELITE MODEL** claims that power is concentrated in a small, wealthy segment of the population.

The **MARXIST POLITICAL-ECONOMY MODEL** claims that our political agenda is determined by a capitalist economy, so true democracy is impossible.

See the Applying Theory table.

pluralist model an analysis of politics that sees power as spread among many competing interest groups

power-elite model an analysis of politics that sees power as concentrated among the rich

Marxist political-economy model an analysis that explains politics in terms of the operation of a society's economic system

Power beyond the Rules

- **REVOLUTION** radically transforms a political system.
- **TERRORISM** employs violence in the pursuit of political goals and is used by a group against a much more powerful enemy.

War and Peace

- The development and spread of nuclear weapons have increased the threat of global catastrophe.
- World peace ultimately depends on resolving the tensions and conflicts that fuel militarism.

political revolution the overthrow of one political system in order to establish another

terrorism acts of violence or the threat of violence used as a political strategy by an individual or a group

war organized, armed conflict among the people of two or more nations, directed by their governments

military-industrial complex the close association of the federal government, the military, and defense industries

463

Sample Test Questions

Multiple-Choice Questions

1. The economy is the social institution that guides
   a. the production of goods and services.
   b. the distribution of goods and services.
   c. the consumption of goods and services.
   d. All of the above are correct.

2. Building houses and making cars are examples of production in which economic sector?
   a. the primary sector
   b. the secondary sector
   c. the tertiary sector
   d. the service sector

3. Which of the following factors is a result of the globalization of the economy?
   a. Certain areas of the world specialize in one sector of economic activity.
   b. Industrial jobs in the United States are being lost to other countries.
   c. More and more products pass through several nations before reaching the consumer.
   d. All of the above are correct.

4. Socialist economies differ from capitalist economies by
   a. being more productive.
   b. creating less economic equality.
   c. creating more economic equality.
   d. making greater use of commercial advertising.

5. The largest 2,568 corporations, each with assets exceeding $2.5 billion, represent about what share of all corporate assets in the United States?
   a. 80 percent
   b. 60 percent
   c. 30 percent
   d. 10 percent

6. Modern societies, including the United States, rely mostly on which type of authority?
   a. charismatic authority
   b. traditional authority
   c. rational-legal authority
   d. no authority at all

7. In which type of political system does power reside in the hands of the people as a whole?
   a. democracy
   b. aristocracy
   c. totalitarianism
   d. monarchy

8. In the 2008 U.S. presidential election, about what share of registered voters actually cast a vote?
   a. 93 percent
   b. 83 percent
   c. 63 percent
   d. 23 percent

9. The Marxist political-economy model suggests that
   a. power is concentrated in the hands of a small "power elite."
   b. an antidemocratic bias is built into the capitalist system.
   c. power is widely spread throughout society.
   d. many people do not vote because they are basically satisfied with their lives.

10. Which of the following wars resulted in the highest loss of life to people in the United States?
    a. Civil War
    b. World War II
    c. Korean War
    d. Vietnam War

ANSWERS: 1(d); 2(b); 3(d); 4(c); 5(a); 6(c); 7(a); 8(c); 9(b); 10(a).

Essay Questions

1. In what specific ways did the Industrial Revolution change the U.S. economy? How is the Information Revolution changing the economy once again?

2. Discuss the pluralist, power-elite, and Marxist political-economy models of political power, explaining how each differs from the others. Which of these models do you think makes the most sense? Why?

Population, Urbanization, and Environment

Population, Urbanization, and Environment

- Why should we worry about the rapid rate of global population increase?

- What makes city and rural living different?

- How is the state of the natural environment a social issue?

Watch the *Core Concepts in Sociology* video "Population Growth and Decline" on **mysoclab.com**

Nina Raingold\Getty Images Inc.,

Looking for a new place to live after you finish college? Crosby, North Dakota, would really like you to call it home. The town's officials will do more than welcome you—they will give you a free piece of land on which to build a house. As a bonus, they will throw in a free membership in the local country club.

The old cattle town of Ellsworth, Kansas, also wants you. The town leaders will match Crosby's offer of free land and go one better, giving you $1,000 cash toward your down payment on a new home.

Perhaps the best deal of all is found in Plainville, another small Kansas town. In addition to free land, you can forget about property taxes for the next ten years!

Why are these towns so eager to attract new residents? The answer is that they are all in the Great Plains, the region of the United States extending from North Dakota all the way down to Texas that has lost much of its population in recent decades. The governments of Crosby (current population 1,100), Ellsworth (2,500), and Plainville (2,000) are offering these incentives because they are worried that unless there is a turnaround, their towns may disappear like hundreds of other nearby communities already have (Greene, 2005).

All across the Great Plains, towns are hanging on by a thread. This chapter investigates population patterns, explaining why people move from place to place, why some cities get so large, and why small towns sometimes die. It will also look at the effects on the physical environment of population change and our way of life.

Demography: The Study of Population

When humans first began to cultivate plants some 12,000 years ago, Earth's entire *Homo sapiens* population was about 5 million, or about the number of people living in Colorado today. Very slow growth pushed the total in 1 C.E. to perhaps 300 million, or about the population of the United States today.

Starting around 1750, world population began to spike upward. We are currently adding nearly 83 million people to the planet each year; the world now holds 6.8 billion people.

The causes and consequences of this drama are the focus of **demography,** *the study of human population.* Demography (from the Greek, meaning "description of people") is a cousin of sociology that analyzes the size and composition of a population and studies how and why people move from place to place. Demographers not only collect statistics but also raise important questions about the effects of population growth and suggest how it might be controlled. The following sections present basic demographic concepts.

Fertility

The study of human population begins with how many people are born. **Fertility** is *the incidence of childbearing in a country's population.* During a woman's childbearing years, from the onset of menstruation (typically in the early teens) to menopause (usually in the late forties), she is capable of bearing more than twenty children. But *fecundity,* or maximum possible childbearing, is sharply reduced by cultural norms, finances, and personal choice.

Demographers describe fertility using the **crude birth rate,** *the number of live births in a given year for every 1,000 people in a population.* To calculate a crude birth rate, divide the number of live births in a year by the total population and multiply the result by 1,000. In the United States in 2008, there were 4.25 million live births in a population of 304 million, yielding a crude birth rate of 14.0 (Hamilton, Martin, & Ventura, 2010).

> **January 18, Coshocton County, Ohio.** Having just finished off the mountains of meat and potatoes that make up a typical Amish meal, our group of college students has gathered in the living room of Jacob and Anna Raber, members of this rural Amish community. Anna, a mother of four, is telling us about Amish life. "Most of the women I know have five or six children," she says with a smile, "but certainly not everybody—some have eleven or twelve!"

demography the study of human population

fertility the incidence of childbearing in a country's population

crude birth rate the number of live births in a given year for every 1,000 people in a population

mortality the incidence of death in a country's population

crude death rate the number of deaths in a given year for every 1,000 people in a population

infant mortality rate the number of deaths among infants under one year of age for each 1,000 live births in a given year

life expectancy the average life span of a country's population

migration the movement of people into and out of a specified territory

sex ratio the number of males for every 100 females in a nation's population

age-sex pyramid a graphic representation of the age and sex of a population

Global Snapshot

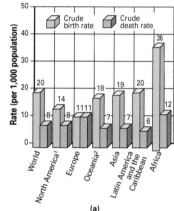

(a)

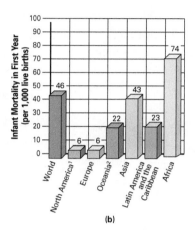

(b)

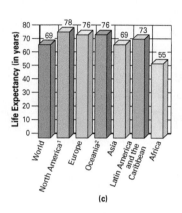

(c)

FIGURE 1   (a) Crude Birth Rates and Crude Death Rates, (b) Infant Mortality Rates, and (c) Life Expectancy around the World, 2009

By world standards, North America has a low birth rate, an average death rate, a very low infant mortality rate, and high life expectancy.

[1] United States and Canada.

[2] Australia, New Zealand, and South Pacific Islands.

Source: Population Reference Bureau (2009).

A country's birth rate is described as "crude" because it is based on the entire population, not just women in their childbearing years. In addition, this measure ignores differences among various categories of the population: Fertility among the Amish, for example, is quite high, and fertility among Asian Americans is low. But the measure is easy to calculate and allows rough comparisons of the fertility of one country or region to others. Part (a) of Figure 1 shows that compared to the rest of the world, the crude birth rate of North Americans is low.

Mortality

Population size also reflects **mortality,** *the incidence of death in a country's population.* To measure mortality, demographers use the **crude death rate,** *the number of deaths in a given year for every 1,000 people in a population.* This time, we take the number of deaths in a year, divide by the total population, and multiply the result by 1,000. In 2008, there were 2.45 million deaths in the U.S. population of 304 million, yielding a crude death rate of 8.1 (Tejada-Vera & Sutton, 2009). Part (a) of Figure 1 shows that in global context, this rate is about average.

A third useful demographic measure is the **infant mortality rate,** *the number of deaths among infants under one year of age for each 1,000 live births in a given year.* To compute infant mortality, divide the number of deaths of children under one year of age by the number of live births during the same year and multiply the result by 1,000. In 2008, there were 27,600 infant deaths and 4.25 million live births in the United States. Dividing the first number by the second and multiplying the result by 1,000 yields an infant mortality rate of 6.49. Part (b) of Figure 1 indicates that by world standards, North American infant mortality is very low.

But remember the differences among various categories of people. For example, African Americans, with three times the burden of poverty compared to whites, have an infant mortality rate of 12.9, more than twice the rate for non-Hispanic whites of 5.7.

Low infant mortality greatly raises **life expectancy,** *the average life span of a country's population.* U.S. males born in 2007 can expect to live 75.4 years, and females can look forward to 80.4 years. As part (c) of Figure 1 shows, life expectancy for North Americans is twenty-three years greater than that typical of low-income countries of Africa.

Migration

Population size is also affected by **migration,** *the movement of people into and out of a specified territory.* Movement into a territory, or *immigration,* is measured as an *in-migration rate,* calculated as the number of people entering an area for every 1,000 people in the

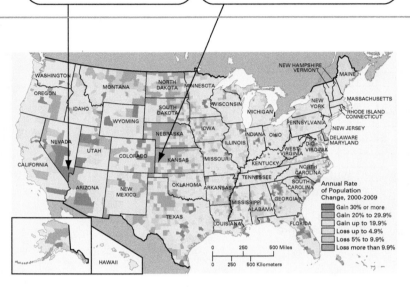

Cheryl Richardson, age 36, has just moved to Las Vegas to work in the expanding tourism industry, which has boosted the region's population.

Tom and Ellen Posten, in their sixties, live in Wichita County, Kansas; like. many other families in the area, their children have all moved out of the county in search of better jobs.

Explore population density in your local community and in counties across the United States on mysoclab.com

Seeing Ourselves

NATIONAL MAP 1

Population Change across the United States

This map shows that since 2000, population has been moving from the heartland of the United States toward the coasts. What do you think is causing this internal migration? What categories of people do you think remain in counties that are losing population?

Explore on mysoclab.com

Source: U.S. Census Bureau (2009).

population. Movement out of a territory, or *emigration,* is measured in terms of an *out-migration rate,* the number leaving for every 1,000 people. Both types of migration usually happen at the same time; the difference is the *net migration rate.*

All nations experience some degree of internal migration, that is, movement within their borders from one region to another. National Map 1 shows where the U.S. population is moving and the places being left behind (as suggested by the chapter opening, notice the heavy losses in the Plains States in the middle of the country).

Migration is sometimes voluntary, as when people leave a small town to move to a larger city. In such cases, "push-pull" factors are usually at work: A lack of jobs "pushes" people to move, and more opportunity elsewhere "pulls" people to someplace new. Migration can also be involuntary, such as the forced transport of 10 million Africans to the Western Hemisphere as slaves or when Hurricane Katrina caused tens of thousands of people to flee New Orleans.

Population Growth

Fertility, mortality, and migration all affect the size of a society's population. In general, rich nations (such as the United States) grow almost as much from immigration as from natural increase; poorer nations (such as Pakistan) grow almost entirely from natural increase.

To calculate a population's *natural growth rate,* demographers subtract the crude death rate from the crude birth rate. The natural growth rate of the U.S. population in 2008 was 5.9 per 1,000 (the crude birth rate of 14.0 minus the crude death rate of 8.1), or about 0.6 percent annual growth.

Global Map 1 shows that population growth in the United States and other high-income nations is well below the world average of 1.2

percent. Earth's low-growth continents are Europe (currently posting no growth) and North America (increasing by 0.6 percent). Near the global average are Oceania (1.1 percent), Asia (1.2 percent), and Latin America (1.4 percent). The highest-growth region of the world is Africa (2.4 percent).

A handy rule for estimating population growth is to divide a society's population growth into the number 70; this yields the *doubling time* in years. Thus an annual growth rate of 2 percent (found in parts of Latin America) doubles a population in thirty-five years, and a 3 percent growth rate (found in some countries in Africa) drops the doubling time to just twenty-three years. The rapid population growth of the poorest countries is deeply troubling because these countries can barely support the populations they have now.

Population Composition

Demographers also study the makeup of a society's population at a given point in time. One variable is the **sex ratio,** *the number of males for every 100 females in a nation's population.* In 2008, the sex ratio in the United States was 97, or 97 males for every 100 females. Sex ratios are ordinarily below 100 because, on average, women outlive men. Because Plainville, Kansas, has an aging population, its sex ratio is 89, or 89 males for every 100 females. In India, however, the sex ratio is 108 because parents value sons more than daughters and may either abort a female fetus or, after birth, give more care to a male infant, raising the odds that a female child will die.

A more complex measure is the **age-sex pyramid,** *a graphic representation of the age and sex of a population.* Figure 2 presents the age-sex pyramids for the United States and Mexico. Higher death rates as people age give these figures a rough pyramid shape. In the

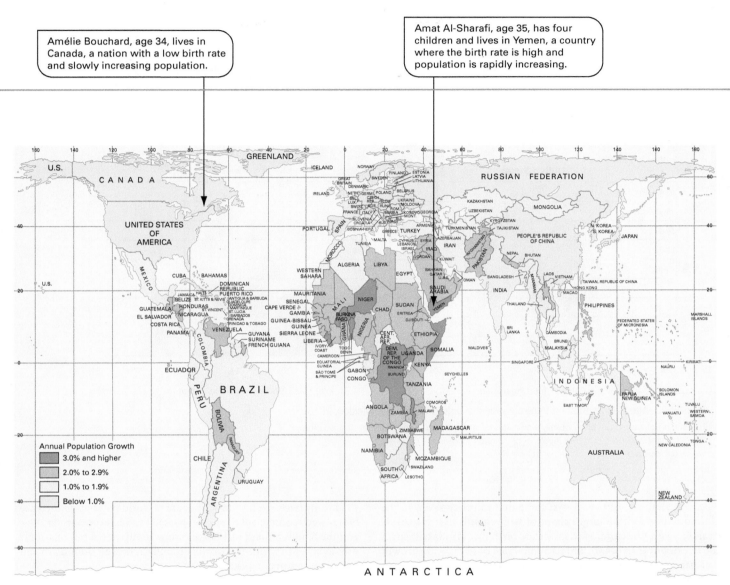

Amélie Bouchard, age 34, lives in Canada, a nation with a low birth rate and slowly increasing population.

Amat Al-Sharafi, age 35, has four children and lives in Yemen, a country where the birth rate is high and population is rapidly increasing.

Annual Population Growth
- 3.0% and higher
- 2.0% to 2.9%
- 1.0% to 1.9%
- Below 1.0%

Window on the World

GLOBAL MAP 1   Population Growth in Global Perspective

The richest countries of the world—including the United States, Canada, and the nations of Europe—have growth rates below 1 percent. The nations of Latin America and Asia typically have growth rates around 1.5 percent, a rate that doubles a population in forty-seven years. Africa has an overall growth rate of 2.4 percent (despite only small increases in countries with a high rate of AIDS), which cuts the doubling time to twenty-nine years. In global perspective, we see that a society's standard of living is closely related to its rate of population growth: Population is rising fastest in the world regions that can least afford to support more people.

Source: Population Reference Bureau (2009).

U.S. pyramid, the bulge near the middle reflects the high birth rates during the "baby boom" from the mid-1940s to the mid-1960s. The contraction for people in their twenties and thirties reflects the subsequent "baby bust." The birth rate of 14.0 in 2008 is still well below its high of 25.3 in 1957.

Comparing the U.S. and Mexican age-sex pyramids shows different demographic trends. The pyramid for Mexico, like that of other lower-income nations, is wide at the bottom (reflecting higher birth rates) and narrows quickly by what we would call middle age (due to higher mortality). In short, Mexico is a much younger society,

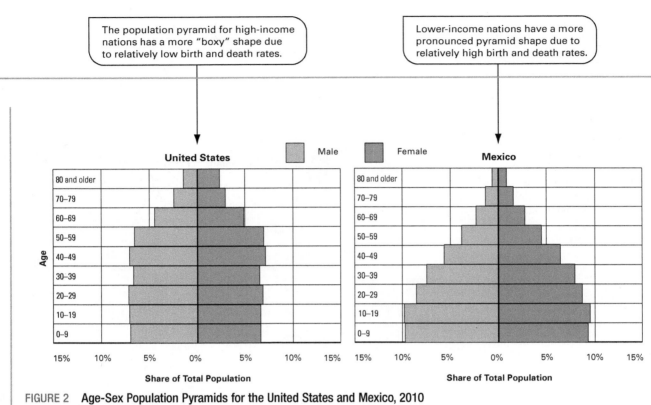

The population pyramid for high-income nations has a more "boxy" shape due to relatively low birth and death rates.

Lower-income nations have a more pronounced pyramid shape due to relatively high birth and death rates.

United States

Male   Female

Mexico

FIGURE 2   Age-Sex Population Pyramids for the United States and Mexico, 2010

By looking at the shape of a country's population pyramid, you can tell its level of economic development and predict future levels of population increase.

Source: U.S. Census Bureau (2010).

with a median age of twenty-six, compared to thirty-seven in the United States. With a larger share of women still in their child-bearing years, therefore, Mexico's crude birth rate (19) is half again the size of our own (14.0), and its annual rate of population growth (1.1 percent) is almost twice the U.S. rate (0.6 percent).

History and Theory of Population Growth

In the past, people wanted large families because human labor was the key to productivity. In addition, until rubber condoms were invented in the mid-1800s, preventing pregnancy was uncertain at best. But high death rates from infectious diseases put a constant brake on population growth.

A major demographic shift began about 1750 as the world's population turned upward, reaching the 1 billion mark by 1800. This milestone (which took all of human history to reach) was matched barely a century later in 1930, when a second billion people were added to the planet. In other words, not only was population increasing, but the *rate* of growth was accelerating. Global population reached 3 billion by 1962 (just thirty-two years later) and 4 billion by

1974 (only twelve years later). The rate of world population increase has slowed recently, but the planet passed the 5 billion mark in 1987 and the 6 billion mark in 1999 and now stands at 6.8 billion. In no previous century did the world's population even double. In the twentieth century, it *quadrupled*.

Currently, the world is gaining almost 83 million people each year; 98 percent of this increase is in poor countries. Experts predict that Earth's population will be more than 9 billion in 2050 (United Nations Population Division, 2010). Given the world's troubles feeding its present population, such an increase is a matter of urgent concern.

Malthusian Theory

The sudden population growth 250 years ago sparked the development of demography. Thomas Robert Malthus (1766–1834), an English economist and clergyman, warned that rapid population increase would lead to social chaos. Malthus (1926, orig. 1798) calculated that population would increase in what mathematicians call a *geometric progression*, illustrated by the series of numbers 2, 4, 8, 16, 32, and so on. At such a rate, Malthus concluded, world population would soon soar out of control.

Seeing Sociology in Everyday Life

Using the age-sex pyramid for the United States shown in Figure 2, why do you think many people are concerned that there will not be enough workers to pay for the retirement of the baby boom generation? How does the pyramid shape change as more and more baby boomers enter retirement?

demographic transition theory a thesis that links population patterns to a society's level of technological development

Food production would also increase, Malthus explained, but only in an *arithmetic progression* (as in the series 2, 3, 4, 5, 6, and so on) because even with new agricultural technology, farmland is limited. Thus Malthus presented a troubling vision of the future: people reproducing beyond what the planet could feed, leading ultimately to widespread starvation and war over what resources were left.

Malthus recognized that artificial birth control or abstaining from sex might change his prediction. But he considered one morally wrong and the other impractical. Famine and war therefore stalked humanity in Malthus's mind, and he was justly known as "the dismal parson."

CRITICAL REVIEW Fortunately, Malthus's prediction was flawed. First, by 1850, the European birth rate began to drop, partly because with industrialization, children were becoming an economic liability rather than an asset and partly because people began using artificial birth control. Second, Malthus underestimated human ingenuity: Modern irrigation techniques, fertilizers, and pesticides have increased farm production far more than he could have imagined.

Some people criticized Malthus for ignoring the role of social inequality in world abundance and famine. For example, Karl Marx (1967, orig. 1867) objected to his view of suffering as a "law of nature" rather than the curse of capitalism. More recently, "critical demographers" have claimed that saying poverty is caused by a high birth rate in low-income countries amounts to blaming the victims. On the contrary, they see global inequality as the real issue (Horton, 1999; Kuumba, 1999).

Still, Malthus offers an important lesson. Habitable land, clean water, and fresh air are limited resources, and increased economic productivity has taken a heavy toll on the natural environment. In addition, medical advances have lowered death rates, pushing up world population. In principle, of course, no level of population growth can go on forever. People everywhere must become aware of the dangers of population increase.

CHECK YOUR LEARNING What did Malthus predict about human population increase? About food production? What was his overall conclusion?

Demographic Transition Theory

A more complex analysis of population change is **demographic transition theory,** *a thesis that links population patterns to a society's level of technological development.* Figure 3 shows the demographic consequences at four levels of technological development. Preindustrial, agrarian societies (Stage 1) have high birth rates because of the economic value of children and the absence of birth control. Death rates are also high due to low living standards and limited

This street scene in Kolkata (Calcutta), India, conveys the vision of the future found in the work of Thomas Robert Malthus, who feared that population increase would overwhelm the world's resources. Can you explain why Malthus had such a serious concern about population? How is demographic transition theory a more hopeful analysis?

medical technology. Outbreaks of disease cancel out births, so population rises and falls with only a modest overall increase. This was the case for thousands of years in Europe before the Industrial Revolution.

Stage 2, the onset of industrialization, brings a demographic transition as death rates fall due to greater food supplies and scientific medicine. But birth rates remain high, resulting in rapid population growth. It was during Europe's Stage 2 that Malthus formulated his ideas, which accounts for his pessimistic view of the future. The world's poorest countries today are in this high-growth stage.

In Stage 3, a mature industrial economy, the birth rate drops, curbing population growth once again. Fertility falls because most

The United States is in this historical stage, with both a low birth rate and a low death rate.

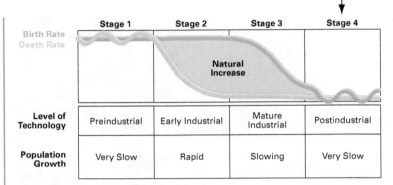

	Stage 1	Stage 2	Stage 3	Stage 4
Birth Rate / Death Rate		Natural Increase		
Level of Technology	Preindustrial	Early Industrial	Mature Industrial	Postindustrial
Population Growth	Very Slow	Rapid	Slowing	Very Slow

FIGURE 3 **Demographic Transition Theory**
Demographic transition theory links population change to a society's level of technological development.

children survive to adulthood, so fewer are needed, and because high living standards make raising children expensive. In short, affluence transforms children from economic assets into economic liabilities. Smaller families, made possible by effective birth control, are also favored by women working outside the home. As birth rates follow death rates downward, population growth slows further.

Stage 4 corresponds to a postindustrial economy in which the demographic transition is complete. The birth rate keeps falling, partly because dual-income couples gradually become the norm and partly because the cost of raising and schooling children continues to increase. This trend, coupled with steady death rates, means that population grows only very slowly or even decreases. This is the case today in Japan, Europe, and the United States.

CRITICAL REVIEW Demographic transition theory suggests that the key to population control lies in technology. Instead of the runaway population increase feared by Malthus, this theory sees technology slowing growth and spreading material plenty.

Demographic transition theory is linked to modernization theory, one approach to global development discussed. Modernization theorists are optimistic that poor countries will solve their population problems as they industrialize. But critics, notably dependency theorists, strongly disagree. Unless there is a redistribution of global resources, they maintain, our planet will become increasingly divided into affluent "haves," enjoying low population growth, and poor "have-nots," struggling in vain to feed more and more people.

CHECK YOUR LEARNING Explain the four stages of demographic transition theory.

Global Population Today: A Brief Survey

What can we say about population in today's world? Drawing on the discussion so far, we can identify important patterns and reach several conclusions.

The Low-Growth North

When the Industrial Revolution began in the Northern Hemisphere, population growth in Western Europe and North America was a high 3 percent annually. But in the centuries since, the growth rate has steadily declined, and in 1970, it fell below 1 percent. As our postindustrial society settles into Stage 4, the U.S. birth rate is at about the replacement level of 2.1 children per woman, a point demographers call **zero population growth,** *the rate of reproduction that maintains population at a steady level.* More than seventy nations, almost all of them rich, are at or below the point of zero population growth.

Among the factors that serve to hold down population in these postindustrial societies are the high proportion of men and women in the labor force, the rising costs of raising children, trends toward later marriage and singlehood, and the widespread use of contraceptives and abortion.

In high-income nations, then, population increase is not the pressing problem that it is in poor countries. On the contrary, many governments in high-income countries are concerned about a future problem of *underpopulation* because declining population size may be difficult to reverse and also because the swelling ranks of the elderly will have fewer and fewer young people to look to for support (Kent & Mather, 2002; United Nations Population Division, 2009).

The High-Growth South

Population is a critical problem in poor nations of the Southern Hemisphere. No nation in the world lacks industrial technology entirely; demographic transition theory's Stage 1 applies only to remote rural areas of low-income nations. But much of Latin America, Africa, and Asia is at Stage 2, with mixed agrarian and industrial economies. Advanced medical technology, supplied by rich societies, has sharply reduced death rates, but birth rates remain high. This is why poor societies now account for two-thirds of Earth's people and 98 percent of global population increase. Read on mysoclab.com

In poor countries around the world, birth rates have fallen from an average of about six children per woman in 1950 to three or four today. But fertility this high will only intensify global poverty. That is why leaders in the battle against global poverty point to the importance of reducing fertility rates in low-income nations. Notice, too, that

Seeing Sociology
in Everyday Life

Typically, immigrants are younger than most people in their new country. What is the likely effect of high immigration on a country's ability to support more and more older people?

zero population growth the rate of reproduction that maintains population at a steady level

a key element in controlling world population growth is improving the status of women. Why? Because of this simple truth: Give women more life choices, and they will have fewer children. History has shown that women who are free to decide when and where to marry, bear children as a matter of choice, and have access to education and to good jobs will limit their own fertility (Axinn & Barber, 2001; Roudi-Fahimi & Kent, 2007).

The Demographic Divide

High- and low-income nations display very different population dynamics, a gap that is sometimes called the *demographic divide*. In Italy, a high-income, very low growth nation, women average just over one child in their lifetimes. Such a low birth rate means that the number of annual births is actually less than the number of deaths. This means that at the moment, Italy is actually *losing* population. Looking ahead to 2050 and even assuming some gains from immigration, Italy's population is projected to be about the same as it is today. The share of elderly people in Italy—now 20 percent—will only increase as time goes on.

Look at how different the patterns are in a low-income nation such as the Democratic Republic of the Congo in Central Africa. There women still have an average of six to seven children, so even with a high mortality rate, this nation's population will triple by 2050. The share of elderly people is extremely low—about 3 percent—and half the country's people are below the age of fifteen. With such a high growth rate, it is no surprise that the problem of poverty is bad and getting worse: About three-fourths of the people are undernourished (Population Reference Bureau, 2009).

In sum, a demographic divide now separates rich countries with low birth rates and aging populations from poor countries with high birth rates and very young populations. Just as humanity has devised ways to reduce deaths around the world, so it must now bring down population growth, especially in poor countries where projections suggest a future as bleak as that imagined by Thomas Malthus centuries ago.

China stands out as a nation that that has taken a strong stand on reducing the rate of population increase. That country's one-child policy, enacted back in the 1970s, has reduced China's potential population by about 250 million. Yet as the Thinking About Diversity box on the next page explains, this policy has been controversial.

In much of the world today, mortality is falling. To limit population increase, the world—especially poor nations—must control births as successfully as it is fending off deaths.

Fertility in the United States has fallen during the past century and is now quite low. But some categories of the U.S. population have much higher fertility rates. One example is the Amish, a religious society living in rural areas of Ohio, Pennsylvania, and other states. It is common for Amish couples to have five, six, or more children. Why do you think the Amish favor large families?

Urbanization:
The Growth of Cities

October 8, Hong Kong. The cable train grinds to the top of Victoria Peak, where we behold one of the world's most spectacular vistas: the city of Hong Kong at night. A million bright, colorful lights ring the harbor as ships, ferries, and traditional Chinese junks churn by. Few cities match Hong Kong for sheer energy: This small city is as economically productive as the state of Wisconsin or the nation of Finland. We could sit here for hours entranced by the spectacle of Hong Kong.

Throughout most of human history, the sights and sounds of great cities such as Hong Kong, New York, and Paris were simply unimaginable. Our distant ancestors lived in small, nomadic groups, moving from place to place as they depleted vegetation or hunted migratory game. The small settlements that marked the emergence of civilization in the Middle East some 12,000 years ago held only a small fraction of Earth's people. Today, the largest three or four cities of the world hold as many people as the entire planet did back then.

● Seeing Sociology
  in Everyday Life

With global population increasing, would you support expanding
the one-child policy to other countries? Why or why not?

○ Making the Grade

As China's economy continues to grow, what would
demographic transition theory predict about that nation's
birth rate?

THINKING ABOUT DIVERSITY: RACE, CLASS, & GENDER

What's Happened to the Girls? China's One-Child Policy

The parents had argued for hours. But the man was determined and the woman was exhausted. The father wrestled the sleeping baby girl from the mother's arms. The decision was now made; the girl had to go. The father put several extra layers of clothing on his daughter and lay the newborn girl in a cardboard box lined with blankets. Next to her, he placed a small bottle of milk. He walked off into the dark night toward the distant village, leaving behind the sobbing of his beloved wife—the baby's mother—who cried out, "Please, I beg you, bring back my baby!"

Yet in her heart, she too knew that this must be done. Half an hour later, the father arrived in the village and found his way to the local school. For the last time, he kissed his daughter goodbye. He set her makeshift crib on the steps of the school's front entrance, knowing that when dawn broke in an hour or so, she would be found and cared for. With tears in his eyes, he said a quick prayer to his ancestors to keep the baby safe from harm. Then he turned and again disappeared into the night, knowing that he would never see or hear from her again.

This story may be heartbreaking, but it is one that has occurred tens of thousands of times in China. What would prompt parents to give up a child? Why would a father abandon his daughter in a public place? The answer lies in China's population control policy and the nation's cultural traditions.

Back in the 1970s, the high Chinese birth rate was fueling an extremely rapid population increase. Government leaders could see that the country's economic development depended on controlling population growth. As a result, they passed a law stating that a family can have only one child. Families who follow the one-child policy can expect rewards such as a better job, a higher salary, and maybe even a larger apartment. On the other hand, parents who violate the law by having a second child face a stiff fine, and their second child may not be eligible for educational and health care benefits.

The government actively promotes the one-child message in the mass media, in popular songs, and in the schools. But education is not the government's only tactic—enforcement officials can be found in most neighborhoods and workplaces. Most Chinese willingly comply with the policy, praising it as good for the country. Those who do not must face the consequences.

Modern China is determined to control population increase. But China is also a country steeped in a tradition of male dominance. If government rules permit only one child, most families would prefer a boy. Why? Parents see boys as a better investment because sons will carry on the family name and must care for their aging parents. On the other hand, girls will end up caring for their husbands' parents, leading most Chinese to see raising daughters as a waste of precious resources. The Chinese government has expanded women's rights and opportunities, but patriarchal traditions are deeply rooted in the country's history, and as is true everywhere, attitudes change slowly.

Around the world, the one-child policy has attracted both praise and condemnation. On the positive side, analysts agree that it has succeeded in its goal of reducing the rate of population increase. This trend, in turn, has helped raise living standards and lifted China to the ranks of middle-income nations. Many one-child families are happy with the added income from women who now work outside the home, and parents now have more to spend on a child's schooling.

But the one-child policy also has a dark side, shown in the story that began this box. Since the law was passed, as many as 1 million girls have "disappeared." In some cases, parents who learn that the woman is carrying a female fetus may choose abortion so they can "try again." In other cases, family members decide to kill a female infant soon after birth. In still other cases, girls survive but are never recorded in the birth statistics so that they grow up as "noncitizens" who can never go to school or receive treatment at a local health clinic. Finally, some parents, like those described earlier, give up or abandon their daughter in the hope that the child may find a home elsewhere.

China's one-child policy has certainly held population increase in check. But it has had a dramatic toll on the female population of China. In one recent year, the nation's birth records showed almost 1 million fewer girls than boys. The Chinese population is now about 250 million lower than it would have been without the one-child policy, but it is also steadily becoming more and more male.

WHAT DO YOU THINK?

1. Point to the reasons China's one-child policy has attracted praise and also blame. On balance, do you think this is a good policy? Can you think of a better way to control population? Explain.

2. What about cases where parents think they can afford additional children? Should family size be a couple's decision? Or does government have a responsibility to look out for the entire country's well-being?

3. Do you now understand why almost all of the babies U.S. parents adopt from China are girls?

China's one-child policy is advertised on billboards throughout the country.

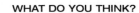

Sources: Hesketh & Lu (2005), Baochang et al. (2007), and Yardley (2008).

Population, Urbanization, and Environment

Seeing Sociology in Everyday Life

As the sections describing preindustrial and industrial cities explain, the size and shape of a city provides clues to a society's technology and culture.

Urbanization is *the concentration of population into cities.* Urbanization both redistributes population within a society and transforms many patterns of social life. We will trace these changes in terms of three urban revolutions: the emergence of cities beginning 10,000 years ago, the development of industrial cities after 1750, and the explosive growth of cities in poor countries today.

The Evolution of Cities

Cities are a relatively new development in human history. Only about 12,000 years ago did our ancestors begin founding permanent settlements, which paved the way for the *first urban revolution.*

The First Cities

Hunting and gathering forced people to move all the time; however, once our ancestors discovered how to domesticate animals and cultivate crops, they were able to stay in one place. Raising their own food also created a material surplus, which freed some people from food production and allowed them to build shelters, make tools, weave cloth, and take part in religious rituals. The emergence of cities led to both specialization and higher living standards.

The first city that we know of was Jericho, which lies to the north of the Dead Sea in what is now the West Bank. When first settled 10,000 years ago, it was home to only 600 people. But as the centuries passed, cities grew to tens of thousands of people and became the centers of vast empires. By 3000 B.C.E., Egyptian cities flourished, as did cities in China about 2000 B.C.E. and in Central and South America about 1500 B.C.E. In North America, however, only a few Native American societies formed settlements; widespread urbanization did not take place until the arrival of European settlers in the seventeenth century.

Preindustrial European Cities

European cities date back some 5,000 years to the Greeks and, later, the Romans, both of whom formed great empires and founded cities across Europe, including Vienna, Paris, and London. With the fall of the Roman Empire, the so-called Dark Ages began as people withdrew within defensive walled settlements and warlords battled for territory. Only in the eleventh century did Europe become more peaceful; trade flourished once again, allowing cities to grow.

Medieval cities were quite different from those familiar to us today. Beneath towering cathedrals, the narrow, winding streets of London, Brussels, and Florence teemed with merchants, artisans, priests, peddlers, jugglers, nobles, and servants. Occupational groups such as bakers, carpenters, and metalworkers clustered in distinct sections or "quarters." Ethnicity also defined communities as people sought to keep out those who differed from themselves. The term "ghetto" (from the Italian word *borghetto,* meaning "outside the city walls") was first used to describe the neighborhood into which the Jews of Venice were segregated.

Industrial European Cities

As the Middle Ages came to a close, steadily increasing commerce enriched a new urban middle class called the *bourgeoisie* (French, meaning "townspeople"). Earning more and more money, the bourgeoisie soon rivaled the hereditary nobility.

By about 1750, the Industrial Revolution triggered a *second urban revolution,* first in Europe and then in North America. The tremendous productive power of factories caused cities to grow bigger than ever before. London, the largest European city, reached 550,000 people by 1700 and exploded to 6.5 million by 1900 (A. F. Weber, 1963, orig. 1899; Chandler & Fox, 1974).

Cities not only grew but changed shape as well. Older winding streets gave way to broad, straight boulevards to handle the increasing flow of commercial traffic. Steam and electric trolleys soon crisscrossed the expanding cities. Because land was now a commodity to be bought and sold, developers divided cities into regular-sized lots (Mumford, 1961). The center of the city was no longer the cathedral but a bustling central business district filled with banks, retail stores, and tall office buildings.

With a new focus on business, cities became ever more crowded and impersonal. Crime rates rose. Especially at the outset, a few industrialists lived in grand style, but most men, women, and children barely survived by working in factories.

Organized efforts by workers eventually brought improvements to the workplace, better housing, and the right to vote. Public services such as water, sewer systems, and electricity further improved urban living. Today, some urbanites still live in poverty, but a rising standard of living has partly fulfilled the city's historical promise of a better life.

The Growth of U.S. Cities

As noted, most of the Native Americans who inhabited North America for thousands of years before the arrival of Europeans were migratory people who formed few permanent settlements. The spread of villages and towns came after European colonization.

Colonial Settlement, 1565–1800

In 1565, the Spanish built a settlement at Saint Augustine, Florida, and in 1607, the English founded Jamestown, Virginia. However, the first lasting settlement came in 1624 when the Dutch established New Amsterdam, later renamed New York.

New York and Boston (founded by the English in 1630) started out as tiny villages in a vast wilderness. They resembled medieval towns in Europe, with narrow, winding streets that still curve through

Looking at the table below, imagine how the lives of people who lived a century ago differed from what we experience today. What are some differences?

metropolis a large city that socially and economically dominates an urban area

suburbs urban areas beyond the political boundaries of a city

megalopolis a vast urban region containing a number of cities and their surrounding suburbs

Table 1   Urban Population of the United States, 1790–2040

Year	Population (in millions)	Urban Portion
1790	3.9	5.1%
1800	5.3	6.1
1820	9.6	7.3
1840	17.1	10.5
1860	31.4	19.7
1880	50.2	28.1
1900	76.0	39.7
1920	105.7	51.3
1940	131.7	56.5
1960	179.3	69.9
1980	226.5	73.7
2000	281.4	79.0
2020*	290.7	84.9
2040*	342.6	88.8

*Projection.

Sources: U.S. Census Bureau (2009) and United Nations Population Division (2009).

lower Manhattan and downtown Boston. When the first census was completed in 1790, as Table 1 shows, just 5 percent of the nation's people lived in cities.

Urban Expansion, 1800–1860

Early in the nineteenth century, towns sprang up along the transportation routes that opened the American West. By 1860, Buffalo, Cleveland, Detroit, and Chicago were all changing the face of the Midwest, and about one-fifth of the U.S. population lived in cities.

Urban expansion was greatest in the northern states; New York City, for example, had ten times the population of Charleston, South Carolina. The evolution of the United States into the industrial-urban North and the agrarian-rural South was one major cause of the Civil War (Schlesinger, 1969).

The Metropolitan Era, 1860–1950

The Civil War (1861–1865) gave an enormous boost to urbanization as factories strained to produce weapons. Especially in the North, waves of people deserted the countryside for cities in hopes of finding better jobs. Joining them were tens of millions of immigrants, most from Europe, forming a culturally diverse urban mix.

In 1900, New York's population soared past the 4 million mark, and Chicago, a city that had scarcely 100,000 people in 1860, was closing in on 2 million. Such growth marked the beginning of the **metropolis** (Greek for "mother city"), *a large city that dominates an urban area socially and economically.* Metropolises became the economic centers of the United States. By 1920, urban areas were home to a majority of the U.S. population.

Industrial technology pushed city populations higher and higher. In the 1880s, the tallest buildings, supported by steel girders and equipped with mechanical elevators, were ten stories high. In 1930, New York's Empire State Building was hailed as an urban wonder, soaring 102 stories into the clouds.

Urban Decentralization, 1950–Present

The industrial metropolis reached its peak about 1950. Since then, something of a turnaround, called *urban decentralization,* has occurred as people have left downtown areas for outlying **suburbs,** *urban areas beyond the political boundaries of a city.* The old industrial cities of the Northeast and Midwest stopped growing, and some lost considerable population in the decades after 1950. The urban landscape of densely packed central cities evolved into sprawling suburban regions.

Suburbs and Urban Decline

Imitating European nobility, some of the rich in the United States split their time between town houses in the city and country homes beyond the city limits. But not until after World War II did ordinary people find a suburban home within their reach. Thanks to more and more cars in circulation, new four-lane highways, government-backed mortgages, and inexpensive tract homes, suburbs grew rapidly. By 1999, most of the U.S. population lived in suburbs, where they frequented nearby shopping malls rather than the older downtown shopping districts (Pederson, Smith, & Adler, 1999; Macionis & Parrillo, 2010).

As many older cities of the Snowbelt—the Northeast and Midwest—lost higher-income taxpayers to the suburbs, they struggled to pay for expensive social programs for the poor who remained. Many cities fell into financial crisis, and inner-city decay became severe. Especially to white suburbanites, the inner cities became synonymous with slum housing, crime, drugs, unemployment, the poor, and minorities (Stahura, 1986; Galster, 1991).

The decline of central cities has also led to a decline in the importance of public space (Goldberger, 2002). Historically, city life was played out on the streets. The French word for a sophisticated person is *boulevardier,* which literally means "street person." However, this term has a negative meaning in the United States today. The activity that once took place on public streets and in public squares now takes place in shopping malls, the lobbies of cineplex theaters, and gated residential communities—all privately owned spaces. Further reducing the vitality of today's urban places is the spread of television, the Internet, and other media that people use without leaving home.

Sunbelt Cities and Urban Sprawl

As the older Snowbelt cities fell into decline, Sunbelt cities in the South and West grew rapidly. The soaring populations of cities such

Seeing Sociology in Everyday Life

Is there a class difference in people's use of the streets as a place to meet and greet others? For example, do you think working-class people are more likely to use the streets in this way than middle-class suburbanites?

Making the Grade

The megalopolis, edge cities, and the "rural rebound" are all aspects of population decentralization as cities spread outward after 1950.

as Los Angeles and Houston reflected a population shift to the Sunbelt, where 60 percent of people in the United States now live. In addition, most of today's immigrants enter the country in the Sunbelt region. In 1950, nine of the ten largest U.S. cities were in the Snowbelt; in 2008, seven of the top ten were in the Sunbelt (U.S. Census Bureau, 2010).

Unlike their colder counterparts, these cities came of age after urban decentralization began. So while Snowbelt cities have long been enclosed by a ring of politically independent suburbs, Sunbelt cities have pushed their boundaries outward to include suburban communities. Chicago covers 227 square miles; Houston is more than twice that size, and the greater Houston metropolitan region covers almost 9,000 square miles—an area the size of the state of New Hampshire.

The great sprawl of Sunbelt cities has its drawbacks. Many people in cities such as Atlanta, Dallas, Phoenix, and Los Angeles claim that unplanned growth results in traffic-clogged roads leading to unattractive developments and schools that cannot keep up with the inflow of children. Not surprisingly, voters in many communities across the United States have passed ballot initiatives seeking to limit urban sprawl (Lacayo, 1999; Romero & Liserio, 2002; W. Sullivan, 2007).

In recent decades, many U.S. cities in the Sunbelt have spread outward in a process called urban sprawl. Los Angeles, for example, now covers about 500 square miles, and even with a vast system of freeways, people moving around the city often find themselves stuck in slow-moving traffic. What are other disadvantages of urban sprawl?

Megalopolis: The Regional City

Another result of urban decentralization is urban regions, or regional cities. The U.S. Census Bureau (2010) recognizes 374 *metropolitan statistical areas* (MSAs). Each includes at least one city with 50,000 or more people. The bureau also recognizes 581 *micropolitan statistical areas,* urban areas with at least one city of 10,000 to 50,000 people. *Core-based statistical areas* (CBSAs) include both metropolitan and micropolitan statistical areas.

The biggest CBSAs contain millions of people and extend into several states. In 2008, the biggest CBSA was New York and its adjacent urban areas in Long Island, western Connecticut, northern New Jersey, and eastern Pennsylvania, with a total population of more than 22 million. Next in size is the CBSA in southern California that includes Los Angeles, Riverside, and Long Beach, with a population of almost 18 million.

As regional cities grow, they begin to overlap. In the early 1960s, the French geographer Jean Gottmann (1961) coined the term **megalopolis** to designate *a vast urban region containing a number of cities and their surrounding suburbs.* Along the East Coast, a 400-mile megalopolis stretches all the way from New England to Virginia. Other supercities cover the eastern coast of Florida and stretch from Cleveland west to Chicago.

Edge Cities

Urban decentralization has also created *edge cities,* business centers some distance from the old downtowns. Edge cities—a mix of corporate office buildings, shopping malls, hotels, and entertainment complexes—differ from suburbs, which contain mostly homes. The population of suburbs peaks at night, but the population of edge cities peaks during the workday.

As part of expanding urban regions, most edge cities have no clear physical boundaries. Some do have names, including Las Colinas (near the Dallas–Fort Worth airport), Tyson's Corner (in Virginia, near Washington, D.C.), and King of Prussia (northwest of Philadelphia). Other edge cities are known only by the major highways that flow through them, including Route 1, which runs through Princeton, New Jersey, and Route 128 near Boston (Garreau, 1991; Macionis & Parrillo, 2010).

The Rural Rebound

Over the course of U.S. history, as shown by the data in Table 1, the urban population of the nation has increased steadily. Immigration has played a part in this increase because most newcomers settle in cities. There has also been considerable migration from rural areas to urban places, typically by people seeking greater social, educational, and economic opportunity.

The rural rebound has been most pronounced in towns that offer spectacular natural beauty. There are times when people living in the scenic town of Park City, Utah, cannot even find a parking space.

Michael Smith\Getty Images Inc.

However, in the 1990s, three-fourths of the rural counties across the United States gained population, a trend analysts have called the "rural rebound." Most of this gain resulted from migration of people from urban areas. This trend has not affected all rural places: As the opening to this chapter explains, many small towns in rural areas (especially in the Plains States) are struggling to stay alive. But even in these areas, the losses have slowed in recent years (K. M. Johnson, 1999; D. Johnson, 2001).

The greatest gains have come to rural communities that offer scenic and recreational attractions, such as lakes, mountains, and ski areas. People are drawn not only to the natural beauty of rural communities but also to their slower pace: less traffic, a lower crime rate,

and cleaner air. A number of companies have relocated to rural counties as well, which has increased economic opportunity for the rural population (K. M. Johnson, 1999; Johnson & Fuguitt, 2000).

Urbanism as a Way of Life

Early sociologists in Europe and the United States focused their attention on the rise of cities. We briefly examine their accounts of urbanism as a way of life.

Ferdinand Tönnies: *Gemeinschaft* and *Gesellschaft*

In the nineteenth century, the German sociologist Ferdinand Tönnies (1855–1937) studied how life in the new industrial metropolis differed from life in rural villages. From this contrast, he developed two concepts that have become a lasting part of sociology's terminology.

Tönnies (1963, orig. 1887) used the German word **Gemeinschaft** ("community") to refer to *a type of social organization in which people are closely tied by kinship and tradition.* The *Gemeinschaft* of the rural village, Tönnies explained, joins people in what amounts to a single primary group.

By and large, argued Tönnies, *Gemeinschaft* is absent in the modern city. On the contrary, urbanization creates **Gesellschaft** ("association"), *a type of social organization in which people come together only on the basis of individual self-interest.* In the *Gesellschaft* way of life, individuals are motivated by their own needs rather than by a desire to help improve the well-being of everyone. By and large, city dwellers have little sense of community or common identity and look to other people mainly when they need something. Tönnies saw in urbanization the weakening of close, long-lasting social relations in favor of the brief and impersonal ties or secondary relationships typical of business.

Emile Durkheim: Mechanical and Organic Solidarity

The French sociologist Emile Durkheim agreed with much of Tönnies's thinking about cities. However, Durkheim countered that urbanites do not lack social bonds; they simply organize social life differently than rural people do.

Durkheim described traditional, rural life as *mechanical solidarity,* social bonds based on common sentiments and shared moral values. With its emphasis on tradition, Durkheim's concept of mechanical solidarity bears a strong similarity to Tönnies's *Gemeinschaft.* Urbanization erodes mechanical solidarity, Durkheim explained, but it also generates a new type of bonding, which he called *organic solidarity,* social bonds based on specialization and interdependence. This concept, which parallels Tönnies's *Gesellschaft,* reveals an important

●─ Seeing Sociology
in Everyday Life

How would Simmel explain cases of people turning away
from others in need on the grounds that they simply "don't
want to get involved"?

●─ Making the Grade

Tönnies's concept of *Gemeinschaft* corresponds to Durkheim's
mechanical solidarity; *Gesellschaft* corresponds to organic
solidarity.

Pieter Breughel the Elder (c. 1525/30-1569), *Peasant Dance*, c. 1565, Kunsthistorisches
Museum, Vienna/Superstock, Inc.

Lily Furedi (1896-1969) American, *Subway* ca. 1934. Oil on canvas, 39 in. x 48 1/4 in. (99.1 x
122.6 cm). Transfer from the U.S. Department of the Interior, National Park Service. Smithsonian American Art Museum, Washington, DC, USA, Art Resource, NY

Peasant Dance (left, c. 1565), by Pieter Breughel the Elder, conveys the essential unity of rural life forged by generations
of kinship and neighborhood. By contrast, Lily Furedi's *Subway (right)* communicates the impersonality common to
urban areas. Taken together, these paintings capture Tönnies's distinction between *Gemeinschaft* and *Gesellschaft*.

Pieter Breughel the Elder (c. 1525/30–1569), *Peasant Dance*, c. 1565, Kunsthistorisches Museum, Vienna/Superstock. Lily Furedi, American. *Subway*.
Oil on canvas, 99 x 123 cm. National Collection of Fine Arts, Washington, D.C./Smithsonian Institute.

difference between the two thinkers. Both felt that the growth of
industrial cities weakened tradition, but Durkheim optimistically
pointed to a new kind of solidarity. Where societies had been built
on *likeness,* Durkheim now saw social life based on *difference.*

For Durkheim, urban society offers more individual choice,
moral tolerance, and personal privacy than people find in rural villages. In sum, Durkheim thought that something is lost in the process
of urbanization, but much is gained.

Georg Simmel: The Blasé Urbanite

The German sociologist Georg Simmel (1858–1918) offered a micro-
level analysis of cities, studying how urban life shapes individual experience. According to Simmel, individuals see the city as a crush of
people, objects, and events. To prevent being overwhelmed by all this
stimulation, urbanites develop a *blasé attitude,* tuning out much of
what goes on around them. Such detachment does not mean that city
dwellers lack compassion for others; they simply keep their distance
as a survival strategy so that they can focus their time and energy on
the people and things that really matter to them.

The Chicago School:
Robert Park and Louis Wirth

Sociologists in the United States soon joined the study of rapidly
growing cities. Robert Park (1864–1944), a leader of the first U.S.

sociology program at the University of Chicago, sought to add a street-
level perspective by getting out and studying real cities. As he said of
himself, "I suspect that I have actually covered more ground, tramping about in cities in different parts of the world, than any other living man" (1950:viii). Walking the streets, Park found the city to be
an organized mosaic of distinctive ethnic communities, commercial
centers, and industrial districts. Over time, he observed, these "natural areas" develop and change in relation to one another. To Park, the
city was a living organism—a human kaleidoscope.

Another major figure in the Chicago School of urban sociology
was Louis Wirth (1897–1952). Wirth (1938) is best known for blending the ideas of Tönnies, Durkheim, Simmel, and Park into a comprehensive theory of urban life.

Wirth began by defining the city as a setting with a large, dense, and
socially diverse population. These traits result in an impersonal, superficial, and transitory way of life for city dwellers. Living among millions of others, urbanites come into contact with many more people
than residents of rural areas. Thus when city people take notice of others at all, they usually know them not in terms of *who they are* but *what
they do*—as, for instance, the bus driver, the pharmacist, or the grocery
store clerk. These specialized urban relationships are sometimes pleasant for all concerned, but we should remember that self-interest rather
than friendship is the main reason behind the interaction.

The impersonal nature of urban relationships, together with the
great social diversity found in cities today, makes city dwellers more

urban ecology the study of the link between the physical and social dimensions of cities

○ Making the Grade

Urban ecology was a significant part of urban sociology until about 1970; after that, it declined in importance as urban political economy gained the attention of sociologists.

THINKING ABOUT DIVERSITY: RACE, CLASS, & GENDER

Minorities Now a Majority in the Largest U.S. Cities

According to the 2000 census, minorities—Hispanics, African Americans, and Asians—were now a majority of the population in 48 of the 100 largest U.S. cities, up from 30 in 1990, and the number has surely increased since then.

What accounts for the change? One reason is that large cities have been losing their non-Hispanic white populations. For example, by 2000, Santa Ana, California, had lost 38 percent of the white population it had in 1990; the drop was 40 percent in Birmingham, Alabama, and a whopping 53 percent in Detroit, Michigan. The white share of the population of all 100 of the largest cities fell from 52.1 percent in 1990 to 43.8 percent in 2000, as the figure shows.

But perhaps the biggest reason for the minority-majority trend is the increase in immigration. Immigration, coupled with higher birth rates among new immigrants, resulted in a 43 percent gain in the Hispanic population (almost 4 million people) of the largest 100 cities between 1990 and 2000. The Asian population also surged by

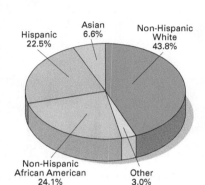

Population Profile for the 100 Largest U.S. Cities, 2000

Racial and ethnic minorities make up a majority of the population of this country's 100 largest cities.

Source: U.S. Census Bureau (2001).

40 percent (more than 1.1 million people). The African American population was steady over the course of the 1990s.

Political officials and other policymakers examine these figures closely. Clearly, the future vitality of the largest U.S. cities depends on meeting the needs and taking advantage of the contributions of their swelling minority populations.

WHAT DO YOU THINK?

1. Why are the minority populations of large U.S. cities increasing?

2. What positive changes and challenges does a minority-majority bring to a city?

3. Before Hurricane Katrina, African Americans represented 60 percent of the population of New Orleans; afterward, the share was about 40 percent. What difference might this change make in the city's immediate future?

Sources: Schmitt (2001) and U.S. Census Bureau (2009).

tolerant than rural villagers. Rural communities often jealously enforce their narrow traditions, but the heterogeneous population of a city rarely shares any single code of moral conduct (T. C. Wilson, 1985, 1995).

○ **CRITICAL REVIEW** In both Europe and the United States, early sociologists presented a mixed view of urban living. Rapid urbanization troubled Tönnies and Wirth, who saw personal ties and traditional morality lost in the anonymous rush of the city. Durkheim and Park emphasized urbanism's positive face, pointing to more personal freedom and greater personal choice.

One problem with all of these views is that they paint urbanism in broad strokes that overlook the effects of class, race, and gender. There are many kinds of urbanites—rich and poor, black and white, Anglo and Latino, women and men—all leading distinctive lives (Gans, 1968). As the Thinking About Diversity box explains, the share of racial and ethnic minorities in the largest U.S. cities increased sharply during the 1990s. We see social diversity most clearly in cities, where various categories of

people are large enough to form visible communities (Macionis & Parrillo, 2007).

○ **CHECK YOUR LEARNING** Of these urban sociologists—Tönnies, Durkheim, Park, and Wirth—which were more positive about urban life? Which were more negative? In each case, explain why.

Urban Ecology

Sociologists (especially members of the Chicago School) developed **urban ecology,** *the study of the link between the physical and social dimensions of cities.* For example, why are cities located where they are? The first cities emerged in fertile regions where the ecology favored raising crops. Preindustrial people, concerned with defense, built their cities on mountains (ancient Athens was perched on an outcropping of rock) or surrounded by water (Paris and Mexico City were built on islands). With the Industrial Revolution, economic considerations placed all major U.S. cities near rivers and natural harbors that facilitated trade.

Go to the Multimedia Library at **mysoclab.com**
to view the *Core Concepts in Sociology* video
"Challenges Facing Cities"

Seeing Sociology in Everyday Life

The decline of industrial production is evident in the decline of industrial cities, such as Detroit.

Urban ecologists also study the physical design of cities. In 1925, Ernest W. Burgess, a student and colleague of Robert Park's, described land use in Chicago in terms of *concentric zones*. City centers, Burgess observed, are business districts bordered by a ring of factories, followed by residential rings with housing that becomes more expensive the farther it is from the noise and pollution of the city's center.

Homer Hoyt (1939) refined Burgess's observations, noting that distinctive districts sometimes form *wedge-shaped sectors*. For example, one fashionable area may develop next to another, or an industrial district may extend outward from a city's center along a train or trolley line.

Chauncy Harris and Edward Ullman (1945) added yet another insight: As cities decentralize, they lose their single-center form in favor of a *multicentered model*. As cities grow, residential areas, industrial parks, and shopping districts typically push away from one another. Few people want to live close to industrial areas, for example, so the city becomes a mosaic of distinct districts.

Social area analysis investigates what people in particular neighborhoods have in common. Three factors seem to explain most of the variation in neighborhood types: family patterns, social class, and race and ethnicity (Shevky & Bell, 1955; R. J. Johnston, 1976). Families with children look for areas with large apartments or single-family homes and good schools. The rich seek high-prestige neighborhoods, often in the central city near cultural attractions. People with a common race or ethnic heritage cluster in distinctive communities.

Brian Berry and Philip Rees (1969) tied together many of these insights. They explained that distinct family types tend to settle in the concentric zones described by Burgess. Specifically, households with few children tend to cluster toward the city's center, and those with more children live farther away. Social class differences are primarily responsible for the sector-shaped districts described by Hoyt; the rich occupy one "side of the tracks" and the poor the other. And racial and ethnic neighborhoods are found at various places throughout the city, consistent with Harris and Ullman's multicentered model.

Urban Political Economy

In the late 1960s, many large U.S. cities were rocked by major riots. As public awareness of racial and economic inequality increased, some analysts turned away from the ecological approach to a social-conflict understanding of city life. The *urban political-economy model* applies Karl Marx's analysis of conflict in the workplace to conflict in the city (Lindstrom, 1995). ● Go to **mysoclab.com**

Political economists reject the ecological approach's view of the city as a natural organism with particular districts and neighborhoods

The industrial revolution created great cities across the United States. In recent decades, however, the movement of industry abroad has brought decline to Detroit and other older cities in the "rustbelt." From this abandoned warehouse, we see the headquarters of General Motors, which, in 2009, declared bankruptcy. What do you see as the future of such cities?

Paul Sancya/AP Wide World Photos

developing according to an internal logic. Instead, they see city life as defined by people with power: corporate leaders and political officials. Capitalism, which transforms the city into real estate traded for profit and concentrates wealth in the hands of the few, is the key to understanding city life. From this point of view, the decline in industrial Snowbelt cities after 1950 was the result of deliberate decisions by the corporate elite to move their production facilities to the Sunbelt (where labor is cheaper and less likely to be unionized) or move them out of the country entirely to low-income nations (Molotch, 1976; Castells, 1977, 1983; Lefebvre, 1991; Jones & Wilson, 1999).

CRITICAL REVIEW The fact that many U.S. cities are in crisis, with widespread poverty, high crime, and barely functioning schools, seems to favor the political-economy view over the urban ecology approach. But one criticism applies to both: They focus on U.S. cities during a limited period of history. Much of what we know about industrial cities does not apply to preindustrial towns in our own past or the rapidly growing cities in many poor nations today. It is unlikely that any single model of cities can account for the full range of urban diversity.

CHECK YOUR LEARNING In your own words, explain what the urban ecology theories and the urban political-economy theory teach us about cities.

Making the Grade

Be sure you understand when and where the three urban revolutions occurred.

ecology the study of the interaction of living organisms and the natural environment

natural environment Earth's surface and atmosphere, including living organisms, air, water, soil, and other resources necessary to sustain life

ecosystem a system composed of the interaction of all living organisms and their natural environment

environmental deficit profound long-term harm to the natural environment caused by humanity's focus on short-term material affluence

Urbanization in Poor Nations

> **November 16, Cairo, Egypt.** People call the vast Muslim cemetery in Old Cairo the "City of the Dead." In truth, it is very much alive: Tens of thousands of squatters have moved into the mausoleums, making this place an eerie mix of life and death. Children run across the stone floors, clotheslines stretch between the monuments, and an occasional television antenna protrudes from a tomb roof. With Cairo gaining 1,000 people a day, families live where they can.

Twice in its history, the world has experienced a revolutionary expansion of cities. The first urban revolution began about 8000 B.C.E. with the first urban settlements and continued until permanent settlements were in place on several continents. About 1750, the second urban revolution took off; it lasted for two centuries as the Industrial Revolution spurred rapid growth of cities in Europe and North America.

A third urban revolution is now under way. Today, 75 percent of people in high-income countries are already city dwellers. But extraordinary urban growth is occurring in low-income nations. In 1950, about 25 percent of the people in poor countries lived in cities. In 2008, the world became mostly urban for the first time in history, with more than half of humanity living in cities (Population Reference Bureau, 2009).

Not only are more people urban, but cities are also getting bigger. In 1950, only seven cities in the world had populations over 5 million, and only two of these were in low-income countries. By 2007, forty-nine cities had passed this mark, and two-thirds of them were in less developed nations (Brockerhoff, 2000; United Nations, 2008).

This third urban revolution is the result of many poor nations entering the high-growth Stage 2 of demographic transition theory. Falling death rates have fueled population increases in Latin America, Asia, and especially Africa. For urban areas, the rate of increase is *twice as high* because in addition to natural increase, millions of people leave the countryside each year in search of jobs, health care, education, and conveniences such as running water and electricity. As cities grow, so do suburbs.

Cities do offer more opportunities than rural areas, but they provide no quick fix for the problems of escalating population and grinding poverty. Many cities in less developed nations—including Mexico City, Egypt's Cairo, India's Kolkata (formerly Calcutta), and Manila in the Philippines—are simply unable to meet the basic needs of much of their population. All these cities are surrounded by wretched shantytowns, settlements of makeshift homes built from discarded materials. Even city dumps are home to thousands of poor people, who pick through the waste hoping to find enough to eat or sell to make it through another day.

Environment and Society

The human species has prospered, rapidly expanding over the entire planet. An increasing share of the global population now lives in large, complex settlements that offer the promise of a better life than that found in rural villages.

But these advances have come at a high price. Never before in history have human beings placed such demands on the planet. This disturbing development brings us to focus on the interplay of the natural environment and society. Like demography, **ecology** is another cousin of sociology, formally defined as *the study of the interaction of living organisms and the natural environment.* Ecology rests on the research of natural scientists as well as social scientists. We shall focus on the aspects of ecology that involve familiar sociological concepts and issues.

The **natural environment** is *Earth's surface and atmosphere, including living organisms, air, water, soil, and other resources necessary to sustain life.* Like every other species, humans depend on the natural environment to survive. Yet with our capacity for culture, humans stand apart from other species; we alone take deliberate action to remake the world according to our own interests and desires, for better and for worse.

Why is the environment of interest to sociologists? Environmental problems, from pollution to global warming, do not arise from the natural world operating on its own. Such problems result from the choices and actions of human beings, making them *social* problems.

The Global Dimension

The study of the natural environment requires a global perspective. The reason is simple: Regardless of political divisions between nations, the planet is a single **ecosystem,** which encompasses *the interaction of all living organisms and their natural environment.*

The Greek meaning of *eco* is "house," reminding us that this planet is our home and that all living things and their natural environment are interrelated. A change in any part of the natural environment sends ripples through the entire global ecosystem.

Consider, from an ecological point of view, our national love of eating hamburgers. People in North America (and, increasingly, around the world) have created a huge demand for beef, which has greatly expanded ranching in Brazil, Costa Rica, and other Latin American nations. To produce the lean meat sought by fast-food corporations, cattle in Latin America feed on grass, which uses a great deal of land. Latin American ranchers clear the land for grazing by cutting down thousands of square miles of forests each year. These

Population, Urbanization, and Environment

○ Making the Grade

I = PAT is an important environmental idea; be sure you understand its meaning.

○ Seeing Sociology
in Everyday Life

Can you identify ways in which the mass media and our popular culture (music, films, and television) encourage people to support the logic of growth?

tropical forests are vital to maintaining Earth's atmosphere. Deforestation ends up threatening everyone, including the people back in the United States enjoying their hamburgers (N. Myers, 1984a).

Technology and the Environmental Deficit

Sociologists point to a simple formula: $I = PAT$, where environmental impact (I) reflects a society's population (P), its level of affluence (A), and its level of technology (T). Members of simpler societies—the hunters and gatherers described—hardly affect the environment because they are few in number, are poor, and have only simple technology. Nature affects all aspects of their lives as they follow the migration of game, watch the rhythm of the seasons, and suffer from natural catastrophes, such as fires, floods, droughts, and storms.

Societies at intermediate stages of sociocultural evolution have a somewhat greater capacity to affect the environment. But the environmental impact of horticulture (small-scale farming), pastoralism (the herding of animals), and even agriculture (the use of animal-drawn plows) is limited because people still rely on muscle power for producing food and other goods.

Human control of the natural environment increased dramatically with the changes brought about by the Industrial Revolution. Muscle power gave way to engines that burn fossil fuels: coal at first and then oil. The use of such machinery affects the environment in two ways: It consumes more natural resources and releases more pollutants into the atmosphere. Even more important, humans armed with industrial technology are able to bend nature to their will, tunneling through mountains, damming rivers, irrigating deserts, and drilling for oil in the arctic wilderness and on the ocean floor. This explains why people in rich nations, who represent just 23 percent of humanity, account for half of the world's energy use (World Bank, 2009).

Not only do industrial societies use more energy, but they produce 100 times more goods than agrarian societies do. Higher living standards are good in some ways, but they increase the problems of solid waste (because people ultimately throw away most of what they produce) and pollution (industrial production generates smoke and other toxic substances).

From the start, people recognized the material benefits of industrial technology. But only a century later did they begin to see its long-term effects on the natural environment. Today, we realize that the technological power to make our lives better can also put the lives of future generations at risk, and there is a national debate about how to address this issue. Seeing Sociology in the News describes one high school's efforts to address environmental issues.

Evidence is mounting that we are running up an **environmental deficit,** *profound long-term harm to the natural environment caused by*

Wilfried Krecichwost/Zefa\CORBIS- NY

The most important insight sociology offers about our physical world is that environmental problems do not simply "happen." Rather, the state of the natural environment reflects the ways in which social life is organized—how people live and what they think is important. The greater the technological power of a society, the greater that society's ability to threaten the natural environment.

humanity's focus on short-term material affluence (Bormann, 1990). The concept of environmental deficit is important for three reasons. First, it reminds us that environmental concerns are *sociological,* reflecting societies' priorities about how people should live. Second, it suggests that much environmental damage—to the air, land, and water—is *unintended.* By focusing on the short-term benefits of, say, cutting down forests, strip mining, or using throwaway packaging, we fail to see the long-term environmental effects. Third, in some respects, the environmental deficit is *reversible.* Inasmuch as societies have created environmental problems, societies can undo many of them.

Culture: Growth and Limits

Whether we recognize environmental dangers and decide to do something about them is a cultural matter. Thus along with technology, culture has powerful environmental consequences.

Rolling Stone

Boyz Under the Hood

BY DAVID KUSHNER
December 18, 2008

Even among the roughest schools in the country, West Philadelphia High School stands out. Situated among boarded-up abandoned buildings and graffiti-covered crack houses, the school has had dozens of arson fires. A Spanish teacher was beaten bloody with a fire extinguisher. A music instructor got a broken jaw after being slugged by a pupil for trying to take away a cell phone. One 15-year-old girl was left for dead after having her face slashed while waiting for her school bus. She survived, but needed 114 stitches.

But in the automotive shop class in a garage next door, a group of African American students and their scrappy white teacher are making their school famous for something else: building the world's greenest car. Kids in baggy jeans and sideways hats mill around a sleek purple car they built that runs on biodiesel. Sparks fly from a chainsaw as one boy cuts through an aluminum plate, his long afro held back by the strap of his scuffed goggles.

Behind a windowed wall, half a dozen girls are busy at their iMacs. Samantha Wright . . . boots up a solar charging station she designed using an image of a rundown Philadelphia parking lot from Google Earth, and augmented it with green roofs and cars. "The photoactive panels convert the sunlight into direct energy," she explains, pointing to a carport onscreen. "We're changing the world, man. I never expected to be doing that."

Like the other kids in the shop, Wright, the daughter of a phone sex worker and absentee dad, overcame incredible odds to find a haven here at the Electric Vehicle X Club, an after-school program that has been turning these cars and kids around, and that's not all. While Washington and Detroit hit the skids on delivering alternative fuel cars for the masses, these inner-city teens are churning out some of the most badass and competitive eco-wheels on the planet for as little as $15,000. As the blog Treehugger puts it, they're "sending a message to the major U.S. auto manufacturers: if we can do it, why can't you?"

In addition to clocking their suburban opponents at state science fairs, the EVX Club has crushed colleges and high-financed corporate start-ups with back-to-back titles in the coveted Northeast Sustainable Energy Association's Tour De Sol, a prestigious eco-car challenge. They modified a Saturn to run on soybean fuel, and transformed a Slovakian kit car into a wildly sporty hybrid called the Hybrid X. "Hybrids don't have to be slow and ugly like a Prius," says 18-year-old EV member, Lawrence Jones-Mahoney. "They can be efficient and cool."

Now the team is racing to prove their cars—and themselves—to the world. They're the dark horse entrants in the Progressive Automotive X-Prize: a worldwide contest to build a car, suitable for mass production, that gets 100 miles per gallon. The contest runs through summer 2010, and the winner gets $10 million. . . .

Simon Hauger, the 38-year-old neighborhood hero who runs the West Philly High auto school, is working overtime with his students to win. But the checkered flag is theirs. "The fact that

The Logic of Growth

When you turn on the television news, you might hear a story like this: "The government reported bad economic news today, with the economy growing by only half a percent during the first quarter of the year." If you stop to think about it, our culture defines an economy that isn't growing as "stagnant" (which is bad) and an economy that is getting smaller as a recession or a "depression" (which is *very* bad). What is "good" is *growth*—the economy getting bigger and bigger. More cars, bigger homes, more income, more spending—the idea of *more* is at the heart of our cultural definition of living well (McKibben, 2007).

One of the reasons we define growth in positive terms is that we value *material comfort,* believing that money and the things it buys improve our lives. We also believe in the idea of *progress,* thinking that the future will be better than the present. In addition, we look to *science* to make our lives easier and more rewarding. In simpler terms, "having things is good," "life gets better," and "people are clever." Taken together, such cultural values form the *logic of growth.*

An optimistic view of the world, the logic of growth holds that more powerful technology has improved our lives and that new discoveries will continue to do so in the future. Throughout the history of the United States and other high-income nations, the logic of growth has been the driving force behind settling the

wilderness, building towns and roads, and pursuing material affluence.

However, "progress" can lead to unexpected problems, including strain on the environment. The logic of growth responds by arguing that people (especially scientists and other technology experts) will find a way out of any problem placed in our path. If, for example, the world runs short of oil, scientists will come up with hydrogen, solar, or nuclear engines or some as yet unknown technology to meet the world's energy needs.

Environmentalists counter that the logic of growth is flawed because it assumes that natural resources such as clean air, fresh water, and fertile soil will always be plentiful. We can and will exhaust these *finite* resources if we continue to pursue growth at any cost. Echoing Malthus, environmentalists warn that if we call on the planet to support increasing numbers of people, we will surely destroy the environment—and ourselves—in the process.

The Limits to Growth

If we cannot invent our way out of the problems created by the logic of growth, perhaps we need another way of thinking about the world. Environmentalists therefore counter that growth must have limits. Stated simply, the *limits-to-growth thesis* is that humanity must put in place policies to control the growth of population, production, and the use of resources in order to avoid environmental collapse.

Population, Urbanization, and Environment

486

we've come this far," Hauger says, looking around the room, "we've already won." . . .

When a go-kart was donated to the school, Hauger decided to start an after-school science group that would work on building an electric motor for the kart. He called it the Electric Vehicle Club. One by one, kids trickled in after school—gang members, drug dealers. One kid had a 150 IQ, but a mom on crack and a dad dying of AIDS. The kid was bouncing between foster homes and stealing credit cards on the side. But when Hauger slapped a wrench in the kid's hand, he was transformed. "When he would work on a project, he would block out all the crap in his life," Hauger recalls, "and he became a mad scientist. Working on this made all the math and science hands on." . . .

As word of Hauger's club spread, kids got turned on not only by getting under the hood, but by making cars that can better the planet—and busting labels along the way. "There's a stereotype that urban kids are just violent and don't care about anything," says Wright, "but we know the environment is important, and we can do something about it."

For the EV club's next project, they modified a silver Jeep Wrangler to go electric. Clueless how to proceed, they hit the Net—downloading instructions from an obscure eco-geek magazine called *Mother Earth.* With Hauger guiding them and improvising plenty, they ripped out the gas engine and stored 217 lead acid batteries in a custom aluminum casing. When they drove their electric hot rod Jeep into the city's science fair of microscopes and Bunsen burners, jaws dropped. "The judges didn't know what to do with it," Hauger recalls. Then they gave West Philly High the top prize. . . .

As the current 15 kids on the EVX team mill around the garage, talk turns to the plans for the Auto X prize. "As crazy as it sounds, I think we have a shot at winning," Hauger says. While the competition is focusing on high-priced cars that look like the Jetsons, the EVX team is taking a decidedly more accessible—and they hope—winning approach. . . .

. . . The EVX team's legacy is already spreading among those in the eco-car pursuit. "It's inspiring that a contest can inspire a group like that to

compete," says Darryl Siry, spokesperson for Tesla, "it says something about who they are. I recommend they not listen to people who tell them this is how it's done. Innovation comes from figuring out solutions and answers to problems in new ways."

WHAT DO YOU THINK?

1. Do you think that many people think of environmental issues as the concerns mainly of more well-off people? Explain.

2. Would you make environmental study part of the curriculum of every school in the country? Why or why not?

3. What specific strategies or policies would you suggest to encourage greater environmental understanding on the part of this country's young people?

Adapted from the original article, "Boyz Under the Hood" by David Kushner, from RolllingStone.com, December 18, 2008, copyright ©2008 Rolling Stone LLC. All rights reserved. Reprinted by permission.

In *The Limits to Growth,* a controversial book that played a large part in launching the environmental movement, Donella Meadows and her colleagues (1972) used a computer model to calculate the planet's available resources, rates of population growth, amount of land available for cultivation, levels of industrial and food production, and amount of pollutants released into the atmosphere. The model reflects changes that have occurred since 1900 and projects forward to the end of the twenty-first century. The authors concede that such long-range predictions are speculative, and some critics think they are plain wrong (Simon, 1981).

But right or wrong, the conclusions of the study call for serious consideration. The authors claim that we are quickly consuming Earth's finite resources. Supplies of oil, natural gas, and other energy sources are declining and will continue to drop, a little faster or more slowly depending on the conservation policies of rich nations and the speed with which other nations such as India and China continue to industrialize. Within the next 100 years, resources will run out, crippling industrial output and causing a decline in food production.

This limits-to-growth theory shares Malthus's pessimism about the future. People who accept it doubt that current patterns of life are sustainable for even another century. Perhaps we can all learn to live with less. This may not be as hard as you might think: Research shows, for example, that as material consumption has gone up in

recent decades, there has been no increase in levels of personal happiness (D. G. Myers, 2000). In the end, environmentalists warn, either make fundamental changes in how we live, placing less strain on the natural environment, or widespread hunger and conflict will force change on us.

Solid Waste: The Disposable Society

Across the United States, people generate a massive amount of solid waste—about 1.4 billion pounds *each and every day.* Figure 4 shows the composition of a typical community's trash.

As a rich nation of people who value convenience, the United States has become a *disposable society.* We consume more products than virtually any other nation, and many of these products have throwaway packaging. For example, fast food is served in cardboard, plastic, and Styrofoam containers that we throw away within minutes. But countless other products, from film to fishhooks, are elaborately packaged to make them more attractive to the customer and to discourage tampering and theft.

Manufacturers market soft drinks, beer, and fruit juices in aluminum cans, glass jars, and plastic containers, which not only use up finite resources but also create mountains of solid waste. Countless items are intentionally designed to be disposable: pens, razors, flashlights, batteries, even cameras. Other goods, from lightbulbs to

● Seeing Sociology
in Everyday Life

Do you think that having more, in a materialistic sense, is the
path to personal happiness? Why or why not?

● Seeing Sociology
in Everyday Life

Think about how specific ways we live put more or less strain
on the natural environment.

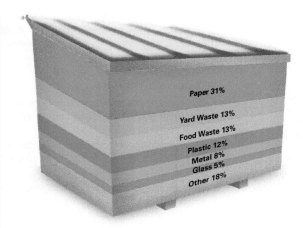

FIGURE 4   Composition of Community Trash

We throw away a wide range of material, with paper the single largest
part of our trash.

Source: U.S. Environmental Protection Agency (2009).

automobiles, are designed to have a limited useful life, after which
they become unwanted junk. As Paul Connett (1991) points out,
even the words we use to describe what we throw away—*waste, trash,
refuse, garbage, rubbish*—show how little we value what we cannot
immediately use. But this was not always the case, as the Seeing Sociology in Everyday Life box explains.

Living in a rich society, the average person in the United States
consumes hundreds of times more energy, plastics, lumber, and other
resources than someone living in a low-income nation such as
Bangladesh or Tanzania (and nearly twice as much as someone living in many other high-income countries such as Japan or Sweden).
This high level of consumption means that we in the United States
not only use a disproportionate share of the planet's natural resources
but also that we generate most of the world's refuse.

We like to say that we throw things "away." But more than half
of our solid waste never goes away. It ends up in landfills, which are,
literally, filling up. Material in landfills can also pollute groundwater
stored under Earth's surface. Although in most places laws now regulate what can be discarded in a landfill, the Environmental Protection Agency has identified 1,269 dump sites across the United States
containing hazardous materials that are polluting water both above
and below the ground. In addition, what goes into landfills all too
often stays there, sometimes for centuries. Tens of millions of tires,
disposable diapers, and other items that we bury in landfills each
year do not decompose and will be an unwelcome legacy for future
generations.

Environmentalists argue that we should address the problem of
solid waste by doing what many of our grandparents did: turn
"waste" into a resource. One way to do this is through *recycling*,
reusing resources we would otherwise throw away. Recycling is an
accepted practice in Japan and many other nations, and it is becoming more common in the United States, where we now reuse about
33 percent of waste materials. The share is increasing as more munic-
ipalities pass laws requiring reuse of certain materials such as glass
bottles and aluminum cans and as the business of recycling becomes
more profitable.

Water and Air

Oceans, lakes, and streams are the lifeblood of the global ecosystem.
Humans depend on water for drinking, bathing, cooling, cooking,
recreation, and a host of other activities.

According to what scientists call the *hydrologic cycle,* the planet
naturally recycles water and refreshes the land. The process begins as
heat from the sun causes Earth's water, 97 percent of which is in the
oceans, to evaporate and form clouds. Because water evaporates at
lower temperatures than most pollutants, the water vapor that rises
from the seas is relatively pure, leaving various contaminants behind.
Water then falls to the Earth as rain, which drains into streams and
rivers and finally returns to the sea. Two major concerns about water,
then, are supply and pollution.

Water Supply

Less than one-tenth of 1 percent of Earth's water is suitable for drinking. It is not surprising, then, that for thousands of years, water rights
have figured prominently in laws around the world. Today, some
regions of the world, especially the tropics, enjoy plentiful fresh water,
using only a small share of the available supply. High demand, coupled with modest reserves, makes water supply a matter of concern in
much of North America and Asia, where people look to rivers rather
than rainfall for their water. In China, deep aquifers are dropping rapidly. In the Middle East, water supply is reaching a critical level. Iran
is rationing water in its capital city. In Egypt, people can consume
just one-sixth as much water from the Nile River today as in 1900.
Across northern Africa and the Middle East, as many as 1 billion people may lack the water they need for irrigation and drinking by 2025
("China Faces Water Shortage," 2001; International Development
Research Center, 2006).

Rising population and the development of more complex technology have greatly increased the world's appetite for water. The
global consumption of water (now estimated at almost 4,000 cubic
kilometers, or 140 trillion cubic feet, per year) has doubled since
1950 and is rising steadily. As a result, even in parts of the world that
receive plenty of rainfall, people are using groundwater faster than

SEEING SOCIOLOGY IN EVERYDAY LIFE

Why Grandma Macionis Had No Trash

Grandma Macionis, we always used to say, never threw away anything. She was born and raised in Lithuania—the "old country"—where growing up in a poor village shaped her in ways that never changed, even after she came to the United States as a young woman and settled in Philadelphia.

In her later years, when I knew her, I remember the family traveling together to her house to celebrate her birthday. We never knew what to get Grandma because although she didn't have all that much, she never seemed to need anything. She lived a simple life and had simple clothes and showed little interest in "fancy things." She used everything until it wore out. Her kitchen knives, for example, were worn narrow from decades of sharpening. And she hardly ever threw anything away—she recycled all her garbage as compost for her vegetable garden.

After opening a birthday present, she would carefully save the box, wrapping paper, and ribbon, which meant as much to her as whatever gift they surrounded. We all expected her to save every bit of whatever she was given, smiling to each other as we watched

her put everything away, knowing she would find a way to use it all again and again.

As strange as Grandma sometimes seemed to her grandchildren, she was a product of her culture. A century ago, there was little "trash." If a pair of socks wore thin, people mended them, probably more than once. When they were beyond repair, they were used as rags for clean-

Grandma Macionis, in the 1970s, with the author.

ing or sewn, along with other old clothing, into a quilt. For her, everything had value, if not in one way, then in another.

During the twentieth century, as women joined men working outside of the home, income went up and families began buying more and more "time-saving" products. Before long, few people cared about the home recycling that Grandma practiced. Soon cities sent crews from block to block to pick up truckloads of discarded material. The era of "trash" had begun.

WHAT DO YOU THINK?

1. Just as Grandma Macionis was a product of her culture, so are we. What cultural values make people today demand time-saving products and "convenience" packaging?

2. Do you recycle drink containers, paper, or other materials? Why or why not?

3. In what ways does this box demonstrate that the state of the natural environment is a social issue?

---

it can be replenished naturally. In the Tamil Nadu region of southern India, for example, people are drawing so much groundwater that the local water table has fallen 100 feet over the past several decades. Mexico City—which has sprawled to some 1,400 square miles—has pumped so much water from its underground aquifer that the city has sunk 30 feet in the past century and continues to drop about 2 inches per year. Farther north in the United States, the Ogallala aquifer, which lies below seven states from South Dakota to Texas, is now being pumped so rapidly that some experts fear it could run dry in just a few decades.

In light of such developments, we must face the reality that water is a valuable and finite resource. Greater conservation of water by individuals (the average person in the United States consumes 3 million gallons in a lifetime) is part of the answer. However, households around the world account for just 10 percent of water use. We need to reduce water consumption by industry, which uses 20 percent of the global total, and farming, which consumes 70 percent of the total for irrigation.

Perhaps new irrigation technology will reduce demand for water in the future. But here again, we see how population increase, as well as economic growth, strains our ecosystem (Postel, 1993; Population Action International, 2000; United Nations World Water Assessment Programme, 2009; U.S. Geological Survey, 2009).

Water Pollution

In large cities from Mexico City to Cairo to Shanghai, many people have no choice but to drink contaminated water. Infectious diseases such as typhoid, cholera, and dysentery, all caused by waterborne microorganisms, spread rapidly through these populations. In addition to ensuring ample *supplies* of water, we must protect the *quality* of water.

Water quality in the United States is generally good by global standards. However, even here the problem of water pollution is steadily growing. Across the United States, rivers and streams absorb hundreds of millions of pounds of toxic waste each year. This pollution

● Seeing Sociology
in Everyday Life

Have you experienced changes in your own world resulting
from global warming or other issues discussed here?

rain forests regions of dense forestation, most of which circle the globe close to
the equator

global warming a rise in Earth's average temperature due to an increasing
concentration of carbon dioxide in the atmosphere

environmental racism patterns of development that expose poor people,
especially minorities, to environmental hazards

results not just from intentional dumping but also from the runoff of agricultural fertilizers and lawn chemicals.

A special problem is *acid rain*—rain made acidic by air pollution—which destroys plant and animal life. Acid rain (or snow) begins with power plants burning fossil fuels (oil and coal) to generate electricity; this burning process releases sulfuric and nitrous oxides into the air. As the wind sweeps these gases into the atmosphere, they react with the air to form sulfuric and nitric acids, which turns atmospheric moisture acidic.

This is a clear case of one type of pollution causing another: Air pollution (from smokestacks) ends up contaminating water (in lakes and streams that collect acid rain). Acid rain is truly a global phenomenon because the regions that suffer the harmful effects may be thousands of miles from the source of the pollution. For instance, British power plants have caused acid rain that has devastated forests and fish in Norway and Sweden, 1,000 miles to the northeast. In the United States, we see a similar pattern as midwestern smokestacks have harmed the natural environment of upstate New York and New England.

Air Pollution

Because we are surrounded by air, most people in the United States are more aware of air pollution than contaminated water. One of the unexpected consequences of industrial technology—especially the factory and the motor vehicle—has been a decline in air quality. In London, fifty years ago, factory smokestacks, automobiles, and coal fires used to heat households all added up to what was probably the worst urban air quality in the world. The fog that some residents jokingly called "pea soup" was in reality a deadly mix of pollutants: In 1952, an especially thick haze that hung over London for five days killed 4,000 people.

Air quality improved in the final decades of the twentieth century. Rich nations passed laws that banned high-pollution heating, including the coal fires that choked London. In addition, scientists devised ways to make factories and motor vehicles operate much more cleanly. The cleanest of today's automobiles emit only a small percentage of the pollutants released by the typical car in 1960.

If people in high-income countries can breathe a bit more easily than they once did, those living in poor societies face problems of air pollution that are becoming more serious. One reason is that people in low-income countries still rely on wood, coal, peat, or other "dirty" fuels to cook their food and heat their homes. In addition, nations eager to encourage short-term industrial development may pay little attention to the longer-term dangers of air pollution. As a result, many cities in Latin America, Eastern Europe, and Asia are plagued by air pollution as bad as London's pea soup back in the 1950s.

The Rain Forests

Rain forests are *regions of dense forestation, most of which circle the globe close to the equator.* The largest tropical rain forests are in South America (notably Brazil), west-central Africa, and Southeast Asia. In all, the world's rain forests cover some 1.5 billion acres, or 4.5 percent of Earth's total land surface (United Nations Environment Programme, 2009).

Like other global resources, rain forests are falling victim to the needs and appetites of the surging world population. As noted earlier, to meet the demand for beef, ranchers in Latin America clear forested areas to increase their supply of grazing land. We are also losing rain forests to the hardwood trade. People in rich nations pay high prices for mahogany and other woods because, as the environmentalist Norman Myers (1984b:88) puts it, they have "a penchant for parquet floors, fine furniture, fancy paneling, weekend yachts, and high-grade coffins." Under such economic pressure, the world's rain forests are now less than half their original size, and they continue to shrink by at least 1 percent (58,000 square miles) annually, which amounts to about one acre every second. Unless we stop this loss, the rain forests will vanish before the end of this century, and with them will go protection for Earth's biodiversity and climate.

Global Warming

Why are rain forests so important to our natural environment? One reason is that they cleanse the atmosphere of carbon dioxide (CO_2). Since the beginning of the Industrial Revolution, the amount of carbon dioxide produced by humans (mostly from factories and automobiles) has risen sharply. Much of this CO_2 is absorbed by the oceans. But plants also take in carbon dioxide and in the process expel oxygen. This is why the rain forests—our largest concentration of plant life—are vital to maintaining the chemical balance of the atmosphere.

The problem is that production of carbon dioxide is rising while the amount of plant life on Earth is shrinking. To make matters worse, rain forests are being destroyed mostly by burning, which releases even more CO_2 into the atmosphere. Experts estimate that the atmospheric concentration of carbon dioxide is now 40 percent higher than it was 150 years ago (Gore, 2006; United Nations Environment Programme, 2009; National Oceanic and Atmospheric Administration, 2010).

High above Earth, carbon dioxide acts like the glass roof of a greenhouse, letting heat from the sun pass through to the surface while preventing much of it from radiating away from the planet. The result of this *greenhouse effect,* say ecologists, is **global warming,** *a rise in Earth's average temperature due to an increasing concentration of carbon dioxide in the atmosphere.* Over the past century, the global temperature has risen about 1.3° Fahrenheit (to

Go to the Multimedia Library at **mysoclab.com** to listen to the NPR report "Sources of Global Warming"

● Seeing Sociology
in Everyday Life

Do you worry much about global warming? Why or why not?
Do you think global warming could affect you personally? How?

an average of 58° F.). Scientists warn that it could rise by 5° to 10° F. during this century. Already, the polar ice caps are melting, and scientists predict that increasing temperatures could melt so much ice that the sea level would rise to cover low-lying land all around the world. Were this to happen, water would cover all of Bangladesh, for example, and much of the coastal United States, including Washington, D.C., right up to the steps of the White House. On the other hand, the U.S. Midwest, currently one of the most productive agricultural regions in the world, probably would become arid.

Some scientists point out that we cannot be sure of the consequences of global warming. Others point to the fact that global temperature changes have been taking place throughout history, perhaps having little or nothing to do with rain forests. A few are optimistic, suggesting that higher concentrations of carbon dioxide in the atmosphere might speed up plant growth (because plants thrive on this gas), and this increase might correct the imbalance and nudge Earth's temperature downward once again. But the consensus of scientists is clear: Global warming is a serious problem that threatens the future for all of us (Kerr, 2005; Gore, 2006; International Panel on Climate Change, 2007; National Oceanic and Atmospheric Administration, 2010). ● Go to **mysoclab.com**

Dave Amit/Reuters\Landov Media

Water is vital to life, and it is also in short supply. The state of Gujarat, in western India, has experienced a long drought. In the village of Natwarghad, people crowd together, lowering pots into the local well, taking what little water is left.

Declining Biodiversity

Our planet is home to as many as 30 million species of animals, plants, and microorganisms. As rain forests are cleared and humans extend their control over nature, several dozen unique species of plants and animals cease to exist each day.

But given the vast number of living species, why should we be concerned about the loss of a few? Environmentalists give four reasons. First, our planet's biodiversity provides a varied source of human food. Using agricultural high technology, scientists can cross familiar crops with more exotic plant life, making food more bountiful and more resistant to insects and disease. Thus biodiversity helps feed our planet's rapidly increasing population.

Second, Earth's biodiversity is a vital genetic resource used by medical and pharmaceutical researchers to provide hundreds of new compounds each year that cure disease and improve our lives. For example, children in the United States now have a good chance of surviving leukemia, a disease that was almost a sure killer two generations ago, because of a compound derived from a tropical flower called the rosy periwinkle. The oral birth control pill, used by tens of millions of women in this country, is another product of plant research, this one involving the Mexican forest yam.

Third, with the loss of any species of life—whether it is the magnificent California condor, the famed Chinese panda, the spotted owl, or even a single species of ant—the beauty and complexity of our natural environment are diminished. And there are clear warning signs: Three-fourths of the world's 10,000 species of birds are declining in number.

Finally, unlike pollution, the extinction of any species is irreversible and final. An important ethical question, then, is whether people living today have the right to impoverish the world for those who will live tomorrow (N. Myers, 1991; E. O. Wilson, 1991; Brown et al., 1993).

Environmental Racism

Environmental problems threaten us all. But most environmental issues harm some people more than others. Conflict theory has given birth to the concept of **environmental racism,** *patterns of development that expose poor people, especially minorities, to environmental hazards.* Historically, factories that spew pollution have stood near neighborhoods housing the poor and people of color. Why? In part, the poor themselves were drawn to factories in search of work, and their low incomes often meant they could afford housing only in undesirable neighborhoods. Sometimes the only housing that fit their budgets stood in the very shadow of the plants and mills where they worked.

Population, Urbanization, and Environment

○ Making the Grade

With its focus on inequality, environmental racism is linked to the social-conflict approach.

ecologically sustainable culture a way of life that meets the needs of the present generation without threatening the environmental legacy of future generations

Nobody wants a factory or dump nearby, but the poor have little power to resist. Through the years, the most serious environmental hazards have been located near Newark, New Jersey (not in upscale Bergen County), in southside Chicago (not in wealthy Lake Forest), or on Native American reservations in the West (not in affluent suburbs of Denver or Phoenix) (Commission for Racial Justice, 1994; Bohon & Humphrey, 2000).

Looking Ahead: Toward a Sustainable Society and World

The demographic analysis presented in this chapter points to some disturbing trends. We see, first, that our planet's population has reached record levels because birth rates remain high in poor nations and death rates have fallen just about everywhere. Reducing fertility will remain a pressing issue throughout this century. Even with some recent decline in the rate of population increase, the nightmare of Thomas Malthus is still a real possibility, as the Controversy & Debate box explains.

Further, population growth remains greatest in the poorest countries of the world, which cannot support their present populations, much less their future ones. Supporting 83 million additional people on our planet each year, 81 million of whom are in poor societies, will take a global commitment to provide not only food but also housing, schools, and employment. The well-being of the entire world may ultimately depend on resolving the economic and social problems of poor, overpopulated countries and bridging the widening gulf between "have" and "have-not" nations.

Urbanization is continuing, especially in poor countries. People have always sought out cities in the hope of finding a better life. But the sheer numbers of people who live in the emerging global supercities, including Mexico City, São Paulo (Brazil), Kinshasa (Democratic Republic of the Congo), Mumbai (India), and Manila (Philippines), have created urban problems on a massive scale.

Throughout the world, humanity is facing a serious environmental challenge. Part of this problem is population increase, which is greatest in poor societies. But part of the problem is the high levels of consumption in rich nations such as our own. By increasing the planet's environmental deficit, our present way of life is borrowing against the well-being of our children and their children. Globally, members of rich societies, who currently consume so much of Earth's resources, are mortgaging the future security of the poor countries of the world.

The answer, in principle, is to create an **ecologically sustainable culture,** *a way of life that meets the needs of the present generation without threatening the environmental legacy of future generations.* Sustainable living depends on three strategies.

First, we need to *bring population growth under control.* The current population of 6.8 billion is already straining the natural environment. Clearly, the higher world population climbs, the more difficult environmental problems will become. Even if the recent slowing of population growth continues, the world will have 9 billion people by 2050. Few analysts think that Earth can support this many people; most argue that we must hold the line at about 7 billion, and some argue that we must *decrease* population in the coming decades (Smail, 2010).

A second strategy is to *conserve finite resources.* This means meeting our needs with a responsible eye toward the future by using resources efficiently, seeking alternative sources of energy, and in some cases, learning to live with less.

A third strategy is to *reduce waste.* Whenever possible, simply using less is the best solution. Learning to live with less will not come easily, but keep in mind that as our society has consumed more and more in recent decades, people have not become any happier (D. G. Myers, 2000). Recycling programs, too, are part of the answer, and recycling can make everyone part of the solution to our environmental problems.

Valery Hache/Agence France Presse/Getty Images

If human ingenuity created the threats to our environment we now face, can humans also solve these problems? In recent years, a number of designs for small, environmentally friendly cars show the promise of new technology. But do such innovations go far enough? Will we have to make more basic changes to our way of life to ensure human survival in the centuries to come?

CONTROVERSY & DEBATE

Apocalypse: Will People Overwhelm the Planet?

NUSHAWN: I'm telling you, there are too many people already! Where is everyone going to live?

TABITHA: Have you ever been to Kansas? Or Wyoming? There's plenty of empty space out there.

MARCO: Maybe now. But I'm not so sure there'll be all that room for our children—or their children. . . .

Are you worried about the world's rapidly increasing population? Think about this: By the time you finish reading this box, more than 1,000 people will have been added to our planet. By this time tomorrow, global population will have risen by more than 200,000. Currently, as the table shows, there are four births for every two deaths on the planet, pushing the world's population upward by almost 83 million people annually. Put another way, global population growth amounts to adding another Germany to the world each year.

It is no wonder that many demographers and environmentalists are deeply concerned about the future. Earth has an unprecedented population: The 2.8 billion people we have added since 1974 alone exceed the planet's total in 1900. Might Thomas Malthus—who predicted that overpopulation would push the world into war and suffering—be right after all? Lester Brown and other *neo-Malthusians* predict a coming apocalypse if we do not change our ways. Brown (1995) admits that Malthus failed to imagine how much technology (especially fertilizers and plant genetics) could boost the planet's agricultural output. But he maintains that Earth's rising population is rapidly outstripping its finite resources. Families in many poor countries can find little firewood, members of rich countries are depleting the oil reserves, and everyone is draining our supply of clean water and poisoning the planet with waste. Some ana-

lysts argue that we have already passed Earth's "carrying capacity" for population and that we need to hold the line or even reduce global population to ensure our long-term survival.

But other analysts, the *anti-Malthusians*, sharply disagree. Julian Simon (1995) points out that two centuries after Malthus predicted catastrophe, Earth supports almost six times as many people who, on average, live longer, healthier lives than ever before. With more advanced technology, people have devised ways to increase productivity and limit population increase. As Simon sees it, this is cause for celebration. Human ingenuity has consistently proved the doomsayers wrong, and Simon is betting that it will continue to do so.

WHAT DO YOU THINK?

1. Where do you place your bet? Do you think Earth can support 8 or 10 billion people? Explain your reasoning.

2. Almost all current population growth is in poor countries. What does this mean for the future of rich nations? For the future of poor ones?

3. What should people in rich countries do to ensure the future of children everywhere?

Sources: Brown (1995), Simon (1995), Scanlon (2001), and Smail (2007).

Global Population Increase, 2009

	Births	Deaths	Net Increase
Per year	138,949,000	56,083,000	82,866,000
Per month	11,579,083	4,673,583	6,905,500
Per day	380,682	155,652	227,030
Per hour	15,862	6,402	9,460
Per minute	264	107	158
Per second	4.4	1.8	2.6

In the end, making all three of these strategies work depends on a more basic change in the way we think about ourselves and our world. Our *egocentric* outlook sets our own interests as standards for how to live; a sustainable environment demands an *ecocentric* outlook that helps us see that the present is tied to the future and that everyone must work together. Most nations in the southern half of the world are *underdeveloped*, unable to meet the basic needs of their people. At the same time, most countries in the northern half of the world are *overdeveloped*, using more resources than Earth can sustain over time. The changes needed to create a sustainable ecosystem will not come easily, and they will be costly. But the price of *not*

responding to the growing environmental deficit will certainly be greater (Brown et al., 1993; Population Action International, 2000; Gore, 2006).

Finally, consider that the great dinosaurs dominated this planet for some 160 million years and then perished forever. Humanity is far younger, having existed for a mere 250,000 years. Compared to the rather dimwitted dinosaurs, our species has the gift of great intelligence. But how will we use this ability? What are the chances that humans will continue to flourish 160 million years—or even 160 years—from now? The answer depends on the choices made by just one of the 30 million species living on Earth: human beings.

Seeing Sociology in Everyday Life

Population, Urbanization, and Environment

Why is the environment a social issue?

As this chapter explains, the state of the natural environment depends on how society is organized, especially the importance a culture attaches to consumption and economic growth.

> **HINT** If expansion is "good times," then contraction is a "recession" or perhaps even a "depression." Such a worldview means that it is normal—or even desirable—to live in a way that increases stress on the natural environment. Sustainability, an idea that is especially important as world population increases, depends on learning to live with what we have or maybe even learning to live with less. Although many people seem to think so, it really doesn't require a 6,000-pound SUV to move around urban areas. Actually, it might not require a car at all. This new way of thinking requires that we do not define social standing and personal success in terms of what we own and what we consume. Can you imagine a society like that? What would it be like?

Richard B. Levine/Newscom

We learn to see economic expansion as natural and good. When the economy stays the same for a number of months, we say we are experiencing "stagnation." How do we define a period when the economy gets smaller, as happened during the fall of 2008?

David Cooper/Toronto Star\ZUMA Press

What would it take to convince members of our society that smaller (rather than bigger) might be better? Why do we seem to prefer not just bigger cars but bigger homes and more and more material possessions?

Applying SOCIOLOGY in Everyday Life

1. Here is an illustration of the problem of runaway growth (Milbrath, 1989:10): "A pond has a single water lily growing on it. The lily doubles in size each day. In thirty days, it covers the entire pond. On which day does it cover half the pond?" When you realize the answer, discuss the implications of this example for population increase.

2. Draw a mental map of a city familiar to you with as much detail of specific places, districts, roads, and transportation facilities as you can. Compare your map to a real one or,

better yet, a map drawn by someone else. Try to account for the differences.

3. As an interesting exercise, carry a trash bag around for a single day, and collect everything you throw away. Most people are surprised to find that the average person in the United States discards close to 5 pounds of paper, metal, plastic, and other materials daily (over a lifetime, that's about 50 tons).

Making the Grade

Population, Urbanization, and Environment

Demography: The Study of Population

Watch on mysoclab.com

✓ *Demography analyzes the size and composition of a population and how and why people move from place to place. Demographers collect data and study several factors that affect population .*

FERTILITY
- Fertility is the incidence of childbearing in a country's population.
- Demographers describe fertility using the **crude birth rate**.

MORTALITY
- Mortality is the incidence of death in a country's population.
- Demographers measure mortality using both the **crude death rate** and the **infant mortality rate.**

MIGRATION
- The **net migration rate** is the difference between the in-migration rate and the out-migration rate.

Explore on mysoclab.com

POPULATION GROWTH
In general, rich nations grow as much from immigration as from natural increase; poorer nations grow almost entirely from natural increase.

POPULATION COMPOSITION
Demographers use **age-sex pyramids** to show graphically the composition of a population and to project population trends.

demography the study of human population

fertility the incidence of childbearing in a country's population

crude birth rate the number of live births in a given year for every 1,000 people in a population

mortality the incidence of death in a country's population

crude death rate the number of deaths in a given year for every 1,000 people in a population

infant mortality rate the number of deaths among infants under one year of age for each 1,000 live births in a given year

life expectancy the average life span of a country's population

migration the movement of people into and out of a specified territory

sex ratio the number of males for every 100 females in a nation's population

age-sex pyramid a graphic representation of the age and sex of a population

History and Theory of Population Growth

- Historically, world population grew slowly because high birth rates were offset by high death rates.
- About 1750, a demographic transition began as world population rose sharply, mostly due to falling death rates.
- In the late 1700s, Thomas Robert Malthus warned that population growth would outpace food production, resulting in social calamity.
- **Demographic transition theory** contends that technological advances gradually slow population increase.
- World population is expected to exceed 9 billion by 2050.

demographic transition theory a thesis that links population patterns to a society's level of technological development

zero population growth the rate of reproduction that maintains population at a steady level

✓ *Currently, the world is gaining 83 million people each year, with 98% of this increase taking place in poor countries .*

Urbanization: The Growth of Cities

Read on mysoclab.com

The **FIRST URBAN REVOLUTION** began with the appearance of cities about 10,000 years ago.
- By about 2,000 years ago, cities had emerged in most regions of the world except North America and Antarctica.
- Preindustrial cities have low buildings; narrow, winding streets; and personal social ties.

A **SECOND URBAN REVOLUTION** began about 1750 as the Industrial Revolution propelled rapid urban growth in Europe.
- The physical form of cities changed as planners created wide, regular streets to allow for more trade.
- The emphasis on commerce, as well as the increasing size of cities, made urban life more impersonal.

urbanization the concentration of population into cities

metropolis a large city that socially and economically dominates an urban area

suburbs urban areas beyond the political boundaries of a city

megalopolis a vast urban region containing a number of cities and their surrounding suburbs

IN THE UNITED STATES, urbanization has been going on for more than 400 years and continues today.
- Urbanization came to North America with European colonists.
- By 1850, hundreds of new cities had been founded from coast to coast.
- By 1920, a majority of the U.S. population lived in urban areas.
- Since 1950, the decentralization of cities has resulted in the growth of suburbs and edge cities and a rebound in rural population.
- Nationally, Sunbelt cities—but not the older Snowbelt cities—are increasing in size and population.

Urbanism as a Way of Life

✓ *Rapid urbanization during the nineteenth century led early sociologists to study the differences between rural and urban life. These early sociologists included, in Europe, Tönnies, Durkheim, and Simmel, and in the United States, Park and Wirth.*

FERDINAND TÖNNIES built his analysis on the concepts of *Gemeinschaft* and *Gesellschaft*.

- *Gemeinschaft*, typical of the rural village, joins people in what amounts to a single primary group.
- *Gesellschaft*, typical of the modern city, describes individuals motivated by their own needs rather than the well-being of the community.

EMILE DURKHEIM agreed with much of Tönnies's thinking but claimed that urbanites do not lack social bonds; the basis of social solidarity simply differs in the two settings.

- **Mechanical solidarity** involves social bonds based on common sentiments and shared moral values. This type of social solidarity is typical of traditional, rural life.
- **Organic solidarity** arises from social bonds based on specialization and interdependence. This type of social solidarity is typical of modern, urban life.

GEORG SIMMEL claimed that the overstimulation of city life produced a blasé attitude in urbanites.

ROBERT PARK, at the University of Chicago, claimed that cities permit greater social freedom.

LOUIS WIRTH saw large, dense, heterogeneous populations creating an impersonal and self-interested, though tolerant, way of life.

Gemeinschaft a type of social organization in which people are closely tied by kinship and tradition

Gesellschaft a type of social organization in which people come together only on the basis of individual self-interest

urban ecology the study of the link between the physical and social dimensions of cities

Urbanization in Poor Nations

- The world's first urban revolution took place about 8000 B.C.E. with the first urban settlements.
- The second urban revolution took place after 1750 in Europe and North America with the Industrial Revolution.
- A third urban revolution is now occurring in poor countries. Today, most of the world's largest cities are found in less developed nations.

Environment and Society

The state of the **ENVIRONMENT** is a social issue because it reflects how human beings organize social life.

- Societies increase the **environmental deficit** by focusing on short-term benefits and ignoring the long-term consequences brought on by their way of life.
- The more complex a society's technology, the greater its capacity to alter the natural environment.

- The *logic-of-growth thesis* supports economic development, claiming that people can solve environmental problems as they arise.
- The *limits-to-growth thesis* states that societies must curb development to prevent eventual environmental collapse.

ecology the study of the interaction of living organisms and the natural environment

natural environment Earth's surface and atmosphere, including living organisms, air, water, soil, and other resources necessary to sustain life

ecosystem the interaction of all living organisms and their natural environment

environmental deficit profound long-term harm to the natural environment caused by humanity's focus on short-term material affluence

rain forests regions of dense forestation, most of which circle the globe close to the equator

global warming a rise in Earth's average temperature due to an increasing concentration of carbon dioxide in the atmosphere

environmental racism patterns of development that expose poor people, especially minorities, to environmental hazards

ecologically sustainable culture a way of life that meets the needs of the present generation without threatening the environmental legacy of future generations

ENVIRONMENTAL ISSUES include

- *Disposing of solid waste:* More than half of what we throw away ends up in landfills, which are filling up and which can pollute groundwater under Earth's surface.
- *Protecting the quality of water and air:* The supply of clean water is already low in some parts of the world. Industrial technology has caused a decline in air quality.
- *Protecting the rain forests:* Rain forests help remove carbon dioxide from the atmosphere and are home to a large share of this planet's living species. Under pressure from development, the world's rain forests are now half their original size and are shrinking by about 1% annually.
- *Global warming:* Increasing levels of carbon dioxide in the atmosphere are causing the average temperature of the planet to rise, melting the ice caps and bringing other dramatic changes to the natural environment.
- *Environmental racism:* Conflict theory has drawn attention to the fact that the poor, especially minorities, suffer most from environmental hazards.

Sample Test Questions

Multiple-Choice Questions

1. *Demography* is defined as the study of
   a. democratic political systems.
   b. human culture.
   c. human population.
   d. the natural environment.

2. Which region of the world has both the lowest birth rate and the lowest infant mortality rate?
   a. Latin America
   b. Europe
   c. Africa
   d. Asia

3. Typically, high-income nations grow mostly from _____, while low-income nations grow from _____.
   a. immigration; natural increase
   b. emigration; natural increase
   c. natural increase; immigration
   d. internal migration; natural increase

4. In general, the higher the average income of a country,
   a. the faster the population increases.
   b. the slower the population increases.
   c. the lower the level of immigration.
   d. the lower the level of urbanization.

5. In the United States, urban decentralization has caused
   a. the expansion of suburbs.
   b. the development of vast urban regions.
   c. the growth of edge cities.
   d. All of the above are correct.

6. Which of the following concepts did Ferdinand Tönnies use to refer to people coming together on the basis of individual self-interest?
   a. mechanical solidarity
   b. organic solidarity
   c. *Gesellschaft*
   d. *Gemeinschaft*

7. The world's third urban revolution is now taking place in
   a. the United States.
   b. Europe and Japan.
   c. middle-income nations.
   d. low-income nations.

8. The *environmental deficit* refers to
   a. long-term harm to the environment caused by a shortsighted focus on material affluence.
   b. the public's lack of interest in the natural environment.
   c. the fact that natural scientists ignore the social dimensions of environmental problems.
   d. the lack of funding for important environmental programs.

9. Which of the following statements reflects the limits-to-growth thesis?
   a. People are rapidly consuming Earth's finite resources.
   b. Whatever problems technology creates, technology can solve.
   c. Quality of life on Earth is getting better.
   d. Higher living standards today will benefit future generations.

10. *Environmental racism* is the idea that
    a. few minorities are represented within the environmental movement.
    b. prejudice is the major cause of pollution and other environmental problems.
    c. environmental dangers are greatest for the poor and minorities.
    d. All of the above are correct.

ANSWERS: 1(c); 2(b); 3(a); 4(b); 5(d); 6(c); 7(d); 8(a); 9(a); 10(c).

Essay Questions

1. According to demographic transition theory, how does economic development affect population patterns?

2. According to Ferdinand Tönnies, Emile Durkheim, Georg Simmel, and Louis Wirth, what characterizes urbanism as a way of life? Note several differences in the ideas of these thinkers.

When Activists Win: The Renaissance of Dudley Street

Jay Walljasper

Margaret Mead once said, "Never doubt that a small group of thoughtful, committed citizens can change the world. Indeed, it is the only thing that ever has." The dramatic revitalization of Dudley Street in Boston, Massachusetts, shows the wisdom in Mead's statement. When a philanthropic foundation joined forces with Dudley Street residents, an ethnically diverse neighborhood devastated by crime, drug abuse, and other urban problems was transformed into a safe, close-knit, urban community.

The neighborhood surrounding Dudley Street, an avenue winding through Boston's Roxbury district, is one of the poorest in Massachusetts, with per capita income half that of Boston as a whole and unemployment at least twice as high. Thirty-five percent of families live below the poverty line, and it's not hard to spot crack dealers slinking past shabby apartment buildings on the side streets. But you also see giggling kids walking home from school, old ladies tending flower patches in their side yards and neighbors chatting over fences behind tidy white wood-frame houses. The town common hosts a farmer's market and a bandstand.

Nearby is Davey's Market, which serves as a gathering spot for anyone seeking the latest neighborhood news. Conversations may be

---

"When Activists Win: The Renaissance of Dudley Street," by Jay Walljasper, reprinted from *The Nation*, March 3, 1997, pp. 11–12,14,16–17.

in Spanish, Cape Verdean or the melodious accents of the Caribbean, but you still sense something of the idealized America found on Norman Rockwell's *Saturday Evening Post* covers.

What's going on here? The answer can be found just down the street from Davey's Market in the cramped storefront office of the Dudley Street Neighborhood Initiative (D.S.N.I.). During the afternoon, it stands in for the corner soda fountain as kids wander in to say hello and see who else might be around. The busy staff usually finds time to talk and joke with them, and when there really is a reason for the kids' visit, they listen carefully. One afternoon when I was there, Ros Everdell, a D.S.N.I. organizer, counseled 16-year-old Jason Webb about an algebra class with no regular teacher. "Get all the kids in the class to go with you and say you need a real teacher, and that you need to make up all the material you've already missed."

The Dudley Street Neighborhood Initiative has been at work in this corner of Roxbury since 1985, pursuing local residents' vision of their community as a safe, lively and close-knit urban village. Dudley Street residents will tell you they've seen significant changes in the neighborhood, achieved against considerable odds. "It's been slow," says Olivio Teixera, co-owner of the Ideal Sub Shop right on Dudley Street, "but that's because it's big work. It's so much nicer around here now."

Besides the usual problems of inner-city neighborhoods—poverty, redlining, unemployment, racism, inadequate public services, pollution, poor schools, crime, drugs, neglect by government officials—Dudley Street has faced some unique challenges. Many landlords in the neighborhood had reacted to plummeting property values by torching their houses for the insurance money, killing several people and leaving the area pockmarked with vacant land. More than 20 percent of the lots in the one-and-a-half-square-mile Dudley Street neighborhood were empty. These soon became dumping grounds, not only for midnight drop-offs of old refrigerators and construction debris but for illegal garbage transfer stations that operated in the light of the day. The neighborhood also had to overcome problems associated with an ethnically fragmented population, including many immigrants with a limited command of English.

African-Americans make up 40 percent of the neighborhood's 24,000 residents, with Latin Americans, mostly from Puerto Rico and the Dominican Republic, at 30 percent. Cape Verdeans, from islands off the coast of West Africa that were a Portuguese colony until 1975, account for another 24 percent of the population, and whites, mostly elderly Irish and Italians who've lived here since the fifties, make up 6 percent.

The revitalization of Dudley Street began when La Alianza Hispana, a local social service agency, interested a small Boston-based trust in taking on the neighborhood as a major program. But when the Riley Foundation unveiled its plans at a community meeting in St. Patrick's Catholic Church on Dudley Street, it was greeted with skepticism. Distrust of outsiders ran strong in Dudley Street because many residents had been forced out of the adjacent South End neighborhood in the seventies by city-sponsored gentrification. Only a few seats on the proposed twenty-three-member board were slated for residents. Che Madyun, a mother of three with a background in the performing arts and a commanding presence, stood up, stared straight at the assembled panel of redevelopment experts and, as she recalls, "I asked how many of the people up there lived in the neighborhood." Not one. And then I asked, "How can you say the residents are going to be represented when there are only three of us on the board?" Other voices quickly joined her. Robert Holmes, a trustee of the Riley Foundation and an attorney with the prestigious downtown Boston law firm of Warner and Stackpole, remembers: "She scared the daylights out of me. I was looking at the door at the back of the room, thinking about how do I leave."

Reeling from its reception at the meeting, the Riley Foundation decided to fund improvements in the Dudley Street neighborhood without maintaining direct control of the project—a show of support rarely seen in philanthropic circles. "We allowed the neighborhood process to happen on its own," Holmes says. "Some people thought we were crazy. They thought we were throwing away our grant money."

Residents make up a majority on the D.S.N.I. board and were joined by representatives from area social service agencies, churches and businesses. The board then hired Peter Medoff, a savvy community organizer who had grown up in Boston, to head the project. Medoff, firmly committed to residents controlling the process yet with surprisingly good contact at City Hall, proved an excellent choice. Emphasizing that D.S.N.I.'s foremost goal was organizing the neighborhood as a political force rather than becoming another developer of low-income housing or broker of social services, he and the board launched several campaigns that resulted in immediate success: restoring rail service to an abandoned commuter train stop on the edge of the neighborhood and improving safety conditions at the hazardous intersection of Dudley Street and Blue Hill Avenue. By setting achievable goals, D.S.N.I. kept the level of participation high even though the bigger things like getting the dumps out of Dudley Street and providing affordable housing were slow in coming.

The organization's active membership has grown steadily over the past decade, and now numbers 2,500. Its biggest accomplishment has been imbuing Dudley Street residents with the sense that things are looking up. From the start, the group's members devoted considerable time and energy to envisioning what they wanted for Dudley Street. More than 150 people met to plot out the future of their neighborhood in an eight-month series of meetings that were conducted in Spanish and Cape Verdean as well as English. They came up with a wide-ranging plan that emphasized building community spirit as much as erecting new houses. Bike paths, apple orchards, outdoor cafes, community gardens, fountains, art programs and a town common with concerts were identified as goals alongside pressing economic needs like jobs.

"The only way to make things happen is to dream," explains Gertrudes Fidalgo, who participated in the original visioning process as a youngster and became a D.S.N.I. organizer after college. "Dreams are your best resources." This visioning process has gone on for ten years, and results from the latest round are taped to the wall in

D.S.N.I.'s conference room, testifying to people's powerful yearning for community—and ice cream. An ice cream parlor figures in many of the scenarios of Dudley Street's future that were jotted down on big sheets of paper, along with dreams like this: "People Walking. People Talking. People Laughing. Saying Hello to Everyone We Meet." Another reads: "I want affordable housing and schools with beautiful green playgrounds."

"A lot of these urban programs do only housing," notes Gus Newport, the former Berkeley, California, mayor who succeeded Medoff as executive director of D.S.N.I. from 1988 to 1992. "I think planners take it for granted that poor people don't need culture, vital businesses or beauty. If you had those things in inner cities, you'd have a lot less crime. You have to get inside the heads of people who live here, see what they want. They want more than houses. Beauty—no matter how small it is, just a few flowers—is what matters most."

Newport, who now lectures and consults on urban issues around the country and is still involved with D.S.N.I., notes that the concept of urban villages has become fashionable recently among progressive architects and planners. "But these people didn't get the idea from academics," he says. "What you have here are a lot of people who grew up in the rural South and the Cape Verde Islands and the Caribbean. They want to work with the land. They want open spaces for kids to play in. They don't want to live in tall buildings. They want to know their neighbors. They understood all by themselves that they wanted to get back to the village."

Standing in the way of these dreams of a thriving urban village, however, have been some very real problems, beginning with dozens of wrecked cars abandoned on the neighborhood's streets each week and regular shipments of other people's garbage, including rotten meat. "You had to hold your nose when you drove down the road," remembers Che Madyun, who became D.S.N.I.'s board president in 1986. "It was terrible." Madyun and Medoff guided the Don't Dump on Us campaign, which strong-armed Boston Mayor Raymond Flynn to do something about all the illegal dumping. Flynn, who had campaigned for mayor against African-American activist Mel King as a populist representative of Boston's neighborhoods in 1983 but had virtually no support in minority communities, was looking for ways to boost his popularity in Roxbury. He immediately saw the political advantages of siding with a scrappy neighborhood group and offered some city resources to assist D.S.N.I., going so far as helping Madyun padlock the gates of one illegal garbage transfer station before rolling TV cameras. "People were galvanized in seeing that they could change things," remembers Ros Everdell.

The next question was what to do with the empty land. The city had acquired about half of it through tax delinquency, and, after some prodding, Flynn agreed to deed it over to D.S.N.I. The rest, however, was owned by individuals, among them real estate speculators, who hoped that some giant urban renewal scheme would net them a handsome profit. Redevelopment plans were hindered by the checkerboard pattern of land ownership. D.S.N.I. then decided to boldly go where no community group has ever gone before, to undertake a controversial move: eminent domain.

This is the legal tool that has been used to devastate many urban neighborhoods, where people are forced to sell their homes and businesses to make way for freeways, convention centers and other megaprojects. Could it be used to help rebuilt a neighborhood? After convincing City Hall to grant it that power and four years of challenges in courts, D.S.N.I. gained the right to buy any empty land in the neighborhood.

The time tied up in court wasn't wasted because the organization still needed to come up with funding to buy the land. The Riley Foundation's support of D.S.N.I. has been limited, amounting to $1.4 million through the years. (Riley contributed more than $1.5 million to social service agencies in the neighborhood as well as making arrangements for considerable pro bono legal work on the eminent domain case and other matters.) Other local and national foundations have contributed smaller amounts. But it would take a sizable chunk of cash to purchase the land. Since banks and other conventional lenders steer clear of projects like this in poor neighborhoods, finding the money was a formidable task. Finally, the Ford Foundation agreed to make a $2 million loan.

Besides working to build affordable housing, D.S.N.I. has been busy with numerous other projects and partnerships. An annual neighborhood cleanup was launched, dozens of community gardens planted and a multicultural festival and a network for family daycare providers established. When drug dealers set up shop at the playgrounds in Mary Hannon Park, the community retook the park by establishing regular youth activities and sports programs. Working with planning professionals, residents translated the ideas of a sociable, walkable urban village into a master plan that was accepted by the city. More than 300 units of housing in the area have been rehabbed. A special effort was made to draw young people into the project, including designating youth seats on the board and bringing on a special organizer. State and municipal money was secured to construct the lovely town common, which opened last June, and plans are under way to remodel an old municipal building into a community center. Renovations for the nearby Orchard Park public housing project (childhood home of soul singer Bobby Brown) have been announced by the Boston Housing Authority, with much of the money coming from Washington. Playgrounds will be built by the authority for residents of the development, and an old cabinet factory on Dudley Street was acquired and will eventually house D.S.N.I., along with a new charter school and a small furniture manufacturer.

Leveraging money from municipal, state and federal authorities as well as foundations has been a key ingredient of D.S.N.I.'s success. Starting with Medoff, who had critical ties into City Hall, and then Newport, who had a national reputation as an urban advocate, on through current director Greg Watson, who served as Commissioner of Agriculture under Michael Dukakis and current Republican Governor William Weld, the organization has made the most of its political and philanthropic connections.

Winning a few early campaigns and publicizing them also positioned Dudley Street as a "success story." Foundation officials, politicians and government agencies—weary of what felt like the intractable problems of urban ghettos—were more than eager to join enthusiastic inner-city residents on what looked to be a wining team. Newport says, "Once you have people who are positive and working toward a goal themselves, then it's easy to get pro bono services and other kinds of support. Make things happen in the neighborhood and you can make things happen other places, too."

D.S.N.I. also got involved with some projects outside the Dudley Street area, joining protests against redlining by Boston banks and sponsoring regular classes for groups who wanted to rehab apartment buildings and low-income people who wanted to buy houses. One of the people signing up for the home-buying class was Debra Wilson, a 39-year-old caseworker for the welfare department. That's how she heard about Dudley Street's Winthrop Estates, which comprises the first thirty-eight of 225 new housing units rising from what was vacant land. Wilson now lives there with her two teenage sons and grandmother. Walking me through her town house, which is modeled on traditional New England houses with clapboard-style siding and a bay window that looks out on one of the new parks, she says, "When I first came here it was all overgrown with weeds, old tires, abandoned cars everywhere. I couldn't imagine this as a neighborhood like it is now. It still surprises me."

Winthrop Estates was developed by D.S.N.I. with funding from various foundations and government programs. The houses can be bought by families with incomes as low as $18,000, in part because the land is owned by a trust. The adjacent Stafford Heights development offers co-ops for families with incomes as low as $15,000. Although only three years old, these houses already feel like a rooted neighborhood, and not just because of newly fashionable old-fashioned touches like front porches and wooden columns at the doorways. Winthrop Estates and Stafford Heights avoid the suburban look of many urban redevelopment projects by emphasizing classic city features like sidewalks, compact lots and narrow streets. Because residents guided the planning process, the usual cookie-cutter subdivision designs were tossed out in favor of plans that fit their vision of an urban village. You see kids racing in front of the houses and hear folks calling out to one another.

The new neighborhood has already pulled together several times to deal with problems in the area: a nearby crack house, speeding drivers, noise from a twenty-four-hour gas station. Thanks to prodding from residents, police drove the crack dealers out. In response to residents' petitions, the city made several streets one-way to discourage drivers from taking shortcuts through the neighborhood. And picketing pressured the gas station owner to quiet his customers, "All of us here realized that this is the first time we had ever spoken up," Wilson says. "We didn't know things could change."

Wilson is involved with a D.S.N.I. committee promoting economic development. "We just had a meeting about what we wanted on the Main Street. In two or three years we'll see the businesses coming back—places to eat outside, a bakery, restaurants where you can take the family."

Promoting small businesses is one of the strategies adopted by residents to increase employment in Dudley Street. So far the construction and rehabbing projects have provided a few jobs for local people, and the reopening of the commuter rail stop provided better access to opportunities downtown, but economic development has lagged behind other D.S.N.I. goals. "It's a much tougher nut to crack," admits D.S.N.I. organizer Everdell. "The answer is not just jobs in the neighborhood but all over the metro area."

So what is it that's brought a new sense of hope to a place whose poverty and deterioration once marked it as a lost cause in the eyes of city officials and even many residents? "There's a tremendous core here, it's not just two or three heroic people," explains journalist Holly Sklar, author, with Peter Medoff (who died in 1994), of a history of the Dudley Street project, *Streets of Hope* (South End Press). She adds that D.S.N.I.'s efforts were effective because they transcended racial and ethnic differences and reached out to young people. "The foundations and government agencies became partners, not patrons," she says. "And the residents are really the leaders."

But Sklar goes on to offer a cautionary note: "Some people will say this shows you don't need government programs. If every neighborhood was just good enough, we wouldn't need government. But you can't duplicate this around the nation on the basis of foundation money. There's millions of dollars of federal, state and municipal money here. You can't do this instead of changing U.S. policies, instead of raising the minimum wage, instead of full employment policies, instead of improving the educational system. No village is an island. Even here they're going to be hit hard because of changes in the welfare bill and the immigration bill."

Dudley Street's significance as a symbol of hope for America's hard-hit urban neighborhoods is not that it represents a magic way to mend problems without spending taxpayers' money. Rather it points to what can be done to make sure that both public and private money invested in low-income areas truly makes a difference in people's lives. Much of the backlash against social spending in inner cities stems from middle-class people's doubts that it does any good. Billions of dollars have streamed into ghettos since the sixties, and poverty and hopelessness persist. The most important message from Dudley Street is that conditions in inner-city neighborhoods can actually improve if revitalization efforts inspire the enthusiastic involvement of people who live there.

Urban revitalization plans are usually cooked up in a foundation office or government agency, and then neighborhood residents are invited to participate in the process—almost as an afterthought. Because many inner-city residents are poor, undereducated, immigrants, minorities or plain out-of-luck, some planners assume they have little to offer. Yet, in one sense, they are the real experts on inner-city life. Gus Newport notes, "This doesn't mean that you can't use professionals. But you must remember that community people know a lot. Here in Dudley Street, they looked over everything that came from the planners and analyzed it. They asked a lot of good questions and offered a lot of good ideas."

Politicians go on about "personal responsibility" as the key for inner-city residents in turning around their lives. The success of Dudley Street proves this true, but not in exactly the sense that Bill Clinton or William Weld means it. Because residents were in complete charge of the planning process for D.S.N.I. they assumed responsibility for where the neighborhood was headed and they tapped unrecognized resources. Local teenagers for instance, volunteered to help the architects on design for housing. Che Madyun and a number of other residents proved to be talented leaders. This would never have happened with a top-down project, even a more lavishly funded one. Some housing might have been built and some services provided but there would have been no boost for the neighborhood's sense of itself. As a result of this experience, folks in Dudley Street began to view politics differently: as a way to get things done not just as something that does things to them. That, as much as the foundation and government money, made a difference in this corner of Roxbury.

Of course, Dudley Street is not safe from the storms of federal policy and the global economy. What happens in Washington and Wall Street directly affects this neighborhood. But the lasting impact of a project like D.S.N.I. is that it strengthens the neighborhood's ability to withstand such assaults. They have more resources to figure out how to deal with the effects of the draconian welfare bill and anti-immigrant legislation. These policies will hurt people on Dudley Street, but not as much as they would if D.S.N.I. wasn't there. Community-based organizing is not a substitute for the hard political work of pulling America back from its rightward course. But the success of this project strengthens the case for progressive policies by showing that public concern and taxpayer money can make a real difference.

There are unique elements of Dudley Street's story that limits its applicability to other urban neighborhoods—empty land strewn with garbage but also providing a catalyst for redevelopment, immigrants struggling with language skills but still enjoying the strengths of extended families, a local foundation willing to invest in a neighborhood rather than just a project. But the overriding theme of Dudley Street applies anywhere. The people living in a neighborhood were called on to make the decisions about its future. And they responded with enthusiasm, outrage, hope, creativity, patience and lots of energy. . . .

◉ ◉ ◉

Questions

1. Why was it important for the D.S.N.I. to initially focus on setting and achieving small, achievable goals?

2. What is an urban village? How was creating one of these accomplished in the Dudley Street neighborhood?

3. What are some key reasons that the D.S.N.I.'s efforts were successful?

4. Use what happened on Dudley Street to illustrate that social problems do not exist in isolation. That is, clarify why D.S.N.I. not only focused on affordable housing, but also on daycare, neighborhood cleanup, closing down drug dealers, and other projects.

5. Does the success on Dudley Street mean that government programs established to solve social problems are unnecessary? Explain your answer.

6. Suppose you are a sociologist who is hired as a consultant to revitalize an inner-city neighborhood. You are about to make a presentation to the City Council, in which you will make recommendations. What would you tell them?

Urbanism as a Way of Life

Louis Wirth

In this selection, Louis Wirth argues that urbanism is the defining feature of modern society. Because the development of large cities has freed us from the forces of "society's natural selection," Wirth contends that urbanism is more important than industrialization or capitalism. This article explains how and why the size, density, and heterogeneity of cities have changed the nature of our social relationships—and not always for the better.

. . .

For sociological purposes a city may be defined as a relatively large, dense, and permanent settlement of socially heterogeneous individuals. On the basis of the postulates which this minimal definition suggests, a theory of urbanism may be formulated in the light of existing knowledge concerning social groups.

A Theory of Urbanism

. . .

In the pages that follow we shall seek to set forth a limited number of identifying characteristics of the city. Given these characteristics we shall then indicate what consequences or further characteristics follow from them in the light of general sociological theory and empirical research. We hope in this manner to arrive at

"Urbanism as a Way of Life," by Louis Wirth, reprinted from *The American Journal of Sociology,* Vol. 44, No. 1, July 1938, The University of Chicago Press. pp. 1–24.

the essential propositions comprising a theory of urbanism. Some of these propositions can be supported by a considerable body of already available research materials; others may be accepted as hypotheses for which a certain amount of presumptive evidence exists, but for which more ample and exact verification would be required. At least such a procedure will, it is hoped, show what in the way of systematic knowledge of the city we now have and what are the crucial and fruitful hypotheses for future research.

. . .

⚇ Size of the Population Aggregate

Ever since Aristotle's *Politics*, it has been recognized that increasing the number of inhabitants in a settlement beyond a certain limit will affect the relationships between them and the character of the city. Large numbers involve, as has been pointed out, a greater range of individual variation. Furthermore, the greater the number of individuals participating in a process of interaction, the greater is the *potential* differentiation between them. The personal traits, the occupations, the cultural life, and the ideas of the members of an urban community may, therefore, be expected to range between more widely separated poles than those of rural inhabitants.

That such variations should give rise to the spatial segregation of individuals according to color, ethnic heritage, economic and social status, tastes and preferences, may readily be inferred. The bonds of kinship, of neighborliness, and the sentiments arising out of living together for generations under a common folk tradition are likely to be absent or, at best, relatively weak in an aggregate the members of which have such diverse origins and backgrounds. Under such circumstances competition and formal control mechanisms furnish the substitutes for the bonds of solidarity that are relied upon to hold a folk society together.

Increase in the number of inhabitants of a community beyond a few hundred is bound to limit the possibility of each member of the community knowing all the others personally. Max Weber, in recognizing the social significance of this fact, pointed out that from a sociological point of view large numbers of inhabitants and density of settlement mean that the personal mutual acquaintanceship between the inhabitants which ordinarily inheres in a neighborhood is lacking.[1] The increase in numbers thus involves a changed character of the social relationships. As Simmel points out:

> [If] the unceasing external contact of numbers of persons in the city should be met by the same number of inner reactions as in the small town, in which one knows almost every person he meets and to each of whom he has a positive relationship, one would be completely atomized internally and would fall into an unthinkable mental condition.[2]

The multiplication of persons in a state of interaction under conditions which make their contact as full personalities impossible produces that segmentalization of human relationships which has sometimes been seized upon by students of the mental life of the cities as an explanation for the "schizoid" character of urban personality. This is not to say that the urban inhabitants have fewer acquaintances than rural inhabitants, for the reverse may actually be true; it means rather that in relation to the number of people whom they see and with whom they rub elbows in the course of daily life, they know a smaller proportion, and of these they have less intensive knowledge.

Characteristically, urbanites meet one another in highly segmental roles. They are, to be sure, dependent upon more people for the satisfactions of their life-needs than are rural people and thus are associated with a greater number of organized groups, but they are less dependent upon particular persons, and their dependence upon others is confined to a highly fractionalized aspect of the other's round of activity. This is essentially what is meant by saying that the city is characterized by secondary rather than primary contacts. The contacts of the city may indeed be face to face, but they are nevertheless impersonal, superficial, transitory, and segmental. The reserve, the indifference, and the blasé outlook which urbanites manifest in their relationships may thus be regarded as devices for immunizing themselves against the personal claims and expectations of others.

The superficiality, the anonymity, and the transitory character of urban-social relations make intelligible, also, the sophistication and the rationality generally ascribed to city-dwellers. Our acquaintances tend to stand in a relationship of utility to us in the sense that the role which each one plays in our life is overwhelmingly regarded as a means for the achievement of our own ends. Whereas, therefore, the individual gains, on the one hand, a certain degree of emancipation or freedom from the personal and emotional controls of intimate groups, he loses, on the other hand, the spontaneous self-expression, the morale, and the sense of participation that comes with living in an integrated society. This constitutes essentially the state of *anomie* or the social void to which Durkheim alludes in attempting to account for the various forms of social disorganization in technological society.

• • •

In a community composed of a larger number of individuals than can know one another intimately and can be assembled in one spot, it becomes necessary to communicate through indirect mediums and to articulate individual interests by a process of delegation. Typically in the city, interests are made effective through representation. The individual counts for little, but the voice of the representative is heard with a deference roughly proportional to the numbers for whom he speaks. . . .

◉ Density

As in the case of numbers, so in the case of concentration in limited space, certain consequences of relevance in sociological analysis of the city emerge. Of these only a few can be indicated.

As Darwin pointed out for flora and fauna and as Durkheim[3] noted in the case of human societies, an increase in numbers when area is held constant (i.e., an increase in density) tends to produce differentiation and specialization, since only in this way can the area support increased numbers. Density thus reinforces the effect of numbers in diversifying men and their activities and in increasing the complexity of the social structure.

On the subjective side, as Simmel has suggested, the close physical contact of numerous individuals necessarily produces a shift in the mediums through which we orient ourselves to the urban milieu, especially to our fellow-men. Typically, our physical contacts are close but our social contacts are distant. The urban world puts a premium on visual recognition. We see the uniform which denotes the role of the functionaries and are oblivious to the personal eccentricities that are hidden behind the uniform. We tend to acquire and develop a sensitivity to a world of artifacts and become progressively farther removed from the world of nature.

We are exposed to glaring contrasts between splendor and squalor, between riches and poverty, intelligence and ignorance, order and chaos. The competition for space is great, so that each area generally tends to be put to the use which yields the greatest economic return. Place of work tends to become dissociated from place of residence, for the proximity of industrial and commercial establishments makes an area both economically and socially undesirable for residential purposes.

Density, land values, rentals, accessibility, healthfulness, prestige, aesthetic consideration, absence of nuisances such as noise, smoke, and dirt determine the desirability of various areas of the city as places of settlement for different sections of the population. Place and nature of work, income, racial and ethnic characteristics, social status, custom, habit, taste, preference, and prejudice are among the significant factors in accordance with which the urban population is selected and distributed into more or less distinct settlements. Diverse population elements inhabiting a compact settlement thus tend to become segregated from one another in the degree in which their requirements and modes of life are incompatible with one another and in the measure in which they are antagonistic to one another. Similarly, persons of homogeneous status and needs unwittingly drift into, consciously select, or are forced by circumstances into, the same area. The different parts of the city thus acquire specialized functions. The city consequently tends to resemble a mosaic of social worlds in which the transition from one to the other is abrupt. The juxtaposition of divergent personalities and modes of life tends to produce a relativistic perspective and a sense of toleration of differences which may be regarded as prerequisites for rationality and which lead toward the secularization of life.

The close living together and working together of individuals who have no sentimental and emotional ties foster a spirit of competition, aggrandizement, and mutual exploitation. To counteract irresponsibility and potential disorder, formal controls tend to be resorted to. Without rigid adherence to predictable routines a large compact society would scarcely be able to maintain itself. The clock and the traffic signal are symbolic of the basis of our social order in the urban world. Frequent close physical contact, coupled with great social distance, accentuates the reserve of unattached individuals toward one another and, unless compensated for by other opportunities for response, gives rise to loneliness. The necessary frequent movement of great numbers of individuals in a congested habitat gives occasion to friction and irritation. Nervous tensions which derive from such personal frustrations are accentuated by the rapid tempo and the complicated technology under which life in dense areas must be lived.

☺ Heterogeneity

The social interaction among such a variety of personality types in the urban milieu tends to break down the rigidity of caste lines and to complicate the class structure, and thus induces a more ramified and differentiated framework of social stratification than is found in more integrated societies. The heightened mobility of the individual, which brings him within the range of stimulation by a great number of diverse individuals and subjects him to fluctuating status in the differentiated social groups that compose the social structure of the city, tends toward the acceptance of instability and insecurity in the world at large as a norm. This fact helps to account, too, for the sophistication and cosmopolitanism of the urbanite. No single group has the undivided allegiance of the individual. The groups with which he is affiliated do not lend themselves readily to a simple hierarchical arrangement. By virtue of his different interests arising out of different aspects of social life, the individual acquires membership in widely divergent groups, each of which functions only with reference to a single segment of his personality. Nor do these groups easily permit of a concentric arrangement so that the narrower ones fall within the circumference of the more inclusive ones, as is more likely to be the case in the rural community or in primitive societies. Rather the groups with which the person typically is affiliated are tangential to each other or intersect in highly variable fashion.

Partly as a result of the physical footlooseness of the population and partly as a result of their social mobility, the turnover in group membership generally is rapid. Place of residence, place and character of employment, income and interests fluctuate, and the task of holding organizations together and maintaining and promoting intimate and lasting acquaintanceship between the members is difficult. This applies strikingly to the local areas within the city into which persons become segregated more by virtue of differences in race, language, income, and social status, than through choice or positive attraction to people like themselves. Overwhelmingly the city-dweller is not a home-owner, and since a transitory habitat does not generate binding traditions and sentiments, only rarely is he truly a neighbor. There is little opportunity for the individual to obtain a conception of the city as a whole or to survey his place in the total scheme. Consequently he finds it difficult to determine what is to his own "best interests" and to decide between the issues and leaders presented to him by the agencies of mass suggestion. Individuals who are thus detached from the organized bodies which integrate society comprise the fluid masses that make collective behavior in the urban community so unpredictable and hence so problematical.

Although the city, through the recruitment of variant types to perform its diverse tasks and the accentuation of their uniqueness through competition and the premium upon eccentricity, novelty, efficient performance, and inventiveness, produces a highly differentiated population, it also exercises a leveling influence. Wherever large numbers of differently constituted individuals congregate, the process of depersonalization also enters. This leveling tendency inheres in part in the economic basis of the city. The development of large cities, at least in the modern age, was largely dependent upon the concentrative force of steam. The rise of the factory made possible mass production for an impersonal market. The fullest exploitation of the possibilities of the division of labor and mass production, however, is possible only with standardization of processes and products. A money economy goes hand in hand with such a system of production. Progressively as cities have developed upon a background of this system of production, the pecuniary nexus which implies the purchasability of services and things has displaced personal relations as the basis of association. Individuality under these circumstances must be replaced by categories. When large numbers have to make common use of facilities and institutions, an arrangement must be made to adjust the facilities and institutions to the needs of the average person rather than to those of particular individuals. The services of the public utilities, of the recreational, educational, and cultural institutions must be adjusted to mass requirements. Similarly, the cultural institutions, such as the schools, the movies, the radio, and the newspapers, by virtue of their mass clientele, must necessarily operate as leveling influences. The political process as it appears in urban life could not be understood without taking account of the mass appeals made through modem propaganda techniques. If the individual would participate at all in the social, political, and economic life of the city, he must subordinate some of his individuality to the demands of the larger community and in that measure immerse himself in mass movements.

. . .

Endnotes

[1]Park, R. E., Burgess, E. W., et al. (1925). *The city*. Chapter i. Chicago..

[2]Simmel, G. (1903). Die Grossstädte und das Geistesleben," In T. Petermann (Ed.), *Die Grossstadt* (pp. 187–206) Dresden.

[3]Durkheim, E. (1932). *De la division du travail social.* Paris, p. 248.

☻ ☻ ☻

Questions

1. According to Wirth, what is a city?

2. How might spatial segregation contribute to the development of social problems? Which social problems do you think are most likely to emerge due to segregation?

3. Wirth says that urban contacts are impersonal, superficial, transitory and segmental. How might this contribute to the emergence of social problems?

4. Is the heterogeneity of the city related to the development of particular social problems? Explain your answer.

5. Think about the community in which you live. Describe it in terms of size, density, and heterogeneity. How do these features influence your degree of satisfaction with life in that community?

Social Change: Modern and Postmodern Societies

From Chapter 16 of *Society: The Basics*, 11/e. John J. Macionis. Copyright © 2011 by Pearson Education. All rights reserved.

Social Change: Modern and Postmodern Societies

- Why do societies change?

- How do social movements both encourage and resist social change?

- What do sociologists say is good and bad about today's society?

 Watch the *Core Concepts in Sociology* video "Defining Social Movements" on **mysoclab.com**

Chapter Overview

This chapter explores social change, explaining how modern societies differ from earlier, traditional societies. The chapter discusses many causes of change, including disasters and social movements.

Laimute Druskis\Pearson Education/PH College

The five-story red brick apartment building at 253 East Tenth Street in New York has been standing for more than a century. In 1900, one of the twenty small apartments in the building was occupied by thirty-nine-year-old Julius Streicher; Christine Streicher, age thirty-three; and their four young children. The Streichers were immigrants, both having come in 1885 from their native Germany to New York, where they met and married.

The Streichers probably considered themselves successful. Julius operated a small clothing shop a few blocks from his apartment; Christine stayed at home, raised the children, and did housework. Like most people in the country at that time, neither Julius nor Christine had graduated from high school, and they worked for ten to twelve hours a day, six days a week. Their income—average for that time—was about $35 a month, or about $425 per year. (In today's dollars, that would be slightly more than $11,000, which would put the family well below the poverty line.) They spent almost half of their income for food; most of the rest went for rent.

Today, Dorothy Sabo resides at 253 East Tenth Street, living alone in the same apartment where the Streichers spent much of their lives. Now eighty-seven, she is retired from a career teaching art at a nearby museum. In many respects, Sabo's life has been far easier than the life the Streichers knew. For one thing, when the Streichers lived there, the building had no electricity (people used kerosene lamps and candles) and no running water (Christine Streicher spent most of every Monday doing laundry using water she carried from a public fountain at the end of the block). There were no telephones, no television, and of course no computers. Today, Dorothy Sabo takes such conveniences for granted. Although she is hardly rich, her pension and Social Security amount to several times as much (in constant dollars) as the Streichers earned.

Sabo has her own worries. She is concerned about the environment and often speaks out about global warming. But a century ago, if the Streichers and their neighbors were concerned about "the environment," they probably would have meant the smell coming up from the street. At a time when motor vehicles were just beginning to appear in New York City, carriages, trucks, and trolleys were all pulled by horses—thousands of them. These animals dumped 60,000 gallons of urine and 2.5 million pounds of manure on the streets each and every day—an offensive mixture churned and splashed by countless wheels onto everything and everyone within a stone's throw of the streets (Simon & Cannon, 2001).

It is difficult for most people today to imagine how different life was a century ago. Not only was life much harder back then, but it was also much shorter. Statistical records show that life expectancy was just forty-six years for men and forty-eight years for women, compared to about seventy-five and eighty years today, respectively (Xu et al., 2010).

Over the course of the past century, much has changed for the better. Yet as this chapter explains, social change is not all positive. Change has negative consequences too, causing unexpected new problems. Early sociologists had a mixed assessment of *modernity*, changes brought about by the Industrial Revolution. Likewise, today's sociol-ogists point to both good and bad aspects of *postmodernity*, the transformations caused by the Information Revolution and the postindustrial economy. One thing is clear: For better or worse, the rate of change has never been faster than it is now.

What Is Social Change?

In earlier chapters, we examined relatively fixed or *static* social patterns, including status and role, social stratification, and social institutions. We also looked at the *dynamic* forces that have shaped our way

Social Change: Modern and Postmodern Societies

• Seeing Sociology
  in Everyday Life

What would you say have been the two or three most
important changes to our society that have occurred during
your lifetime? Explain your answer.

social change the transformation of culture and social institutions over time

of life, ranging from innovations in technology to the growth of bureaucracy and the expansion of cities. These are all dimensions of **social change,** *the transformation of culture and social institutions over time.* This complex process has four major characteristics:

1. **Social change happens all the time.** People used to say that the only sure things in life were "death and taxes." Yet our thoughts about death have changed dramatically as life expectancy in the United States has nearly doubled in the past century. And back in the Streichers' day, people in the United States paid little or no taxes on their earnings; taxation increased dramatically over the course of the twentieth century, along with the size and scope of government. In short, just about everything in life, even the "sure things," is subject to the twists and turns of change.

   Still, some societies change faster than others. Hunting and gathering societies change quite slowly; members of technologically complex societies, by contrast, can witness significant change within a single lifetime.

   It is also true that in any society, some cultural elements change faster than others. William Ogburn's theory of *cultural lag* asserts that material culture (that is, things) changes faster than nonmaterial culture (ideas and attitudes). For example, genetic technology that allows scientists to alter and perhaps even create life has developed more rapidly than our ethical standards for deciding when and how to use the technology.

2. **Social change is sometimes intentional but often unplanned.** Industrial societies actively promote many kinds of change. Scientists seek more efficient forms of energy, and advertisers try to convince us that we cannot live without the latest electronic gadget. Yet rarely can anyone envision all the consequences of changes as they are set in motion.

   Back in 1900, when the country still relied on horses for transportation, people looked ahead to motor vehicles that would take a single day to carry them distances that used to take weeks or months. But no one could see how much the mobility provided by automobiles would alter life in the United States, scattering family members, threatening the environment, and reshaping cities and suburbs. Nor could automotive pioneers have predicted the more than 37,000 deaths that occur in car accidents each year in the United States alone (National Highway Traffic Safety Administration, 2009).

These young men are performing in a hip-hop dance marathon in Hong Kong. Hip-hop music, dress style, and dancing have become popular in Asia, a clear case of cultural diffusion. Social change occurs as cultural patterns move from place to place, but people in different societies don't always attach the same meanings to these patterns. How might Chinese youth understand hip-hop differently from the young African Americans in the United States who originated it?

3. **Social change is controversial.** The history of the automobile shows that social change brings both good and bad consequences. Cars brought an end to the muck of urine and manure on city streets, but they spewed carbon monoxide into the air. In the same contradictory way, capitalists benefited from greater production and profits made possible by the Industrial Revolution at the same time that workers pushed back against the machines that they feared would make their skills obsolete.

   Today, as in the past, people disagree about how we ought to live and what we should welcome as "progress." We see this disagreement every day in the changing patterns of social interaction between black people and white people, women and men, and homosexuals and heterosexuals that are celebrated by some people and opposed by others.

4. **Some changes matter more than others.** Some changes (such as clothing fads) have only passing significance; others (like the invention of computers) may change the world. Will the Information Revolution turn out to be as important as the Industrial Revolution? Like the automobile and television, computers have both positive and negative effects, providing new kinds of jobs while eliminating old ones, isolating people in offices while linking people in global electronic networks, offering vast amounts of information while threatening personal privacy.

Social Change: Modern and Postmodern Societies

Martina Serfass, age 54, is a nurse who lives near Decorah, Iowa; most of the people in her community have lived there all their lives.

Serge Smith-Heiser, age 27, lives in an apartment complex in Fort Lauderdale, Florida, and thinks of his city as a place where people come and go. He arrived two years ago in search of a new job.

Explore residential stability in your local community and in counties across the United States on mysoclab.com

Seeing Ourselves

NATIONAL MAP 1

Who Stays Put? Residential Stability across the United States

Overall, only about 15 percent of U.S. residents have not moved during the past thirty years. Counties with a higher proportion of "long-termers" typically have experienced less change over recent decades: Many neighborhoods have been in place since before World War II, and many of the same families live in them. As you look at the map, what can you say about these stable areas? What accounts for the fact that most of these counties are rural and at some distance from the coasts?

Explore on mysoclab.com

Source: U.S. Census Bureau (2000).

Causes of Social Change

Social change has many causes. In a world linked by sophisticated communication and transportation technology, change in one place often sets off change elsewhere.

Culture and Change

We have identified three important sources of cultural change. First, *invention* produces new objects, ideas, and social patterns. Rocket propulsion research, which began in the 1940s, has produced sophisticated spacecraft that can reach toward the stars. Today we take such technology for granted; during the present century, a significant number of people may well have an opportunity to travel in space.

Second, *discovery* occurs when people take notice of existing elements of the world. For example, medical advances offer a growing understanding of the human body. Beyond their direct effects on human health, medical discoveries have extended life expectancy, setting in motion the "graying" of U.S. society.

Third, *diffusion* creates change as products, people, and information spread from one society to another. Ralph Linton (1937a) recognized that many familiar aspects of our culture came from other lands. For example, the cloth used to make our clothing was developed in Asia, the clocks we see all around us were invented in Europe, and the coins we carry in our pockets were devised in what is now Turkey.

In general, material things change more quickly than cultural ideas. For example, breakthroughs such as the science of cloning occur faster than our understanding of when—and even whether—they are morally desirable.

Conflict and Change

Inequality and conflict within a society also produce change. Karl Marx saw class conflict as the engine that drives societies from one historical era to another. In industrial-capitalist societies, he maintained, the struggle between capitalists and workers pushes society toward a socialist system of production.

In the more than 125 years since Marx's death, this model has proved simplistic. Yet Marx correctly foresaw that social conflict arising from inequality (involving not just class but also race and gender) would force changes in every society, including our own, to improve the lives of working people.

Ideas and Change

Max Weber also contributed to our understanding of social change. Although Weber acknowledged that conflict could bring about change, he traced the roots of most social changes to ideas. For example, people with charisma (Martin Luther King Jr. is an example) can carry a message that changes the world.

Weber highlighted the importance of ideas by revealing how the religious beliefs of early Protestants set the stage for the spread of industrial capitalism. The fact that industrial capitalism developed primarily in areas of Western Europe where the Protestant work ethic was strong proved to Weber (1958, orig. 1904–05) the power of ideas to bring about change.

Demographic Change

Population patterns also play a part in social change. The typical U.S. household was almost twice as large in 1900 (4.8 people) as it is today

○● Seeing Sociology
　　in Everyday Life

Look at the various changes in the United States over the past
century. In each case, think about how the change affected
everyday social life.

●
social movement an organized activity that encourages
or discourages social change

(2.6 people). Women are having fewer children, and more people are living alone. Change is also taking place as our population grows older. Thirteen percent of the U.S. population was over age sixty-five in 2008, three times the proportion back in 1900. By the year 2030, seniors will account for 20 percent of the total (U.S. Census Bureau, 2009). Medical research and health care services already focus extensively on the elderly, and life will change in countless other ways as homes and household products are redesigned to meet the needs of growing numbers of older consumers.

Migration within and between societies is another demographic factor that promotes change. Between 1870 and 1930, tens of millions of immigrants entered the industrial cities in the United States. Millions more from rural areas joined the rush. As a result, farm communities declined, cities expanded, and by 1920 the United States had for the first time become a mostly urban nation. Similar changes are taking place today as people moving from the Snowbelt to the Sunbelt mix with new immigrants from Latin America and Asia.

Where in the United States have demographic changes been greatest, and where have they been less pronounced? National Map 1 provides one answer, showing counties where the largest share of people have lived in their present homes for thirty years or more.

Social Movements and Change

A final cause of social change lies in the efforts of people like us. People commonly band together to form a **social movement,** *an organized activity that encourages or discourages social change.* Our nation's history includes all kinds of social movements, from the colonial drive for independence to today's organizations supporting or opposing abortion, gay rights, and the death penalty.

Social movements are about connecting people who share some political goal. Computer technology, including smartphones and social networking Internet sites, has made it possible for people to connect as never before. Seeing Sociology in the News on takes a closer look at the power of networking sites such as Facebook to support effective social movements.

Types of Social Movements

Researchers classify social movements according to the type of change they seek (Aberle, 1966; Cameron, 1966; Blumer, 1969). One variable asks, Who is changed? Some movements target selected people, and others try to change everyone. A second variable asks, How much change? Some movements seek only limited change in our lives; others pursue a radical transformation of society. Combining these variables results in four types of social movements, shown in Figure 1.

Alterative social movements are the least threatening to the status quo because they seek limited change in only part of the population. Their aim is to help certain people *alter* their lives. Promise Keepers is one example of an alterative social movement; it encourages men to live more spiritual lives and be more supportive of their families.

Redemptive social movements also target specific individuals, but they seek more radical change. Their aim is to help certain people *redeem* their lives. For example, Alcoholics Anonymous is an organization that helps people with an alcohol addiction achieve a sober life.

Reformative social movements aim for only limited change but target everyone. The environmental movement seeks to interest everyone in protecting the natural environment.

Revolutionary social movements are the most extreme of all, working for major transformation of an entire society. Sometimes pursuing specific goals, sometimes spinning utopian dreams, these social movements, including both the left-wing Communist party (pushing for government control of the entire economy) and right-wing militia groups (seeking the destruction of "big government") seek to radically change our way of life.

Claims Making

In 1981, the Centers for Disease Control and Prevention began to track a strange disease that was killing people, most of them homosexual men. The disease came to be known as AIDS (acquired immune deficiency syndrome). Although AIDS was clearly a deadly disease, it was given little public or media attention. Only

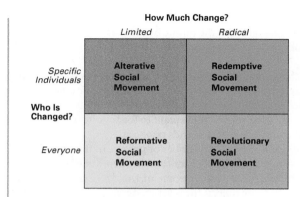

FIGURE 1　**Four Types of Social Movements**

There are four types of social movements, reflecting who is changed and how great the change is.

Source: Based on Aberle (1966).

JSA Today

Facebook Helps Spark Movements

BY DAVID UNZE

March 25, 2010

Austin Lee spent three years advocating for a skate park in St. Cloud, Minnesota, before he turned to Facebook.

The seventeen-year-old used to work the phones to keep his friends and supporters updated about his efforts. But when he took his campaign to the social networking site, he says his message really started to take off. The site's value as a grassroots organizing tool was never more clear to Lee than when sixty of his 1,085 followers confirmed within a day of getting an update from him that they would be able to attend a key City Council meeting on the project.

"Facebook, I think, made a huge impact," he said.

The effort paid off. The council approved a $500,000 skate plaza last month and council members agreed the Facebook community played a role. John Libert, vice president of the St. Cloud City Council, said he's never gotten more e-mails and other communications about a single issue than the skate plaza in his four years on the council.

"It was definitely effective. It did influence me, to the extent that the number of people who were out there supporting it" was so large, he said. Facebook is becoming a core component for social movements, from constituent outreach for political campaigns to building support for causes, says Andrew Noyes, manager of public policy communications for Facebook.

A growing number of people are discovering that Facebook, with its 350 million members, "is about way more than simply connecting with friends," Noyes said.

The use of Facebook to rally political support got a huge boost when President Obama relied on it during his candidacy to get his message out, Noyes said. Newly elected Senator Scott Brown, R-Mass., embraced Facebook during his campaign, Noyes said, an illustration of how the GOP is waking up to the power of social media. . . .

Levi Russell, communications director for Tea Party Express, the planned national bus tour that will host rallies across the nation to promote fiscal conservatism and protest Obama administration policies between March 27 and April 15, says the group started its first Facebook page a little less than a year ago, and has been growing by the thousands.

"Facebook allows us to promote and organize events in a whole new way," he said. "While it is not our primary communication tool, it is one of the most targeted and flexible tools we use. Our supporters are able to really take ownership of events in their area by sharing, discussing, and inviting their friends in a very visual and tangible format."

College students looking to get support for issues have also turned to Facebook.

Casey Allen Sears, a student at The College of William and Mary in Williamsburg, Virginia, helped start a Facebook group this month in opposition to Virginia Attorney General Ken Cuc-

cinelli's letter about discrimination policies at state public universities. Cuccinelli wrote that Virginia's public universities could not adopt policies that prohibit discrimination based on sexual orientation "absent specific authorization from the General Assembly."

The Facebook group promoted a protest against Cuccinelli's assertion that public universities should back away from policies against discrimination on the basis of sexual orientation.

"In the forty-eight hours from the creation of the event, we had more than 700 people saying they were attending," Sears said. "It's really easy to organize a mass movement." . . .

WHAT DO YOU THINK?

1. According to the article, why are Facebook and other computer-based networking systems becoming a "core component for social movements"?

2. Do you think the use of Facebook for political purposes will make this country more democratic? Why or why not?

3. Have you ever used Facebook or a similar networking site as part of an effort to organize a political demonstration or other social movement activity? Explain.

Adapted from "Facebook Helps Spark Movements" by David Unze. Source: *USA Today*, a division of Gannett Co., Inc. March 25, 2010. Reprinted with permission.

about five years later did the public begin to take notice of the rising number of deaths and start to think of AIDS as a serious social threat.

The change in public thinking was the result of **claims making,** *the process of trying to convince the public and public officials of the importance of joining a social movement to address a particular issue.* In other words, for a social movement to form, some issue has to be defined as a problem that demands public attention. Usually, claims making begins with a small number of people. In the case of AIDS, the gay community in large cities (notably San Francisco and New York) mobilized to convince people of the dangers posed by this deadly disease. Over time, if the mass media give the issue attention and public officials speak out on behalf of the problem, it is likely that the social movement will gain strength.

Considerable public attention has now been given to AIDS, and there is ongoing research aimed at finding a cure. The process of claims making goes on all the time for dozens of issues. Today, for example, a movement to ban the use of cell phones in automobiles has pointed to the thousands of automobile accidents each year related to the use of phones while driving; six states have now passed laws banning the use of handheld phones, and debate continues in others (McVeigh, Welch, & Bjarnason, 2003; Governors Highway Safety Association, 2010; Macionis, 2010).

Explaining Social Movements

Sociologists have developed several explanations of social movements. *Deprivation theory* holds that social movements arise among people who feel deprived of something, such as income, safe working conditions, or political rights. Whether you feel deprived or not, of course, depends on what you expect in life. Thus people band together in response to **relative deprivation,** *a perceived disadvantage arising from some specific comparison.* This concept helps explain why movements for change surface in both good and bad times: It is not people's absolute standing that counts but how they perceive

Social Change: Modern and Postmodern Societies

claims making the process of trying to convince the public and public officials of the importance of joining a social movement to address a particular issue

relative deprivation a perceived disadvantage arising from some specific comparison

○ Making the Grade

Review the discussion to see how we use reference groups to decide whether we are being deprived or not.

their situation in relation to the situations of others (J. C. Davies, 1962; Merton, 1968).

Mass-society theory, a second explanation, argues that social movements attract socially isolated people who join a movement in order to gain a sense of identity and purpose. From this point of view, social movements have a personal as well as a political agenda (Melucci, 1989).

Resource mobilization theory, a third theoretical scheme, links the success of any social movement to the resources that are available to it, including money, human labor, and the mass media. Because most social movements begin small, they must look beyond themselves to mobilize the resources required for success (Valocchi, 1996; Zhao, 1998; Passy & Giugni, 2001; Packer, 2003).

Fourth, *culture theory* points out that social movements depend not only on money and other material resources but also on cultural symbols. People must have a shared understanding of injustice in the world before they will mobilize to bring about change. In addition, specific symbols (such as photographs of the World Trade Center towers engulfed in flames after the September 11, 2001, terrorist attacks) helped mobilize people to support the U.S. military campaigns in Afghanistan and Iraq (McAdam, McCarthy, & Zald, 1996; J. E. Williams, 2002).

Fifth, *new social movements theory* points out the distinctive character of recent social movements in postindustrial societies. Rather than being local matters, these movements are typically national or international in scope, and most focus on quality-of-life issues, such as the natural environment, world peace, or animal rights, rather than more traditional economic issues. This broader scope of contemporary social movements results from closer ties between governments and between ordinary people around the world, who are now linked by the mass media and new information technology (Kriesi, 1989; Pakulski, 1993; Jenkins & Wallace, 1996).

Sixth and finally, *political economy theory* is a Marxist approach that claims that social movements arise in opposition to the capitalist economic system, which fails to meet the needs of the majority of people. Despite great economic productivity, U.S. society is in crisis, with millions of people unable to find good jobs, living below the poverty line, and surviving without health insurance. Social movements arise as workers organize to demand higher wages, citizens rally for a health policy that protects everyone, and people march in opposition to spending billions to fund wars while ignoring basic needs at home (Buechler, 2000).

Stan Honda/Agence France Presse/Getty Images

Political debate is a matter of claims making by various organizations. After the insurance giant AIG was saved from collapse by a massive government bailout, executives took millions of dollars in bonuses for themselves, claiming this served the interest of the company. The action prompted one organization to visit the executives' homes, denouncing the bonuses as little more than greed and demanding that the money be returned.

Stages in Social Movements

Social movements typically unfold in four stages: emergence, coalescence, bureaucratization, and decline. The *emergence* of social movements occurs as people begin to think that all is not well. Some, such as the civil rights and women's movements, are born of widespread dissatisfaction. Others emerge as a small group tries to mobilize the population, as when gay activists raised public concern about AIDS.

Coalescence takes place when a social movement defines itself and develops a strategy for attracting new members and "going public." Leaders determine policies and decide on tactics, which may include demonstrations or rallies to attract media attention.

As it gains members and resources, a social movement may undergo *bureaucratization.* As a movement becomes established, it depends less on the charisma and talents of a few leaders and more on a professional staff, which increases the chances for the movement's long-term survival.

Finally, social movements *decline* as resources dry up, the group faces overwhelming opposition, or members achieve their goals and lose interest. Some well-established organizations outlive their original causes and move on to new crusades; others lose touch with the idea of changing society and choose instead to become part of the "system" (Piven & Cloward, 1977; F. D. Miller, 1983).

Seeing Sociology
in Everyday Life

Many people, including fishermen, who lost their ability to work
in the wake of the 2010 oil spill in the Gulf of Mexico believed
that neither BP nor government officials did all they could to help
them. How can such a belief intensify the effects of a disaster?

aster an event, generally unexpected, that causes extensive
harm to people and damage to property

Barry Lewis\Alamy Images

AFP Photo/Eitan Abramovich/Newscom

Salah Omar/AFP\Getty Images, Inc. - Agence France Presse

Sociologists classify disasters into three types. The 2010 earthquake in Haiti, which claimed several
hundred thousand lives, is an example of a natural disaster. The 2010 oil spill in the Gulf of Mexico is an
example of a technological disaster. The slaughter of hundreds of thousands of people and the
displacement of millions more from their homes in the Darfur region of Sudan since 2003 is an example of
an intentional disaster.

Disasters: Unexpected Change

Sometimes change results from events that are both unexpected and
unwelcome. A **disaster** is *an event, generally unexpected, that causes
extensive harm to people and damage to property.* Disasters are of three
types. Floods, earthquakes, forest fires, and hurricanes (such as Hurricane Katrina, which devastated the Gulf Coast in 2005) are examples of *natural disasters* (Erikson, 2005a). A second type is the
technological disaster, which is widely regarded as an *accident* but is
more accurately the result of our inability to control technology
(Erikson, 2005a). The nuclear accident at the Chernobyl power plant
in Ukraine in 1986 and the spilling of millions of gallons of oil in the
Gulf of Mexico in 2010 were technological disasters. A third type is the
intentional disaster, in which one or more organized groups deliberately harm others. War, terrorist attacks, and the genocide that took
place in Yugoslavia (1992–95), Rwanda (2000), and the Darfur region
of Sudan (2003–10) are examples of intentional disasters.

The full scope of the harm caused by disasters may become evident only many years after the event. The Thinking Globally box

describes a technological disaster that is still affecting people and
their descendants more than half a century after it took place.

Kai Erikson (1976, 1994, 2005a) has investigated disasters of all
types and has reached three major conclusions about the social consequences of disasters. First, we all know that disasters harm people and
destroy property, but what most people don't realize is that disasters
also cause social damage by disrupting human community. When a
dam burst and sent a mountain of water down West Virginia's Buffalo
Creek in 1972, it killed 125 people, destroyed 1,000 homes, and left
4,000 people homeless. After the waters had gone and help was stream-
ing into the area, the people were paralyzed not only by the loss of family members and friends but also by the loss of their way of life. Even
four decades later, they have been unable to rebuild the community life
that they once knew. We can know when disasters start, Erikson points
out, but we cannot know when they will end.

Second, Erikson explains that the social damage is more serious
when an event involves some toxic substance, as is common with
technological disasters. As the case of radiation falling on Utrik Island
shows us, people feel "poisoned" when they have been exposed to
a dangerous substance that they fear and over which they have no

● Seeing Sociology
in Everyday Life

What social damage do you think was caused by the 1986 explosion and massive radiation leak at the Chernobyl nuclear plant in Ukraine?

modernity social patterns resulting from industrialization

modernization the process of social change begun by industrialization

THINKING GLOBALLY

A Never-Ending Atomic Disaster

It was just after dawn on March 1, 1954, and the air was already warm on Utrik Island, a small bit of coral and volcanic rock in the South Pacific that is one of the Marshall Islands. The island was home to 159 people, who lived by fishing much as their ancestors had done for centuries. The population knew only a little about the outside world—a missionary from the United States taught the local children, and two dozen military personnel lived at a small U.S. weather station with an airstrip where a single plane touched down each week.

At 6:45 A.M., the western sky suddenly lit up brighter than anyone had ever seen, and seconds later, a rumble like a massive earthquake rolled across the island. Some of the Utrik people thought the world was coming to an end. Their world, at least as they had known it, had changed forever.

About 160 miles to the west, on Bikini Island, the United States military had just detonated an atomic bomb, a huge device with 1,000 times the power of the bomb used at the end of World War II to destroy the Japanese city of Hiroshima. The enormous blast vaporized the island and sent a massive cloud of dust and radiation into the atmosphere. The military expected the winds to take the cloud north into an open area of the ocean, but the cloud blew east instead. By noon, the radiation cloud had engulfed a Japanese fishing boat ironically called the *Lucky Dragon*, exposing the twenty-three people on board to a dose of radiation that would eventually sicken or

kill them all. By the end of the afternoon, the deadly cloud spilled across Utrik Island.

The cloud was made up of coral and rock dust, all that was left of Bikini Island. The dust fell softly on Utrik Island, and the children, who remembered pictures of snow shown to them by their missionary teacher, ran out to play in the white powder that was piling up everywhere. No one realized that it was contaminated with deadly radiation.

Three-and-one-half days later, the U.S. military landed planes on Utrik Island and informed all the people that they would have to leave

CORBIS- NY

immediately, taking nothing with them. For three months, the island people were held at another military base, and then they were returned home.

Many of the people who were on the island that fateful morning died young, typically from cancer or other diseases associated with radiation exposure. But even today, those who survived consider themselves and their island poisoned by the radiation, and they believe that the poison will never go away. The radiation may or may not still be in their bodies, but it has worked its way deep into their culture. More than half a century after the bomb exploded, people still talked about the morning that "everything changed." The damage from this disaster turns out to be much more than medical—it was a social transformation that left the people with a deep belief that they are all sick, that life will never be the same, and that the people who live on the other side of the world could have prevented the disaster but did not.

WHAT DO YOU THINK?

1. In what sense is a disaster like this one never really over?

2. In what ways did the atomic bomb test change the culture of the Utrik people?

3. What does this account lead us to expect about the long-term consequences of other disasters such as Hurricane Katrina, which damaged much of the Gulf Coast in 2005?

Source: Based on Erikson (2005a).

control. People in Ukraine felt much the same way after the 1986 explosion and radiation leak at the Chernobyl nuclear plant.

Third, the social damage is most serious when the disaster is caused by the actions of other people. This can happen through negligence or carelessness (as in technological disasters) or through willful action (intentional disasters). Our belief that "other people will do us no harm" is a foundation of social life, Erikson claims. But when others act carelessly (as in the case of an oil spill) or intentionally in ways that harm us (as in the case of genocide in Darfur), survivors typically lose their trust in others to a degree that may never go away.

Modernity

A central concept in the study of social change is **modernity,** *social patterns resulting from industrialization.* In everyday terms, *modernity* (its Latin root means "lately") refers to the present in relation to the past. Sociologists use this catchall concept to describe the many social patterns set in motion by the Industrial Revolution, which began in Western Europe in the 1750s. **Modernization,** then, is *the process of social change begun by industrialization.* The timeline inside the back cover of this book highlights important events that mark the emergence

Social Change: Modern and Postmodern Societies

various changes in the United States over the past
as summarized in the table below. In each case, think
out how the change affected everyday social life.

○ Making the Grade

Be sure you understand the four traits of modernization
identified by Peter Berger.

Table 1   The United States: A Century of Change

	1900	2000
National population	76 million	281 million
Share living in cities	40%	80%
Life expectancy	46 years (men), 48 years (women)	74 years (men), 79 years (women)
Median age	22.9 years	35.3 years
Average household income	$8,000 (in 2000 dollars)	$40,000 (in 2000 dollars)
Share of income spent on food	43%	15%
Share of homes with flush toilets	10%	98%
Average number of cars	1 car for every 2,000 households	1.3 cars for every household
Divorce rate	about 1 in 20 marriages	about 8 in 20 marriages
Average gallons of petroleum products consumed	34 per person per year	1,100 per person per year

of modernity. Table 1 provides a summary of change in the United States over the course of the twentieth century.

Peter Berger (1977) identified four major characteristics of modernization:

1. **The decline of small, traditional communities.** Modernity involves "the progressive weakening, if not destruction, of the . . . relatively cohesive communities in which human beings have found solidarity and meaning throughout most of history" (1977:72). For thousands of years, in the camps of hunters and gatherers and in the rural villages of Europe and North America, people lived in small communities where life revolved around family and neighborhood. Such traditional worlds gave each person a well-defined place that, although limiting range of choice, offered a strong sense of identity, belonging, and purpose.

   Small, isolated communities still exist in the United States, of course, but they are home to only a tiny percentage of our nation's people. These days, their isolation is only geographic: Except among those who are extremely poor, cars, telephones, television, and computers give rural families the pulse of the larger society and connect them to the entire world.

2. **The expansion of personal choice.** People in traditional, preindustrial societies view their lives as shaped by forces beyond human control—gods, spirits, fate. As the power of tradition weakens, people come to see their lives as an unending series of options, a process Berger calls *individualization*. For instance, many people in the United States choose a particular "lifestyle" (sometimes adopting one after another), showing an openness to change. Indeed, it is a common belief that people *should* take control of their lives.

3. **Increasing social diversity.** In preindustrial societies, strong family ties and powerful religious beliefs enforce conformity and discourage diversity and change. Modernization promotes a more rational, scientific worldview as tradition loses its hold and people gain more individual choice. The growth of cities, the expansion of

impersonal bureaucracy, and the social mix of people from various backgrounds combine to encourage diverse beliefs and behavior.

4. **Orientation toward the future and a growing awareness of time.** Premodern people focus on the past; people in modern societies think more about the future. Modern people are not only forward-looking but also optimistic that new inventions and discoveries will improve their lives.

   Modern people organize daily routines down to the very minute. With the introduction of clocks in the late Middle Ages, Europeans began to think not in terms of sunlight and seasons but in terms of hours and minutes. Focused on personal gain, modern people demand precise measurement of time and are likely to agree that "time is money." Berger points out that one good indicator of a society's degree of modernization is the share of people who keep track of time by continually glancing at their wristwatches (or nowadays, their cell phones).

Finally, recall that modernization touched off the development of sociology itself. The discipline originated in the wake of the Industrial Revolution in Western Europe at a point when social change was proceeding rapidly. Early European and U.S. sociologists tried to analyze the rise of modern society and its consequences, both good and bad, for human beings.

Ferdinand Tönnies: The Loss of Community

The German sociologist Ferdinand Tönnies produced a lasting account of modernization in his theory of *Gemeinschaft* and *Gesellschaft*. Like Peter Berger, whose work he influenced, Tönnies (1963, orig. 1887) viewed modernization as the progressive loss of *Gemeinschaft*, or human community. As Tönnies saw it, the Industrial Revolution

Making the Grade

Durkheim's concepts match up with those of Tönnies, but be sure to get it right: Mechanical solidarity corresponds to *Gemeinschaft,* and organic solidarity is the same as *Gesellschaft.*

Read "Bowling Alone: America's Declining Social Capital" by Robert D. Putnam on mysoclab.com

weakened the social fabric of family and tradition by introducing a businesslike emphasis on facts, efficiency, and money. European and North American societies gradually became rootless and impersonal as people came to associate with one another mostly on the basis of self-interest—the state Tönnies termed *Gesellschaft.*

Early in the twentieth century, at least some parts of the United States could be described using Tönnies's concept of *Gemeinschaft.* Families that had lived for many generations in small villages and towns were bound together into a hardworking and slowly changing way of life. Telephones (invented in 1876) were rare; not until 1915 could one place a coast-to-coast call. Living without television (introduced commercially in 1933 and not widespread until after 1950), families entertained themselves, often gathering with friends in the evening to share stories, sorrows, or song. Lacking rapid transportation (Henry Ford's assembly line began in 1908, but cars became common only after World War II), many people knew little of the world beyond their hometown.

Inevitable tensions and conflicts divided these communities of the past. But according to Tönnies, the traditional spirit of *Gemeinschaft* meant that people were "essentially united in spite of all separating factors" (1963:65, orig. 1887).

Modernity turns society inside out so that, as Tönnies put it, people are "essentially separated in spite of uniting factors" (1963:65, orig. 1887). This is the world of *Gesellschaft,* where, especially in large cities, most people live among strangers and ignore the people they pass on the street. Trust is hard to come by in a mobile and anonymous society in which people put their personal needs ahead of group loyalty and a majority of adults believe "you can't be too careful" in dealing with people (NORC, 2009:1811). No wonder researchers conclude that even as we have become more affluent, the social health of modern societies has declined (D. G. Myers, 2000). Read on mysoclab.com

CRITICAL REVIEW Tönnies's theory of *Gemeinschaft* and *Gesellschaft* is the most widely cited model of modernization. The theory's strength lies in its synthesis of various dimensions of change: growing population, the rise of cities, and increasingly impersonal interaction. But modern life, though often impersonal, still has some degree of *Gemeinschaft.* Even in a world of strangers, modern friendships can be strong and lasting. In addition, some analysts think that Tönnies favored—perhaps even romanticized—traditional societies while overlooking bonds of family and friendship that continue to flourish in modern societies.

CHECK YOUR LEARNING As types of social organization, how do *Gemeinschaft* and *Gesellschaft* differ?

George Tooker's 1950 painting *The Subway* depicts a common problem of modern life: Weakening social ties and eroding traditions create a generic humanity in which everyone is alike yet each person is an anxious stranger in the midst of others.

Source: George Tooker, *The Subway,* 1950, egg tempera on gesso panel, 18 1/8 × 36 1/8 inches, Whitney Museum of American Art, New York. Purchased with funds from the Juliana Force Purchase Award, 50.23. Photograph © Whitney Museum of American Art
George Tooker (b. 1920), *The Subway,* 1950, egg tempera on gesso panel, 18 1/8 x 36 1/8", Whitney Museum of American Art, New York, purchased with funds from the Juliana Force Purchase Award, 50.23. Photograph courtesy of The Whitney Museum of American Art

Emile Durkheim: The Division of Labor

The French sociologist Emile Durkheim shared Tönnies's interest in the important social changes that resulted from the Industrial Revolution. For Durkheim (1964a, orig. 1893), modernization was marked by an increasing **division of labor,** or *specialized economic activity.* Every member of a traditional society performs more or less the same activities; modern societies function by having people perform highly specific jobs.

Durkheim explained that preindustrial societies are held together by *mechanical solidarity,* or shared moral sentiments. Members of such societies view everyone as basically alike, doing the same work and belonging together. Durkheim's concept of mechanical solidarity is virtually the same as Tönnies's *Gemeinschaft.*

With modernization, the division of labor (job specialization) becomes more and more pronounced. To Durkheim, this change means less mechanical solidarity but more of another kind of tie: *organic solidarity,* mutual dependency between people engaged in specialized work. Put simply, modern societies are held together not by likeness but by difference: All of us must depend on others to meet most of our needs. Organic solidarity corresponds to Tönnies's concept of *Gesellschaft.*

Despite obvious similarities in their thinking, Durkheim and Tönnies viewed modernity somewhat differently. To Tönnies, modern *Gesellschaft* amounted to the loss of social solidarity because people lose the "natural" and "organic" bonds of the rural village, leaving only the "artificial" and "mechanical" ties of the big city. Durkheim

Social Change: Modern and Postmodern Societies

Go to the Multimedia Library at mysoclab.com to hear author John Macionis discuss "What Is Distinctive about the Modern World?"

RBIS- NY

Photos.com

In traditional societies, such as Amish communities in the United States, everyone does much the same work. These societies are held together by strong moral beliefs. Modern societies, illustrated by urban areas in this country, are held together by a system of production in which people perform specialized work and rely on one another.

had a different view of modernity, even reversing Tönnies's language to bring home the point. Durkheim labeled modern society "organic," arguing that modern society is no less natural than any other, and he described traditional societies as "mechanical" because they are so regimented. Durkheim viewed modernization not so much as a loss of community as a change from community based on bonds of likeness (kinship and neighborhood) to community based on economic interdependence (the division of labor). Durkheim's view of modernity is thus both more complex and more positive than Tönnies's view.

CRITICAL REVIEW Durkheim's work, which resembles that of Tönnies, is a highly influential analysis of modernity. Of the two, Durkheim was more optimistic; still, he feared that modern societies might become so diverse that they would collapse into anomie, *a condition in which society provides little moral guidance to individuals.* Living with weak moral norms, modern people can become egocentric, placing their own needs above those of others and finding little purpose in life.

The suicide rate, which Durkheim considered a good index of anomie, did in fact increase in the United States over the course of the twentieth century, and the vast majority of adults report that they see moral questions not in clear terms of right and wrong but as confusing "shades of gray" (NORC, 2009:478). Yet shared norms and values seem strong enough to give most people a sense of meaning and purpose. Whatever the hazards of anomie, most people value the personal freedom modern society gives us.

CHECK YOUR LEARNING Define mechanical solidarity and organic solidarity. In his view of the modern world, what makes Durkheim more optimistic than Tönnies?

Max Weber: Rationalization

For Max Weber, modernity meant replacing a traditional worldview with a rational way of thinking. In preindustrial societies, tradition acts as a constant brake on social change. To traditional people, "truth" is roughly the same as "what has always been" (1978:36, orig. 1921). To modern people, however, "truth" is the result of rational calculation. Because they value efficiency and have little reverence for the past, modern people adopt social patterns that allow them to achieve their goals.

Echoing Tönnies's and Durkheim's claim that industrialization weakens tradition, Weber characterized modern society as "disenchanted." The unquestioned truths of an earlier time had been challenged by rational thinking. In short, said Weber, modern society turns away from the gods just as it turns away from the past. Throughout his life, Weber studied various modern "types"—the scientist, the capitalist, the bureaucrat—all of whom share the forward-looking, rational, and detached worldview that he believed was coming to dominate humanity. ● Go to mysoclab.com

CRITICAL REVIEW Compared with Tönnies and especially Durkheim, Weber was very critical of modern society. He knew that science could produce technological and organizational wonders, yet he worried that science was carrying us away

Social Change: Modern and Postmodern Societies

○ Making the Grade

Be sure you see what, from Weber's point of view, the scientist, the capitalist, and the bureaucrat (all pictured below) have in common.

○ Making the Grade

Marx claimed capitalism was the foundation of modern society; Weber claimed that capitalism (along with science and bureaucracy) rests on a more basic foundation—rationality.

from more basic questions about the meaning and purpose of human existence. Weber feared that rationalization, especially in bureaucracies, would erode the human spirit with endless rules and regulations.

○ **CHECK YOUR LEARNING**   What did Weber mean by describing the modern world as "disenchanted"? In what ways are scientists, capitalists, and bureaucrats all "disenchanted"?

Some of Weber's critics think that the alienation Weber attributed to bureaucracy actually stemmed from social inequality. This issue leads us to the ideas of Karl Marx.

Karl Marx: Capitalism

For Karl Marx, modern society was synonymous with capitalism; he saw the Industrial Revolution primarily as a *capitalist* revolution. Marx traced the emergence of the bourgeoisie in medieval Europe to the expansion of commerce. The bourgeoisie gradually displaced the feudal aristocracy as the Industrial Revolution gave it control of a powerful new productive system.

Marx agreed that modernity weakened small communities (as described by Tönnies), increased the division of labor (as noted by Durkheim), and encouraged a rational worldview (as Weber claimed). But he saw these simply as conditions necessary for capitalism to flourish. According to Marx, capitalism draws population away from farms and small towns into an ever-expanding market system centered in the cities; specialization is needed for efficient

factories; and rationality is illustrated by the capitalists' endless pursuit of profit.

We have painted Marx as a spirited critic of capitalist society, but his vision of modernity also includes a good bit of optimism. Unlike Weber, who viewed modern society as an "iron cage" of bureaucracy from which there was no escape, Marx believed that social conflict in capitalist societies would sow the seeds of revolutionary change, leading to an egalitarian socialism. Such a society, as he saw it, would harness the wonders of industrial technology to enrich people's lives and rid the world of social classes, the source of conflict and so much suffering. Although Marx's evaluation of modern capitalist society was highly negative, he imagined a future of human freedom, creativity, and community.

○ **CRITICAL REVIEW**   Marx's theory of modernization is a complex theory of capitalism. But he underestimated the dominance of bureaucracy in shaping modern societies. In socialist societies, in particular, the stifling effects of bureaucracy have turned out to be as bad as, or even worse than, the dehumanizing aspects of capitalism. The upheavals in Eastern Europe and the former Soviet Union in the 1990s revealed the depth of popular opposition to oppressive state bureaucracies.

○ **CHECK YOUR LEARNING**   Of the four theorists just discussed—Tönnies, Durkheim, Weber, and Marx—who comes across as the most optimistic about modern society? Who was the most pessimistic? Explain your choices.

Max Weber maintained that the distinctive character of modern society was its rational worldview. Virtually all of Weber's work on modernity centered on types of people he considered typical of their age: the scientist, the capitalist, and the bureaucrat. Each is rational to the core: The scientist is committed to the orderly discovery of truth, the capitalist to the orderly pursuit of profit, and the bureaucrat to orderly conformity to a system of rules.

Social Change: Modern and Postmodern Societies

● Seeing Sociology
in Everyday Life

Identify five examples of "mass culture" that are the same throughout the United States. Name five more that differ from region to region.

...tural-Functional Analysis: ...dernity as Mass Society

November 11, on Interstate 275. From the car window, we see BP and Sunoco gas stations, a Kmart and a Walmart, an AmeriSuites hotel, a Bob Evans, a Chi-Chi's Mexican restaurant, and a McDonald's. This road happens to circle Cincinnati, Ohio. But it could be in Boston, Saint Louis, Denver, San Diego, or almost anywhere else in the United States.

The rise of modernity is a complex process involving many dimensions of change, reviewed here in the Summing Up table. How can we make sense of so many changes going on at once? Sociologists have two broad explanations of modern society, one guided by the structural-functional approach and the other based on social-conflict theory.

The first explanation, guided by the structural-functional approach and drawing on the ideas of Tönnies, Durkheim, and Weber, understands modernity as the emergence of a *mass society* (Kornhauser, 1959; Nisbet, 1969; Berger, Berger, & Kellner, 1974; Pearson, 1993). A **mass society** is *a society in which prosperity and bureaucracy have weakened traditional social ties.* A mass society is productive; on average, people have more income than ever. At the same time, it is marked by weak kinship and impersonal neighborhoods, leaving individuals to feel socially isolated. Although many people have material plenty, they are spiritually weak and often experience moral uncertainty about how to live.

The Mass Scale of Modern Life

Mass-society theory argues, first, that the scale of modern life has greatly increased. Before the Industrial Revolution, Europe and North America formed a mosaic of rural villages and small towns. In these local communities, which inspired Tönnies's concept of *Gemeinschaft,* people lived out their lives surrounded by kin and guided by a shared heritage. Gossip was an informal yet highly effective way of ensuring conformity to community standards. Such small communities tolerated little social diversity—the state of mechanical solidarity described by Durkheim.

For example, before 1690, English law demanded that everyone participate regularly in the Christian ritual of Holy Communion (Laslett, 1984). On the North American continent, only Rhode Island among the New England colonies tolerated any religious dissent. Because social differences were repressed in favor of conformity to established norms, subcultures and countercultures were few, and change proceeded slowly.

Increasing population, the growth of cities, and specialized economic activity driven by the Industrial Revolution gradually altered this pattern. People came to know one another by their jobs (for example, as "the doctor" or "the bank clerk") rather than by their kinship group or hometown. People looked on most others simply as strangers. The face-to-face communication of the village was eventually replaced by the impersonal mass media: newspapers, radio, television, and computer networks. Large organizations steadily assumed more and more responsibility for the daily needs that had once been fulfilled by family, friends, and neighbors; public education drew more and more people to schools; police, lawyers, and courts supervised a formal criminal justice system. Even charity became the work of faceless bureaucrats working for various social welfare agencies.

Geographic mobility, mass communication, and exposure to diverse ways of life all weaken traditional values. People become more tolerant of social diversity, defending individual rights and freedom of choice. Treating people differently because of their race, sex, or religion comes to be defined as backward and unjust. In the process, minorities at the margins of society gain greater power and broader participation in public life. The election of Barack Obama—an African American—to the highest office in the United States is surely one indicator that ours is now a modern society (West, 2008).

The mass media give rise to a national culture that washes over the traditional differences that used to set off one region from another. As one analyst put it, "Even in Baton Rouge, La., the local kids don't say 'y'all' anymore; they say 'you guys' just like on TV" (Gibbs, 2000:42). Mass-society theorists fear that the transformation of people of various backgrounds into a generic mass may end up dehumanizing everyone.

The Ever-Expanding State

In the small-scale preindustrial societies of Europe, government amounted to little more than a local noble. A royal family formally reigned over an entire nation, but in the absence of swift transportation and efficient communication, even absolute monarchs had far less power than today's political leaders.

As technological innovation allowed government to expand, the centralized state grew in size and importance. At the time of independence, the U.S. government was a tiny organization, its primary function being national defense. Since then, government has assumed responsibility for more and more areas of social life: schooling, regulating wages and working conditions, establishing standards for products of all sorts, and providing financial assistance to the elderly, the ill, and the unemployed. To pay for such programs, taxes have soared: Today's average worker in the United States labors more than four months each year just to pay for the broad array of services the government provides.

In a mass society, power resides in large bureaucracies, leaving people in local communities with little control over their lives. For

⌐○ Making the Grade

This table is a good summary of trends that define our modern society.

⌐○ Making the Grade

As you read about mass society theory, keep in mind the theories of Tönnies, Durkheim, and Weber on which it is based.

SUMMING UP

Traditional and Modern Societies: The Big Picture

Elements of Society	Traditional Societies	Modern Societies
Cultural Patterns		
Values	Homogeneous; sacred character; few subcultures and countercultures	Heterogeneous; secular character; many subcultures and countercultures
Norms	Great moral significance; little tolerance of diversity	Variable moral significance; high tolerance of diversity
Time orientation	Present linked to past	Present linked to future
Technology	Preindustrial; human and animal energy	Industrial; advanced energy sources
Social Structure		
Status and role	Few statuses, most ascribed; few specialized roles	Many statuses, some ascribed and some achieved; many specialized roles
Relationships	Typically primary; little anonymity or privacy	Typically secondary; much anonymity and privacy
Communication	Face to face	Face-to-face communication supplemented by mass media
Social control	Informal gossip	Formal police and legal system
Social stratification	Rigid patterns of social inequality; little mobility	Fluid patterns of social inequality; high mobility
Gender patterns	Pronounced patriarchy; women's lives centered on the home	Declining patriarchy; increasing share of women work in the paid labor force
Settlement patterns	Small-scale; population typically small and widely dispersed in rural villages and small towns	Large-scale; population typically large and concentrated in cities
Social Institutions		
Economy	Based on agriculture; much manufacturing in the home; little white-collar work	Based on industrial mass production; factories become centers of production; increasing white-collar work
State	Small-scale government; little state intervention in society	Large-scale government; much state intervention in society
Family	Extended family as the primary means of socialization and economic production	Nuclear family still has some socialization functions but is more a unit of consumption than of production
Religion	Religion guides worldview; little religious pluralism	Religion weakens with the rise of science; extensive religious pluralism
Education	Formal schooling limited to elites	Basic schooling becomes universal, with growing share of people receiving advanced education
Health	High birth and death rates; short life expectancy because of low standard of living and simple medical technology	Low birth and death rates; longer life expectancy because of higher standard of living and sophisticated medical technology
Social Change	Slow; change evident over many generations	Rapid; change evident within a single generation

example, state officials mandate that local schools must meet educational standards, local products must be government-certified, and every citizen must maintain extensive tax records. Although such regulations may protect people and enhance social equality, they also force us to deal more and more with nameless officials in distant and often unresponsive bureaucracies, and they undermine the autonomy of families and local communities.

⌐○ **CRITICAL REVIEW** The growing scale of modern life certainly has positive aspects, but only at the cost of our cultural heritage. Modern societies increase individual rights, have greater tolerance of social differences, and raise living standards (Inglehart & Baker, 2000). But they are prone to what Weber feared most—excessive bureaucracy—as well as to Tönnies's self-centeredness and Durkheim's anomie. The size, complexity, and

Social Change: Modern and Postmodern Societies

...rade

expansion of the modern state,
encourage dehumanization.
...ore positive view of the expanding
reduce social inequality.

...of diversity of modern societies all but doom traditional ...and families, leaving individuals isolated, powerless, and ...rialistic. Voter apathy is a serious problem in the United States. ...ut should we be surprised that individuals in vast, impersonal societies such as ours end up thinking that no one person can make much of a difference?

Critics sometimes say that mass-society theory romanticizes the past. They remind us that many people in the small towns of our past were eager to set out for a better standard of living in cities. This approach also ignores problems of social inequality. Critics say mass-society theory attracts social and economic conservatives who defend conventional morality and are indifferent to the historical inequality of women and other minorities.

CHECK YOUR LEARNING In your own words, state the mass-society analysis of modernity.

Social-Conflict Analysis: Modernity as Class Society

The second explanation of modernity derives mostly from the ideas of Karl Marx. From a social-conflict perspective, modernity takes the form of a **class society,** *a capitalist society with pronounced social stratification.* While agreeing that modern societies have expanded to a

Social-conflict theory sees modernity not as an impersonal mass society but as an unequal class society in which some categories of people are second-class citizens. This Arizona family, like many Native Americans, lives on a reservation, where poverty is widespread and many trailer homes do not have electricity or running water.

mass scale, this approach views the heart of modernization as an expanding capitalist economy, marked by inequality (Habermas, 1970; Harrington, 1984; Buechler, 2000).

Capitalism

Class-society theory follows Marx in claiming that the increasing scale of social life in modern times has resulted from the growth and greed unleashed by capitalism. Because a capitalist economy pursues ever-greater profits, both production and consumption steadily increase.

According to Marx, capitalism rests on "naked self-interest" (Marx & Engels, 1972:337, orig. 1848). This self-centeredness weakens the social ties that once united small communities. Capitalism also treats people as commodities: a source of labor and a market for capitalist products.

Capitalism supports science not just as the key to greater productivity but also as an ideology that justifies the status quo. Modern societies encourage people to view human well-being as a technical puzzle that can be solved by engineers and other scientific experts rather than through the pursuit of social justice. For example, a capitalist culture seeks to improve health through advances in scientific medicine rather than by eliminating poverty, despite the fact that poverty is a core cause of poor health.

Businesses also raise the banner of scientific logic, trying to increase profits through greater efficiency. Capitalist corporations have reached enormous size and control unimaginable wealth as a result of global expansion. From the class-society point of view, the expanding scale of life is less a function of *Gesellschaft* than the inevitable and destructive consequence of capitalism.

Persistent Inequality

Modernity has gradually worn away some of the rigid categories that divided preindustrial societies. But class-society theory maintains that elites persist in the form of capitalist millionaires instead of nobles born to wealth and power. In the United States, we may have no hereditary monarchy, but the richest 5 percent of the population controls about 60 percent of all privately held property (Keister, 2005; Wolff, 2009).

What of the state? Mass-society theorists argue that the state works to increase equality and fight social problems. Marx disagreed; he doubted that the state could accomplish more than minor reforms because, as he saw it, real power lies in the hands of the capitalists who control the economy. Other class-society

○ Making the Grade

Both mass- and class-society theories are critical of modernity: the first because of what is lost (traditional social ties), the second because of what remains (persistent social inequality).

○ Seeing Sociology in Everyday Life

Have you ever felt difficulty deciding "who you are"? Do you try to be a different person in different settings? If you answer "yes" to such questions, how might you link such experiences to modernity?

SUMMING UP

Two Interpretations of Modernity

	Mass Society	Class Society
Process of modernization	Industrialization; growth of bureaucracy	Rise of capitalism
Effects of modernization	Increasing scale of life; rise of the state and other formal organizations	Expansion of the capitalist economy; persistence of social inequality

theorists add that to the extent that working people and minorities do enjoy greater political rights and a higher standard of living today, these changes were the result of political struggle, not government goodwill. Despite our pretensions of democracy, they conclude, most people are powerless in the face of wealthy elites.

○ **CRITICAL REVIEW** Class-society theory dismisses Durkheim's argument that people in modern societies suffer from anomie, claiming instead that most people deal with alienation and powerlessness. Not surprisingly, the class-society interpretation of modernity enjoys widespread support among liberals and radicals who favor greater equality and seek extensive regulation (or abolition) of the capitalist marketplace.

A basic criticism of class-society theory is that it overlooks the increasing prosperity of modern societies and the fact that discrimination based on race, ethnicity, religion, and gender is now illegal and is widely regarded as a social problem. In addition, most people in the United States do not want an egalitarian society; they prefer a system of unequal rewards that reflects personal differences in talent and effort.

Based on socialism's failure to generate a high overall standard of living, few observers think that a centralized economy would cure the ills of modernity. Many other problems in the United States—including unemployment, industrial pollution, and unresponsive government—are also found in socialist nations.

○ **CHECK YOUR LEARNING** In your own words, state the class-society analysis of modernity. What are several criticisms of it?

The Summing Up table compares views of modern society offered by mass-society theory and class-society theory. Mass-society theory focuses on the increasing impersonality of social life and the growth of government; class-society theory stresses the expansion of capitalism and the persistence of inequality.

Modernity and the Individual

Both mass- and class-society theories look at the broad patterns of change since the Industrial Revolution. From these macro-level approaches, we can also draw micro-level insights into how modernity shapes individual lives.

Mass Society: Problems of Identity

Modernity freed individuals from the small, tightly knit communities of the past. Most members of modern societies have the privacy and freedom to express their individuality. However, mass-society theory suggests that so much social diversity, widespread isolation, and rapid social change make it difficult for many people to establish any coherent identity at all (Wheelis, 1958; Berger, Berger, & Kellner, 1974).

Previously we explained that people's personalities are mostly a product of their social experiences. The small, homogeneous, and slowly changing societies of the past provided a firm, if narrow, foundation for building a personal identity. Even today, Amish and Mennonite communities that flourish in the United States teach young men and women "correct" ways to think and behave. Not everyone born into an Amish community can tolerate such rigid demands for conformity, but most members establish a well-integrated and satisfying personal identity (Kraybill & Olshan, 1994; Kraybill & Hurd, 2006).

Mass societies are quite another story. Socially diverse and rapidly changing, they offer only shifting sands on which to build a personal identity. Left to make many life decisions on their own, people—especially those with greater wealth—face a confusing range of options. The freedom to choose has little value without standards to guide the selection process; in a tolerant mass society, people may find little reason to choose one path over another. As a result, many people shuttle from one identity to another, changing their lifestyles, relationships, and even religions in search of an elusive "true self." Given the widespread relativism of modern societies, people without

social character personality patterns common to members of a particular society

tradition-directedness rigid conformity to time-honored ways of living

other-directedness openness to the latest trends and fashions, often expressed by imitating others

○ Making the Grade

Riesman's tradition-directedness corresponds to Tönnies's *Gemeinschaft* and Durkheim's mechanical solidarity. Other-directedness is linked to *Gesellschaft* and organic solidarity.

a moral compass lack the security and certainty once provided by tradition.

To David Riesman (1970, orig. 1950), modernization brings changes in **social character**, *personality patterns common to members of a particular society.* Preindustrial societies promote what Riesman calls **tradition-directedness**, *rigid conformity to time-honored ways of living.* Members of such societies model their lives on those of their ancestors, so that "living the good life" amounts to "doing what people have always done."

Tradition-directedness corresponds to Tönnies's *Gemeinschaft* and Durkheim's mechanical solidarity. Culturally conservative, tradition-directed people think and act alike. Unlike the conformity often found in modern societies, the uniformity of tradition-directedness is not an effort to imitate a popular celebrity or follow the latest trend. Instead, people are alike because they all draw on the same solid cultural foundation. Amish women and men exemplify tradition-directedness; in the Amish culture, tradition ties everyone to ancestors and descendants in an unbroken chain of righteous living.

Members of diverse and rapidly changing societies define a tradition-directed personality as deviant because it seems so rigid. Modern people prize personal flexibility, the capacity to adapt, and sensitivity to others. Riesman calls this type of social character **other-directedness**, *openness to the latest trends and fashions, often expressed by imitating others.* Because their socialization occurs in societies that are continuously in flux, other-directed people develop fluid identities marked by superficiality, inconsistency, and change. They try on different "selves" almost like new clothing, seek out role models, and engage in varied performances as they move from setting to setting (Goffman, 1959). In a traditional society, such "shiftiness" marks a person as untrustworthy, but in a changing, modern society, the chameleonlike ability to fit in almost virtually anywhere is very useful.

In societies that value the up-to-date rather than the traditional, people look to others for approval, using members of their own generation rather than elders as role models. Peer pressure can be irresistible to people without strong standards to guide them. Our society urges people to be true to themselves, but when social surroundings change so rapidly, how can people develop the self to which they should be true? This problem lies at the root of the identity crisis so widespread in industrial societies today. "Who am I?" is a nagging question that many of us struggle to answer. In truth, this problem is not so much us as the inherently unstable mass society in which we live.

Class Society: Problems of Powerlessness

Class-society theory paints a different picture of modernity's effects on individuals. This approach maintains that persistent inequality undermines modern society's promise of individual freedom. For some people, modernity serves up great privilege, but for many others, everyday life means coping with economic uncertainty and a gnawing sense of powerlessness (K. S. Newman, 1993; Ehrenreich, 2001).

For racial and ethnic minorities, the problem of relative disadvantage looms even larger. Similarly, although women participate more broadly in modern societies, they continue to run up against traditional barriers of sexism. This approach rejects mass-society theory's claim that people suffer from too much freedom; according to class-society theory, our society still denies a majority of people full participation in social life.

The expanding scope of world capitalism has placed more of Earth's population under the influence of multinational corporations. As a result, 80 percent of the world's income is concentrated in high-income nations, where just 23 percent of its people live. Is it any wonder, class-society theorists ask, that people in poor nations seek greater power to shape their own lives?

The problem of widespread powerlessness led Herbert Marcuse (1964) to challenge Max Weber's claim that modern society is rational. Marcuse condemned modern society as irrational for failing to meet the needs of so many people. Although modern capitalist societies produce unparalleled wealth, poverty remains the daily plight of more than 1 billion people. Marcuse added that technological advances further reduce people's control over their own lives. The advent of high technology has generally conferred a great deal of power on a core of specialists—not the majority of people—who now dominate discussion of when to go to war, what our energy policy should be, and how people should pay for health care. Countering the popular view that technology *solves* the world's problems, Marcuse believed that science *causes* them. In sum, class-society theory asserts that people suffer because modern societies have concentrated both wealth and power in the hands of a privileged few.

Modernity and Progress

In modern societies, most people expect and applaud social change. We link modernity to the idea of *progress* (from the Latin, meaning "moving forward"), a state of continual improvement. We equate stability with stagnation.

Given our bias in favor of change, members of our society tend to regard traditional cultures as backward. But change, particularly toward material affluence, is a mixed blessing. As the Thinking Globally box shows, social change is too complex simply to equate with progress.

Even getting rich has both advantages and disadvantages, as the cases of the Kaiapo and Gullah show. Historically, among people in

┌─○ Making the Grade

In a sense, mass-society theory claims that modern people
have too much freedom and choice; class-society theory
claims that we have too little.

┌─○ Seeing Sociology
in Everyday Life

In 1970, Alvin Toffler coined the phrase "future shock" to
describe the effect of social change that comes so rapidly that it
overwhelms us. Do you think the pace of change has become
overwhelming? Does our world need more change, or do we
have too much already? Explain your answers.

Mass-society theory relates feelings of anxiety and lack of meaning in the modern world to rapid social change
that washes away tradition. This notion of modern emptiness is captured in the photo at the left. Class-society
theory, by contrast, ties such feelings to social inequality, by which some categories of people are made into
second-class citizens (or not made citizens at all), an idea expressed in the photo at the right.

the United States, a rising standard of living has made lives longer and
more comfortable. At the same time, many people wonder whether
today's routines are too stressful, with families often having little
time to relax or to spend time together. Perhaps this is why, in the
United States, measures of happiness have declined (D. G. Myers,
2000; Inglehart, Welzel, & Foa, 2009).

Science, too, has its pluses and minuses. People in the United
States are more confident than people living in most other indus-
trial societies that science improves our everyday lives (Inglehart &
Welzel, 2010). But surveys also show that many adults in the United
States feel that science "makes our way of life change too fast"
(NORC, 2009:1329).

New technology has always sparked controversy. Just over a century ago, the introduction of automobiles and telephones allowed
more rapid transportation and more efficient communication,
improving people's lives. At the same time, such technology also
weakened traditional attachments to hometowns and even to families.
Today, people might wonder whether computer technology will do
the same thing: giving us access to people around the world but
shielding us from the community right outside our doors; providing
more information than ever before but in the process threatening
personal privacy. In short, we all realize that social change comes
faster all the time, but we may disagree about whether a particular
change is good or bad for society.

Modernity: Global Variation

> **October 1, Kobe, Japan.** Riding the computer-
> controlled monorail high above the streets of Kobe or
> the 200-mile-per-hour bullet train to Tokyo, we see
> Japan as the society of the future, in love with high
> technology. Yet the Japanese remain strikingly traditional in
> other respects: Few corporate executives and almost no politi-
> cians are women, young people still show seniors great respect,
> and public orderliness contrasts with the relative chaos of
> many U.S. cities.

Japan is a nation both traditional and modern. This contradiction
reminds us that although it is useful to contrast traditional and modern
social patterns, the old and the new often coexist in unexpected ways. In
the People's Republic of China, ancient Confucian principles are mixed
with contemporary socialist thinking. In Saudi Arabia and Qatar, a love
of the latest modern technology is mixed with respect for the ancient
principles of Islam. Likewise, in Mexico and much of Latin America,
people observe centuries-old Christian rituals even as they struggle to
move ahead economically. In short, although we may think of tradition
and modernity as opposites, combinations of traditional and modern
are far from unusual, and they are found throughout the world.

○ Making the Grade

The importance of a global perspective is seeing that "tradition" and "modernity" are not simply opposites but are often found in unexpected combinations in societies around the world.

postmodernity social patterns characteristic of postindustrial societies

THINKING GLOBALLY

Does "Modernity" Mean "Progress"? The Kaiapo of the Amazon and the Gullah of Georgia

The firelight flickers in the gathering darkness. Chief Kanhonk sits, as he has done at the end of the day for many years, ready to begin an evening of animated talk and storytelling (Simons, 2007). This is the hour when the Kaiapo, a small society in Brazil's lush Amazon region, celebrate their heritage. Because the Kaiapo are a traditional people with no written language, the elders rely on evenings by the fire to pass along their culture to their children and grandchildren. In the past, evenings like this have been filled with tales of brave Kaiapo warriors fighting off Portuguese traders in pursuit of slaves and gold.

But as the minutes pass, just a few older villagers assemble for the evening ritual. "It is the Big Ghost," one man grumbles, explaining the poor turnout. The "Big Ghost" has indeed descended on them; its bluish glow spills from windows throughout the village. The Kaiapo children—and many adults as well—are watching sitcoms on television. Buying a television and a satellite dish several years ago has had consequences far greater than anyone imagined. In the

end, what their enemies failed to do with guns, the Kaiapo may well do to themselves with prime-time programming.

The Kaiapo are among the 230,000 native peoples who inhabit Brazil. They stand out because of their striking body paint and ornate ceremonial dress. During the 1980s, they became rich from gold mining and harvesting mahogany trees. Now they must decide if their newfound fortune is a blessing or a curse.

Mauri Rautkari

To some, affluence means the opportunity to learn about the outside world through travel and television. Others, like Chief Kanhonk, are not so sure. Sitting by the fire, he thinks aloud, "I have been saying that people must buy useful things like knives and fishing hooks. Television does not fill the stomach. It only shows our children and grandchildren white people's things." Bebtopup, the oldest priest, nods in agreement: "The night is the time the old people teach the young people. Television has stolen the night" (Simons, 2007:522).

Far to the north, half an hour by ferry from the coast of Georgia, lies the swampy island community of Hog Hammock. The seventy African American residents of the island today trace their ancestry back to the first slaves who settled here in 1802.

Walking past the brightly painted houses that stand among yellow pine trees draped with Spanish moss, a visitor can easily feel transported back in time. The local people, known as Gullahs (or in some places, Geechees), speak a

Postmodernity

If modernity was the product of the Industrial Revolution, could the Information Revolution be creating a postmodern era? A number of scholars think so, and they use the term **postmodernity** to refer to *social patterns characteristic of postindustrial societies.*

Precisely what postmodernism is remains a matter of debate. The term has been used for decades in literary, philosophical, and even architectural circles. It has moved into sociology on a wave of social criticism that has been building since the spread of left-leaning politics in the 1960s. Although there are many variations of postmodern thinking, all share the following five themes (Hall & Neitz, 1993; Inglehart, 1997; Rudel & Gerson, 1999):

1. **In important respects, modernity has failed.** The promise of modernity was a life free from want. As postmodernist critics see it, however, the twentieth century was unsuccessful in solving

social problems such as poverty because many people still lack financial security.

2. **The bright light of "progress" is fading.** Modern people look to the future expecting their lives to improve in significant ways. Members (and even leaders) of a postmodern society are less confident about what the future holds. The strong optimism that carried society into the modern era more than a century ago has given way to widespread pessimism, especially in recent years due to the weak economy.

3. **Science no longer holds the answers.** The defining trait of the modern era was a scientific outlook and a confident belief that technology would make life better. But postmodern critics argue that science has failed to solve many old problems (such as poor health) and has even created new problems (such as air and water pollution and declining natural resources).

Postmodernist thinkers discredit science, claiming that it implies a singular truth. On the contrary, they maintain, there

Social Change: Modern and Postmodern Societies

○ Making the Grade

Just as the Industrial Revolution marks the onset of modernity, the new postindustrial economy (or Information Revolution) marks the onset of postmodernity.

○ Making the Grade

An important sociological insight is that social change always has both positive and negative consequences, so it is simplistic to equate change with "progress."

creole, a mixture of English and West African languages. They fish, living much the same as they have for hundreds of years.

But the future of this way of life is now in doubt. Few young people who are raised in Hog Hammock can find work; beyond fishing and making traditional crafts, there are simply no jobs to do. "We have been here nine generations and we are still here," says one local. Then, referring to the nineteen children who now live on the island, she adds, "It's not that they don't want to be here; it's that there's nothing here for them—they need to have jobs" (Curry, 2001:41).

Just as important, with people on the mainland looking for waterside homes for vacations or year-round living, the island is now becoming prime real estate. Not long ago, one larger house went up for sale and the community was shocked to learn of an asking price over $1 million. The locals know only too well that higher property values will mean high taxes that few can afford to pay. In short, Hog Hammock is likely to become another Hilton Head, once a Gullah community on the South Carolina coast that is now home to well-to-do people from the mainland.

The odds are that before long, the people of Hog Hammock will be selling their homes and moving inland. But few people are happy at the thought of selling out, even for a good price. On the contrary, moving away will mean the end of their cultural heritage.

Kelly-Mooney Photography\CORBIS- NY

The stories of the Kaiapo and the people of Hog Hammock show us that change is not a simple path toward "progress." These people may be moving toward modernity, but this process will have both positive and negative consequences. In the end, both groups of people may enjoy a higher standard of living with better shelter, more clothing, and new technology. But their newfound affluence will come at the price of their traditions. The drama of these people is now being played out around the world as more and more traditional cultures are being lured away from their heritage by the affluence and materialism of rich societies.

WHAT DO YOU THINK?

1. Why is social change both a winning and a losing proposition for traditional people?

2. Do the changes described here improve the lives of the Kaiapo? What about the Gullah community?

3. Do traditional people have any choice about becoming modern? Explain your view.

is no one truth. This means that objective reality does not exist; rather, many realities result from social construction.

4. **Cultural debates are intensifying.** Many people have all the material things they really need, which allows ideas to take on more importance. In this sense, postmodernity is also a postmaterialist era in which issues such as social justice, the environment, and animal rights command more and more public attention.

5. **Social institutions are changing.** Just as industrialization brought sweeping transformation to social institutions, the rise of postindustrial society is remaking society all over again. For example, the Industrial Revolution placed *material things* at the center of productive life; the Information Revolution emphasizes *ideas.* Similarly, the postmodern family no longer conforms to any one pattern; on the contrary, individuals are choosing among many family forms.

○ **CRITICAL REVIEW** Analysts who claim that the United States and other high-income nations are entering a postmodern era criticize modernity for failing to meet human needs. In defense of modernity, there have been marked increases in longevity and living standards over the past century. Even if we were to accept postmodernist views that science is bankrupt and progress is a sham, what are the alternatives?

○ **CHECK YOUR LEARNING** In your own words, state the defining characteristics of a postmodern society.

Looking Ahead: Modernization and Our Global Future

Imagine the entire world's population reduced to a single village of 1,000 people. About 230 residents of this "global village" are from high-income countries. Another 196 people are so poor that their lives are at risk.

Social Change: Modern and Postmodern Societies

Seeing Sociology in Everyday Life

Do you think there is too much of a "me first" attitude in today's world? Explain your view.

Seeing Sociology in Everyday Life

Does the balance between individual freedom and personal responsibility differ for men and women? If so, how, and why?

SEEING SOCIOLOGY IN EVERYDAY LIFE

Personal Freedom and Social Responsibility: Can We Have It Both Ways?

SAMUEL: I feel that being free is the most important thing. Let me do what I want!

SANJI: But if everyone felt that way, what would the world be like?

DOREEN: Isn't there a way to be true to ourselves and also take account of other people?

One issue we all have to work out is making personal decisions that take proper account of other people. But what, exactly, do we owe others? To see the problem, consider an event that took place in New York in 1964.

Shortly after midnight on a crisp March evening, Kitty Genovese drove into the parking lot of her apartment complex. She turned off the engine, locked the car doors, and headed across the blacktop toward the entrance to her building. Out of nowhere, a man holding a knife lunged at her, and as she screamed in terror and pain, he stabbed her repeatedly. Windows opened above as curious neighbors looked down to see what was going on. The attack continued for more than thirty minutes until Genovese lay dead in her doorway. The police never identified her killer, and the follow-up investigation revealed a stunning fact:

Jim West\Alamy Images

In today's world, people can find new ways to express age-old virtues such as extending a helping hand to their neighbors in need. In the wake of Hurricane Katrina, thousands of college students from across the country converged on New Orleans to help repair the damage to the stricken city. Are there opportunities for you to get involved in your own community?

Not one of the dozens of neighbors who witnessed the attack on Kitty Genovese went to her aid or even called the police.

Decades after this tragic event, we still confront the question of what we owe others. As members of a modern society, we prize our individual rights and personal privacy, but we sometimes withdraw from public responsibility and turn a cold shoulder to people in need. When a cry for help is met by indifference, have we pushed our modern idea of personal freedom too far? In a society of expanding individual rights, can we keep a sense of human community?

These questions highlight the tension between traditional and modern social systems, which is evident in the writings of all the sociologists discussed in this chapter. Tönnies, Durkheim, and others concluded that in some respects, traditional community and modern individualism don't mix. That is, society can unite its members as a

---

The tragic plight of the world's poor shows that some desperately needed change has not yet occurred. We have presented two competing views of why 1 billion people around the world are so poor. *Modernization theory* claims that in the past, the entire world was poor and that technological change, especially the Industrial Revolution, enhanced human productivity and raised living standards in many nations. From this point of view, the solution to global poverty is to promote technological development and market economies around the world.

For reasons suggested earlier, however, global modernization may be difficult. Recall that David Riesman portrayed preindustrial people as *tradition-directed* and likely to resist change. So modernization theorists claim that rich nations should help poor countries grow economically. Industrial nations can speed development by exporting technology to poor regions, welcoming students from these countries, and providing foreign aid to stimulate economic growth.

The review of modernization theory discussed previously points to some success for these policies in Latin America and more dramatic results in the small Asian countries of Taiwan, South Korea, and Singapore and in Hong Kong (part of the People's Republic of China). But jump-starting development in the poorest countries of the world poses greater challenges. Even where dramatic change has occurred, modernization involves a trade-off. Traditional people, such as Brazil's Kaiapo, may gain wealth through economic development, but only at the cost of losing their traditional identity and values as they are drawn into a global "McCulture," which is based on Western materialism, pop music, trendy clothes, and fast food. One Brazilian anthropologist expressed optimism about the future of the Kaiapo: "At least they quickly understood the consequences of watching television. . . . Now [they] can make a choice" (Simons, 2007:523).

But not everyone thinks that modernization is really an option. According to a second approach to global stratification, *dependency*

Seeing Sociology in Everyday Life

Think of people you admire. Do you admire them for their personal achievement, social responsibility, or a combination of the two?

Seeing Sociology in Everyday Life

After reading the box below, think of ways your campus encourages a sense of community and social responsibility.

moral community only by limiting their range of personal choices about how to live. In short, although we value both community and freedom, we can't have it both ways.

The famed sociologist Amitai Etzioni (1993, 1996, 2003) has tried to strike a middle ground. The *communitarian movement* rests on the simple idea that with rights must come responsibilities. Put another way, our pursuit of self-interest must be balanced by a commitment to the larger community.

Etzioni claims that modern people have become too concerned about individual rights. We expect the system to work for us, but we are reluctant to support the system. For example, we believe that people accused of a crime deserve their day in court, but fewer and fewer of us are willing to perform jury duty; similarly, we are quick to accept government services but reluctant to support these services with our taxes.

The communitarians advance four proposals toward balancing individual rights with public responsibilities. First, our society should stop the expanding "culture of rights" by which we put our own interests ahead of social responsibility. The Constitution, which is

quoted so often when discussing individual rights, does not guarantee us the right to do whatever we want. Second, we must remember that we cannot take from society without giving something back. Third, the well-being of everyone may require limiting our individual rights; for example, pilots and bus drivers who are responsible for public safety may be asked to take drug tests. Fourth, no one can ignore key responsibilities such as obeying the law and responding to a cry for help from someone like Kitty Genovese.

The communitarian movement appeals to many people who believe in both personal freedom and social responsibility. But Etzioni's proposals have drawn criticism from both sides of the political spectrum. To those on the left, problems ranging from voter apathy to street crime cannot be solved by some vague idea of "social responsibility." As they see it, what is needed is expanded government programs to protect people and lessen inequality.

Conservatives, on the political right, see different problems in Etzioni's proposals (Pearson, 1995). As they see it, the communitarian movement favors liberal goals, such as confronting prejudice and protecting the environment, but

says little about conservative goals, such as strengthening religious beliefs and supporting traditional families.

Etzioni responds that the criticism coming from both sides suggests he has found a moderate, sensible answer to a serious problem. But the debate may also indicate that in a society as diverse as the United States, people who are so quick to assert their rights are not so ready to agree on their responsibilities.

WHAT DO YOU THINK?

1. Have you ever failed to come to the aid of someone in need or danger? Why did you not take action?

2. Half a century ago, President John F. Kennedy stated, "Ask not what your country can do for you; ask what you can do for your country." Do you think people today support this idea? Why or why not?

3. Are you willing to serve on a jury? Do you mind paying your fair share of taxes? Would you be willing to perform a year of national service after you graduate from college? Explain your answers.

theory, today's poor societies have little ability to modernize, even if they want to. From this point of view, the major barrier to economic development is not traditionalism but global domination by rich capitalist societies.

Dependency theory asserts that rich nations achieved their modernization at the expense of poor ones, by taking their valuable natural resources and exploiting their human labor. Even today, the world's poorest countries remain locked in a disadvantageous economic relationship with rich nations, dependent on wealthy countries to buy their raw materials and in return provide them with whatever manufactured products they can afford. According to this view, continuing ties with rich societies will only perpetuate current patterns of global inequality.

Whichever approach you find more convincing, keep in mind that change in the United States is no longer separate from change in the rest of the world. At the beginning of the twentieth century,

most people in today's high-income countries lived in relatively small settlements with limited awareness of the larger world. Today, the world has become one huge village because the lives of all people are increasingly interconnected.

The twentieth century witnessed unprecedented human achievement. Yet solutions to many problems of human existence—including finding meaning in life, resolving conflicts between societies, and eliminating poverty—have eluded us. The Seeing Sociology in Everyday Life box examines one dilemma: balancing individual freedom and personal responsibility. To this list of pressing matters new concerns have been added, such as controlling population growth and establishing an environmentally sustainable society. In the coming years, we must be prepared to tackle such problems with imagination, compassion, and determination. Our growing understanding of human society gives us reason to be hopeful that we can get the job done.

Social Change: Modern and Postmodern Societies

Seeing Sociology in Everyday Life

Is tradition the opposite of modernity?

Conceptually, this may be true. But as this chapter explains, traditional and modern social patterns combine in all sorts of interesting ways in our everyday lives. Look at the photographs below, and identify elements of tradition and modernity. Do they seem to go together, or are they in conflict? Why?

> **HINT** Although sociologists analyze tradition and modernity as conceptual opposites, every society combines these elements in various ways. People may debate the virtues of traditional and modern life, but the two patterns are found almost everywhere. Technological change always has social consequences—for example, the use of cell phones changes people's social networks and economic opportunities; similarly, the spread of McDonald's changes not only what people eat but where and with whom they share meals.

These young girls live in the city of Istanbul in Turkey, a country that has long debated the merits of traditional and modern life. What sets off traditional and modern ways of dressing? Do you think such differences are likely to affect patterns of friendship? Would the same be true in the United States?

Paul Prescott\Alamy Images

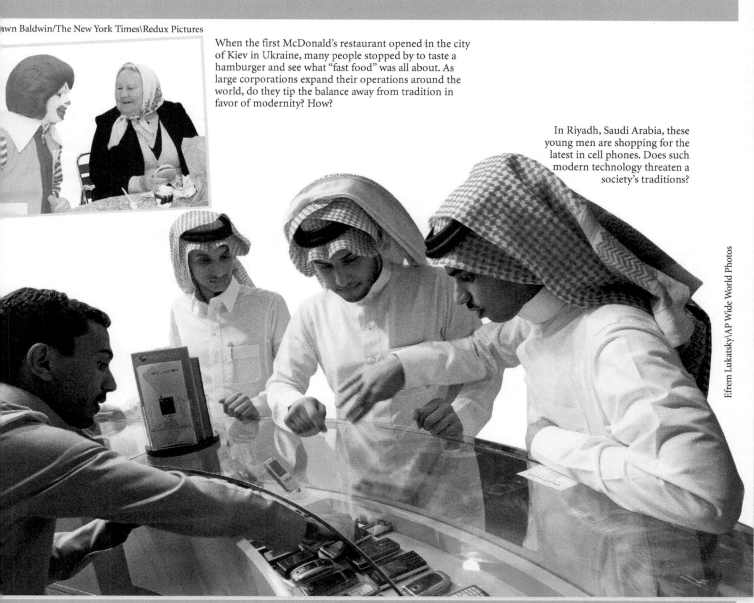

awn Baldwin/The New York Times\Redux Pictures

When the first McDonald's restaurant opened in the city of Kiev in Ukraine, many people stopped by to taste a hamburger and see what "fast food" was all about. As large corporations expand their operations around the world, do they tip the balance away from tradition in favor of modernity? How?

In Riyadh, Saudi Arabia, these young men are shopping for the latest in cell phones. Does such modern technology threaten a society's traditions?

Efrem Lukatsky\AP Wide World Photos

Applying SOCIOLOGY in Everyday Life

1. How do tradition and modernity combine in your life? Point to several ways in which you are traditional and several ways in which you are thoroughly modern.
2. Ask people in your class or friendship group to make five predictions about U.S. society in the year 2050, when today's twenty-year-olds will be senior citizens. Compare notes. On what issues is there agreement?
3. Do you think the rate of social change has been increasing? Do some research about modes of travel—including walking, riding animals, bicycles, trains, cars, airplanes, and rockets. At what point in history did each of these ways of moving come into being? What pattern do you see?

Making the Grade

Social Change: Modern and Postmodern Societies

👁 Watch on mysoclab.com

What Is Social Change?

SOCIAL CHANGE is the transformation of culture and social institutions over time. Every society changes all the time, sometimes faster, sometimes more slowly. Social change often generates controversy.

> **social change** the transformation of culture and social institutions over time

Causes of Social Change

CULTURE
- *Invention* produces new objects, ideas, and social patterns.
- *Discovery* occurs when people take notice of existing elements of the world.
- *Diffusion* creates change as products, people, and information spread from one society to another.

SOCIAL CONFLICT
- Karl Marx claimed that class conflict between capitalists and workers pushes society toward a socialist system of production.
- Social conflict arising from class, race, and gender inequality has resulted in social changes that have improved the lives of working people.

IDEAS
Max Weber traced the roots of most social changes to ideas:
- The fact that industrial capitalism developed first in areas of Western Europe where the Protestant work ethic was strong demonstrates the power of ideas to bring about change.

DEMOGRAPHIC FACTORS
Population patterns play a part in social change:
- The aging of U.S. society has resulted in changes to family life and the development of consumer products to meet the needs of the elderly.
- Migration within and between societies promotes change.

> **social movement** an organized activity that encourages or discourages social change
>
> **claims making** the process of trying to convince the public and public officials of the importance of joining a social movement to address a particular issue
>
> **relative deprivation** a perceived disadvantage arising from some specific comparison
>
> **disaster** an event, generally unexpected, that causes extensive harm to people and damage to property.

Disasters

Disasters cause unexpected social change:
- *natural disasters* (example: Hurricane Katrina)
- *technological disasters* (example: nuclear accident at the Chernobyl power plant)
- *intentional disasters* (example: Darfur genocide)

⊕ Explore on mysoclab.com

Social Movements

TYPES OF SOCIAL MOVEMENTS
- *Alterative social movements* seek limited change in specific individuals (example: Promise Keepers).
- *Redemptive social movements* seek radical change in specific individuals (example: Alcoholics Anonymous).
- *Reformative social movements* seek limited change in the whole society (example: the environmental movement).
- *Revolutionary social movements* seek radical change in the whole society (example: the Communist party).

EXPLANATIONS OF SOCIAL MOVEMENTS
- *Deprivation theory:* Social movements arise among people who feel deprived of something, such as income, safe working conditions, or political rights.
- *Mass-society theory:* Social movements attract socially isolated people who join a movement in order to gain a sense of identity and purpose.
- *Resource mobilization theory:* Success of a social movement is linked to available resources, including money, labor, and the mass media.
- *Culture theory:* Social movements depend not only on money and resources but also on cultural symbols that motivate people.
- *New social movements theory:* Social movements in postindustrial societies are typically international in scope and focus on quality-of-life issues.

What Is Modernity?

MODERNITY refers to the social consequences of industrialization, which include the decline of traditional communities, the expansion of personal choice, increasing social diversity, and a focus on the future.
- **Ferdinand Tönnies** described modernization as the transition from *Gemeinschaft* to *Gesellschaft*, characterized by the loss of traditional community and the rise of individualism.
- **Emile Durkheim** saw modernization as a society's expanding division of labor. *Mechanical solidarity*, based on shared activities and beliefs, is gradually replaced by *organic solidarity*, in which specialization makes people interdependent.
- **Max Weber** saw modernity as the decline of a traditional worldview and the rise of rationality. Weber feared the dehumanizing effects of rational organization.
- **Karl Marx** saw modernity as the triumph of capitalism over feudalism. Capitalism creates social conflict, which Marx claimed would bring about revolutionary change leading to an egalitarian socialist society.

> **modernity** social patterns resulting from industrialization
>
> **modernization** the process of social change begun by industrialization
>
> **division of labor** specialized economic activity
>
> **anomie** Durkheim's term for a condition in which society provides little moral guidance to individuals

📖 Read on mysoclab.com

Theoretical Analysis of Modernity

STRUCTURAL-FUNCTIONAL THEORY: MODERNITY AS MASS SOCIETY

- According to **mass-society theory,** modernity increases the scale of life, enlarging the role of government and other formal organizations in carrying out tasks previously performed by families in local communities.
- Cultural diversity and rapid social change make it difficult for people in modern societies to develop stable identities and to find meaning in their lives.

SOCIAL-CONFLICT THEORY: MODERNITY AS CLASS SOCIETY

- According to **class-society theory,** modernity involves the rise of capitalism into a global economic system resulting in persistent social inequality.
- By concentrating wealth in the hands of a few, modern capitalist societies generate widespread feelings of alienation and powerlessness.

mass society a society in which prosperity and bureaucracy have weakened traditional social ties

class society a capitalist society with pronounced social stratification

See the Summing Up tables.

Modernity and the Individual

Both mass-society theory and class-society theory are macro-level approaches; from them, however, we can also draw micro-level insights into how modernity shapes individual lives.

social character personality patterns common to members of a particular society

tradition-directedness rigid conformity to time-honored ways of living

other-directedness openness to the latest trends and fashions, often expressed by imitating others

MASS SOCIETY: PROBLEMS OF IDENTITY

- Mass-society theory suggests that the great social diversity, widespread isolation, and rapid social change of modern societies make it difficult for individuals to establish a stable social identity.

David Riesman described the changes in social character that modernity causes:

- Preindustrial societies exhibit **tradition-directedness:** Everyone in society draws on the same solid cultural foundation, and people model their lives on those of their ancestors.
- Modern societies exhibit **other-directedness:** Because their socialization occurs in societies that are continuously in flux, other-directed people develop fluid identities marked by superficiality, inconsistency, and change.

CLASS SOCIETY: PROBLEMS OF POWERLESSNESS

- Class-society theory claims that the problem facing most people today is economic uncertainty and powerlessness.
- Herbert Marcuse claimed that modern society is irrational because it fails to meet the needs of so many people.
- Marcuse also believed that technological advances further reduce people's control over their own lives.
- People suffer because modern societies have concentrated both wealth and power in the hands of a privileged few.

Modernity and Progress

Social change is too complex and controversial simply to be equated with progress:

- A rising standard of living has made lives longer and materially more comfortable; at the same time, many people are stressed and have little time to relax with their families; measures of happiness have declined in recent decades.
- Science and technology have brought many conveniences to our everyday lives, yet many people are concerned that life is changing too fast; the introduction of automobiles and advanced communication technology have weakened traditional attachments to hometowns and even to families.

Modernity: Global Variation

Although we often think of tradition and modernity as opposites, traditional and modern elements coexist in most societies.

Postmodernity

POSTMODERNITY refers to the cultural traits of postindustrial societies. Postmodern criticism of society centers on the failure of modernity, and specifically science, to fulfill its promise of prosperity and well-being.

postmodernity social patterns characteristic of postindustrial societies

Sample Test Questions

Multiple-Choice Questions

1. Sociologists use the term "modernity" to refer to social patterns that emerged
   a. with the first human civilizations.
   b. with the founding of cities.
   c. after the Industrial Revolution.
   d. along with the Information Revolution.

2. Which of the following are common causes of social change?
   a. the invention of things, ideas, and social patterns
   b. diffusion from one cultural system to another
   c. the discovery of existing things
   d. All of the above are correct.

3. Karl Marx highlighted the importance of which of the following factors in the process of social change?
   a. immigration and demographic factors
   b. ideas
   c. social conflict
   d. cultural diffusion

4. Max Weber's analysis of the rise of rational, modern society highlighted the importance of which of the following factors in the process of social change?
   a. invention
   b. ideas
   c. social conflict
   d. cultural diffusion

5. Which term did Ferdinand Tönnies use to describe a modern society?
   a. *Gesellschaft*
   b. *Gemeinschaft*
   c. mechanical solidarity
   d. organic solidarity

6. According to Emile Durkheim, modern societies have
   a. respect for established tradition.
   b. widespread alienation.
   c. common values and beliefs.
   d. an increasing division of labor.

7. The 2010 Gulf of Mexico oil spill is one recent case of
   a. a natural disaster.
   b. a technological disaster.
   c. an intentional disaster.
   d. an everyday disaster.

8. Which of the following statements about modernity as a mass society is *not* correct?
   a. There is more poverty now than in past centuries.
   b. Kinship ties have become weaker.
   c. Bureaucracy, including government, has expanded in size.
   d. People experience greater moral uncertainty about how to live.

9. Sociologists who describe modernity in terms of class-society theory focus on which of the following?
   a. rationality as a way of thinking about the world
   b. mutual interdependency
   c. the rise of capitalism
   d. the high risk of anomie

10. David Riesman described the other-directed social character typical of modern people as
    a. rigid conformity to tradition.
    b. eagerness to follow the latest fashions and fads.
    c. highly individualistic.
    d. All of the above are correct.

ANSWERS: 1(c); 2(d); 3(c); 4(b); 5(a); 6(d); 7(b); 8(a); 9(c); 10(b).

Essay Questions

1. Discuss how Tönnies, Durkheim, Weber, and Marx described modern society. Point out the similarities and differences in their understandings of modernity.

2. What traits lead some people to call the United States a "mass society"? Why do other analysts describe the United States as a "class society"?

Fixing the Bungled U.S. Environmental Movement

ROBERT BRULLE

J. CRAIG JENKINS

The United States has done little to address environmental problems at home or around the world. For example, gas efficiency standards remain where they were set 20 years ago due to a loophole that exempts SUVs and light trucks. Moreover, Congress doesn't have the political will to increase efficiency standards. The United States has also failed to move forward to address even small environmental problems due to political obstacles. In this selection, Robert Brulle and J. Craig Jenkins ask, "Where is the U.S. environmental movement in all of this?"

Senators John McCain and John Kerry slumped in chairs outside the Senate Chamber on March 13, 2002, having just lost a critical vote to increase the fuel efficiency of every vehicle on America's roadways. It was an especially difficult defeat. In conjunction with vigorous lobbying and a major public campaign by environmental organizations, Kerry and McCain had hoped to start the United States on the road toward dealing with global climate change.

But a lack of support and heavy opposition (from autoworkers, manufacturers, and the oil lobby, among others) resulted in the measure's defeat, ensuring the continued decline in the overall fuel efficiency of the U.S. automobile fleet. As a result, gas efficiency standards today remain where they were set more than 20 years ago, and a loophole that exempts light trucks and SUVs remains in effect.

Reprinted from *Contexts* 7, no. 2 (spring 2008), by permission of American Sociological Association.

Courtesy of AP/Wide World Photos

Sen. John Kerry (D–Massachusetts), left, and Sen. John McCain (R–Arizona) in 2002.

This outcome, which came on the heals of the Senate's rejection of the Kyoto Protocol in 1999 by an overwhelming 95-0 vote, demonstrates the political obstacles that stand in the way of even the most basic baby steps toward addressing environmental problems at home and around the world. If Congress can't generate the political will to raise domestic fuel efficiency standards, then dealing with global climate change seems almost impossible.

What do these recent political defeats say about the state of environmentalism in the United States? More to the point of the present analysis, where is the U.S. environmental movement in all this?

When it comes to activists and organizers, the current situation stands in marked contrast to the 1970s, when the environmental movement displayed an extraordinary ability to mobilize support in Congress and created an impressive infrastructure of safety agencies and regulatory oversight. But despite a strong organizational base and widespread public support, most critics agree the movement's political clout has declined over the past decade. Some even claim environmentalism is dead.

Sociological research suggests the environmental movement's seeming lack of influence stems from some fundamental changes in the culture of its organizations and in the traditions of organizing itself. It also may be the result of a mismatch between movement ideals and actual environmental problems and associated public policy options. Recognizing these shortcomings is crucial to translating the energies, passions, and principles of the movement into concrete legislative outcomes and policy solutions.

◉ Early Successes, Present Failures

Like the civil rights, women's, peace, and other movements, environmentalism was reborn in the 1960s. Building on the earlier conservationist, public health, and preservationist movements, the decade saw a flourishing of new ideas about environmental problems and how to address them.

Intellectuals like Rachel Carson and Barry Commoner developed and promulgated a new perspective that later became known as "environmentalism." They helped the general public understand the links among environmental degradation, ecosystem processes, and human health. Environmental organizations then repackaged these ideas in an effort to energize activists and the general public, thereby bringing about major policy changes.

The first Earth Day in April 1970 showcased an extraordinary mobilization over environmental issues and consolidated momentum that, in the few short years that followed, produced an impressive record of legislative victories. During the 1970s, environmental organizations appeared regularly before Congressional hearings and passed between 20 and 30 major bills every year with relatively limited challenge from corporations and other counterinterests.

Congress passed the Clean Air Act in 1970, the Clean Water Act in 1972, and the Endangered Species Act in 1973. Legislators extended or strengthened many such landmark bills soon thereafter. By the end of the 1970s, environmental activists and legislators had created a system of federal regulatory oversight and safety agencies that included the U.S. Environmental Protection Agency (EPA), the Nuclear Regulatory Agency, and the National Oceanic and Atmospheric Administration. States also set up their own counterparts to the national laws, policies, and agencies.

These landmark laws and organizational networks significantly improved environmental quality across the nation. For example, in 1972 the Clean Water Act—passed by Congress a matter of hours after a presidential veto—required that all waters in the United States be swimmable, drinkable, and fishable by 1983, and that the discharge of pollutants into U.S. waters end by 1985. This significant, hard-hitting legislation required real changes to the standard operating procedures in nearly every American community.

But this legislation and enforcement of it was far from perfect. Indeed, 34 years after the Clean Water Act passed, more than half of U.S. waters remain significantly degraded and EPA found in a 2006 study of streams that only 28 percent were in "good" condition. Also according to EPA, more than 146 million residents live in areas with unhealthy levels of air pollution.

These disappointing and unexpected outcomes were part of a larger, quite unsettling trend in the 1980s in which the policy advances of the previous decade suffered from a lack of enforcement or retrenchment, and few new advances. In part this was a result of the "wise use" countermovement, in which corporations launched new advocacy organizations, such as the Capital Research Center and the Mountain States Legal Foundation, to attack environmental initiatives. Playing on the media's reporting balanced accounts, these countermovements successfully cast doubt on scientific studies documenting environmental problems.

Political transformations also played a role. Since the mid-1990s, in fact, legislative successes for the environmental movement have been few and far between. After Republicans took control of the House of Representatives in 1994, environmentalists virtually disappeared from Congressional hearings and won passage of less than a dozen priority bills per year.

In any case, the results are clear when examining the continuing, unsustainable growth of America's "ecological footprint" (right). The footprint collects the use of all non-renewable natural resources—imported oil being the major source—and compares it against the ecological productive capacity of the United States since 1961. In 1968, the United States moved beyond existing resources; in other words, we began exporting our environmental problems abroad by consuming imported, non-renewable resources. Overall, the U.S. ecological footprint has increased by more than 240 percent over the 40-year period.

◉ Strong Movement, Lacking Clout

The environmental failures and shortcomings of recent years belie what appears to be a strong and vibrant movement, at least institutionally speaking. More than 10,000 tax-exempt environmental organizations are registered with the Internal Revenue Service, and they boast a combined support base of approximately 15 percent of the U.S. population. Based on our recently completed analysis published in *Mobilization*, the movement has a total annual income of more than $2.7 billion and assets of more than $5.8 billion. More than 100 new organizations are formed each year to address a wide spectrum of environmental problems.

A March 2007 Gallup poll found fully 70 percent of Americans are either active in or sympathetic to the environmental movement. Since 1980 membership in environmental groups has grown from 5.1 percent to 15.9 percent of U.S. adults and those donating time has grown from 1.4 percent to 8.8 percent, according to the World Values Surveys from 1980, 1990, and 2000.

Yet, for all this support and organizational strength, the political clout of the environmental movement appears to have eroded steadily since the early 1990s. Indeed, most critics agree the environmental movement is at best currently on the defensive—and this at a time when we face growing and perhaps irreversible environmental degradation.

Part of the problem is that the environmental successes of the 1970s were over issues that might be considered "low-hanging fruit"—easy wins against problems that were plain as day to the average citizen and politician. Dumped chemicals caused rivers to catch fire, major cities' air quality was so poor you could see it in the sky and feel it in your lungs, and waterways simply weren't suitable for fishing or swimming.

Beginning in the 1980s, the issues facing environmentalists became more complicated and challenging. A new set of environmental problems emerged that didn't fit into the 1960s environmental paradigm and prototype. Global warming, loss of biodiversity, tropical deforestation, ozone depletion, and acid rain were global, far more abstract, and less tractable problems. They were also outside the authority of the existing regulatory agencies, and thus required new types of political mobilization and policy solutions. For example, no single agency has jurisdiction over tropical deforestation or ozone depletion, so it's difficult to know who or what to target in lobbying and public-policy making.

The movement responded with public education projects, monitoring, lobbying for international treaties, and promoting "green" consumerism, but these have yet to make major institutional inroads. Indeed, critics suggest that the movement has become "Chicken Little," trumpeting an ever-growing litany of doomsday warnings without offering concrete solutions.

In 2004, environmental activists Michael Shellenberger and Ted Nordhaus published a widely circulated article titled "The Death of Environmentalism." They contended "the environmental movement's foundational concepts, its method of framing legislative proposals, and its very institutions are outmoded!" Substantial evidence supports their claims.

A major problem is the lack of deep public support for initiatives with major economic costs. Despite broad public support for environmental protection, the depth of this support is modest when it comes to actually paying for environmental protection or sacrificing economic growth. The figure at right shows the drop since 2000 in members of the general public willing to pay for environmental protection with decreased economic growth. Contemporary environmental challenges, such as global warming, species loss, and tropical deforestation, can't be addressed without significant economic sacrifices. How these will be paid and by whom is a major political challenge. Moreover, most are transboundary problems, which means they require international cooperation, and thus considerable political clout.

Scholars have long argued that social movements and movement organizations have a tendency to become timid and conservative with

U.S. ecological footprint

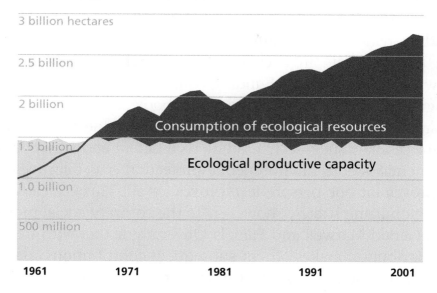

U.S. Ecological Footprint

U.S. attitudes toward environment and economy

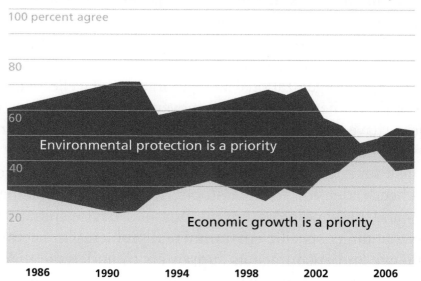

U.S. Attitudes Toward Environment and Economy

age. Today's environmental movement seems to have become complacent and overly bureaucratic, a movement dominated by "protest businesses" that substitute professional advocacy for citizen action. Few of the leading national environmental organizations offer members the chance to participate in a concrete, meaningful way. Members are check-writers, not activists. Funding comes from foundation and corporate grants, wealthy donors, and "checkbook activists." The majority of grassroots members simply come along for the ride.

Some scholars suggest "free riding" is inherent and even effective in environmental action. Environmental protection is a collective good—if it improves for one person, it improves for all. This is clearly not an optimal mobilizing strategy, however. To the contrary, social movement scholars Gerald Marwell and Pamela Oliver argue that with free riding "each contribution makes others' subsequent contributions less worthwhile, and thus less likely." And indeed today one of the paramount problems of the movement is the perception among potential supporters that their individual contributions won't make a difference.

Shellenberger and Nordhaus argue that the environmental movement needs to reframe its agenda to appeal to core progressive values and create a broader, more engaged political coalition. This "respinning" of the environmental message might help generate a new, more committed grassroots constituency, but our research suggests another change is needed as well.

The movement's other crucial ailment is a failure to translate general public support and organizational strength into specific effective actions. Though not dead, the environmental movement's organizations, ideals, and projects have failed to speak to or match current environmental challenges, legislative priorities, and public policy realities.

The task for the environmental movement, therefore, is not just to be a cheerleader for the grassroots, rank-and-file membership, but also—and perhaps more importantly—to devise initiatives and proposals that target specific environmental problems and actors, and then challenge and encourage its supporters to undertake them.

Successful campaigns in the movement's earlier years were organized around the workplace, schools, and churches and largely by volunteer activists. But they focused on specific, meaningful issues and targets.

Today's movement has some of these types of networks (the Sierra Club and local environmental justice groups, for instance) but lacks the projects and initiatives connected to people's lives and the relevance in the political culture required to mobilize real action and change.

Engaging citizens in the contemporary environmental movement in the United States will require instituting local democracy and fostering civic engagement, broadening commitments and agendas, and linking environmentalism to social justice, workplace equity, and broader social protections. It ultimately could require restructuring civic politics in America—focusing not only on passion and mobilization but also on law and public policy. But in the final, sociological analysis, getting Americans involved in a movement that will affect real environmental change will require reorganizing the environmental movement, shifting from a "top-down" structure to a grass-roots approach emphasizing concrete social problems and real-world, public policy solutions.

❧ An Opportunity for Revitalization

The environmental movement has recently attempted to mobilize around the issue of global warming, with the mass media playing a leading role. In May 2004 the fictional dramatic film *The Day After Tomorrow* was released. Then came Al Gore's *An Inconvenient Truth*, which gained a wide audience (and helped secure him a Noble Prize). Television coverage shows a marked increase in coverage of global warming.

In the wake of the November 2006 elections and the Republican loss of Congressional control, many environmentalists were excited about the prospects for environmental legislation, especially on the topic of global warming. Gone from the chairmanship of the Senate Committee on Environmental and Public Works was James Inhofe (R–Oklahoma), who once called global warming the "greatest hoax ever perpetrated on the American people." In his place was Barbara Boxer (D–California), a legislator with an impressive national profile and strong environmental record. In her first statements after the election Boxer promised swift and strong action to deal with global warming.

Recent polling still shows little change in public opinion in the aftermath. Every month Gallup asks what respondents consider the "most important problem" facing the nation. Over the past 10 years they've mentioned the environment no more than 2 percent of the time. A November 2007 Gallup poll showed the environment ranks 14th in major problems, with only 1 percent saying environmental improvement is our country's most important problem. Opposition to strong measures, such as instituting a carbon tax, is high. Fully 68 percent of those polled in March 2006 opposed a policy to "increase taxes on gasoline so people either drive less, or buy cars that use less gas." Moreover, 81 percent opposed a policy that would "increase taxes on electricity so people use less of it." A soft majority of 52 percent responded to the 2006 Gallup poll that they supported environmental protection over economic growth.

So despite strong scientific consensus on the basics of global warming theory, a Gallup poll from as recently as March 2006 showed 62 percent of the U.S. public still did not believe global warming was a problem. Perhaps it isn't surprising that Congress has been slow to act or that the presidential nomination debates have essentially ignored global warming. A carbon tax may be unpopular, but it's impossible to imagine significant reductions in carbon emissions in the near future that don't entail increased energy costs. However, the groundwork may be coming into place.

Environmental activists—working with scientists and politicians as well as writers and reporters—are not only continuing to raise public attention about global warming, they are beginning to think seriously about public policy innovations in the United States and elsewhere. As concrete analyses and political solutions come into circulation, we may well find ourselves in a situation similar to the period from 1963 to 1967—Rachel Carson's *Silent Spring* had been published and there was a great deal of media interest in her book, but it was only beginning to translate into the increased environmental mobilization of the late 1960s and early 1970s.

The United States needs a movement that leads away from the path of continued degradation and toward ecological sustainability. But without a paradigm shift from the top-down approach where members of environmental organizations are treated as budget funders to a grassroots focus that will engage citizens to take specific actions that stem the tide of environmental degradation, our environmental movement won't have the right approach to get us there.

Organizationally and in terms of broad public support, the environmental movement has been a remarkable success. But in terms of political clout for tackling the big issues, the movement is weak, losing critical policy battles while failing to provide strategies that can transform potential public support into environmental action. This makes it all the more incumbent on the environmental movement to help the general public connect the dots between their personal, local concerns and the dramatic, global threats to which environmental groups devote their resources and energy.

Recommended Resources

Christopher J. Bosso. *Environment Inc.: From Grassroots to Beltway* (University of Kansas Press, 2005). Shows the process by which the U.S. environmental movement shifted from a grassroots effort to an inside-the-beltway lobby.

Robert J. Brulle and J. Craig Jenkins. "Foundations and the Environmental Movement: Priorities, Strategies, and Impact," in *Foundations for Social Change: Critical Perspectives on Philanthropy and Popular Movements* (Rowman & Littlefield, 2005). Details the nature and amount of foundation funding of the U.S. environmental movement, and how this funding has impacted its strategy and tactics.

F. Buell. *From Apocalypse to Way of Life: Environmental Crisis in the American Century* (Routledge, 2004). An historical and textual analysis of the anti-environmental movement and the decline of the U.S. environmental movement.

Aaron M. McCright and Riley E. Dunlap. "Defeating Kyoto: The Conservative Movement's Impact on U.S. Climate Change Policy," *Social Problems* 50 (2003): 348–373. Describes the rise and impact of the anti-global warming political coalition.

David S. Meyer. "How Social Movements Matter," *Contexts* 2 (2003): 30–35. Provides an excellent overview of the factors that affect a social movement's effectiveness.

⚉ ⚉ ⚉

Questions

1. List some of the early successes of the environmental movement. Why have these successes lead to failures?

2. Explain why people are so reluctant to address contemporary environmental problems. What role do free riders play in this situation?

3. What must be done to revitalize the environmental movement?

4. According to Gallup Poll reports, the environment ranked 14th in major problems, with only 1% saying it was the nation's most important problem. Ask people on your campus what they consider to be the most important problem facing the nation. How do your results compare?

ndex

Page references followed by "f" indicate illustrated figures or photographs; followed by "t" indicates a table.

233, 289-291